I0754989

In the hope of immortality

A. Campbell

POPULAR

LECTURES AND ADDRESSES.

BY

REV. A. CAMPBELL.

PHILADELPHIA:
JAMES CHALLEN & SON.
J. B. LIPPINCOTT & CO......CINCINNATI: H. S. BOSWORTH......BETHANY, VA.: A. CAMPBELL.
1863.

STEREOTYPED BY L. JOHNSON & CO.
PHILADELPHIA.

TO

Selina Huntington Campbell,

MY DUTIFUL AND AFFECTIONATE WIFE,

WHO HAS GREATLY ASSISTED ME IN MY LABORS IN THE GOSPEL,

AT HOME AND ABROAD,

THIS VOLUME OF PUBLIC ADDRESSES,

LONG SOLICITED BY MANY FRIENDS, IS

Dedicated,

AS AN HUMBLE TOKEN OF MY ESTEEM AND AFFECTION.

BETHANY, VA., 1861. A. CAMPBELL.

PUBLISHERS' PREFACE.

We take great pleasure in presenting to the public this superb work, containing the Lectures and original Essays of Alexander Campbell, President of Bethany College and Minister of the Gospel of Christ. They have been carefully revised and prepared for the press, and now, for the first time, put in a form acceptable to all. They have been collected from his periodicals, covering a space of nearly forty years past, and were delivered and read to large and select audiences in different parts of the United States, and have frequently been required by those who have heard them or have known any thing of his intellectual strength and ability.

No man of the present age has been more frequently before the public, both in his addresses, debates, and writings, than Alexander Campbell; and the impress of his mind he has left on the age, and will leave to future generations.

No one can read these Lectures and Essays without being struck with the wonderful powers of reasoning he possesses, the ease with which he masters the most recondite subjects, and the boldness and originality with which he contemplates and handles them. He throws new light upon whatever he touches; and, as he thinks profoundly and clearly, he brings within the comprehension of all the weighty matters which he discusses. He has labored zealously and successfully to redeem the world from the authority of great names to the truth of things, and from the fanciful systems of theorists to the established principles of philosophy, morality, and religion. He never substitutes the speculations of men for authenticated facts, nor reasonings for faith, but confines himself within the area of nature, society, and religion in their truest, broadest, and largest extent. His works show that he has been no gleaner in the fields of science or of art, no winnower in the waste and rubbish of ages, but has entered the great harvest-fields of truth and observation and has brought home the riches of his herculean labors.

This work does not attempt to give the author's views on the subject of the Christian religion at large: these may be found in his numerous publications already before the people, and which have been extensively circulated and read both in Europe and America. His thoughts on collateral themes—literary, educational, philosophic, and moral—are here presented, embracing a wide range of subjects and elaborated in his own masterly and profound manner.

We think that no private or public library can well afford to dispense with this work. Every one who wishes to know what one of the most original minds and profound thinkers of the age has said and written on subjects of the greatest interest to our race, will avail himself of the reading and study of this volume.

The distinct themes discussed in the book will be found in its opening pages and a full and copious index, alphabetically arranged, at its close. No pains or expense have been spared by the publishers to get it up in a style and form most acceptable to the reader.

The portrait is one of the finest, by J. C. Buttre, of New York, from a recent superior photograph, given at our urgent request.

We commit it to the public in the full confidence that its just merits will be appreciated by it, and that it will take its place along with the standard publications in the English language.

THE PUBLISHERS.

PHILADELPHIA.

CONTENTS.

POPULAR LECTURES AND ADDRESSES.

ADDRESS

ON

THE ANGLO-SAXON LANGUAGE:

ITS ORIGIN, CHARACTER AND DESTINY.

CINCINNATI, O., 1849.

BEFORE we can appreciate our own vernacular, we must have some knowledge of language in general, and of other dialects of speech besides our own. It is, on all hands, agreed, that reason, language and religion, are God's greatest and best gifts to man; and that the cultivation and knowledge of these are essential to the development of our nature, and the enjoyment of ourselves and one another. With the immortal Newton, therefore, we say: "God gave to man reason and religion, by giving to him speech." This being admitted, language is a subject worthy of the highest consideration and regard. Hence, in the judgment of the wisest and best of men, much of our early life is devoted to the acquisition and cultivation of this ennobling faculty of speech; this divine art of acquiring and communicating knowledge, sentiment and feeling; this mysterious and sublime instrument of enjoying religion, society and truth.

To this most interesting theme, then, we ask your indulgent attention, while we endeavor to place it before you in a few of its more important attitudes and relations to ourselves, our country and the world.

Language, then, is either oral or written. Oral language, or language proper, consists of articulate sounds addressed to the ear; written language consists of stipulated symbols addressed to the eye. With the

2

absent and with the deaf, we intercommunicate by symbols addressed to the eye; with those present, by sounds addressed to the ear.

These, however, are but definitions of the terms as we use them. What is the thing itself?

As applied to man, language is pictured or embodied thought, feeling and emotion. It is an embodiment of ideas, volitions and feelings, in audible sounds, or in visible forms, addressed to others. It is, indeed, the aerial and sensible impersonation of human spirits in communion with one another. It is not the mere giving of a name, or a local habitation, to an idea, emotion or volition; but it is the imparting to that idea, emotion or volition, the power of reproducing itself in the mind of another. It is that ethereal instrument, that spiritual symbol, by which one spirit operates upon another, in simultaneously producing views, feelings and emotions, corresponding with its own.

It is, indeed, an endowment of unbounded influence for weal or for woe, bestowed on man, for which he is more accountable than for any other social influence conferred upon him. No uninspired man has given such a picture of the power of human language, for good or for evil, as that drawn, in a few words, by the eloquent Apostle James. To that great instrument of speech he ascribes a transcendent potency. Of an unruly tongue, he says: "The tongue is a fire, a world of iniquity; it defileth the whole body, and setteth on fire the course of nature, and is set on fire of hell. Every kind of beasts, and of birds, and of serpents, and of things in the sea, is tamed, and hath been tamed by mankind; but the tongue can no man tame; it is an unruly evil thing, full of deadly poison. By it," indeed, "we bless God;" but by it, also, "we curse man, created in the image of God. Out of the same mouth proceedeth a blessing and a curse. Brethren, these things ought not so to be."

From this high source we learn that there are two kinds of eloquence —the eloquence infernal, and the eloquence supernal. We occasionally hear of the fire of eloquence, but are not always informed whence it comes. It may, indeed, emanate from the fire beneath as well as from the fire above, and is, therefore, all potent in blessing or in cursing man.

But, if the tongue is sometimes set on fire by hell, it is sometimes set on fire by heaven; and hence men are both blessed and cursed by the faculty of speech. How much good feeling and tender affection spring up within us, and gush from our lips, on hearing the kind, and courteous, and sympathizing compellations of some kindred spirit—of some estimable and affectionate friend! If, from wicked words, some hearts burn with rage, from kind and benevolent words other hearts overflow with love. But our own words react upon ourselves, according to their import; and hence we are sometimes wrought up to a pathos, a fervor, an ecstasy, indeed, by the mysterious sound of our own voice upon ourselves, as well as by that of others, to which we never could have ascended without it. Hence the superior eloquence of extemporaneous speaking over that of those who read or recite what they have coolly or deliberately thought at some other time and in some other place. Indeed, our most sincere and pious emotions are stirred up—a more soul-subduing piety is developed—and a height of bliss enjoyed in the fervor of expressed admiration and praise, addressed to the throne of God, under the influence of our own voice, in private and in social worship, than could be produced in silent meditation, prayer or praise. Even the raptures of heavenly bliss are but the sublime consummation of expressed adoration, and the sweetest bliss of heaven is but the effect of a heavenly concert in some lofty ecstasy, uttered by seraphic tongues to the unwasting Fount of universal good.

Language is, indeed, a most sublime machinery, by which a man can raise himself, and those whom he addresses, to the loftiest conception of nature and of nature's God, and to the highest personal and social pleasure of which his nature is capable. Volumes have been written in commendation of it, and of the great masters of this divine art; but who, in his most happy moments, and in his loftiest strains of admiration, has ever equalled the transcendent theme? It has been the subject of many a volume, and the theme of many a speech. Sages, philosophers, fabulists and poets, have exhausted their stores of learning and eloquence in commendation and in admiration of the gifts and achievements of human speech. Of Grecian eloquence, an English poet has said:—

> "Resistless eloquence that fulmined o'er Greece,
> *And shook the way to Xerxes' and Artaxerxes' throne.*"

And what is eloquence, but language properly applied?

But we need not the fictions of the fabulist, nor the high-wrought eulogies of the poet; we need but the great fact, that language has ever been the great minister of civilization and of redemption. It was by the gift of tongues that nations were subdued to the obedience of faith. It was the spirit of wisdom and of eloquence that gave to HIM that spoke as mortal man never did, a power, intellectual, moral and spiritual, transcendent over the destinies of the world.

Its power is not only felt on the thrones of kings and on the tribunals of justice, but on the throne of God itself. It electrifies the heavenly hosts, and opens the fountains of sympathetic feeling and of profound devotion, in the loftiest spirits that environ the celestial throne. It has awakened emotions in the human heart, and kindled raptures in the soul, that, rising to heaven, have caused the earth to tremble under the knees of adoring saints, and have brought angels down on missions of mercy to mankind. The piety of the saint, and the zeal of the martyr, have, under its hallowed influence, achieved the most splendid victories inscribed on the rolls of time, and have effected revolutions and deliverances on earth that have caused enraptured silence amongst the adoring legions of the skies.

But it is not to pronounce an eulogy on its ineffable powers; it is not to argue its human or divine origin, or discuss the comparative excellence of any one of the dialects of earth in contrast with the claims of any or of every other, that we now appear before you. It is rather to assert the claims of our own vernacular to our especial regard and attention, as destined to pervade the world, and to carry civilization and salvation to the human race.

True, indeed, in attempting this, we must occasionally glance at other tongues; and it may be due to the occasion to avow, at least, our own conviction, that language, as much as religion, is the special gift of God to man. But to propound the question, *Was language human or divine in its origin?* as a subject of grave discussion in this enlightened land, in the midst of the nineteenth century, and especially in this city of schools and colleges, would seem to me as inapposite as uncomplimentary to my auditors. Suffice it, then, on the present occasion, to assume it to be a special gift of God to man.

That the first man could not have taught himself to speak; that language, like faith, comes by hearing; that it could not have been conventional; that, without it, assemblies could not have been convened or the subject debated; that mankind were not, as Lucretius and Horace sung, sanctioned by the first of Roman orators, a *mutum et turpe pecus*—a dumb and brutal race—is self-evident. It would, indeed, require an unusual amount of patience to reason with men who begin by assuming that—

> "Men out of the earth of old,
> Dumb and beastly vermin, crawled;"

that from this state of brutal barbarism they degenerated into civilization; that they apostatized from their primitive state into learned and eloquent men; that from error and vice they fell away into learning and virtue, and give, for proof, that water is purer in the stream than in the fountain! From such philosophers, or rather philosophists, we must dissent, and confidently assume that language was originally a divine gift to man.

The only question, then, is:—WAS IT GIVEN TO MAN BY INSPIRATION? or, DID GOD TEACH MAN, *viva voce*, TO SPEAK?

Reason and faith concur in affirming that all things begin in miracle. The course of things is nature; their beginning supernatural, or miraculous. Of two miracles supposable in the case, we choose the less. That God conversed with man, and taught him, VIVA VOCE, is not only rational, but scriptural, and less marvellous than that he taught himself to speak, or that God simply inspired him with wisdom and learning to invent it. God made the human ear for a guide to the human tongue. Hence, the deaf are always dumb. No one ever spoke that did not first hear another speak. Inventing speech is, therefore, in its nature, impossible. Speech is imitation, not invention nor discovery. Hence, we individually and nationally have a mother tongue—a vernacular. But there was one man that never was an infant, that never had a VERNA, a nurse, or a mother. He had no mother tongue. But he had a father. He must, then, have had a father tongue. That man was Adam, and his father God. The most natural or rational conclusion is, that God taught him to speak, to give names to things and his conceptions of them. God, then, not only gave to man ears and a tongue, but he also taught him to use them; not by inspiration, but by example.

According to Moses,—and he is not only the most ancient, but the most learned authority in the world,—God spoke before he made his son Adam. He created the Universe by the power of speech. And is not this the most lofty conception that we can form of the grandeur and divinity of speech—that God, of all means in his power, chose language as the envelop of omnipotence, and ushered the universe into being by the divine eloquence of words? He said, "*Let there be light, and there was light.*" At the sound of his voice darkness became the parent of light, and Nothing the mother of all things. He said, and it was done; he commanded, and the universe began to be; he spoke, and truth was born. The first speech continued, at intervals, for six days. When it ceased, creation was perfect and complete, and ever since but echoes back the voice and the praise of the Lord.

From this miniature view of the gift of speech, and its divine origin, we advance another step toward our vernacular. The human family were all of "one language and of one speech" for almost eighteen hundred years. Since that time the history of language has not been fully written. Still, amidst the confusion of tongues and the traditions of antiquity, and especially from the structure of different dialects of nations, we may arrive at a good degree of certainty as to the lineage and descent of the Saxon and Anglo-Saxon tongues. But to discuss all questions that might be propounded on such an exuberantly fruitful theme, could we respond to them, would be rather the burthen of a volume than the mere item of a popular address.

There is no question that the ancient Chaldee or Hebrew was the only language spoken by mankind from Adam to the erection of the Temple of Babel, in the year of the world 1775. This unfortunate and infamous pyramidal temple, rather than the surrounding city, was, we presume, the procuring cause of this sad calamity. The anathema then inflicted upon mankind is immortalized in the name of this ill-fated pile, intended, by its apostate founders, for a centre of attraction; but, in pursuance of a divine malediction, it became a centre of repulsion and dispersion. The causes of this eternal mark of divine disapprobation are not so evident to all as to preclude a doubt whether a refusal to spread themselves over the earth, and locate in different regions, according to a divine intimation, or a desire to erect a temple in honor of some embodiment of divinity, as a form of God, which they or some of their immediate ancestors had vainly imagined, became the cause of this confusion of language and dispersion of mankind. The fact of a flagrant apostasy from the divine will is indisputably evident, explain it as we may. They either refused to obey the patriarch Noah, allotting, by inspiration, to each family of his great-grandsons, then amounting to seventy-two incipient tribes, such a portion of the earth as God, in his all-superintending wisdom and providence, had allotted to them; or forgetting, in the vanity of their minds, that God was a Spirit, they sought to embody their conceptions of him in some sensible form, for which they devised a temple, and for themselves a city. To discuss such subjects as these would be foreign to our purpose. It sufficeth our purpose to note the melancholy fact that the language which God and Adam spoke in his primeval innocence; which Abel, Enoch, Methuselah and Noah spoke; the vernacular of Shem, Ham and Japheth, gave way to a confusion of language, to new sounds and signs, unheard and unknown in the years before the flood.

Into what, and how many, forms, human language was now cast, is a subject in which the most learned antiquarians do not altogether harmonize. Some assume *three*, others sixteen, and others seventy-two new dialects of speech. Those who assume three, allot one to each of the three sons of Noah; those contending for sixteen, give one to each of his grandsons; while those who oppose both, assign one to each of his seventy-two great-grandsons. But all these assume that, in journeying from the east to this new location, the posterity of Shem accompanied Ham and Japheth; that, indeed, all the families of the earth, leaving their former residences in the east, set out in quest of a new location. This is not probable, nor does it so well accord with the subsequent details of sacred history. The stronger probability is that the posterity of Shem had no part in the erection of this tower to Belus, or to whatever divinity it was designed to honor; and, consequently, were not implicated in this grievous apostasy, but, retaining their language and their religion, continued their abode around the location of their venerable father, Noah.

Sir William Jones—no mean authority—argues that mankind are divided into three races, corresponding with the three races of Noah, and that each of these had its own distinctive and independent tongue. These he presumes to have been Hindoos, Arabs and Tartars; and their three unconnected and original tongues were, the Sanscrit, Arabic and Slavonian.

The Indian, or Hindoo race, comprehends the ancient Persians, Ethiopians, (whether Asiatic or African,) the Phenicians, Tuscans, Greeks, Chinese, Goths, Celts, Japanese, Burmans, Egyptians, Syrians, Peruvians and Romans. This race anciently spoke the Sanscrit, the great parent of the Gothic and Celtic, afterwards blended with the old Ethiopic, Persian and Armenian. It is alleged that the traditions of Homer are found in Sanscrit poetry, and that, unquestionably, the Greek and Roman tongues are derived from it.

The Arabic race located themselves between the Red Sea and the Persian Gulf, and from them the Jews, Arabs and Assyrians derived their respective dialects of speech; rather a modernized form of the ancient and once universal Chaldee, which, with slight variations, is called Aramean, Arabic, Hebrew, Samaritan, Syriac, Coptic.

The Tartar race located in the vast regions of Tartary, spreading themselves over Russia, Poland and Hungary. Their language was the Slavonic, whence sprang various dialects of Northern Asia and Northeastern Europe. Coinciding with these views, we are gratified to have the latest and most eminent writers on the subject; amongst whom we place Bryant, Sir William Jones, and the distinguished Faber.

Notwithstanding the confusion of speech, it would not be difficult to prove one ancient original tongue. We have only to take a few prominent terms, and trace them through all the more ancient tongues down to the modern. Take, for example, the first imperative uttered by the Creator:—God said, "Let there be light, and there was light." In the old Chaldee, the word rendered light is UR, translated light, or fire. In the Sanscrit, OUR signifies day, in contrast with night. In all the Eastern languages it signifies light and fire. In the Coptic or Egyptian, OR indicates the sun, or light. The Greek AEER is sometimes rendered air, sometimes light. In Latin, AURA, in Irish, AEER, are formed from the same root. From the same source the Greek has PUR, for which we have substituted FIRE. Many such examples could be given; but enough, you will say, of the endless genealogy, transference and transformation of words.

We shall, then, leave Asia, and travel to Europe; but before we leave this cradle of the world, this nursery of the human race, we must remind you that all that is great and good and venerable in human history commenced in Asia. God made the first man of Asiatic clay. There he located Paradise; there he planted the Tree of Life; and when, for the sin of man, he deluged the Old World, he commenced the New in Asia: Noah's ark was anchored there. In Armenia, the smoke of the first postdiluvian sacrifice ascended to heaven. There lived the renowned Patriarchs of the world. The Bible was written first in Asia. In Asia repose the ashes of Bible heroes, saints, martyrs, prophets, apostles and evangelists. There the Saviour of the world was born, lived, died, and rose again. There the first Christian Church was founded. There the Kingdom of the Messiah was first established. From Asia, indeed, religion, language and civilization spread over the world.

But there is one section of Asia on which our eye lingers with peculiar interest. Between the Euxine Sea and the Caspian lie the Caucasian Mountains, whence migrated our remote ancestors. Of the five distinct races of men that now people the globe, it is agreed, at least by ourselves, that in all the great attributes that elevate and adorn human nature, the Caucasian race is chief. The people of the seven Caucasian Mountains have filled a thousand volumes with their fame. Some trace to them seventy, others three hundred nations, and almost as many dialects of speech. Without debating these claims and assumptions, we are pleased to be assured that they are our progenitors. For great men and beautiful women, their praise resounds through all lands. And in proof that we have not degenerated, we are pleased to learn that seven nations, yet possessing these extensive ranges, still preserve the ancient type of their superiority, and thus confirm our pretensions. Providentially, they have always been the most prolific, enterprising and wide-spreading people in the world. They anciently swarmed over the best portions of Asia and Europe. The Circassians and Georgians, yet residing in those regions, are, at this day, the finest physical models of our species. And we think we do not exaggerate when we say that, for stateliness of person, vigor of intellect, loftiness of imagination, moral capacity and energy of character, they stand pre-eminent amongst all forms and races of human kind.

From them sprang the venerable Pelasgic Chiefs, first residents of Greece; and from them, too, the Romans are proud to count descent. Persians, Germans and Gaulatians, are scions from that stock. But there is a higher cause than the cloud-capt eminences of Caucasus and its fertile slopes, for this illustrious race of men. God gave these lofty regions to the sons of Japheth, the first-born of Noah, the great progenitor of seven-sixteenths of the human race. His patrimony was the northern highland regions of Asia, and all Europe.

His sons encompassed the Euxine Sea and the Caucasian Mountains. Gomer, his first-born, the vigorous germ of a mighty progeny, is most evidently the father of the ancient Gomerians or Germans, sometimes called the *Cimmeri* or *Cimbri*. Faber learnedly contends that those first called Cimmeri are called the Cimbri, and the Umbri of Gaul and Italy, and the Cimri, Cambri and Cumbri of Wales and Cumberland, at the present day. Moreover, sundry ancient authors identify with them the Galatæ, of Asia Minor, and assign to them the Gaels, Gauls and Celtæ of ancient Europe. Josephus, also, alleges that the Galatæ were called *Gomeriani*, from their great ancestor Gomer.

After very considerable research into the antiquities of both European and Asiatic history, I acknowledge that it is very difficult, if not impossible, to trace, in a continuous and unbroken line, the ancestry and regular descent of any nation in the world down to our day, one only excepted. The Jews, because of one descended from them, of universal interest to the human race, are the only people whose nationality, language and religion, can be traced, in one unbroken chain, from Abraham to the present time.

The Anglo-Saxon people of all the Japhetic, Caucasian or Gomerian race, are, through Teutones, Goths, Celts, Gauls, Angles, Saxons and Normans, as traceable as any modern nation known to us; and with all that certainty of evidence necessary to our present purpose, though, perhaps, not sufficient according to our modern codes and courts of law, to establish their claims to England, or the United States, if these countries had been exclusively willed to them by their very great-grandfather, Gomer.

I am aware that Tacitus, a historian of the highest Roman fame, endeavors to supply the place of history by a peculiar grammatic etymology of the term German, as simply indicating a *war-man*. Warmen they certainly were, but that fact will not supply the place of history. Some other critic might, from the appellative German affixed to cousin, as logically affirm that the Germans were a nation of cousins. But had he known Jewish history as well as he knew Roman, Tacitus would not have taken a current local meaning of a word to indicate its original import. He would, moreover, have found in Jewish history that *places*, as well as *nations*, had given quite another etymology. Some of the school of Tacitus have sought in a similar manner for the meaning of the term Euxine, applied to the sea, around which Japheth's sons erected their first settlements. One Greek etymologist derives it from *axenos*, inhospitable, because he did not like the climate. With him the Euxine was an *in*hospitable sea. Another Greek, as learned as he, but more enamored with the sea, discovered that while *a* prefixed to *xenos* was negative, *eu* prefixed was affirmative of hospitality; and, consequently, he concluded that *euxenos*, or Euxine, meant the hospitable sea. But to a student of the Bible and of ancient history, neither the one nor the other is true, or necessary in the case; for *Askenos*, a son of Gomer, had located first on the coast, and from him, according to very ancient custom, it received its name. But still more confirmatory of this, other sons of Japheth have given their names to settlements—such as Magog, *Madai*, *Riphath*, *Tubal*, *Meshech*. Thus we have the Riphaen mountains, from Riphath—Ezekiel collocates Magog, Tubal and Meshech, sons of Japheth—Greece is called *Javan* by Daniel, and all Christendom assign the Medes to *Madai*. I hold it, then, to be established, beyond a doubt, that the Caucasians derive their superiority, not so much from the mountains from which they receive their name, as from their ancestry.

There is a promise of *enlargement* in the very name Japheth. Hence half the world has been allotted to Japheth, and with much probability, as may yet be shown, half the human race. No physiological writer has yet fully discussed the laws of human increase. But one fact is more or less evident to all, that certain predominating qualities long continue in families, tribes and nations. To this it was providentially owing that Japheth had seven sons—while Shem had but five, and Ham four. Presuming on this principle, I heard a living Bible interpreter once say, that could we obtain a correct census of the world, he did not doubt, that as Noah had only sixteen grandsons, it might be found that seven-sixteenths were from Japheth, five-sixteenths from Shem, and four-sixteenths from Ham.

A year after, an estimate of the present population of the globe, collected from the best statistics, appeared in some of our annuals. The author of it had no allusion to this view of the subject; yet, strange to say, no other denominator or common measure but sixteen, would measure or proportionably divide them. The result gave exactly, or with a very inappreciable remainder, the aforesaid ratios of *seven*-sixteenths to Japheth, *five* to Shem, and *four* to Ham!

It is not, however, in fruitfulness only, but in other distinguishing characteristics, both physical and mental, that posterity, for many generations, resemble not merely their immediate, but also their very remote ancestry. The Jews, the Arabs, the Germans, the French, the Spaniards, and last, though not least, the Anglo-Saxons, have, for ages, preserved, and to this day more or less distinctly exhibit, those attributes and peculiarities on account of which their progenitors were distinguished.

Some nations, known to history, had their peculiar characters as fully and as clearly drawn a thousand years ago, as they have to-day. Paul once said, and he felt himself authorized to say it, not merely on the authority of the poet Epimenides, but from tradition and observation, that "the Cretans were always liars, evil beasts, lazy bodies."

"As the twig is bent the tree's inclined," is as true of nations, in their infancy, minority and manhood, as it is of the individuals that compose them. Were it otherwise, all history would be fable, and all prognostications of the future delusive and vain. We, therefore, feel ourselves fully warranted to anticipate the career and to estimate the future character and destiny of a people from their past and present history. At present, however, we merely allude to the history of Japheth, for the sake of one of his sons.

The seven sons of Japheth, after their dispersion, spreading over Northern Asia, over Scythia and Tartary, as well as through the South and West of Europe, forming new centres of association, as circumstances indicated, did constitute and establish new settlements, and, consequently, in the natural course of things, acquired new names and designations. Hence, in process of time, some of them were called Goths, some Teutones, some Celts, some Gauls, some Cimbri, some Angles, some Saxons, some Normans. Often, too, the same tribes and nations were called by different names. No living man, therefore, can now trace their progress or fully write their history. We are too dependent upon the Romans for the history of this portion of the earth, and its manners and affairs. Unfortunately, they never were famous for impartial truth. Roman glory had such brilliancy, in their eyes, that those who most devoutly sought, or cultivated, or gazed upon it, could see no living glory anywhere else. They are not, then, to be regarded as wholly impartial historians. But, so far as our present object requires, we can find materials enough in their own concessions, or independent of them. Indeed, we have almost enough already.

Julius Cæsar, from Gaul, sometimes called Gallia Celtica, invaded Britain in the 55th year before the Christian era. On his arrival there, he found much of the same population he had subdued in Gaul. He found those called Celts, not from their blood, but from their having long been inured to living in dense forests; others called Belgæ, from their border wars and love of fight; Cimbri, from a corrupted or abbreviated ancestral name; Gauls, from the country in which they had long resided; Germans, or Gomerans, from their original founder.

But in Britain he also found various tribes of them; and, had he then visited Ireland, he could have found other shades of Celts, and other varieties of Asiatic growth, for which we cannot now find an appropriate name. In process of time, however, and after many a hard-fought field, he Romanized them, as the Germans before had Germanized the old Celtic Britons—a more ancient tenantry of the island.

After a struggle of almost five centuries, the Britons called for foreign aid, and obtained it. The Jutes, the Angles and the Saxons, promptly obeyed the summons. The Jutes and the Angles then dwelt in the Cimbric Chersonesus, a peninsula of Jutland, (now within the confines of Denmark,) and a portion of Schleswig and Holstein, the province and territory of the Angles. In Holstein there is a district still called Anglen, the true and veritable Old England; a small kingdom, indeed, but the prototype of a larger and more illustrious dominion. The Saxons, of Scythian blood and spirit, formerly called Sacæ, true sons of Japheth, possessed a large territory south of the Jutes and Angles, reaching from the Weser to the Delta of the Rhine, and occupying countries now called Westphalia, Friesland, Holstein, and a portion of Belgium. They had, Japheth-like, "ENLARGED," or spread themselves from the Baltic to the British Channel, and had not to perform a protracted voyage to aid their friends in Britain. They were known to the Celtic Britons to be as brave as themselves,—alike bold and daring on sea and on land,—a portion of a larger stock issuing from the Gothic and Teutonic hive, and, like all that race, great lovers of the sea,—delighting in storms and tempests,—honored with the very graphic and imposing title of "SEA-KINGS." To this parentage England owes as much her passion for the ocean, and her success upon it, as she does her Anglo-Saxon tongue. The result of the alliance was the conquest and expulsion of the Romans, the Saxonizing of South Britain, and the changing of its name into Angland, or England.

Upon the whole premises which history lays before us, as to the true character of our Pagan Anglo-Saxon forefathers, we must, in all candor, say that they were what we would now-a-days call "sea-pirates" and "land-pirates." But, as they had now got as far as they could go westwardly, and finding much in Britain to suit their taste, especially around its coasts, and much congeniality in its population, who, like themselves, had wandered from the East in quest of new adventures, they very readily, after a time, coalesced, and formed, indeed, the most land-loving and the most expert sea-faring nation in the world, greatly softened and subdued by their embracing, after a time, the Christian faith.

Although the Roman army was ultimately driven from England by the Britons and their new allies, there still remained a remnant of that people in Wales, and along its borders, retaining their mother tongue, of which many words and phrases were blended with the language of the victors. Nor is it to be supposed that a people possessing so much of the island for five hundred years would not leave at least some fragments of their vernacular amongst them. To this mixture, again, were added, both before and after the Norman conquest, many words and phrases of Danish, Norwegian, and Norman extraction. So that, in truth, even their own language was rather of an *eclectic* than of an original character, although essentially of Anglo-Saxon origin.

Having, so far, ascertained the origin of the Anglo-Saxon tongue, and quite enough for our purpose, we are prepared to consider its peculiar and distinctive CHARACTER.

This we may easily accomplish, by making ourselves somewhat familiar with its structure. It is, in one sentence, a language of languages, whose terminology is mainly selected from almost all the ancient and most finished tongues of the civilized world. A rich, a broad and lofty tongue; a splendid composite; a greatly diversified, curiously inwrought, and highly polished Mosaic composition, which can embody and present every form, color and gradation of thought, sentiment and emotion. In religion, ethics, politics, sciences and arts, it has drawn upon Hebrew, Greek, Latin, German—upon all parent languages of every nation known to the Anglo-Saxon people, or their ancestors, far back as any living monument, or any written document now extant, attests.

But the great end and use of language must be clearly perceived, and, indeed, comprehended by every one who presumes to assert the comparative merit of any tongue, living or dead. That language which can most directly, clearly, fully and impressively utter all the soul, and render transparent to an attentive mind every emotion, thought or desire, is decidedly the best.

The Anglo-Saxon possesses all these qualities in as high a degree, and to as full an extent, as any tongue, living or dead. But why should it not possess all conceivable perfection? The language of any people is but the exponent of the mind and character of that people. And what is the comparative standing of the Anglo-Saxon people in Europe and America at the present day? This, with me, if not the most logical, is the most popular and appreciable way of deciding the question.

It is conceded that the language of every people is but the embodied and pictured mind of that people. The Hebrew, Greek, Roman, French, German or English mind, is all extant, and fully developed, in their respective tongues.

If we thought that any one denied or doubted the assumption, that the language of a people is the exponent or measure of the mind of that people, we would make an effort to prove it. But at present, not presuming this, I do not volunteer, in advance of the public demand, to perform such a work of supererogation.

If any one, however, has a lingering doubt of this fact, I will propound to him but one question, on answering which he may settle it to his own satisfaction. That question is, Why is there not found in Hebrew, Greek, Latin, or any other dead language, a single word or phrase to represent a printing-press, an electric machine, a steam-engine, a mariner's compass, &c. &c.? Because, he must respond, the Hebrew, Greek or Latin mind had not such an idea in it. He may propound the same question to himself in reference to every Pagan nation now extant, not having the Christian religion. Why, in a hundred dialects of Asia, Africa and America, is the name of Jesus Christ not found? The answer is as prompt: Because he is not in the mind of these nations. We have, we presume, carried our main point, viz.:

that the mind and language of a people are commensurate; that the character of the one is essentially the character of the other. The Anglo-Saxon language is, therefore, the most comprehensive language ever spoken on earth: because the people whose language it is, have the most enlightened, comprehensive, and, consequently, the most energetic mind of any people now speaking any living tongue in the Old World or in the New. Think not, however, my respected auditors, that, in affirming this conviction, I have either forgotten or contemned other nations of high respectability, such as Germany, France, Prussia, Russia, &c. We give them all due credit for every demonstration of intellect and moral greatness which they have given to the world. In saying this, we only affirm their own convictions or concessions. They do homage to the Anglo-Saxon mind; not merely as we do homage to certain master-spirits amongst them, by transferring their works into our language, but in laying aside their own sciences, arts and inventions, and in adopting ours. Of many proofs of this fact, a few instances must suffice.

Let me, then, ask, why did Peter the Great disguise himself, and spend four years in England, learning the art and mystery of ship-building? Why did he send his emissaries abroad, in quest of Anglo-Saxon arts and sciences? Why does the present Autocrat of all the Russias clandestinely send his emissaries to peep into our work-shops, our manufactories, our schools and colleges? Why does he, indirectly, carry home our ploughs, carts, wagons, implements of husbandry, and the useful arts of Old England or New England? Why employ, at the present time, an American engineer to project and consummate the highways, the railways of his great empire? Not because he has not some rude form and conception of some of them, but because he has not any one of them, in all its improvements and adaptations, in his own mind. He has neither the ideas nor the appropriate terms in his own language, and, therefore, our vernacular is, at least in these points, himself being judge, before his own. What Anglo-Saxon visits the continent of Europe in quest of new discoveries in useful arts and sciences? We go there to contemplate the ruins of empires, and to learn the causes of their decline and fall, not to acquire new ideas in the sciences and arts of our own age.

But again: the Anglo-Saxon mind, wherever found, is greater—that is to say, it is more acute, comprehensive and vigorous—than the French, the German or the Russian, because it has a more acute, comprehensive and vigorous language; a more polished machinery of thought; better instruments to work with; for, while mind generates language, language generates and polishes mind. In arguing thus we do not, indeed, reason in a circle, any more than when Cæsar said, "money will raise soldiers, and soldiers will raise money." In the same sense, ideas create language, and language creates ideas. This is farther proved by the great discoveries and improvements made by the American and English mind. Whence came the complete, yet simplified, steam-engine, and its accompanying machinery? Whence came the spinning-jenny, the power-loom, the electric telegraph, and all they have given birth to? It is not the spirit of the age, for these have created a new age. They are our contemporaries. We think, we speak, we act, before the age, else a new age would never come.

Once more: the Saxon language is the language of PROTESTANTISM. I might have said, and I beg leave to correct myself, the ANGLO-Saxon language is the language of Protestantism. Luther, it is true, was a Saxon, but John Wickliffe was an ANGLO-Saxon. Calvin was a Frenchman, but William Tyndal was an Anglo-Saxon. The Germans and the French became reformers; but the Anglo-Saxons were the first translators and commenders of the Bible, and of universal Bible-reading. These were the morning star, the rising dawn of the Protestant Reformation. These were the harbingers that pioneered the way and furnished the arms and munitions of that great political and ecclesiastic, as well as spiritual, war.

The very word PROTESTANT implies thought, examination, dissent and self-reliance. Who protests without reflection, comparison, deduction, and some degree of mental independence, as well as of self-reliance? These, too, are verily the elements of all human greatness, of all comparative excellence. The Protestant Reformation, notwithstanding all that can be said against it, was the regeneration of literature, science, art, politics, trade, commerce, agriculture. Hence, the more Protestant a people, the more elevated in all the elements of modern civilization. Self-thinking—pardon the anomalous expression, for there are millions who possess not the art or mystery of self-thinking; when they think, their minds are only listening to some other one thinking, speaking or moving within them—I say SELF-THINKING and SELF-RELIANCE are the two main elements of personal, social, national greatness and goodness. These are the pillars of true religion, true learning, true science, true prosperity, true greatness. By self-thinking and self-reliance, I do not mean confidence in the flesh, pride, self-conceit; I mean the confident application of our minds to the means of intellectual, moral, political and religious improvement, in the hope of improving ourselves and our condition.

Every country, and nation, and people, rise above their contemporaries and competitors, every thing else being equal, in the direct ratio of their Protestantism. Who needs to be informed when he passes out of a Protestant into a Romish community? Every thing he looks at attests the fact. This strikes every man of observation, when he passes out of the Papal into the Protestant cantons of Switzerland; out of Papal Ireland into Protestant Ireland; out of Papal America into Protestant America. Freedom of thought, freedom of speech, mental independence, self-thinking, self-relying, give to Protestant communities a spirit, a character, an elevation, that deeply imprint themselves on all the products of their mind, on all the labors of their hands.

They imprison no one for affirming that stars do not fall; that the earth moves. They exile no one for thinking that there may yet be a new continent, that the number of worlds is incalculable, or that the Pope may err. They put no one to torture or to death for thinking for himself on religion, science or the arts; therefore, they continually progress, and leave far in the distance behind, those who allow or license one man to think for millions, and sternly command acquiescence in his dogmas.

But we have not yet asserted all the claims of our vernacular, nor do we mean to assert them all on this occasion. We limit ourselves to one object. Nor do we wish to institute invidious comparisons between Protestants and Romanists, ourselves and the French, the Germans or the ancient Saxons. They are, in blood and affinity, our nearest relations. We do not plead this cause from vanity or pride, or personal or national interest or honor, but for suffering humanity. The sequel will demonstrate.

We will only add, on this topic, that the stature and structure of our language are gigantic. Its capacity is immense. For strength of frame it has the bone and muscle of the Romans, the Goths and the Saxons. It has the patience and endurance of the German and the Dutch, both High and Low. It partakes of the vivacity of the French, of the genius of the Italian, the wit and sprightliness of the Greek and the Celt. For comprehension, if for nothing else, our language is chief amongst all the dialects of earth. There is nothing written —poetry, philosophy, history, or in the form of literature, ancient or modern—that cannot be translated, body, soul and spirit, into our language. Who of the ancients or moderns, in any one department of science or art, has given to the world an idea that cannot be perspicuously and fully set forth in Anglo-Saxon? But could all our learning now be expressed in Hebrew, Greek, Latin, or any language heretofore spoken by man? Nay, could it all be transferred to any purely Asiatic, African or American tongue now extant? We have been obliged to fabricate a myriad of new words from dead languages, and to form thousands of new combinations of the words of dead and living tongues, to express all our Anglo-Saxon sciences, arts and literature. But we can translate all their learning into our tongue, and do it so perfectly that the translation is fully equal to the original. As some one said of Pope's Homer: "If all records were obliterated, and the chronology of nations lost, a time might come when the wonder would be, whether Pope translated Homer, or Homer Pope;" so might it be said of all the most polished works of the most polished nations of antiquity, when set forth in a good suit of Anglo-Saxon words. As Dryden said of Homer, Virgil and Milton—

> "Three poets, in three distant ages born,
> Greece, Italy and England did adorn;
> The first in loftiness of thought surpass'd;
> The next in majesty, in both the last;
> The force of nature could no further go—
> To make a third, she join'd the former two."

So we may say, with more than equal truth, the "force of nature" has not yet brought forth any tongue equal to our vernacular; and whether she can, is yet a problem to be demonstrated.

There are, indeed, many large and beautiful streams and rivers between the Alleghanies and the Rocky Mountains, wending their courses towards the Valley of the Mississippi, on which are borne the products of millions of acres; but what are these, severally, to the "king of waters," on whose deep current fleets and navies may float, and on whose broad bosom the annual products of whole States and Territories are carried to the ocean? As the Amazon of South America, the Mississippi and the St. Lawrence of North America, to all other streams on this continent, so is the Anglo-Saxon to the dialects and tongues which have ministered to its origin, its structure and vast comprehension.

It is a strange fact in the history of Pagandom, corroborative of what we have said, that while all the conquerors of its constituent nations always gave their religion to the conquered, except in the solitary case of the Jews, the Romans at last received the religion of the nations professing Christianity, whom they had subdued. In that case only, the victors received the religion of the vanquished. So of the languages of the world. In the case of those Pagan nations that vanquished the preceding occupants of both England and Ireland, instead of doing as all other conquerors of nations had done—impose their language on the conquered—they, for once, received the language of the conquered. Now, is it not as strong a proof of the superiority of the language of our ancient Saxon progenitors, as it is of the superiority of Christianity to any form of Paganism, that those ancient invaders of England and Ireland, after giving them laws, condescended to receive from them both language and religion? But it may be alleged, that they received the language of the conquered because that language had in it a religion more evidently true and rational than their own. Grant it, and what follows? THAT OUR RELIGION WILL BE A PASSPORT YET TO OUR LANGUAGE INTO ALL THE NATIONS OF THE EARTH. The probability of this conclusion is just the point I wish to carry in the present address. Thus we gain, rather than lose, by the admission.

Now, as I was led, as I supposed naturally and logically, from the very meagre sketch I have given of the *origin* of our vernacular, to make a few remarks upon its *character*, I am now under the same necessity, to be consistent with myself, and to carry the point all-transcendent and important to my mind, to offer you a few thoughts on the *destiny* of the Anglo-Saxon.

The destiny of our language is to be inferred from the following facts and considerations:

I. From the energy of character of those who speak it.

II. From the number of those who at present speak it, and are likely to speak it, in our own country and in Great Britain.

III. The extent of country now possessed and occupied by the Anglo-Saxon people.

IV. The naval and maritime, all-spreading commercial power of those who speak it.

V. The many great discoveries and improvements made by the Anglo-Saxon people in the sciences and arts of the world, treasured up in that language.

VI. The religion of those who now speak it.

VII. The Anglo-Saxon missionary spirit now pervading all the nations of Christendom.

Here is matter for a volume; but we must despatch these items with comparatively a very few remarks.

First: a few words on the energy of the Anglo-Saxon people. We have only, my highly respected audience, to remind you that the meaning of the name of our father Japheth is ENLARGEMENT and

PERSUASION. Our father's children have never, since the flood, been at rest. They have, in the age of whip and spur, first galloped over the earth, to see how large it was; then they went to sea, to ascertain the countries it contained; then they went to fighting for them; and I have sometimes opined, that, if God had not set them to speaking a language called GIBBERISH, our great-grandfather Japheth, and his seven sons, would long ago have driven Shem and Ham, and all their children, into the sea, and, in the reign of Paganism, have drowned them all. But their energies having been thus restrained, they have busied themselves to make a fortune and a name. A genuine, unsophisticated Yankee, from the centre of New England, if we could ever find him at home, is the best representative and embodiment of a genuine, uncorrupted Anglo-Saxon descendent of Japheth. But it would be easier to find him in Oregon, California, or in Commodore Franklin's Northern Expedition, than to find him where he was born.

And such are his notions, his enterprise, and his success, as to have warranted the late Lord Jeffrey, the founder of the Edinburgh Review, or some of his coadjutors, to say, that he believed if a liberal reward were offered for the best translation of the Septuagint, some Yankee, who did not yet know a Greek letter, would go to work in the Grecian mines of literature, and gain the prize.

Let us, then, contemplate the Island of Great Britain for one or two centuries, as affording a demonstration of Anglo-Saxon energy. She had a small territory—a crowded population. She set them to mining, levelling mountains, digging canals, building highways, erecting cities, walling out the sea, constructing quays, harbors and wharves, building ships, furnishing navies, raising armies, stretching out her arms to Asia, Africa, America; founding new colonies, or attempting to do it, from Nova Zembla to the Cape of Good Hope, from the Ganges to the Oregon, from Newfoundland to New Zealand, from Labrador to the Falkland Isles.

But she lost too much time in travelling on business, and set about devising a more expeditious system. Immediately she moves, with eagle speed, along an iron railway, and traverses the island of Great Britain in a few hours. Next, the ocean is too broad, and voyages too long protracted. She must narrow its width or contract time. Anon the same principle is applied, with equal success, to her packets, and the Atlantic is crossed in a week or ten days. But her thirst for early news increases. Her sons of genius at home and abroad, in England and America, are tributary to her will, and she wings intelligence, not with the wings of a tempest, but with the lightnings of heaven. But the provinces abroad have created work for her people at home, and she needs more operatives to supply them. She needs a generation that will neither eat, nor drink, nor sleep, nor tire; and an Arkwright, in his creative genius, furnishes her with millions of wooden, iron and brazen men, and animates them with steam.

The work is done; old things have passed away; a new age is born. Empires change masters, and invention is tortured to preserve them. Wars must cease, or rage with more fury. The people must be employed. The same passions burn eternally in the human breast, and who can quench them? An agrarian spirit has gone abroad, and who can restrain it? There is a superabundance of energy, but a great deficit of benevolence. Other new settlements must be formed, new outlets for industry must be created, and more security of reward must be guaranteed. Intelligence and virtue must be cultivated and more extensively diffused, that invention and energy may be still further glorified in warding off evil and diffusing new and greater blessings amongst men.

They are at work devising new schemes of diffusing knowledge, competence and contentment, amongst those that plough and those that "guide the shuttle and direct the loom." The gospel, and its philanthropy, alone can dispel the clouds that sometimes lower over the too thickly peopled regions of the old world, in consequence of the too great energy of the Anglo-Saxon race.

But the destiny of the Anglo-Saxon tongue is neither to be estimated nor anticipated merely by the energy of those who speak it. True, indeed, that directly tends to multiply those who must learn it, and to extend the territories over which it must bear rule. But the number of those who now speak it must be taken into the account. This, then, is a second point of inquiry.

There are in North America, it is presumed from the last census, at least twenty-five millions who speak the Anglo-Saxon. I include the British Provinces and the United States, and feel confident that I will be sustained by the census of 1850. There are in England, Ireland and Scotland, twenty-seven millions; and should we add three millions more in all her provinces and new settlements, including those on the ocean, in her ships, navies and armies abroad, we should have thirty millions in her empire—making the aggregate, now speaking the Anglo-Saxon, fifty-five millions. And this, so far as Christian civilization, in any of its forms, is contemplated, is the greatest number of persons speaking one language in the world. In Russia there are fifty-five or sixty millions, subjects of the Autocrat, but they speak forty dialects. In Austria there are thirty-five millions of subjects, but only six millions who speak the German. Other Slavonian dialects are spoken in Austria, Hungary, Poland and Russia.

Our third topic is the extent of territory or country over which the Anglo-Saxon people bear rule. In America we have three millions of square miles, and in British America two millions three hundred thousand square miles—an aggregate of five millions three hundred thousand square miles. The British possessions in India are immense. There is the maritime Bengal, with its Ganges, Burrampooter and Dummoda, containing one hundred thousand square miles; the interior Bahar, intersected by the Ganges, the Coosey and the Soane; the more interior province of Allahabad, containing twenty thousand square miles, bordered by the Neibudda; the provinces of Orissa, the Northern Circars, five provinces on the Bay of Bengal. To this we must add the seacoast Carnatic country, stretching over eight degrees of latitude, intersected with numerous rivers. Besides these, there are the allies of Great Britain; Rajahs of Mysore, Madeira, Tanjore and Travancore, giving more than one hundred millions of our species to the control of the little island of Great Britain, containing only eighty-eight thousand square miles.

In Africa, too, the Anglo-Saxon is spoken. There is the Cape of Good Hope, with its one hundred and twelve thousand square miles of territory, and the colonies of Liberia and Sierra Leone. Then there is another territory, almost equal to all Europe, belonging to Great Britain—Australia, and its circumjacent islands, containing two millions three hundred thousand square miles. Thus giving to Britain, in all, more than six millions square miles, with one hundred and fifty millions of inhabitants. Hence, the Anglo-Saxon people, in the old world and the new, bear rule over some *one-fourth* of all the habitable territory of the globe.

But to this we must add their dominion and power on the rivers, the lakes, the seas and the oceans of the world. Here, by common consent, the Anglo-Saxon race is all-predominant. Their canvas whitens every sea, and is swelled by every breeze. It is no longer Britannia, but Britannia and America, that rule the seas.

The commerce, too, of the Anglo-Saxons, greatly trancends that of any other people on the face of the globe; and of all the elements of national greatness and power, this is chief. Without this great auxiliary, both agriculture and manufactures are comparatively unavailing, in giving power to a people.

Nothing, indeed, contributes more than commerce to extend the language, as well as to increase the wealth and greatness of a people. The commerce of these two countries, internal and external, if I am not mistaken, is some seven times as great as it was at the commencement of the present century; and, from their rapidly increasing creative power, we have much reason to think that it will long continue to increase in similar ratios.

But we must not look merely at the European, American, Asiatic and African territory possessed by the Anglo-Saxons. We must also consider the present unoccupied room on these territories for population, compared with that of any other portions of the habitable globe, and also the well-authenticated ratios of the increase of that population.

On a careful consideration of the most authentic reports on this subject, we confess that we are rather startled at the conclusions which they seem to warrant. The population of England alone, in the first forty years of the present century, doubled, or nearly doubled, itself. In the same time, that of the United States has more than trebled itself. We are aware of all the difficulties attending the different theories of the increase of population; of the errors of Franklin, Malthus, and some other rather visionary speculators on this subject, upon which, of course, we cannot now enter. The means of subsistence, and the labor by which they are acquired, are, indeed, on all hands, agreed to be the most important conditions of its increase. In our own country, therefore, its ratios of increase must inevitably transcend those of any other country on the globe. But still, we dare not think that they will or can continue one century and a half at the present ratio of trebling every forty years; for, in that case, we should have on our Anglo-Saxon portion of America alone, more than double the present population of the globe. For example, say that we are, or will be, in 1850, only twenty-five millions; then, in 1890, we should be seventy-five millions strong. This is, indeed, very reasonably to be expected, from broad views of our condition and that of the civilized world. In forty years more—that is, in A.D. 1930—we should be, on the same ratio, two hundred and twenty-five millions. This is startling, but yet by no means impossible. But in the next forty, or A.D. 1970, we should be six hundred and seventy-five millions. This is too much for either our faith or our hope. And in forty years more —that is, in A.D. 2015—we should be 2025,000,000! But on what could they subsist, unless one-half of them lived on the fish of the sea and the fowls of the air? Our past and present ratios arithmetically give these results. But should we deduct one-half, and give away the

British Isles into the bargain, the Anglo-Saxon race and language would still be—A.D. 6000—a thousand millions strong. Reasoning from the past and present energies, genius and general talents—physical, intellectual and moral—of the Anglo-Saxon people at the end of the current millennium, in the year of the world 6000—now distant only one hundred and fifty years—they must direct and control the energies and the destiny of the world. Come short we may of this aggregate, in the insoluble problem of the increase of population; but if we do, other nations in the old world must, in their relative force, come much further short of their present proportional ratios.

On these premises the tongue of skepticism must falter, and its face turn pale. All must concede to Noah the spirit of inspiration, as well as to the Apocalyptic John. By what other spirit could Noah have said, "God will enlarge Japheth, and he shall dwell in the tents of Shem, and Canaan shall be his servant"? By what other spirit could the Apostle John have foretold the rise, the progress and the fall of empires, and a Christian triumph over all her foes? Neither history nor our own experience, neither reason nor philosophy, can subtract aught from faith in Noah and in John. "If weak thy faith, why choose the harder side?"

But, beyond all the advantages yet named, there is a power in our vernacular to extend itself by other means than natural generation. It is animated by a mighty proselyting spirit and power, arising from the innumerable stores of learning, science, art and new discoveries treasured up in it—the rich behests of Anglo-Saxon genius.

If the Greek and Latin tongues, though dead for ages, have, merely for the sake of their elegant diction and polished style, been studied to the present, in all the schools of Christendom, without any internal spirit or rich veins of science contained within them, to reward the labor of five or seven years' study, how much more our vernacular, full of the soundest learning, the truest science, the richest treasures of salutary intelligence to man! What rich legacy have the Platos, the Socrateses, the Aristotles, of Greek philosophy, bequeathed to the human race, compared with those of a Bacon, a Locke, a Newton? What moral and useful instruction in the poetry of Homer or Hesiod, compared with that of Milton, or Young, or Shakspeare? What has Demosthenean or Ciceronian eloquence achieved for man, more than that of Sheridan, and Burke, and Curran, and Wilberforce, and Webster, and Clay? But where are the Franklins, the Watts, the Fultons, the Arkwrights, or men of that class, to be found amongst Grecian and Roman benefactors? They had a Cincinnatus, it is true, but we have had a Washington. They had a cloud-compelling Jupiter; but we have had a host of air and earth and sea compelling heroes —compelling air, and earth, and water, and fire, and their innumerable elements, to minister to the health, and wealth and happiness of man.

These great revealers and masters of nature have been found in hosts among the Anglo-Saxon race, and almost exclusively among them. These are the great benefactors of man—the great reformers of the world. They have transformed the rugged hills and mountains into Sharon and Carmel; they have made "the wilderness and the solitary place glad," and have compelled "the desert to rejoice and blossom as the rose."

But again: we argue the destiny of the Anglo-Saxon language from the Anglo-Saxon religion. The Anglo-Saxons that conquered and possessed England, were Pagans. But they afterward yielded to the religion of the conquered. They received from Rome the Roman gospel; but the Roman church then gloried, as she yet glories, in being the LATIN church. She still prays and worships in the Latin tongue. But, as before noted, early in the 13th century the Anglo-Saxon Wickliffe was born. He taught that men might read the Bible and pray in Anglo-Saxon. Hence, a controversy arose. It was, in fact, in those days a grave question whether in public worship men might read and pray in Anglo-Saxon, and instead of repeating *Pater noster qui es in cœlis*, they might say, "Our Father who art in heaven."

Wickliffe, like all other innovators, was scoffed at, dishonored and proscribed. Fortunately, however, after his death, the Roman church dug up his bones and burned them; a very striking symbol that he would yet enlighten the world in that identical tongue.* Tyndal was of the same faith, and, to prevent a second similar illumination, crossed the seas, and printed his Anglo-Saxon version on the Continent. Soon after the Anglo-Saxon spirit revived. Then Luther, of Saxony, was born, who, with a pen more puissant than the club of Hercules, entangled the Roman Bull, caught him by the horns, and exorcised him.

* "The bones of Wickliffe were dug out of his grave seventy-five years after his death, and burned for heresy. His ashes were thrown into a river in Warwickshire, on which some prophet of that day said:

The Avon to the Severn runs,
The Severn to the sea;
And Wickliffe's dust shall spread abroad
Wide as the oceans be."

We never can place in more striking contrast the spirit of Luther and the spirit of Papal Rome, than by contemplating, in their symbolic import, his throwing his inkstand at the devil, presuming to terrify him, as he thought; and their digging up and burning the bones of Wickliffe. They intended to extinguish the light and the spirit of Wickliffe; but Luther resolved to write down the evil spirit, by illuminating the world with pen and ink, or by the labors of the press. Hence, after a grand model conception of bringing light out of darkness, he cast his inkstand at the devil and drove him from his cell.

From that day to this the Anglo-Saxon spirit, genius and learning have been, with gigantic strides, advancing and rising in the wonder and admiration of the world. Now, this presuming to read the Bible and to pray in Anglo-Saxon, like our Declaration of Independence, though apparently at first a small matter, like an avalanche, is ever progressing with increasing magnitude and accumulating force, till it has shaken the foundation of the Roman States, and now causes Italy to tremble even to the strongholds of Gaeta.

It is worthy of special notice, that as England began to rise soon after she presumed to dissent from the Latin church, and substituted the Anglo-Saxon church, she has continued to rise in all the elements of greatness, so far as she has advocated an Anglo-Saxon Bible, psalter and prayer book. Although she has not at home yet carried out her principles and professions, still, under it she has gained a transcendent influence over the world, that throws into the shade Austria, France and all other nations and powers that prefer the ecclesiastic Latin to Queen Victoria's English. The Bible translated into all dialects, circulated freely amongst all the people, and read by every one, in whatever version he prefers, is the brightest gem that adorns the coronal of the British queen, and the strength and glory of her august government—the wisest and the most puissant in the old world.

But, finally, we argue the destiny of the Anglo-Saxon tongue from the Anglo-Saxon missionary spirit. This is truly a catholic spirit. It embraces the human race, and knows neither language nor caste according to the flesh. "The frozen Icelander and the sun-burned Moor" are equally embraced and cherished in the generous bosom of its large philanthropy. Britain sends the Bible and the missionary to every island and territory she calls her own. Feigned or unfeigned, political or philanthropic the spirit, the work is done. In accomplishing this, she is strengthening and enlarging her empire, and alluring the world by the moral grandeur of her professed humanity.

But one improvement in her missionary operations is suggested, approbated, and, indeed, tested by the wisest and best of her ambassadors of peace. Instead of depending so much on the labors of missionaries addressing the natives in their own tongues, they are qualifying and sending out school-masters, to instruct the heathen children in the Anglo-Saxon tongue, that they may learn to understand the Anglo-Saxon Bible. This is as sound philosophy as it is genuine philanthropy. It gives to the young an incalculable advantage over the old, and interposes a great barrier between them and their parents, to prevent opposition to what they preach.

We cannot but anticipate its general adoption; and, in that event, who cannot anticipate the spread of the Anglo-Saxon tongue all over the world?

Thus, without indulging in a romantic spirit, we may hope that, as there was at first but one language, there will be at last but one language amongst the sons of Adam. To this, indeed, the pages of prophecy seem to look, when they reveal the glorious fact, that in the day of the triumph of Christianity, there will be acknowledged all over the earth but one Lord. "For," as saith the prophet, "the Lord shall be King over all the earth, and in that day there shall be one Lord, and his name one." "For then," saith another prophet, "I will turn to the people a pure language, that they may all call upon the name of the Lord, to serve him with one consent."

Now, it may be presumed that if "the Lord shall be King over all the earth, and if his name shall be one," and only one; and if all nations are "to serve him with one consent," they will address him in one and the same tongue, and under one and the same name celebrate his lofty praise.

And is not this the tendency of things under the reign of Christ? Already many languages have died. Others are dying. Of the hundreds of ancient American and Asiatic tongues, how many have been absorbed or perished from the earth? And if neither the once boasted universality of the Greek and Roman sceptres and the Greek and Roman tongues, nor the classic beauty and polish of these model languages, could give them perpetuity and extension, what other language can reasonably hope to survive its own nationality, merely from the number or respectability of them who speak it?

Heaven has already frowned on the four great empires claiming universality, because, as we presume, of their unnatural lusts and debasing idolatries. But there are in the Anglo-Saxon tongue elements and treasures of infinite value to mankind; the noblest specimens of Christian genius, learning, science, true religion and pure morality, ever communicated in human speech or treasured up in any dialect spoken by man. Hence we strongly affirm the conviction, that for the sake of these, and in honor of those who, by Bible-translation, Bible-distribution, in all lands and languages, missionary enterprise, missionary zeal, and missionary success in the cause of human advancement and human redemption, the Anglo-Saxon tongue will ultimately triumph. The Lord Almighty, who has now girdled the earth from east to west with the Anglo-Saxon people, the Anglo-Saxon tongue, sciences, learning and civilization, by giving a colossal power and grandeur to Great Britain and the United States over the continents and oceans of earth, will continue to extend that power and magnificence until they spread from north to south, as they have already from east to west, until, in one vernacular, in one language and with one consent, they shall, in loud acclaim and in hallowed concert, raise their joyful and grateful anthem, pealing over all lands and from shore to shore, from the Euphrates to the ends of the earth. Then will "they hang their trumpet in the hall, and study war no more." Peace and universal amity will reign triumphant. For over all the earth there will be but one Lord, one faith, one hope and one language.

But in order to do this, what duties and obligations has the Lord of the universe imposed on us? or what part are we American Anglo-Saxons to act in this great moral revolution?

We must answer this question by taking an inventory of our means of doing good, and of the wants and condition of society at home and abroad; for, while charity begins at home, it does not continue at home, but goes abroad on missions of love and mercy to all mankind. But education, intellectual and moral, at home, in the Sunday-school, in the common school, in the academy, in the college, in the church, are amongst the most obvious, the most important, the most essential, the most puissant means to our advancement—to the filling up of our duties, our usefulness, our glory and our happiness.

God having given to the Anglo-Saxon people the largest portion of the earth vouchsafed to any one people speaking one language and professing one religion; and not only the largest portion of the earth, but the only really new, fruitful and salubrious portions of the earth—indeed, the only portion of it that can, for one hundred and fifty years to come, afford space for a population increasing in the current ratios of Britain and America, to such a point as would either equal the present population of the whole earth, or, at least, certainly place the population of the whole earth under the control of the Anglo-Saxon race, language, politics and religion. For the same purpose he has given to us the great oceans of the globe and the means of managing the seas, as if to furnish us for this great work abroad as well as at home. No event in the future, next to the anticipated millennial triumph, appears more natural, more probable, more practicable or more morally certain and desirable, than this Anglo-Saxon triumph in the great work of human civilization and redemption.

But, in this view of the subject, in what a sublimely grand and fearfully responsible attitude we are placed! To us are the moral destinies of the human race committed. Our horizon is fearfully, gloriously, transcendently extended beyond the conception of any living man. Numerous races and generations of men yet unborn, swarming not only over this grand continent, but over the newly acquired Asiatic possessions of our Anglo-Saxon relations on the old homestead, in Western Europe, are to be moulded, controlled and destined by us.

Becomes it not, then, a most imperious duty to preserve and transmit, uncorrupted and unimpaired, the institutions, civil, literary, moral and religious, which high Heaven has allotted to us? Never before lived a people possessing such birthrights—such an unbounded horizon of greatness and glory—as that which spreads itself before the enraptured vision of every enlightened American citizen. Should the great Anglo-Saxon family of families fall out by the way; should this great nation of nations, this hallowed and august union of so many sovereign and independent States of one political faith, of one rich and noble eclectic language, and of one divinely true and supremely grand religion, be sacrificed at the demon shrine of any sectional idol, then, indeed, would the measure of our disgrace be complete; our folly, our fall, would be an eternal shame—an everlasting reproach—the greatest political and moral catastrophe that time could record, involving, in its details, all the vital and grand interests, temporal, spiritual and eternal, not of our country only, but of the whole human race. IT CANNOT BE! Grant it, then, it cannot be. But should we not stand so far aloof from even the appearance of it, as not to encourage a single hope in any tyrant's breast that we, too—a living refutation of all the pretensions and claims of absolutism, as now displayed in the mouldering and tottering thrones of the old world—will yet subscribe its creed, recant our errors, and reconstruct the despotisms of the old world? Let us regard ourselves, and teach our children to regard themselves, as God's own depository of all the great blessings of civilization and salvation for the new world, and as his co-operants with all the master-spirits on the eastern continent, with every nation and people who will accept our aid in the great work of disenthralling, evangelizing, redeeming and ennobling mankind. Let us teach them that we regard it our greatest honor to have deposited with us blessings so numerous, so various and so grand, and that we esteem it to be our greatest glory to be faithful in the high and holy trust.

ADDRESS

ON THE

AMELIORATION OF THE SOCIAL STATE.

LOUISVILLE, KY.

Ladies and Gentlemen:—

It is not always that the *subject* and the *object* of an address can be made to harmonize. The good of the state, or the glory of God, has been the subject of many a speech; while, alas! too often the object has been the speaker's own.

In popular addresses, my predilections are generally on the side of having the subject and the object to agree. On the present occasion, therefore, after considerable indecision, I have chosen the AMELIORATION OF THE SOCIAL STATE as the *subject;* and, however I may succeed in my endeavors, I do assure you that it is the *object* of my present address.

There is also, I am happy to think, a congruity between my subject and the object of the association at whose solicitation I have the honor, on this occasion, to appear before you. The object of that course of lectures, of which this is but the introductory one, as it is of the gentlemen who have volunteered in this cause, is, the improvement of the social condition of man. They have very justly decided that an elevation of the standard of intellectual and moral excellence would be eminently conducive to a higher cultivation and refinement of the social feelings of our nature, and, consequently, to the amelioration of the social state. In pursuance of these views and convictions, they have instituted this series of addresses—not so much, perhaps, to enlighten your understandings, as to enlist your affections, and secure your efforts in the noblest and most benevolent of human undertakings—the positive advancement of the moral conditions of our social existence.

But the term *society* is somewhat vague, and the thing itself covers an area as variegated and diverse as it is immense. Society is not the mere juxtaposition of ten, or ten thousand persons; it is, in its full comprehension, the union of a simple plurality, or of a multitude, or of the human race in all common interests. It is not the local or personal nearness of those who may inhabit the same city, the same village, the same house, the same room, (for these often have as much society with their antipodes as with one another;) but it is the union, communion and copartnery of a few, or of the whole race with one another, in all that is human and divine in our nature.

But we sometimes speak of society in a less strict and philosophic sense. We use the term as commensurate with the term community, the entire population of a given district—those united in mere local and political interests. Such masses of our species are frequently styled societies only in reference to some two or three general interests, which may be as diverse from one another as the countries and the climates which they inhabit. There is, indeed, in our nature, such a tendency to assimilation, that those societies which inhabit the same quarter of the globe, or have any the least intercourse with one another, do, in process of time, exhibit such points of common resemblance as easily to distinguish them from those who seldom or never have any intercourse with them. Hence those prominent differential attributes of Asiatic, African, European and American societies.

Society, indeed, even in reference to these more prominent points of common interest, is continually in motion, in transition from one state to another, insomuch that in a few centuries the inhabitants of the same country differ from their ancestors in their interests, manners, customs and social rites, as much as the child differs from the sage, or the natives of Nova Zembla from those of the Cape of Good Hope. When, however, we speak of an amelioration of the social state, we have not exclusive reference to that little community of which we may happen to be a component part; but to that great community of communities which fills up the whole circle of our national intercourse. And for our encouragement in the work of amelioration, it is an exhilarating truth that no person's influence is necessarily limited to that society in which he moves. Individuals have often, through their immediate society, acted upon other societies, and have thus extended their influence from city to city, and from nation to nation, to the utmost extent of an extensive empire. In this way it came to pass that Aristotle, the philosopher of Stagira, Plato of Athens, Paul of Tarsus, and Luther of Saxony, have stamped their image not only upon their own city, their own country or generation, but upon nations and empires for an indefinite series of ages.

But it would be necessary to the full completion of our purpose, and it would be as curious as it is necessary, to contemplate society both *as it was*, and *as it now is*, in some given district, with special reference to what it *ought to be* in regard to the entire demands of human nature in its best attainable state in this world. This, indeed, in all its amplitude, would be a sweep by far too large for a single address. For the sake of a few facts and documents as data, we must, however, glance, very briefly indeed, at the causes that have conspired in giving to modern Europe and to these United States their present civilization, their present superiority over their more remote ancestors, and over all other portions of the human race.

The present state of society in this commonwealth, in the United States, in England, in Europe, in the world, is the effect of a thousand causes, both co-operative and antagonist, the history of which it is impossible to trace. These causes, first hidden in the deep and unexplored recesses of human nature, work for a time, as the secret fires under the mountains, unnoticed, unobserved, till on some favorable crisis they produce a shaking, an earthquake, a revolution; then, and only then, they impress themselves upon the observation of man, excite his admiration, call forth his philosophy, and direct his energies into correspondent action. Such, indeed, have been all the primary causes, facts and events that have conspired and amalgamated in the present improvements of European and American society. But as the geographer sees not the atoms that compose the mountains which he describes, so the historian perceives not that infinity of little facts, feelings, motives, actions, which co-operated and combined in one of those grand and prominent facts or events which he records. His task it is to trace these minor agencies who would understand the mysteries of human revolutions from civilization to barbarism, and again from barbarism to civilization.

The fall of the Roman Empire, the last of the four imperial Pagan despotisms, was indeed an awfully sublime and transcendent fact, and essentially connected with the state of society in the city of Louisville at this very moment. But who can trace with persuasive accuracy to the original fountains that memorable series of stupendous revolutions which, in little more than thirteen centuries, broke to atoms that "splendid fabric of human greatness"? Who can trace every little rill, and brook, and stream and river that swelled the current of that mighty flood which swept from the earth those colossal monuments of human genius, science, art and enterprise?

The historian faithfully records that wonderful succession of triumphs which, in seven full centuries, raised the municipality of Rome —a single city—to be the mistress of the world. He records, with admiration, the profound policy of its senate, the emulation of its consuls, the valor and heroism of its soldiers, which subjected to the imperial sceptre of Augustus that immense region reaching from the Euphrates on the east to the Atlantic on the west, and from the Rhine and the Danube on the north to the sandy deserts of Arabia and Africa on the south. He tells also of its further extension in the first century—of the conquest of Dacia, of Britain, even to the Highlands of Scotland, and of provinces beyond the Tigris and the Euphrates in the East.

As faithfully he records the grand facts that hastened its decline and precipitated its fall; the disastrous defeats which, in rapid succession, humbled its pride and ultimately left scarce a vestige of its former strength and glory. But, in doing all this, how many occult causes are unobserved; how many secret facts are untold; how many fortuitous but concurring agencies are unnoticed; how many recondite workings of the human heart are never known, which, though not the immediate, were nevertheless the true and active sources of all that is told by the historian, or commented on by the philosopher!

Notwithstanding these difficulties in our way to comprehend the phenomena of many of the acts in the great drama of states and empires; of the revolutions and counter-revolutions of society; he who would understand the past, or anticipate the future, by looking minutely into all that is written, examining and comparing the actors and the actions, and reasoning from the facts passing before him in his daily converse with himself and his fellows, may have a general and a correct, though not a complete, knowledge of the remote and proximate causes of the overthrow and ruin of the ancient states, as well as of the elements and forces that have given, as their natural and proper result, the present society in which we are all so deeply and so necessarily interested.

Our American society is the result of Spanish, German, French and English civilization—that is, the result of European civilization—that is, the consequence of the downfall of the Roman Empire, itself originally composed of the most civilized and improved portions of Asia, Africa and Europe: that fall was the effect of the incursions of those immense swarms of Northern barbarians, which, like a torrent from the mountains, rolled, wave after wave, over the whole face of the Roman Empire, from the banks of the Danube to the shores of the Atlantic, and placed itself in whole nations in the finest portions of the subjugated lands of the Western Empire.

Now, he who would possess just and comprehensive views of American society—of that singular compound of race, of genius and of character which now individualizes, distinguishes and elevates the American family—must not only begin with the decline and fall of the Roman Empire, but he must push his inquiries to the ancient lands of the Huns, the Goths, the Vandals, the hundred tribes and nations of ancient Germany and Asiatic Scythia; he must visit the plains beyond the Oxus and the Jaxartes; he must go to Mount Caucasus, and trace the meanderings of a hundred rivers, along plains five thousand miles in length and one thousand in breadth, before he finds the germs of his own greatness—the root and origin of his own family—and the causes of the political institutions, manners and customs of his own country. This, indeed, is a work as far beyond the ambition as it is beyond the means and opportunities of a vast majority of our contemporaries.

Monsieur Guizot, one of the ablest of the statesmen of France—one of the wisest of her philosophers—in his recent general history of the civilization of modern Europe, a work of great erudition and of thrilling interest, in tracing the immediate elements of European society, commences with the fall of the Roman Empire. He finds the rudiments of all European institutions and improvements in a few great facts, of which he speaks with great familiarity and precision. From Rome he supposes we have got the archetypes of all our municipal and imperial ideas. From the barbarians that destroyed it and located themselves within its bounds, we have got our greatest polish—our ideas of liberty, independence and loyalty.

Modern civilization, according to this historian, was, at its origin and throughout its whole history, "diversified, agitated and confused." At the beginning of the fifth century he has found "Municipal society, Christian society, Barbarian society;" these three agonizing in the same field, and struggling for the ascendant. To use his own words: "We find these societies very differently organized, founded upon principles totally opposite, inspiring men with sentiments altogether different. We find the love of the most absolute independence by the side of the most devoted submission; military patronage by the side of ecclesiastic domination; spiritual power and temporal power everywhere together: the canons of the church—the learned legislation of the Romans—the almost unwritten customs of the barbarians—everywhere a mixture, or rather co-existence, of nations, of languages, of social institutions, of manners, of ideas, of impressions the most diversified."

To the confusion, the tossings and jostlings of these elements, he assigns the slow progress of Europe, the storms by which she has been buffeted, and the miseries to which she has often been a prey. These, however, are with him the real elements of European civilization.

Like a mass of heterogeneous ingredients thrown into the same vessel, by their intestine motion, their antagonistic operations, the soft and more ethereal particles rareified and subtilized ascend, while the grosser and more feculent materials sink to the bottom and leave the pure liquor to be drawn off by itself; so these remains of ancient society, thrown together into the European chaldron, worked, fermented, effervesced, till, drawn off in various casks, the new wine of European civilization is found in many nations, and still greatly improved by being shipped across the Atlantic and racked off into so many sovereign and independent States.

The ruling passion and principle of Roman society was the city corporation—the municipal mode of life. Indeed, the Roman Empire, first, midst and last, was but a confederacy of cities. Ancient Italy alone contained eleven hundred and ninety-seven cities; Gaul boasted of twelve hundred; Spain, of three hundred and sixty; three hundred African cities at one time acknowledged the authority of Carthage; and in the time of the Cæsars, Asia Minor alone counted five hundred populous cities. Here are but five members of the Roman Empire, a mere fraction of its territory, containing three thousand five hundred and fifty-seven cities. On the other hand, the conquerors of Rome came from the immense plains of Scythia, or from the deep and dense forests of ancient Germany—wandering tribes—nations in camps, whose delights were the wild mountains, the deep valleys, the extended plains, the mighty rivers, the ocean's roar, the tented fields, the forest chase, unbounded freedom, the independence of unmeasured tracts of land. In the beginning of the fifth century the Christian religion had been corrupted into a hierarchy—it had become a state engine; it had, therefore, lost its spirit, its purity, its original power; yet, as an ecclesiastic institution, it had power over the empire, conquered its conquerors, and was, beyond doubt, the most puissant element of the new compound.

Such was the crisis of the dissolution of the Roman Empire, and such was the commencement of the new process. In Europe was then found the democratic, the aristocratic, the monarchical, the imperial, the despotic, the theocratic principle at work, in proximity, in amalgamation, in compromise and in strife, struggling for precedency. Violence ruled the day. There was no legitimacy but might! All claimed something else—antiquity, priority, reason, justice, right; yet it actually was *might* that gave *right* to all.

For some six or seven centuries the territory of the ancient Roman Empire was one immense wreck—a perfect chaos—"a universal jumble:" nothing was permanent, nothing systematic: the Koran and the sword in the East; the Roman hierarchy, legitimacy and persecution, feudalism, despotism, anarchy, mutation, in the West; freemen, fideles, freedmen, and slaves, made up the four chief masses of the new nations. But all was in motion; "no man continued long in the same rank; no rank continued long the same." Every thing triumphs in its turn: feudalism triumphs, the church triumphs, monarchy triumphs, the right of compulsion in religion triumphs, the amalgamation of spiritual and temporal power in the same hands triumphs, barbarism triumphs. Again, free cities rise, charters rise, new classes rise, central government and the centralization system rise in public esteem,—Peter the Hermit is born,—the Crusades are planned,—all Europe for the first time sympathizes—the spirit of the recovery of the holy sepulchre, the deliverance of the holy city, inspires all Europe, animates all classes, kings and beggars, church and state, savage and civilized. Millions of men and money are put in motion; immense armies are raised, commanded by kings in person; a hundred years scarce quench the fervors of this holy war. But it finally expired. The Koran and the scimetar were too strong for an imagination and a mad impulse, or rather the spirit of the age had changed; the causes, moral and social, that had thrown Europe into Asia ceased to exist; new views, new feelings, new objects, seized the European minds. During the Crusades the laity had been too often in Rome; they had seen too much of the character of their own priesthood, the nakedness of the land appeared, the selfish and worldly spirit of their own pastors in contrast with those of the Turks astonished them. Their newly acquired knowledge inspired them with a freedom of thought, a boldness hitherto unknown in Europe, their souls were enlarged, "more political freedom and more political unity characterized the subsequent age." The compass —printing and gunpowder—the Lutheran reformation and the English revolution, changed the entire aspect of society in those countries that gave the original nucleus of American society.

"The history of European society may be thrown," says Guizot, "into three great periods: first, a period which I shall call that of *origin* or *formation*, during which the different elements of society disengage themselves from chaos, assume an existence, and show themselves in their native forms, with the principles by which they are animated: this period lasted till almost the twelfth century. The second period is a period of experiments, attempts, groping: the different elements of society approach and enter into combinations, feeling each other, as it were, without producing any thing general, regular, or durable: this state of things, to say the truth, *did not terminate till the sixteenth century.* Then comes the period of development, in which human society in Europe takes a definite form, follows a determinate direction, proceeds rapidly and with a general movement towards a clear and precise object: this is the period which began in the sixteenth century and is now pursuing its course."

After this general—alas! too general—sketch of the progress of social improvement, you will perhaps be curious to know the opinion of so eminent a philosopher and historian as to the present state of civilization in the most polished nations in Europe—in the world. It is an opinion in which I cordially concur—an opinion in which many of the greatest and most cultivated minds acquiesce. It is this:—

"*Society and civilization are yet in their childhood.* However great the distance they have advanced, that which they have before them is incomparably, is infinitely greater." Thus speaks one who, as he imagines, lives at "the centre, at the focus of the civilization of Europe;" who has made himself intimately acquainted with its past history, and with its present condition.

Ladies and gentlemen, after such a declaration you will, perhaps, expect from me a definition of this term; you will ask, What is meant by *civilization?* Our historian regards civilization as a *fact;* "two circumstances are necessary to its existence—it lives upon two conditions—it reveals itself by two symptoms—the progress of society—the progress of individuals—the amelioration of the social system, and the expansion of the mind and faculties of man. Wherever the exterior condition of man becomes enlarged, quickened, improved, and wherever the intellectual nature of man distinguishes itself by its energy, its brilliancy and its grandeur, wherever these two signs concur—and they often do so, notwithstanding the greatest imperfections in the social system—there man proclaims and applauds civilization." So says our philosopher.

But, perhaps, for some minds it may be too abstruse—the definition is more unintelligible than the term itself. Well, we shall contrast civilization with barbarism. Savages of all ages, it is agreed, have a common character. Two demons divide the empire of the savage heart—*selfishness* and *terror:* lust, hatred and revenge minister to the former; while credulity, superstition and cruelty attend upon the latter. The description given of our savage ancestors, the Huns, the Goths, the Scythians, the Scandinavians, that overran all Europe, from the Caspian Sea to the Thames, admirably illustrates the savage character, and demonstrates these simple but strong passions, variously combined and excited by surrounding circumstances, to be the true criteria of barbarism. Now, as we recede from these we advance in civilization.

Civilization is not, therefore, merely intellectual culture, refinement of taste, high advances in criticism, eloquence, philosophy; nor is it eminence in the fine arts of poetry, music, painting, sculpture, architecture. The Greeks and Romans equalled, if not excelled us far, in most of these attainments; yet, compared with many of this community, they were an uncivilized and barbarous people. They lived and died under the tyranny of selfishness and terror. Their amusements, their exhibitions, their amphitheatres, their gladiator feats and pastimes were cruel, inhuman—full of lust, hatred and revenge. In fact, man, fully civilized, is wholly rescued from the tyranny of selfishness, lust, hatred, revenge, terror, cruelty, credulity and superstition. Till this is accomplished, society has not reached that intellectual, benevolent, pacific, moral and blissful goal, to which it has been advancing, with slow but steady pace, since the commencement of the sixteenth century.

Man is fully civilized when all the powers of his animal, intellectual, moral and religious nature are fully developed in subordination to his ultimate and eternal destiny; and society is perfectly civilized when all the members of it, in their respective places, stations and conditions, fully receive and reciprocate all the genuine feelings and expressions of benevolence, brotherly-kindness and charity, dictated by a refined sensibility and guided by an enlarged and cultivated understanding.

Thus, by a long and circuitous route, I have arrived at the main subject of my address. I now especially invite your attention to the influence of woman and of the Bible in carrying forward the begun amelioration of the social state.

There are two facts pretermitted, two powers unappreciated, by Monsieur Guizot and by all writers on civilization known to me. These are the two superlative agencies in the amelioration of the social state; they are woman and the Bible; or if any pleases to make but one out of two, it is *the Bible in the hand and heart of woman.*

I admit that the philosopher gives great power to the church, and makes it the chief element of European civilization. But with him it has not more power than the Koran and the Mosque among the

Moslems; or the temples, altars and priests among the Pagans. The hallowed fanes among the Druids, the altars among the Pagans, and the Mosque among the Mohammedans, have led the way in their civilization quite as much as the church of Rome in the dark ages has led the way in ours. Nevertheless I concur with our philosophic historian in giving to the church the precedence in all that appertains to our civilization: for I am persuaded that take that element out of his own compound agencies, and we would have all been barbarians still. But I mean more than the Church as defined by him, when I speak of woman and the Bible. Permit me then to explain myself.

Woman, with me, is to society what the spirit is to the body; for as the body without the spirit is dead, society without woman is dead also. She is then the quickening, animating, conservative element of society. If man on this terraqueous ball be the glory of God, most certainly woman is the glory of man. She is the life, the beauty, the ornament, the glory of society. What a simple, powerful and sublime preface has God written to the volume of her history! "It is not good," said he, "that man should be alone;" and instantly out of his side, and by his side, stood blooming, smiling, lovely woman. Never was any being more appropriately named than this woman. She is called *Eve,* which in our own language is equivalent to her being called *life.* And Adam called her *life,* because she is the mother of all living. She is then the fountain and source of society.

Now, her intellectual and moral culture, her elevation to her own proper rank, which is not to sit at the *foot,* but to stand by the *side,* of man, is of supreme importance to the State, to the Church, to the world, and to the amelioration of the social system. But this subject has never yet taken hold of the head, the heart or the hand of man in the ratio of its importance; because, perhaps, the power of woman for good or evil, for weal or for woe, has not yet appeared in its full proportions to the mental vision of even the sages and the learned of our race. She is, indeed, in some points of view, rightly called "the weaker vessel" of the twain; but in this her weakness are found some of the main springs of her power.

It is essential to our argument, so far as the logic of it is concerned, that we first form a clear and definite idea of *the power of woman.* But how shall this be done convincingly? Not by reasoning hypothetically nor speculatively, but inductively. As we find out the power of any agent in nature, so learn we the power of woman. The power of electricity, of the tempest, of the flood, is seen in their effects; the power of woman is seen and felt in her deeds—I do not say in her *good* deeds only, but in her *bad* deeds also; for she, too, as well as man, has some bad deeds. Still, it is fair logic to infer the power of doing good, from her power of doing evil; and in placing this matter before you, ladies and gentlemen, you will allow me to avail myself of a fair specimen of female achievements both on the side of virtue and of vice.

It is not necessary that we examine the whole history of the sex to be convinced of the potency of woman. The first melancholy proof, and perhaps as striking a proof as universal history affords, of the power of woman is found at the close of the first act of the great drama of human existence—she persuaded her husband to rebel against his God. Adam seems to have been so perfectly fascinated by her charms and bewitched by her blandishments, as to have lost both his reason and his loyalty at the moment that she stretched out her enchanting hand to his lips. "He was not deceived" by the serpent, as Paul affirms. May we not thence infer that he was allured and captivated by his wife? How unspeakably great, then, was that power which overcame man in the glory of his strength and prostrated his understanding and his resolution in the very presence of the pledge of inevitable ruin!

Since that moment of triumph of Satan over woman, and of woman over man, who can tithe the spoils of history, or form even a miniature view of her power over human destiny? She never had any pretensions to physical superiority over man—to physical equality; but really some of the brightest triumphs of genius, of intellect, of contrivance, of policy, of the arts both of peace and of war, that brighten the annals of human greatness, and throw a halo of glory over our nature, are found in the memoirs of woman.

In the first two thousand years of human history, and in all the sacred records of twenty centuries, the names of but five women, good or bad, have escaped the general wreck and oblivion of ancient times. Of these five, Eve, the mother of all living, is the first; and Sarah, the mystic mother of all the faithful, is the last. Her faith and her virtues, her conjugal affection and devotion, not only overcame the course of nature itself, and gave to her husband and the world "the child of promise," but also furnish one of the most perfect models of domestic excellence, of maternal worth and of female complaisance which sacred history affords. Why there should have been so great silence from Adam to Moses of the sayings and doings of woman, is only to be explained on the hypothesis that the dark shade which in an evil hour her folly had entailed upon herself, her husband and posterity, seems to have fallen upon her own history for almost one-third the whole flight of time. The influence of woman is, indeed, a second time adduced in the annals of the antediluvian world; but there, alas! it is in unison with a second catastrophe of human kind—a second witness, but too strictly accordant with the first, that woman's power in doing evil, in congenial circumstances, is not easily exaggerated. "The sons of God," says the divine historian Moses, a heavenly style for the faithful of all ages,—"the sons of God intermixed with the daughters of men," making their beauty, without regard to moral excellence, the supreme attraction; till the world was filled with personal combat, murder and rapine, (all couched in the word violence,) and became, even to the long-suffering of Heaven, intolerably wicked. This state of things superinduced that tremendous deluge whose monuments are stereotyped in the deep valleys and on the lofty mountains that diversify the four quarters of the globe.

Opening the postdiluvian pages of sacred and profane history, we are, indeed, occasionally furnished with a bright display of feminine power, culminating over the highest summits of masculine ambition. In ascending the stream of Assyrian history almost to its fountain, we see the memory of her greatness, engraven on the proudest trophies of human grandeur. Do we commence our inquiries with the first and most magnificent of earthly empires—the Assyrian?—we shall find her mighty deeds contemporaneous with its origin. Who laid the foundation of mighty Babylon, the city of eternal fame, the wonder of the world—the metropolis of that gigantic empire that stretched from the fountains of the Tigris and the Euphrates to the oceans of the East and of the West—that mighty emipre that withstood the tossings of a thousand tempests, the swellings of angry seas, the tumults of incensed and impassioned multitudes for more than fourteen hundred years—who before the Macedonian hero led an army of three and a half millions of troops across the Indus to extend her dominions in the East, and for the long term of forty years gave laws to the fairest and best portions of the human race? I say, do we put these questions to the historians of ancient times? They give us the name of Semiramis, the widow of the founder of Nineveh, the Queen of the Queens of the East. In the life and achievements of this peerless heroine of fortunes so various and splendid, though ultimately disastrous, we discover faculties as enlarged, policies as profound, energy as unbounded, perseverance as untiring, courage as dauntless, ambition as towering, as ever distinguished an Assyrian, Persian or Grecian chief.

But if woman have power to create and raise up families, cities, states and empires, she has power to destroy them. Thus, if Babylon rose, Troy fell, by a woman. The ill fortunes and overthrow of the Trojan commonwealth are as intimately associated in fame with the beauty and perfidy of Helen, as are the rise and glory of Babylon with the intrepidity, energy and varied talents of Semiramis. I am of opinion that there never was a nation, a state or an empire—not even an administration, save that of General Jackson—that was not more or less reared or ruined, strengthened or weakened, controlled or managed, by the policy, the skill or the dexterity of woman.

Should any one doubt this opinion, let him examine the records of the Assyrian, Persian, Grecian, Roman or modern European women; he will find there were other Rebeccas, Miriams, Deborahs, Delilahs, Jaels, Jezebels, Athaliahs, Esthers, Herodiases, than those written in sacred history. Should he wish for a few samples of the dark as well as the bright side of the picture, let him contemplate the deeds of vengeance, barbarity and general inhumanity of Amestris, wife of the Persian Xerxes. Her demand at a royal banquet for the wife of Masistus, and her treatment of that woman, in more points than one, resembles that of the vengeful Herodias towards John the Harbinger. Let him consider the workings of jealousy and ambition in the bloody and horrible deeds of the queen mother of Cyrus. Let him examine the confederated strength of these evil passions in the proceedings of Queen Parysites, both sister and wife of Darius Nothus, towards the no less cruel Queen Statira, daughter of Darius II. A bear robbed of her whelps was milder far than Queen Parysites towards those who were accessory to the slaughter of Cyrus, her son. Let him read, if he can without inexpressible horror, her cruelties to a Carian soldier, to Mithridates, to Mesabates, consummated in the murder of her own daughter-in-law, the beautiful but cruel and murderous Queen Statira.

And should he wish for a perfect sample of all this category of attributes, we would refer him to the history and fortunes of the Egyptian Queen Cleopatra, the ninth of that name distinguished in ancient history. This celebrated woman far excelled all her contemporaries in the rarest assemblage of extraordinary endowments and splendid crimes; possessing wit, imagination, genius, in no ordinary measures, superlative in beauty of person, in all the bewitching blandishments of elegant manners, in all the captivating arts of fascination, she was the slave of passion, vain, deceitful, ambitious, tyrannical, cruel. Under all her unrivalled charms was concealed a demoniacal heart, full of malignant passions, stratagems, plots, amours, murders, suicide. She permitted herself to be carried into the presence of Julius Cæsar that she might subdue him by her charms. She did so. She also beguiled and ruined the unfortunate Anthony. Her voyage to Tarsus is one of the most pompous and glittering pageants in ancient history. It is said that the stern of her ship flamed with gold, its sails were purple, its oars inlaid with silver. Her pavilion on deck was of golden cloth, in which she sat robed like Venus, surrounded by the most beautiful virgins of her court, some representing the Nereiades, and others the Graces; instead of trumpets were heard flutes, hautboys, harps and innumerable instruments, warbling the softest airs, to which the oars kept time and completed the harmony; perfumes smoked upon the deck; while the banks of the river, lined with countless multitudes of spectators, gave to the spectacle a brilliancy and pomp never surpassed. The end of this voyage was to captivate the heart of Anthony, in which she was, for him, alas! too successful. She boasted to Anthony that she could spend a million of livres at a single supper. This, indeed, she wellnigh did, by snatching from one of her ears the costliest pearl in the world, worth about that incredible sum, and casting it into a cruse of vinegar, dissolved it, and thus drank the health of the grandson of Cicero, one of the triumvirate of Rome.

The Romans, indeed, always acknowledged the mighty sway of woman. Faustina, daughter of the pious Antonine, celebrated for her beauty and gallantries, so ruled her husband Marcus, that he not only elevated her lovers to the highest honors, but also so influenced the Senate as to declare her a goddess, and, with the attributes of Juno, Venus and Ceres, to have divine honors paid to her in her temples.

Julia Mæsa, by her genius and her largesses, raised her grandson, the execrable Bassianus, sometimes called Antoninias, but better known by the name of Elagabalus, a Syrian by birth, first to be the High-Priest of the Sun, and next to be the Emperor of Rome. After he had careered the dark and dismal race of every folly, and covered himself with the infamy of every monstrous deed that could disgrace humanity, murdered by his own indignant prætorians and cast into the Tiber, she still had the address to raise her second grandson by another mother to the imperial throne; and placed Alexander Severus on the list of Roman Emperors, while his mother Mamæa really empired over Rome.

But lest we should seem to draw from the records of Pagan times too many proofs of woman's ill-fated empire over the destiny of man, before we open the annals of modern Europe we shall give another and a somewhat different picture of female greatness, in the person of the Queen of Palmyra, pupil of "the Sublime Longinus," well skilled in the Latin, Greek, Syriac and Egyptian tongues.

After avenging the murder of her husband, Zenobia herself filled the vacant throne, and, with the most manly counsel, governed Palmyra, Syria and the East for five years. The Roman Senate for a time in vain attempted to curb her power; she repulsed their general, and sent him back to Rome alike denuded of his army and his fame. Arabia, Armenia and Persia solicited her alliance. To the dominions of her husband by her prudence she added the populous and fertile kingdom of Egypt.

But the Emperor Aurelian with an immense army invaded Asia, and decided the fortunes of the Queen of the East in two hard-fought battles. Besieged at last in her own beautiful city of Palmyra, renowned for its splendid temples, palaces and porticos of Grecian architecture, she was compelled to yield, not by capitulations, but by flight—she was carried to Rome a splendid trophy of Aurelian's good fortune and valor. On entering the city, as Gibbon relates, "the beauteous figure of Zenobia was confined by fetters of gold, a slave supported the gold chain which encircled her neck, and she almost fainted under the intolerable weight of jewels. She preceded on foot the magnificent chariot in which she once hoped victoriously to have entered the gates of Rome." So fades the glory of this world. She was, indeed, treated honorably by the emperor, who, because of his admiration of her splendid talents and public virtues, presented her with a beautiful villa on the bank of the Tiber, about twenty miles from Rome, where the Syrian queen insensibly sunk into a Roman matron. Her daughters married into noble families, and her race continued till the fifth century.

But what shall I say of the illustrious women of modern Europe, whose noble deeds, whose splendid follies, whose heroic achievements, whose mighty genius or whose public virtues have thrown a lustre on almost all the principal kingdoms of Europe? Time would fail me to tell of Margaret, Queen of Denmark, the Semiramis of the North, mistress of three kingdoms—of Margaret of Valois, mother of Henry IV., an authoress, a poetess, a queen—of another Margaret, mother of Henry VII., a patroness of learning, a founder of two colleges, although allied and related to thirty kings and queens, who spent her leisure hours not in courtly pastimes, but in translating from the French such pious books as A Kempis on Imitating Christ—of Maria Theresa, Empress Queen of Hungary, daughter of Charles VI., whose brilliant achievements and whose varied fortunes astonished Europe for forty years—of her daughter Marie Antoinette, Archduchess of Austria and Queen of France, wife of the unfortunate Louis. Voluptuous and criminal, her prodigality and bad counsels, opposing the convocation of the States, terminated in her own ruin and in that of her husband king, and precipitated the reign of terror—the triumph of atheism in France.

I again repeat, time would fail me to tell of the Catharines of France and Russia—the Elizabeths, the Marys, the Annes of England, and a thousand other noble and illustrious names. But I will be asked, Why enumerate so many of regal dignity, of high and elevated place, of illustrious fortune, in exemplifying the power of woman? Because, I answer, amongst these we have the best educated of the sex—those invested with the most ample means of showing off to advantage the leading attributes of female character, and those whose deeds are best known in human history. How much more familiar to the million are Josephine, Maria Louisa, Anne Boleyn, Joan of Arc, Lady Jane Grey and the present Victoria, than females of less conspicuous station!

To know the force of character of any individual, he must be placed in a position on a theatre where he has room to act his part fully. Few persons ever know themselves or their most intimate friends and relatives, because of the want of opportunity of developing themselves. If a prophet foretold our future exploits, more than Hazael would exclaim, "Is thy servant a dog, that he should do such a deed?" One reflection forces itself upon us while these premises are present. Had the females above named enjoyed as much *moral* as intellectual culture, and been as much under the government of the moral sentiments, as they were under the control of animal passions, how different from what it now is, might have been the fortunes and the character of the world at this hour!

But there are four aspects which I shall henceforth call *the four cardinal points* of woman, in which she must be contemplated before her all-controlling influence in society can be duly appreciated, especially her power of doing good. There is no need now-a-days to talk of her talents, nor of her susceptibilities of the most polished intellectual and moral culture. These are no longer matters of doubtful disputation. Notwithstanding the defects in her education, (and, till recently, they were neither few nor small,) she has not merely occasionally, but in fact often, astonished, dazzled, delighted us with the rich and varied resources of her genius, the splendid efforts of her understanding, the finished productions of her taste. She has gathered laurels on Mount Parnassus and wreaths of flowers on Mount Helicon. She has sat in the cells of the philosophers, and walked in the groves of the Academies, and strewed all her paths with flowers of the sweetest odors and of the most beauteous tints.

We need not go back to the days of Aspasia, whose genius in poetry and romance Socrates himself, with all his philosophic gravity, could not but admire; nor to the time of Sappho, the poetess of Mytilene, almost coeval with Rome, whose delicious effusions and richly varied odes obtained for her the honors of the tenth muse. Nor need we call up the memory of Corinna and her fifty books of epigrams, to show what gifts Pallas, Apollo and Mercury have bestowed on woman. Our own times, alike removed from the ages of superstition and of romance, furnish clearer, more striking, richer and more varied examples, not merely of her power to attain to eminence, but of her successful competition in general literature, science, and in the fine arts of poetry, music, painting, and of living well.

I need not speak of the celebrity of Miss Edgeworth as a writer of moral tales; of Miss Baillie as a tragedian; of Madame de Staël as a miscellaneous writer of much wit and vivacity; of Miss Martineau as a tourist; of Mrs. Bowdler as a moralist; and of Miss Sedgwick as a moral instructor. These are not our best models of female excellence even in the didactic art. Nor need I refer to the celebrity of Mrs. Hemans, now commensurate with English literature; nor to that of Mrs. Sigourney, commensurate with our own; nor to the miscellaneous and moral productions of Mrs. Hannah More, or Miss Beecher, all excellent in their kind. These are becoming as familiar in our country as weekly visitors or household words. They, indeed, are all honorable vouchers of what woman might be under a more philosophic, rational and moral system of education; and, together with a thousand names of equal renown, show that the female mind only needs the proper appliances of good education to shine with a lustre, on a general scale, transcending far the humble standards fixed for it in ages, we hope, forever past.

But the four cardinal points in woman are quite of a different category from that of talents and susceptibilities. These are the points of mighty influence from which she radiates her powers over the world. They are those of *daughter*, *sister*, *wife* and *mother*. A woman is first a daughter—then a sister—then a wife—and then a mother; and under these potent and enchanting names she exercises all her transforming influence on human destiny.

As a *daughter*, she re-acts on her parents; she opens new springs of pleasures in their hearts, new hopes, new joys, new fears, which have a mystic influence over their characters; either in subduing their spirits to moral influences, or in stimulating their career in the paths of pride, avarice and ambition.

As a *sister*, she either softens, subdues, mollifies and polishes the manners of her brothers; or she excites them to deeds of chivalrous daring, to bold adventures in the ways of false pride, false shame, false honor. It has been sometimes observed by those who attend more philosophically to what passes under their observation, that it is always a misfortune to a brotherhood to have no sister in the family. Such persons are generally more rude, more awkward, more unpolished; more uncivilized in their modes and manners, than, all things else being equal, those fraternities are that enjoy the communion of sisters—

> "Whose company has harmonized mankind,
> Soften'd the rude and calm'd the boisterous mind."

As a *wife*, when properly educated, her power is not to be computed. The weaker vessel though she may be, in all that appertains to mere intellectual power; yet in the department of feeling, sensitiveness, promptness, decision, tenderness of affection and self-denying devotion to her husband, she is generally his superior. Her counsels, if not uniformly infallible, are always sincere and cordial. Her motives can never be suspected, though her wisdom may; one, too, so intimately acquainted with his weak as well as his strong side, (for most husbands have two sides,) cannot fail to obtain incalculable ascendency. There is no covenant like the nuptial covenant—no copartnery like the oneness of the matrimonial contract. It is the identification of all the temporalities of two persons for life—an amalgamation of all natural interests, which places the parties in a position supremely to influence one another. But the recondite secret of a wife's power is only found in the superiority of her love. She conquers and reigns by love. Therefore, in the ratio of her affections and her good sense there must ever be her ascendency.

As a *mother*, however, her power is paramount. On that throne she is supreme. The whole world is in her hands, in her arms, in her bosom, while she is intrusted with the moulding of the soft clay of humanity, and forming it after her own image. The discreet and affectionate mother lives forever in the heart of her children. They never can throw off all their allegiance to her, nor rise above her sovereign sway, if indeed she only knows how to wield that potent sceptre which the God of nature has put into her hands.

I believe there never was a man both good and great, that adorned with brilliant virtues our fallen race, that did not owe it to his mother.

Her wisdom, her piety, her example, led him into the straight paths of true wisdom, goodness and greatness, else his feet had not found them. So true it is, that if a child be brought up in the way that he should go, he will not in advanced years desert it, that it became a proverb in Israel three thousand years ago; and who can find in the annals of ancient or modern biography an exception to it, or a person of distinguished excellence who had not an excellent mother?

Ladies and gentlemen, this is just the point in which we can demonstrate woman's power to do good in society. I doubt not you were disappointed when I was instancing, by some names illustrious in history, her power of doing evil, that I did not at least balance the account by giving more bright examples of her power to bless and to do good. The reason, you will soon discover, is, I was not then in the proper place to find such examples. Woman was not made to found cities and empires, to command armies and navies, to enter the arena of political strife, to figure in camps, in tilts and tournaments, to mingle in the intrigues and cabals of kings and courts. She was made for other ends, to move in other circles, and to exert an influence more pure, more powerful, more lasting. She was made to have an empire in the heart of man, and to wield a mild and gracious sceptre over the moral destinies of our race. Hence the domestic circle is the area of which she is the power, the light, the life, the glory. But though this circle be small, it has a paramount sway over every other circle in which man lives and moves. Hence the family institution gives laws to the school, the college, the university, the church, the state, the world. And so it comes to pass that woman's power is confined within this narrow circle that it might be the more concentrated and rebound with more force on all the interests of humanity.

And here, while we have the four cardinal points of woman's true and proper sphere before us, and are dwelling on the last and paramount of these, her power as a *mother*, it will not be difficult or tedious to demonstrate her illimitable power of doing good. The giving to the world a Moses, a Samuel, a David, a Josiah, a Luther, a Franklin, a Washington, is doing more than did all the Pharaohs, the Ptolemies, the Alexanders, the Cæsars, the Gregories, the Bourbons, the Tudors, the Stuarts, the Hanoverians, the Guelphs, the Napoleons, that ever lived. There is no power in numbers nor in mathematics to compute the amount of good effected by a Luther or a Washington. Not Saxony only, but Germany, Switzerland, Holland, England, Europe, America, the world, temporally, spiritually and eternally, have been advantaged by the deeds of Luther. The annals of eternity alone can unfold all the good effects of the life of that reformer. And yet a single bias given by his mother may have been, and doubtless was, the fountain, the mainspring of all this incalculable series of advantages to our race! Is not the mother of our own Washington the root and origin of all the blessings, civil and social, accruing to this country and to the human race for an indefinite series of ages? When, like the pious Hannah, a mother undertakes to train a child for the Lord and the human race, and brings him up in the tabernacles of piety, she aims at a power of doing good that reaches far beyond the landmarks of time—she may anoint the head and the heart of more kings than did the son of Hannah, and with a holier and more fragrant oil than that which from the prophet's horn was poured upon the head of Saul, or on that of the son of Jesse. There is no decree which saith to woman's sway, either as a daughter, a sister, a wife or a mother, as God hath spoken to the waves of the sea, "Hitherto shalt thou come, and no farther, and here let all thy efforts be stayed." No, thank Heaven's eternal King, there is no limit set to her power. It may be temporal, spiritual, eternal. If woman has vanquished Samson the strongest of men, Solomon the wisest of men, and Adam the greatest of men, she has been made the mother of the *Saviour of men*, and may, through the religion of her Son and of her Lord, exert a transcendent power over the destiny of man. She may bless a family, a nation, a generation, a world—not only for a jubilee, an age, a few centuries, but forever and forever.

But I said something of the Bible in her heart and in her hand, as next to her, or in conjunction with her, the mightiest and best means of civilizing, refining, elevating and ennobling human nature. I presume so much upon the intelligence and good taste of my audience, as not to have allotted much space or time to the elucidation of this point.

It is certainly well known to you, ladies and gentlemen, that women are more susceptible of religious impressions than men. All classic, all Pagan, all political, all sacred history, may be appealed to in proof that female piety is larger in quantity as well as of a finer quality than that of man. Woman figures more eminently in all the walks of piety in New Testament history. Not only in the days of the Christian chief were women most ardent in their attachment to him, more devoted in all their attentions to him, waiting upon his person, ministering to his wants—"last at the cross and earliest at his grave;" but after his resurrection they rallied in greater numbers to his cause, embraced it with warmer affections, endured persecution with greater constancy, often courting rather than shunning the pains of martyrdom. There is everywhere at this moment a preponderating amount of female devotion, and a very striking numerical superiority of female communicants at all the altars in our land.

The reason of this is found in the superior sensitiveness of woman—in the delicacy of all her susceptibilities of moral influence—and in her seclusion from the corrupting influences, the collisions, the revelries and jarring interests of a commercial, political and worldly spirit. As some one has very beautifully said, "The current of female existence runs more within the embankments of home." But home is the centre and the throne of the sanctities as well as of the charities of life. The duties of a mother or of the mistress of a family all tend to piety by warming and softening the intellect and the affections. Women, therefore, are usually the appointed guardians of domestic religion. They are removed at a more salutary distance from the stirring business, from the ambitions that engross the heart of man and the passions that devour it, and the undeviating processes which fix upon it day by day a thicker and a thicker crust of icy selfishness.

Add to this, women need more of the comforts of religion, depend more upon its aid, confide more in its protection, and derive from it more of their real charms and loveliness than from any other source whatever. A pious lady, well educated, (and none are well educated that are not pious, that do not fear God and keep his commandments,) has a power above every other female of the same circumstances, of the same personal accomplishments, not only over the good and excellent, but even over the irreligious themselves. Many irreligious, and even profane men, cannot love a woman without religion. When they think of marrying, they always think of a pure, and virtuous, and religious woman. Such only they regard as a crown of glory and honor; and only under the presidency of such a wife, and mother, and mistress of a house would they dare to commit the destinies of a family. It is, indeed, a noble testimony to religion, that not only good men, but bad men themselves, acknowledge its excellency and prefer an alliance with its friends rather than with those who are destitute of its ornaments and guardianship, or opposed to its purity and power.

Religion is, then, the true dignity of woman. The Bible in her heart, on her lips, and in her hand, imparts to her an excellency, a majesty and a power that renders her the most efficient of all the agencies in the universe, to improve, to civilize and bless the world with the highest moral excellence, with the most refined and exalted social pleasures of which our species is susceptible in this state of trial and discipline.

I have said *the Bible in her heart,* and have I exaggerated the influence of that wonderful volume when inscribed upon the female heart? This I presume to be impossible. There is no hyperbole here. That book widens, deepens, enlarges, strengthens and elevates the intellectual and moral capacities of human nature, of the male and female mind, above all other books, and sciences, and arts ever taught man or woman. The *fact* is one thing, and the philosophy of it another. But so clear is the evidence of the fact, that the destiny of a nation might be staked upon it. Let two females of equal natural development, of equal capacity for mental and moral improvement, be selected; let one of them have the Alexandrian or London library at her command, *without the Bible;* and the other *the Bible only;* and let each of them devote for any definite number of years so many hours, daily, to reading and reflection. She who makes the Bible her choice will as certainly excel the other in all the points of which we now speak, as the Bible itself excels all other books in the world: provided only, that she reads it without prejudice, and subject to the same canons of interpretation to which all other books of distant ages and countries are to be subordinated.

We have now no time on hand to eulogize the book of God; nor is it necessary to this audience. It is a very common theme. It is, however, a noble—a sublime one. It might well occupy the talents of an angel—the descriptive powers of a cherub. It is the book of the Divine nature; it is, indeed, the book of God—and the book of man. Other books have nations or individual men, or specific sciences or arts, for their subject; this is the book of man. Human nature is here as fully revealed as the Divine. They are revealed in comparison, in contrast, in things similar, in things dissimilar. The fountains of the great deep of human thought, of human motives, of human action, are broken up; and man, inward and outward, is contemplated not in the dim taper light of time, but in the strong bright light of eternity; not merely as respects his position on the terraqueous globe, nor in human society, but as respects all his positions and attributes in a whole universe, a boundless future, a vast eternity. The *speaker* is God; the *hearer,* man; the *subject,* human nature, human relations, human destiny; the *object,* eternal life, immortal glory.

The divine mind, the eternal Spirit, breathes through the signs of that book—through its words, its types, its figures, its principles, its precepts, its examples—upon our moral nature. It quickens, animates, purifies, enlarges, elevates, and dignifies it by an assimilation of it to an incarnation of the Divinity itself; and capacitates man and woman for higher joys, purer delights, and a more efficient agency in imparting bliss to others, than all the documents, volumes, facts and events in all the other records of man, or developments of God visible to mortal eye. But I said I intended neither comment nor encomium on the Bible: I therefore hasten to the capital and closing point of my address.

Society is not yet fully civilized. It is only beginning to be. Things are in process, in progress to another age—a golden—a millennial—a blissful period in human history. Selfishness, violence, inordinate ambition, revenge, duelling, even tyranny, oppression and cruelty, are yet exerting a pernicious influence in society. These are the real drawbacks on human happiness—the loud calls on genuine philanthropy. Woman, I believe, is destined to be the great agent in this grandest of all human enterprises—an effort to advance society to the acme of its most glorious destiny on earth.

Already she exerts a great influence in all works of benevolence. In the visiting societies, in quest of the destitute, the sick, the wounded, the miserable—in the labors of the Sunday-school—in the active and constant charities of the Christian church, her reputation is commensurate with the institutions themselves, and her influence is universally acknowledged. These, too, are acts of eternal renown. The great Benefactor gave a fame lasting as time and the human race to the sister of Martha for such an act of love. Such ladies as Mrs. Chaupone, Mrs. Trimmer, Mrs. Carter, Mrs. Barbauld, Mrs. Hannah More, Mrs. Hemans, &c., have an extensive fame and an extensive usefulness; but the space which they occupy is but a speck compared with that filled with the Mary that anointed the Lord for his sepulture. The labors of Mrs. Fry, or of the Sisters of Charity, are not those of genius, poetry, imagination, but of genuine benevolence. It is not the shedding of a few sympathetic tears over some high-wrought imaginative tale of woe, found in books of fiction, in the volumes of romance, but the pouring of the oil and the wine, the genuine tears of benevolence, into the real wounds of the sons and daughters of anguish, that is inscribed in the book of Heaven's heraldry, and to be divulged in celestial ears with angelic admiration and delight.

But we ask, because we expect, more than this. We ask for a female cordon to stretch through the whole length of this land, against the appalling progress of fashionable vices, not merely against the luxurious extravagances of costly raiment, splendid furniture and sumptuous modes of living, which in themselves are great evils, and fast precipitating this nation against that fatal rock on which the proudest empires have been dashed to pieces; but against the remains of barbarism still existing amongst us—duelling, revenge, violence, oppression, &c.

Am I interrogated on what I mean by a female cordon? I answer, that all ladies of education, of elevated standing, of moral excellence, shall, with one consent, frown from their presence those who delight in such deeds—who either perpetrate them, or take pleasure in those that do them; that they show a profound veneration for the philanthropic Author of our religion, who has peremptorily, and on pain of eternal ruin, forbidden all malice, violence, revenge, cruelty, murder and oppression.

They can do more than all legislative enactments, than all human codes and punishments, to exterminate these horrible remains of savage paganism, so incongruous with the doctrine and principles of the *Prince of Peace.* Were it, for example, to be known and depended upon, as certain as death, that every one concerned in a duel was to be enrolled as a coward—as one that feared a whimsical, imaginative, unwritten, unintelligible code of honor, more than the laws of the eternal God—as one that dreaded the scorn of the wicked more than the scorn of all in the heavens, was to be debarred the company of ladies, and to be excluded from the participation of their smiles, I am confident that we should never again hear of a single rencounter of the sort, that the soil of such a community would not again be polluted by the tread of one that in time of peace had passionately, revengefully and recklessly shed the blood of his brother.

But before such consolidated virtue can be warrantably hoped for, the standard of female education must be greatly elevated and improved. Incomparably more attention, than at present, must be paid to the training and development of the moral sentiments. The *heart,* rather than the *head,* the *affections,* rather than the *intellect,* must be the centre of the whole circle of education, on which must operate all the scholastic forces from the lessons of the nursery up to those of the sage philosopher. The dignity of human nature, its sublime origin, its godlike organization, its magnificent and glorious destiny, its mysterious and spiritual relations to an immense universe, to high orders of intelligences, to the principalities, authorities and hierarchies of the heavens, must be standing topics in the every-day bill of intellectual and moral fare, from the abecedarian up to the seniors of the highest school in the land.

Every subject, every object of thought in all the regions of mind and matter, in literature, science and art, must be laid under tribute to religion and morality. If there be design, utility, beauty, loveliness, apparent in any thing, it must be traced up to the eternal Source of all wisdom, goodness, beauty and loveliness, and made a text to show forth his infinite excellencies to the opening genius of the youthful inquirer. Every thing must be taught and learned in all its connections with the being, perfections and designs of the Creator. The archetypes of the universe must be found in his infinite and eternal intelligence, and every beauty, melody and harmony in nature and society, must be made to engage the affections more and more to him—"Him first, him last, him midst and without end;" all nature, science, art and learning, must be made to reveal and extol. This course will, under the dews, the rains and the sunshine of heavenly and divine influence, secure the heart to all that is good, and honorable, and excellent in earth and heaven.

Finally, ladies and gentlemen, be it remembered that it is only when woman is viewed in her first cardinal point, that she is within the circle of direct didactic influence. It is only as a *daughter* that she is immediately under parental education and discipline. She must, while only sustaining this position to the family, be made to comprehend all that is indicated in that very dear and interesting title. But for our consolation it ought to be distinctly and emphatically stated, that when a daughter is so trained and educated as to understand all that is implied in filling up the whole measure of the duties of a daughter, she is an accomplished sister, will make a good wife, an excellent mother. A good daughter must inevitably be a good sister, a good wife, a good mother. If, then, proper care be taken of our daughters, and their education be conducted on rational and moral principles, no person need fear to endorse for the reputation, excellency and moral worth of the sister, the wife or the mother.

Who is it, then, who desires a deep and more thorough reformation of public manners and customs, or who is it that seeks for social pleasures of the highest earthly order, and would advance the amelioration of the social state to the highest point within the grasp of rational or religious anticipation? Let him turn his attention to more rational, scientific, liberal and moral education of woman. Let him bear in mind that she must take the precedence as the most puissant leader in every work of moral reform in society. Hers is the delightful task, as well as the sovereign power, to mould human nature after a divine model. She sows the seed, she plants the germs of human goodness and human greatness. She infixes the generous purpose, the salutary and noble principles in the youthful heart. She makes the men and women of future times, and shapes the character and destinies of posterity even to the third, and to the fourth, and sometimes to the tenth generation. Ought not, then, every patriot, every philanthropist, every good citizen, every Christian in the land to rally all his forces, to summon all his energies, to co-operate in the great cause of female education? It is not the education of the daughters of the affluent and honorable only, or chiefly, of which we speak—it is the education of all—it is common, it is universal female education, and to a more liberal extent than has yet been imagined—for which we speak, when we plead for that female education indispensable to the full and proper amelioration of the social state.

Individual, family or national wealth never can be more advantageously appropriated, than in the mental and moral education of all the sons and daughters of the States. We owe it, then, to ourselves, to our children, to our country, to the world, to bestir ourselves in this most useful, honorable and beneficent of mortal undertakings. Let us, then, awaken to our responsibilities, and to our power of blessing others, and of being blessed, and place our energies and our influence, along with our other means, on the side of woman's high advancement in all the paths of literature and science, of religion and morality. Then must we greatly enhance and sweeten the charms of home—of the social hearth—the domestic circle—the city—the church—the world. Then may we anticipate a day of richer blessings, of purer pleasures, of more lasting joys to the human race; and, on the well-fledged wings of vigorous and healthful hope, we may glide down the whole vista of time, to those eternal scenes of holier delight, of more refined ecstasy, which fill the raptured vision of the saint, in those climes of eternal peace and social bliss, where every eye is filled with uncreated light, and every heart with love.

ADDRESS

ON THE

RESPONSIBILITIES OF MEN OF GENIUS.

TO THE

MEMBERS OF THE UNION LITERARY SOCIETY OF MIAMI UNIVERSITY, OHIO, 1844.

MR. PRESIDENT AND GENTLEMEN,

Members of the Union Literary Society of Miami University:—

SOON as I had obtained my own consent to appear before you on the present occasion, in pursuance of the very polite and flattering invitation I had received from you, I immediately laid all my powers of invention under tribute to furnish a subject worthy of your attention. But, to my great disappointment, I never knew them pay any tax imposed upon them with so much reluctance. Weeks passed away before I could even fix upon any topic; and after I had resolved upon one, new, unexpected and inexorable calls upon my time and labor, so crowded upon me as to leave but a few fragments to devote to a subject which, in my humble opinion, deserves a year rather than a few hours, and a volume rather than a single address.

Accustomed only to read what is written, or to speak extemporaneously, and not at all to recite from memory, I have sketched a few thoughts upon the RESPONSIBILITIES OF MEN OF GENIUS; which, without further introduction or apology, I now submit to your most kind and candid consideration.

Human responsibility, gentlemen, is a momentous theme, and of transcendent importance to the world. In the amplitude of its comprehension it contemplates man in every power and capacity of his nature, and in all the conditions of his existence. It views him in all his relations to that mysterious and incomprehensible whole, of which he is so important a part, indicated by the all-engrossing terms of *Creator* and *creature*. A complete and perfect knowledge of the subject, were it made dependent upon our own exertions, would require an intimate and perfect acquaintance with the universe. But in this it may be said to correspond with every other subject of thought; as no one ever yet understood an atom of the universe who did not understand it all. We are not, however, made dependent for the science of our duty upon our ability to acquire a knowledge that is wholly unattainable. The divine precept happily comes to our relief, and rescues man from a difficulty absolutely insurmountable.

Men, indeed, are not generally satisfied with a clear, broad precept. They are curious to know the reason why it is so commanded. This they have not, in any case, perfectly succeeded in ascertaining; and, in most instances, never can. Still it is some satisfaction to know any of the reasons, and to comprehend the more immediate causes of things, involving either duty or happiness. Hence the pleasure felt in an excursion into the regions of fancy and abstract speculation, even on the most familiar subjects. There is sometimes a very great satisfaction in discovering an end of all human attainments, and in perceiving that there is a fixed goal beyond which even imagination itself cannot stretch its wings.

Still reason has something to do with the ascertainment and comprehension of human responsibility; and it is important just to know how much lies within its lawful precincts, and what lies beyond them. But even this view of the subject is too large for the present occasion; and we have therefore confined our efforts to a single branch of the mighty theme—viz. *the responsibilities of men of genius.*

I do not, however, expect to escape the difficulties which lie upon the whole subject of human responsibility, by asking your special attention to a single branch of it. This special department cannot, indeed, be considered without a general view of the whole subject. We must have just, if not adequate, conceptions of the responsibilities of man, before we can form a correct estimate of the responsibilities of a particular class of men. But as it is my aim to give a proper direction, if need be, to a particular class of mind, I prefer to solicit your attention, gentlemen, to this very prominent branch of the great subject.

And, in the first place, it would, in accordance with well-established usage, seem to be incumbent on me to define a man of genius, as well as our acceptation of the term *responsibility.* When not in a very great haste to arrive at a given point, or when in quest of entertainment as well as of business, I sometimes indulge in a circuitous rather than in a direct approach to the precise point in hand.

Allow me, then, to remark that the development of genius as well as of responsibility, has much to do with the proper comprehension of that most mysterious and sublime something called *mind.* I speak not of its essence. The whole doctrine of essences, whether of mind or of matter, is contraband in every province of legitimate philosophy. No sane person, trained in the schools of useful learning, in this our age of reason, presumes to scan any essence or quintessence whatever. The doctrine of the fifth essence is now-a-days not more ridiculous than the doctrine of the first essence. If at any time we should be seized with a fit of the Muses, we might with Milton sing of

> "Ethereal light, quintessence pure,
> Sprung from the deep."

Or, if wrapt in the visions of an hypothetical philosophy, we might, with the genius of Stagyra, speculate upon "the quintessential purity of a heavenly body immutable." But this matter-of-fact inductive age disdains such idle dreams, and repudiates the ideas and almost the name of *essence* and of *quintessence*, with all the retinue of imaginative properties, accidents and ends. The rigid Baconians, to a man, are willing to acknowledge that there are three topics, once the darling themes of all the sons of hypothesis, which now lie beyond the limits of true philosophy. These are the *origin*, the *essence* and the *end* of any thing, mental or material.

The phenomena of mind and of matter come honorably and fairly within the empire of observation and of reason. Many of their attributes we can and do apprehend, while their essences will forever remain a *terra incognita*—a subject so metaphysically abstruse that no mind can grasp it in any one of its predicaments. The mind, indeed, may seize any thing as gross as ether, or the subtle fluids that roll their invisible currents through the channels of a vein infinitely minute; but the *sanctum sanctorum* of its own awful residence is not to be approached, much less entered, by the ablest, the most profound and erudite of human kind. Its capacity and elasticity are, indeed, appreciable by those who attentively consider its operations. It grasps a universe, and yet may be filled with a single idea. Like the human eye, at one time it seizes a hemisphere, and at another it sees only a single animalcule. Its spirituality is demonstrated by the celerity and compass of its movements. When we spread out upon the largest canvas which the most vigorous imagination has stretched, a universe composed of one hundred millions of suns and two thousand millions of attending planets, moving in orbits wide as those that fill the area of our solar system, the mind finds no difficulty in sweeping the uttermost circle of such a universe, and of still ranging through fields of space far beyond its precincts, from which subtracted, the existing universe would seem to be but an atom.

But the celerity of its movement is no less wonderful than the almost illimitable extent of its comprehension. Light itself, that bounds eight millions of miles in a minute, moves as the sloth, "compared with the speed of its flight." Infinite duration and boundless space are the immense fields through which it gambols with ineffable pleasure. Nor do the unapproachable heights or the unfathomable depths of nature lie beyond its sublime aspirations. These indeed, though beyond an angel's ken and its own comprehension, are nevertheless the only areas that seem to afford it room to spend its mighty energies, or fatigue itself in impetuous sallies.

That Pagan philosophers should have regarded the human mind as an emanation from the Supreme Divinity, is by no means an irrational or absurd hypothesis; yet it is an undefined and undefinable speculation, and explains not at all the mysteries of its awful existence. It is a *creature*, and therefore no part of the Creator; and it is a creature of every day's manifestation. Like sparks stricken off from Nature's eternal and unwasting Sun, there are every moment myriads of them ushering into existence, commencing a career boundless as space and lasting as the years of eternity.

While the realms of matter have all been filled up and peopled with their appropriate orbs, so that no new star has been born since the first Sabbath, nor a single new atom added to the masses of the original creation, during the progress of all the ages of time, mind is constantly springing into existence, but never going out; so that the machinery of nature seems to be but one grand laboratory for the continuance, production and manifestation of these new creations; while all its vast dominions seem to constitute but one splendid and magnificent theatre on which individual minds are to be the eternal actors.

Creation, gentlemen, is a very grand and sublime subject. It had its beginning, but where shall it end? In its alphabet it has no *omega*, and within its vocabulary the word *annihilation* is not found. It is matter first, and mind second; and these combined constitute all its wonders. Now, as the forms of matter are exceedingly variant and numerous, what shall we think of the mysterious and multiform diversities of mind and character! Of these developments one there is to which the ancients have consecrated the name *genius;* and it is to this manifestation of mind your attention is now specially solicited.

What then, gentlemen, mean we by the word *genius?* Shall we regard it as a supernal spirit suddenly inspired, or a guardian angel allotted to a good or great man? This family of genii, it would seem, is now extinct. Once, indeed, it was a large and powerful family, and of illustrious fame; but, like other great families, it had its own feuds and broils. Two parties were formed, each calling itself the *good genii* and the other the *evil genii.* A furious war arose between them; and, after a hundred battles, they agreed to divide between themselves the empire of the world—allotting to every individual a guardan genius, good or evil, as he desired or deserved. But, like other mystic agents, they have gone the way of all fictions, and now gently repose in the bosom of oblivion.

Since that time the etymology of the name has been the amusement of the critics. Some would have it, and the word *giant,* of kindred Grecian extraction, because both alleged to be the offspring of *gignomai,* regularly descended from the venerable *Geno,* alias *Geino,* of prolific memory. From denoting a sort of sub-divinity, it thus became the representative of a highly gifted man. But, as *gigno,* one of its ancestors, means *to beget,* it rather indicates one class of great men, of which there are, at least, two illustrious categories—the great in reason, and the great in fancy. Conception and comparison distinguish the former—imagination and invention the latter. These are the men of genius—those the men of talents. Men of genius soar on eagles' pinions to worlds of fancy; while men of talents, Atlas-like, stand under the real world. The loftier regions of fiction and romance delight the former, while the realities of earth and its mighty destinies engross the attention and command the energies of the latter. Men of genius create new worlds—men of talents carry them. Strength (for so *talentum,* from *talao,* would seem to indicate) characterizes the one; while activity and celerity of movement distinguish the operations of the other. While, then, invention is the boast of genius, execution is the glory of talent. Combined, they make earth's great ones; and, leagued with virtue, constitute the real nobility of human nature.

Example, however, is always more intelligible, and generally more eloquent, than definition. We shall, then, summon its aid. Genius, we have said, is distinguished by invention, creation, origination; talent by effort, enterprise and great achievements. Energy is prime minister to talent; the love of admiration, to genius.

Homer excelled in genius; Virgil in talent; Shakspeare and Milton in both. In the fine arts of painting, sculpture and music, as well as in poetry, oratory, and even in the useful arts, that have contributed to the progress of civilization and comfort, we have numerous happy illustrations of both genius and talent. Raphael in his cartoons, Michael Angelo in his frescoes, and our own Benjamin West in his historic paintings, are, par excellence, models of genius in the department of painting. In sculpture, Phidias, Praxiteles and Polydore are as bright a constellation of genius as Demosthenes, Cicero or Sheridan, in oratory; or as Milton, Pope or Byron, in poetry. In the useful arts a Fulton and an Arkwright afford as fine specimens of genius as a Mozart in music, or a Scott in romance. On the other hand, we discover in a Butler, a Luther, a Franklin, a Washington, the mighty power of talent; and in a Locke, a Bacon or a Newton, the still superior force of genius and talent combined.

Before dismissing the definition of a man of genius, it deserves to be noted that in the question of responsibility we give precedence to genius, not in contrast with talent, but because a man of genius is always more or less possessed of talent; whereas a man of talent is not necessarily a man of genius. Genius, then, in this view, comprehends talent; while talent does not necessarily comprehend genius.

It is now expedient that we advance more into the interior of our subject, and endeavor to form some conception of the term *responsibility*.

The doctrine of responsibility is the doctrine of moral relations between an inferior and a superior—between a dependent and an independent being; as well as between such co-ordinates as enter into any social compact implying or involving obligations to each other. It is, therefore, a doctrine of paramount importance, in the social system, to every individual member of it. It is, indeed, the doctrine of human destiny, involving the whole subject of human happiness and human misery.

As there is not one lawless atom in the material universe, so there is not one irresponsible agent in the social system. The order of material nature is, indeed, the outward symbol of the order of spiritual nature, and that is the order of obedient dependence. We shall, then, enter the holy place of moral obligation by passing leisurely through the outer court of physical obligation.

In the material universe all the inferior masses are under law to the superior. One of the sublime designs of the Creator is, that all the central masses of the universe shall not only be the largest masses in their respective systems, but also radiating centres to their systems. Thus he has constituted the great masses perennial fountains of beneficence to all the subordinate masses that move round them. Our own bright orb, representative of all the suns of creation, is an unwasting fountain of life to its own glorious system. No sooner does he show his radiant face than floods of life teem from his bosom upon some thirty attendant planets, which, in sublime majesty and in expressive silence, ceaseless move around him. Light, heat, life and joy emanate from him. These are the sensible demonstrations of his bounty to his waiting retinue of worlds. What other emanations of goodness he vouchsafes to those who obey him are yet unknown, and perhaps unknowable to us while confined to this our native planet. In the purer and more elevated regions of ether he may perhaps generate and mature the ultimate and more recondite elements of the vital principle, which, combining with our atmosphere, quicken it with all the rudimental principles of animal existence.

In the realms of matter, so far as fact, observation and analogy authenticate any conclusion, the law is universal, viz. that the minors must be subject to the majors; that the inferior masses shall depend on the superior for all that gives them life and comfort. But that the satellites of all systems and of all ranks requite their suns in some way by receiving from them their beneficence, and thereby maintaining, through their respective gravities, their central positions and perpetual quiescence, while they all move forward in one grand concert around the throne of the Eternal, in awful grandeur musing his praise, is not to be questioned or doubted by any one conversant with God's grand system of designs. On these sublime though simple principles are suspended the order, beauty and felicity of the universe. Destroy this, and a scene of disorder, confusion and destruction would instantly ensue, that would not leave an atom of the universe unscathed.

Such is also the order of the intellectual system. One great mind, nature's spiritual and eternal sun, constitutes the mighty centre around which, in their respective orbits, all pure minds, primary or secondary—angelic or human—revolve. In this system the great minds as certainly govern the inferior, as in material nature the large masses govern the less. Now, as the power of mind consists in intelligence, educated mind must as certainly govern uneducated mind, and the more vigorous and talented the less favored, as the great material masses govern the inferior.

Some, indeed, argue that all power is in mind, and that volition is the cause of all motion. Phrenologists, moreover, depose that there is no organ for the will. Hence volition is the mind moving in a certain direction. It is the whole mind in action to effect a change in some person or thing. Hence all changes, all motions in the universe, are but the volitions of an intelligent agent. So God willed light; and his *fiat*, or *will expressed in words*, gave it being. And as the same volition, guided by intelligence, that created the masses, still upholds them in being and directs all their movements, may we not affirm that *intelligence governs the universe?* Educated mind, or intelligence, is, then, the supreme power in every department of nature. Hence, men of genius must always, every thing else being equal, direct and govern those not so highly gifted as themselves. May we not then conclude that it is Heaven's own law that superior minds must always govern the inferior?

But this reasoning supposes mental inequalities; and who believes that all men (*i.e.* all minds) are equal, either by nature, education or art? If the sun and planets were all equal, the material universe would stand still. If all minds were equal, there would be no government in the world. But it might need none. If so, however, it certainly could not move. The sun never would set in one half of the world, and consequently never rise in the other, if it depended on human volition, and if one half of the world had just as much power as the other half.

The beauty as well as the happiness of the universe requires inequality. Equal lines, smooth surfaces and eternal plains have no beauty. We must have hill and dale, mountain and valley, sea and land, suns of all magnitudes, worlds of all sizes, minds of all dimensions, and persons and faces of divers casts and colors, to constitute a beautiful and happy world. We must have sexes, conditions and circumstances—empires, nations and families—diversities in person, mind, manners, in order to the communication and reception of happiness. Hence, our numerous and various wants are not only incentives to action, but sources of pleasure, both simple and complex—physical, intellectual and moral.

Hence the foundation and the philosophy of unequal minds—unequal in power, in capacity and in taste—unequal in intelligence, activity and energy. The inequalities of mind are numerous and various as the inequalities of matter. One mind sports with worlds—another, with atoms. One man perches himself on Mount Chimborazo and communes with the stars—another delves into the earth in search of hidden treasures, and buries himself in mines and minerals. One man moves along with the tardiness of the ox in the drudgery of life—another ascends in a balloon and soars above the clouds. Here we find a Newton measuring the comet's path, a Franklin stealing fire from heaven, a Columbus in search of a new world; and there a sportsman with his hounds in quest of a fox. One delights in his revelling and song, in riotous living and the giddy dance—another, in locking up his golden pelf in an iron chest. Talk we, then, of minds equally endowed by nature or improved by art! No such minds ever composed any community. Varieties, all manner of varieties, are essential to society. The world needs the rich and the poor—the young and the aged—the learned and the unlearned—the healthy and the infirm—the cheerful and the melancholic. These call forth all our energies, open channels for all the social virtues, lay the basis of our various responsibilities, and constitute much of the happiness of this life. They furnish opportunities for communicating and receiving benefits.

The positive and the negative belong as much to society as to electricity. These relative states belong to all earth's categories. Some are positive, and some negative, in health, wealth, genius, learning, cheerfulness, contentment; the one imparts, and the other receives, blessings, and thus the circle of social happiness is completed.

But the world that now is, in more senses than one, is the offspring of a world that once was. We have derived more than our flesh, blood and bones from our ancestors. We speak their language, read their books, learn their customs, imbibe their spirit, copy their manners, and are the complex result of all their institutions. Our language, religion and morality, are alike hereditary. We shall just as soon invent a new language as a new religion, objectively considered. Of all creatures, man is the most imitative. His whole person, head, face and hands, body, soul and spirit, are, more or less, shaped through the influence of this mysterious law of transformation. We do not only speak the language of our own country, but the provincialisms of our nurseries. The gift of all tongues did not, because it could not, annul the Galilean brogue. Nor does the casual interchange of nations deface the national head, form of person, or gait, of early education and youthful association.

Need we further proof that men are, to an extent involving all their essential interests, subject to the law of imitation, and, consequently, example and precept are the two grand formative influences of human destiny? From this point, then, we may look more earnestly, as well as more intelligently, on the whole subject of human responsibilities. If, indeed, as could be clearly shown, it is most certain that the physical, intellectual and moral constitution of one generation essentially depends upon the intelligence, religion and morality of its immediate predecessor; and if parents, teachers, and men of more advanced age, unavoidably impress their image on those brought into life, and up to manhood, under their influence; follows it not, that men of transcendent genius have a mighty influence, and are awfully responsible to God for the application of that intellect and influence delegated to them?

It is a startling proposition, that a truly intelligent and religious community could, according to the laws of our own being, gradually introduce a more vigorous, long-living, intellectual and moral population, than is possible to any ignorant and immoral people in existence; yet it is not more startling than true.

But let us, for the sake both of argument and illustration, look for a moment at some of the men of genius that have lived in the world. A mere specimen or two of those of the last and present century must, for the present, suffice.

In works of genius and general literature, no writer of the eighteenth century obtained a higher conspicuity or a greater celebrity than Voltaire. Distinguished from infancy with superior intellectual endowments, a sprightly imagination, great versatility of genius, a ready and sparkling wit; he is said to have written poetry while yet in his cradle. When passing through the College of Louis the Great, comet-like, he dazzled with the lustre of his genius, and the brilliancy of his path, not only his fellow-students, but all the great masters of science and literature which then adorned that royal college. In admiration of his powerful intellect, and captivating eloquence, and in anticipation of his future greatness, Ninon de l'Enclos bequeathed to him two thousand livres to purchase a library.

The vivacity of his wit and humor, as well as his devotion to the muses, early drew him away from the study of the law, gave him a passport to the society of men of learning, and introduced him to the courtiers of Louis XIV. Even in his youth he became a favorite both of the tragic and of the comic muse. He successively shone, a star of the first magnitude, amongst the courtiers of St. Cloud, St. James and those of Berlin. His ascendency over the French king, over George I. and his queen Caroline, and afterwards, over the Prussian monarch, from whom he received a pension of two-and-twenty thousand livres, are to be regarded as the trophies of his genius; as monuments of his extraordinary endowments.

In proof of his powers of satire, and that against the government too, the Bastille was honored with his company for one whole year. And had it not been for the admiration of his Œdipus, the first-fruits of his tragic muse, on the part of the Duke of Orleans, he might have been doomed to a longer imprisonment. This admonition did not long restrain the impetuosity of his mind, its recklessness of the moral consequences of its career. His *Lettres Philosophiques*, so profane and dissolute in their witticism, soon obtained the honor of a public conflagration at the hand of the public hangman, and that, too, by order of the Parliament of France. Despite of all these marks of public displeasure, by the singular merits of his Mahomed, Merope and Alzire, he obtained the honor of the first dramatic poet of the age, and was again introduced to the Court of France, as the peculiar favorite of Madame de Pompadour.

His other works, published while in Geneva, at Ferney and at Paris, both comic and tragic, both philosophical and literary, gave him a very high rank amongst the men of literature and of taste; so that in the esteem of admiring myriads, he commanded the homage and guided the taste of the literati of the whole French Empire, during the last half of the eighteenth century. While at Ferney, in the midst of his little colony of artisans, abounding in wealth, and rich in fame, he was not only in the continual receipt of the adulations of philosophers and princes, but also of princely presents, and liberal gifts from some of the sovereigns of Europe. Dissatisfied with these rewards of his genius and labors, and wearied with the luxurious ease of that delightful abode, he languished for the daily incense of praise, and the admiring plaudits of the French capital. Even in his gray hairs, and at the advanced period of fourscore and four years, he returned to the metropolis, as he said, "to seek glory and death." Honors extraordinary were crowded thick upon him on his arrival in Paris. The learned critics emulated each other in the despatch with which they offered incense at his shrine; and, finally, he was crowned with the poetic wreath in a full theatre, amidst applauding thousands. The excitement, however, was too powerful for his enfeebled constitution. The weight of so many honors oppressed him. The complimentary visits of Parisian ceremony stole away sleep from his pillow, and compelled him to resort to opium for relief; one large dose of which finally took away his senses, and immediately despatched him from the worship of infidels to the presence of his God.

Thus perished this extraordinary genius; the founder of a new sect of philosophers, distinguished more for their wit and their licentiousness, than for the profundity of their science or their influence in the cause of civilization. Thus perished the author of seventy-one octavo volumes, not one of which was seasoned with one pure emotion, with a single tribute to religion or pure morality; all of them, however, characterized by a great versatility of genius, a glowing imagination, a peculiar ease and fluency of style, and for a great variety of knowledge, such as it is; much of it, indeed, incorrect, little of it useful, and all of it poisoned with the seeds of anarchy, libertinism and irreligion. Thus perished the fickle-minded, wavering and inconstant Voltaire, who, as some one has justly said, was a free-thinker in London, a courtesan at Versailles, a Christian at Nantz and an infidel at Berlin. Assuming at one time to be a moralist, pleading for toleration, and dissuading from war; at another, acting the buffoon; now writing a tragedy, then a farce; to day a philosopher, cold as Diogenes; to-morrow an enthusiast, ardent as Peter the Hermit; to-day a parasite, fulsome as Tertullus; to-morrow a satirist, severe as Juvenal; now a voluptuary, feasting in princely style, again a miserable ascetic, worshipping mammon; now as modest as a sage, anon as bold as an atheist, denouncing the Messiah, and contemning the hope of immortality.

Such was the man whose anarchical theories, whose polished libertinism, whose atheistic reasonings, more than those of any other, polluted almost all the illustrious youth of France during the reigns of Louis XV. and XVI. Such was the master-spirit of the master-spirits of the French Revolution;—that reign of terror whose infamous annals are destined to demonstrate to the human race the madness of atheism, the weakness of philosophy, the desolating tumults of passion, and the necessity of religion and righteousness to the prosperity, the honor and the happiness of every nation and people.

But on what canvas can be grouped, and by what historic pencil sketched, the ruined myriads, deluded, polluted and destroyed, by the conversation, writings and examples, of such a genius as that of Voltaire, Volney, Diderot, or that of our own less gifted, but equally morally distempered and licentious, Paine? His "Common Sense," and his "Rights of Man," are but the charm through which he fascinated and beguiled untold thousands into the downward paths of ruin and disgrace;—temporal, spiritual and eternal. He, too, was but the deluded votary of a more gifted and still more depraved genius.

And who were the Dantons, the Marats, the Robespierres, of the age of despotism, the triumph of anarchy? Men of the school of Voltaire, Diderot and Gabriel Mirabeau. It will remain a secret to the development of the Great Day, how much poison has been infused into society through the intoxicating cup of a false, though fascinating philosophy, sparkling with the brilliant display of elevated genius, administered by such men as the speculative Hume, the eloquent Gibbon or the accomplished Rousseau.

Our two great historians, before they commenced their proud monuments of elevated genius, had travelled through France; and one of them both wrote and spoke the language of Voltaire as fluently and as eloquently as his own vernacular. These men had themselves drunk deeply of the continental philosophy—had become too familiar with the licentious principles of the eighteenth century. The first impulse to delineate the fortunes of England seems to have sprung up in the bosom of a skeptic, who had first conceived a false theory of the genius of human nature, and afterwards sought, in the annals of his country, facts to prove it. Such, it appears, was the character of David Hume. Destined to the law by his parents, "he preferred Virgil and Cicero to Voet and Vinnius," while his taste for philosophy led him to write an "Inquiry into the Principle of Morals," a "Treatise on Human Nature," and an essay on "Natural Religion," before he completed a single volume of his history of England. A man of distinguished talents, and an elegant historian, he certainly is; but the spirit and tendency of his writings are most clearly, though most insidiously, irreligious and immoral. His sentiments are often clothed in equivocal and fallacious language, and are intended indirectly to sap and mine the influence of the Bible. With all "the careless inimitable beauties of Hume," as Gibbon calls them—*i.e.* "his solecisms, his scotticisms, his gallicisms, his violations of the rules of English grammar," severely exposed by Dr. Priestley in his philosophical disquisitions, he is still, in language and style, the beau ideal of all English historians. But this is a small matter compared with the sly narcotic poison of his infidelity; which has, in truth, perverted the facts of his history, and rendered it rather a panegyric of skepticism than a faithful record of facts. Like Voltaire, as one of our late reviewers has said, "Hume adopted history as the vehicle of opinions which he could make palatable to the million in no other way." His *suppressio veri*, and his *suggestio falsi*, have beguiled other writers into very great errors, distortions and suppressions of fact. Keightley, in his "Outlines of History," Gleig, in his "Family History," and even Mrs. Markham, in her history, so admirably adapted, in many respects, to children, have been imposed on by Hume; and that, too, when his infidelity perverted his genius, and discolored the facts which lay before him in the annals of the world. All this, and perhaps more, might be said of the still more highly endowed and more eloquently accomplished author of the "Decline and Fall of the Roman Empire."

Gifted by nature, and adorned by art, no historian either in our language or in any other known to us, possessed a much more fascinating style of narration than Edmund Gibbon. If, indeed, second to any English historian, he is second only to the more learned and polished Robertson; not, indeed, in the rich easy and flowing eloquence of his splendid periods, but in the more sublime, more chaste, nervous and classic character of his general style and manner. But the subtle poison of an insidious skepticism is infused into the whole performance; and ere the youthful reader is aware of it, he is beguiled into an indefinable incertitude and dubiety on the whole subject of historical veracity, and charmed into an unutterable suspicion that Christianity and polytheism are but modifications of the same superstitious credulity of poor human nature.

I presume not to descant upon the history of those mighty chiefs—the men of high renown—whose genius, like that of Byron, or that of Napoleon, have been the subject of a thousand comments—orations—eulogies. Those rare prodigies, like comets of stupendous magnitude, seldom appear in our own horizon, and when they do, are so far beyond the aspiration of our youth as to afford no very strong incentive to their ambition. As those burning mountains of lofty summit, seldom trodden by human foot, need no parapet to prevent the too near approach of the unwary traveller, so these giants of enormous stature are placed so far above all aspiration, as not to seduce by their example one in a hundred millions of our race. Still their history is a part of the history of humanity, and, as such, is not without its use. Their towering ambition, transcendent success and tragic end, together with the tendency of their course, are beacons, not without a moral influence to the human mind. The evils they have done while they lived, and the evils they are still doing, and yet to do, cannot be easily computed.

The good or evil that men do while they live, lives after them; neither the one nor the other is "always interred with their bones." Their example lives, and in the long series of cause and effect, in the complex and mysterious concatenation of things, their actions are pregnant with effects on human destiny that whole centuries do not always either unfold or annihilate.

Can any one compute the expenditures of human life, the number of widows, orphans and bereaved parents, occasioned by the insatiate ambition of the late Emperor of the French? What tears and groans and agonies, did each of his hundred battles cost the nations in which he sought that harvest of renown, which, for a few years, he reaped in the admiration of the world! But who can fix, either in time or place, the last effect which his wild career of glory shall have entailed upon the human race?

But it is not the military chiefs, the ambitious aspirants after civil or military renown, with whom we have to do. A Voltaire, a Paine, a Byron or a Scott come more legitimately within the precincts of our subject. These all were men of high responsibilities, because of the greatness of their talents, their lofty genius, their rare attainments. But whither tended the labors of their lives? Of the two former, but one opinion obtains amongst all Christians—their whole influence was decisively against religion, morality and good government. The French Revolution is a lesson known to all men, demonstrating the indissoluble connection between atheism, anarchy and misrule. It was as certainly the offspring of atheism, as the Spanish Inquisition was the child of the Papacy, or the temple of Jupiter Olympus the creation of Paganism.

Men reason against both common sense and philosophy, when they argue either themselves or others into the hallucination, that a good civil government can anywhere exist without sound religion and sound morality; or, indeed, that a people can be moral, in the proper sense of the word, without religion. Without temples, altars, priests and religion by civil law established, they may, indeed, be intelligent, religious, moral, and, consequently, prosperous; but without true religion no state can be moral, prosperous and permanent. All empires that have fallen, all states and nations that have passed away, have perished through irreligion, immorality and vice.

Now, as the master-spirits of the French Revolution were the disciples of Voltaire and his associates, we read the power, the character and the tendency of their genius and talent in that momentous event, prolific of instruction, not only to the living, but to ages yet unborn. If England in the days of her Commonwealth was a proof of the genius of her Cromwell, or if the riches and glory of Israel, at the era of the erection of their temple, constituted a proof of the wisdom and sound policy of their Solomon, so was France in the days of her Pantheon, during the tyranny of her Danton, Robespierre, Marat, &c., a proof of the philosophy, policy and virtues of her Voltaire, Volney and Gabriel Mirabeau.

But why, it may be asked, mention in the same chapter such men as Byron, Burns and Scott? This, indeed, demands an explanation. They are not, then, at all to be classed with such men as Voltaire, Volney or Mirabeau, except as men of genius and favorites of public fame. Still the influence of a Byron, a Burns, a Scott, may be as greatly mischievous as their genius was transcendently great and admirable. That they have all said many beautiful things—that they have expressed the purest and the noblest sentiments and views in the finest style, in language the most chaste, the most classic and the most exuberantly rich and fascinating, is admitted, with the greatest pride of English literature and of Englishmen. That much of their poetry and fiction is deeply imbued with sentiments of piety and humanity, is also most cheerfully conceded; and that most men may improve their language, their taste and their style by the perusal and the study of their admirable productions, we also admit. And if any one please to add, that three such men almost contemporaneous have not adorned any nation, ancient or modern, with richer specimens of rare genius of the finest texture and the most exuberant growth, I will not at all dissent from him; and yet I must say, that in view of the tendency, the whole tendency of the products of their genius, and in my estimate of human responsibility, I would not, for "all that wealth or fame e'er gave," be the author of their works. I cannot but view them as decidedly tending to impiety, and consequently to immorality. They may not, indeed, Bulwer-like, have made the libertine a successful adventurer, or the licentious rake a man of honor and of good fortune. They may not have decorated vice with the charms of innocence, or thrown around the sensualist the robes of virtue; they may not have commended to juvenile fancy a plausible prodigal, or introduced to the favorable regard of unsuspecting youth some amorous knight of easy virtue: still they have so mingled up virtue and vice, piety and impiety, wisdom and folly, moral beauty and moral deformity, as to confound the understanding and blunt the pure sensibilities of our nature. They have created false virtues, and if they have not called good *evil* and evil *good*, they have made certain vices of much less frightful mien, under the names of gallantry, patriotism, chivalry, heroism, &c. Human nature is exaggerated, discolored, misrepresented, in many points. A wrong direction is given to the mind, false motives are inspired, unworthy principles instilled in the minds of the less discriminative readers of their works, and wrong conceptions of honor, greatness and goodness inculcated upon all. In some respects the author of Waverley is to be excepted from this sweeping censure. Of a better temperament, of a more moral constitution and of a more religious education, more historic too and descriptive than merely fanciful or imaginative, he is more conversant with fact and reality, and generally more nearly approaches nature and truth, than most of his contemporaries or predecessors. Still he occasionally outrages the moral sense and good taste, by making his outlaws heroic, noble and honorable men; thus creating false virtues and dishonoring the true.

That as life was eking out he condemned his course, the prostitution of his admirable genius and unparalleled powers of description, is to my mind a gratification, though no extenuation of the aberrations of his otherwise splendid and unparalleled career.

I have not arrayed before you, gentlemen, a per contra list of the great reformers and benefactors of mankind; I have not laid before you any samples of the men of genius selected from prophets, apostles, saints or martyrs; I have not told you of the inventors of useful arts, of the founders of benevolent institutions, or of the great and splendid discoveries of men of science. Nor have the Christian poets, writers, orators, reformers, missionaries, been arrayed before you. We have not spoken of the wide-spread and long-enduring influence of a Claude, a Wickliffe, a Luther, or a Calvin, or of the bright deeds of illustrious fame of a Barnard, a Howard, or a Robert Raikes. No, these are common and familiar as household words. Yet the last mentioned of these, though of no remarkable genius, by setting on foot the Sunday-school system, has done for the world more than all the conquerors of nations, founders of empires and great political demagogues whose names are inscribed upon the rolls of fame. Eternity alone can develop the wide-spreading and long-continued series of good and happy consequences, direct and indirect, resulting from their schemes of benevolence and deeds of mercy. Their noble influence may be compared in its beginnings to the salient fountain of some of earth's grandest rivers, which, though not ankle-deep, issuing from beneath a little rock on some lofty mounttain's brow, after wending its serpentine way for thousands of miles through many a rich valley and fertile plain, and receiving the contributions of numerous tributary streams, finally disembogues its deep broad flood into the ocean, carrying on its majestic bosom the products of many climes and the wealth of many nations. So, in the course of ages, the labors of the more distinguished benefactors of mankind, at first humble and circumscribed, yield largely accumulating revenues of glory and felicity; and carry down, not only to the remotest times and to the most distant nations, manifold blessings; but occasionally, transcending the boundaries of earth and time, they flow into eternity itself, carrying home to God and the universe untold multitudes of pure and happy beings.

But, gentlemen, to escape the imputation of merely theorizing on this subject in the form of vague generalities, allow me to press the subject on your attention in the more practical form of a few leading specifications.

First, then, it is a paramount responsibility resting upon all persons having talents—upón every one possessing genius, to cultivate those noble powers which God has bestowed upon them. The gift of genius is a special call upon its possessor to cultivate and improve it to the highest possible degree. It is already established that men of superior intellect and moral power must govern the world. Men might as successfully legislate against the Ten Commandments, or enact statutes against conjugal affection or filial reverence, as to think of legislating against the subordination of inferior to superior minds. God has so constituted the world. As, then, it must be so, how great the responsibility resting upon those possessed by nature of the higher mental endowments, to cultivate them to the utmost perfection! The marble in the quarry, the ore in the mountain, or the diamond in the sand, is not susceptible of greater improvement and polish by art, than is the human mind, especially a highly gifted mind. Education adorns as well as enlarges and strengthens the human soul. Demosthenes might always have stammered in his father's blacksmith-shop but for his devotion to intellectual improvement.

But it is not *intellect* alone, however highly cultivated, that commands either the admiration or the reverence of mankind. It is not mere intellect that governs the world. *It is intellect associated with moral excellence.* Hence the necessity of the proper cultivation of the moral nature of man. That the divine similitude of man consists more in his moral than in his merely intellectual constitution, needs neither argument nor proof. And that the Supreme Lawgiver and Governor of the universe reigns over the empire of mind by goodness, justice and truth, rather than by mere intellect, whether called knowledge, wisdom or power, is equally plain to all who can reason, or indeed think on what passes before them in the developments of nature, society and religion.

That the moral nature of man is, therefore, to be sedulously and constantly cultivated, is not more obviously evident than is the still more interesting fact, that in the direct ratio of its importance is the facility with which it may be accomplished, provided it be submitted to the proper means, timously commenced, and perseveringly prosecuted when most susceptible of moral impressions. It is in this department that the law of improvement is necessarily the law of healthful exercise, whose immutable tendency is enlargement and corroboration. He, then, that would gain the full advantage of his talents, and secure the legitimate rewards of genius, must pay a supreme regard to the cultivation and high development of his moral nature. In this way only can he obtain and wield an influence commensurate with all his powers of blessing and being blessed. Had Demosthenes, the model orator and statesman of both Greece and Rome, devoted his mighty genius to the moral as well as the intellectual improvement of his mind, the bribe of Harpalus, the parasite of Alexander, would not have tempted him; nor would he have terminated his days by poison, obscuring the glories of his great name by self-murder, the greatest and meanest of mortal sins.

But, in the second place, it is supremely incumbent on all men of genius that they choose a calling most favorable to the promotion of the best and greatest interests of human kind. In the social system there are many offices to be filled, many services to be performed, and consequently many persons needed to perform them. Of these offices there are all degrees of comparison—the needful, the more needful, the most needful—the honorable, the more honorable, the most honorable. The scale of utility is, indeed, the scale of honor. That calling is always the most honorable that is the most useful; and that is the most useful which is the most necessary to the completion and perfection of human happiness. "The glory of God," (a phrase more current than well understood,) the glory of God can best be promoted by promoting the happiness of man. Indeed, it can be promoted in no other way. Now, as man is susceptible of individual and social happiness—of animal, intellectual and moral gratifications and pleasures—that happiness is to be regarded the highest which comprehends the greatest variety and the largest amount of blessedness.

It so happens, however, that whatever produces the greatest amount of moral felicity also yields the greatest variety of enjoyment. This is founded upon the fact that moral pleasure is not only most exquisite in degree, but is itself founded upon the harmonious fruition of our entire constitution. Hence the virtuous man is always the most happy man, because virtue is essential to the entire enjoyment of his whole animal, intellectual and moral nature. The restraints which virtue imposes upon the minor gratifications are laid only for the purpose of securing the major both in variety and degree.

Now, as intellect and society are essential to morality and virtue, those offices and callings which have most to do with these, are most productive of human happiness. From conceptions of this sort arose the preference given to what are usually called the learned professions. But law, physic and theology are but chapters in this great category; they are not, in my opinion, the component parts of it; they do not engross the learned professions. For unfortunately it does not always follow that those who engage in these three professions are either learned men or learned in their respective professions, nor is it true that these are the only callings that require much learning. Some of the mechanical arts, politics and agriculture, require as much learning as either law or medicine. The school-master's vocation and that of the professor of language and science ought to be not only regarded, but actually constituted, learned professions. Indeed, all professions would be the better of a little more learning than is usually thought indispensable. A learned carpenter and cordwainer there might be, as well as a learned blacksmith, without any detriment to those callings or to the learned professions. And as all men are in this community, in virtue of our political institutions, constituted politicians, lawgivers, judges and magistrates, whenever the people pronounce their sovereign *fiat*, the number of learned professions might be at least doubled, and perhaps quadrupled, without any detriment to the state or any jeopardy of human happiness.

In this allusion to learned callings it may be regarded as a culpable omission should I not name the military and naval professions. True, indeed, so far as any callings are purely belligerent, they are not very nearly allied to the theory of human happiness, how important soever they may be to that of human safety. The preservation and enjoyment of human life, rather than the scientific destruction of it, fall more directly within the purview of our present remarks. Generals, heroes and conquerors are very illustrious men in the esteem of the more rude and barbarous nations of the world, but as civilization advances they uniformly fall back into the rank and file of Nimrod, Tamerlane, Alaric and Company.

One of the greatest misfortunes entailed upon society is the opinion that great generals are great and noble men, and that those callings which have the most gunpowder, lead, epaulettes and music about them, are the most splendid, honorable and useful. False views of glory and greatness are not indeed confined to those circles of earth's great ones, but are unfortunately extended to other circles connected as much with the animalism of human nature as they. Political chiefs and successful demagogues are everywhere hailed as men of great parts and good fortunes. Every senator is an *honorable* man, and every governor is an impersonation of *excellency*. The worship paid to these political dignitaries deludes the unwary into the idolatry of such offices and officials, and turns their judgment awry from the oracles of reason and the true philosophy of human greatness and human happiness. Indeed, such is the mania for political honors and political office, that more seem to desire the honor of an office than to be an honor to the office.

We would not, indeed, divest useful offices of their proper honor. To serve a society faithfully, whether as a scavenger of Rome or as a king of the French, is an honor to any man. But to serve society in any capacity promotive of its moral advancement, is the highest style and dignity of man. True, indeed, that in the great category of moral improvement there are numerous departments, and consequently many offices. There are authors, teachers of all schools, ministers of all grades, missionaries of all mercies, ambassadors of all ranks, employed as conservators, redeemers and benefactors of men. These, in the tendencies and bearings of their respective functions, sweep the largest circles in human affairs. They extend not only to the individual first benefited, not only to those temporally benefited by him, in a long series of generations, but breaking through the confines of time and space, those benefits reach into eternity and spread themselves over fields of blessings, waving with eternal harvests of felicity to multitudes of participants which the arithmetic of time wholly fails to compute, either in number or in magnitude. The whole vista of time is but the shaft of a grand telescope through which to see, at the proper angle, the teeming harvests of eternal blessedness flowing into the bosoms of the great moral benefactors of human kind. To choose a calling of this sort, is superlatively incumbent on men of genius. As Wesley said of good music, so say we of good talents. The devil, said the reformer, shall not have all the good tunes; and we add, nor the law, nor politics, nor the stage, all the good talents.

If men are held responsible, not only for all the evil they have done, but also for all the good they might have done—as undoubtedly they will be; and if they are to be rewarded, not for having genius and talent, but for having *used* them in accordance with the Divine will, and the dictates of conscience, then what immense and overwhelming interests are merged in the question—to what calling should men of great parts and of good education devote themselves? Taste, inclination and talent are altogether, and always, to be taken into the account in a matter of such thrilling interest. But we are speaking of men of genius in general, and not of a particular class. The historic painter may, like our great West, give us Bible characters and Bible scenes. We may as well have the patriarchal scenes, tabernacle and temple scenes, official personages and festivals upon the walls of our rooms and museums, as the island of Calypso, or the ruins of the Capitol, or the Pantheon, or the panorama of Mexico, Paris or Waterloo. The poet may sing of Zion, and Siloam, of Jerusalem and its King, as well as of the wrath of Achilles, the siege of Troy, or the adventures of Eneas. An orator may as well plead for God as for man, for eternity as for time, for heaven as for earth; he may as well plead for man's salvation, as for his political rights and immunities; and the same learning and eloquence that gain for a client a good inheritance or a fair reputation, might, also, have gained for him an unfading crown, and an enduring inheritance. It depends upon the taste of the man of genius of any peculiar kind, to what cause he may supremely devote it. It is his duty, however, to bring it to the best market, and to consecrate it to the noblest and most exalted good.

But, finally, it is not only incumbent on men of genius that they cultivate their talents to the greatest perfection, and that they select the noblest and most useful calling, but that they also prosecute them with the greatest vigor, and devote themselves to them with the most persevering assiduity. It is not he that enters upon any career, or starts in any race, but he that runs well, and perseveringly, that gains the plaudits of others, or the approval of his own conscience.

Life is a great struggle. It is one splendid campaign, a race, a contest for interests, honors and pleasures of the highest character, and of the most enduring importance. Happy the man of genius who cultivates all his powers with a reference thereunto, who chooses the most noble calling, and who prosecutes it with all his might. Such a one, ultimately, secures to himself the admiration of all the great, the wise, the good. Such a one will always enjoy the approbation of his own judgment and conscience: and, better still, the approbation of his God and Redeemer. How pleasing to him who has run the glorious race, to survey from the lofty summit of his eternal fame, the cumulative results of an active life, developed in the light of eternity! How transporting to contemplate the proximate and the remote, the direct and the indirect beatific fruits of his labors reflected from the bright countenances of enraptured myriads, beaming with grateful emotion to him as the honored instrument of having inducted them into those paths of righteousness which led them into the fruition of riches, honors and pleasures boundless as the universe and enduring as the ages of eternity! That such, gentlemen, may be your happy choice and glorious destiny, is the sincere desire of your friend and orator.

ADDRESS.

IS MORAL PHILOSOPHY AN INDUCTIVE SCIENCE?

DELIVERED BEFORE THE CHARLOTTESVILLE LYCEUM, 1840.

MR. PRESIDENT AND GENTLEMEN OF THE LYCEUM:—

The desire of knowledge, and the power to acquire it, are, by a benevolent provision of the great Author of Nature, jointly vouchsafed to man. The centripetal principle of self-preservation which pervades every atom of the universe, the great globe itself, with every thing that lives and moves upon it, is not more universal than is the desire *to know*, in every being that has the power to know. This is the soul of the soul of man,—the energizing principle, which stimulates into action his whole sensitive, perceptive and reflective powers; and were it our duty to collect and classify the criteria by which to appreciate the intellectual capacity of an individual, we would give to his desire of knowledge an eminent rank among the evidences of his ability to acquire it.

To direct into proper channels, and to control within rational limits, the desire of knowledge, have always been paramount objects in every government, human and divine, which has legislated on the subject of education, or sought the rational happiness of man. Indeed, the Divine Father of our race, in the first constitution given to man, suspended his destiny on the proper direction and government of this desire. He was pleased to test the loyalty of his children by imposing a restraint, not so much upon their animal appetites as upon their desire to know. The God of reason hereby intimates to all intelligences, that the power to control this master passion is the infallible index of man's power of self-government in every thing else. How wisely and how kindly, then, did he denominate the forbidden tree, "the tree of knowledge of good and evil"! And perhaps it is just at this point, and from this view of the subject, that we acquire our best conceptions of the reason of high intelligences—of the fall of that mighty spirit whose desire to know, transcended the law of his being and the object of those sublime endowments bestowed upon him. That he was experimentally acquainted with this paramount desire of rational nature, is obvious from the policy of the temptation which he offered. Its point was to stimulate, not the animal, but the intellectual appetite of our mother Eve, by dogmatically affirming that God forbade the fruit, because he knew that if they should eat it, "they would be as gods, *knowing* both good and evil."

But while it appears most probable that all intelligences, angelic and human, embodied and disembodied, are superlatively fallible and vulnerable in this one point, and that their catastrophe was so far, at least, homogeneous, as to afford plausible ground of inference that the not holding or employing any power bestowed upon us in abeyance to the will of the donor, is the radical sin of our nature, and the prolific fountain of all the follies and misfortunes of man; still the desire of knowledge is one of the kindest and noblest instincts and impulses of our nature. Without it, the power to know would have been comparatively, if not altogether, useless to man.

The physical wants of the infant do not more naturally nor necessarily prompt his first animal exertions to find relief, than does this innate principle, this natural desire of knowledge, urge the mind into the pursuit of new ideas. The ineffable pleasure of the first conception only invites to a second effort; and success in that, stimulates to a third; and so on, in increasing ratios, till the full-grown man, on his full-fledged wings of intellectual maturity, soars aloft, as the eagle from the mountain-top, in quest of new and greater discoveries. And never did the miser's love of gold bear a more direct proportion to his success in accumulating it, than does the desire of knowledge in the bosom of the successful aspirant after new ideas keep pace with his intellectual attainments.

This again suggests to us a good reason for the variety and immensity of creation. Man needs such a universe as this, and the universe needs such a being as man, not merely as a component part, but as the worthy guest of it. Every thing that exists is to be enjoyed by a being who has the power of understanding and admiring it. Now, as the human power to know and to enjoy is naturally cumulative and progressive, the objects to be known and enjoyed must be proportionably vast and illimitable. And here again arises a new proof of design and adaptation in this grand and eloquent universe of God. For it is not only in the infinitude and variety of its parts—in its physical, intellectual and moral dimensions; but in the immeasurable aggregate of its provisions, as respects variety, extent and duration, that it is so adapted to the human constitution—to this unquenchable thirst for knowledge—this eternally increasing intellectual power of knowing and enjoying, bestowed on our rational and moral nature.

In all the language of celestial or terrestrial beings, there is no word of more comprehensive and transcendent import than the term *universe.* In its mighty grasp, in its boundless extent, it embraces Creator and creature—all past, all present, all future existences within the revolving circles of time, and the endless ages of eternity. Our finite minds, indeed, with all their gigantic powers of acquisition, cannot compass infinite ideas, but they can divide and subdivide the mighty whole into such small parts and parcels as come within their easy management. We have, therefore, divided the universe into innumerable solar systems spread over fields of space so immense as to make imagination herself flag in her most vigorous efforts to survey them. These systems we have again divided into planets, primary and secondary; and these again into various kingdoms—mineral, vegetable, animal, intellectual. These we have further distributed into genera, species and individuals, until a single individual becomes a distinct theme of contemplation. Even *that* we often find an object too large for our feeble efforts, and set about separating an individual existence into the primary elements of its nature, the attributes, modes and circumstances of its being, before it comes within the easy grasp of a special operation of our minds.

But the feast of the mind, the joy of the banquet, is not found in these distributions and classifications of things, but in viewing every organ and atom of every creature in reference to itself, and to the creature of which it is a part; then that creature as related to other creatures of its own species and genera; and these again in reference to other ranks and orders belonging to the particular world of which they are atoms; and that world itself as connected with others; and then all as related to the Supreme Intelligence, the fountain and source of all that is wise, and great, and good, and beautiful and lovely—the Parent of all being and of all joy; and thus to look through universal nature, and her ten thousand portals and avenues, up to nature's uncreated and unoriginated Author.

It is, indeed, a sublime and glorious truth that this to us unsearchable and incomprehensible universe can all be converted into an infinite and eternal fountain of joy, an inexhaustible source of pure and perennial bliss, commensurate with the whole capacity of man. But this, to us, is yet in the boundless future, and must depend upon the proper direction given to our desires and pursuits in the contemplation and study of the universe. The fields of science are innumerable. But few of them have ever passed under the observation of our greatest masters. Not one of them is yet understood. The whole universe, indeed, is yet to be studied; and with such care and attention that the worlds, and systems of worlds—of ideas within us, shall exactly correspond to the worlds and systems of worlds without us. As exactly as the image in the mirror resembles the face before it, so must the ideas within us correspond to the things without us, before we can be said to understand them. What ages, then, must pass over man, before the single system to which he now belongs shall have stamped the exact image upon his soul, and left as many sciences within him as there are things cognate and homogeneous without him! Before this begins to be accomplished, the seven sciences of the ancients will not only have multiplied into the seventy times seven of the moderns, but into multitudes that would bankrupt the whole science of numbers to compute. If Socrates, the great master of Grecian philosophy, could only boast that he had attained so much knowledge of the universe as to be confident that he knew nothing about it—comprehended no part of it—how much of that science of ignorance ought we to possess, to whom so many fountains of intelligence have been opened from which the sage of Athens was debarred!

But as there is nothing isolated or independent in all the dominions of God, so there cannot be an isolated or detached science in any mind, save that in which the original archetypes of all things were arranged before one of them was called into existence. And this is now, and always has been, the insuperable obstacle to the perfect comprehension of any one science, the basis of which is in the realms of mind or matter.

Still the desire to know rises with the consciousness of our ignorance, and even of our present inability, and we promise ourselves a day of grace in which we shall not only know in part, and prophesy in part, but shall see clearly, comprehend fully and know as we are known. Till then we must be content to study the primer of Nature and learn the elements of things around us, as preparatory to our admission into the high-school of the universe. Indeed, the greatest genius, the most gifted and learned in all human science, rises but to the portico of that school, the vestibule of that temple, in which the true science of true bliss is practically taught, and rationally communicated to man.

There is one science, however, in which it is possible to make great proficiency in this life, and which, of all the sciences, is the most popular, and withal the least understood. It has been a favorite in all the schools of the ancients, and of the moderns, but has never been successfully taught by Grecian, Roman, Indian or Egyptian philosophy. It is, indeed, neither more nor less than the *science of happiness—than the philosophy of bliss.* But some of you will immediately ask, "Where shall that science be found? In what temple does she deign to dwell? By what rites are her ears to be propitiated to our prayers? And by what less ambiguous name shall she be called?"

To introduce her, without proper ceremonies, to your acquaintance, would be as impolitic on my part as it would be perplexing to my inventive powers to find for her a pleasing and familiar name. But, in the absence of such a designation, I will state the *five points* of which she treats.

Whether it is because we have only five senses, five fingers on each hand, or because there are five points in Calvinism, and as many in Arminianism, that this divine science has only five points, I leave it to more learned doctors and sages than your humble servant to decide. But so it is: she has five points peculiarly her own, which no other science in the universe has ever been able to develop with either certainty or satisfaction to any man. These five points are—*the origin, the nature, the relations, the obligations and the destiny of man.*

Many, indeed, of the teachers, admirers and votaries of a science sometimes called "*moral philosophy,*" as taught by the ancients and by the moderns, have, with a zeal and devotion truly admirable, and worthy of a better cause, inculcated upon the youth of past and present times the sufficiency of human reason, or of human philosophy, to clear up all doubts and uncertainty upon every subject connected with man's relations and responsibilities to the universe.

That there are sciences physical, mental and moral, truly and properly so called, I doubt not; but that the science sometimes called "moral philosophy," which professes, from the mere light of nature, to ascertain and establish—indeed, to originate and set forth—the origin, nature, relations, obligations and destiny of man—is a true science of the inductive order, founded upon facts, upon observation and experiment, and not upon assumption, plagiarism, imagination, I cannot admit. If, then, we cannot set forth the science of happiness, nor find for it, at this time, an appropriate name; we shall attempt to expose, in part at least, the fallacy and imposition of all human science (especially of moral philosophy, which in this particular arrogates to itself more than every other science) in attempting to settle or develop any one of these five points with any degree of certainty, authority or evidence, either salutary or satisfactory to any man of sense.

This is neither the time nor the place for mere definitions, metaphysical arguments, nor for abstract reasonings. A definition or two we may have occasion to offer; but we shall rely much more upon a safer and more palpable evidence in demonstrating the perfect impotency of philosophy and human reason, however cultivated, possessing only the mere light of nature, to decide and enforce any one of these five cardinal points.

It will, I presume, be conceded by all persons of education and good sense, that human happiness demands the full enjoyment of all our powers and capacities, in harmony with all our relations and obligations to the creation of which we are a part, and that a knowledge of those relations and obligations is essential to the fulfilment and enjoyment of them; consequently there is a very great intimacy between the knowledge of these points and the philosophy of bliss.

It will also be conceded that the knowledge of our obligations and relations presupposes a knowledge of our origin and destiny; and, therefore, whatever system of reasoning, whatever science, fails to reveal these, cannot possibly develop those. These things premised, I hasten to show, that while moral philosophy proposes to do all this, *she has never done it in any one instance*—her greatest masters and most eloquent and powerful pleaders being accepted as credible testimony in the case.

That moral philosophy assumes to teach man his obligations and relations to Creator and creatures, and to make him virtuous and happy, is first to be proved. Whose testimony, then, shall we hear? That of the greatest of Roman philosophers—the most learned of her scholars—the most profound of her reasoners—the most eloquent of her orators—the most accomplished of her citizens—the unrivalled Cicero? He was, indeed, an honor to human nature; and, without exaggeration, in my opinion, the greatest man Pagan Rome ever produced. Many a fine encomium on philosophy may be gleaned from his numerous writings; but a few sentences will suffice to imprint his views on every mind. "Philosophy," says he, "is the culture of the mind that plucketh up vice by the roots—the medicine of the soul that healeth the minds of men. From philosophy we may draw all proper helps and assistance for leading virtuous and happy lives. The correction of all our vices and sins is to be sought for from philosophy.

O Philosophy!" adds he, "the guide of life—the searcher out of virtue and the expeller of vice, what would we be, nay, what would be the life of man, without thee! Thou wast the inventress of laws, the mistress of morals, the teacher of discipline! For thee we plead—from thee we beg assistance. One day spent according to thy precepts is preferable to an immortality spent in sin."* So spake the gigantic Roman, standing on the shoulders of the more gigantic Greek philosophers, Socrates, Plato, Aristotle, Zeno, and a hundred others of minor fame.

We shall next hear the oracle of modern philosophers who filled the chair of Dugald Stewart, the greatest of metaphysicians. "Philosophy," says he—quoting the most renowned of the stoics of Roman fame, the distinguished Seneca—"Philosophy forms and fashions the soul, and gives to life its disposition and order, which points out what is our duty to do, and what is our duty to omit. It sits at the helm, and in a sea of peril directs the course of those who are wandering through the waves." "Such," says our model philosopher in American schools, Brown of Edinburgh, "is the great practical object of all philosophy." "It comprehends," adds this standard author, "the nature of our spiritual being, as displayed in all the phenomena of feeling and of thought—the ties which bind us to our fellow-men and to our Creator, and the prospect of that unfading existence, of which life is but the first dawning gleam." (Vol. i. ch. 14.) Such, then, are the pretensions of philosophy, mental and moral, in the esteem of Christian as well as in that of Pagan sages.

I believe this to be the orthodox creed of all the popular schools in Britain and in America. Indeed, both Hartley and Paley might be quoted as going still further, in ascribing to moral philosophy an almost superior excellence in some points even to Revelation itself. But we need not such exaggerated views. The preceding will suffice for a text.

We shall now look for the exemplification of the fruits of this boasted and boastful philosophy in the admissions, declarations and acts of its teachers, and in the lives and morality of its students and admirers.

The witnesses to be heard in this case are the Grecian and Roman lawgivers and philosophers. We have not time to hear them depose singly and separately: we shall therefore examine them in companies.

The Greek philosophy is all arranged in three lines; as the learned,

* See Cic. Tuscul. Disputations, lib. 2, caps. 4 and 5; lib. 3, cap. 3; lib. 4, cap. 38; lib. 5, cap. 2.

since and before the revival of literature, have conceded. These three great lines are the Ionic, the Italic and the Eleatic. The Ionic was founded by the great Thales of the Ionian Miletus; the first natural philosopher and astronomer of Greece, who divided the year into three hundred and sixty-five days; observed the diameter of the sun; and foretold eclipses, about the middle of the sixth century before Christ. The Italic was founded by that great lawgiver and philosopher, Pythagoras, who established a school in Italy a little after the middle of the fifth century before Christ. The Eleatic was founded by Leucippus and Parmenides, of Elæ, early in the fifth century before Christ; the chiefs of which may be alluded to in the sequel. These schools are all named from the country or place in which they were originally located.

The Eleatic school was wholly atheistic, root and branch. Leucippus first taught the doctrine of atoms, afterwards adopted by the learned and facetious Democritus. While Heraclitus, the great Ephesian philosopher, wept over the follies of men, Democritus laughed at them, and taught that the universe was but the fortuitous concourse of atoms. The more refined and accomplished Epicurus speculated at great length upon the same theories, somewhat modified; and each of these great names headed a sect of atheists, who, while they agreed in the essential doctrine, differed in minor points. The essential doctrines of all the sects of the Eleatic school were, that the world was made by the god Chance—a fortuitous concourse of atoms; that it is governed by no intelligence, ruled by no governor and preserved by no providence. That the soul, if there be any, dies with the body; consequently there is no future life. That there is neither virtue nor vice, moral good nor moral evil by nature, or any other law than that of custom and public utility. That pleasure is the chief good, and pain the greatest evil, to man.

With the moral theories of this school other distinguished philosophers concurred, amongst whom Laertius ranks Theodorus, Archelaus and Aristippus, teaching that upon fit occasions (that is, when not likely to be detected) theft, sacrilege, and other enormities which we cannot name, might be committed, because nothing was by nature or of itself base, but by law and custom. I shall certainly be allowed to dismiss this school without further hearing, without a more formal proof that moral philosophy, in their hands, was not what our great moral philosophers, from Cicero down to Stewart and Brown of Scotch and American fame, have affirmed, viz. "The guide of life, the standard of virtue, the path to happiness."

We shall now hear the second school—the Italic. Pythagoras himself, the great Grecian father of the Metempsychosis, and his distinguished pupil, the Locrian Timæus, have opened the mysteries of this line in their leading differential attributes. This school believed in souls, and taught their immortality too. But curious souls they were, and unenviable their immortality. "The soul of the world," said they, "is an immortal soul, and human souls are but emanations from it; to which, after some ages of transmigrations, they return and are reabsorbed." This is a miniature of the darling peculiarity of Pythagoreanism. These emanation souls were, by an insuperable necessity, to make the tour of some definite number of human bodies—clean and unclean; and on their return to the *anima mundi*, to lose their individuality and identity, and to be amalgamated with it. This soul of the world, moreover, was, by the god Necessity, compelled to change worlds. Hence a succession of new worlds and of new transmigrations of the soul of the world was to fill up the series of infinite ages. This was illustrated by a bottle of sea-water, well corked, tossing about in the tumults of the ocean until the cork decayed, or till the bottle dashed upon a rock. In either event its soul, or the water within, mingled with the water of the ocean, and so lost its identity; yet it was as immortal as the ocean, because a part of it. If the illustration was good, the proof was better. This learned lawgiver and philosopher, blessed with a retentive memory, was able to prove his doctrine by narrating his own various and numerous transmigrations, antecedent to the name and body of Pythagoras. His delighted followers heard of his curious and brilliant intrigues and singular freaks while his soul was tabernacling in other mortal tenements.

If any one can find reasons of morality or of piety, motives to virtue or sources of joy in this school, he must excel the ingenious Ovid himself, who had to amend it in one or two points to suit the licentiousness of his own poetry. If not elegantly, he is correctly translated in the following lines, taken from his fifteenth book:—

"O you whom horrors of cold death affright,
Why fear you Styx? vain name! and endless night,
The dreams of poets, and feign'd miseries
Of forged hell, whether last flames surprise
Or age devour your bodies: they ne'er grieve,
Nor suffer pain. Our souls forever live,
Yet evermore their ancient houses leave
To live in new, which them as guests receive."

But need we ask, How can human souls enjoy or suffer any thing with a reference to the past, having first lost every feeling of personal identity? This school, then, was as ineffectual a guide of life—as whimsical a standard of virtue—as fallacious a way of happiness, as the Eleatic.

There yet remains another school—the Ionic school, more ancient, and therefore more orthodox, than either of the former two. Thales, its founder, was followed by Anaximander and Anaximenes: these were followed by Anaxagoras, the instructor of Pericles, and Archelaus, the alleged master of Socrates. These all, down to Socrates, devoted themselves to physics and not to morals; therefore they are out of our premises. Not so Socrates: of him Cicero has said, "He was the first to call philosophy from the heavens, to place it in cities, and to introduce it into private houses: that is, to teach public and private morals." He was, indeed, the first and the last of all the Grecian philosophers that wholly devoted himself to morals.

Plato and Xenophon were his immediate pupils; Aristotle and Xenocrates theirs. The Ionic school, in its theological and moral departments, was now merged in the Socratic; but that soon branched off into several sects—the Platonic, or old Academic; the Aristotelian, or Peripatetic; the Stoic, founded by Zeno; the middle Academy, by Arcesilaus; and the new Academy, by Carneades. Between these two last Academies there was no real nor permanent difference. If not in all their conclusions, they were, in all their modes of reasoning, skeptical. Their discriminating principles were, that "nothing could be known," and that "*every thing was to be disputed;*" consequently, nothing was to be assented to, said the absolute skeptic. "No," said the Academics, "the *probable*, wherever you find it, must be assented to, but, till it be found, you are to doubt." And the misfortune was, they rarely or never found the *probable;* and in effect the Academics and followers of Pyrrho, the absolute skeptic, were equally atheists all their lives. Meanwhile, as said the learned Bishop of Gloucester, "they talked perpetually of their *verisimile* and of their *probabile*, amidst a situation of absolute doubt, darkness and skepticism—like Sancho Panza of his island on the *terra firma!*" Pyrrho dogmatically affirmed that "no one opinion was more probable than another," and that there were no moral qualities or distinctions. Beauty and deformity, virtue and vice, happiness and misery, had no real cause, but depended on comparison—in one word, that "*all was relative.*"

The lights of all Pagan philosophy are now reduced to the three sects of the Socratic school—the Platonic, the Peripatetic and the Stoic. If we find no surer, no clearer moral lights in these three, all

Grecian, all Roman philosophy is a varied and extended system of skepticism, so far as the origin, moral obligations and destiny of man are involved.

The Stoic, (for we shall take the last first,) so called, not from Zeno, their founder, nor from his city; but from the *painted porch* in Athens, from which he promulged his doctrines, by another route arrived at the same goal with Epicurus. In their abstractions they discovered, I had almost said, that pain was pleasure; at least, that pain was no evil. Epicurus taught that pleasure was the only good—Zeno, that virtue alone was bliss—Epicurus, that virtue was only valuable as the means of pleasure. Both agreed in demanding from their disciples an absolute command over their passions, and both supposed it practicable. They both boldly asserted that the philosophy which they taught was the only way to happiness; and yet both agreed that there was no future state of happiness or misery, and equally justified self-murder.

Could any evidence dissipate the delusion of the competency of philosophy to be either the standard of virtue or the guide of life, methinks it might be found in this best of Pagan schools. Amongst its brightest ornaments were Chrysippus, Cato of Utica, Epictetus, Seneca and Marcus Antoninus the Pious. Plausible in many of their dogmata, prepossessing in their displays of certain virtues, fascinating in some of their theories, most ingenious in all their speculations, they breathed contempt both of pleasure and pain, commanded the extinguishment of passion and appetite, eulogized temperance and self-government, and extolled the dignity of virtue and the rules of modesty and piety; while themselves were addicted to vicious indulgences, sensual pleasures, and even to gross intemperance itself. Zeno drank to excess, and killed himself rather than endure the pain of a broken finger; Chrysippus died of a surfeit of sacrificial wine; Cleanthus followed his example; while Cato of Utica thrust the dagger into his own heart; Epictetus gave to the human will a power almighty, above that of the gods themselves, and advised suicide in certain cases; Seneca taught that no man ought to fear God—that a virtuous man equalled him in happiness; he justified the drunkenness of Cato, and plead for self-murder; while many of them indulged in the grosser and more nameless vices of the Pagan world. Of none of the Stoics could as much in truth be said as Cowley says of Epicurus:—

"His life he to his doctrine brought,
And in a garden's shade that sovereign pleasure sought;
Whoever a true Epicure would be
May there find cheap and virtuous luxury."

The Peripatetic school, so denominated from the *peripaton*, or walk of the Lyceum in which Aristotle taught his philosophy, next claims our attention. With the moral part of his theory our demonstration lies. Aristotle, then, with all his prodigious parts, great erudition and various and profound studies, was a polytheist. He asserted the eternity of the world both in matter and form. He, indeed, held a supreme abstract Intelligence, which he called the Supreme God—pretty much the *anima mundi* of Pythagoras. This Supreme God was the life and soul of all the gods inferior; for all the stars were, with him, true and eternal gods. He denied that Providence ever stooped beneath the moon, and, consequently, superintended not human affairs. His moral sentiments and theories, as a matter of course, corresponded with his theological views. He not only approved but prescribed the exposing and destroying of weak and sickly children. He encouraged revenge. Vacillating in all his theories of the soul, he doubted at one time its future existence, and finally concludes the ninth chapter of his third book of Ethics with these words: "Death is the most dreadful of all things; for that is the *end of our existence:* for to him that is dead there seems nothing further to remain, whether good or evil." Dicæarchus, one of his most learned followers, whom Cicero extols, wrote books to prove that souls are mortal; and many of his followers compared the soul to the harmony of a musical instrument, which has no existence when the instrument is destroyed. The Platonic school, or the old Academic, is not much better than the Peripatetic. Plato is designedly obscure in all his speculations on divinity. He affirms one Supreme God, but he had no concern in the creation or government of the world, and recommended the people to worship a plurality of inferior deities. He extols the oracles, and advises the consultation of them in all matters of religion and worship. He prescribed great licentiousness of manners; allows, and sometimes commands, the exposing and destroying of children. He declares that on proper occasions lying is not only profitable, but lawful. He argues the immortality of the soul, and speaks of the rewards and punishments of a future life. He sometimes, however, equivocates on this subject, and seems to believe in the transmigration of souls; while again he will have the soul immortal from a necessity of nature, or from an antecedent immortality. He taught the Greeks to love themselves and hate the barbarians as enemies; by which term he denoted all other nations.

But yet there remains Socrates himself, the father of the Greek moral philosophy. Though not followed in the best part of his speculations by even his own Plato, who, nevertheless, with the exception of Xenophon in some points, followed him more closely than any other disciple of the Socratic school, he clearly asserted and boldly taught one God, the immortality of the soul and future retributions. Paradoxical, however, though it be, he did not fully believe the doctrine which he taught. Sometimes he believed it; at other times, his reasonings not fully proving it, he seems to doubt it. He appears, indeed, to have died a skeptic. He both taught and practised polytheism, and amongst his last words ordered a sacrifice to the god of physic.

As Plato represents him in his *Phædon*, the more nearly he approached death, the more he doubted his own doctrine. To his surrounding friends he says, "I hope that I shall go to good men after death; but this I will not absolutely affirm." But as to his going to the gods he is positive. "If," says he, "I could affirm any thing, concerning matters of such a nature, I would affirm this." Again, "That these things are so, as I have represented them, it does not become any man of understanding to affirm; though, if it appear that the soul is immortal, it seems reasonable to think that either such things, or something like them, are true with regard to our souls and their habitations after death; and that it is worth making a trial, for the trial is noble."

To his judges he says, "There is much ground to hope that death is good; for it must necessarily be one of the two: either the dead man is nothing, and hath not a sense of any thing, or it is only a change or migration of the soul hence to another place—according to *what we are told*"—

Κατα τα λεγομενα.

Finally, he says, "Those who live there are both in other respects happier than we, and also in this, that ever after they are immortal." *If the things which are told us are true, Ειπερ τα λεγομενα αλεθε εστιν.* Such are the triumphs of philosophy. Such is its power to guide the life, the piety, the morality, the destiny of man.

But we are about still further to despoil it of the little light that it has, and divest it of all its glory, even in the points in which the three mightiest of Grecian philosophers—Socrates, Plato and Aristotle—most deserve and have most enjoyed the admiration of the world.

Remember the last words of Socrates—"*If, indeed, the things that have been told us are true.*" Who, then, will have the temerity to affirm that moral philosophy is a true science; that it builds upon its own foundation and uses only its own materials; while its father and founder at last shifts it off the basis of reason and its own researches, and seeks for a foundation in the traditions of former times?

Tradition, then, and not induction, originated in the minds of the Socratic school all the light of the origin, moral obligations and destiny of man, which this school and the Grecian and the Roman world from it enjoyed.

The history of the whole matter is this:—The Romans borrowed from the Greeks, the Greeks stole from the Egyptians and Phenicians, while they borrowed from the Chaldeans and Assyrians, who stole from the Abrahamic family all their notions of the spirituality, eternity and unity of God, the primitive state of man, his fall, sacrifice, priests, altars, immortality of the soul, a future state, eternal judgment and the ultimate retribution of all men according to their works.

We might, indeed, pursue the same course in reference to the Persians, the Egyptians, the Indians, the ancient Gauls, and trace all the light in them to the same common origin.

The Indians, Egyptians, Phenicians, Greeks, Romans, made very great advances in geometry, astronomy, natural history, philosophy, language, politics, oratory, and the fine arts of architecture, sculpture, painting, poetry and music. But in the points before us they degenerated into superstition, mythology, licentiousness and barbarity.

As we examine and compare all the systems of moral philosophy and theology, ascending the streams of antiquity we find the Druids among the Gauls, the Magi among the Persians, the Brahmins among the Indians, the philosophers among the Greeks and Romans, all borrowing from one original and universal tradition. The writings of Confucius and Zoroaster, of Borosus and Sanchoniathon, and every ancient monument which has escaped the wreck of time, bear inscribed upon them the same unequivocal testimony.

Thus the lawgivers, philosophers and sages of Greece travelled into Egypt and the East in quest of knowledge. Amongst the Grecian lawgivers and sages who visited this ancient and celebrated country in search of new ideas, were Orpheus, Rhadamanthus, Minos, Lycaon, Triptolemus, Solon, Pythagoras, Plato, &c.; by whom the Greeks, as generally acknowledged by themselves, imported from Egypt their theology, philosophy and learning.

Philosophy, or human reason, as may appear in the sequel, is very inadequate to the discovery of ideas on any of the great points involved in the origin, obligations and destiny of man. Hence, sensible and learned men of former times and of the present day assign to tradition or revelation, handed down orally, and neither to "natural religion" nor moral philosophy, all knowledge upon these subjects. Great and learned names may be found in abundance, to sanction the conclusion to which we are forced to come, from the facts now standing in our horizon. These will say, with the distinguished Puffendorf, in his Law of Nations,* "It is very probable that God himself taught the first men the chief heads of natural laws, which were preserved and spread abroad by means of education and custom." "Nature," says Plutarch, in his treatise on Education, "nature without learning or instruction is a blind thing." "Vice can have access to the soul by many parts of the body; but virtue can lay hold of a young man only by his ears." And "Man," says Plato, "if not properly educated, is the wildest and most untractable of all earthly animals." And, declare a host of close observers, "No man has ever been found possessed of a spiritual conception by the mere exercise of his own powers."

But, to complete our premises, two things are yet wanting—a just view of *tradition*, and of the comparative claims of reason and faith as faculties or powers of acquiring knowledge of the highest and most important character. On these we have time for but a few remarks. And, first, of *tradition* as the first and chief source of knowledge to man.

Before an effort to sketch the history of ancient tradition, we must define the term. According to Milton—a name of high renown—"tradition is any thing delivered orally from age to age." But, in its more enlarged signification, it denotes any thing—fact, event, opinion—handed down to us, whether by word or writing. Still, the ancient traditions being accounts of things delivered from mouth to mouth, without written memorials, while speaking of them I shall use the term as defined by Milton—*Things delivered orally from age to age.*

Few of us have paid much attention either to the nature or the amount of that knowledge possessed in the remotest ages of the world, or to the safe and direct manner by which it was communicated from one generation to another. It was a true and practical knowledge of those five elements which was essential to the science of happiness. On no one of these points did man, *could* man, begin to speculate or philosophize till tradition was corrupted by fable, and men began to doubt. Hence the era of philosophy, mental and moral, was the era of skepticism. For, in the name of reason, why should a man institute a demonstration *a priori* or *a posteriori* to ascertain a fact for which he had direct, positive and unequivocal evidence?

---

* Vol. ii. chap. iii. sect. 20.

That the first man never was an infant, reason and philosophy are compelled to admit; and that he was *spoken to* before *he* spoke, and that by a superior Being, are postulates which will be no sooner demanded than conceded by every man having any pretensions to science or reason. Of course, then, the adult Adam received knowledge orally from its fountain—knowledge of his origin, nature, relations, obligations and destiny. If he did not fully comprehend each or all of these, he could not possibly be ignorant of any one of them. He lived for nine hundred and thirty years, an adult life all the time; and certainly was the oracle of the world for the first thousand years of its history.

But there were two witnesses from the beginning; and two witnesses most credible, because every feeling of human nature compelled Adam and Eve to give a true history of their experience to their own children. Methuselah, who lived to the age of nine hundred and sixty-nine—the very year of the deluge—conversed with Adam for two hundred and forty-three years; and with Shem, the son of Noah, for almost one hundred years. Thus, not only all the experience, all the acquisitions, of these two great and learned sages, (for great and learned they truly were,) but all the science of the antediluvian world was carried down to Shem by the lips of one man. Now, as Shem lived five hundred years after the flood, he must have been the greatest of moral oracles that ever lived. All antiquity, from Adam to himself, came to his ears by one man, corroborated too by the concurrent testimony of many others.

The amount and variety of knowledge which Methuselah possessed and communicated would, without much reflection, be almost incredible to any one who has not closely looked into the fragments of sacred history which are extant at this hour. Besides, their knowledge of geology, astronomy, natural history, chronology and general physics was much more extensive than we imagine.

Enoch, the father of Methuselah—the most enlightened and perfect man that lived during the first two thousand years of human history—was a most gifted teacher of the science of morals. He taught a future judgment, the coming of the Lord, with ten thousand of his saints, to punish the wicked; and, in his translation to heaven—body, soul and spirit—forty-four years before Seth, the immediate son of Adam, died, gave an exemplification of the immortality of the saints to all his contemporaries and to posterity through all generations. At the time of his translation, Seth, Enos, Cainan, Mahalaleel, Jared, Methuselah and Lamech were all of mature age and reason; so that all the generations between Adam and Noah had the advantage of the doctrine, manner of life and translation of Enoch. The origin of the universe and of man—his nature, relations, obligations and destiny—were, therefore, matters of fact or direct testimony amongst the antediluvians, and faithfully communicated from the mouth of one individual, corroborated by many concurrent witnesses, into the ears of Shem. Shem, too, became an oracle of the postdiluvians for five hundred years; spending one hundred and fifty years of his life with Abraham, and fifty with Isaac, his son. Thus the entire experience of Adam came to Shem through one individual, and passed through him to Isaac; so that from the tongue of Methuselah the words of Adam fell upon the ears of Shem, and from the tongue of Shem may have fallen upon the ears of Abraham and Isaac.

The vast knowledge of ten antediluvian generations, with the subsequent details of four hundred years—a period of two thousand one hundred and fifty-six years—is transferred to Isaac through two persons.

But, while I thus speak of two persons, I would not be understood as making them the sole depositaries of all the learning and knowledge of twenty generations of men. In keeping the chronicles of the world, Adam was aided eight hundred years by his son Seth; almost seven hundred by his grandson Enos; six hundred by Cainan; five hundred by Mahalaleel; four hundred by Jared; three hundred by Enoch; two hundred by Methuselah; and sixty-four, by Lamech, the father of Noah and grandfather of Shem. Shem, also, after the deluge, was aided by ten generations of men with whom he conversed; for, of the twenty generations of our Lord's ancestors whose history he could give, he had seen with his own eyes twelve. How vast and varied, then, were the stores of tradition and of personal experience possessed by this most learned of all the sages of mankind! A fit person, indeed, in the character of the King of Salem and priest of the Most High God, to bless the patriarch Abraham, the holder of the promises.

But, to trace the history of tradition down to Moses: Isaac, it will be remembered, lived long enough with Shem to have learned it all from him. He also conversed not only with Jacob, but for more than fifty years with Levi. Levi told the story to his son Kohath; Kohath told it to his son Amram; and Amram to his son Moses. So that all ancient knowledge reached Moses from Adam down to his own times —a period of two thousand four hundred and thirty-three years—by only *six persons*.

Meanwhile, the knowledge of the true and only God and of these cardinal points was in Egypt, from other sources of tradition, when Abraham first reached it. Other branches of the human family besides that of Shem took notes of facts and events. And we know that all the knowledge of Shem, communicated to Jacob, Joseph and Levi, went down into Egypt with these persons as early as the year of the world 2298.

Now, we learn from profane history that Cadmus, with his Phenician colony, founded Thebes, and Cecrops and Danaus, with their Egyptian relations, founded Athens and Argos, about the time of Moses. Carrying with them the science and learning of Egypt into these new states, we can easily discover how the knowledge of the East came into Europe, and how the traditionary revelation in Abraham's family became a common fountain of knowledge to the whole human race.

With regard to the correctness and authority of these traditions, moderns generally entertain very erroneous conceptions. We suppose them to be of no higher authority than many of the legendary tales of more modern times. But this is owing to our want of a little philosophy, and to our confounding the character of the traditions after the confusion of speech and the dispersion of mankind with those which existed while the world was all of one language and of one speech.

Could we place ourselves among the antediluvians while all mankind spoke one language, and then among the postdiluvians after the confusion of speech, the contraction of human life and the wide dispersion of mankind over the earth, we should find some *data* by which to appreciate the all-important difference between the *ancient* and the *most* ancient traditions.

Can any one, the least acquainted with human nature, possessing a little of the philosophy of himself, imagine that Adam and Eve would not freely communicate to every son and daughter, to the tenth generation, who visited them, all they had orally learned from their Creator, or by subsequent revelation, on the three great questions which human reason and human philosophy frankly confess they cannot answer, viz. *What am I? Whence came I?* and *Whither do I go?* Would not the venerable pair most cheerfully and faithfully narrate their experience to their own offspring—give a clear and full record of the past—and intimate all their anticipations of the future? With what thrilling interest would they detail the incidents of the patriarchal state, and the sad series of events accompanying and subsequent to their eventful catastrophe!

Or can any one suppose that during the latter centuries of this chief patriarch, when his progeny had grown up into nations, multitudes of the most virtuous of them, even from the remotest settlements, would not continually visit him as an oracle, and learn from his own lips the whole history of time, the origin of the race, and the antiquities of nature herself?

Who of us moderns would not make a pilgrimage half round the globe to see the first man; to look in the face and to hear the voice of the great prototype of humanity; and to listen to his narration, not only of what he had seen and heard of the Creator himself, or learned in latter days of his works and will; but to hear him relate his conceptions and ecstasies when first the breath of life swelled the purple current in his veins—when wonder, love and praise struggled within him for utterance, while he gazed upon the Father of his spirit, and the new-born glories of a universe smiling upon him with brighter beams of joy and bliss than ever the rapt vision of the most inspired of human bards has yet conceived!

I say, who of us would not have curiosity enough to encounter toils and dangers of the first magnitude, to have it to tell to our children that we had seen and heard the unborn man—the father of a world—the origin of mankind—and his divinely formed wife, an after-creation from himself—the mother of all the loveliness and beauty, of all the grace and excellency, of all the intelligence and taste, of all the delicacy and sensibility which have adorned the untold millions of her deceased and living daughters!

We have only to bring the matter home to ourselves to be assured that the whole history of the first nine centuries, which had in it the elements not only of society, but of religion, morality and all natural science, so far as Adam was concerned, (and no man's experience ever equalled his,) would have been told by him ten thousand times, and as often repeated by his faithful sons and daughters. This would also be true of Shem and of his wife, who stood in a similar relation to the postdiluvian world. They had to tell not only what they had heard from Methuselah, Lamech, and a thousand others of the old world, but had the marvellous record of the deluge, by which a world was lost, and a new order of things begun.

Now, can there be any thing more obvious than that narrations so often delivered by the same persons, should be engraved upon their memories with the clearness and fidelity of words deep cut in marble, or engraved on plates of brass? No translations or spurious readings could vitiate or corrupt that text, written on the tablets of hale and undegenerate memories, and kept as within the ark of the covenant, in the *sanctum sanctorum* of their hearts.

We need no oracle to declare or to decide, that men walked by faith before philosophy, or that there was no place for speculation or hypothesis during the first two thousand years of time; for who could have been so crazy as to state a hypothesis about the origin or nature, the relations or obligations of man, or about the origin of the universe, while Adam lived! or about the deluge or antediluvian state of our planet, while Noah, Shem or Japheth yet lived! Such a speculator would have been laughed out of society, and excommunicated from the habitations of the sane and rational of mankind.

Some of the events of the first age of the world were, moreover, of such a nature as to attract extraordinary attention; to occasion more reflection and elicit more light than we can now fully appreciate. The martyrdom of Abel, the death of Adam and the translation of Enoch were of this class. Hence many conversations on the questions, Whither went Enoch? What came of Abel? Why was he slain? Where now is Adam? Of what use is an altar, a priest, a victim? Why count time by weeks? What means the promised seed? What means the threatened bruising of the serpent's head? &c. &c. Among the faithful line of the ancestry of our Lord these were topics familiar and often discussed.

Hitherto we have spoken of but one line of tradition—that which has given all true light, civilization and refinement to human nature. But there was, and still is, another line, whence came hypothetical philosophy, ignorance and barbarity. Cain was the head of this line. Of him it is said, that after he had slain his brother Abel he went out from the presence of the Lord, or from the dwellings of the righteous, and east of Eden settled in the land of Nod. His line is heard through his descendants, Enoch, Jared, Mehujael, Methusael, Lamech, and his sons Jabal, and Jubal, and Tubal-Cain, seven generations. Cain founded the first city on earth, called after his son, the city of Enoch. Having gone away from the presence of the Lord, and busied himself in worldly employments to drown reflection, and his descendants all following his example, it is not likely that he would often visit the paternal dwelling. The blood of Abel still haunted him, and rendered him in fact a fugitive and vagabond on the earth. His descendants also gave themselves up to animal and temporal pursuits, and became distinguished for their inventions in tent-building, musical instruments, in brazen and iron implements and weapons, and for introducing polygamy and war.

The destiny of man is never a pleasant theme to such spirits; and as guilt is the natural parent of fear and the immediate progenitor of a refuge of lies and hatred of the light, such persons would be at more pains to vitiate the ancient traditions than to preserve them pure and incorrupt. Intermarrying with these on the part of the other line, superinduced the deluge.

After that catastrophe, either through the wives of Ham and Japheth, or from the inherited depravity and corruption of the old world, they again apostatized from God. Ham immediately dishonored himself, and brought upon his family a paternal and prophetic malediction. Japheth, too, removed from the residence of his father; and in their wanderings, and subsequently in the confusion and wide dispersion of their offspring, they lost their veneration for the paternal customs and traditions concerning their relations, moral obligations and destiny. Among them the truth began to be mixed up with fable, and so metamorphosed that it lost all its redeeming influence upon these two branches of the family of Noah.

The posterity of Japheth, called by the Greeks *Japetus*, comprehended the ancient Cimbrians, Phrygians, Scythians, Medes, Persians, Macedonians, Iberians, Greeks, Romans—indeed, all the ancient European and northern tribes of Asia, and probably some of the American tribes; while the posterity of Ham peopled some portions of Arabia, all Egypt and Canaan, Seba, Shebah, Shinar, much of Africa, and some parts of Asia.

Among these, fable, mythology and hypothesis began. Oral tradition, much corrupted indeed, continued amongst them till the time of Hesiod, Homer, and, I might say, to the time of Pherecydes of Scyros, the preceptor of Pythagoras—himself the pupil of Pittacus and the oldest of the Greek prose writers. But as the history of the Greeks consisted of oral and incoherent traditions, kept for thirteen centuries before they had a written history of themselves, little or nothing certain can be known of them, except their original extraction and their plagiarisms on Egypt and the posterity of Shem; for, of all people that ever lived, the Greeks were the greatest literary thieves, and had the best art of concealing the theft.

The word *philosophy*, and the profession of philosopher, began with Pythagoras, when tradition was involved in doubt owing to the causes already mentioned—the contraction of human life to seventy or eighty years, the confusion of human speech, the multiplications and wide dispersion of nations, and especially the gigantic iniquity, violence and crime which almost universally prevailed. Polytheism, mythology, hypothesis, skepticism and licentious manners, were the legitimate fruits of departing from the sacred traditions truly and faithfully kept in the line of Seth, Enoch, Noah and Shem, down to Moses, the divine historian and lawgiver of the Jews.

Thus far the history of the most ancient traditions is placed in contrast with the pretensions of hypothetical philosophy. It remains for us to cast a glance upon two or three points in the human constitution, to ascertain whether man was made to be led by philosophy or tradition in matters pertaining to the science of happiness: for certain it is, if man was not made to be led by philosophy, in vain she pretends to be his guide.

The question now before us is, *How is man constituted as respects the faculty of acquiring knowledge?* or with what powers of knowing the universe is he endowed? for, as before observed, the universe must be known before it can be enjoyed. I ask not what are his powers of retaining knowledge, nor what are his powers of applying or of enjoying knowledge; but what are his powers of acquiring it? With the most liberal philosophers they are four—*Instinct, Sense, Reason, Faith.* Some philosophers, indeed, are not so generous; none, however, give him more; and we are willing that he should appear with all his armor on—with all his intellectual apparatus in full requisition, that we may demonstrate that he was made to be led, pre-eminently and supremely, by a power that despoils speculative philosophy of all its proud assumptions, and gives to tradition, in its broadest and fullest sense, a very elevated standing amongst the sources of intelligence accessible to man.

Let us then briefly survey these powers. Instinct has never been definitely and satisfactorily explained by any man. The theories on the subject are innumerable, but speculation and inquiry are as rife as ever. Nothing is decided except that it is a law or rule of life conferred by the Creator on every animated existence, animal or vegetable, by which such acts are performed as are essential to its existence and well-being. But it is of a much higher order in the animal than in the vegetable kingdom, and in some animals it appears to be so nearly assimilated and related to intelligence as to be with difficulty distinguished from it. It is, however, very different from sensation and reason; for it is found to exist where there is neither of them.

In reference to my object, it is enough to say, that by instinct we mean that innate or natural rule of life, which God has written upon and incorporated with the nature of every animal; by which it is enabled to govern itself, in order to the full enjoyment of all its powers and susceptibilities, and so much of the universe as is suited to its nature. So far it is a perfect and infallible rule of life to it, in all that respects its nature and the end of its existence. It may be impaired by physical disease; it may also be deteriorated, but it cannot be improved by education. It is as perfect the first as the last hour of animal or vegetable existence. It gains nothing by experience or observation: hence the swallow builds her nest, the beaver his dam, the bee its cell, and the ant her cities and storehouses, as they were wont to do six thousand years ago.

Now, man has little or no instinct; and, in this point, is more neglected by his Creator than any other creature; and would, indeed, perish from the earth the first day of his existence, if left to the guidance of all his instinctive powers—an evident proof that he was not made to be led by it, as the law of his animal, intellectual or moral existence.

By *sense* we mean those external organs, usually denominated the five senses, through which we become acquainted with the sensible properties of all the objects around us. In this endowment man is not singular. All terrestrial beings of much importance to man have as many senses as he has. And if, in some of his senses, he is superior to some of them, in others, some of them are greatly superior to him.

But he has intellect—he has reason; and this greatly compensates for those inferiorities; and yet there are many creatures that seem to possess it in some good degree: still it is man's great perfection, by which he rises far above the beasts that perish. Some philosophers have almost deified reason, and given to it a creative and originating power. They have so eulogized the light of reason and the light of nature, that one would imagine reason to be a *sun*, rather than an eye; a revelation, rather than the power of apprehending and enjoying it. But when accurately defined, it is only a power bestowed on man, of comparing things, and propositions concerning things, and of deducing propositions from them. It is the faculty of discriminating one name, or thing, or attribute from another, and of forming just conceptions of it. It is not, then, a creative power. It cannot make something out of nothing. It is to the soul what the eye is to the body. It is not light, but the power of perceiving and using it. And as the eye without light, so reason without tradition or revelation would be useless to man in all the great points which the inductive and true philosophy of nature and of fact humbly acknowledges she cannot teach. She modestly avows her inability to unfold, or even to ascertain the origin, nature or end of any thing. Her verdict in the case before us is, that he who presumes to walk by the light of reason in these great matters is not more eminently insane, than he who assumes to walk by his eyes in the midst of utter darkness.

But the ennobling faculty of man is *faith*. This puts him in possession of the experience of all other men by believing their testimony. Instinct, sense and reason, however enlarged in their operations, are confined to a single individual of the race, and that within a very narrow circle, a mere atom of creation, and but for a moment of time; while faith encompasses the area of universal experience, and appropriates to its possession the acquisitions of all men in all ages of time.

Human knowledge, properly so called, consists of but two chapters. Our own individual experience furnishes the one, and faith the other.

Faith, therefore, is to instinct, sense and reason, as the experience of all mankind is to that of a single individual—the experience of a thousand millions to one. And were we to add to the experience of all living men that of all who have lived and died, or that of all who shall hereafter live, and superadd to this the experience of all angels, and all other orders of intelligences hereafter to be made, accessible to faith, how inconceivably immense the disproportion between reason and faith, as the means of enlarging the capacity and of storing the mind of man with true knowledge! In one word, then, from an invincible necessity of nature, we are indebted to faith for millions of ideas, for one obtained by our own personal sensations, observations or reflections.

How preposterous, then, was it for the learned and ingenious author of the "Treatise on Human Nature," to elaborate an essay to prove that no man could rationally believe the testimony of any number of persons affirming a supernatural fact; because, as he imagined, their testimony was contrary to universal experience! The eloquent author of the History of England seems not to have perceived the delusion he was imposing on himself, in making his own individual experience, or that of a few others, equal to that of all mankind in all ages of the world, a ten-thousand-millionth part of which he, nor no other person, ever heard or knew! No man ever had universal experience, consequently no man could believe it. On such a splendid sophism, on such a magnificent assumption, however, is founded the capacious temple of French, English, German and American infidelity.

While we have our definitions of instinct, sense, reason and faith before us, and this ingenious class of doubting philosophers in our eye, we must enter another demur to the sanity of their intellects, or of their logic. We have seen that instinct is a divine and infallible rule of life given to the mere animal creation—and, indeed, to the vegetable also, (as might be demonstrated were this the proper place,) for the purpose of guiding the actions of those creatures in benevolent subordination to the end of their being. Now, of this endowment man is of all creatures the most destitute: therefore, if he have not an infallible rule somewhere else, he is more slighted than any other creature; nay, he is the only creature wholly neglected by his Creator, in the most important, too, of all communicated endowments. But he has not this infallible rule in his five senses—he has it not in his powers of reasoning; and unless he have it in his faith in divine testimony, in a revelation internal and external, he is an anomaly in creation—the solitary exception to a law which, but for him, would be universal. But what makes this hypothesis still more extravagantly absurd is the fact, that, of all sublunary creatures, man is the favorite of his Maker—the head and "lord of the fowl and the brute." Now, to have granted the meanest insect a perfect rule of life; to have remembered every other creature and forgotten only man, in a point the most vital to his enjoyment of himself and of the universe, is an assumption, a result more incredible and marvellous than any other assumption on the pages of universal history. This is, indeed, to swallow a camel while straining out a gnat.

Another assumption of this speculative philosophy, another point deeply affecting the pretensions of revelation, and the most ancient and veritable traditions of the infancy of time and of nations, is equally at fault with the instances now given, and demands a special notice. It objects to a system of religion and morals founded upon faith rather than upon philosophy, as not in harmony with human nature, on account of its liabilities to deception in all matters depending upon human testimony. It dogmatically affirms that man is more liable to be deceived by *faith* than by *reason.*

This is a direct assault upon nature, and consequently upon the Author of it. For what can be more evident than that every human being is by an insuperable necessity compelled to make the very first step in life, intellectual and moral, if not physical, by faith? Must an infant wait the impulses of instinct or the decisions of reason for instruction in what to choose, or what to refuse, in the nursery or infant school? Or must it depend on its own observation, experience and reason, or upon oral tradition, for light upon food, and medicine, and poison? Must it experiment with the asp, the adder, the basilisk, the fire, the flood, the innumerable physical dangers around it, or implicitly believe its nurse, and walk by faith in her traditions? When it enters the infant school, must it prove by reason, or receive upon testimony, the names and figures of all the vowels and consonants of the alphabet? Can it by reason or instinct learn any grammar, speak any language, or make one step in human science or literature? It is just as true in nature as in religion, that he that believeth not shall be destroyed. There is no salvation to the infant man from natural evils—from ignorance, vice and misery—any more than to the adult sinner, from guilt and ruin, but by faith in tradition, oral or written. The voice of nature and that of the gospel speak the same language—*he that believeth not shall perish.* Man, then, is so constituted that he must walk by faith if he walk at all. He must do this long before reason has commenced its career of examination. Now, to affirm that reason is a better guide than faith, is to charge our Creator with folly in subjecting man to an inferior guide, even in the incipient and moulding period of his being, while his mind is assuming a character, and being fashioned for future life. To do this on a model, too, that forever gives to his ears an ascendency over sense and reason, as the channel of light and knowledge, unless he intended that faith should always have the superiority in guiding the actions of man, is, in fact, to interpose an insuperable obstacle to his own designs, and to defeat himself in any after-measure to restore him to reason, from aberrations supposed to be attendant on the exercise of faith as an incompetent rule of moral action. Man, however, reason as we may, is by an insuperable necessity compelled to make the first step in physical, intellectual and moral life by faith in tradition; and well would it have been for immense multitudes had they continued to walk by faith in the oral traditions of those moral instructors to whom God in the first ages of the world, confided the temporal and eternal destiny of mankind.

Lest, however, it should seem as if faith and reason were rival claimants for the absolute government of man, and, like other aspirants, were seeking to rise, each upon the ruin of his competitor, to this high office, the province of reason should be distinctly noted and understood. Permit me, then, to say in behalf of reason, that she assumes to be only a minister to faith, as she is to religion and morality. She examines the testimony, and decides upon its pretensions. In this sense, intellect and reason are as necessary to faith as they are to moral excellence; for a creature destitute of reason is alike incapable of faith, morality and religion. Reason, then, in one word, examines the tradition and the testimony, whether it be that of our five senses, our memory, our consciousness, or that of other persons; faith receives that testimony, and common sense walks by it.

From the definitions, facts and inferences now before us, may we not, gentlemen, conclude that if the physical sciences—natural philosophy in all its branches—be true sciences, because all founded on their own facts, observations and inductions, that science usually called moral philosophy is not a true science, because not founded on its own facts, observations and inductions, but on assumptions and plagiarisms from tradition and divine revelation; borrowing, instead of originating and demonstrating, all its fundamental principles?

If our mode of examining its pretensions be fair and logical, as we humbly conceive it is, does it not appear, by a liberal induction of witnesses from the best Pagan schools, that it has never taught, with the clearness and fulness of persuasion, nor with the authority of law or demonstration, the true doctrine of man's origin, nature, relations, obligations and destiny? And from a careful consideration of all our powers of acquiring knowledge, is it not equally evident that he is not furnished with the power of ascertaining any one of these essential points, without the aid of a light above that of reason and nature?

And may I not further appeal to your good sense, whether we could have instituted and pursued a fairer or more honorable course than to state the pretensions and claims of moral philosophy in her own terms, as used by her greatest and most approved masters—Grecian, Roman and English; and then inquire singly of all her schools and renowned teachers, whether in their own experience, and in their candid concessions and acknowledgments, philosophy, in life and in death, has redeemed her pledges, fulfilled her promises and sustained the expectations of her friends and admirers?

When hard pressed on these points, observing that she herself relied more on tradition than on her own resources, fastening her hopes more on the basis of what was handed down to her by the ancients, than upon all her own discoveries and reasonings, became it not expedient that we also should turn our thoughts to tradition, examine its history and canvass its pretensions, so far at least as to institute a comparison between it and philosophy on the points in discussion?

Having thus placed these two great sources of intelligence in contrast and comparison, and finding on the side of tradition, as defined by us, incontestable and decided advantages, incomparably superior claims and pretensions, what more natural and conclusive than to examine the human constitution, with special reference to these two; and, if possible, to ascertain whether the Creator intended man to walk by hypothetical philosophy or authentic tradition? Such, then, has been our method; and what now, on summing up the whole, are the legitimate results and conclusions?

Does it not appear that moral philosophy never removed any doubts except those which she had created? Like the spear of Achilles, she healed only the wounds which herself had inflicted. That it cast not a single ray of light upon a single cardinal point in the whole science of happiness! That it failed in all the three great lines of the Ionic, Italic and Eleatic orders; and most essentially failed, even in the best branches of the Ionic school, even in the hands of the great masters—Socrates, Plato, Aristotle, Zeno and Epicurus.

Nay, does it not appear that the age of doubting was the era of philosophy?—that men never began to start hypotheses till they had lost their way?—that mankind walked safely by the light of tradition from a divine origin for many years before philosophy was born?—that those ancient traditions were kept pure for thousands of years in one great line of the human race, but were finally corrupted by priests, and disguised by poets, and thus became the basis of the Chaldean, Indian, Phenician, Egyptian, Persian, Grecian and Roman philosophy?

And is it not most of all evident, that man is not constituted by his Creator to be led by instinct, sense or reason; but by faith in infallible tradition, in all these points of vital importance in the philosophy of bliss; and that such arrangement is in good keeping with the pre-eminent superiority of the most ennobling of all the endowments of man, whether we consider the immense compass, the infinite variety of its acquisitions, or that high certainty and assurance to which it often rises, and to which we may attain, on all essential points, when accompanied with that candor and inquisitiveness indispensable to the detection of truth, in all matters of vital interest to man?

My object now is gained, even although I may not have carried conviction to every heart. The science of human happiness is now before us; and if I have not shown where it may be learned, I have certainly shown where it never has been and where it never can be learned.

And may I now be permitted to add, that the study of these five points opens to the human mind the purest, sweetest and most copious fountains of delight? They connect themselves with the whole universe of God, and place it all under tribute to our happiness.

With the telescope of faith to our eye, looking back to our *origin*, beyond the solar system, beyond all the systems of the heavens, we descry the archetype of our being in the remote and unfathomable depths of the bosom and mysterious nature of that divine and transcendent Being whose temple is the Universe, and whose days are all the ages of Eternity.

While man stands upon this earth and breathes this material breath of life, and sees and feels in his outward frame much in common with the beasts that perish, he feels within himself an unearthly principle—an inward man—a heaven-descended mind—a nature more than ethereal—a spirit ever panting, thirsting, longing after the affinity of his Father's spirit, whence, as a spark of intelligence, it was stricken off, and made to illumine its little mansion in the vast temple of creation.

The intellectual nature vouchsafed to man communes with the Supreme Intelligence in all his various and boundless works; and such is its love of new ideas, of new conceptions of the almighty source of its being and bliss, that if it could only imagine any fixed summit of its attainments, even in the heavens, beyond which it could add no new discoveries, that summit would be the boundary of its career of glory and of bliss; and, repining, as did the Grecian chief, that no new worlds were yet to be conquered, heaven itself would cease to be the place of infinite delight, the ultimate and eternal home of man.

The *relations* of man are, as a necessary consequence, equally sublime and comprehensive with his origin and nature. He touches every point in the universe, whether material or immaterial, animal, intellectual or moral—temporal, spiritual or eternal. He not only derives pleasure from all these sources, but feels that he is related to God, angels and all natures, by ties, and sympathies, and nice dependencies, from which arise innumerable pleasures, duties and obligations; each of which becomes a new source of delight to him who, reconciled to the government of the rightful Sovereign, seeks the enjoyment of all things in subordination to HIS will.

The destiny of man is in harmony with his nature, relations and origin. True, indeed, there is a dark, cheerless and gloomy mansion, to which his mortality is for a season confined. But should he learn in this life the science of happiness, and regulate his actions according to the philosophy of bliss; beyond that land of darkness and of night, that dreary bourn of his follies, misfortunes and sins, "there is a land of pure delight," a more blissful paradise than that of ancient Eden, in which man will freely eat of the fruit of a more delicious tree of life, breathe a purer air, see a brighter sun, and enjoy, without the intervention of a cloud, the light of that divine and glorious countenance which illumines all the suns of all the systems of universal nature. There, in the midst of kindred spirits of a celestial mould, of a divine temper—the mighty intellects, the refined and cultivated genii of the skies—the true nobility of creation—he will converse, and in the seraphic pleasures of a taste and an imagination of which all terrestrial objects are inadequate types, he will view the bright and more perfect displays of creative power, wisdom and goodness in the palace of the universe; in that holiest of all, where beauty and loveliness in their most divine forms, unseen by mortal eye, shall be displayed in the superlative of glory, amidst the enraptured gratulations of innumerable multitudes of holy spirits, assembled not only from all earthly nations and all mundane ages, but from all the celestial dominions, states and communities of the empire of God.

To contemplate an eternity past—to anticipate an eternity yet to come—with full-developed minds of celestial stature, dwelling in spiritual and incorruptible bodies of unfading beauty and immortal youth, to survey the past creations of God—to witness the new—to commune with one another, and with all intelligences, on all the manifestations of the divinity—and above all, to trace all the acts of the great drama of man's redemption as developed by the Divine Author and Perfecter of a remedial economy—to read the library of heaven, the volumes of creation, of providence and redemption—to intercommunicate the sentiments and emotions arising from such themes, interrupted only by heavenly anthems, and fresh glories breaking on our enraptured vision—will constitute a proper employment for a being of such endowments, capacities and aspirations as man.

Need I add, to disclose such secrets—to reveal such mysteries—and to guide man in a path that leads to such a destiny, is not the province of philosophy—of the mere light of nature or of reason; but the peculiar and worthy object of a communication supernatural and divine? and such a volume we have in that much neglected, but incomparably, sublime and awful volume—the BIBLE.

ADDRESS.

LITERATURE, SCIENCE AND ART.

DELIVERED AT NEW ATHENS COLLEGE, TO THE STUDENTS OF THAT INSTITUTION, 1838.

YOUNG GENTLEMEN:—

Were I asked what element or attribute of mind confers the greatest lustre on human character, I would not select it from those most conspicuous in the poet, the orator, the philosopher, or the elegant artist; I would not name any of those endowments which are usually regarded as superlative in adorning the reputation of the man of genius or of distinguished talent; I would not call it memory, reason, taste, imagination; but I would call it *energy*. I am sorry that it has not a more expressive and a more captivating name; but, gentlemen, that *something* which we call *energy*, is the true *primum mobile*—the real mainspring of all greatness and eminence among men. Without it, all the rarer and higher powers of our nature are useless, or worse than useless. The genius of a Milton, a Newton, a Locke or a Franklin, would have languished and expired, without achieving any thing for them, their country, or the human race, but for this peculiar *vis a tergo*—this active, operative and impulsive ingredient in the human constitution. Sustained and impelled by this impetus or power, endowments very moderate may accomplish—nay, have accomplished—more for human kind, than the brightest parts have ever done without it. That power, or element of our constitution, which makes humble talents respectable; respectable talents, commanding; commanding talents, transcendent; and without which the most splendid powers can effect nothing—may, we presume, be regarded as chief of the elements of human nature.

Were I again asked what power, or art, or habit, most of all accelerates and facilitates the acquisition of knowledge, which most of all widens, deepens and enlarges the capacity of the human mind; feeling myself sustained by the oracles of reason and the decisions of experience, with equal promptitude I would allege that it is that undefined and undefinable something, which no one comprehends, but which every one understands, usually called the faculty or art of *attention*—a power, indeed, not often appreciated, not easily cultivated, and never enough commended, even by the most devoted sons of literature and science. But a small remnant, an elect few of our race, have ever known how to use their eyes, their ears or their hands in the pursuit and acquisition of useful knowledge, much less how to direct and govern the operations of their own minds in the application of it.

Of a great majority it may truly be said, though not in the identical sense of the Great Teacher, "Eyes they have, but they see not; ears they have, but they hear not; and powers of understanding, but they perceive not." They know not, indeed, how to use their senses, or their reason, on material nature; and therefore perform the whole journey of life with a few vague, indistinct, incomplete and misshapen conceptions; and finally embark for eternity without a clear, definite or correct idea of their relations to the universe, or of their responsibilities to Creator or creature.

Some might consider this use of our perceptive powers as what is usually called *observation*. But what is observation? Another name for the attentive application of our minds, through the senses, to whatever passes before us in the operations of nature and society. And this again depends upon what the new school of mentalists have agreed to denominate *concentrativeness*. They have discovered, or think they have discovered, that there is a native, original and distinct power of the mind by which the other powers are concentrated, commanded or continued on the objects around us. This they have very aptly denominated our concentrativeness. Be this true or false in theory, one thing is evident—that without attention nothing is perceived, and consequently nothing learned; while by it, all nature and society, as they pass before us, find a way into the chambers of the human mind and are safely lodged in the spacious apartments of our intellectual nature, whence they diffuse themselves through all the avenues of human life and human action.

And were I still further interrogated what other habit, art or power completes the measure of the comparative superiority of individual greatness, I would as decidedly and, I think, as rationally answer that it is the faculty or habit of classifying our acquisitions and conceptions under proper heads. It is the power of properly labelling every new thought, and of marshalling all our ideas under their proper captains on every emergency. It is the power of generalizing and of abstracting whatever is foreign to some grand idea, or some particular system or law or principle of nature. Every man will be eminent amongst his compeers in the ratio of his readiness and power to classify the objects of nature, society, art and religion; or, what is the same thing, his views of them according to any given attribute or property which they may possess, or according to any end or object he may have in view.

To a person well disciplined and practised in classification, all nature, society, literature, science, art, ever stand in rank and file before him, according to his intimacies with them. In the philosophy and skill of the greatest military chieftain that ever lived, *he* can assemble the greatest force to a given point in the shortest time. He, too, superlatively enjoys his own knowledge, just as the prudent mistress of a household, who has a place for every thing and every thing in its place, enjoys all her resources. He also sees order, harmony, variety, fitness, beauty, from a thousand points inaccessible to one destitute of this sovereign art.

He that looks at the universe with a generalizing eye, looks at it with a discriminating perspicacity more individuating than his who rarely ascends from an individual to a species, or from a species to a genus; for, however paradoxical it may appear, the habit of generalizing is the habit of individuating; and he who classifies most expertly individuates most readily; and, therefore, he who best understands the species most clearly discerns the individual; and he most clearly perceives the species who best comprehends the genus under which it stands; just as he whose vision commands the largest horizon most distinctly discriminates the objects which it contains.

To illustrate and enforce this important point is, gentlemen, a primary object of this address; and, to make it as useful as possible, I shall select three generic words as a proper theme for such a development. These are, LITERATURE, SCIENCE, ART. A definition of these terms—their comprehension, mutual dependence, and the connection of all true science with religion—shall constitute the outlines of my practical remarks at present.

And how shall we define the generic term *literature?* You anticipate me, and, with one accord, reply, "*The knowledge of letters.*" It is, gentlemen, neither more nor less than the knowledge of *letters;* but it is generic, and comprehends all sorts of letters—words, signs, languages. Contradistinguished from science and art, it simply means language and its laws. These principles or laws may, however, be classified and arranged into the form of a science—such as grammar, logic, rhetoric; and, according to our mode of considering or using them, they become to us either sciences or arts. As subjects of study or contemplation, they are *sciences;* but, as precepts and rules of thought or of speech, they are *arts.* Hence they are called sciences or arts just as we approach them and use them. We must, however, keep to our definitions; and, having agreed that literature is the knowledge of letters and that a literary man is only a man of letters, we must hasten to our second definition.

What is *science?* You answer, "*The knowledge of things.*" You mean the constitution, attributes, operations and states of all the individual subjects on which we think, reason or discourse. True, very true, gentlemen; hence we may have sciences based on things themselves, or on their attributes—their operations and relations. Of these we presume not to fix the limits. You can convert any part of speech into a noun by making it the subject of a verb: so you can convert literature, art, or any thing on which you think, contemplate, reason, discourse, into a science. Still, however, science, properly so called, denotes that knowledge of things—their properties, operations, laws, relations—founded upon demonstration or certain and indubitable evidence.

In former and less enlightened ages, we had but "*seven sciences,*" "*four elements*" and "*ten categories.*" Those ages have, however, been added to the years beyond the flood; and elements and categories and sciences have multiplied exceedingly, and replenished the earth with many valuable and splendid improvements.

In this age of simplification and true science, *a science* means the accurate and certain knowledge of some particular subject. Thus, astronomy is the knowledge of the heavenly bodies and their laws. But, as we cannot be said to have the knowledge of any thing without knowing its laws or the changes to which it is subject, we may simplify still further, and say that astronomy is the knowledge of stars; geology, the knowledge of the earth; mineralogy, the knowledge of minerals; botany, the knowledge of trees and plants; zoology, the knowledge of animated beings, &c.

And what is *art?* Art is the application of science, or it is the rules of some particular practice or calling, or it is the practice itself. Every science has its own peculiar and corresponding art; and, indeed, the use and end of all the sciences are the useful and liberal arts to which they give rise and for the sake of which they are acquired and cultivated. Thus, we naturally associate science and art, theory and practice, faith and obedience, as correlate terms—as mutually implying each other—especially the latter as presupposing the former; for art without science, practice without theory, and obedience without faith, would be as anomalous and unnatural as an effect without a cause, fruit without blossoms, or a child without a parent.

Our terms are now defined. Literature is the knowledge of the signs of thought; science, the knowledge of the things of thought; and art, the application of these signs and things to the numerous and varied ends of individual and social life. Each of these terms, as already observed, is generic, and represents a class—one grand abstract idea—from which all that is common to other ideas, and not individual, is separated. Literature, therefore, includes all that pertains to language or signs of ideas, ancient or modern, natural or artificial, from the alphabet of Cadmus down to the *belles-lettres* productions of the present day. The arts of reading, writing, speaking, grammar, logic, rhetoric, are but the practice of the theory of literature; for, like every thing else, literature has both its theory and practice. A mere literary person, however, is conversant only with letters or signs of thought, without regard to science or the useful and liberal arts. Could you accurately and elegantly speak and write all the languages of the world, living and dead, ancient and modern, from the hieroglyphics of Egypt to the apocalyptic symbols of unaccomplished prophecy, you would be only literary men—skilled in the names of things, the symbols of thought, the signs of ideas. It is freely admitted that in so much intercourse with books, so much attention to the signs of thought, much useful knowledge of men and things may be acquired, and that a literary man of high attainments will necessarily possess much valuable information in the study of ancient and modern dialects of thought; still, we must plead that such a person is greatly inferior to the man of science in point of really useful and practical knowledge, as he who can only name a horse in ten languages is greatly inferior in the knowledge of that useful and noble animal to the keeper of a livery-stable, who can only name the animal in his vernacular. Believe me, young gentlemen, a man with one language and many sciences, or even useful arts, is much more likely (for he is better prepared) to be a valuable and useful member of society, than he who has many languages and only one or two sciences. Except it may be in the departments of a translator or an interpreter, or in preparing others for those services, such persons are greatly overrated in society.

But, as science, rather than literature or art, is the burden of our address, and as we have more in view than simple definition—combining, as far as we can, the definitions of important terms with the laws of classification, and thus illustrating and commending its value—we shall hasten to the classification of science, properly so called.

The great end to be gained in classification is the proper distribution of all knowledge under proper heads, with a single reference to the easy acquisition and communication of it. A good and rational classification, then, is that which collects all that appertains to any one subject under a suitable designation, and clearly separates it from all that belongs to another category or subject. There are two great difficulties in perfecting such a classification of science: one, radical and as yet insuperable, is that no one science is so insular in its position, so separate and distinct from all others, as to be perfectly independent of them—so as never to borrow or lend a single idea. Such a science would be as singular as Robinson Crusoe, or Alexander Selkirk, in the island of Juan Fernandez: yet even he had his man Friday. A science perfectly isolated is not yet known; therefore our classifications are not bounded by insuperable barriers or mountain landmarks: they rather resemble the charters given by the kings and queens of England to the principal American colonists, setting forth the eastern, the northern and southern boundaries, but ending in the vague terms, "thence west to the Pacific Ocean," "the Lake of the Woods," or some unknown terminus in the midst of Indian tribes. Hence, as our western limits are yet undetermined, so one side of all our sciences is yet unsurveyed. The best classifications hitherto made are therefore imperfect.

The other difficulty is found in the unfortunate fact that we have not yet acquired a perfect scientific language. All our vocabularies and nomenclatures are defective, and unfit for close and accurate definition or reasoning. Still, the best classification of science, in the absence of a perfect one, is that which collects all our knowledge of one subject under the best title and distinguishes it from every other.

Mr. Locke, the great mental philosopher, was duly sensible of this, and sought to divide the whole world of ideas into provinces separate and distinct from each other. He so generalized ideas as to place them all under three distinct heads. These three *genera generalissima*, or grand generic ideas, are,—*things, actions, signs;* that is, *things*, as they are in themselves knowable; *actions*, as depending on us, in reference to our happiness; and *signs*, as they may be used in reference to our knowledge as regards both clearness and accuracy. According to this eminent Christian philosopher, all science pertains to these three, or these three engross all the science in the world:—"For," says he, "a man can employ his thoughts about nothing but either the contemplation of *things* themselves for the discovery of truth; or about the things in his own power, which are his own *actions*, for the attainment of his own ends; or the *signs* he would make use of both in the one and the other, and the right ordering of them for his clearer information."

The modern schools of Britain have sought to improve upon this view of the matter by reducing all science to two chapters. The head of the one is, "WHAT IS;" the head of the other is, "WHAT OUGHT TO BE." The *what is* and the *what ought to be*, say they, are the sum total of all our knowledge. This is within one step of the ontological abstraction, which makes the word BEING the *genus generalissimum*, the highest and most comprehensive term in universal language. This is, however, too sublimated for practical purposes. The ontology and the deontology, or the *what is* and the *what ought to be*, of the most approved schools, would, I think, make five chief heads of science, or five chapters of sciences of sciences; for we are now seeking not for a particular science, but for a science of sciences. Following both Locke and the moderns, so far as they both can be followed by one person, or rather putting them together and forming a *tertium quid*, a new compound, we would have five sciences of sciences, or five general sciences, which would include the whole area of human knowledge; and if we must continue the old nomenclature, we should call them physics, metaphysics, mechanics, ethics and symbolics. By *physics* I mean natural truth, or truth in the concrete, as it is found in material nature; by *metaphysics* I mean artificial or abstract truth, or truths not found in nature, but inferred or generalized from nature; by *mechanics* we would denote truths that are simply useful; by *ethics* we intend truths moral and good in their operation; and by *symbolics* we mean the signs which are employed in acquiring and communicating these truths. We would thus represent truth as the matter of all science, and name the science from the nature or character of the truth of which it treats. Thus we would have truth in the concrete, truth in the abstract, truth as connected with simple utility, truth as connected with human happiness, and lastly, the signs of truth; or particular truths, general truths, useful truths, happifying truths, and the signs of truth.

But, gentlemen, I will be told that this is too multiform an abstract of science reduced to five chapters, and that the inductive sciences are already well divided into *natural, mental, moral;* or, to speak more learnedly, into physical, psychological and ethical. With all due deference to the men of enlarged and liberal science, I object to this division as quite indistinct, confused and defective. We have had physical and metaphysical sciences, natural and moral, speculative and practical, material and mental, and I know not how many other classifications, all, in my judgment, either too indefinite, too defective or too confused. The best of these, perhaps, is the natural, mental and moral; but do not these most wantonly run into each others' territories? The specific idea which is as essential to a science of sciences as to a particular science, is lost,—as, for instance, do we not find the specific idea of the mental in the natural, and the specific idea of the natural both in the mental and the moral? and does not this division leave out the science of signs altogether? If not, wherein does it excel the ontological and the deontological division already defined?

In the classification of science, as in the arts and business of life, we seek some generic idea; and having found it, we arrange all things that have that idea in them, under the term or name which represents that idea. For example, if we contemplate sciences with regard to the subjects on which they treat, we prefix to them the name of that idea. That science which treats of simple being for the sake of discovering general or abstract truth, is properly called *ontology*, because that Greek compound represents the law, or reason, or nature of *being* in general. We call this science sometimes a *speculative* science, because it is a mere exercise of our intellectual powers—itself, too, the result of speculative reasoning and discussion upon simple existence, rather as a matter of intellectual or moral gratification, than of practical utility. It is, therefore, purely metaphysical. But those sciences which treat of the masses of matter that compose the universe, the structures and relations of all those parts that compose the immense whole, we properly call the physical sciences, contrasted with the former, which is properly metaphysical. Again, those sciences which treat of *actions* with a reference to *utility*—as the construction of all the necessaries and conveniences of life—are properly called *mechanical* by the mechanicians of the world. Those, however, that contemplate actions in reference to *right*, or to human happiness, are called moral, or ethical, from the earliest ages of philosophy. Thus, according to the division now contemplated, we would have two chapters of science on *things*, two chapters on *actions*, and one on *signs;* and this, after all, is but the perfection of Locke's views.

These five chapters of science, namely, *physics*, *metaphysics*, *mechanics*, *ethics* and *symbolics*, cover the whole ground of English and American sciences, and are the completion of all the improvements from Locke to the present day. The two first concern being and truth, or things particular and general; the next two contemplate actions as useful and good; and the last one treats of the signs of all our ideas in every department of our knowledge. They are, indeed, dependent on one another as much as the intellectual powers of man are dependent on his active or effective powers, and his active powers upon his intellectual.

We shall now briefly notice the principal sciences that are found under these general heads or classes:—

1. In the science of sciences called *Physics*, or physical sciences, we make seven primary sciences, viz. astronomy, geology, geometry, mineralogy, botany, zoology, chemistry. Gentlemen, neither approve nor disapprove this division till we have examined it. Our process of thinking and reasoning in making out this distribution is, we think, very *natural*. It is as follows:—In physics the generic idea is material nature. We then proceed to the specific sciences, which are the integral parts of it. This we do in the following manner:—1st. We look at the whole universe as composed of innumerable masses of matter spread out over infinite space, moved and moving by certain powers or laws, and tending to some grand result. The science that treats of all these masses and their laws we call astronomy. Of these systematic masses we select one, called the solar system; and of that system we again select one planet, our earth. Then comes, in the second place, the science of the composition and organization of our earth, called *geology*. But we cannot proceed any further in the study of the universe without some scaffolding; for the ideas of quantity, extension, magnitude, number, rush upon us, and so completely overwhelm us, that we set about measuring our earth that we may measure the universe; and hence arises, just at this point, the science of *geometry*, a word indicating the measurement of the earth; for we soon discover, with the ancients, that God has made the universe geometrically, by line, scales, weight and measure. Geometry, then, although an abstract science, is indispensable to the study of astronomy, geology, or even the geography of the earth. After the geology of the earth come its minerals, vegetables, animals. Each of these become separate and distinct subjects of science. Its minerals occupy the precincts of mineralogy; its trees, shrubs, plants, flowers, fruits, constitute the science of botany; and all animated beings become the subject of its zoology. Finally, the elements and simple substances, which form all its creations, and of which the terraqueous sphere is composed, and all its inhabitants, form the substratum of the immense and sublime science of chemistry. Chemistry, indeed, is a system of

science in itself, and extends its jurisdiction, as a sort of supreme court, over all the physical sciences, geometry alone excepted. Whatever is not explained or understood in geology, mineralogy, botany, zoology, whatever *caput mortuum*, whatever *residuum* these sciences leave, is within the jurisdiction of chemistry, which has for its rich and extensive domains the elements, the simple substances, the combinations and uses of all the bodies in or upon this terraqueous ball. Like the Germanic Empire, a cluster of principalities, of little kingdoms, it is a subgeneric which might count almost seven times seven individual sciences, such as the science of light, caloric, oxygen, azote, hydrogen, carbon, &c. &c.; nay, it disputes the ground with what was formerly called "natural philosophy," and claims the old sciences of optics, dioptrics, catoptrics, pneumatics, hydrostatics; it takes the fossils, the minerals, the metals, the earths, the salts, the atmosphere itself, the solids, the liquids, the gases of our earth, under its care and keeping. Plants and animals are not wholly beyond its assumptions. Such is the seventh of the first series, or the last verse of the first chapter of the science of sciences.

Such, my young friends, is the process of reasoning from which sprang the division of physics into astronomy, geology, geometry, mineralogy, botany, zoology, and chemistry. I wish you to bear in mind that *man*, in his physical constitution, belongs to the science of zoology; and, under this head, we may, perhaps, contemplate him at some other time.

2. *Metaphysics* are not confined to any kingdom of nature, not even to the material universe; but in their daring and presumptuous flight speculate on time, space and eternity; on being, truth and goodness; on God, angels, and demons; on moral good and evil; on free agency and necessity; on mind and matter; on thought and language. We have the metaphysics of every science, such as speculative theology, speculative morality, speculative language, speculative philosophy, &c. &c.

3. *Mechanics.*—Trigonometry, mensuration, surveying, navigation, gauging, dialling, architecture, sculpture, painting, &c. are chief among the sciences called mechanical. These sciences are often regarded as arts; but they are sciences first and arts afterwards.

4. *Ethics* call for the whole science of man, and send us back to zoology for his animal existence. He is chief of the science of zoology. Of animated nature he is the consummation, as well as the head. But he is not all found in any one department of nature. There is a spiritual system as well as a material system. The science of Pneumatology, or of spiritual existence, is as comprehensive as the science of astro-

nomy. But as in physics, so in pneumatology. After speaking of astronomy, we take our earth, on which, and from which, to reason astronomically; so, after speaking of pneumatology, we take man, on whom, and from whom, to reason pneumatologically. For in man alone, of all physical beings, is there a distinct and an unequivocal portion of a spiritual system. But this view exhibits man as the subject of many sciences. Of all the physical sciences he is a part and portion, and he is himself the engrossing theme of a respectable number. His animal and human nature, in the hands of the physician, make him the subject of several sciences—such as anatomy, physiology, osteology, neurology, nosology, pathology and pharmacology.

Besides these, in the hands of the jurisconsult he becomes the subject of the sciences of politics, of jurisprudence, of municipal, civil and criminal law. In the hands of the theologian he is also the subject of the canon law, the ecclesiastical law, the moral law and the Christian law.

His perceptive, reflective, affective, communicative and mechanical powers make him the subject of the sciences of phrenology, grammar, logic, rhetoric, mechanics, ethics and religion.

From these premises we may easily survey the sciences that properly range under the general head of Ethics. According to our best schools, they are—*Natural Theology*, as it is called, or the being and perfections of the Deity, as manifested in all the designs of material nature; *Moral Science*, properly so called; *Political Science*, properly so called; the *Theory of a Future Life*—Human Rights, Wrongs, Obligations and Responsibilities, &c. But, as Christians, we would abandon the doctrine of the schools, and substitute the Bible, the Law, the Gospel, the Adamic, Abrahamic and Christian institutions, as furnishing not merely a perfect code, but the proper motives and incentives to good morals.

5. *Symbolics.*—This is our fifth and last head, and, as might have been inferred from our previous remarks on literature, we would enumerate seven distinct sciences as comprehended under this head. These are orthography, orthoepy, grammar, prosody, logic, rhetoric and every species of engraving or chirography. This is usually the first branch of science taught, but it ought also to be the last. The acquisition and the communication of knowledge being the chief end of education, that part which most subserves this high end ought to be first, midst and last.

Gentlemen, after having made the tour of so many sciences, and ranged at large over a field so extensive, we have no time to descant upon the arts. I will only say that they are both the useful and the fine or liberal arts. On the useful or mechanical arts there is no need that I detain you; and I will only say that the *fine arts* are not contrasted with the useful, as in opposition to them; but to distinguish them from such as are necessary or useful only. They are generally regarded as six; but I will add one to them. They are poetry, music, painting, sculpture, engraving, architecture of the different orders—to which I will add *good manners*.

There remains but one point to consummate our plan—the connection of science, all true science, with religion. One might as rationally seek to comprehend an effect without any knowledge of its cause, as to comprehend any part of the science of the universe without some knowledge of its Author. God and his works are the basis of all the science in the world. But as the universe is not without God, nor God now without his universe, so no science, physical or ethical, can be thoroughly learned without the revealed knowledge of God. We study man in his works and in his word, and we contemplate our Creator through the medium of what he has done and said.

The works of God are his first and most ancient revelation of himself; and had not man, by his apostasy, lost the art of reading and studying the works of God, he would not have stood in need of any other medium of knowing him, or of communicating with him, than this wonderful and greatly diversified volume of nature. And, even as it is, the intelligent Christian makes the greatest proficiency in studying nature and the Bible by making them subservient to each other—sometimes interpreting the Bible by nature, and at other times expounding nature by the Bible. They are two voices speaking for God—two witnesses of his being and perfections; but neither of them is wholly adequate to meet all the variety of human circumstance without the other.

But we need no more striking evidence of the intimate connection between science and the Bible than the well-established fact, that all the great masters of science were believers in the Bible and cherished the hopes which it inspires. Bacon, the founder of the inductive philosophy; Locke, the great mental and moral philosopher; and Newton, the interpreter and revealer of nature's secrets, are known to the religious as well as to the scientific world as believers in the Bible and expounders of its doctrine, its precepts, types and promises. They are as eminent for their homage to the Bible as for their devotion to the studies of nature. Philosophy, with them, and Christianity were not at variance.

They saw the immutable and inimitable traces and characters of one and the same Supreme Intelligence clearly and boldly written on every page of the volumes of Creation, Providence and Redemption. They were persuaded that the still small voice which whispers in every star and in every flower speaks aloud in the language of authority and of love in all the precepts and promises of the law and of the gospel. Such were the great founders of the reigning philosophy and sciences of the present day. But I speak not of the first class only; for it seems as if the Father of Lights had vouchsafed all useful sciences, discoveries and arts to those who acknowledged his being and perfections, and to none else. So general, if not universal, is this feature of his providence, that I know not the name of the founder of any science, or the inventor of any useful art, or the discoverer of any great master-truth in any department of human thought, who did not acknowledge the God of the Bible and cherish the hope of a future life.

I have permitted my mind to take a long retrospect into the annals of the great inventors and discoverers, the authors and founders of those sciences and arts that have since the dark ages new-modelled society and the world, to see if there was any one of them who had divorced nature and religion, or who had rejected the being, perfections and providence of God, or denied the authenticity and inspiration of his word. By the examination I have been greatly confirmed in my theory, that "the secrets of the Lord are with them that fear him," even the great secrets of nature, as well as of his purposes and will in reference to the future. Beginning with the invention of the mariner's compass, in the early part of the fourteenth century, by Flavio Gioia, born A.D. 1300, and descending in a direct line down to Sir Humphry Davy, who but a few years since passed the Jordan of time, I observe that all the sciences and arts that have been introduced or perfected during the last five hundred years—which have made this century so unlike the year 1300—have been given to us by men who looked through nature, society and art up to nature's God.

Of this sort were Dr. Fust, or Faust, a goldsmith of Mentz, who invented the art of printing on wooden blocks, and gave it to the world in 1430; Schæffer, his son-in-law, who, in 1442, invented the casting of metallic types; Christopher Columbus, born at Genoa, 1442, who discovered a new world in 1492; Copernicus, born at Thorn, in Prussia, 1472, who proved the errors of the Ptolemaic system of the universe, and suggested the elements of the present demonstrative system; Tycho Brahe, of Sweden, born in 1546, and Kepler, of Weil, of Würtemberg, born 1571, who, though of somewhat conflicting opinions in some branches of the Copernican system, greatly advanced it by their discoveries; Galileo, born at Florence, 1564, who first discovered the gravity of the air and sundry new astronomical truths, inventor of the pendulum and of the cycloid, and an able defender of the Copernican system; Descartes, too, a native of Touraine, born 1596, though erroneous in his docrine of the vortices and in some metaphysical speculations, nevertheless in mathematics, algebra and in his Analytics greatly advanced the cause of science, and became the founder of the Cartesian philosophy, now reviving in some of its branches in Europe; Boyle, inventor of the air-pump,* born in 1626—one of the most retiring and devout of philosophers; Isaac Barrow, the light of the age in mathematics, philosophy and theology—the instructor of Newton—born in England, 1630. Passing over the famous epocha of Sir Francis Bacon, born 1561, Locke, born 1632, and Newton, born ten years after, 1642, we will only name Franklin, the American sage and distinguished philosopher, born 1706; Euler, born 1707; Ferguson, born 1710; Sir William Herschel, born 1738; James Watt, LL.D., born 1730, improver of the steam-engine first invented by the Marquis of Worcester, 1660, and author of various useful inventions; Robert Fulton, the inventor and constructor of the steamboat, born in Pennsylvania, 1765; and Sir Humphry Davy, born 1778, the enlarger and perfecter of the science of chemistry—all mighty men in science, or in the useful arts and discoveries which have really new-modelled the world. These, however, are not all the men of renown that should be mentioned in a catalogue of public benefactors in science and art. Some, indeed, might plausibly think that we ought to have begun with Roger Bacon, almost a century before the age of Gioia, and have given him and Schwartz a conspicuity in this class of renowned and noble spirits—Bacon, for his many new discoveries; and Schwartz, for his invention of gunpowder; but we have been rather too particular, our object being only to name the mighty chiefs in each department, and to adduce them in proof of this important point—that true science and religion are intimately associated both in theory and practice: otherwise we should have embellished our cloud of witnesses with the names of such men as Harvey, Gall, Spurzheim, &c. &c.

There is but the name of La Place concerning whom infidelity itself could have the hardihood to complain. It might be said that the atheist La Place is worthy of a rank amongst the greatest of philosophers; but I ask, What new truth or science, or new art, did he discover or teach? Newton opened the door and led the way for him into the study of nature.

---

* Generally conceded to Otto Guericke.

"But Franklin," says the skeptic, "belonged to us." Strange arrogance, indeed! Read the epitaph on his tombstone, sketched by his own hand; and see his hope of a future life and his acknowledgment of his Creator and Benefactor unequivocally expressed therein.

It was observed that one of the principal difficulties in the proper classification of science and of human knowledge is found in the fact that all the sciences run into each other, and are separated rather by gradations than by clear and prominent lines of demarcation. Now, if this be true in physics or ethics, it is most certainly and evidently true of their connection and intimacy with religion. In the natural sciences we cannot advance a single step without the perception of adaptation and design. The cosmical adaptations are so numerous, obvious and striking, that we are compelled to notice them, and to see that, like the leaves that envelop the rose-bud, from the inmost petal that enfolds the germ to the outermost covering, they are all shaped and fitted, not only to one another, but to the central stamina, for whose protection they seem to have been made. Thus the whole solar system seems to exist for our earth; our earth for its vegetable and animal productions; and these, again, for man. Our earth, however, appears to be adapted to the universe as the universe is to it; and after it has subserved human existence as its ultimate end, it again repays to the system of nature the aids and advantages furnished it by its neighboring planets. Thus the whole universe, both in its general laws and in its particular arrangements, is one immense system of means and ends, suggesting to the true philosopher one great First Cause and one grand Last End, between which all things exist.

It is as impossible, then, to understand any portion of such a system with a clear comprehension, viewed apart from this great First Cause and Last End of all things, as it would be to understand a human finger without a human hand, a hand without an arm, an arm without a body, a human body without a mind, a mind without the Supreme Intelligence.

If it be folly, plain, palpable folly, to pronounce an opinion upon a part, when ignorant of the whole to which that part belongs, what shall we say of his philosophy who dogmatically pronounces upon science in general, who has not studied any one fully; or of him who has studied but a single chapter in the volume of nature, and yet presumes to judge the whole library of the universe! And is not this, gentlemen, his character who would presume to divorce the study of nature from the knowledge of its First Cause, or from the science of the Bible, on the pretence that it is unnecessary, or, which is the same thing, that any one science may be as fully comprehended without, as with, the knowledge of Him who is himself, his being, perfections and will, the sum and substance, the Alpha and Omega of them all?

But who, of unperverted reason and of uncorrupted affections, could wish to study science without tracing its connection and its intimacies with the most magnificent, sublime and interesting of all sciences—the knowledge of God, of our own origin, destiny and duty? If there be beauty, grandeur, sublimity, immensity, infinity in this stupendous temple of the universe, how infinitely beautiful, lovely, grand and glorious must be that august and adorable One who had from all eternity the archetypes of every system, and of every creature, existing in his own mind, unexpressed; awaiting the moment which infinite wisdom, power and benevolence had fixed upon as the most fitting to speak them forth into being! To make the universe and all its science the way, the means to know him, appears to us the true wisdom and the true happiness of man. He clothes himself with light as with a garment; nay, he has clothed himself with his own creations, insomuch that the clear intelligence of them is the clear intelligence of himself.

To me it has ever been a paradox, a mystery, how any one can feast on nature, or luxuriate in the high enjoyment of the arcana which science reveals—how any one can in ecstasy and rapture contemplate the celestial and the terrestrial wonders of creation, and yet be indifferent either to the character or will of Him who is himself infinitely more wonderful and glorious than they—how any one can admire the developments of the Creator, and forbear himself to adore. Assuredly there is something wrong, some superlative inconsistency or mistake in this matter; else it would be impossible to delight in the works and neglect or despise the workman.

When education shall be adapted to the human constitution and conducted in full reference to the rank and dignity of man, then will the connection of science and religion, of nature and God, be made not merely the subject of an occasional lecture, but a constant study; the universe will then be but a comment on the Supreme Intelligence; the being, perfections, providence and will of the Almighty Father will always be the text; and every science but a practical view of Him in whom we live and are moved and have our being, and of our responsibilities and obligations to Him who has endowed us with these noble faculties and powers, on account of which we rejoice and triumph in existence.

Meanwhile, young gentlemen, I would remind you that there is one science, and one art springing from it, which is the chief of all the sciences and of all the arts taught in all the schools under these broad heavens. That science, as defined by the Great Teacher, is the knowledge of God and of Jesus Christ whom he has commissioned. This, he says, is eternal life. And that art which springs from it is the noblest and the finest in the universe: it is the art of doing justly, of loving mercy, and of walking humbly with our God.

SUPERNATURAL FACTS.

AN ADDRESS TO THE MAYSVILLE LYCEUM, 1839.

GENTLEMEN:—

In testimony not merely of my sense of the honor you have done me in unanimously electing me an honorary member of your institution, nor of the high regard which I entertain for such of your association as I have the pleasure personally to know, but rather in proof of the high estimate I have formed of the great and useful objects of your lyceum, do I at this time appear before you. On every other account, I should certainly at this time have declined a task for which I am so ill qualified. Fatigued as I am with the labors of a six months' tour, only closed this forenoon in this city, and not having had an hour to arrange my thoughts on any subject since I received from your committee an invitation to address you, I should, in justice to myself, as well as to the expectations expressed by the large assemblage before me, have deferred this address to a more convenient and propitious season. But, as in the routine of the reigning manners and customs of society we sometimes make visits of friendship as well as fashionable visits, I prefer to appear before you in the guise of the former rather than in the disguise of the latter. In the one case, dress and display are supreme; in the other, the frank and unadorned congratulations and communications of friendship and of the social feelings have the ascendency. Without the corsets and trappings of a set speech and a fashionable address, I propose, then, gentlemen, to offer you a few practical remarks connected with the great object of your association—viz. "*Mental and Moral Improvement.*"

Among the useful institutions of this age of improvement, I think the village and city lyceums occupy a very prominent and a very large space. When well conducted and in reference to the object you propose, they offer, in my judgment, at least half the advantages of a collegiate course of instruction. Aided by a good library and governed by the decorum of a polite and rational administration, young men especially may derive from them many and great advantages, not only in compensation of the want of a liberal education, but even in superaddition to all the benefits usually derived from it.

Well, then, gentlemen, as you have very wisely organized with a true regard to your mental and moral advancement, permit me to invite your attention to a subject of transcendent importance, involving in it the genuine radices of all intellectual and moral superiority. That subject is *the nature and use of supernatural facts.* This, as you have no doubt frequently observed, is an age of facts against hypotheses, and of the inductive process of inferring the laws of things from facts observed and classified; and, therefore, all that is now dignified with the name of science is the knowledge of facts and of the inferences logically drawn from them. As there is but one great truth in the universe, and all truths are but fractional parts of that sublime and incomprehensible truth; so there is, indeed, but one science, of which all the varieties of human knowledge are but so many component parts. There is neither an isolated fact nor science in this great universe. They run into each other, and mutually lend or borrow light, illustration or proof from one another.

The classification of science most convenient and philosophical is that which arranges human knowledge according to the facts of which it treats. Thus, as we have physical, intellectual and moral facts, generically speaking, we can only have physical, mental and moral sciences. The knowledge of things physical, mental and moral is, therefore, the measure and boundary of all our scientific attainments.

But, besides these facts, which are the basis of all human science, there is another class of facts, mysterious and sublime beyond comparison, which, for the want of a more distinctive name, we have called *supernatural facts.* These, as have been stated, constitute the theme of our present address.

How, then, shall we define this word *supernatural?* You say, gentlemen, "It literally means *above nature.*" But still the wonder grows, and we are asked, "What is *nature?*" The answer commonly given is, "*The usual course,*" or, "*The established order of things.*" Supernatural, then, would indicate something above the reach or power of the established connection of things. The established order of things is not to be trenched upon, nor violated, nor even suspended, by any one who is himself a subject of those laws. Hence, none but the Author of nature, or a being not a subject of the laws of nature, can either suspend or control any of her laws or arrangements.

Supernatural facts are, then, facts superior to the powers of nature—facts above the established order of things, and which can only be performed by a hand that can control, suspend or annihilate the laws of nature. All facts, therefore, that are clearly not the effect of any law of nature, but contrary or superior to those laws, we call supernatural; such as a person's walking in the midst of a burning fiery furnace without the slightest injury, or upon the tops of the waves of a tempestuous sea as upon a rock, or curing natural diseases or raising to life a dead person by speaking a word.

I need not tell you, gentlemen, that the reality of such facts is denied, and that, too, by some of our shrewd and speculative philosophers; nay, further, there are some who teach that if such facts did happen, no sort of evidence could sustain them, because it is more probable and more credible that the witnesses are mistaken than that the event or fact reported should have occurred. With a few there is no power above nature—nature is omnipotent, self-existent and eternal. These are not to be reasoned with; and, therefore, they are not at present within our jurisdiction. We now reason with those who contemplate nature not as a first cause—"a cause uncaused"—but as an effect of one intelligent and almighty agent.

Next to Newton, La Place ranks in the philosophy of nature. He is decidedly skeptical. He denies supernatural facts altogether. So does David Hume. These are the two greatest names on the list of skeptics. Their philosophy is standard and canonical in all the high schools of infidelity. If, then, we can show their philosophy to be at fault, false and chimerical, foolish and absurd, on this subject, we shall, I trust, be excused from wrestling with inferior spirits—mere freshmen in their school. On this occasion, then, we shall contend with none but these two great masters of the hosts of skepticism. I have to prove the existence of supernatural facts; and my first task shall be to show that the skeptical philosophy is based on a false hypothesis, and, consequently, a gross and even a palpable delusion.

We shall first hear La Place state his own argument against revelation:—"The probability of the *continuance* of the laws of nature is, in our estimation, superior to every other evidence, and to that of historical facts the best established. One may judge, therefore, the weight of testimony necessary to prove a suspension of those laws, and how fallacious it is in such cases to apply the common rules of evidence.'

Now, the strength and point of this philosophy is, that the probability that the laws of nature have always continued and shall continue as they are, is superior to the evidence of sense, the evidence of testimony, and every other evidence by which we prove any fact whatever. If, then, we had walked through the channel of the Red Sea after Moses, or had seen the rock Horeb turned into a fountain of water at the bidding of the prophet; if we had seen the three sons of the captivity walking in the midst of the fiery furnace, breathing in flame; or Lazarus rising out of his grave, on the fourth day, at the command of the Christian Lawgiver; we should rather believe that our eyes and ears and senses had deceived us, than doubt the probability that the laws of nature continued in these cases to operate as they had always done. Is there not, then, but one short step between the assumption of La Place and absolute and universal skepticism of even the laws of nature themselves? For, let me ask even the sons of skepticism, On what sort of evidence does our assent to this "probability" rest? or, rather, By what sort of evidence do we learn the laws of nature? Is it not by the testimony of our senses? If, then, I believe my senses while they at one time attest the regularity of the laws of nature, why should I disbelieve them when, in a particular case or in a number of cases, they depose that the laws of nature are suspended, violated or changed? Why should the senses in this arbitrary way be metamorphosed into true or false witnesses to suit the emergency of a philosopher? Now, we—who believe in supernatural facts, or facts above the regular continuance of the laws of nature, and which those laws can by no possibility achieve—admit the testimony of our senses as true and faithful in both cases. Judge, then, gentlemen, which of the two schemes is most rational and consistent—that which uniformly credits the senses as faithful witnesses, or that which, according to the emergency of the case, whimsically and arbitrarily makes them true or false witnesses at the demand of a favorite theory. And is it not evident that he who discredits the testimony of the senses in any case, in which they unequivocally and concurrently depose a fact, natural or supernatural, aims a fatal blow at the foundation of all certainty, natural and moral —at the foundation of all science, material and mental?

But, to come to still closer quarters with this great sage of nature's laws, let me ask, Whence the evidence of the probability of the continuance of these laws of nature? Is not the skepticism of the philosopher in supernatural facts clearly based upon a most fallacious hypothesis? Who has proved the uninterrupted continuance or the much boasted uniformity of the laws of the universe? It is a baseless assumption, and obviously contrary to the evidence of both sense and reason, especially when they are permitted to extend their researches through all the fields of human science, limited though they be.

If nature's laws are uniform and permanent without the intervention of a supernatural agency; if all things continue as they were from eternity—all science is hypothetical—astronomy and geology, with all the physical sciences, are without facts and without reason. But they are not; therefore we have all the physical facts against the hypothesis of the skeptic, and in proof of facts supernatural. Let us, then, hear what the sciences already named depose against the skeptical hypothesis. What saith Geology? Does she prove that all things continue as they were? Does she testify to the uninterrupted continuance of the laws of nature?

We shall first hear the testimony of Mr. Lyell, the President of the British Geological Society, in his anniversary address to the society for 1837:—*

"All geologists will agree with Dr. Buckland, that the most perfect unity of plan can be traced in the fossil world, the modifications which it has undergone, and that we can carry back our researches distinctly to times antecedent to the existence of man. We can prove that man had a beginning, and that all the species now contemporary with man, and many others which preceded, had also a beginning; consequently, the present state of the organic world has not gone on from all eternity, as some philosophers have maintained."

To this I may add the testimony of Dr. Buckland himself, author of the Bridgewater Treatise on this most interesting science. His words are, "All observers" of the mechanism of the earth "admit that the strata" of which it is composed "were formed *beneath the waters*, and have been subsequently converted into dry land." (p. 44.)

To these two distinguished witnesses we shall add the testimony of a still more deservedly renowned name—one of the three greatest men of the present century that have flourished in the French metropolis, and near the court of that great nation. I allude to Cuvier, and his distinguished friends MM. Cousin and Guizot. These three deserve the admiration and the gratitude of that nation and all lovers of religion and science. Gentlemen, let me recommend to you the late work of M. Guizot on the Progress of European Civilization. I have read it with pleasure and profit. It traces, with the hand of a master, the agencies and elements that have conspired in the present civil-

---

* Not having the works herein quoted with me, the substance was only given from my recollections in the extemporaneous address.

ization of the world. While I would not endorse every sentiment in the works of these great masters in philosophy and science, I cannot but regard them and their works as a blessing to that volatile, vivacious but great and distinguished nation. They have greatly contributed to redeem France from the theoretic atheism of the Voltaire and Volney school, and to convert its seminaries to a theism not only tending to good morals and good government, but to emancipate the people from the superstition and follies of the Papacy, and to propitiate their ears to the religion of the Bible. And, ladies, permit me to say for your consolation and encouragement that all the piety of these great authors, and the good tendency of their numerous and elegant productions, are to be traced to the religious affections and pious trainings of the mother of one of them, Madame Cuvier, at whose house the other two, when lads, were accustomed to visit in the days of their juvenile amusements. She was accustomed to take every occasion to imbue their minds with a deep and abiding sense of the being and perfections of God as displayed in all his works and in his word—and to lead them "to look through nature up to nature's God."

From this digression let us turn to the testimony of Cuvier in his most splendid System of Geology:—

"The lowest and most level parts of the earth exhibit nothing, even when penetrated to a very great depth, but horizontal strata or layers composed of substances more or less varied, and containing almost all of them innumerable marine productions. Similar strata, with the same kind of productions, compose the lesser hills to a considerable height. Sometimes the shells are so numerous as to constitute of themselves the entire mass of the rock; they rise to elevations superior to every part of the ocean, and are found in places where no sea could have carried them at the present day, under any circumstances; they are not only enveloped in loose sand, but are often enclosed in the hardest rocks. Every part of the earth, every hemisphere, every continent, every island of any extent, exhibits the same phenomenon. It is the sea which has left them in the places where they are now found. But this sea has remained for a certain period in those places; it has covered them long enough and with sufficient tranquillity to form those deposits, so regular, so thick, so extensive, and partly so solid, which contain those remains of aquatic animals. The basin of the sea has therefore undergone one change at least, either in extent or in situation: such is the result of the *very first search* and of the *most superficial examination*."

"The traces of revolutions become still more apparent and decisive when we ascend a little higher, and approach nearer to the foot of the great chains. There are still found many beds of shells; some of these are even thicker and more solid; the shells are quite as numerous and as well preserved, but they are no longer of the same species. The strata which contain them are not so generally horizontal; they assume an oblique position, and are sometimes almost vertical. While in the plains and low hills it was necessary to dig deep in order to discover the succession of the beds, we here discovered it at once by their exposed edges, as we followed the valleys that have been produced by their disjunction."

"These inclined strata, which form the ridges of the secondary mountains, do not rest upon the horizontal strata of the hills which are situate at their base, and which form the first steps in approaching them; but, on the contrary, dip under them, while the hills in question rest upon their declivities. When we dig through the horizontal strata in the vicinity of mountains whose strata are inclined, we find these inclined strata reappearing below; and even, sometimes, when the inclined strata are not too elevated, their summit is crowned by horizontal ones. The inclined strata are therefore older than the horizontal strata; and as they must necessarily, at least the greatest number of them, have been formed in a horizontal position, it is evident that they have been *raised*, and that this change in their direction has been effected before the others were superimposed upon them."

"Thus the sea, previous to the disposition of the horizontal strata, had formed others, which, by the operation of problematical causes, were broken, raised and overturned in a thousand ways; and as several of these inclined strata which it had formed at more remote periods rise higher than the horizontal strata which have succeeded them and which surround them, the causes by which the inclination of these beds was effected had also made them *project above the level of the sea*, and formed islands of them, or at least shoals and inequalities; and this must have happened whether they had been *raised* by one extremity or whether the depression of the opposite extremity had made the waters subside. Thus is the second result not less clear nor less satisfactorily demonstrated than the first, to every one who will take the trouble of examining the monuments on which it is established."—*Cuvier's Theory of the Earth*, vol. v. pp. 8–10.

May we not now ask, How can these plain, sensible and incontrovertible facts of geology, stereotyped in rocks and mountains, clearly legible to the eye of science, be reconciled with the hypothesis of the skeptic—that "the probability of the continuance of the laws of nature is superior to every other evidence"—when, in fact, we find no evidence of the continuance of the said laws of nature for any great length of time; but rather the tokens of a series of supernatural facts, answering to the series of creative acts recorded by Moses? He says, "The earth was without form and void, and darkness was upon the face of the deep; and the Spirit of God moved upon the face of the waters. And God separated the waters, and the dry land appeared." Peter says, when speaking of our present scoffers, that this wilfully escapes those who say that "all things continue as they were from the beginning of the creation:"—"This wilfully escapes them, that by the word of God the heavens were of old, and the earth standing out of the water and in the water; by which water the old earth perished," &c. Geology is proving this by tables of rock, by stratas of earths, by the indurated remains of progressive creations, showing that at least six grand generic *fiats* originated and ordered the dominions of nature so far as pertains to our terraqueous inheritance. There is no bribing of these fossil witnesses—no counterfeiting of these imprinted rocks—these tables engraven by the finger of God; a portion of which, exclusively a petrifaction of sea-shells, I picked up the other day in this county of Mason; and if I were permitted to conclude from the pavements of your streets and the excavations from the bottoms of your wells, I would say that you, gentlemen and ladies, live and move and have your being on an immense bed of sea-shells deposited ages since by the movements of a shoreless ocean, now converted into limestone;* whose upper surface, by the action of atmospheric agents, has mouldered down to dust; and from which, mingled with vegetable deposits, the beautiful frames around me have, by another marvellous process, been reared and animated by the omnipotent hand of the Creator. Yes, gentlemen, I read on the deeply imprinted volumes of God's earth, in your own city and county, the refutation of the theory of La Place, and all of that school, who affirm that all things have continued in one uniform system of nature from some dateless eternity, alike unknown to reason and record.

From the geological premises now before us, and I believe they are the most scientifically orthodox, though as nothing compared with the masses of documents and stratas of evidence within our reach; still, from these premises the following conclusions are inevitable:—

1. *The present earth was formed under water.* Geology, and the Bible, Moses and Peter agree in this testimony. This truth is most

* The primitive name of Maysville.

prolific of facts subversive of the skeptical philosophy. For, in the second place, the vegetable and animal structures and creations, requiring atmosphere, did not, could not possibly, exist from the beginning. Therefore a new class of supernatural facts, or a new series of supernatural operations, must have succeeded the first system of nature, before the *fiat* which separated the waters above and under the firmament, and which caused the dry land and the pure air to appear.

2d. The creation, then, of all the vegetable genera and species, each of which is a special operation, a new suspension, violation or deviation of the then laws of nature, next ensued, and became a distinct category of supernatural facts—a new system of nature.

3d. Then, when the vegetable dominions were finished, the earth clothed and filled with provisions for animal creations, a new series of supernatural interpositions was required to fill the air, the sea and the earth with inhabitants, requiring vegetable productions mediately or immediately for their subsistence. This occasioned more supernatural facts.

4th. And even yet the work was not complete; for there was no being of earthly creation that could read, or understand, or enjoy either the Creator or his creation; and this called forth those divine energies that brought man into existence.

Without further details, you will perceive, gentlemen, how baseless the hypothesis that nature's laws, operations and powers have continued always as they now are. Nothing can be more absurd. Consequently, nothing can be plainer to the candid, unsophisticated mind, than that there is a class of facts as properly styled supernatural, or miraculous, as that there are physical facts for the foundation of physical science. What more evident than that there was one man who was never born—a person that spoke who had never been spoken to by man—an oak that never sprang from an acorn—and trees innumerable that never sprang from seeds? Or, will the skeptic prefer to say that there was a child without a father—speech before persons—eggs before birds—and seeds before trees? On either hypothesis, miracles or supernatural facts are conceded as true and undeniable; and therefore La Place's hypothesis of the uniformity and continuance of the laws of nature falls prostrate to the dust. Dare any philosopher affirm that nature continues to operate as she began? Why, then, does she not annually cast up new genera and species, and begin new races of plants, animals and men? May we not then conclude that the probability of the long continuance of the present system of nature is fairly shown to be a fond hypothesis rather than an ascertained fact?

But the facts of geology are sustained and illustrated by astronomical observations; so far, indeed, as the conglomeration of our planet, and, I might add, so far as the Mosaic account of the creative processes are implicated.

The two Herschels, Sir William and Sir John, have greatly enriched astronomical science by their many splendid discoveries and speculations on the construction and architecture of the heavens. By the aid of their immense telescopes, of from ten to forty feet in length, they have ascertained that stars are still forming, and the remote fields of space are filling up with new systems of suns and their satellites. "A shining fluid," rare and cloud-like, or nebulous, in immense masses, sometimes of a pale milky appearance, diffused over millions of miles, and of immense depth, like a curdling liquid, thickens, and, from being "without form and void," gradually assumes a globular appearance, thickens down into less dimensions, and finally shines as a star occupying but a speck, a shining point in a region which it once filled with its cloud-like appearance. Stars are counted up to thousands, in different states of perfection, from shapeless masses of nebulæ to sparkling orbs of various magnitudes. They are said to resemble one another in their approaches to perfection, as an infant in its annual progress to manhood resembles a perfect man. "In the first and rudest state," Nichol in his Architecture of the Heavens has said, "the nebulous matter is characterized by great *diffusion;* the milky light is spread over a large space so equally that scarcely any peculiarity of construction or arrangement can be perceived." The perfectly chaotic modification of this matter on its first appearance, or original form, resembles vapor thinly spread, some spots thicker and more luminous than others. So Moses describes our planet:—"And the earth was without form and void, and darkness was upon the face of the mass; and the Spirit of God moved upon the face of the waters."*

We cannot now detail what astronomers have said on the gradual condensation of these amorphous nebulosities into globular masses, or of the increased brilliancy which follows a change of structure. Suffice it to say, their matter seems gradually to fall under the same laws of gravitation and motion which govern our system; but in the first instance one of their diurnal revolutions may occupy thousands

* Keith, after quoting from Nichol as above, says, "Nebulæ or nebulous matter, *i.e.* cloud or cloudy, may be said to be identified with waters, designated as without form and void. Water in a void or diffused state is vapor or cloud; hereby denoting a harmony of expression between Moses and the astronomers for a state of matter for which human language, as they confess, has no name."

of years, while as they condense into more solid masses, their motion increases, until their days, like those of our planet, from thousands of years are reduced to a few hours. Hundreds of instances given by our greatest astronomers confirm the truth of this statement, and show that the matter of these stars, by this rotatory motion, is separated and gradually solidified into a globe.

If any one should doubt the power of glasses to bring such objects under our vision, to him we should say that the largest telescopes do penetrate into distances perfectly beyond the limits of even our imaginations. The diameter of the orbit of our earth is about one hundred and ninety millions of miles; and, making it a sort of measuring-rod, it is calculated that our most powerful glasses can descry luminous objects almost four hundred times more remote than Sirius, which is distant from our earth about thirty-six billions of miles.

It would be foreign to our object to institute a comparison between the discoveries of modern astronomers and the record of Moses concerning the first state of the heavens and the earth, and the gathering together of our globe. I will only say that, as in geology, so in astronomy, the nearer we approach the truth, the more complete is the evidence that no person in the times of Moses could have given such a description of the heavens and the earth, unless guided by the unerring hand of omniscient wisdom.

We have made this reference to the diffused nebulosities, those chaotic vaporous masses which contain within them the seeds and elements of new suns and systems, and which in process of time are rolled up, condensed and solidified into globes like ours, and fitted up for the production and residence of numerous and greatly-diversified inhabitants, to show that when Moses says the old earth was without form and void, and enveloped in darkness, and that God separated the waters above and below the firmament, and darkness and light, and finally made the dry land appear, he only speaks in accordance with the modern discoveries of the great masters of astronomical science; and for another purpose of greater interest with many—with a reference to the length of the six days, or the much higher antiquity that some geologists assign to our earth, comprred with what is understood to be the Mosaic account of this matter. It is alleged that the fossil remains, deposits and formations discovered in this earth argue an antiquity many thousand years beyond the period which Moses assigns to its origin, not yet full six thousand years. But to say that the time from darkness to darkness, or from light to light, called "evening and morning," is necessarily of one length, is as unwarranted from the Bible as it is from analogy, or from the changes which must have happened to the vaporous mass, formless and void, of which this globe was formed. Is there any ball in motion—any wheel in the universe, that performs its first rotatory motion in the same time in which it performs even its second, to say nothing of its motion when under the full influence of all the agencies and impulses which are then in co-operation upon it? This would be a supernatural fact indeed! The earth now revolves upon its axis in twenty-four hours; but that it must have occupied no more time when it was an immense volume of vapor spread over a thousand millions of times its present occupancy of space, and uninfluenced by the same laws that now govern it, would be a preposterous conclusion, a supernatural fact of marvellous import. While, then, the last days of the creation-week may have been no more than twenty-four hours, the first two or three may have been twenty-four thousand years, for any thing which science or the Bible avers on the subject.

But all this is a free-will offering, uncalled for by the oracles of faith or of reason—by the word of God or the scientific researches in either of the departments of geology or astronomy. When any one argues from the length of time necessary to the formation of all the strata of earths and rocks with which the earth abounds, against its being created in six common days, he resembles a brother skeptic who argues against the fact of the first man's being an adult the first moment he saw the sun, because the formation of the bones and sinews, the muscles, arteries and nerves of an adult requires some twenty-five or thirty years to develop and confirm. To such drivelling philosophers we say, if God by one word could raise up in perfection one man, could he not by one word raise up this earth in all its developments—though now, as in the case of man, many years might be necessary, by the operations of the common laws of nature, to such a wonderful consummation? We conclude, then, that there is nothing in true philosophy or in true science against supernatural facts, on the ground assumed by La Place, in his false hypothesis concerning the continuance of the laws of nature; but, on the contrary, that both geology and astronomy, when fairly and impartially considered, compel the conclusion that various systems of nature must have preceded the present; and that to the commencement of each a divine or supernatural interposition was absolutely necessary.

As an astronomer, La Place deposes against himself; for, according to him, "the primitive fluidity of the planets is clearly indicated by the compression of their figure conformably to the laws of the mutual attraction of their molecules; it is moreover demonstrated by the regular diminution of gravity as we proceed from the equator to the poles. The state of primitive fluidity to which we are conducted by astronomical phenomena is also apparent from those which natural history points out."*

As La Place endorsed for David Hume, alleging that he was the first writer who had fairly and correctly propounded the connection between the evidence drawn from universal experience and the evidence of testimony—who had, in one word, declared that *miracles are incredible because the laws of nature are inviolable*—we need not assign much place to the consideration of his objections to supernatural facts, they being identical with those of the great materialist already examined. Still, as Hume is the real author of that philosophy which makes it equally impossible for God to work a miracle as for man to believe it, he deserves a more formal notice at our hand than we have yet given him. La Place's immutable and eternal continuance of the laws of nature, and Hume's inviolability of those laws, are identical propositions. If, then, the Creator of man desired to communicate with him, either by word or sign, on the assumption of these two mighty infidel chiefs, whose dogmas are the boast of all the French and English skeptics of the present day, he could not do it: for that would be to violate the inviolable laws—that would be to break up their eternal continuance. Revelation is, therefore, impossible to God himself; and the glorious consummation of the philosophy of this school is, that man has more power to reveal himself to man, or even to the animals around him, than God himself. Man, then, is condemned to eternal ignorance of his origin and destiny, and of the will of his Creator, if nature's laws are inviolable, and God cannot suspend them. This, we think, would be absurd enough for even the skeptical philosophers themselves.

But Mr. Hume could not "*believe any testimony that is contrary to universal experience,*" *because it is infinitely more probable that the witnesses are mistaken, than that the laws of nature have been violated.* This is the marrow and strength of his essay against miracles, or supernatural facts. This sophistry has been so ably exploded by the justly celebrated Dr. George Campbell, that it would seem a work of supererogation again to notice it. But as many still rest in the delusion, who do not love truth so well as to listen to the other side of any question, for their sakes I would briefly ask Mr. Hume, if he were present, or any of his friends, How do you come into the possession of that which

* La Place's System of the World, vol. ii. p. 365.

you call universal experience? By what evidence do you acquire the assurance that the laws of nature are *inviolable?* Your own observation? Your own senses? A narrow horizon, truly, from which to infer the uniformity and the inviolability of the laws of nature! And is this your boasted philosophy, to infer from the evidence of your own senses, for some half-century exercised on an atom of the universe—not a hand's-breadth of creation—the inviolable character of its laws through infinite space and eternal duration? A mole, a gnat, an insect, may, then, from the image of this great world painted on the retina of its eye, philosophically depose that the universe is self-existent and eternal!

But, stranger still, do you call your own observations universal experience? Is not universal experience the experience of all men in all places and at all times? And have your five senses given you the assurance of the experience of all persons in all places and at all times? It is absurd. You can know only the experience of one man in one place and at one time. The rest is all memory, or all faith. You believe the experience of all men, and know only your own. Your own experience is knowledge, other men's experience is with you faith. Yes, gentlemen, your own personal experience is all that you know of this great universe; all the rest is mere belief of the testimony of others. And so it comes to pass that Mr. Hume could not believe the testimony of *some men*, because their testimony was contrary to the testimony of *all men!!* But had he heard and examined the testimony of all men before he concluded himself in actual possession of universal experience? No, not a millionth part of the testimony of all men: yet on this veriest fraction of universal experience he presumes to erect a house of refuge for all the outlaws of the universe, and calls it the Castle of Universal Experience! Mr. Hume's "splendid, unanswerable and most philosophic argument," as his disciples call it, against supernatural facts, when analyzed, is simply this:—"I cannot believe the testimony of some men, because it is contrary to my own experience and to that of a millionth part of all men, whose experience is, in my judgment, universal experience!" And so deposes the Emperor of Siam:—"I cannot believe one word that an Englishman utters, because he says that in England men and cattle walk upon water congealed into ice, which certainly is a glaring falsehood, because contrary to my experience and to that of all the good people of the torrid zone, which is the universal experience of all mankind in all ages and in all places!"

But if it were allowable further to expose this shameless sophistry,

I would yet ask, Why does Mr. Hume believe the testimony of any man on any subject? Because his own experience and that man's exactly tally with one another? Then his own individual experience is the standard of all truth! Who can believe that? Mr. Hume, in his elegant but insidious History of England, shows that he believed ten thousand facts without, or contrary to, his own experience. This, then, was mere credulity, his own philosophy being in the chair. But his vouchers were honest men, veracious and competent witnesses. And have we not as honest men—as veracious and competent witnesses of supernatural facts, as they? And if we rely upon the eyes and ears of one class of witnesses, why not upon the eyes and ears of another class, who are even more disinterested and capable than they? men who sealed their testimony of supernatural facts by laying down their lives calmly and deliberately in proof of what they alleged?

We admit that it requires good, strong and unimpeachable testimony to establish a suspension or violation of the laws of nature. And we admit that the uniformity of the laws of nature must be well established in order to the credibility of a supernatural fact: for were the laws of nature frequently suspended, or were not their uniformity, except by the interposition of the Creator, fully sustained, then the proof of a supernatural fact would be impossible. The Christian philosopher contends strongly for the uniformity and inviolability of the laws of nature, unless the Author of nature interpose, and that on an occasion worthy of such an interference; for with Horace he will say—

——— Nec Deus intersit,
Nisi dignus vindice nodus.

(Let not a god appear in the piece, unless upon an occasion that calls for his presence.)

But we are persuaded, from the sciences already named, that occasions have occurred in which the Divinity has interposed; for the tables of nature, as well as the oracles of prophets, have made it most evident; and if it were expedient for the Creator to interpose on any occasion in reference to the creation of man, reason says, with her ten thousand tongues, more necessary it is that he interpose to save man from ruin, that this creation, this mundane system, might not issue in a perfect abortion! We Christians thank all the philosophers, and amongst them the two master-spirits now before us, for their efforts to establish the uniformity and inviolability of the laws of nature; for we need their arguments to establish ours; but with one of their own school, the eloquent though visionary Rousseau, we will say, "Can God work miracles? that is to say, Can he derogate from the laws which he has established? The question, treated seriously, would be impious, if it were not absurd."

Having seen that philosophy, from all her treasures and with all her talents, not only inefficiently assails, but even corroborates and illustrates the certainty of supernatural facts; we shall define a miracle with a reference to its utility in religion and morals; for with us miracles or supernatural facts are as necessary to true morals as to true religion. Evidence and authority are demanded alike by conscience and by reason, before we make a perfect surrender of ourselves to the dictates of piety and humanity

A MIRACLE, *in the Jewish and Christian sense, is a display of supernatural power in attestation of the truth of a message from God.* To seal a message, or to attest a messenger, is essential to the credit and acceptance of them. Now, miracles are the seal of a message. "Witness my hand and seal" is the philosophy of the whole matter. "God the Father *sealed* Jesus;" Moses and Jesus were *sealed* messengers of God. The former was the minister of law; the latter the minister of grace: "for the law was given by Moses; but the grace and the substance came by Jesus Christ."

Now, as there are two sorts of supernatural power, there are two sorts of supernatural facts—physical and mental. Miracles, then, may be displays of the one or the other, or of both conjointly, as the nature of the case may demand. The person who controls, violates or suspends any of the laws of physical nature,—curing disease by a word, healing the sick, restoring the maimed, raising the dead, or dispossessing demons, gives evidence that he is sustained by the hand of Omnipotence. He performs physical miracles; he overpowers physical nature. This is what we mean by a display of supernatural physical power.

He who foretells a future event, depending on no known or ascertainable cause, such as the fortune of a man, a family, a nation, at any given future period, displays a mental power equally supernatural and miraculous. This is a display of supernatural mental power. Physical miracles are, then, primarily addressed to the reason and senses of living witnesses; intellectual miracles to the reason and senses of those who shall hereafter live. One class, it may be said, are primarily designed for contemporaries; the other for posterity.

Thus we who now live are made equal to those who lived in the times of the apostles in point of assurance of the truth of the Christian religion. They saw some miracles, and believed others; we see some miracles, and believe others. The miracles which they saw, we believe; the miracles that we see, they believed. One half of our supernatural evidences grows weaker, the other half grows stronger, by time. This, with me, is a point of great moment; permit me therefore, gentlemen, to make myself fully understood. The power that infallibly foretells a future event, depending on no laws known to mortals, but upon a thousand contingencies beyond human calculation, is as clearly supernatural as that power which reanimates at a bidding the dust of a dead man. Not, however, the uttering of a prediction, but the accomplishment of it, constitutes the proof of omniscience.

Now, the longer the interval between the prediction and the event foretold, the clearer the evidence of supernatural knowledge: whereas the longer the interval between a reported miracle, and the more numerous the hands through which it has been transmitted to us, the fainter or more obscure the evidence. Thus, while for the sake of argument it might be admitted that the evidence of the miracles of Moses and of Christ, at the distance of two or four thousand years, is weaker than it was a single century after they occurred; surely it will be conceded that their clear predictions of events two or four thousand years future, is a stronger proof of their inspiration, or divine mission, than the foretelling of events only fifty or a hundred years distant. Thus, while the evidence of physical miracles daily grows lighter, the evidence of mental miracles or prophecy daily grows heavier. And he that lives to see a prediction fully and clearly accomplished as certainly sees a miracle as he that by his natural eyes saw Lazarus revive and leave the sepulchre at the command of Jesus of Nazareth.

To illustrate:—Suppose any one should arise amongst us in the character of a divine messenger, having some communication from Heaven of transcendent importance to the human race: it would not be sufficient that he solemnly affirm his mission: he must prove it; he must show the hand and seal of Heaven attached to it. Nothing like omnipotence or divine power so naturally addresses itself to the human understanding through the senses in evidence of inspiration. He performs physical miracles: this satisfies contemporaries, and they report it to posterity. But posterity would like to *see* as well as to *believe* a miracle. Well, he is willing that posterity as well as his contemporaries should be blessed. He, therefore, in the presence of many witnesses, at diverse times and places, foretells some future events which shall in the different ages of the world sensibly and intelligibly occur: for example, among other predictions, he foretells that the inhabitants of a certain Spanish island shall, in fifty years from this time, possess this whole continent; that their language, laws, customs and religion shall be everywhere predominant; and that our children, excepting such as migrate to some distant region, shall be extirpated by them. Now, suppose this prediction be made a matter of state record, placed among the archives of the nation and copied and translated into different languages; and, finally, should this event, with all its circumstances, so strange, so unexpected, so contrary to all human probability, actually occur: I ask, would not those who then lived see as great a miracle, having the prediction in their eye, as we who saw the same prophet raise the dead? While, then, we his contemporaries see some miracles and believe others, our posterity believe the miracles that we see, and see the miracles that we believe; and thus the more improbable the events foretold, and the longer the interval, the stronger the assurance of the mission of him that uttered them.

Such, gentlemen, are the supernatural facts recorded in the Bible, and such their *use*. And, when the subject is examined with the candor and the care which its infinite importance demands, it will undoubtedly appear to all that we who live in the year of grace 1839 have prophecies accomplishing, miracles occurring before our eyes, which were registered in the records of nations and translated into different languages thousands of years before we were born; and therefore we have as good reason to believe that Jesus is the Saviour of the world as they who witnessed his miracles in Judea.

Indeed, the Bible is the only book in the world that ever did presume to foretell the fortune of the whole human race. It has, so to speak, one great prophetic meridian-line which surrounds the destinies of our globe; and, when we intelligently bring up any particular place or epoch to that line, upon it we read its fortunes at that hour. But this requires some intelligence in that book and in the history of the world: it requires that both be read and understood—just as it required the Jews to walk with Jesus to the tomb of Lazarus, and to look and listen, to see and believe that miracle. It therefore behooves us to go with the prophets, geographically and chronologically, and to listen and look that we may see and understand the miracles submitted to us. The same candor and attention that could have seen and believed a miracle then, can see and believe a miracle now.

I can illustrate by only an instance or two these remarks on the second class of miracles—those displays of supernatural intellectual power in attestation of the great proposition. I will select a single specification from each Testament. That from the Old will be found in the writings of Moses—the most ancient of historians—delivered at a time when his own people were standing around him on their way from Egypt to Canaan. In anticipation of their breaking covenant with God, the prophet Moses states (Deut. xxviii. 46–68) certain "curses which should be upon them for a miracle and perpetual wonder." These are among the specifications:—

1. A far foreign nation, swift as eagles fly, should come from the ends of the earth—a nation of a foreign and to them a barbarous speech, of warlike character, fierce and unrelenting to old or young—and should devour their good land with all its products, and then besiege them in all their cities.

2. The details of the sieges are then given with a minuteness that ends with the account of a delicate lady eating her own infant secretly in the distress and straitness which should come upon them.

3. They should afterwards be reduced in number, from immense multitudes to comparatively a very few, and driven from their own land.

4. Then they were to be scattered among all people from one end of the earth to the other, and should serve them and their gods of wood and stone.

5. And, while among these nations, they should have no ease, no rest for the sole of their feet, but should be seized with a trembling heart, failing of eyes and sorrow of mind.

6. Yet they should not be absorbed by those nations; for, as saith the Lord by Jeremiah, "they should never, while sun, moon and stars existed, cease from being a nation before him." Jer. xxxi. 35, 36.

These are but a few—not a hundredth part—of the clear, literal, unfigurative predictions of that miraculous people: a standing miracle, indeed, they have ever been, from the supernatural birth of Isaac to the present hour; which go to prove that Moses and their prophets spoke by a divine and supernatural wisdom and intelligence. Now, as they who lived in the times of the siege of Jerusalem saw the verification of so much of the prediction as pertained to that epoch, so we who now live see another portion of it literally accomplishing: we see the Jews in our own land preserved a separate and distinct people—not yet amalgamated and absorbed by any nation on earth, though dispersed through Asia, Africa and Europe, as among us, without a home, a resting-place, or national institutions—yet still a people; while the Assyrians, Medo-Persians, Greeks and Romans, who, ages after the prediction was delivered, tyrannized over them, and rose to the government of the world, have long since been absorbed, amalgamated and lost in the ocean of humanity. Now, that Moses wrote in Hebrew more than three thousand three hundred years ago, and was publicly and by national authority translated into Greek more than two thousand years ago, are facts as veritable and certain as that there were once Assyrians, Medes, Persians, Greeks, Romans; and that is all that is necessary to perfect this miracle. For, let me ask, was it within the power of human reason or intellect to foretell, with such minuteness, with a singularity of incident unparalleled in the history of the world, the present fortunes of any people some two, three or four thousand years ago? If this be not a display of supernatural intellectual power —a real miracle—a palpable supernatural fact—we confess ourselves incompetent judges of the attributes of any fact, ordinary or extraordinary.

Take another example. Paul (in the second chapter of Second Thessalonians) foretells a man of sin, with such a variety of circumstances as wholly transcends all human prescience, as much as the removal of a mountain exceeds all human volition. Within thirty years of the crucifixion of the Messiah, he describes one who should sit in the Christian church, assuming a power over all political magistrates and rulers; that this personage could not appear till an apostasy from the apostles' doctrine should occur, and until the Roman Pagan magistracy was taken out of the way, as a hindrance to his full revelation. He also foretells the *consumption* of this son of perdition, his final ruin, &c. And have we not this fact now before our eye? That apostasy came: Christian emperors mounted the throne of the Cæsars; Christian priests made for themselves a *Pontifex Maximus*—a great High-Priest—a Pope, who now sits in what he claims to be the temple of God, and who has oft assumed all the powers before described over all princes and rulers. And has not the *consumption* of his power commenced? and do we not see, ever since the Protestant Reformation, the waning and gradual diminution of his authority? Surely, we have this fact before our eyes at this moment. Now, that the prediction is eighteen hundred years old, is proved from the ancient Syriac and Latin versions, and all authentic records concerning the commencement and progress of Christianity, Jewish, Pagan and Christian. And need I say that nothing was or could be more unlikely to happen than that the alleged vicar of one then so recently crucified should rise to a transcendency of power eclipsing the glory of all Roman, of all Pagan magistracy—not for a moment, but for a series of ages, amounting to almost thirteen centuries?

In the extemporaneous address of an hour, gentlemen, it is not possible to set this matter forcibly and clearly before you. We rather submit to you these facts and observations as a subject of your own examination and development. To give to one of these supernatural facts the demonstration of which it is susceptible would require more time than we have now occupied on the whole premises before us. With me, I assure you, this is an important subject. True religion and true morals are, like all true science, founded on homogeneous facts. Christianity is a supernatural institution for man in a preternatural condition, and it is itself—both its proposition and its proof—a superhuman system. That God should have permitted his Son to die for his rebellious creatures, in open war engaged, is itself a moral miracle, and demands supernatural attestations. It is unique. The proposition, the proof, and the issue, are alike supernatural and transcendent.

In bringing this subject before you, gentlemen, I had another object: I desired to contribute my mite to the proof of another proposition not fully stated in this address—that all the discoveries in science are favorable to Christianity. The voice of nature will never contradict the voice of revelation. Nature and the Bible are both witnesses for God—they are consistent witnesses, and mutually corroborate each other. But they must be understood.

Some novices in religion are alarmed at every new discovery in science, lest it should militate against the Bible. Astronomy, geology, phrenology, have all been proscribed, like Galileo, by some untaught and unteachable ecclesiastics. We fear nothing from true science. Phrenology herself, when she takes her seat in the temple of true science, will lift up her voice for the necessity of the Bible and of religion. She does it already by showing that man is made to worship and adore, to be both righteous and religious, just and generous; that in order to be happy, he must know and reverence and delight in the true God. She proves man, as he now is, to be a religious animal, and in need of a revelation from God; and leaves to reason and conscience to prefer truth to error—Christianity to idolatry—reality to fable.

That you, gentlemen, individually and collectively, may not only attain to the true science of God, but to the true enjoyment of a religion based on supernatural facts; that you may be prepared for the enjoyment of an immortal life in a new creation; is the unfeigned desire of your friend and fellow-citizen, long devoted with you to the great work of mental and moral improvement.

ADDRESS

THE DESTINY OF OUR COUNTRY:

DELIVERED BEFORE THE

PHILO-LITERARY SOCIETY OF CANONSBURG COLLEGE, PENNSYLVANIA, AUGUST 3, 1852,

BEING ITS FIFTIETH ANNIVERSARY.

GENTLEMEN :—

No one can really understand any thing, who does not know something of every thing. Circles, cycles and centres compose the machinery of the universe. Suns, moons and stars have their respective centres, their orbits and their cycles. But there is one centre that regulates and that governs all other centres; for every centre is both attractive and radiating. It communicates and it receives. It supports and is supported. There must, then, be one self-sustaining centre, and that centre must be forever at rest. It is both the centre of gravity and the centre of motion. And that centre is not God himself, for he is everywhere. He is himself a circle, whose centre is everywhere, and whose circumference is nowhere.

There is a reason for every thing, if there be any reason in any thing. Of what use light, if there be not an eye? And of what use an eye, if there be not light? Creator and creature are correlates. The one implies the other. There is, therefore, in the human mind, a necessity for the being and perfections of God. His existence is essential to ours; but our existence is not essential to his. We *are*, because he *was*. Had he not been, we never could have been. We are not self-existent. He must, then, be self-existent; consequently, infinite, eternal and immutable.

But there is in God something passive, as well as something active. A human muscle is passive without a nerve of motion. A nerve of motion is passive without a will; and, therefore, *will*, and will only, is the *primum mobile*—the first cause and the last end of this universe. For God's pleasure, or will, we are and were created.

How much philosophy find we, then, in that beautiful word UNIVERSE! It is a *versus in unum. It is every thing in motion around one thing, which is immovably fixed.* The true centre of gravity is, then, the true centre of motion. But there is not much gravity in a volition. Volitions are very ethereal entities. Oh for Ithuriel's spear, to dissect one of them! Oh that we could place ourselves yonder, "where fields of light and liquid ether flow"!

But here we must place ourselves upon an assumption. We do not like that word *assumption.* We shall, therefore, call it a *postulatum.* But its very assertion is its proof. It is this: THE UNIVERSE IS FOUNDED UPON A MORAL IDEA. God did not create the universe because he had wisdom to *design* it. He did not create the universe because he had *power* to create it. For both wisdom and power are passive instruments. Goodness alone is necessarily, eternally, immutably active. It is essentially and perpetually communicative. It is communicative when it radiates and when it attracts. It is the cause of all motion. But for it, nothing would ever have been. The universe is, therefore, a necessary existence. *It must be, because God was.* It must be, because Jehovah was God—the absolute Good One. It is but a temple, in which goodness lives, moves and has its being—its local habitation and its home. For its glory all things are and were created. This, and this only, is physical, intellectual, moral and religious orthodoxy. It is orthodoxy in essence, in form, in substance. It is the philosophy of philosophy, and the religion of religion. It is the immovable centre of all the centres of the universe. And here we place our foot upon the Rock of Ages. Our only postulatum is the "*Rock of Ages.*"

Man having been created in the image of God, and cradled in a universe in perpetual motion, his mind is necessarily active. As soon as man begins to think, he begins to construct circles of thought around some perception or idea; and these, according to their specific nature, are formed into what are properly called *systems*, or sciences. He has an ideal *ontology* and a *deontology*, before he knows the meaning of a single word. His primordial conceptions are, first, *being*, then *relation*, then *dependence*, then *duty*, then *pleasure*, then *pain.* These are all arranged before he understands a word or a thing. These are the centres of his thoughts, his volitions and his actions. But he is surrounded by bad teachers, and has a fallen and, consequently, a shattered constitution. He is passive, and easily led astray. His mind is perverted by bad teachers and bad associations. He soon finds himself in error, and sets about correcting it. He again finds an error in his mode of correcting it; and so the conflict between truth and error, good and evil, begins long before he knows any one thing. This is an inherent calamity, consequent upon an ancestral catastrophe.

He is necessarily obliged to classify perceptions, reflections, volitions, actions and their consequences. He is born with a pope in his stomach, and that is a very indigestible substance. Hence the dogmatism of children, simpletons and charlatans. Of these *big children* we have yet a sample in every family of science. I say *family of science*, for these families have grown and multiplied, and replenished the whole earth. Our great-great-grandfathers had but *seven* sciences—the number of perfection. But we have seventy sciences; and yet we want another. With the great Hooker, we will say, that "no science doth make known the first principles on which it buildeth." But in this age of progress, any art, or species of knowledge, is called a *science*. Any one *specific* idea may become the centre of a science. Indeed, we have, without knowing it, been moving forward to a new nomenclature on the grand subject of sciences, sects and schisms, in all the knowledges of earth, of time, of the universe. The time may come, if it be not already come, when every generic and specific idea shall become the foundation of a science, a sect, a party and a school. Take the following words—*Papist, Protestant, Episcopalian, Presbyterian, Congregationalist, Methodist, Baptist, Monarchist, Aristocrat, Democrat, &c.* Does not each one of these terms indicate one specific idea? And is not that one idea, to all within its circle, a centre of attraction, and to all beyond it, a centre of repulsion?

General assemblies, synods, diets, councils, conventions, &c. are constituted, held and perpetuated upon the sub-basis of one idea, which is the one only essential and differential attribute or idea of the school or party. These ought to be styled the centripetal and centrifugal ideas of all bodies. They are the souls of all ecclesiastical and political corporations. Not one of these bodies has two souls, nor any of these souls two bodies. And just at this corner, this *punctum saliens*, I place my Jacob's staff on every survey I make of the ecclesiastical and political plantations in our beloved country.

The body of a democrat differs but in a few accidents from the body of an aristocrat. The essential difference is in their souls. This idea is the living, moving, acting, essential idea which gives them animation, name, action and reaction.

There is but a paper wall, say some in Scotland, and some in England, and but one idea inscribed upon it, between prelatic and papal episcopacy. And they retort with equal zeal and evidence, that there is but one idea between episcopacy and the moderator of a general assembly. And the Congregationalist says there is but one idea between Old England and New England Congregationalism and Scotch and English Presbyterianism. And all the umpires on the walls of Zion say Amen! But that one idea—that dear, divine and glorious idea, is as centripetal and centrifugal as the law that guides and compacts the spheres of the natural universe. We place it upon our armorial—it is inscribed upon our flag. Its associations are as dear as life and stronger than death. But further on this subject deponent saith not. My charity hopeth all things, and your charity, my respected auditors, endureth all things. And now for the *destiny* of our divinely favored and beloved country.

Every word I have yet spoken has been spoken with a single reference to our country, our beloved country, and its destiny. Individuals constitute families, families make tribes, tribes constitute nations, nations empires, and empires a world. Nations and empires stand to each other as members of an individual family stand to one another.

A well-developed family is a miniature world. The duties we owe our superiors, inferiors and equals, and the privileges we derive from them in the family circle, contain in them all the elements that enter into all the relations, duties, obligations, rights, privileges, honors and rewards of the most enlarged communities and corporations, civil or ecclesiastic. And as the individual members of a family have each an individual destiny involved in that of the whole family, each individual has also a mission into that family, upon the perfect or imperfect accomplishment of which his own destiny, for good or for evil, for weal or for woe, must inevitably depend. This is a law of reason, a law of experience; and, above all, it is a law of God.

When the God of Israel sold Israel, or sent them into captivity under an Assyrian yoke, he enjoined them by his prophet "to seek the good of the country into which he had caused them to be delivered into captivity," and added, as a reason or motive, "for in the peace thereof you shall enjoy peace." Their condition, at that time, was a very special and peculiar providence; ours is equally so now. That nation had one great idea committed to it for the benefit of the world. It was the unity, spirituality and ubiquity of God. It was his inflexible justice, his immaculate purity and his inviolate truthfulness, as specially the God of the Jews, and generally the God of the whole family of man.

All Christendom has its special condition, and its special commission into the world. In this designation we comprehend the Greek, the Roman and the Protestant States of Europe, in whatever country or of whatever language. Their mission is very different from that of God's ancient people, the Jews. Polytheism was the damning sin of Pagandom. Gods many, created by the human imagination, against one only living and true God, was their apostasy and their ruin. Polytheism never winked at, and polygamy merely tolerated in certain cases, became the fountains of iniquity, injustice and inhumanity, during the patriarchal and Jewish epocha of the world. Christianity, the consummation of Divine wisdom and benevolence, at a proper period of human experience, at the manhood of the world, was introduced, and gradually and gloriously developed and confirmed. It was not a mere *family* religion, like the Patriarchal, nor was it a mere *national* religion, as the Jewish. It was *œcumenical,* or universal. It recognized neither Jew nor Greek, neither Barbarian nor Scythian, neither bond nor free, neither male nor female; but made the same gracious tender of remission, justification, reconciliation, adoption and glorification, on the principle of sovereign favor, through the absolute merit of the sacrifice of the great Redeemer, and through the sanctification of the Holy Spirit, who, on the formation of the Church of Christ, became its *Holy Guest.*

As the admission of many gods constituted the damning sin of the Patriarchal and Jewish ages of the world, so the introduction of many mediators, many altars, priests and sacrifices, constitutes the damning sin under the benignant reign of grace, usually styled the Remedial Dispensation. And thus we approach the destiny of our country. But there is yet another step.

The Popedom, in its long, dark despotism over Europe and Asia, took away the key of knowledge from the Christian Church, read prayers in an unknown tongue, substituted for Christian ordinances unmeaning and idle ceremonies, consecrated relics, erected holy crosses, hallowed forbidden altars, mitred their priests, girdled a representative of Peter with the keys of paradise, handed to the priests alone the golden chalice of their spiritually medicated wine, established an empty ceremonial, paganized Christian doctrine through an empty and deceitful philosophy, and with unblushing effrontery prated against the dangers of thinking for one's self, of liberty of speech and freedom of action. Thus was consummated the long, dark night of Papal supremacy, during which the immortal Luther was born.

Protestantism was the legitimate consummation of Lutheranism. Yet had it not been for the threatening attitude of the Turks, Charles the Fifth would not have called a diet at Speyer, A.D. 1529, to ask help from the German princes; and had not Ferdinand, Archduke of Austria, and other Popish princes in this diet, decreed that in the countries in which Luther's views had been received, they should be merely tolerated till a general council could meet, and that during the interval no Roman Catholic should be allowed to turn Lutheran, in other words, to think differently from Archduke Ferdinand, and that during the interval the Reformers should not attack the pure and unadulterated doctrine of Popery, Protestantism might never have been born.

Six Lutheran princes and thirteen deputies of imperial towns, solemnly *protested* against this gag law,—this Papal ordinance against thinking or speaking contrary to the dicta of one man and his ecclesiastic advisers. Thus Protestantism was born, and although Lutherans were the first occasion of the decree, Calvinists and all other dissenters —that is, *thinkers* and *talkers* against his infallible excellency—became heirs in common of all the rights, titles, honors and emoluments of the name and style of *Protestants*.

Having given an historical definition of the word *Protestant*, we must form a clear conception of its import. It is neither a Lutheran nor a Calvinist, as such ; neither an Arminian nor a Methodist; neither a high church man nor a low church man; neither an Episcopalian nor a Presbyterian, a whig nor a tory, a monarchist nor a republican. It is a mere *generic* term. These are all specific terms. A true and well-defined Protestant might enter his protest against any one and all of these, and be a better Protestant than any one or all of them. A reverend gentleman educated, I think, within these walls, once said to his congregation, "Brethren, there is a *blue*, and a better *blue;* but, brethren, we are the true blue." So there are three degrees of comparison amongst Protestants.

But there are two species of Protestantism. There is ecclesiastic Protestantism, and there is political Protestantism. These, indeed, have more than a chemical affinity.

There are, indeed, three species of Protestantism. There is political, ecclesiastic and spiritual Protestantism. These are the positive, comparative and superlative degrees of an abstract, anomalous noun substantive. At its commencement church and state were so mixed and confounded that there was not a metaphysician in Rome or out of it, that could tell where the state ended and the church began. They had the same geographical and astronomical metes and boundaries. Lands intersected by a narrow frith, or river, hated each other for

God's sake and man's sake; for their State polity and their church polity were lodged in the same crazy vessels. In the purest casks of ancient Protestantism, there was a considerable sediment of worldly prudence and temporal policy. But the fierce ordeal and fiery trial of the sixteenth and seventeenth centuries, separated much of the worldly of the times of Luther, and Puritanism began to have a local habitation and a name. The Mayflower ferried over the Atlantic the seeds gathered from the early harvests, the choicest first-fruits of European Protestantism. Brought directly from Old England, they were planted in New England. The soil and climate, however rugged for the germs of earth, were most fertile and happy for the new seeds, and, consequently, rich harvests rewarded the labors of the puritanic husbandmen. God sent them to a new world, that they might institute, under the most favorable circumstances, new political and ecclesiastic institutions. Such, most assuredly, was their Divine mission. Their influence was direct and reflex. It gave life, and vigor, and enterprise to the mother land and those they left behind them, and planted deep and sowed broadcast the seeds of a great, and populous, and mighty empire. England lost at home, but, by her commerce and her missionaries abroad, she planted in the East, the far East, a population and principles homogeneous, more or less, with her American colonies. She became still more Protestant at home and more Protestant abroad. Her canvas whitened every sea, and wherever British power was felt, it might be said, mankind felt her mercies, too. From the days of Luther until now, her throne, her navies and her armed bands, have directly, or indirectly, been the bulwarks of Protestantism. With all her faults, and they are not few nor small, we love her still; because God has been her shield and buckler, her stay and strength. We are her children, and, according to the fifth commandment, we must honor our parents; though, as duteous sons, we may wish that our fathers had been more wise.

But Britain and America are of one paternity, of one religion, of one language and of one destiny. They stood by Luther, by the first Protestants, in the times that tried men's souls; and however occasionally perverted in judgment upon and around the throne, the heart of England has ever sympathized with young America, and with all the Protestant States of Europe. From untold myriads of family altars, morning and evening prayers and praises for young America and her infant institutions, and for infant Protestantism, have ascended into the ears of the Lord of Hosts. Councils of States against England and Protestantism, alliances abroad, armies on the continent, armadas on the seas, and treasons at home, have been thwarted, confounded and annihilated, in answer to her prayers.

To the Saxons in Europe, to the Anglo-Saxons in Britain, to the American Anglo-Saxons on this continent, God has given the sceptre of Judah, the harp of David, the strength of Judah's Lion, and the wealth of the world. He has given to them the oceans of earth, the golden regions of the far West, and the golden regions of the far, far East. California and Australia pour their treasures into their coffers, and Anglo-American arts, and sciences, and language, pervade the earth, and permeate the populations of the civilized world. To Britain and America God has granted the possession of the new world; and because the sun never sets upon our religion, our language and our arts, he has vouchsafed to us, through these sciences and arts, the power that annihilates time and annuls the inconveniences of space. Doubtless these are but preparations for a work which God has in store for us,—a great, a mighty, a stupendous work, that will bring into requisition the arts, the sciences and the resources with which he has so richly, so simultaneously and so marvellously endowed England and America.

There are means to ends, great and small, wisely and irrevocably established in all the cosmical and terrestrial operations, which are perpetually in progress. He gave to the mammoth and the mastodon bones, muscles, nerves, tools, and a covering adapted to their localities and to their work, in their day and generation. He does so still to all the existing species that people earth, or sea, or air. The eagle mounts above the clouds, and Leviathan ploughs the mighty deep, with as much ease as the gossamer constructs her filmy balloon or as the spider weaves his slender web. The beaver builds his dam, and the honey-bee constructs his waxen honey-cells, with as much science and art as man displays in his stately palaces or in his golden temples.

Divine providence and moral government equally attest the same power, wisdom and goodness. These, associated with other moral excellencies in the government of the world, as in its creation, to the cultivated mind, with equal assurance, attest his condescending care and providence, in anticipation of all the changing scenes of man's earthly destiny. Coming events cast their shadows before them, while those that have passed away fling their shadows behind them. Hence the value of prophecy and history.

Men of reflection are wont to conceive of their mission into the world from an attentive survey of their own capacities, circumstances and opportunities. It was doubtless intended that it should be so. Hence, individual accountability will depend much on the use every one makes of those endowments, circumstances and opportunities, which the Governor of the world has vouchsafed to him in reference to the country, population and age in which God has located him.

The *kairon gnoothi* of Pittacus, is only second to the *gnoothi seauton* of Solon. To "*know an opportunity*," is only second in importance to "*know thyself*." He is both a wise and a prudent man, that can combine in his own life and action these two. But should he add to these the oracle of Periander, *meletee to pan*—"nothing is impossible to industry"—he must, if the elements of greatness be in him, become a great man. These, to my taste, the wisest of the wise sayings of the Grecian sages, have, in modern times at least, been more eminently displayed in Britain and in the United States than amongst any other people on earth. And this I ascribe, not so much to soil or climate, or national superiority, or blood, as I do to the fact that these are the lands of Bibles and of Protestantism.

There is a nobility, a moral grandeur of soul, in saying, *I protest against* such a law or statute. To protest innocence, is sometimes just and necessary. To protest *against* political tyranny, is often expedient; but to protest against religious usurpation and ecclesiastic despotism, caps the climax of human nobility and grandeur. And none but Heaven's own noblemen can, *ex animo*, make such a sublime protestation. Hence temporizers, sycophants, aspirants after worldly honor and influence, could not, in the days of Luther, have protested against a Roman pontiff, when all Roman power and grandeur were leagued in favor of Papal aggrandizement and monopoly.

From all my premises, I am compelled to think that there is much of moral grandeur in the very name *Protestant*. There is a moral heroism in non-conformity to unjust laws and unholy requirements for the sake of five barley-loaves and two small fishes. These seven principles and the men who adopt them, will be condemned, now, henceforth and forever, before the bar of enlightened reason, of a generous philanthropy and of a just judgment. It was, in the esteem of Philosopher Locke, a fatal act of uniformity to the English hierarchy, which, on St. Bartholomew's day, ejected two thousand non-conformist ministers, alias uncompromising Protestants, from the national pulpits. Hence, it may be logically inferred that there may be occasionally a hypocrite even among Protestants.

But, in speaking of Protestantism we speak not of a pretended Protestantism, but of a true, real and unsophisticated Protestantism. And what is *Protestantism*, but a solemn negation of all human dictation and usurpation over man's understanding, conscience and affections; over his personal liberty of thought, of speech and of action, in reference to each and every thing pertaining to himself, his fellows, his God and his Redeemer?

Education, religion, morals and politics are, therefore, the fields and realms over which Protestantism, *de jure divino*, presides.

Man's whole destiny in this world is comprehended in these four words, education, religion, morals and politics. I own the ambiguous use of these four cardinal points of human destiny. Volumes without number have been written, and our shelves are burdened with ponderous folios, quartos, octavos and duodecimos, on each and every one of these great centres of thought. And still they come. Yes, they come, and not in single file, but in platoons, extended wings and hollow squares, terrible as an army with banners. But, under a good intellectual and moral power-press, how meagre their solid contents! If even gold, as Newton affirmed, has more pores than particles, and water forty times more pores than solid parts, how beautifully gaseous must these volumes be!

Education is the development of a man's physical, intellectual and moral constitution; religion, his moral and spiritual obligations to God; morals, his duties and obligations to man; and politics, his duties and obligations to the state, or social compact, in which he lives and moves and has his being. In each and all of these Protestantism affirms he must think, will and act of and from himself, according to the free and unbiassed dictates of his own best thoughts and understanding.

Popery says of this grand principle of human responsibility, of free and voluntary action, of self-government, of merit and demerit, that it is, in essence, impiety, insubordination—a Pandora's box of ills and evils, intolerable and accursed. To Protestants, and in Protestant communities, they exclaim, How gross and infamous this calumny! See how resolutely, boldly and cheerfully *Saint* Carrol, of Maryland, and other distinguished Romanists, took active part in the Revolutionary War; "how they bared their breasts, and shed their generous blood," in support of the cause of American independence! Yes; but was this the real motive? Did they love England less, or Rome more, than American independence? Did they not, in other words, hate England ineffably more than they loved either church or state independence?

On landing in Philadelphia, a day after the commencement of the Revolutionary War, an honest son of the Emerald Isle, on hearing the news, taking his companion by the hand, exclaimed, "By Saint Patrick, Jack, I'll 'list and fight for nothing, for nothing, sir, against old Johnny Bull." He was an unsophisticated exponent of the part taken in the war of the Revolution by Romanists for American independence. It is not possible, or, in other words, it is not in human nature, to love liberty, freedom of thought, of speech and of action, in the state, and to hate it in the church; or to love it in the church and to hate it in the state. The love of liberty is a law or principle as uniform and immutable as the law of gravity. I mean liberty—rational, moral, social liberty; not licentiousness, recklessness, lawlessness. I mean not lust nor passion, the love of plunder and robbery. It is a moral principle, founded upon the perception and approbation of justice and humanity. If a Protestant becomes a tyrant, he is a hypocrite or a freebooter. And if a Romanist becomes a true republican, the *man* has triumphed over his religion, and cares not for it.

Do you think of the French Revolution? Do you say, France was then Catholic, and did she not array her power against tyranny and oppression? If you think so, you are not enlightened, and have never read with discrimination the history of the French Revolution.

Roman Catholicism had converted France into a nation of infidels, seared the national conscience, and inspired the masses with the spirit of murder and rapine. It was vengeance and freebooting, not benevolence and freedom, that erected bastilles and guillotines during the Reign of Terror. France, as a nation, was then infidel. She is so now, and has been so during the whole reign of Napoleon. Spain, Portugal, Italy and Austria, too, in the main, are infidel, much more than Roman Catholic. The whole heart of Popedom is gangrenous. Italy and Rome are but the centre of European infidelity and atheism. Nothing but French cannon and French bayonets has kept Pio Nono in St. Peter's worm-eaten chair. She took the sword, and Messiah's word is pledged that she shall perish by the sword. Be the day near or remote, Rome, eternal Rome, the Rome of the Cæsars, the Rome of the Pontiffs, shall be baptized in blood and drenched with the gore of human sacrifice. There are still some names in Sardis that have not received the mark of the beast, and so we humbly hope a remnant may be saved.

But if any one desires to know Roman Catholicism, we advise him to go to Rome or to Paris. View it at home. Did I wish an inhabitant of the mountains of Wales or of Scotland to see our Indian corn in all its mid-summer or autumnal grandeur, should I invite him to the Valley of the Penobscot or to the Valley of the Mississippi, to view it in its glory? As impolitic in any American to judge of Romanism as it appears in New York, in Baltimore, in Cincinnati, in New Orleans, or in Mexico. Let him go to the meridian of St. Peter's, on the banks of the Tiber, and see it at home in all its glory. We ask no more.

That Protestantism is essential to political liberty, is the best-substantiated fact in the annals of European nations. It is endorsed by the most enlightened and philosophic journalists and essayists of the present day. Take a single passage from Blackwood's Magazine. Although itself anti-republican, and an apologist for Toryism, it utters the truth on this vital subject. Weigh the following sentences:—

"The Papist demands religious liberty. The words, in a Papist's lips, are jargon. He has never had it in any country on earth. Has he it in Rome? Can a man have the absurdity to call himself a freeman when the priest may tear the Bible out of his hand? when, without a license, he cannot look into the Book of Life? when, with or without license, he cannot exercise his own understanding upon its sacred truths, but must refuse even to think except as the priest commands? when, for daring to have an opinion on the most essential of all things—his own salvation—he is branded as a heretic? and when, for uttering that opinion, he is cast into a dungeon? when the priest, with the *Index Expurgatorius* in his hand, may walk into his house and strip it of every book displeasing to the caprice, insolence and ignorance of a *coterie* of monks in the Vatican?

"We affirm, in the most unequivocal manner, that, to be free, nations must be Protestant. The Popish religion is utterly incompatible with freedom in *any* nation. The slave of the altar is essentially the slave of the throne. We prove this by the fact that no Popish country in the world has been able to preserve, or even to have a conception of the simplest principles of civil liberty. If we are told France is free, the obvious reply is, that though France is the least of all Popish countries, it is wholly under military government; it has no *habeas corpus;* and no journalist can discuss any subject without exposing himself to Government by giving his name. Would this be called liberty in England?"

And yet this would be our American liberty if Romanism should ever gain the day in America. The holy, infallible, apostolic Church of Rome is essentially immutable. This is her boast. The reign of Popery ever must be a reign of terror to all who love liberty of thought and freedom of speech.

To Protestant America and Protestant England, young gentlemen, the world must look for its emancipation from the most heartless spiritual despotism that ever disfranchised, enslaved and degraded human kind. This is our special mission into the world as a nation and a people; and for this purpose the Ruler of nations has raised us up and made us the wonder and the admiration of the world.

A nation—a nation great and mighty and prosperous—has been

born in a day. Compared with other nations, we have had no childhood. We were born and nurtured and developed in a day, some seventy-five years ago. And now I stand in the midst of the first literary society ever instituted in the immense Valley of the Mississippi. And this, strange to tell, is its fifty-fourth anniversary, and the first semi-centennial anniversary of Jefferson College, under whose generous maternal auspices it has been nurtured and matured.

And what an imposing scene presents itself here to the philosopher and the philanthropist! Here, on the environs of the Monongahela, on whose waters, just eighty years ago, the first white man's cabin was reared and the first Christian hymn was sung amidst the solemn stillness of the deep, dense forests in which, till then, had only echoed the warwhoop and the Indian's yell. The white man, moccasined with his deer-skin boots, wrapped in his hunting-shirt, with a tomahawk suspended from his girdle on his right side, and a scalping-knife, sheathed in a deer-skin scabbard, dangling on his left, with rifle on his shoulder, his faithful dog by his side, sallies forth from his cabin or his fort, at early dawn, and, with cautious step and listening ear, surveys his environs. If neither savage man nor savage beast greets his watchful eye, he grounds his rifle, seizes his axe, and begins to girdle the forest-tree, or, with mattock in hand, engages in grubbing the virgin earth in quest of his daily bread. Gathering courage as he proceeds, day after day the forests bow beneath his sturdy strokes, and an opening is made through which the sun penetrates the newly-opened soil and quickens into life the precious seeds which, with so much parsimony, he had hopefully deposited in the bosom of his mother earth. Thus began, twice forty years ago, the settlements around us. And what a change!

On every side around us, far as the eye can reach, a thousand hills and valleys, waving in rich harvests or covered with green pastures, overspread with bleating flocks of sheep or lowing herds of cattle, interspersed with beautiful villas and romantic hamlets, shaded with venerable oaks, the remains of ancient forests, or enclosed with evergreens of other climes, that vie with each other in lending enchantment to the scenes that environ the homesteads of the rugged pioneers of the great and mighty West, present themselves to our enraptured vision. They are alike the trophies of bold adventure, of successful enterprise, and the imposing evidence of industry, morality and good taste.

And what shall we say of the sons and daughters of those brave and magnanimous pioneers? We are unable to do them justice. The beautiful towns and cities spread all over the new western world, "with glistening spires and pinnacles adorned," pyramidal trophies of industrial art, monuments of generous liberality, piety and good sense, in solemn and majestic silence, speak their praise. Thrones of justice, solemn temples, stately residences, colleges, male and female seminaries, everywhere attest their good taste, their liberality, patriotism and genuine philanthropy.

The Americans very generally seem to have made a new and valuable discovery. They strongly affirm that good mothers make good sons, and that good fathers make good daughters. Hence the prudence and policy of educating both sexes with equal generosity.

Solomon long since discovered that a *man's* wisdom made his face to shine, but went no farther. The Yankees, however—a very shrewd people—with equal clearness discovered that a woman's learning made *her* face to shine with superior lustre. They went to work on this sound theory, and what has been the result? We look around us here and everywhere, on all public occasions, on crowds of ladies whose faces shine with such beauty that it is always dangerous for them to travel abroad unveiled. It is not the lily and the rose that vie with each other for precedence on their fair faces, but it is the sparkling, intellectual eye, the philosophic smile and the graceful assenting nod. So imposing are their charms and their influence, the fascinations of their imagination and the poetry of their manners, that no heart of man is proof against their charms. They have a decided and controlling influence upon all our seminaries of learning for young men. Students in our colleges grow pale over the midnight lamp, and are distilling the nectar of poetry and philosophy from Greek and Roman springs, to render themselves acceptable, in prose and verse, to the refined sensibilities, the chaste imaginations, the good sense and mellifluent eloquence of American ladies in general, and of Western American ladies in particular.

But, gentlemen, I know that you are not insensible to their charms. You are not such stoics or book-worms as not to lay down Plato or Socrates, Newton or Euclid, even Milton or Shakspeare, to hang in profound attention upon their soul-subduing disquisitions, their profound dissertations upon the higher magnetism and centripetal tendencies of the sublimer sentimentalities of their philosophy, which pauses not in the outer court of humanity, but reposes only in the penetralia of the human heart.

We have, young gentlemen, been involuntarily borne away from the plumb and square of a strictly logical address. But even the stars in their courses cannot move in perfect circles. The orbits of all planets are elliptical; and we are all but planets—not wandering stars, I hope, nor meteors of the night. Besides, this is a semi-centennial occasion and a semi-centennial address—the first of the kind ever pronounced in any college of the great West—the great and mighty West. And you, gentlemen, are the oldest literary association in the vast Valley of the Mississippi—an area sweeping through twenty degrees of north latitude and thirty degrees of west longitude—an area of arable land and hospitable climate not greatly inferior, when all proper subtractions of seas and mountains are made, to all inhabitable Europe.

Your society lacks but twenty days of being fifty-four years old. Your regular members are fourteen hundred and eight, and your honorary members two hundred and twenty-nine; amongst which you have been pleased to place my humble name. In looking over your proper membership, we notice many eminent men, now filling high and important stations in both church and state. Amongst your honorary members we see a constellation of the most dignified and honored names in the annals of our country; men known all over Christendom, pre-eminent in the national executive department, on the bench, in the Cabinet, in the Senate, in the legislative halls and on the field of war. In this great valley, your college will continue to hold in the future, as it has done in the past, a pre-eminent place. Its destiny is not only onward, but upward. Its career will be still more brilliant in the future than it has been in the past. You will not only leave behind you, but you will carry with you in all the walks of life, an influence favorable to its usefulness and its honor.

The cause of education—of rational, moral, philosophical, religious education—is the most transcendent cause in any and every community. On it depend the prosperity, the influence, the honor and the happiness of every state and of every people. It has, therefore, intrinsically, the strongest claims upon the liberality, the fostering care, the aids, the smiles, the prayers and the patronage of both church and state. It is a law of God and it is a law of society, paramount and insuperable, that educated mind shall govern the world. It has done it, it now does it, and it will continue to do it till the last pulse of time, despite the clamors of ignorance and the thunders of the Vatican. How necessary, then, that it be conducted according to the genius of true religion and true humanity! How important that it be founded on the Bible—that great library of heaven, the combined product of four thousand years, the result of the labors of a constellation of forty divinely-inspired men, embracing a period of sixteen centuries, and holding positions the most dignified and honorable amongst men!

Of the one hundred and twenty-one colleges in the United States, ninety have been chartered since Jefferson College. But some thirty colleges are older than it. Of this aggregate, twelve are Roman Catholic. All the others are Protestant, or, what is the same thing, State institutions. Besides these, we have, in the American Union, forty-two theological schools, all Protestant. Romanists have no theological schools. Their colleges being wholly under the influence of their theology and church, they are, upon the whole, more theological than literary, and, more than either, scientific. Protestants, therefore, have the literature, the science and the arts of the country, we may say, exclusively under their direction. The whole literary and theological force of Romanists is, therefore, concentrated in twelve colleges. Indeed, Romanism is their body, soul and spirit. They are sold to the Pope and absolutism. With them, the church and state are one idea. Proportional to their number and their population, they are stronger, richer and more centralized than the Protestant institutions. They are conducted, too, with more secrecy than ours. They are pure crystallizations of selfishness, and, like all secret societies, more to be feared than to be loved.

Their influence is the only portentous cloud in our horizon. It is seen charged with an electricity ominous to our destiny, because ominous of mischief to liberty of thought, of speech and of action on all the vital interests of such a community as ours. In a community based on universal suffrage, unless that community be enlightened, moral and religious, there is no guaranty of a prosperous and glorious career. A Protestant conscience is essential to political and religious liberty, and as necessarily tends that way as all the rivers of earth ultimately disembogue themselves into the ocean. And a Protestant conscience is the legitimate consequence of Bible literature and Bible institutions.

The star of our destiny is that star which attracted the attention of the Persian Magi, and directed their steps and their offerings to "the new-born King of the Jews," now the King of kings and Lord of lords, "by whom all the kings of the earth do reign, and all the princes thereof do decree justice." Philo-literary institutions, under Protestant colleges, under Protestant auspices, and Bible literature and morals, are the solid sub-basis of a free and an enlightened government, in the church and in the state—the real Jachin and Boaz—the antitypes of the right and left brazen pillars which Solomon reared in the porch of the Temple, to emblazon its solemn and august entrance.

As through our verdant valleys flow the limpid rivulets that make our creeks, our rivers and our seas, on whose bosom float the gallant navies which, under the Stripes and Stars, the symbolic ensign of our nation's destiny, command the respect, the homage and the admiration of all the nations of the earth, so from your literary institutions, and from all similar ones in our colleges, flow those healing streams which swell the rivers that fill the ocean of literature that shall bless the world.

In our country's destiny is involved the destiny of Protestantism, and in its destiny that of all the nations of the world. God has given, in awful charge, to Protestant England and Protestant America—the Anglo-Saxon race—the fortunes, not of Christendom only, but of all the world. For this purpose he has given to them all the great discoveries and improvements in the arts and sciences that have made the wilderness and the solitary places glad, and that have caused the deserts to rejoice and blossom as the rose. He has vouchsafed to them "the splendor of Lebanon," and added "the excellency of Carmel and Sharon," and "has caused them to see the glory of the Lord and the excellency of our God."

To us, especially, he has given the new world and all its hidden treasures, with all the arts and sciences of the old. Europe, Asia and Africa look to Protestant America as the wonder of the age, and as exerting a preponderating influence on the destinies of the world. We have, then, a fearful and a glorious responsibility. Let us cherish in our individual bosoms this feeling of personal as well as national responsibility; and not only enter upon, but *prosecute*, the duties which we owe to ourselves, our country and the human race. Thus, and thus only, will our career be glorious, our end victorious, and our destiny, and that of our country, "fair as the moon, clear as the sun," and to our enemies "terrible as an army with banners."

But there is yet one position which, because of its importance—its transcendent importance—I would make stand out before you in bold relief, and leave it with you in solemn charge, as the paramount duty of every American citizen, and especially of the educated and talented youth of our country, who, from a benevolent and insuperable law of the Great Philanthropist, must ever hold in their hands the casting vote on each and every great question in every grand crisis that may involve its future weal or woe. The position which I have in my eye is founded on one strongly affirmed, viz. *that educated mind must govern the world.* It is the grand corollary of my address, first in intention, though last in execution. It is more than a corollary. It is the *corolla* itself. It is the flower that contains the seed that yields the fruit of the political tree of life to every community on earth, and more especially in a community to which God has given in solemn charge the key that opens the chest that holds the covenant of future peace and happiness to man, as a social and immortal being.

Not to prolong, nor to increase your suspense, I must reiterate an aphorism early announced on this occasion—that God created the universe, not because of his wisdom or power to do it, but to find a vent for his goodness. Now, the object and aim of goodness is happiness—prolonged, not momentary happiness; increasing, not stationary happiness; multiform, not uniform happiness. Hence it is that the perpetuity and prosperity of a people, or nation, are wholly dependent upon their goodness, their humanity, their philanthropy. And what is either individual or social goodness or humanity, but the proper combination of three ingredients—justice, truth and piety? No nation ever survived the death of these three principles, and no nation ever can die, or will die, till these principles become, with them, a dead letter. A Roman once said, *Fiat justitia, ruat cœlum;* we say, *Fiant justitia, veritas, et benevolentia, et non ruet cœlum in sæcula sæculorum.* Let our nation, then, be just, true and benevolent to all nations and to herself, and it will stand while time endures. These are bright stars—a glorious constellation—and they will be the unwaning and unsetting stars of her destiny, and that of every other nation and people. The Jews, the monumental nation—God's ancient elect kingdom—would have remained till the final trumpet, the paragon of nations, had they continued true to these principles. The Saviour once said that Sodom and Gomorrah, on certain principles, might have remained till his coming. Righteousness exalteth a nation, but sin is a reproach and a desolation to any people. It must be so, because the laws of nature and the laws of God were all fashioned and established under the dynasty or supremacy of the moral sentiments. The pulse of time and of human life is not merely indicative of, but absolutely dependent upon, the action of the heart. The universe was conceived and born in the bosom of absolute, eternal and immutable benevolence. Benevolence has for its sisters righteousness and truth. This being the moral character of the divine being, is immutable and eternal. On these principles our country stands; and on these principles alone she can stand, and rise, and flourish, to meet not only her own wishes and her own happiness, but the expectations and the prayers of all the great and wise and good of mankind.

Let it, then, be so established and published to the world, that we are the stern, uncompromising advocates of human rights; that America is not only "the home of the brave," but "the land of the free;" that we supremely love equal rights, and bow to no sovereignty but to that of God and the moral sentiments; that with open arms and warm hearts we welcome to our shores the oppressed and down-trodden of all nations and languages; and that while the old world is pouring into our harbors and into our homes her ignorant, superstitious and down-trodden serfs and masses, we will, by common schools and common ministrations of benevolence, dispossess them of the demons of priestcraft and kingcraft, and show them our religion by pointing to our common schools, our common churches, our common colleges, and our common respect for the Bible, the Christian religion and its divine and glorious Founder—the Supreme Philanthropist. But you may ask me what special bearing have these views and sentiments on you, gentlemen, as members of the Philo-Literary Institute. Think for a moment of the moral, as well as of the literal, import of your name.

The founders of your society, gentlemen, were peculiarly happy in the selection and adoption of its name—a name so apropos to the condition of this great locality, when first they met *sub tegmine fagi*, and resolved to call it the *Philo-Literary Society* of Jefferson College. The name of Jefferson, had it no other association than the reputation of the memorable and justly celebrated Declaration of the Independence of the American colonies, will descend to the latest generations in that halo of glory which encircled the sun of our destiny on the first morn of its rising. But that, gentlemen, is not the point, nor the association of ideas on which I would congratulate you, nor from which I would argue with you. It is the special name of your own society, the *Philo-Literary Society*. And here, for a moment, let us pause and formally propound the question, What is *literature?* "The knowledge of letters," you promptly respond. But this is a definition too etymological for my taste, or for my use on the present occasion. Literature, in its rhetorical use, denotes not mere letters. It is, indeed, learning. But in its usual and well-defined distinctive sense, while it excludes the *positive* sciences, it embraces languages, history, grammar, rhetoric, logic, criticism, belles-lettres and poetry. Be it so, then, according to our most approved lexicography. In literature we have, therefore, all the machinery of positive science, without which we could, in fact, have no real science of any sort whatever.

In my youthful days I sometimes wondered why, in the Scotch universities, this form of literature, or the study of these dead tongues, was called humanity, or, rather, humanities. I ultimately discovered the philosophy of this portion of their nomenclature. The Scotch, you know, are a nation of long heads, while the English, at least of the Puritan stamp, were called round heads, probably more from the cut of the hair without, than from the form of the brains within. Be this as it may, the Scotch early discovered that the gift of tongues, or of languages, was located in the forehead. They imagined that, language being the symbol of ideas, a man of much language had many ideas. Amongst that people, the arts of acquiring and communicating knowledge were highly appreciated and cultivated. Of them they said—

> "These polish'd arts have humanized mankind,
> Soften'd the rude, and calm'd the boisterous mind."

Consequently, they had professors of the humanities called grammar, logic, rhetoric, poetry.

Literature is, indeed, in its proper import, a lever of prodigious arm. It wants but the *Δος Που Στο* of Archimedes, to lift a world from earth to heaven. But this affirmation might over-stimulate some weak and nervous heads, and therefore it ought to be diluted according to the ratios of our modern panaceas, in the ratio of one grain of sense, two of reason and four of faith.

Religion and morals come to us *objectively*, through literature. Yet literature is no more religion or morals, than lead is water because the water passes through it. Still it happens, if you have not the leaden pipe, you can have no water in the cup. Now, as religion comes to us through the Bible, or through literature, if you have not some Divine literature in your heads or ears, you will never have Divine love in your hearts. Literature is not paper or parchment. It is that which is inscribed upon it. The envelope of a letter, any more than the paper on which it is written, is not the letter. The letter is the written word. And yet the written word is itself but an envelope. The power that smites the conscience, that melts the heart, that cheers the broken spirit, is not the paper, the ink, the written symbol, but something that underlies the whole. It is the mind, the idea, the spirit, the conception, clothed, embodied, uttered, perceived, received, accredited, that agonizes or consoles, that softens and subdues, that purifies and ennobles the heart, that transforms the man, and adorns him with the beauty of purity, the true graces of religion and morality.

We have not yet, gentlemen, capped the climax of the honors due and actually vouchsafed to literature. The Eternal Spirit employed literature in creating light, heaven's own symbol of knowledge, purity and love. How passing strange, beautiful and sublime, the commendation given to language in the first paragraph of the oldest book in the world! God not only *said*, "Let there be light," but he created all things by language or by words; and what are words, but the utterances of ideas, emotions, volitions? All literature is but the pictured symbols of vocables. Language, rudimentally, is literature, fashioned by the tongue, guided by the ear. Hence the deaf can manufacture no language, can articulate no ideas. Language is fashioned by the ear, addressed to the ear, enters into the brain, and thence enters into the understanding, the conscience and the heart. From the heart again it responds by the tongue and the lips, and enters into the ear, the understanding, the conscience and the heart. Language is, therefore, the spiritual or intellectual and moral currency between man and man, between nation and nation, between ancestors and their descendants; by which, though dead, they commune with us and we with them. This is the whole circuit of language that decorates, enriches and beautifies the halls of literature, science and religion.

As all the learning, science and religion in the world, are thus embodied in language, those who are initiated into these sciences, as the graduates of our colleges are presumed to be, go out into the world like a regular army, panoplied *cap-à-pie*, for a grand and solemn mission; for a sacred warfare against ignorance and error in all their forms. They are, by their education, to become the captains and leaders of the people, especially the uneducated masses, which in all countries, even in our own, constitute the great and fearful majority. Associated with moral excellence and moral character, they are prepared to be the great benefactors of their country and of their contemporaries. When we consider what one well-educated mind has achieved in any one of the departments of literature, of science, or of art, for his country and the world, we are not prepared to estimate or anticipate what may be accomplished, for weal or for woe, by the mighty hosts that are annually pouring forth from all our halls of science, literature and religion, in the great fields of humanity which spread out before us.

Approve or disapprove it who may, it is a law of reason, a law of God, that the educated portion of every community must direct and form public opinion. In theology, in law, in politics, in physics and metaphysics; in all the errors and diseases of the head, the conscience, the heart, as well as in the body natural, the body ecclesiastic, the body politic, they must exercise an immense power. Approve or disapprove it who may, it is as immutable and uncontrollable as the law that governs the spheres and regulates the seasons of the year.

Have not a few distinguished individuals, well educated in almost all the fields of literature, science, politics and religion, indelibly stamped their image upon a nation, an age, an empire, a world? These are facts so obvious, so uncontrollable, that to controvert them would be only to stultify one's self, or to falsify the annals of nations and the history of the world. When, then, we speak of the destiny, the special destiny of our beloved country, we cannot but contemplate it through the medium of our schools of learning, of science, politics and religion. Our schools, then, one and all, should command and occupy the profound, the patriotic, the religious deliberation, consideration and supervision of the combined wisdom, talent and learning of the age. Every patriot, every philanthropist, and every Christian, will say from his heart, Amen. Seeing it is a law of God, a principle incorporated in the very constitution of society, it must be wisely, cheerfully and gratefully acquiesced in and submitted to. It must also be regulated and managed with a care, a wisdom, a diligent supervision, commensurate with the immense and eternal interests involved in it.

Patriotism, it is conceded, has no special place in the Christian religion. Its founder never pronounced a single sentence in commendation of it. The reason is, I presume to say, that the world was his field, and as patriotism is only an extension of the principle of selfishness, he deigned it no regard; because selfishness is now the great and damning sin of mankind. Still, the very test of morality is self-love. We are commanded to love our neighbor as we love ourselves, neither more nor less. And in his enlarged mind and heart, our neighbor is every man in the world. Charity, it is said, begins at home, but at home it does not stay. It goes abroad, and radiates its blessings according to its strength, to the utmost domicile of man. But few men can extend their charity, in its special currency, beyond their village, their parish, or their church. Still, when the frozen Icelander or the sunburned Moor comes within our sphere of doing good, we will, as we ought, pour into his wounds and bruises the soothing and mollifying ointment of Christian benevolence. Our country, then, for the most part, engages our attention, and exhausts all our means of doing good. But in promoting its moral excellence, its wealth, its honor, its character, we increase its power and extend its means of communicating blessings which, without it, no Christian man could bestow upon his species.

The United States of America, as they grow in learning, in the arts and sciences, and in all the elements of human wealth and power, can extend blessings to many nations; indeed, to the four quarters of the world. In promoting her health, her wealth and greatness, especially that natural characteristic of a paramount regard for the freedom, amelioration, civilization, as well as the evangelization of foreign lands, we lay for her prosperity, for our own, for that of our children, for that of the human race, the most solid, substantial and enduring basis, pregnant, too, with the civilization and advancement of the great family of man. In this way, too, we secure for ourselves and for our posterity the richest inheritance which mortals can secure in heaven or on earth. Philanthropy, like honesty, is the best national, as it is the best individual, policy. It acts and reacts; it blesses and is blessed; it glorifies and is glorified. If, then, as a nation and a people we stand out upon the canvas of time as the most generous, magnanimous and benevolent nation, we will, as certainly as the sun radiates and attracts, bless the nations and be blessed by them, and grow in every element and characteristic of a great, a mighty, a prosperous and a happy people.

Now, my young friends, in forming your beau ideal of your individual duty, honor and happiness, should you concur with these views and principles, you will carry with you, in all the private or public walks of life, an influence most benignant and beatific. You will guide the less favored of mankind, because they cannot but look up to you. You will thus form their views, guide their aims and elicit their suffrage, on every question you advocate for the public interest, honor and happiness. And that you may do so—be blessed in blessing, be elevated in elevating, be honored in honoring—is not only the wish of your humble orator, but, doubtless, that of every one who takes any real interest in your true and real happiness, in that of your country and of the human race.

ADDRESS.

PHRENOLOGY, ANIMAL MAGNETISM, CLAIRVOYANCE, SPIRITUAL RAPPINGS, ETC.

DELIVERED AT WASHINGTON COLLEGE, PA., 1852.

GENTLEMEN:—

Humanity, in its grand and awful amplitude—in its height and depth—in its length and breadth—in all its relations to the past, the present and the future, to things seen and unseen, to the finite and to the infinite—is the theme of themes, most recondite, mysterious and sublime; transcending far the astronomies, the geologies, the physiologies, thereunto appertaining. We have never seen any thing so wonderful, so mysterious, so awful, as man. In the elements of his constitution he is a microcosm—a world in miniature—an abbreviated system of the universe. In the truthful yet awful and sublime conception of his being, he is an embodiment of all the essences of things, animate and inanimate, in unison with an emanation of Divinity—a manifestation of which stirs within him, imparting to him a sublime and awful personality, constituting him a terrestrial representative of the Self-Existent, who fills with varied life and beauty the awful circles of time, space and eternity; himself the last, the greatest and the most wonderful volition and operation of the absolute and incomprehensible Divinity.

Self-knowledge, of all the knowledges of earth, is *par excellence*, and by common consent, the most desirable, the most useful, and yet the most difficult to obtain. Few students ever become *bachelors*, much less *masters*, of this science and of this art—the greatest of all the sciences and of all the arts, whether called useful or ornamental.

Still, it is possible to rise to very considerable eminence in this art, and to save ourselves from the labyrinths and mazes of folly into which a fond but, ofttimes, a blind parental tenderness, precipitates the dearest objects of its solicitude and affection. How many young men, and young ladies too, have mistaken both themselves and their mission into this world; and though in mind and manners, as well as in birth and circumstances, fitted to have acceptably and honorably filled a conspicuous niche in the great temple of humanity, are found at last amongst the broken ware and lumber of six thousand years, and "crammed into a space we blush to name"!

Old-bachelor mistakes of this sort are comparatively innocent and harmless, because they die childless, and entail not their follies or their misfortunes on others. But when an ambitious father or a vain mother takes a stripling by the hand, and whispers into his ear some romantic notion of his great parts and eminent capacity for this or that elevated dignity and place, they propagate errors lasting as life and reaching beyond its goal into the awful infinite of future destiny. True, in this life we sometimes reap the first-fruits of these follies in painful years of anguish and disappointment.

How many sprightly youths, that might have figured acceptably to themselves and others behind a counter, in an artist's or mechanic's shop, or on a luxuriant farm, have been, unfortunately, thrust into some of the falsely-imagined more honorable and respectable callings of life! Here one is found culling simples, compounding panaceas or nostrums for all the maladies of human life, and thereby only "adding to the bills of mortality." Another pushes, or is pushed, into the musty lore of Roman or English pandects of laws, antique, and sometimes as arbitrary and whimsical, as any one of the five hundred and thirty-four decisions of the Justinian Code, to which the Roman emperors gave the force of law. And yet those fifty volumes of legal judgments contained but a part of their civil law.

By such aids, an ingenious youth sometimes acquires the unprofitable art of making the worse appear the better reason; or, by subtleties of learned quibbling, hangs up in chancery to doomsday the justice or the right, which unperverted reason or unperplexed justice and common sense would have immediately awarded.

Another, perhaps even more unfortunate, is taught to regard a "pulpit of wood," or a "sacred desk," as more honorable than the Æsculapian art, or the costliest ermine that ever decorated a supreme tribunal, and paralyzes both his head and his heart in conning over the voluminous decisions of synods and councils, or in mastering the Fabrician lore of the Augsburg or some other time-honored formula of Christian faith.

Still, we have yet a *quantum sufficit* of the salt of reason and of faith, that may conserve all that is good and true, so long as we cherish the Bible and the Baconian creed. The inductive science has prevailed over the Platonic and the Aristotelian, and, under its guidance and that of Heaven's own book of light and love, we are, or may be, safe from every relic of Roman hermeneutics and of Roman prescription, whether Pagan or Papal. This is of right, and ought to be, the constellation of our destiny.

There is in the true light of true science and of true religion a stimulating efficiency that energizes and enlarges the human soul. The superiority of all the bloods and races of men on the verdant earth, as to mental energy and activity, is to be traced more to the influence of the Bible and Protestantism, than to any peculiar tincture or element in the blood or marrow of the Caucasian, or of any other race.

This opinion is not the mere result of any learned *a priori* ratiocinations. It is a well-established fact, the result of *a posteriori* demonstration, from the fullest annals of nations now extant in every well-assorted library in the world. The Bible-reading, Protestant States of Europe and America are confidently appealed to in evidence of this affirmation. Compare the Papal and the Protestant States of the same languages and genealogies, in any and every empire in the world. From such comparison we fear nothing against our position.

Why, in the long race of four thousand years, did the Jews, in peace and in war, excel not only all the Pagan nations, but also all the other Shemitish nations and dialects of earth, in all that aggrandizes and ennobles human nature? Why excel the Protestant States of Europe the Papal States?—the Protestant cantons of Switzerland the Papal cantons of Switzerland; Protestant Ireland Papal Ireland; Protestant America Papal America? Have the annals of nations ever more univocally answered any appeal?

Patriarchs, Jews and Christians, with one God, one altar, one sacrifice, one faith, one Lord, one Spirit and one hope, against gods many, lords many, mediators many, altars, priests and victims innumerable, have, in every conflict, ultimately triumphed. The great and awful religious and moral truths of revelation naturally energize and invigorate the human soul, as bread and water energize and invigorate the human body. Hence the superior civilization and force of character of the Protestant Anglo-Saxon race, whether found in Asia, Europe or America. We neither reason nor decide from partial premises or from a few solitary examples. We rest upon the concurrent developments and demonstrations in the long race of three or four thousand years. Compare Hesiod or Homer with David or Solomon; Solon or Lycurgus with Moses; Pythagoras, Plato or Socrates with the Bible sages—the Jewish prophets, from Isaiah to Malachi. In one focal point compare continental Europe with Great Britain; even their representatives at this hour, the drift-wood of European and American civilization in Australia and California, contending with all other nations and people for the empire of gold. Is it not a moral demonstration, more resembling, from its brilliancy and power, a mathematical demonstration than any other logical comparison ever instituted by man? We fear no mind, however enlightened, no array of historical facts and documents, however large and respectable, in any controversy on these premises.

While yet standing in the outer court of our subject, I would further premise, that every thing very good in society originates in, and emanates from, true religion and true philosophy; and that every thing very evil originates in, and emanates from, false religion and false philosophy. There is a true and a false philosophy of God and man, as there is of nature and society. The true philosophy is only to be acquired from the profound study of God's own library—the rich and ample volumes of Creation, Providence and Redemption.

Your Pantheon, gentlemen, Pagan though it be, proves this assumption. Its *daimoon kakon* was the *fons et principium*, the real fountain, of all evil; while its *daimoon agathon* was the *fons et principium*, the true and real source, of all personal and social good. In all the forms of polytheism, when resolved into their constituent elements, these were the proximate or remote causes of all Grecian and Roman moral good and moral evil.

In Christendom there are, it is true, many modifications of Christianity, but they are all resolvable into two, and only two, essentially distinct forms. In their essence, matter and form, they are either *Papistical* or *Protestant*. They are politically and ecclesiastically contemplated under the popular designations of *absolutism* and *republicanism*. The Papacy is sheer, bald absolutism. Protestantism is the negation of this idea or assumption, and the affirmation of freedom of thought, of conscience, of speech and of action, in harmony with the law of God, as every one understands it. Protestantism is essentially republican, and elective in all its tendencies. False religion may, indeed, in its licentiousness, fitfully become a fierce and bloody democracy, a heartless oligarchy, or an absolute despotism. But in the last it finally reposes, as its legitimate goal. Every rudimental idea or element in our political, literary and moral institutions is of the essence and spirit of Protestantism.

There is, in my opinion, no more perfect and complete antagonism on earth than that between Papalism and Protestantism. They never can amalgamate. One or the other must ultimately triumph in every community. No oaths, no tests, no forms, no covenants of naturalization can ever assimilate, unite or identify them. Oil and water, light and darkness, good and evil, are not more discordant and heterogeneous than Protestantism and Romanism. While Protestantism has the majority, we will inevitably continue republican. And should Romanism obtain the majority—which may the Lord forbid!—we should, as certainly, come under an absolute despotism. He is a simpleton, or unread in Romanism and in the history of Christendom, that can otherwise think.

Tell us not of the European Republic of Venice, with its aristocratic government. It has long since waned, and is now a portion of the kingdom of Italy. There is no real republic in Europe, and certainly none in the bosom of the holy mother Church. We have no ancient dynasties, no standing armies, no chartered aristocracies, no state religions. European States, the freest and the best, have these, and, therefore, are not free.

But it is in this new world, and in this new world only, that Protestantism fully develops itself. It is in the United States of America alone, that the free discussion of every question involving freedom of thought, freedom of speech and freedom of action, in all the relations of life—political, moral or religious—is guaranteed and fully enjoyed by every citizen. And hence the American Union is becoming, is perhaps even now, the cradle of new ideas of all sorts, home-bred and foreign. Here they are nurtured, cherished and perfected, with equal generosity, magnanimity and benevolence. Let any one desirous to know or comprehend the prolific genius of full-bred, Americanized, Protestant Anglo-Saxons, make a special visit to Washington City, and spend one leap-year in the Patent-Office and its correlate museums, and if his head is not pregnant with more new notions than he could nurse and develop in a century, I will concede that I am no philosopher, and still less a phrenologist. There is every thing in this large world of inventions, from the cranium of an Indian trapper down to the trap of a spiritual-rapper of the Rochester school. It is in these rare galleries, and with Gall, Spurzheim, George Combe, the Messrs. Fowler, Elias W. Capron, and Henry D. Barron, for your guides, that you can, with the aid of correlate spiritual spectacles, get a genuine, unsophisticated peep into the cabinet of true and unsophisticated spiritualism, with all the knocks, bumps and echoes essential to a comprehension of the spiritual spheres of the upper and nether worlds of our present hemisphere. On retiring from your first lessons, you'll say—

> "There are more things in heaven and earth, Horatio,
> Than are dream'd of in your philosophy."

But you must hold fast to the idea of *matter*, as well as *spirit*, else you may—

> "Upwhirled aloft,
> Fly o'er the back side of the world far off
> Into a *limbus puerorum* large and broad."

And here we will premise one of our favorite aphorisms, which is as sage as it is brief:—

> "'Tis through the known, and only through the known,
> That any man can learn the things unknown."

You must also, at your commencement, cautiously and carefully survey the true metaphysical sphere. It is a most mysterious and sublime sphere. According to my telescope, it is bounded on the north by *matter*, on the south by *spirit*, on the east by *eternity*, and on the west by *infinity*. It is canopied by *imagination*, and founded upon *abstraction*. I have taken its position and bearings from my spiritual observatory, under very favorable circumstances, and presume it to be philosophically correct, according to the true Baconian faith and the oracles of Plato.

From these introductory and initiatory speculations, we may proceed to descant somewhat freely upon the tendencies of phrenology, mesmerism, clairvoyance, and the spiritual rappings—all of which come fairly within the purview of the new philosophies, theoretic and experimental, of the nineteenth century. I cannot now enter upon these themes either learnedly or at length. I am not profoundly read in any one of them. But I have ciphered just so far as to see all the bumps, without seeing through them. Consequently, in ascending these stairs, I place my left hand on the baluster of common sense, and my right hand on the baluster of faith, with my eyes directed to my feet. At the top of the first flight I pause, and ponder on George Combe's Phrenology. The bumps and the brains are all right, according to Dr. Spurzheim and Dr. Bell. But he builds his theory upon one fatal assumption. He affirms the proposition, that "the constitution of this world appears to be arranged, in all its departments, on the principle of slow and progressive improvements." He and Moses, unfortunately, are in direct antithesis on this great point, and wholly irreconcilable. *Man never fell, but rather grows better, according to the philosophy of George Combe.* Against this capital error, if I mistake not, his own brother, Andrew Combe, strongly remonstrated, as well as the distinguished W. Scott, Esq., once President of the Phrenological Society of the great city of Edinburgh. Phrenology is, therefore, not chargeable with the aberrations of George Combe. Against his assumptions, we have collected and collated four, as we think, unanswerable arguments:—

I. That universal history furnishes not a single fact in proof that any barbarous tribe or nation, by any innate elements in its constitution, or by its own unassisted efforts, ever made one step in the career of intellectual and moral improvement.

II. That from all monumental evidence, and from universal history, it is demonstrable that the most ancient nations were farther advanced, in moral and intellectual attainments, than their successors.

III. That the analogies drawn from geological facts, on which Combe and others too fondly rely, so far from favoring his assumption, directly prove the contrary.

IV. That the present civilization of Great Britain, like that of the more civilized nations of the Old World, is the product, not of unassisted barbarism, but of successive conquests and intermixtures with other nations; and especially of the early introduction of Christian principles and a Christian people. And this applies to our own country as much as to any other. The proofs and documents confirmatory of these facts are voluminous and unanswerable.

Indeed, his own geological statistics demonstrate a fact which subverts all his reasonings, viz. That, so far from the gradual evolutions of time improving man, animal or plant, it required various successive exertions of creative power "before the jarring elements were reduced to order;" that no less than *five successive races of plants and four successive races of animals* appear to have been *created* and swept away by the physical revolutions of the globe before the system became so permanent as to be fit for man.

To enter formally into the details of facts, evidences and arguments, illustrative and confirmatory of these statements, would be more tedious than necessary or profitable on such an occasion as the present. This has been well and ably done by more skilful hands. It is fully shown by the researches of geologists, that no race of animals was ever derived from an antecedent or contemporary species, or was gradually perfected. And certainly the history of three thousand years furnishes not a single fact corroborative of such an assumption.

As to the history of man, it appears from all the records of earth that he has accomplished mightier and more astonishing works, in ages the most remote, than he has achieved since the ages of authentic history began. Of the four great empires of time, the Babylonian excelled the Medo-Persian, the Medo-Persian the Grecian, the Grecian the Roman, in the great achievements of earth that give character to the human mind. The great elementary principles that terminate in a higher civilization originated amongst the primitive nations, and, in an unbroken chain, have been handed down to us. We may, in all safety, commit the question to the more enlightened portions of our own or of any other civilized community, whether Moses and his people have not contributed more to the civilization of the world than all the kings and heroes from the days of the Pharaohs down to Napoleon the Great!

Still, these objections, subtracted from all the arguments and evidences, do not essentially impair the superstructure. The materialism of the system, as dispensed by the Messrs. Fowler, is a still greater objection. Yet despite the erroneous reasonings and fallacious assumptions of some of its advocates and defenders, there is sufficient evidence that the mind of man incarnate, commonly, but not always, acts, and is acted upon, by the nervous machinery of the brain; and that the brain and its developments in the cranium, with the physiology of the human body, afford an index to the mind within.

Dr. George Combe, the great apostle of phrenology in Scotland, is more transparently infidel than most of his American brotherhood. Still, as a class, they are not entirely above suspicion. There is, indeed, more to fear than to hope, from the tendencies and developments of both the American and European schools of phrenology, mesmerism, clairvoyance and spiritual rappings, especially amongst an uneducated population. Christianity, however, fears nothing from any true science of body or soul, matter or spirit. But there is now, as well as in former ages, much that is called science, which is "science falsely so called."

One of the worst symptoms of certain European and American phrenological schools, is a prevailing and pervading disposition to test the claims of the Bible by an appeal to phrenology, rather than to test the claims of phrenology by an appeal to the Bible. This, indeed, has created a prejudice against phrenology which is more benevolent than rational. Weak, indeed, is the faith of any man in the Bible, who fears any thing for it from any quarter whatever. If any man has true faith in his own personal identity, and true faith in the Bible, he could not be persuaded that it is a lie, though one rose from the dead and so affirmed. Paul spoke as a true philosopher when, on a certain occasion, he said, "Though we or *an angel from heaven* preach any other gospel to you than that which we have preached, *let him be accursed.*" No man that truly (that is, rationally) believes the gospel, fears any thing in the name of science, learning or wisdom, whether called phrenology, pneumatology, psychology or physico-theology.

When any proposition is proved to be true, the universe could not prove it false. If twelve veracious men, *compos mentis,* sound in mind and body, should, on the scaffold, swear, at the jeopardy of their lives, that they saw a man murdered, cut to pieces, buried, laid in the grave, and on the third day after rise again whole and sound, walk about, eat, drink and converse with them during forty days, could any speculations, *a priori* reasonings, or theorizings upon body or spirit, stultify, falsify or annihilate the united testimony to a plain matter of fact, reported by them, and for which deposition they laid down their heads and suffered them to be cut off? *Credat Judœus Apella, non ego!*

None but a skeptic at heart could fear any thing from any alleged science, true or false, against the Bible facts, precepts and promises. Times without number it has been assailed, by all sorts of men and by all sorts of arguments. It has been laughed at, ridiculed, caricatured, anathematized, banished, inhibited, imprisoned, burned, dragged through the streets of Paris by a common hangman, as though it were an execrable felon; and yet it not only lives, but reigns and triumphs in the hearts and lives of the greatest, the wisest and the best of mankind. It is being translated into all the dialects of earth. It is borne on the wings of every wind to every point of the compass. It is penetrating Australia, New Zealand, the isles of the Pacific, and the coasts of both continents, despite the Vatican and all its thunderings and voices and trumpets. It is reinvading Italy, and is secretly sold or bestowed in the very metropolis of Popery, within sight of St. Peter's. It has almost invaded the palace of Pio Nono himself, and terrified the pretended vicar of Christ.

Dr. Combe, in Edinburgh, and other phrenologists in New York and elsewhere, may *doubt* whether death be a *punishment* consequent upon the sin of Adam, or whether it entered our world in pursuance of any moral aberration, or merely as the inevitable result of the wear and tear of the physical forces upon all organic life. They may even honestly assume and teach that the pains of parturition are no more connected with Eve's transgression than are those of the fowl and the brute. They may propose the improvement of the physical constitution of man, as the only means of his moral and spiritual health, and pity those who endeavor to improve the physical by the moral. They may write and preach hygeia and the laws of health and life, and make the present eating, drinking and sleeping of man his paradise and his heaven. They may regard prayers and thankgivings for special providences and special deliverances, like the doctrine of the fall and the contamination of sin, as one and all but the innocent speculations of poets or the fables of philosophers, for the benefit of the uneducated, but entirely below the respect of phrenologists of the higher schools, being merely the remains of ancient traditions—the hoary fables of a remote and unwritten age.

They speak eloquently and reverently of the "dear, blessed Bible, the family Bible, *that lay on the stand*," gilded with gold and covered with dust. They sincerely regret that it is of so little account, because so "obscure," so "corrupted" in the text, "having so many doubtful readings," and requiring so "many learned and consecrated interpreters." Still it is a good book, and worthy of one or two careful readings during life. But, as Dr. Combe deeply regrets, its requirements are so high, and its oracles and precepts so sublime, that to command obedience to them is like commanding a horse to fly to heaven, without even the wings of a bat. The doctrine of the fall, he must think, is "*a fundamental error* of the divines," which, "because of their entire ignorance of the laws of nature, and of a true system of mental philosophy, they were obliged to adopt." He would, therefore, benevolently advise the Christian ministry to turn their churches into lecture-rooms, and to preach the laws of eating and drinking, of sleeping and working, more philosophically; and of studying the physical economy of life as the true doctrine of salvation, and the only scientific path to good health, a good stomach and a good, plump, fat, round old age.

Thus, walking on stilts with rapid strides, *phrenology* has almost made the tour of Christendom within the memory of one generation. It has selected for its special companions a cohort of craniologists, with their craniometers, examining *craniums*. These philosophers deliver lectures in four sciences, which sprang from one egg. They are, scientifically, denominated craniology, craniognomy, craniometry and cranioscopy. There is a good deal of bone, as well as of marrow, in these sciences of the solid contents of human craniums, which, by the aid of the scalpel and the scalping-iron, furnish ample materials for very profound disquisitions on this pre-eminently metaphysico-physical subject.

In older times, our revered fathers taught that man's thinking-power was in his head, and his feeling-power in his heart. Hence, wise men in former years died of "nervous headaches," and all disappointed lovers died of "broken hearts." What simpletons they were!

In good old Scotland, I formerly heard disquisitions upon the philosophy of man, both in college and from the pulpits of the orthodox. These learned men could show the exact difference between the south and the southwest side of a hair. But in speaking of man, they always reduced him to *three heads*, as they called them: we would rather say *three points*. They gave him a *body*, a *soul* and a *spirit*. This was his entire outfit for the pilgrimage of earth. They were very learned doctors, and gave us Hebrew, Greek and Latin for every thing, sacred and divine.

They discriminated between the *soul* and the *spirit*, and affirmed that Hebrews, Greeks and Romans had an appropriate name for each. The Hebrews, for example, had *ruach* for the spirit, and *nepesh* for the soul; the Greeks, *pneuma* for the spirit, and *psuchee* for the soul; while the good old Romans had *animus* and *spiritus* for the mind or spirit, and *anima* for the soul. Paul himself, it was alleged, spoke and wrote in this philosophic style. With him, there was a species of trinity in man. One of his prayers was quoted: "*Αὐτὸς δὲ ὁ Θεὸς τῆς εἰρήνης ἁγιάσαι ὑμᾶς ὁλοιελεῖς· καὶ ὁλόκληρον ὑμῶν τὸ πνεῦμα, καὶ ἡ ψυχὴ, καὶ τὸ σῶμα.*" (See 1 Thess. v. 23.) In English: May God sanctify you wholly,—1st, the *pneuma*, or spirit; 2d, the *psuchee*, or soul; 3d, the *sooma*, or body. These constitute the positive, comparative and superlative of man—three *natures* in one *personality*.

The whole divine philosophy of man, according to Paul, is thus condensed or concentrated into a nutshell. It is this: Man's spirit by his soul, and his soul by its organ of many nerves, (the brain,) operates upon a world within him; and his spirit by his soul, and his soul by its organ, (the brain,) and the brain by its organ, (the body,) operates upon a world without him. The formulas of this faith are very brief. *Acti agimus.* Acted upon, we act. *Actus, me invito factus, non est meus actus.* An act done against my will is not my act. *Actus non facit reum nisi mens sit rea.* The act does not make a man guilty unless the mind be also guilty. This was and is the short metre of the soundest religious and moral orthodoxy! Who of us, the sons of such philosophic sires, would not endorse it?

Having paid a passing tribute of respect to phrenology, we are, in common courtesy, constrained to compliment, not her cousin-german, but her German cousin, *mesmerism.*

Frederic Anthony Mesmer, of the past and present century, a German physician, having been some time psychologically sojourning among the planets, till electrified by their serene influence, so long ago as 1766 gave to the world a thesis on planetary influence, endeavoring to show that these heavenly bodies diffused through this nether universe a subtle fluid, acting upon and impregnating the nervous system of all animate terraqueous beings. He founded the new philosophy of Animal Magnetism about the beginning of the present century. He lived and died on this side of the science of psychomancy. He did not consult the souls of the dead, but only the souls of the living.

The science and art of mesmerism is simply the science and art of communicating a peculiar species of sleep, either by the eye or the hand, so affecting the human body as to leave the mind active and intelligent—wide awake and watching; even more intuitive and penetrating under the conquest of the animal energies than when encumbered with the working of its own machinery and with the sights and sounds of earthly realities.

This new art and mystery—science it cannot be called—is in rapid progress of cultivation at the present time. Its metes and boundaries are, however, nearly, if not altogether, ascertained. Its vocabulary is strange and mysterious. With its votaries, the word *see* indicates a new and strange idea. We, in common parlance, see by the means of light, and by an organ we call the eye. But they profess to see without light, and with closed eyes, or without eyes. We see while awake, but they only see mesmerically when asleep. How, then, can men, who only see with eyes open, and by means of light, understand their visions, and sights, and revelations? Neither prophets nor apostles, in ancient times, saw earthly things, read letters, or saw their antipodes through ocean spectacles encased and underlaid with earth and granite. We are thus fairly lost and bewildered in the premises, by terms and phrases which no dictionary of earth expounds. They can, in their vernacular, equally see a mountain, and, through a mountain, a spirit on the other side, without the aid of sun, or lamp, or eyes. Their doctors dispense medicines, and examine pulses, by looking through a man's skin, and flesh, and bones, into and through the marrow in his bones, and count, compare and analyze the nerves of every tissue from the centre of the brain to the centre of the heart. These are clairvoyants with a vengeance, whom any man of mere common sense and common faculties would fear to encounter! They claim to possess a new species of omnipresence and omniscience, or what is equal to both.

A mesmerized lady takes the hand of a person, and travels with him in mind from Philadelphia to Paris in less than four seconds, and with him walks through the Louvre, and with him contemplates the portraits and pictures, one by one, and, in less than the twinkling of an eye, returns to Philadelphia and reveals the vision. And yet the mesmerizer disbelieves in spirits, and only believes in fluids. Who can reason with or against such pretensions? It is neither a subject of reason nor of revelation, and, therefore, we at once surrender, or deny *in toto* the whole pretence, as a demoniacal pretension, or a new art or device of jugglery.

Some of its special pleaders deny the pretence of looking through solid rocks or solid substances, and yet they pretend to travel to Paris or London, in a straight line, through the earth, or so much of it as, in a rectilinear direction, lies to the right or left of a traveller from a room in New York to a room in London or in Paris. The somnambulist may not always, in such excursions, succeed; but if he only once, in any given number of times, succeeds, it is sufficient. The miracle, in that case, is wrought.

Many of the mesmerizers deny both spirits and miracles, as positive entities. *Fluids* and *effluvia* are their spirits and wonder-working agents. Fluids and effluvia, with them, become oral prophets and prophetesses; divine fortunes and narrate them; pry into the future and launch into eternity. Every somnambulist is positively inspired, if not by a spirit, certainly by an effluvium, or some subtle, inappreciable material agency, more refined than any gaseous body known to science or to fame.

But the mysteries of mesmerism transcend all other mysteries; for, while it denies spiritual inspiration, it claims an inspiration and a power above and beyond all the inspiration of prophets and apostles. Its most ingenious advocates even deny the theory of working upon the imagination, and assert that wild bulls, mad dogs, and animals in the agonies of death, have felt its awful power and have been healed. And, strange to tell, while faith in men is essential to its development, brutes, without either faith or reason, are wholly under its power. Nay, even doors and floors are mesmerized by the waving of the hand; and human feet and hands are, *nolens volens*, bound in adamantine chains by its enchanting power.

And, stranger still, connected with phrenology, greater miracles than even these are wrought by its sublime magicians. Even characters are convertible by its mystic power. A gentle wave of a mesmerist's hand over this or that organ gives, for the time-being, a new character. Its subject becomes a churl or a prodigal, a thief or an honest man, a combatant or a coward, veracious or a liar, not as the touch, but as the shadow, of the mesmerist's hand or finger passes near the localities of certain organs of the brain or bumps of the cranium. Young ladies, and even the coyest old maids, are courted and subdued by its mystic charms. Truly it is a terrific and an appalling power in the hands of certain priests and priestesses of either Cupid, the son of Venus and Jupiter, or the son of Erebus and Nox.

But, in certain cases, it is questionable—a matter yet *sub judice*—whether the power of the mesmerist is more in his hand or in his eye. Perhaps it is in both. When doctors differ, pupils may disagree. But it is said that a glove from the hand of a lover may be transmitted, by post, any distance, to his mistress, and become a medium of the most felicitous communication, by what is technically called "*rapport*"—a term for whose meaning, young gentlemen, I must refer you to your best French dictionaries.

This is an improvement in harmony with the telegraphic despatch of the age. Thus, by the aid of mesmerism, a young gentleman at Washington may not only communicate, but hold court, with the mistress of his heart at the distance of a few thousand miles. In this way, the language of his affection, while yet warm from his heart, may reach her eye, and be as efficient of love as the most felicitous *tête-à-tête* demonstration. We are, indeed, very much in doubt—if this alleged science should prove to be any thing but a *lusus naturæ*, an *ignis-fatuus*—whether it would not be infinitely more pregnant of evil than of good to human kind.

But, as yet advised, we are slow to believe its boasted claims and marvellous pretensions. There is one fact of colossal magnitude, strongly asserted by those who, from a large field of observation and innumerable trials made, have a right and an authority to speak which I have not, from any attention which I have paid to the subject. It is this: *No one has ever yet been magnetized in good health when free from any suspicion or apprehension of the operation to which he or she was subjected.* The mind or the imagination must be excited or morbidly affected, from representations made, in order to superinduce a state of feeling in harmony with the mind and intentions of the operator. Now, as conceded on all hands, "*physical agents act of themselves, independent of the will of the subject.*" This is essential to all our conceptions of physical agency in all cases. But not so in moral agencies. In these, the will of the agent and of the subject—the operator and the operated upon—must, in every act, simultaneously sympathize or harmonize. We have, indeed, mental as well as physical invalids in the great family of man. These are rather passive instruments, and, in the hand of every tempter, of every ingenious or enthusiastic operator, an easy prey. The extent of this subtle influence, whether in the hand or in the eye of the charmer and of his prey, has never yet been ascertained either in man or in the brutal tribes of earth.

The true philosophy of mesmerism is to be found in the infirmities of human nature—its morbid sensibility, its credulity, its insatiate curiosity, its love of the marvellous, and the necessary absence of self-government. These render their subjects the easy prey of imagination, and of the faith or of the self-confidence of bold experimentalists, themselves too often as much deceived as deceivers.

A clear and comprehensive conception of the laws of sympathy and of animal influence upon animal bodies, with the different states of the parties, will go a sufficient length to free every one from being a proper subject for the manifestations of the too credulous or too cunning hand of well-practised manipulators. The sinful curiosity to acquire, and the presumption to impart, may, indeed, conspire to yield results as astounding as they may be judicial, on the part of divine government, to furnish those who presume to open the sealed volumes of forbidden knowledge.

As in the cases of those who formerly consulted demons, who had recourse to familiar spirits and to wizards, seeking to unseal the volumes of human destiny and to pry into secrets which God has as kindly hidden as he has benevolently revealed that which man ought to know of himself and of his destiny in order to his true and lasting glory, honor and felicity, God has now given an undiscerning mind, so that a deceived heart has turned multitudes aside; insomuch that none of them can deliver his own soul from the infatuation, and, therefore, can neither see nor say, "Is there not a lie, an error, in my right hand?"

That all *bodies*—the human body as well as every other body, mineral, animal, or vegetable—are the subjects and residences of an electric spirit, no one, tolerably initiated into the secrets of nature, either can or will deny. And what is this electric spirit, permeating, in certain degrees and dispensations, every thing terraqueous, organic and inorganic? Are its mysteries all revealed? Is any one of them all revealed? No: not one. Science—true science—cheerfully puts its finger upon its lip, and nods assent. Ether, atmosphere, water, earth, are its grand and august treasure-houses. These are all distinct bodies, each one severally possessing its own treasures of this mysterious spirit. And yet it is not pure spirit. It is only relatively so called. Not one of its phenomena is perfectly comprehended by any living man. In one class of bodies it is made manifest only by friction; in another class, by sensible communication. Some bodies absolutely refuse to receive electricity by communication; one class becoming electrical by friction only, another only by communication. This, indeed, is not an absolute law. By force of human genius they can be made convertible into each other. Pools of water have been so electrified as, on presentation of the human hand, to yield enough to produce pain. But we must ascend towards heaven to find its proper habitation. Its home is the ether that lies beyond the realms of atmospheric air. Hence, its solemn and sublime chambers never can be entered by the foot of mortal man.

We may talk of the quantities of electricity under the denominations of positive and negative; of its residences, transmigrations, transformations or metamorphoses; but its secret chambers and its domestic laws no son of earth can penetrate till he has shuffled off this mortal coil.

We may call the electricities positive and negative, vitreous or resinous, without increasing our knowledge of either. We may ascertain its immutable laws—such as that the rubbing and the rubbed body always require opposite electricities, and that the intensity of the electric force resembles the law of gravitation, being inversely as the square of its distance. But of its essence and its primordial *modus operandi* the philosopher is yet as ignorant as an Indian from the cliffs of the Andes or a Bedoueen from the deserts of Arabia.

Shall we, then, assume as a fact that a human hand, applied frictionwise to a human body, may abstract from it a substance sensibly affecting the brain, and at the same time dogmatically affirm that, with the fluid abstracted or communicated—the one positive, the other negative—the mind of the subject is perfectly identified with that of the agent? Such an inference would be at open war with every principle and law of sound reason and of human experience. But, that some *physical* effect might and would accrue to one or both, might, on some of the laws of animated nature, be lawfully presumed. If, indeed, the mind of man were a mere fluid—even the most recondite and abstract—the inference would not be so perfectly incongruous, illogical and revolting. But to identify the human understanding, spirit, reason, conscience or affections with matter solid, liquid or gaseous, is alike at war with reason and revelation, as well as with all the canons of a sound and safe philosophy. But all that we have assumed or said is with reference to the spiritual rappings or knockings—the legitimate result of mesmerism and clairvoyance, as developed in the recent conversations with the dead. The links of this chain, however curious, should we attempt now to trace them, would trench alike upon our time and your patience. We prefer, on such premises, to be suggestive rather than dogmatic.

To save time, I will then assume that with a good "*medium*," and a *quantum sufficit* of animal magnetism, the spiritual knockings, first heard in modern times in the house of Rev. John Wesley, believed in by Dr. Adam Clarke, and reported and commented on by Dr. Priestley, are true and veritable facts; that old Jeffrey's ghost did torment the family of the distinguished Wesleys, more or less, during three-and-thirty years; and that the fearful knocks first heard in Hydesville, in the town of Arcadia, New York, in 1847, afterwards tenanted by Mr. and Mrs. Fox, staunch members of the Methodist Episcopal Church; testified to by so many true and veritable citizens in New York; more fully developed in Rochester, Auburn, Skaneateles, and recently in many towns in this Union, according to the prophecy that went before concerning them, through the distinguished Baron Swedenborg, in his prophecies concerning the year 1852, which was to decide the fate of his Church and doctrines, *are all true and veritable facts and documents, of unquestionable truth and verity.* I do hereby, therefore, engross and accept, as veritable and substantially true, with a reasonable discount for the false and hypocritical pretences of some ring-streaked, speckled and spotted goats, that have insinuated themselves, horns off, amongst these true and honest believers, the facts as stated. Having, then, thus cordially admitted the whole premises and facts claimed, I proceed to offer a few reasons and considerations why they ought to be promptly repudiated by all rational and well-informed Christians and citizens, in these United States and elsewhere.

Necromancy is just as true as history, and as much to be believed. It is a universally conceded doctrine of revelation, accredited by all learned Protestants, from Luther down to the present day. It is both a science and an art, true as the Bible. As a science, it develops a portion of the unseen world, as clearly as Newton developed a portion of the seen world. There is a spirit world as well as a material world. There is a world of darkness and death as well as a world of light and life.

Necromancy was taught in Egypt before the birth of Moses. The art of conferring with the dead was well understood in Egypt, whence it travelled all over the earth. Hence, laws concerning it were a part and parcel of the Jewish code. God never enacted laws against absolute non-entities. The fact of his enacting laws against wizards, witches and necromancy as much substantiates and authenticates their reality as that of his enacting laws against sodomy and Sodomites, and against the image-worship of Pagandom, demonstrates their actual existence. Balaam, the enchanter and soothsayer, was as real a character and prophet as Moses. The witch of Endor and her necromancy were as much facts as were King Saul and the prophet Samuel. And that she had power over the dead, is just as veritable as that Samuel had power over the living. Down to the Christian era, witches, familiar spirits and witchcraft obtained all over Asia. Paul was beset by a Pythonic spirit, as truly as Jesus was tempted by Satan in person. These are Bible facts as palpable and as demonstrable as the dispossession of demons or the resurrection of Lazarus. No man, who believes the Bible testimony, can deny it. God commanded Moses to punish with death the witches that troubled Israel. And Paul places witchcraft amongst the execrable sins of his day, and warns Christians against it. Some semi-infidels amongst modern Christians have endeavored to ridicule this belief. Knaves and fools alike have made a mockery of these awful realities, as much as Universalians make a mock of hell. But I never knew a well-educated man, or a man of a vigorous or enlightened mind, who denied or doubted these awful realities.

God has been pleased to restrain, and again to let Satan loose a little season, and now his coming is heralded from Boston to California and Oregon. These indications, as usual, are ridiculed by materialists and atheists of every school. Christians believe, and fear for coming events. These shadows indicate an approaching crisis. Let us, then, be prepared for it. The wise shall understand, while the foolish virgins are asleep and have no oil in their lamps.

Never were actors more true and faithful to their calling than these pretended spirit-rappers. They are always communing with the spirits of the dead. They are asking and obtaining messages from them, but only from the wicked dead. They are lying spirits, pretending to speak from heaven above, but they speak from the earth and below the earth. They are true to their prophetic character; and alas for them that consult these too familiar spirits, whether real or pretended, which peep, and rap, and mutter! They are all genuine Universalians. They take away from sinners the fear of death and hell. Not one of them, so far as I have heard, gives a single intimation of hell. All their communications allure to the belief that the friends of all inquirers are now in Abraham's bosom.

There have always been a few such real or false pretenders, and again they are let loose from prison, and are everywhere busied in deluding those who have not the true faith in their hearts. Since the true gospel has been promulged, and is being promulged, they are exceedingly fierce against it, and take occasion to oppose it by transforming themselves into angels of light. They now say that Christ is in the desert, or, rather, most of them delight to say he is in the secret chambers. How fearfully does this comport with those secret tables, the mediums, and the queries and responses echoing from Rochester to the centre and circumference of this much-favored land of Bibles!

But in all that I have conceded, I have not yet conceded their reality. These are such poor demons, and appear in forms so questionable and mean, that I cannot fully credit their reality. If demons they be, they are the meanest demons, and the most bereft of talent and capacity to speak, I presume to say, in the whole annals of demonology. We have read of demons of respectable character and standing, in former ages; but these New York demons are the veriest liliputian demons I have ever read of. They can speak neither a dead nor a living tongue. They peep, and mutter, and rap, and thump, as the most clownish, ill-bred demons in universal history. They are too exceedingly fond of the ladies, and associate quite too familiarly with them. They even impinge upon their wardrobes, their secret chambers, and have the rudeness to chatter about it at a distance. They come in shapes so questionable, that I have almost concluded they are only hypocritical demons. I have rummaged over one of their most erudite volumes of conversations and communications, and had intended to embellish my address with a few of their flowers of rhetoric, but I am positively so electrified by shame, that I can scarcely bring myself to make a single quotation from their low, vulgar, or clownish responses.

Mr. Wesley's ghost Jeffrey, of Epworth, Lincolnshire, England, was a ghost of some respectability of language and address. And Mrs. Seeress Harper, formerly Miss Emily Wesley, was a lady, every inch of her, and although the ghost Jeffrey haunted her for four-and-thirty years, he was, upon the whole, rather genteel; and she, in all their intercourse, never lost her happy equilibrium.

It is due to my present audience and to those absent spirits, rappers, mediums, and all that wait upon them for illumination, that we cite, from their annals, a few of the new revelations and communications with which they have been favored. We will, therefore, propound a few questions, and give their answers :—

1. When a spirit leaves the human form, how does it look?

DAVIS.—"Spirits retain the same bodily form in the spiritual sphere, and at first they feel as if they were only transformed to a country they know not. It is, however, not long after the transition before the interior senses are opened: then they behold and appreciate the change and the beauties with which they are surrounded."

2. Do embodied and disembodied spirits intercommunicate?

DAVIS, CLAIRVOYANT.—"It is a truth that spirits commune with one another while one is in the body and the other in the higher spheres, even, too, when the person in the body is unconscious of the influence, and hence cannot be convinced of the fact. *This truth will, ere long, present itself in the form of a living demonstration.*"*

3. How will the world receive this new light?

DAVIS.—"The world will hail with delight the ushering in of that era, *when the interiors of men will be opened,* and the spiritual communion shall be established, such as is now being enjoyed by the inhabitants of *Mars, Jupiter and Saturn, because of their superior refinement.*"*

4. Pray, Mr. Davis, as you illustrate by the spiritual communion now enjoyed by the inhabitants of Mars, Jupiter and Saturn, of course you have been there; but we, never having been there, cannot understand you: would you please enlighten us in that point, that we may understand you in this?

DAVIS.—"I cannot communicate with you on that subject."

[*Enter Reverend A. H. Jarvis, of the Methodist Church.*]

MR. JARVIS.—"There are many facts which have come under my observation equally convincing of the intelligence and utility of the communications from these unseen agents, who I now believe are continually about us, and more perfectly acquainted with all our ways, and even our thoughts, than we are with each other. But the fact in reference to my friend Pickard is what you desire. He was at my house on Friday afternoon, April 6th, 1849. None of the Fox family was present. While at the table, we had frequent communications on different subjects. Pickard was requested to ask questions. He desired to know who it was that would answer questions. The answer was, 'I am your mother, Mary Pickard.' Her name, or the fact of her death, was not known to any of us. The next Monday evening he

---

* See Principles of Nature, pp. 658, 675.

(Pickard) was at Mr. G.'s, and tarried there over night. He there received a communication, purporting to be from his mother, saying, 'Your child is dead.' He came immediately to my place, and said he should take the stage for home, (Lockport, sixty miles distant.) He left in the stage at eight or nine A. M. At twelve M. I returned to my house, my wife meeting me with a telegraph-envelop. I broke the seal and read mentally first:—

"'ROCHESTER, April 10, 1849.

"'By telegraph from Lockport, to Rev. A. H. Jarvis, No. 4 West Street. Tell Mr. Pickard, if you can find him, his child *died this morning*. Answer. R. MALLORY.'

"I then read it to my wife, and said, 'This is one of the best and most convincing evidences of the intelligence of those invisible agents;' and then I added, 'God's telegraph has outdone Morse's altogether.'"

Was not this a glorious message from the spirit land?

We will take another specimen, from the New York Tribune, of December 28, 1849:—

"After this report and some discussion on the subject, the audience selected another committee, composed of the following persons:—Dr. H. H. Langworthy, Hon. Frederick Whittlesey, D. C. McCallum, William Fisher, of Rochester, and Hon. A. P. Hascall, of Le Roy. At the next lecture this committee reported that they went into the investigation at the office of Chancellor Whittlesey, and they heard the sound on the floor, on the wall, and door; that the ladies were placed in different positions, and, like the other committee, they were wholly unable to tell from what the sound proceeded or how it was made; that Dr. Langworthy made observations with a stethoscope, to ascertain whether there was any movement with the lungs, and found not the least difference when the sounds were made; and there was no kind of *probability or possibility of their being made by ventriloquism, as some had supposed—and they could not have been made by machinery.*

"This committee was composed of Dr. E. P. Langworthy, Dr. J. Gates, Wm. Fitzhugh, Esq., W. L. Burtis, and L. Kenyon. This committee met at the rooms of Dr. Gates, at the Rochester House, and appointed a committee of ladies, who took the young women into a room, disrobed them, and examined their persons and clothing, to be sure there were no fixtures about them that could produce the sounds. When satisfied on this point, the committee of ladies tried some other experiments, and gave the young ladies the following certificate:—

"'When they were standing on pillows, with a handkerchief tied around the bottom of their dresses, tight to the ankles, we all heard the rapping on the wall and floor distinctly.

(Signed) 'MRS. STONE,
'MRS. J. GATES,
'MISS M. P. LAWRENCE.'

"In the evening the committee, through their chairman, Dr. Langworthy, made a very full report of their examinations during the day. They reported they excluded all friends of the two ladies from the committee-room, and had the examination only in presence of the committee of gentlemen, and ladies chosen by them. Notwithstanding all this precaution, these sounds were heard when the ladies stood on large *feather pillows, without shoes*, and in other various positions, both on the floor and on the wall; that a number of questions were asked, which, when answered, were generally correct. Each member of the committee reported separately, agreeing with, and corroborating, the first statements."

We will adduce only another specimen of these revelations:—

"Thousands of questions have been asked on these points, and have been answered by spirits who purported to be Emanuel Swedenborg, the 'Seeress of Prevorst,' George Fox, Galen, William E. Channing, Nathaniel P. Rogers, John Wesley, Samuel Wesley, Percy Bysshe Shelley, Prof. David P. Page, and many others.

Question.—What is your mission to the world?

Answer.—To do good. The time will come when we will communicate universally.

Question.—Of what benefit will it be to mankind?

Answer.—We can reveal truths to the world, and men will become more harmonious and better prepared for the higher spheres.

Question.—Some persons imagine that the spirits are evil, and that Satan is transformed into an angel of light to deceive us. What shall we say to them?

Answer.—Tell them some of their bigotry will have to be dispensed with before they can believe we are good spirits. Ask them why they refuse to investigate. They are not as wise as they suppose themselves to be.

Question.—Can ignorant spirits rap?

Answer.—Yes. (An ignorant spirit rapped, and the difference was very plain between that and the other.)

Question.—Are these sounds made by rapping?

Answer.—No. They are made by the will of the spirits causing a concussion of the atmosphere and making the sounds appear in whatever place they please.

Question.—Can they make the sounds to all persons?

Answer.—No. The time will come when they can.

Question.—Is there some peculiar state of the body that makes it easier to communicate with some persons than others?

Answer.—Yes."

Such, gentlemen, are the *quasi*-Divine revelations now being made to the world by the spirits in prison, or somewhere else, through these elect gentlemen and ladies. If you desire to have their own explanation of these mysteries, I can give it to you from their own pens. It is all compressed into one period. Here it is :—

"They (clairvoyants) have the full power of sympathy with the spirits, through the medium of the nervous fluid or electricity, which is the only medium of communication between spirits in and out of the body."

On these premises you can philosophize without my aid, and readily appreciate the amount of credulity which the Christian philosopher has now to encounter. From such revolting spectacles and silly pretensions, I am ashamed and mortified to say that we must fix, at no very elevated point, the standard of Christian intelligence and good sense of a great mass of our community who are led away by this solemn mockery.

But, before we close, it may be expedient to suggest a few criteria by which all such pretensions may be tried, however plausible and with whatever show of evidence they may claim the attention of an enlightened community.

1. We either have, or have not, a Divine Revelation, perfectly adapted to the genius and condition of human nature. The educated mind of Christendom, during a period of more than eighteen centuries, has concurred in the belief and assertion of this transcendent fact. The philosophers, poets, orators, legislators, and all the highly gifted and cultivated leaders of public opinion, in the civilized world, have conceded, that, of earth's literature, science and religion, the Bible itself is, *par excellence*, the Book of Books, worthy of the Supreme Intelligence to be its Author, and of man to be its instrument, subject and object. It has passed through every ordeal—through the burning fiery furnace of the most scathing criticism; and, like the pure gold of Ophir, it has come out of that furnace not merely unscathed, but shining with a lustre, a beauty, a glory, that surpasses all the literature, science and religion of all ages, races and generations of men. The arm of flesh will sooner quell the waves of the sea, arrest the winds of heaven, or pluck the sun from the centre of its system, than human wisdom, genius or learning fasten upon any page of this Divine Volume a single characteristic of weakness or folly—of fraud or fiction.

Truth and error have their appropriate characteristics. Nature and art—I mean nature and human art, (for all nature is but art unknown to man)—are distinguishable to every educated age. No honey-bee ever sought honey from an artificial flower in all its bloom of beauty.

No one of perspicacity, who has read with attention the oracles of any Divine prophet or apostle, will for a moment listen to the prosing nonsense and folly of a mesmerized clairvoyant. To listen to such stuff as is printed from the lips of such sages, *as a communication from heaven*, is to give proof positive that the party in attendance has never seen the Sun of Righteousness in his full-orbed glory, and knows nothing of his meridian splendor.

2. But, in the second place, these assumed revelations are private revelations, and from private impulse, and are, consequently, of private interpretation. Of course, then, they are not of any public importance. This is not a *seal*, but a *brand* from heaven, of their imposture. No oracle of God is of any private impulse or private interpretation, for the holy men of olden times spake as they were moved, not by angel or spirit, but by the Holy Spirit. This is, itself, an explicit refutation of them. No divinely-inspired man ever was a fortune-teller, or a communicator of private intelligence for the good or behoof of any individual. Angels have been sent on special errands to special persons, for public interest; but the Divine Spirit never condescended to answer any man's petition concerning his own personal property, domicil, goods or chattels. These spiritual rappers and their spirits, in all their speculations, have stamped upon themselves the brand of their own fraud and imposition, and yet have not sense to read or see it.

3. When God interposes, it is on an occasion worthy of himself. There was always a Moses or a Joshua in the field—a Lawgiver or a Redeemer on the stage—when God "rapped." His voice then shook, not a door, but the earth and the heavens. He needed no lamp nor sensible light, for his own glory veiled the sun and hid the stars from mortal vision.

"When Israel went out of Egypt,
The house of Jacob from a people of strange language,
Judah was his sanctuary,
And Israel his dominion.
The sea saw it, and fled;
The Jordan was driven back;
The mountains skipped like rams,
And the little hills like lambs.
What ailed thee, O thou sea, that thou fleddest?
Thou Jordan, that thou wast driven back?
Ye mountains, that ye skipped like rams,
And ye little hills, like lambs?

The earth trembled at the presence of the Lord,
At the presence of the God of Jacob;
Who turned the rock into a pool of water,
And flint into fountains of water."

In what contrast with these scenes stand the domiciles of Mr. Fox, of Lyman Granger, and of Johnny Grott, of Rochester, Auburn, or Skaneateles, with their young groups of ghostly faces peeping, peering, muttering around a drowsy *medium*, half Mercury, half man, waiting for the news from the spirits in some infernal purgatory beyond some Stygean pool!

It is a canon of Protestantism, worthy of a golden tablet, that to the Bible's last *amen* nothing is to be added by any new revelation or commandment of demon, angel or man. Between the last voice of the Apocalypse and the final trumpet of man's drama, no new oracle, dream or vision is promised by God or expected by any intelligent man.

Indeed, as soon as the drama of redemption was completed, and the keys of the kingdom of heaven given in charge to the Apostle Peter, all subsequent preachers, teachers and inquirers were, by visions or precepts from heaven, sent to hear words from Peter, which all that learn, believe and obey will need no angel, ghost, medium or missionary from another sphere, to teach them any thing which they ought to know, to fill up their mission and destiny of life, or to consummate their own glory, honor and blessedness.

Young gentlemen, we live in an age of wonders, and we Anglo-Saxons are, in fact, a wonderful people. We have, too, *as a people*, a wonderful destiny in this world, beyond our individual personal destiny in an eternal universe, on the mere confines of which we yet stand. You have peculiar privileges, and, consequently, will have peculiar duties, and a peculiar destiny, in this world. The truly educated portions of our country, in the broad and large import of the word *education*, are not one in a thousand of our aggregate population. The credulity of many infidels and skeptics has afforded a somewhat perplexing theme to certain moral philosophers. We allude to it no further, at present, than to express our wonder at the facile belief of some schools of infidelity in new revelations. They reject Moses and the prophets, Jesus and the apostles, and believe in the day-dreams and visions of every new pretender to some new form of supernaturalism. Hence the ready ear and voluntary belief which they yield to every pretence of some new light from the spirit world.

Within a few years there has been a very general excitement amongst this class on the subject of new communications from the dead. We regard this fact as at least a very striking proof of an all-pervading latent interest in the state of the dead, and of the unsatisfyingness of all the mere philosophies of earth upon the unseen and the eternal world. Human nature, in its more rational forms, without a positive and explicit revelation of a future life, has never been, and never can be, at rest. It demands a God, a future judgment, and a future life. It has hopes and fears, however latent, that occasionally develop their positive existence, and cannot, by any possibility, be either eradicated or annihilated. But the misfortune is that men seek to conceal or to secrete this innate dread of the great unseen and the great unknown, rather than to institute an earnest search or inquiry after the great secret of his being, character and will. Man needs a revelation of God as much as he needs the breath of life. The future of himself is always infinitely more interesting to him than all his experiences of the past. Hence the facile ear of even a stern unbeliever in the Christian revelation to every new, and strange, and mysterious indication of a spiritual sphere and of a future life. There are at this very hour, I am constrained to think, myriads of persons more laborious and indefatigable in their inquiries after mesmerism, clairvoyance and spiritual rappings, than they have ever been to investigate the claims of Moses or of the Messiah. This, in my opinion, is a proof that the requirements of Moses and of Christ are inwardly, or at heart, more resisted than the simple fact of their real personality or of their Divine mission. Human nature, fallen and degraded as it is, has more of an innate revulsionary feeling to the doctrine of the Bible, and especially to the self-denial which Christianity enjoins, than it has to the stern realities of a God, a Saviour and a future life. Had Moses and the prophets, Jesus and the apostles, granted impunity to, or delivered oracles in harmony with, the demands of the unbridled lusts and passions of men in the flesh, the whole world would have loved, honored and adored them, and have gladly acquiesced in their mission.

Men in the flesh desire a *heaven*, a pathway to it, and a safe and sure guide, provided that this heaven and its highway suit their taste, and that its guide grant impunity to their inordinate affections. Hence the growing popularity of Universalianism in many parts of our country. It is in good keeping with the tastes and the affinities of a secular population, and the pulsations of a purely animal and worldly spirit.

But without an entire regeneration of body, soul and spirit, what sort of a paradise would heaven be! Mohammed and his elysium lying beyond the seventh heaven, with its snow-white rivers, its crystal fountains, its groves and gardens, more odoriferous than the purest musk, studded with goblets bright and numerous as the stars of heaven, spread over a saffron earth, covered with pearls; women formed of cognate musk, beautiful as angels, lolling in pavilions of hollow pearls, feasting on nectar and ambrosia, tuning their golden lyres to the odes of Venus and Bacchus—the chief divinities of earth—would be the proper heaven, the delightful hope, of the great majority of the most polished circles of London, Paris and Washington City, together with a thousand other towns and cities of inferior fame.

But such is not the hope or the heaven of the Bible and its Author. It is a much more beautiful and glorious heaven. There grows the tree of life. There flows the river of life. There are seen the cherubim and the six-winged seraphim. There are sweeter melodies than mortal ear has ever heard; more heart-ravishing sights than mortal eye hath ever seen. The jasper, the sapphire and the emerald, the beryl, the amethyst and the topaz, and all the diamond brilliancies of earth, are but the image of its beauties and the shadow of its glories. Yet it is, in certain circles, a very unfashionable place. It is even in bad taste, on some splendid occasions, to allude to it. And I am not sure that even here it is in good keeping with the occasion to dwell too long upon it. Pardon me, then, you cynic critics, for trespassing on your forbidden ground. Turn we, then, to the constellation of the Lesser Bear,—

> "Where, perhaps, some other beauty lies,
> The blessed cynosure of neighboring eyes."

And here we shall only add, that, in the midst of all the knocking, rapping spirits of earth, there is a Spirit standing at the door of every heart, knocking for admission, promising to all who open to its call a banquet richer far than earth has ever seen or mortals ever known.

But that Spirit speaks in a style of lofty argument, of moral dignity and Divine grandeur, worthy of a Christian's heaven; of such a being as God, and of such a being as man, viewed in all the sublime and awful outlines of his moral nature, his lofty port and heavenward aspirations, and not in the grimace and silly buffoonery of those spirits that peep and mutter tales unworthy of man, and still more unworthy of woman. From such demons, such silly demons, whether of imagination, fraud or fiction, let every man and woman of self-respect, of good sense and of sound discretion, turn away with scorn and contempt.

ADDRESS.

WOMAN AND HER MISSION.

DELIVERED BEFORE THE HENRY FEMALE SEMINARY, NEWCASTLE, KY., MAY 30, 1856.

I APPEAR before you, young ladies, on this interesting occasion, not to flatter you or your sex, but to contribute to your gratification and that of myself, in suggesting to your consideration some practical views on a subject alike interesting to your sex and to my own. That subject, alike important to us both, is just and adequate views of woman and her mission, and these in reference to her proper education and development. Regarding woman, as I do, as the *octave*, or rather the *diapason*, of the hymn of creation, and as having committed to her the destinies of our species and our planet, she, in the scale of material nature, in unison with the spiritual, is a spectacle alike interesting to Creator and creature—to all intelligences, of all ranks and orders, terrestrial or celestial. If the morning stars in concert sang, and all the sons of God shouted for joy, when the drama of creation culminated in the person of Eve, can she, whose very name is LIFE, in its first impersonation and full-orbed grandeur, ever cease to be not only the dearest object of our earth-born affections, but the most attractive spectacle ever seen, when robed in all the charms and graces of our ransomed and beatified humanity?

I speak not of her as she now is, in any of the generally diversified conditions of her being, superinduced by the enmity, if not the envy, of a fallen seraph. But I speak of her as she was, when she stood at the left side of Adam on the day of her espousals, in the bridal robes of angelic purity and love. 'Twas then, in the ambrosial bowers of Eden's paradise, she stood attired in all the charms of intellectual grandeur, moral beauty and ecstatic bliss. But in an evil hour she hearkened to the deceitful eloquence of Satanic flattery, and touched the alluring fruit of the one only forbidden tree, "whose mortal taste brought death into the world, and all our woe." In this eclipse of reason, in this aberration of heart, the sting of sin transfused its poison through her whole personality,—body, soul and spirit; and instantly the light of joy, and peace, and love, that beamed from her spirit-stirring and soul-subduing eyes, vanished, a cloud of pensiveness sat brooding over her fallen countenance, and, handing the fruit to her admiring husband, he, in the blindness of his devotion to her charms, fascinated and overpowered by her former loveliness, thoughtlessly and recklessly, without a single remonstrance or demur, snatched it, ate it; in consequence of which, all his glory and dignity in a moment vanished away.

And now, born as we are, creatures of mere instinctive appetites and passions, we have become an easy prey to that same insidious tempter, and make our debut amidst the thorns and thistles of the earth, doomed to desolation, without one heavenward aspiration, void of even one desire to know our origin, our relations to the universe, or our destiny in it, in and of ourselves have become the most helpless, the most passive and erratic creatures that figure upon it.

This is the solemn, significant and soul-appalling fact, interpret it, hide it or disregard it as we may. But for it, no tear had ever dimmed the eye of beauty, no anxiety had ever disturbed the human breast, no guilt had ever clouded the understanding or agonized the soul of man.

It is essential to our redemption, that some supernatural interposition should have been originated and instituted, else our escape from this condition would have been, so far as our reason or resources are concerned, wholly impossible.

There are, indeed, a few speculative philosophers who imagine that reason alone could, of its own inherent power, have originated some remedy for those conditions of ignorance, guilt and bondage, under which we languish, sicken and die. But superficial and erratic reasoners they are, who can even imagine any such possibility. Reason but measures, compares and decides upon given premises. Imagination is, indeed, in a certain limited sphere, creative. But the very word itself annihilates its claims to originate. It forms *images*, and only images. It creates not one *original* idea. It can abstract and combine, in new forms and modifications, the images of human experience and observation. But beyond this its power reaches not.

Revelation alone meets the present conditions of our being. And even written revelation commences its career with the *positive* history of the drama of creation. From supernatural revelation alone can we derive any assurance of our origin or of our origination. Enlightened by it, certain philosophers, of a superficial cast, think, or assume to think, that they could prove, *a priori*, the being of God. They have, indeed, demonstrated a power to *materialize* every thing, which only proves that they never could rise to the conception of a *spiritual* first cause of *matter*. Others, the greatest and best of them, too, have confessed that matter could never have been the parent of spirit. Those who have assumed that matter is naturally, necessarily and eternally active, have never yet been able to abstract from it one spiritual *voluntary* agent, nor, by any process of reasoning, to show any possibility of such a process or result.

But even with Bible in hand, there are those now, and there have been those formerly, who presume to say that woman was not created simultaneously, or even on the same day, with man. And this, forsooth, because the special details of her creation are not found in the first, but in the second chapter of Genesis. It is indeed conceded that, in the second chapter, we have a detailed account of her creation,—a minute and graphic history of that mysterious, sublime and adumbrative operation. But to the attentive student of the style and manner of Moses, as an historian, there is no difficulty in the case.

In the first chapter of Genesis, we are informed that on the last working-day of the first week God created *man*. How dull and indiscriminating is that student of Holy Writ who imagines that the word *man* is there used *sexually*, and not *specifically?* Does not Moses say, (chap. i. 27,) that God created man, "a *male* and a *female* created he them?" Indeed, he not only created man on the sixth day of the first week, but on the same day he solemnly enacted matrimony, simultaneously with woman's creation. This was the only marriage in the annals of time unpreceded by courtship; the only marriage, too, celebrated when the parties were not one day old. Every thing on this occasion was, of course, original and unprecedented.

There was something so mysterious and wonderful in the creation of Lord Adam and Lady Eve, that it was deemed both edifying and important to give to them a special account of their instructive and suggestive origin; and therefore Moses, by Divine inspiration, afterwards gives, in the next chapter, a detailed narrative of the whole particulars of this, the most exquisite, peculiar and instructive operation of God. Hence, he resumes the subject in the second chapter; but this is not the only act in the whole drama of creation, upon which he enlarges in the form of details.

A similar misconception we have observed in regard to the "*deep sleep*" into which Adam fell, preparatory to the abstraction of a part of himself, as the material out of which his Eve was formed. For aught that appears in the statement, that deep sleep did not engross one minute. It was supernatural, and the operation may not, in the whole premises, have consumed a second. Many conceive of this operation from that of a surgeon, whose preparations often demand much more time than the work itself. But it was in harmony with all the oracles or *fiats* of the first week. If

> "The modest water, awed with power Divine,
> Beheld its God, and blushed itself to wine,"

can we, shall we, suppose that the creation of Eve occupied any sensible measure of time? We cannot, in harmony with all the operations that constitute the material universe, consummated in six consecutive days. Besides, it must be taken into our premises that, according to the express oracles of God, both in history and in law, he created all things within six days.

In our common version of the Bible, we are also led to think that our mother Eve was created out of, or around the nucleus of, a crooked rib. This does not well comport with her character and sensibilities. The original *Tsela* is, however, a word of two meanings, indicative both of *side* and of *rib*. We presume that there must have been some flesh about it. Adam, indeed, sanctions this opinion; for on her presentation to him, as soon as he recovered his senses, he said, "This creature is now bone of my bone and flesh of my flesh;" and, in attestation and consummation of this fact, he calls her *Woman*. And, still better authority, God himself said on this occasion, that, in holy wedlock joined, man and woman should be *one flesh*, as, no doubt, commemorative of their intimate, mysterious and sublime origin.

There is a pleasing speculation cherished by some fond philosophers, that Adam's left side was opened in the region of his heart, and from this they argue that man's left side became his weak side, because from it woman was extracted; and to this assumption they assign not only the weakness of that side, but also the peculiar love of man for woman. But like many other theories in this our day, it is more ingenious and curious than philosophic or religious.

There is, indeed, a more or less favorable stand-point from which to contemplate any and every object in the universe. And on a subject of such thrilling and soul-engrossing interest to the present and eternal happiness of our species, it is of the greatest importance that we should be placed in such a position, and in such an attitude, as to survey the entire mission and destiny, not of woman only as respects her own person and sex, but of woman in her mission and destiny in the whole creation of God.

And for what, let us inquire, was woman created and made? You anticipate me, no doubt, and would respond, She was created and commissioned to be a help *meet* for man. Man was created in the image of God, and woman was created in the image of man. Man was created to glorify God, and to enjoy him forever; and woman was created to be a help suitable to such a being as man, and to participate in common with him in glorifying God and in enjoying him forever. This is the true position and the true stand-point from which we should contemplate one another, and glorify and beatify one another, in perfect harmony with mutual esteem, affection and admiration, and in a felicitous submission to all the conditions in which our heavenly Father has respectively placed us.

This stand-point is lofty, and commands a very large horizon. But it is not at all a fictitious position, nor an exaggerated importance gratuitously assumed, but is as solid and enduring as the Rock of Ages.

This planet allotted to man, with all the tenantry thereof—of air, and earth and sea—was created for *him;* not for one Adam and one Eve, but for all the varieties, types and manifestations of humanity, conceivable by the Supreme Intelligence.

The simple fact of an *incarnation* of the Supreme Divinity in our humanity, is more suggestive of the space occupied by man in the bosom of his Father and his God, than all the volumes of the highest reason, than all the poetry of the loftiest and most fruitful imagination, unfolds, or can unfold in the largest series of ages yet to come, or conceivable by our contracted vision.

But this, young ladies, in its soul-subduing grandeur, is not a theme within the immediate province of your studies or of your capacities. Still, a glance at it through the telescope of divine revelation is of such stimulating power and efficiency as to justify an allusion to it, to excite in your imagination the importance of qualifying yourselves for higher, holier, happier and more enduring positions in the area of the universe, than you could aspire to without such suggestions.

It is, indeed, quite enough for our present purpose, and for the short space allotted to us, to impress upon your attention that woman was created to be a companion, perfectly suitable to man: hence it is equally her duty, her honor and her happiness, to accomplish herself for this high and dignified position.

It is true, the present types of men, usually called *gentlemen*, are not well read on this subject, and some of them only aspire to be *genteel men*, rather than gentlemen.

Do you smile at this distinction? It is, indeed, somewhat ridiculous. Man, however, being the only creature, save one, that can laugh, he must have something to laugh at, either real or fictitious. Tailors and *mantuamakers* manufacture *genteel* men and *genteel* ladies, according to order; but a *gentleman* and a *gentlewoman* are, according to Paul, the fruit of God's own Spirit; for Paul says that "the fruits of the Spirit are love, joy, peace, *gentleness*," &c. Hence, a true and real *gentleman* must always be a Christian; for if *gentleness* be the fruit of the Spirit, without that fruit and that Spirit no one can ever rise above the rank of a *genteel man*—a polished *gentile*. As for a *lady*, there is only one way of meritoriously achieving that rank and dignity, and that is, *by becoming a dispenser of bread to the poor*. All the first *lords* and *ladies* recognized in Anglo-Saxon literature and history were *bread-givers*—dispensers of bread to the poor and the dependent. True, they occasionally wore some trinkets and ornaments. But these never constituted either *lords* or *ladies*. In time, however, these *bread-givers* died, and those who wore only the trinkets, having no bread to give, and sometimes little to eat, engrossed the honorable title of *lords* and *ladies*.

We citizens of these United States have abjured all factitious and hereditary titles, canonized by the now decaying monarchies, aristocracies and autocracies of the old European world. Still, we have not abolished the desire for them. We Americans inherently, and in virtue of our consanguinity with old Adam and Eve, desire to be *lords* and *ladies*, just as much on our Old Virginia sands and on your rich Kentucky limestone hills and valleys, as do the kings and queens and noble peers, lords and ladies of rich heraldic families, spread over the green hills and valleys of the islands and over some of the continents of the Old World. Here they are *sour* grapes, because inaccessible. And hence we are all *lords* and *ladies*, in fee-simple, now, henceforth and forever, or until our present parchments are moth-eaten, and some Napoleon *le grand* appears in our midst.

From this stand-point, and from these prefatory views, let us glance for a moment at the grand themes which have in them all the potent elements of human development and of human destiny.

To present this subject before you in all its claims, permit me again to inquire, *For what* was woman created and made?

There is much that is suggestive in the name given to her on the day of her espousals. Adam, her lord and husband, gave her, as we have learned, the name *Life*—the most felicitous and appropriate name, and the most suggestive too, bestowed on any creature named by Adam. It is a most beautiful and lovely name. What monosyllable in universal speech indicates an object so dear to man as the idea of his own *Life?* It is a representative of all that we include in the idea of happiness. In its radical conception, in its etymology, it comprehends all *living* creatures; and in special reference to man it indicates *society, company, activity, valor, courage*—even a *host*, an *army*. Adam, in calling his wife Eve, in his unclouded reason indicated the largest conception of human happiness—indeed, of social happiness. And had he stood firm in his loyalty to his Creator, his *Eve*, his Life, would have been to him a source of joy and pleasure—a fountain of strength and moral heroism—greater far than all the sensible beauties and attractions of the Paradise around him.

She was in herself *life*, and to him the *soul* of animated nature. The beauties of Paradise, in all its virgin bloom and delicious fragrance, with all its carolling, warbling, joyful songsters, could not have been so richly enjoyed, or, indeed, enjoyed at all, by such a being as a perfect man, without the companionship of a kindred, admiring, sympathizing heart. At this moment I am reminded of a few most felicitous lines by Mrs. Sigourney on this closing act of the drama of creation:—

"Last came a female form, more soft, more fair,
And Eden smiled to see the stranger there;
Then tones of joy from harps seraphic rung,
The stars of morning in their courses sung;
Earth echoed back a shout of grateful love
From every valley, cavern, stream and grove.
Man, fill'd with praise, in solemn rapture stood,
God bow'd to view his work, and God pronounced it good."

Eve, then, was the crowning act of the last scene of the entire drama of creation, and, so far as our planet is understood, she is, and was, a microcosm of animated nature in a personal and social embodiment, in which Creator and creature are united in the holy bands of an eternal compact, pregnant with all the elements of social being and of social blessedness.

But she is not only the mere life of humanity, in its literal import, but the life and the spirit of all true and genuine civilization. The respect paid to woman, and the interest exhibited in her education and social culture, constitute the index of the civilization of every community under the broad heavens. Hence, the only question as to the comparative civilization of any nation, or people, which is an end of all controversy, is, *How is woman regarded, educated, honored?* This is the sovereign and superlative index of civilization—of comparative civilization; and above it, beyond it, there is no appeal—there can be no appeal. In forming a safe and satisfactory judgment of the *spirit* and progress of civilization, this is our polar star—our ultimate appeal. We test the religion, the morality, the prosperity, the happiness, of every nation and people, by the question, How stands woman amongst them?

We are happy in the conviction, that wherever Protestantism is in the highest ascendency, there is woman in the highest honor and esteem. We fearlessly submit the question—the whole question—of woman's rights, honors, privileges, civilization, to this tribunal; and not this question only, but the questions, In what country, under what form of government, under what profession of Christianity, is woman most honored and most honorable? I do this, too, in the full conviction, in the full assurance, that our own country will in no one point of contrast, in any element of true and genuine civilization, stand second to any other in the broadness of what is usually called the civilized world. Indeed, I may still further avow the conviction, that among Protestant communities themselves, and under free governments—which are indeed the fruit of Protestantism—the more *Protestant* the more civilized, the more honored, the more honorable, is woman, educated woman. This fact, then, is one of the elements of the reason why our father Adam, in his vigorous thought and broad horizon, on the presentation of himself to himself, in a second personality, prospectively, in bright vision of the future, called her LIFE.

But the social nature of man being neither physical nor intellectual alone, neither moral nor religious alone, in another attitude and at another angle, we see that the name *Eve*, or Life, was still more appropriately and felicitously conferred on Adam's bride. There are, in the phenomena of life, many forms and modifications of life. We have political and ecclesiastic life, as well as an animal and spiritual life. And woman is the life of all the forms and institutions of all the compacts and constitutions of society. Adam—I mean Adam the first, in his first estate—possessed an intuitive perspicacity beyond any one of his degenerate posterity. The name that he gave his wife on the morning of their nuptials, is worth all the dissertations on woman ever written by any of Eve's degenerate offspring. In proof of this assumption, we refer the inquisitive to the fact, that God himself assembled the animated tenantry of Eden around his residence, and caused them to pass in review before him to ascertain what he would call them. This seems to have been the final examination of his attainments in the science of zoology in its broadest sense; for all the beasts of the field, and all the fowls of the air, were made to pass before him, and such were his attainments in this great science of sciences, that he failed not in a single instance to give the appropriate name to every species of animated nature around him. Thus he obtained his diploma from the highest authority in the universe. And what a splendid monument it is of the capacity and attainments of our father Adam in the school of animated nature!

God in nature, in providence, in moral government, and in redemption, presents to the senses of man, to the reason of man, to the conscience of man, or to the affections of man, nothing in the abstract, but every thing in the concrete. There is not, indeed, a simple substance, nor an abstract entity, existing alone in the natural universe. Every thing in nature exists in holy wedlock and in family circles. Analysis and synthesis are, therefore, the grand preliminaries to the acquisition of the knowledge of the works of God and the operations of man. The doctrine of relations, affinities, congruities, sympathies, antipathies, attractions and repulsions, has its foundation in this fact—that there is not a single abstract substantive existence in so much of God's universe as has been submitted to the observation, analysis and reflection of man.

Even light—the first-born of heaven, supposed to be one of the most simple, active and sublime agents of the physical universe—is a compound of seven different colors.

The universe is itself a library of God; but to all the pupils in his large school it is legible only in part, and that part imperfectly. But there is one volume in this grand library of the universe peculiarly interesting to every man; and that is his *autobiography*—a work written by himself upon himself, and one, unfortunately, which, when written, he almost always reads with more or less reluctance. He cannot, however, proceed very far in the study of this work until four questions arise in his mind, upon which, if of an inquisitive turn, he feels himself constrained to ponder. These four questions are of soul-absorbing interest. They are—1. *Who am I?* 2. *What am I?* 3. *Why am I?* 4. *Whither go I?* Of these four primordial questions, two are transcendental. These are—*What* am I? and, *Whither* go I?

The last is impliedly answered when the third is satisfactorily decided. "*Why am I?*" is a question too profound for a majority of mankind to answer. Indeed, no man can satisfactorily answer it who does not believe and realize the fact that he has a special mission into the world, and this mission is just why he appears at a particular time, on a particular stage, in a particular scene and in a particular act of the great drama of humanity at his stand-point. Solomon, the wisest of men by a special providence, and inspired, too, by a special wisdom, instituted his *Ecclesiastes*, or became a *preacher*, to develop the question—"*What is that special good which a man, as man, should pursue all his life?*" He occasionally writes as a sage political economist in things of time and sense; but he also writes as an oracle of God in things pertaining to God and man, in spiritual and eternal relations. And to this question what answer does he give?

But we take the privilege to propound to you, young ladies, not, What is man? but, What is *woman?* She is but the one-half of man—only the one-half of humanity. But she is, or may be, the better half. She is of a finer tissue in body, soul and spirit: the last, and, we think—if mortals of such dim vision and within so contracted a horizon dare so think—decidedly the better half—not in muscular power, not in physical strength, not in animal courage, not in intellectual vigor, but in delicacy of thought, in sensitiveness of feeling, in patient endurance, in constancy of affection, in moral courage and in soul-absorbing devotion.

But God did not for her own sake bestow upon her all these distinguishing qualities. He did not, indeed, create her immediately from the earth. Adam was made out of the cold dust of Eden; but Eve was made out of the animated dust and from the left side of Adam—nearest offshoot from his heart. He not only made her out of the left side of the first man, but in holy wedlock he placed her there to protect the wound and vacuum whence her personal being came.

The power of God is not physical nor metaphysical power; it is not spiritual nor animal power, in our conception and use of these symbols of thought. It is divine power in all its elements, operating simultaneously in all these directions, under the control of a simple volition. He only willed, and the universe was; but that will was embodied in a word—an utterance of itself, giving existence, local habitation and form to every beau ideal of goodness, beauty and grandeur, in harmony with his own supreme excellence and majesty. Hence, the well-cultivated mind contemplates God in every thing and every thing in God.

No mere deist, theist, atheist or polytheist ever had one round, clear and strong imprint of divinity upon his understanding, his conscience, his will or his affections. While the well-educated Christian sees God in every thing and every thing in God, the self-conceited theist or atheist or skeptic sees God in nothing and nothing in God.

The philosophy of the universe is a sublime philosophy. It is the philosophy of love. And, pray, what is *love?* How would you, young ladies, define it? Young gentlemen talk about it learnedly, and sometimes philosophically; but they do not comprehend and realize it as you do. Oh, say you, we have not had much experience on that subject, and with us 'tis all theory. Well, a good theory, even on this subject, is better than no theory at all. But we are not inquiring into a theory, good or bad, sound or unsound: we are inquiring into a substantive, real existence.

There is not in the universe a more positive, a more substantive, a more real existence than love; for *God is love.* This is a divine oracle from a most true and veritable source. And the whole universe is but an outburst of love. God did not create the universe because he had wisdom to do it or power to do it; for neither of these has a distinct positive existence. They are mere attributes of love. Love, at the true stand-point of vision, is the only *self-existent* entity or ideality, or conception, or positive principle, or actual, indestructible fact in imagination's boundless, measureless, endless fields of thought. It ever was and is and ever shall be the one only immutable, indestructible, self-existent principle. Two eternal antagonistic principles are wholly beyond the landmarks of reason and sanity. It is the brightest star in the diadem of love that it is, of necessity, the one only self-existent and necessarily indestructible reality in the entire area of rational thought. And, just at this stand-point, we *apprehend*—we do not say *comprehend*—the beauty, the truth and the wisdom of that oracle—that *God is love.* (John iv. 8–16.) Heaven itself is but the theatre of love. There is no other theatre of its full development, manifestation and enjoyment than heaven itself. The most loveless thing in God's vast universe is a haughty spirit; because it is only exorbitant selfishness, attracting nothing, radiating nothing, but repelling every thing coming into competition with itself. Hence, rebellion, anarchy and ruin are the trinity of hatred and the essence of endless perdition.

But, while we thus seek a fulcrum and a lever to lift us up to an adequate conception of love in its essence, its origin and end, we must descend to the atmosphere of earth and to the circles of our fallen humanity, where love is rather a passion than a principle, an impulse than a law of reason, of God, of heaven and of happiness.

We must study *love* in its manifestations. It seems to act in society as attraction or gravity in material nature. It has its affinities, its attractions and repulsions. If it had a *form*, as matter has, we should be compelled to regard it as *globular* in its form. It attracts every thing around it into proximity to itself; and this proximity for the sake of enjoyment, of blessing and of being blessed, of communicating and of receiving felicity in the most direct, immediate, and instantaneous sympathy. It has a philosophy in it the most recondite, the most attractive, the most refining, the most beatifying, the most conservative in the entire area of cultivated reason. It is no less than intellectual, moral, spiritual, divine magnetism, attracting, alluring, radiating, beautifying, beatifying kindred spirits in eternal circles, wide as creation and lasting as eternity.

This is not that short-lived, impulsive, animal thing on which every simpleton talks with the fluency and brilliancy of quicksilver. It is a glorious reality, since *God is love.* The three most splendid and yet the three most simple propositions in all the oracles of God are—1. "*God is Spirit.*" 2. "*God is Light.*" 3. "*God is Love.*" He is not *relatively* a spirit, a light or a love; but he is absolute, infinite, eternal and immutable SPIRIT, LIGHT and LOVE. These are the all-potent, energizing, active and soul-subduing manifestations of Jehovah.

But you, young ladies, may think that these are matters too erudite, too high, too lofty and too far beyond your stature. In one sense—so far as full *comprehension* of them is contemplated—they may be not only beyond *your* comprehension, but of that of the tallest man or the tallest angel in the highest heaven. But is not the law of gravity, is not the essence of light, of electricity, of magnetism, also beyond your comprehension? Not one of them is, however, excluded from your studies or meditations. You study physical science, physiology, pneumatology, and probably some of you have even encountered and vanquished metaphysics. Of one thing we are assured, that these studies are as much within your grasp as they are within that of half the young gentlemen of the present living age. In our galaxies of distinguished females there are some very brilliant stars. I care not though you visit the museums of literature, language, poetry, philosophy, theology, theodicy, metaphysics. In the departments of the highest reason, literature, science, philosophy, religion, they shine with great splendor. What deserved, well-earned reputation have Mrs. Hemans, Mrs. Sigourney, Miss Beecher, Mrs. Charlotte Elizabeth, Madame de Staël, Madame Guyon, Mrs. Ellis, Madame Roland, Hannah More, Joanna Baillie, Mrs. Barbauld, Agnes Strickland, and, better still, the Mrs. Judsons! Young ladies, I especially commend to your most devout study these greatly-gifted, these self-sacrificing Christian ladies last mentioned. They are an evangelical constellation worthy of your special admiration and imitation. We need not remind you of the Bible female heroes, from Sarah down to Electa Cyria; nor tell you of the Hannahs, the Deborahs, the Queen Esthers, the Marys, the Elizabeths; nor of the women who, through faith, received from the dead their departed children—such as the widow of Zarephath, and the Shunamite. (2 Kings iv. 34.) These are more familiar themes, and every day within your reach. The highest and most attractive encomium pronounced in Christian history upon woman is not that she bathed the feet of Jesus in her tears and that she wiped them with the tresses of her hair; it is not that she was last at the cross, in solemn contemplation of the fearful agonies of his death; but that she was first at the sepulchre in the early dawn of the first day of the week, making her way through the Roman guard, with full intent to embalm his lacerated body; in honor of which most affectionate and grateful devotion he presented himself to her in that same body, as the triumphant conqueror of death and of the grave, and commissioned her, as his prime-minister, to announce the gospel of his resurrection to her mourning and disconsolate companions.

The true philosophy of female education has for its proper basis, not merely her person, but more especially her *mission.* That man and woman should be educated in their entire personality—body, soul and spirit—is, at our latitude, not a debatable subject. The full development of each of these departments or constituents of our humanity demands a special education and training. But even this is not enough. There is a still more special education in reference to the special *calling*, or the special *mission*, of each individual. This, too, being conceded by all whose views are of any value to society, is not a debatable subject. Yet we have reason to regret that female education has not generally been conducted more in harmony with the special *mission* of woman, under the conviction that she was intended to be emphatically a *help meet* for man on the whole premises of humanity, and not merely in reference to the accidents and specialties of humanity.

There are in human nature sympathies of joy as well as sympathies of sorrow. Indeed, it is a Christian precept, "rejoice with them that do rejoice," as well as, "weep with them that weep." There are also sympathies of admiration, and sympathies of contempt. We love those who admire what *we* admire, and we love those that contemn what *we* contemn. In each and every element of human nature, of human character and of human conduct, there are sympathies and antipathies, conformities and non-conformities, pleasure and pain. Hence the necessity of imparting and receiving an education in harmony with all these premises, in order to the enjoyment of one another in the most intimate of all the relations of life; and also the propriety of the oracle that preceded the appearance of woman:—Let there be a *help meet* for man. Let every young woman, therefore, be so educated as to be a help suitable to those with whom we would have her united, in all the fortunes and misfortunes, in all the pleasures and pains, in all the joys and sorrows, of earth and of time.

There is a great deal in a name. In some names there is a mixture of history, geography, philosophy and religion. Hence, in the supernatural wisdom of our Father Adam, in his primeval rectitude, all names given by him were essentially characteristic. His nomenclature was so perfect that God sanctioned it. There was reason *in* it all, and a reason *for* it all. Hence the reason given for the name of the first woman was as perfect as herself. She was called LIFE, because she was the life of the world.

But we must study woman in her mission, in order to train her and honor her according to her rank in creation. And is there not a reason given for her name, from a source of unquestionable authority? She was called in Hebrew *Havah*, in Greek *Zoee*, in English *Life*, because she was the life of the world. And does not that reason indicate her mission?

She was an extract of man, in order to form man; in order to *develop, perfect, beautify* and *beatify* man. And hence these four terms comprehend the whole duty, honor, dignity and happiness of woman; consequently, her education should be equal to her mission. Every distinctive element of her sex was conferred upon her in order to her accomplishment for the great work of forming and moulding human nature in reference to human destiny. How important and how true the remark, that the distinguished men who have made their mark in the moral world have been the offspring of religious and exemplary mothers! There is no authority, no influence, no power, of whatever name, equal to that which God has vested in woman, in its conservative and beatifying character and influence on the prosperity and happiness of man. In conferring so much influence on woman, God intended to use it in the moral government of the world. She has, consequently, a mission of transcendent importance—of paramount value to the happiness of man. From these premises we argue the paramount importance of her education, and press its claims upon the patriot, the philanthropist and the Christian.

We use these terms because of their popular currency. The patriot, indeed, is absorbed in the philanthropist, and the philanthropist in the Christian. The full-orbed Christian is, in fact, the sum-total of all human excellency, grandeur and honor. We can imagine nothing noble, or grand, or beatifying in humanity, that is not comprehended and absorbed in the beau ideal of a Christian. Hence, any school, male or female, not based on Christianity—genuine, heaven-born and heaven-descended Christianity—is a wild freak of uncultivated reason, a vagary of an untutored mind. Hence the Christian Scriptures are, and of right ought to be, the daily text-book of every school in Christendom, based on the true philosophy of man, from the nursery up to the university.

Why memorize the grammar of a living or a dead language, why memorize the elements of arithmetic, geography, astronomy or human history, and not memorize the Book of Life—the volume of human destiny in its rudimental lessons? Why memorize the choice selections of human wisdom and eloquence, and not the Sermon of the Messiah upon the Mount, or of Paul a prisoner before a Felix or a King Agrippa? Can any composition on the earthly attitudes of man, on his civil or political relations, equal those on his eternal destiny in a boundless universe? Tell it not in Rome, publish it not in Constantinople, that in the schools and colleges and seminaries in the United States of America the Bible is no more a text-book than the Koran of Mohammed or the Zendavesta of Zoroaster; that Roman and Grecian mythologies are read and studied in our colleges and universities, in the centre of our Christian civilization, while Moses and David and Solomon, while Jesus and Peter and Paul, are seldom or never permitted to be heard or appealed to, any more than the Arabian Nights or the tales of elves and fairies.

Young ladies, such has not been your misfortune. The star of your destiny is infinitely more splendid and felicitous. You have learned that woman, like an angel of mercy, was sent into our world to be queen of the human heart and mistress of the moral destinies of humanity.

A woman became the mother of the King of Heaven, the Lord and Arbiter of the sublime and grand and awful empire of the universe. Yes, the King of Eternity was solaced in the bosom of Mary the Virgin. And through him you have become, or may become, heiresses in common of the empire of the universe. Christianity has infinitely aggrandized your sex, and has conferred on you the sovereignty of the human heart: these constitute the splendid coronal of sanctified woman.

Every one of you that has embraced Christ has a mission from this Sovereign of the human heart. And all of you may labor in it, who sincerely desire it. This missionary field is as broad as the tenanted earth. It is a mission of mercy; and in the ear of enlightened reason it is, in its pleadings, the true sublime of true eloquence.

You stand not in the front rank of the battle-field, in conflicting with the rebel hosts of the great enemy of human happiness. But your task is to minister to their comfort who war a good warfare in the cause of man's redemption. You pour into their wounds the oil of joy and gladness; you solace the sick and the dying with the perfume of your Christian sympathy; and you soothe the parched lips of the expiring Christian with the last cup of water from the perennial fountain of everlasting love.

Yours is a beautiful mission, viewed in its entire amplitude; and in reference to it all your studies should be prosecuted, and all the virtues of Christian excellencies cherished in your hearts and practised in your lives. The treasures of learning and science should now be mastered, and every literary and scientific study prosecuted with a vigorous diligence, in order to your successfully entering upon a career of usefulness so pregnant with enduring blessings to yourselves, so full of promise of laurels that will never wither, of pleasures that will never cloy, and of a reward from the right hand of the final Arbiter of the destinies of the world, richer far than all the treasures of earth, and as enduring as the throne of God and the ages of eternity.

There is no necessity to mount the rostrum, to stand up in public assemblies, to address mixed auditories of both sexes, of all classes and of all orders of society, in order to fill up the duties of *your* mission. If Paul would not have a woman to pray *unveiled* in a Christian church, and if he made long hair a glory to her, because it veiled her beauty and protected her eyes from the gaze of staring sensualists, think you he would have sent her out on a missionary tour, or placed her in a rostrum, surrounded with ogling-glasses in the hands, not of old men and women of dim vision, but of green striplings of pert impertinence? Be assured, not one word of such import ever fell from the lips of prophets or apostles. On the contrary, modesty, shame-facedness and sobriety are the garland of beauty, the wreath of glory and the coronal of dignity and honor, on the person of a Christian woman, who is always in her proper sphere; an "*elect lady;*" not necessarily of the aristocracies of earth, but of the élite and honorable of heaven.

I am one of that feeble minority in this our age and nation who think that Solomon was richer than the Rothschilds, wiser than Benjamin Franklin, and more admirable than Napoleon *le Grand* in the zenith of his power and glory; and yet, having spoken three thousand proverbs, and written more than one thousand songs, and discoursed on trees and plants, from the hyssop on the wall to the cedars of Mount Lebanon, he consummates his literary and philosophic labors with a dissertation on woman and his beau ideal of an accomplished lady in the relation of an amiable and virtuous wife. With the close of his encomium we shall close our address:—

> "She openeth her mouth in wisdom,
> And the law of kindness is on her tongue.
> She observeth the conduct of her household,
> And eateth not the bread of idleness.
> Her children rise up and bless her;
> Her husband, and he praiseth her.
> Many women have done virtuously,
> But thou excellest them all.
> Gracefulness fadeth, and beauty is vain;
> But the woman that feareth Jehovah shall be greatly praised.
> The fruits of her hand shall be given to her,
> And in the assemblies her works praise her."

That you, young ladies, may, each and every one of you, fill up all the excellencies of Christian character, shine in all the splendors of the female virtues, and lead useful, honorable and happy lives, is the sincere wish of your friend and orator.

ADDRESS ON EDUCATION.

CINCINNATI, 1856.

THERE is not, in all the expanded area of human thought, any theme more important or more prolific of good or evil to man, temporal, spiritual or eternal, than is the theme of human education. It has commanded the attention, and more or less engrossed the thoughts, of the most gifted minds and the most philanthropic hearts that have adorned our common humanity. The capacity of man, the dignity of man and the destiny of man have been more or less popular themes in every age, and amongst all the civilized nations of the earth. The three most engrossing questions in every age, in every clime of earth, and in every tongue of man, are, were and ever will be, *What am I? Whence came I? Whither do I go?*

These are the loftiest, the most profound and soul-engrossing themes on which the mind of man can concentrate all its powers and its energies. It is conceded by the highest tribunals of human science and human learning, by the greatest and best of all philosophers, that the only object seen, contemplated and admired by man, which the sun surveys or the earth contains—the only existence within the human horizon—that will never cease to be—is *man*. He of all earth's tenantry had a beginning, but will never, never, never have an end.

It is this view of man, and this view only, that magnifies and aggrandizes the theme of his education, and that, in every age of civilization, has, more than all other themes, engrossed the attention, elicited the energies and commanded the activities of every truly enlightened philanthropist.

But the proper philosophy of man, indicated in his origin, constitution and destiny, is an essential preliminary to a rational disposition and development of this theme. The first question, then, necessarily is, *What is man?* He is neither an angel nor an animal. He has a body, a soul and a spirit. He has a trinity of natures in one personality. While Jehovah has a trinity of personalities in one nature, man has a trinity of natures in one personality. He has an animal nature, an intellectual nature and a moral nature. Hence the prayer of the greatest apostle and ambassador of heaven was, "May God sanctify you wholly"—in body, soul and spirit. These are not two, but three, entities, and these three are in every human being. Man has an animal body, an animal soul and a rational spirit. Two of these are earthly and temporal—one is spiritual and eternal. He is, therefore, not improperly called a microcosm, a miniature embodiment of universal nature, or of the Divine creation.

We do not, then, wonder, standing on the pinnacle of this temple, that there was a Divine interposition in behalf of humanity in its ruins, and none for the angels who kept not their first estate. And this, indeed, is no ordinary attestation of the dignity of man.

Hence the institution of a remedial system, to elevate, dignify and beatify man, was introduced by the Creator himself, and consummated by the incarnation of the Divinity in our humanity. This is the proper stand-point whence to survey the special providence and the special grace vouchsafed to man as he now is, in his lapsed and ruined condition.

Hence the true and enduring sub-basis of a rational and adequate education of a human being, is a just and true conception of man, not as he was, but as he is now, and as he must forever be. Any system not based on these conceptions cannot possibly meet the demands of our nature, or develop and perfect a human being to act well his part in the great drama of human life. The only text-book for such a system, and such a study, and such a perfect development of man, is that inestimable volume, vouchsafed by God himself, in progress of completion some sixteen hundred years. It develops his nature, his origin, his destiny, and counsels his course in life with special reference to his full development and preparation for the highest honors, pleasures and enjoyments of which he is capable. It adapts itself to his highest reason, to the strongest and most enduring cravings of his nature, and reveals to him the only pathway to true glory, honor and immortality. Hence we conclude that this volume should be a standing and a daily text-book in every primary school, academy and college in Christendom.

But this is not all. The true philosophy of man demands that a rational and systematic course of instruction should be instituted and prosecuted with a special reference to the conscience, the heart and the spirit of man, as to the understanding or intellectual powers, the taste and the imagination of the pupil or the student. The whole world within him, as well as the whole world without him, should not only be defined and developed, but cultivated, matured and perfected, in full harmony with his origin and destiny, not only as far as appertains to the present world, but also as relates to the future and the eternal world.

Man was not created for this earth as his whole patrimony. He was destined to be a cosmopolite, not of our planet only, or of our solar system, but to have intercourse, free and cordial, with the tenantry of all worlds, and to be a peer of the highest circles of the highest sphere of God's universe. He is, in fact, through the interposition of the second Adam, made a peer of the highest realms in creation, and a joint heir with Adam the Second, who is himself heir of all things. May we not, then, with still more emphasis and earnestness, inquire, What should his education be?

What then is the meaning of the word *education*, inquire the sparkling eyes around me? It is a Roman word, of etymological composition. It is tantamount to *development*—a complete development. It enlarges, invigorates, beautifies, adorns and beatifies the soul and spirit of man. King Solomon endorses this theory in affirming that "a man's wisdom makes his face to shine;" that "its merchandise is better than silver, its increase than that of fine gold." "It is more precious than pearls; and all the objects of desire are not equal to wisdom." He affirms that "its ways are ways of pleasantness; that all its paths are paths of peace;" that "it is a tree of life to those who possess it, and that happy is he who retains it."

But there is knowledge without wisdom; and there may be, at a certain angle, wisdom without much knowledge. We have occasionally met with persons of much knowledge possessing little wisdom, and with some possessing much wisdom with little knowledge. Education, however, imparts knowledge rather than wisdom; while wisdom uses knowledge with discretion, applying and appropriating it to high and holy purposes. Wisdom and knowledge are of the same paternity, but not of the same maternity. They are, however, eagerly to be sought after; and he that seeketh them with all his heart shall attain to wise counsels. They are the richest gifts of God to mortal man.

Education, we repeat, is the development of what is in man, and, according to Webster, "it comprehends all that series of instruction and discipline which is intended to enlighten the understanding, correct the temper and form the manners and habits of youth, and fit them for usefulness in their future stations." *It is, therefore, physical, literary, moral and religious.* No irreligious man is, therefore, a well-educated man. His head may be large and crowded with ideas; but his heart is dwarfed and cold to God and man. His conscience is callous, if not seared with guilt, and his moral sensibilities morbid, if not paralyzed to death. When we affirm the conviction that every well-educated person must be a genuine Christian, we would not be understood as holding or expressing the idea that a Christian is the mere fruit of a good literary, moral or religious education. Still, without education, in some measure, no man can be a Christian. He must understand in some degree the oracles of God. Since the Bible contains the oracles of God, and since these oracles are written in human language, that language, whatever it may be as a mother tongue, must be the vehicle of all intercommunication between heaven and earth, between God and man. Now, if that language be not understood by any particular person, he cannot come to the knowledge of his God or of himself, so far as God has spoken to man, either of himself or of man, or so far as the most enlightened man can develop in words the being of God, the providence of God, the moral government of God, or the general salvation which he has provided for man in his moral ruin.

Education is, therefore, essential to the salvation of any man in whose hand God, in his moral government or overruling providence, has placed a Bible. This measure of education, essential to a man's self-reliance, his origin, responsibilities and destiny, and to his appreciation of a revelation from God concerning a remedial system, and man's present lapsed and ruined condition, is as indispensable to his immortal spirit and happy destiny as are atmosphere and lungs to his animal life and health. We merely assert these positions, because they are conceded by every man of sound judgment and self-disposing memory. And, therefore, a certain amount of education is absolutely necessary to give to every man the means of possessing and enjoying the life that now is, or that future and everlasting life to come.

For this end, there is in every child an innate craving after knowledge, as constant and as insatiate as the craving for congenial food. There are, indeed, degrees of it discernible in all children; and, as a general rule, in the exact ratio of the cravings for knowledge is the power or faculty of acquiring it.

But of all the knowledges of earth and time, the knowledge of our eternal destiny is rationally the all-absorbing, soul-captivating and soul-subduing craving of humanity. A human being devoid of this is not *compos mentis*, nor, indeed, *compos corporis*. Lungs without atmosphere would not be more useless or worthless than this insatiate craving for light and knowledge without some communication from the Father of our spirits on the soul-absorbing theme of our future and everlasting destiny. This is, after all the disquisitions on the certainty of a revelation from God to man, embracing his future and eternal destiny, the most palpable *a priori* argument in favor of the prince of school-books—the Holy Bible.

But we argue not this question as though it were still a doubtful one. We argue from it as from a fixed fact, fully and cordially and gratefully conceded by those whom we now address. The Bible, indeed, is the tongue of the universe, ever unfolding its mysteries, ever developing the awful and glorious character of that magnificent Architect whose sublime and awful *fiat* broke the solemn silence of eternity, and gave birth and being to a thousand millions of suns, and thirty thousand millions of attendant planets,—

"Forever singing, as they shine,
The hand that made us is Divine."

One of the most obvious and impressive arguments for the intellectual and moral dignity of man, is the fact that nothing short of the infinite, the eternal and the immutable, can meet and satisfy the cravings of his spiritual nature. There is more of philosophical fact than of fable in the tradition that the son of Philip and Olympias—Alexander of Macedon—having conquered the world that then was, hung his sword and trumpet in the hall, weeping that his arm was hampered, and had not room enough to do its work, in a world so small as ours. Ambition reddens at this tale, and hangs its head in solemn contemplation. But the truth, the glorious truth, the soul-subduing truth, is, that nothing but the infinite and the eternal can satisfy the cravings of an enlightened human soul. This thought—*fact* may I call it?—is enough to show to any one of grave reflection, that, whatever may be said of the physical or the intellectual nature of man, the moral and the spiritual are his transcendent glory and felicity. And hence we argue, that any and every system of education that does not contemplate this at a proper stand-point is perfectly at sea, in a boisterous ocean, without sail, compass, or pilot aboard, and, therefore, can never anchor in the haven of safe and happy repose.

Hence our position, our capital position, is, that the Holy Bible must be in every school worthy of a Christian public patronage, and not in the library only, but daily in the hand of teacher and pupil, professor and student. A dwelling-house without a table, a chair or a couch would not, in our esteem, be more unfit for guests, than a primary school, an academy or a college, without a Bible—not in the library only, but daily in the hand of the student, in solemn reading, study and exegetical development.

The most highly educated minds in Christendom will, *nemine contradicente,* with one accord, depose that for simplicity, and beauty, and intelligibility of style, as well as for the grandeur, the majesty and the sublimity of its oracular developments, it has no equal, much less superior, in all the libraries and archives of literature and science, of ancient or modern institution. It stimulates all the energies of the human soul, awakens all its powers of thought, elevates its conceptions, directs its activities, chastens its emotions, and urges it onward and upward in the career of glory, honor and immortality.

There is an unreasonable and an unfortunate prejudice in some regions, touching the introduction of the whole subject of religion, especially of speculative creeds and catechisms, into the public seminaries of this our age and nation. Into the merits or the demerits of this economy and dispensation of religious truth, or of theoretic and speculative disquisitions of a religious bearing, we have neither taste nor time to enter.

Suffice it to say that there is a catholic, as well as a provincial, formula of Divine truth, and that neither of them ought to be placed upon the table, to be theologically dissected or embalmed. *Christianity* is an abstract noun, from the adjective *Christian*, and that from *Christ* the *consecrated.* But the Bible being a book of *facts*, and not of *theories*, it may in these be studied, believed, obeyed and enjoyed, without one speculative oracle, on the part of teacher or pupil.

It is universally conceded by all, whose judgment is mature and worthy of authority amongst the masses, that no man was ever healed, saved or restored to health or life by an assent or subscription to any abstract formula in physics, metaphysics or theology. We live not, we cannot live, on alcohol, or on any distilled spirits whatever; but we can live and enjoy good health on bread and water. And so it is in religion. No man ever entered heaven, according to the Bible, either on physics or metaphysics. It is by *faith*, based on facts, and not by mere *doctrines*, orthodox, assented to, that any one is reformed, sanctified or saved. So the learned, and the truly religious, of all creeds and human platforms, unequivocally proclaim.

Why not, then, rather carry the Bible than the catechism to school? Why not listen to God rather than to man? Are we more safe in the teachings or in the hand of man than of God? Who teaches like Him who possesses not by measure, but without measure, the Spirit of all wisdom and understanding,—who taught on earth, and who speaks from heaven, with the plenary inspiration of the Holy Spirit of all wisdom and understanding? No school, worthy of Christian patronage, ever was or can be founded on a catechism, or on the speculative dogmata of any sectarian formula of opinions. We demand, and the age we live in demands, *facts*, and not *theories*, Divine oracles, and not human dogmata.

Had it been compatible with Divine wisdom and prudence to substitute a formula of abstract doctrine, or to give what we call a synopsis of Christian doctrine and sound orthodoxy, could he not, would he not, have given us an infallible summary—a stereotyped and a divinely patented formula of sound opinions, in mode and form to a scruple? The fact that He who foresaw the end of every institution from the beginning, and who foreknew all the involutions and evolutions of human kind, did not do it, is, to our mind, an unanswerable argument against any effort of man to do it.

In our studies of what is commonly called *nature*, or the material and spiritual universe, we observe that, despite the four elements of the moderns, God in nature, in providence, in moral government, and in redemption, presents nothing to man in the abstract, or absolute elementary form, but every thing in a concrete and relative form. So contemplated, the universe and the Bible bear the demonstrable impress of one and the same mind and will. To the educated eye of sound reason, there is one supreme intelligence everywhere manifest, without a single aberration; and there is, to the cultivated ear of religion, an omnipresent harmony, without one discordant note in all the spheres of God's own universe.

There is no apology for skepticism or infidelity, in heaven, earth or hell. There is not a more demonstrable proposition in the whole area of enlightened reason and cultivated intellect, than that the same mind that projected the universe and created the body, soul and spirit of man, also projected the oracles of Eternal Truth, which constitute the materials of that volume we so emphatically and impressively call the Holy Bible.

The works of the great sculptors, carvers, painters, architects, the Phidiases, the Praxiteles, the Raphaels, the Michel Angelos, of world-wide fame, are not more marked and characterized in the monuments left behind them, than are the shepherds, the husbandmen, the fishermen, the prophets, kings and priests, that were the oracles and the amanuenses of the Holy Spirit of all Divine wisdom and knowledge, embodied and embalmed on the pages of that much-neglected volume emphatically denominated THE BOOK OF LIFE TO MAN.

This is not only the *family* Bible, the *Sunday-school* Bible, the *church* Bible, but should be the common school, the academy, the college and the Congress Bible, and daily read, studied and practised in and by them all.

The Bible is, indeed, the tongue of creation. It inspires sun, moon and stars. It not only echoes in the thunders of heaven, in the tempests, the whirlwinds, the earthquakes and the volcanoes of earth, but it speaks in the still small voice of morning and evening, in the conscience, in the heart and in the soul of man. It was the great moral engine of ancient civilization, so far as it obtained a local habitation and a name amongst human kind.

For the best essay of modern times on the subject of the best means of civilizing the tenantries of the provinces in Great Britain's East India possessions, a rich medal was voted to the author of an essay whose theory of civilization was, "*Give to Pagandom the whole Bible in every man's vernacular, and teach every man to read it.*" The Bible and the schoolmaster are God's two great instrumentalities to enlighten, to civilize and to aggrandize man.

The Assyrian empire was annihilated by the Medo-Persian, the Medo-Persian by the Grecian, and the Grecian by the Roman. But Bible civilization, even in its rudimental elements, fettered by Grecian and Roman philosophies, falsely so called, sapped and mined the bases of Pagan governments, and gradually paved the way to a more rational, humane and dignified civilization.

The whole philosophy of the highest civilization ever exhibited on earth, or, indeed, conceivable in our horizon, is summarily comprehended in two precepts, on which, according to the greatest philosopher that ever appeared amongst men, depend the whole law and the prophets. These two precepts are but two manifestations or applications of one principle. Love to God and love to man, on the part of man, is the gravitating principle conservative of a rational and moral universe. The centres of all systems are attracting and radiating centres. It is so in the physical, the moral and the spiritual universe. The analogies of the physical to the spiritual, or of the spiritual to the physical, universe, so far as observation extends its dominion, aided by the light of the Bible, and what is sometimes called the light of nature, fully and most satisfactorily demonstrate and attest that they are the offspring of one and the same supreme intelligence, and, therefore, they severally, more or less, interpret and sustain one another.

We may change the terminology of whatever constitutes our beau ideal of a perfect social system; but the facts or realities of humanity, in its most extended horizon, are the fruit of a piety based upon a Divine communication. Hence the Bible, daily in the hand of every pupil in every school, is not only the best antidote against the frailties and the follies of man, but is also the sovereign directory in all that constitutes an amiable, honorable and magnanimous man or woman.

A *gentle*-man and a *gentle*-woman may be, and, indeed, often are, confounded, in our current dialect, with a *genteel* man and a *genteel* woman. But these are the mere creatures of the tailor or mantua-maker, the barber or the milliner, possessing the fashionable diction and mannerism of a Bostonian, a Londoner or a Parisian. These, indeed, are the creatures of perverted reason and romantic fancy; often at war with head, and heart, and conscience, alienating the reason, the moral sensibilities and the affections, from all that is truly amiable, estimable and praiseworthy in the legitimate aspirations of man or woman.

Education is a transcendently interesting theme. Its merits, its claims, its achievements, its enjoyments, its honors and its rewards, are not to be told in a few minutes, nor inscribed on a few pages. It is more than mere science, art, literature, philosophy, theology or Christ-ology. It is the perfect development and decoration of man, body, soul and spirit. It develops and adorns his animal, intellectual, moral and spiritual nature. It enthrones reason and conscience within him, and subordinates his animalism to the direction and control of an enlightened conscience and a purified heart.

To achieve these, is the great end and intention of a rational, moral and religious education. And, as assumed in our premises, it must be adapted to our whole constitution, our position in the social compact, and our eternal destiny in the universe of God. Any of these over-looked, neglected or disparaged, must ordinarily, in the common course of human events, terminate unfortunately and unhappily. The individual pupil is, first of all, the loser, but society must, more or less, suffer in every such failure.

We have in all communities, formally or informally, a joint-stock concern. The honest, industrious, frugal and successful operators in the busy hive of humanity do always suffer from, and generally have to pay all the costs of, all the drones, spendthrifts and marauders within their respective localities. More than half the common and necessary expenses of social life are imposed upon us through the neglect of a rational system of universal education, in the perfect development of what legitimately enters into its unsophisticated definition and import.

Were we arithmetically to compute our taxes, annually paid, chargeable to the neglect of a rational system of intellectual, moral and religious education, based upon the mature oracles of reason, of human experience, and the authentic annals of expenditures on account of the drones, loungers, loafers, technically defined, in erecting for them pillories, jails, court-houses, penitentiaries, prison-shops, hospitals, houses of correction, armies and navies, to say nothing of lawyers, judges, courts of oyer and terminer, &c. &c., all of which, or most of which, are the legitimate results of the entire or partial neglect of timely physical, intellectual, moral and religious culture, they would be astounding. These, indeed, are the cardinal points in human education, in reference to which the ship of our humanity must direct its course across the ocean of human ignorance and depravity, at the peril of vessel, cargo and all the hands aboard.

No sage philosopher, no profound political economist, no common philanthropist, no minister of State or of Church, has given to this subject a tithe of the thought and earnest attention which its vital importance and its superlative claims legitimately demand at our hands. That an amelioration of the social system is practicable, and that it is desirable, every man of enlightened reason and sober thought must admit. A cold indifference, indeed a sinful apathy, seems to exist on the part of many who possess an influence which, were it discreetly used and brought to bear on the public mind, might not only stay the progress of this social delinquency, but introduce such a system of moral education, based on the true science of man and of the social system, as would at least prevent the growth or spread of these noxious elements, which ultimately work the degradation and ruin of every people.

We hold it to be a paramount duty of every citizen, to seek the good of that people amongst whom himself and his posterity are, by Divine Providence, located. The *amor patriæ* of the Greeks and of the Romans, of the ancient and modern Jews and Gentiles, though not a virtue wholly disconnected from our native selfishness, is still a duty of paramount importance, not merely to ourselves, but, in its wide-spreading and long-enduring influence, more or less bearing upon the destiny of subsequent generations.

No man on earth, by any Divine or human warrant, lives solely for himself. Others providentially have lived, and do live, for him; and both religiously and morally he is obliged to live for others, or to make his life profitable to them. No man, in any society, lives for himself or dies for himself. This is an oracle both of reason and of revelation. And this fact alone is superlatively suggestive of the premises from which we should reason on the whole subject of education—physical, intellectual and moral. The world is so constituted, that its fortunes or its misfortunes may be materially, if not essentially, changed for the better or for the worse by the education of one individual actor in the drama of one generation. This actor, this agent for good or evil to contemporaries and to posterity, on some scale, large or small, often has been, and may hereafter be, the creature of a propitious or an unpropitious education. Histories and biographies of all sorts—literary, moral, philosophical, political and religious—abound with examples and illustrations of the influence, direct and indirect, of the incalculable good or evil commenced, conducted and consummated, by individuals, clubs, associations, councils and conventions, in each or in all of which, one, two, or three master-spirits, prompting, inspiring, guiding and controlling, have originated, matured and consummated crises of good and evil, in Church and State, in public and in private life, in sciences and in arts, useful and ornamental, the tendencies and bearings of which have continued for generations past, and will continue for generations to come. Old Testament and New Testament history, Chaldean, Persian, Medo-Persian, Grecian, Roman, German, French, English and American histories and biographies, furnish materials for a hundred volumes in proof of the position, that sometimes one, two or three distinguished men have stamped their image, not merely on the coinage of their respective countries, but on the masses that have handled it, and transmitted it, with their manners and customs, during hundreds, if not thousands, of years. The Bible alone, which is, or ought to be, in every man's hands at least once or twice a day, furnishes, in its biographies and narratives, enough, and more than enough, to convince any reasonable man, that education, good or bad, has been the most immediate, and continuous, and potent agency, in the fortunes and misfortunes of mankind, from Adam and Noah down to this present hour.

From this meagre outline of the all-permeating and all-potent agency of education in the affairs and destinies of the tribes, and nations, and empires of earth, we are authorized to conclude, that it is the paramount duty, privilege and honor of every family, tribe, state and empire on earth, to take it under its most special care, direction, supervision and patrimony.

The richest mine in any community is its mind. In it are found the wealth of nations, the honor, the dignity and the aggrandizement of every community on the verdant earth. It is a Divine decree, which should be as familiar as household words, and as oft repeated, *that educated mind must govern, and does govern, the world, and the universe, of which it is a constituent part.*

Our lawgivers, our law-interpreters, our judges, our executives, should know this, feel it, realize it, and patronize national education, to the utmost extent of constitutional limits. Why should we not work this mine with more intensity of interest, with more careful and paternal solicitude, with more liberality of support, with more generosity of endowment, than any other mine of national wealth—than any other fountain of national dignity and prosperity? All those lawgivers and rulers are penny-wise and pound-foolish, whose national coffers are replete with gold, while a majority of their population are steeped in ignorance, and more or less polluted with crime.

To keep within the precincts of one letter of our English alphabet, we ask—How many more Franklins, Fultons, Fausts, Farels, Fauquiers, Fayettes, Fénélons, Fergusons, Fields, Fieldings, Findleys, Flavels, Fleetwoods, Flemings, Fletchers, Forbeses, Fosters, Forces, Francises, Frederics and Fullers, might we, and mother England, have had, provided only, as a people, we had sooner learned that educated mind is the true riches, the true honor and the real estate of any and every people!

But our time and our premises are too much restricted to enter into the development of this theme. But we need not go far abroad in search of argument, illustration, or proof of the incomparable value, benefit and importance of education, in all its bearings upon the destiny of man now, henceforth and forever. In fact, the whole earth, with all its riches, real and personal, was designed by its Creator to be one grand constellation of schools, of every rank and order, for training, developing and perfecting humanity, not merely to eat, drink, frolic, dance and die, but to live, reign, triumph in immortal youth, to bloom and fructify forever in the eternal paradise of God.

From a consideration of this lofty and profound theme, an important and practically interesting question arises in every inquisitive and earnest mind, How is this education to be prosecuted, and, in some degree, perfected? To answer such a question, might occupy the details of a handsome volume. We can only say at present, that the great text-book of humanity, especially in its moral, spiritual and everlasting relations and enjoyments, is emphatically *the Bible;* not on the shelf, nor on the family stand, but daily in the hands, under the eyes and upon the conscience and the heart of every pupil capable of reading it. I do not mean in the nursery, the infant school, the seminary, the academy, the college, the university, but in whatever you may please to call the school, the Bible must be daily, solemnly read, and the attention of the pupils or students concentrated upon it, with corresponding literary and exegetical developments, in harmony with the capacity and attainments of the pupil, whether child or stripling, whether in full manhood or womanhood. We have wrought out this problem to our entire satisfaction during the last fifteen years, in college life; and we previously wrought it out for seven years in academic life, and have proof, strong as Holy Writ, of its practicability, power and efficacy.

In the Holy Bible we have five books in the Christian Scriptures and five primary books in the Jewish Scriptures. These are, in their simple facts and documents, an all-sufficient library for this department of education. We have two other Bibles for two other collateral studies, which constitute and consummate our studies of religion and morality. These are the volumes of the earth and the heavens: the former, the text-book of geology; the latter, the text-book of astronomy. These three infallible volumes severally studied, analytically and synthetically, furnish ample data for any and every student in the great family of man who desires to comprehend himself in his origin, relations and destiny in this magnificent universe.

But, in the details of moral culture, it should be noted with much emphasis, that of those pupils that enter schools of all orders, a fearful majority are beyond the period of successful moral culture. Neglected at home, they enter schools from which they very seldom can receive that culture most essential to the full exhibition of their spiritual and moral constitution. If this be neglected in the nursery and infant school, as it is in a majority—a fearful majority—of cases, there is not that full assurance of hope which we so fondly desire to entertain that it can be done in the most primary school beyond the nursery. There is a seed-time in humanity as well as in the seasons of the year, which, if passed, is rarely, if ever, to be recalled but by the special grace of God. Paul's compliments to Timothy, touching his grandmother Lois and his mother Eunice, are like apples of gold in pictures of silver, and ought to be committed to memory by every mother in Christendom.*

But, When may moral culture most hopefully commence? is a grave

* 2 Tim. i. 5; iii. 15.

question—a most interesting question. Shall we say in grandmother Lois, or in mother Eunice? Before birth, or after it? This is to me, and to you, ladies and gentlemen—Christian ladies and Christian gentlemen—a very grave, serious and highly interesting question. But a word to the wise is sufficient on any thing. It must commence with the commencement of our being, and be continued till the period of our full physical and moral development. So have said our Solomons and our Apostle Pauls, with all the good and great, the learned and wise men of the last three thousand years. *As the twig is bent, the tree's inclined.* But it is not merely to commence with our being, but to be continued, in the female sex, to the age of eighteen, and in the other sex—more slow to learn—till three times seven, or one-and-twenty years.

My old friend, Robert Owen, of Lanark, Scotland—once well known in this city—took the position, and stoutly maintained it, that man in his prime was but the creature of mere circumstances. But, since the era of new spiritual communications, he has learned better, and abandoned the position, and now imagines that there is more in man than flesh, blood and bones, and that there are at least infernal spirits, and that the presumption may now be entertained that there are also supernal spheres, with supernal tenantry, all of which were to him, in by-gone days, less than problematical.

But God's own Book of books is a book of facts, and not at all a book of theories. *Facts* are for children and the great masses of humanity; *philosophies*, speculations and doctrines, abstruse and metaphysical, are for philosophers and dogmatists, and not for the great masses of humanity. Moses begins with facts and palpable documents, and ends with them; so do all other inspired writers. They give us every thing in the concrete and nothing in the abstract. Hence, the divine area of creation, of providence, of moral government and of redemption furnish the proper materials of history and prophecy, which include the contents of both Testaments.

This is the material and the manner of all the inspired documents; and it should be the material and the manner of a useful and practical education. We can discover no good reason why there should be any difference. God is revealed to man by what he has done and what he has said, just as man is revealed to man by what he has done and what he has said. Moral culture is the great end of all human education. This is the polar star of our whole theory. Much experience, and more observation, have most satisfactorily convinced us that this can never be achieved without the instrumentality of God's own Book of Life. Scholastic ethics are *jejune* provisions for an immortal mind. God's Book is the only book of life to man. His oracles are living oracles, and they are also life-giving oracles. The word of God is a *living* and a *life-giving* word. It imparts the light of life to a benighted world. It is a monumental fact, to be read and studied and admired by every reflecting and cultivated mind, that *God created the universe by his word.* In the only infallible and satisfactory account of the origin of the material universe, we are informed that *twice seven fiats* give to it birth and being and location. This antedates all the existing and all the dead philosophies of man by thousands of years.

The Book of God is the only book of life, the only charter of immortality to man. A school, an academy, a college, without the Bible in it, is like a universe without a centre and without a sun. In its hallowed teachings and in its spiritual breathings upon our spirits they are stimulated, energized into all the activities of a moral, a spiritual and an eternal life that satisfies the perpetual cravings of our nature, the longings of our souls for the infinite, the eternal, the unfading joys of a blissful immortality.

We demand no politico-ecclesiastical creed, rubric or platform, no red-book dictated and commanded or recommended by the civil sword or an intolerant priesthood. We want the Holy Bible of Protestant Christendom to be consecrated in the heads, the hearts, the consciences and the lives of our sons and daughters. We, therefore, plead with God, and we plead with man, and especially with the curators, the superintendents, the presidents, the professors, the teachers, of all seminaries of learning, to *permit* their pupils, if not to cause them, duly to listen to God speaking to them, teaching them and directing them in the path of life and honor and blessedness eternal. If, with Blackstone, we say, "The trial by jury is the *palladium* of our civil rights," the Bible in any school in America is the palladium of all our rights, titles and honors, temporal, spiritual and eternal.

If, with the Honorable Soame Jenyns, of England, we place not patriotism among the Christian virtues because our Lord did not, being only social selfishness, we will not withhold that Book of books from any pupil of any school, in any section of humanity, which places *philanthropy* before our eyes in its most attractive forms, and which, indeed, enthrones it in the heart of every well-educated youth, as the queen of all the social virtues. If our humanity be limited or circumscribed by political and social leagues and corporations, let us infuse into every youthful heart that spirit of universal benevolence by the teachings of that Divine Spirit which makes it our duty, our interest, our honor and our happiness to embrace in the bosom of Christian benevolence the whole family of man; in doing which, we practically imitate the Father of all mercies and the God of all grace, who causes his sun to rise upon the good and the evil, and who sends the early and the latter rain on the just and on the unjust.

To the professional teachers of the youth of our country, we would express an opinion which we have long cherished, and which we esteem it both a duty and a privilege, on such occasions as the present, to express. Gentlemen, from many years' experience and observation—at least one-quarter of a century of my life a professional teacher—and familiar with many of the most reputable teachers in the Old World and in the New, for at least half a century, I have come to the conclusion that no class of men, in any department of society, have more of the good or evil destiny of the world in their hands and under their influence than the teachers of our schools and colleges. In forming this opinion, I have taken into my premises that everywhere-appreciated and highly respected and respectable class of men that occupy the pulpit—sometimes called the sacred desk—on at least one day in every week. They have very promiscuous and sometimes very unstable hearers, and they give them but one lesson, or at most two, in one week, and these are not protracted generally beyond the limits of a single hour, while most of you occupy the attention of your pupils more time in one month than they do in a whole year. In point of time and labor, one academic teacher is equal, in this area, to some ten or twelve religious instructors. Besides, you teach with a book in your hand, and the same book is in the hand of every pupil in your class. The preacher takes a verse, and you take a page or a plurality of pages, in a single lesson. You have, besides, this advantage—your classes are children, or young men with good memories, not deeply inscribed with the cares and troubles of life. Of course, then, you have a power paramount in shaping the destinies of mankind, greatly superior to that of the priesthood and clergy of this age. You read the Holy Scriptures, too, in the vernacular, and sometimes in the original; hence, in truth, I must regard you as quite as influential upon the destinies of the world as are the clergy of the living age.

Cherish, then, a high estimate of your noble calling, and estimate your responsibilities in the light of eternity; and act, accordingly, your part as responsible functionaries in planting in the heart, in the dawn of life, the seeds of those holy principles which enlarge the understanding, purify the heart and adorn with high and holy virtues the life of man.

ON COMMON SCHOOLS.

AN ADDRESS DELIVERED AT CLARKSBURG, VA., 1841.

FELLOW-CITIZENS:—

This, I trust, is an auspicious day for the Old Dominion. I hail it as a day long to be remembered, on which, for the first time, a respectable portion of the intelligence, patriotism and philanthropy of Cis-Alpine Virginia have assembled in convention gravely and benevolently to deliberate on the ways and means by which this community shall discharge to itself its paramount and all-transcendent duty. For if there be any truth in the oft-repeated maxim that a representative government depends not merely for its prosperity and perpetuity, but for its very existence, on the intelligence and virtue of its citizens, evident it is that the great and superlative duty of the people and of the Government they have placed over them is to provide for, and secure, that intelligence and virtue, by a system of education not only rational and well adapted in itself, but also coextensive with the entire wants of the whole community. Until this be done, our liberties are not secured, and nothing can be effectually done to perpetuate and extend to our heirs and successors that rich inheritance obtained for us at the expense of so much blood and treasure, and transmitted to us by those noble spirits who for this end imperilled all, and staked their lives, their fortunes and their sacred honor.

Two objects will naturally engross the attention of this convention. The first—What sort of an education is adapted to the common wants of the whole community, to the happiness and prosperity of the State? and the second—How is it to be made truly common and accessible to all?

But as introductory to this discussion, certain great principles ought to be clearly propounded, developed and accredited by those who undertake to effect this great moral revolution in the community. The interest that the State has, purely as a matter of policy, in establishing and sustaining such a system in whole or in part, the duties which devolve upon the Government in reference to the establishment and maintenance of such a system, should be thoroughly laid open to the apprehension and full conviction of all persons of mature age and reason. These points should be elaborated, illustrated and confirmed by facts and documents, plain and undeniable, in all the primary meetings of the people. Lecturers should perigrinate every town, village and hamlet in the State, and awaken the whole community to the consideration of the matter. In arguing the first point—the political interest that the State has in establishing and patronizing universal education—care should be taken to show that educated mind is the *true commonwealth* of every community. This may be done by showing clearly and conclusively that it is mind and society, and only these two, that find any value in the earth above that which the brutal creation enjoy. Of what use, for example, are hills and mountains stored with minerals and metals of the most valuable character, without educated mind to search them out and to convert them into use? Of what value to the Indian are the forests in which he roams, or the mountains and hills of brass and iron on which he treads, destitute as he is of science and educated art to convert them to his use and comfort? Of what value the richest mines of India or Peru, of Margaretta or Potosi, to him who has not skill to work them, and art to fuse, and compound, and mould, and hammer, and polish their products into the conveniencies and comforts and elegances of civilized life? Do not the granite hills and marble quarries of Italy and Egypt—the pearls and hidden treasures of the ocean—the diamond, the ruby and the emerald, with all the precious stones of the earth—acquire even their beauty and lustre, their interest and value, from the mind that science illumines and the hand that education guides in laying them under contribution to the wants of man?

Nay, may it not be shown that the richest valleys and the most luxuriant soils owe their fruitfulness more to the skill and labor of the cultivator, than to their natural and inherent richness?—that the agriculturist, the planter and the manufacturer owe to science and general education the utensils and machinery of their respective callings and pursuits?—that it is educated mind that makes the wilderness and the solitary place glad, and that causes the desert to rejoice and blossom as the rose? Of all the sources of national wealth, may it not be affirmed that not only is the mind, the intellect of the community, the richest and the most considerable part, but that it is that which gives value, and riches, and beauty, and convenience, and comfort, and refinement to every thing else? Viewed as a separate and distinct item of the national domain, it deserves more labor, cultivation and improvement than all the other items of public property in the statistics of a nation's wealth. Of what avail to the world the genius of a Newton, a Franklin, a Fulton, without education? To what do we owe the plough, the sickle and the scythe, the cotton-gin, the shuttle and the loom? To what the ships, the steamboats, the railroads, the thousand-and-one inventions that subdue our forests, that beautify our fields and meadows, our orchards and gardens, that erect and adorn our dwellings, that build our towns and cities and replenish and enrich them with the products of every clime—with the fabrics of every hand? To these and a thousand such inquiries there is but one answer; and that answer is, *Educated mind.* As a single item of a nation's wealth, the political economist, whether he appear in the character of a statesman, a philosopher, a patriot or a philanthropist, is therefore compelled to say that the development and cultivation of the mind, the whole mind, of a community, by a judicious and favorable system of education, is the first and superlative duty of the State. The masses of national wealth that have been accumulated to society by the inventors of the mariner's compass, the steam-engine, the cotton-gin, are worth more than the entire commonwealth of Virginia, real and personal, with all the hereditaments and appurtenances thereunto belonging. And who can tell but that there is at this moment amidst these rough mountains and deep valleys, these gently-sloping hills and wide-extended plains that diversify and beautify Western Virginia, one or more such minds, like marble yet in the quarry or a diamond among the pebbles of Golconda, which, were fair science to smile upon their humble birth, might make them not only gems in a nation's crown of glory, effulgent stars emblazoning her escutcheon, but sources of wealth equalling the resources of many prosperous years, and lessening the toils of many generations?

But it is not only as a portion of a nation's wealth that the public mind is to be contemplated by even the mere political economist, but as a means of a nation's defence, and of its annoyance also. Nations have been *saved,* and they have been *destroyed,* by a portion of their intellect overpowering all the balance. A minority, a very small minority, of a nation's intellect, immorally educated, has often proved the scourge and the ruin of a whole country. A few spirits—a mere trio, like that of Danton, Robespierre and Marat, sustained by a few subalterns moving in humbler circles, but holding places of power, drenched the fields of France in human blood, clothed its millions in the sable garments of mourning, and agonized the hearts of untold multitudes with unutterable pangs of sorrows. What varied mischiefs have a few ambitious marauding Pharaohs, Cæsars, Tamerlanes, Bonapartes, inflicted on mankind! At the shrine of their unhallowed ambition what millions of human beings have been immolated! And what shall we say of the Torquemadas, the Voltaires, the Hastings, the Arnolds, the Burrs, and the lesser monsters that have in various spheres scourged mankind? Men of high intellect, indeed, partially educated, but whose hearts were suffered to grow up the hotbeds of every passion and lust that could degrade and afflict human kind! But, to turn from the darker to the brighter side of the picture, we have some few samples of the power of good intellectual and moral culture combining their happy powers to work out a nation's deliverance. We need not indeed tell of the saviours of other nations, nor of the few small bands that have from time to time risen up to redress a nation's wrongs, to wrest the scorpion-scourge of tyranny from the relentless hand of heartless despotism. We can tell of our own Washington, and the few mighty and noble spirits of that era, his confederates in the council and in the field—who, at the sacrifice of all that men hold dear, dared to redeem a nation from the unjust encroachments and avaricious spoliations of a corrupt Government prompted by a few aspiring and ambitious men. Yet had that Washington and his illustrious compeers been still better educated than was the age in which they lived and from which they took their counsels and their examples, who can tell but that without so much blood and so many years of suffering, by other policies and principles, all that we enjoy might have been secured to themselves and their posterity for many generations! Another Franklin, of another category, might have arisen, who could have stolen from the breast of kings the electric fluid of a monarch's wrath by a conducting-rod that would, without the lurid flash of scathing lightnings and the mighty peals of angry thunders, have sent it secretly and quietly into the bosom of mother earth!

The powers of a proper system of education have never yet been fully developed on a grand scale. Yet, from the developments already made, we may infer that the time is not far distant when we will look to the schoolmaster and the district school, more than to mighty generals, standing armies and immense navies, with all the munitions of war, for the preservation of a nation's peace, a nation's safety, and a nation's honor. It is no freak of fancy, no hallucination of a romantic imagination, but the oracle of substantial truth, derived from the experience of the past, that all will sooner be gained, by good education, in the adjustment of even national wrongs by mediatorial tribunals, which hitherto have cost millions of gold and torrents of human blood.

We are beginning to see that as yet we have too much of Roman barbarism, not only in some of our patrician regulations, but in our rudimental ideas of what is just and honorable, and in our views of what is creditable to ourselves as individuals and as nations. Our political halls and chambers of legislation—our *honorable* rencounters, first in wordy strife, then in polite blackguardism, and finally with powder and lead or Turkish sabre, bowie-knife or stiletto—show that as yet we are but half civilized, and more Pagan than Christian in the inner man. We look in vain to those standing upon the upper rounds of the ladder of human ambition for help to remove it or to change its position and modification. We must begin at the bottom; we must stand upon the soil, and raise up a new species of men, and attach to the high places of the State a ladder of a new and more rational and moral construction.

Learned men and the higher classes, in their more sober and lucid intervals, begin to see that it would be less expensive to educate an infant than to support an aged criminal in a State prison; nay, that a county pauper costs more than a well-educated child. It is therefore becoming a very grave question whether ignorance and crime do not now cost the State more than would expatriate them and introduce intelligence and virtue in their place. If any one were so well educated in the State finances—in the expenditures for jails, pillories, penitentiaries and poor-houses, with all the expenditures in gaming, gambling, immoral speculations, eating tobacco and drinking rum, in idleness and its brood of gigantic vices—as to be able to tell how many millions per annum ignorance and vice cost the nation, I doubt not for a single moment but that it would be found that we are annually paying, in various ways, direct and indirect, more for the present stock on hand of ignorance and vice than would educate every child born on our territory in a good common school, such as patriarchal monarchs in the North of Europe allow their population out of the public purse.

Indeed, there are some conscientious men who are seriously asking the question whether a State government has a right, natural, inherent or divine, to punish the crimes which grow from the ignorance which she creates, rather than removes, by laying taxes on myriads without their consent, and withholding from them that education which is essential to their clear discrimination of right and wrong.

It is no longer debatable whether the great mass of enormities which are daily growing up in this country are not the legitimate offspring of the want of good primary and common school education. From the strictest inquiries and researches which I have been able to make, from our penitentiary reports, and the number of executions for capital offences, it appears that while in our best-educated States the proportion of the whole population that are taught to read varies from more than one hundred to one to twenty-eight to one, the proportion of those in public prisons not educated at all is more than two to one. The difference, then, between the two aggregates in the penitentiaries and out of them, in such States as New York, for example, is as follows:—Out of the penitentiaries, in twenty-nine persons twenty-eight can read for one that cannot; whereas in the penitentiaries, out of twenty-nine persons fifteen cannot read for fourteen that can.

Dr. Julius, after a laborious examination of the principal prisons in the United States, affirms that "*one-third* of the convicts are foreigners. In New York they are frequently *one-half*." Now, these are, for the most part, wholly uneducated persons. A cheering fact occurs in the statistics of the State prisons of New York in demonstration of the influence of education to diminish crime. In the Secretary's report for 1840, it is stated that crimes requiring some education and skill, such as "forgery, perjury, burglary, &c., have been gradually diminishing with the diffusion of education; whereas those the usual concomitants of ignorance and debasement are increasing." "That knowledge," remarks the chaplain of the Connecticut State Prison, "is not very frequently used as an instrument in the commission of crime, appears from the fact that out of sixty-six committed to that prison last year, the crimes of but four were such in commission as required ability to read or write." The Directors of the Ohio Penitentiary state that "it is an erroneous impression that the convicts are intelligent, shrewd men. Nearly the whole number in our prison are below mediocrity in point of information. Of two hundred and seventy-six, nearly all are below mediocrity; one hundred and seventy-five are grossly ignorant, and in point of education scarcely capable of transacting the common business of life." From all the documents that I have had access to, it appears that "*the tendency to crime amongst the ignorant is fourteen times greater than it ought to be on the supposition that education has no power to restrain it.*" Is not this a cheering fact, regarding education as it now is, having generally little or no reference to the heart, but chiefly to the head? If the culture of the heart or moral training were equal to that of the mere intellect, which, on every principle of policy, interest, honor, safety and benevolence, it ought to be, the tendency to crime would be a hundred times greater than it ought to be, on the supposition that education has no power to restrain it. Our theory might carry us much further; but we are content to let it be bounded by what actually has occurred.

From this view of the subject it would seem a fair and logical inference that the rich ought to contribute to the support of common schools in the ratio of their stakes in society; for of what use their superior fortunes, if the sons of their neighbors be thieves and robbers, marauders or murderers? This conclusion is not only fair in logic, but also in fact; for property is uniformly judged most secure and insured for less per cent. in the midst of an orderly and moral society than in one of a different character. But I do not argue this point: I only name a few of the topics from which those will argue in favor of universal education on the part of the State, who contemplate the subject in all its bearings upon the commonwealth, as the prime source of public revenue, as the palladium of national defence, and as a great preservative of the internal peace, safety and prosperity of the whole community.

The accurate reasoner on this great subject will labor to show, that, viewed in all its bearings upon the social compact, education is not only to be universal, but to be adapted equally to the head and to the heart. For, while cultivated intellect necessarily builds up the agricultural, manufacturing and commercial interests of the community, cultivated hearts as necessarily preserve the peace and constitute the safety and happiness of society. The orator, too, will not fail to reason from one of the popular maxims in every republic—that the chief end of government is not to preserve itself, build up its own fortunes and aggrandize itself, but to develop a nation's resources, direct its energies, provide for its exigencies and protect it from intestine rivalries and animosities as well as from encroachments on the part of foreign powers; in one sentence, to protect the people in the full enjoyment of all their rights, natural or conventional. His great and invincible argument from this fundamental view and concession will always be, "If mind be any part of a nation's wealth or resources, or if education be one of the exigencies of the State, or if ignorance and vice are evils from which the people are to be protected, then does it not follow with the light of demonstration that the intellectual and moral improvement of all the mind belonging to the State is the first concern of every intelligent, just and patriotic Government in the world?" Believe me, fellow-citizens, that Government is wanting in the essential ends of its being, in the vital object of its existence, which makes not the education of every child born upon its territory its primary concern.

We should not pause until we have concentrated all the light derived from the voluminous fact—that *intelligence* and *freedom* are but two names for the same thing. An intelligent community will always be free; an ignorant one, never. As we advance education, as we promote universal intelligence, we promote universal freedom. If free government, if liberty of thought, of speech and of action, are privileges, then it behooves all who think so to combine their efforts to extend the blessings of education to all, and to make provision for such a system of mental and moral culture as will insure all that we include in the idea of a great nation—an intelligent, virtuous and prosperous community.

But from these general and fundamental views we must turn to the two points standing directly in the line of an incipient effort to awaken and direct the energies of our fellow-citizens in the present crisis. The first of these is, *What is the character and what are the outlines of that system of education which is properly popular and common, and which ought to be commensurate with the geographical boundaries of every community?*

In sketching the outlines of such a system, a due regard must be had to what the common wants of humanity are, in respect of physical, intellectual and moral development and improvement. Whatever is not in harmony with the human constitution, the position that man occupies not only in society, but in the universe, his nature, relations, obligations and destiny, is not only in itself inadequate and imperfect, but must be subject to continual mutation. Hitherto a perfect system has not been introduced; and hence the endless variety of theories and experiments on the part of authors and teachers. In devising a suitable system, the questions, *What is man? Where is he?* and *What is he destined for?* must be clearly ascertained, and then it will be more competent to man to devise for him a proper system of education. If to the tailor or the cordwainer it be essential that he have the measure of those parts of the human body he would furnish with suitable apparel, as necessary is it to the school-teacher that he should have the dimensions of his pupil as a sentient, intellectual and moral being, before he can furnish him with an education suitable to his nature and in harmony with the conditions of his existence and his ultimate destiny.

Without presuming now or hereafter to say what would be a perfect and complete system, we may remark that there are seven arts that human nature must acquire in a judicious course of primary and fundamental education. These seven arts are as essential to education, as society always was, and is, and evermore shall be constituted, as food and raiment are to the human body in the Valley of the Mississippi. These seven arts must therefore ever be the basis of a good system of primary and common school education. They are as follows:—1st. The art of thinking; 2d. The art of speaking; 3d. The art of reading; 4th. The art of singing; 5th. The art of writing; 6th. The art of calculating; and, 7th. The art of book-keeping. These are the seven essentials of a primary school-system; they are fundamental to the whole system of education—to a series of schools—primary, secondary and ultimate, usually called common schools, academies and colleges. For, be it observed, the common school system is not only to be perfect in itself for those who shall never enter another school, but also perfect so far as it goes with reference to every other species of school in the most civilized and highly-improved community.

But I will be asked, Is the system of primary and common school education to consist only of these seven arts, or of any number of arts? Is there nothing worthy of the name of science in all this? I answer, These seven arts are, like all other arts, useful or ornamental, founded on science. Hence, in acquiring these arts the following sciences will necessarily have to be taught to greater or less extent:—orthography, orthoepy, grammar, arithmetic, elements of geometry, algebra, music and elocution. I am aware that some persons will be startled at this range of science in common schools, especially those whose views are bounded by spelling, reading, writing and ciphering to the end of the rule-of-three. But to these I will only say, first, that we do not comprehend the entire range of those sciences as forming a part of common school education, but merely hold that certain portions of them are essential; and, in the second place, that whenever the State sets about finding teachers by founding normal schools to manufacture rational and competent instructors, she will find that all this and more can be taught in the time usually spent in the common schools now in operation under the monarchical governments of the Old World and some portions of our own country.

I have not added the word *correctly* to each of these seven arts. I have not said, indeed, that the art of thinking correctly is to be taught before the art of speaking correctly, though I am of opinion that their natural order is in the position in which I have placed them. We regard some of these arts as necessarily facilitating improvement in the others, and all of them as existing on such terms of intimacy and friendship as will mutually aid advancement in all. It may also be objected that few adults have learned to think correctly, and that this is rather the work of a college than of a primary and incipient school. To which I answer that the reason that comparatively so few adults ever learn to think correctly, is that they never enjoyed the advantage of a good common school education. It is not often in adult years that men become proficients in those branches of education which have been wholly neglected in youth. Hence we find hundreds of graduates issuing from respectable colleges, who could not spell correctly all the monosyllables in the book of Proverbs were their lives staked upon it. But in teaching youth to think correctly, I mean no more than the communication of the simple art, which consists in the habit of accurate observation, comparison and deduction—an art, indeed, which, to be satisfactorily communicated, demands assiduous attention on the part of a competent instructor from the very commencement of the alphabet to the end of the course of primary instruction.

In addition, however, to these seven all-important arts, and so much of the sciences as are necessary to their acquisition, there are other branches of scientific knowledge essential to a rational and useful common school course of instruction, viz. the geography of our planet, a knowledge of material and animated nature, natural history, together with the elements of society, our own social compact, constitution and laws, a sketch of ancient and modern history, especially the history of our own country; and, above all, the admirable science of self-knowledge, an intimate acquaintance with our sentient, intellectual and moral nature, which is to be a portion of every day's instruction, from the abecedarian class to the last lesson in the elementary departments. All this knowledge may be found in a very few elementary books which are now constantly issuing from the press, with the accompanying instructions and explanations of a properly-qualified instructor. "THE HOUSE I LIVE IN," by Dr. Alcott, contains a fund of knowledge on the anatomy of the human system, adapted to an infant-school. This, with "*The Laws of Physical Health*," forms a school-book of incalculable importance to youth; for those things ought to be first and most thoroughly learned that are most essential to the preservation of health and the formation of proper habits. Mr. Taylor, of New York in his admirable work on the District School, in sketching the glaring defects of the common school and common education, very appositely complains:—

"This useful and intensely interesting subject is almost entirely neglected in our common schools. Not one pupil in a thousand eve learns a single lesson in either the mineral, vegetable or animal kingdoms. The young farmer learns nothing of the varieties of soil, its nature and composition, and its peculiar preparation for different grains; he obtains no knowledge of the nature and growth of vegetables; or the properties and influence of the 'life-giving air.' The most important information for his business the school does not give him.

"The little knowledge that he acquires of his business he is obliged to get by ignorant experience and blind observation. The mechanic does not study the nature, pliability and uses of the minerals and metals, nor does he learn the beauty, strength and durability of the various timbers. The laborer in his experiments has no science to assist him: he is preparing nature to administer to his necessities, without knowing her rules of action. He knows nothing—for his school has given him no opportunity to know—of his own physical nature, or of the properties of the natural world around him.

"He cannot, therefore, conform his life and conduct to the relations which exist between matter and his physical nature. He has no means of foreseeing the infringement of the organic laws. In his school he has never learned the most common and simple truths in physiology or anatomy. The structure and uses, the layers, the mucous coat, &c. of the skin, the common school student learns nothing of.

"He is not told that the skin is the seat of perspiration, the regulator of animal heat, and the seat of absorption. He does not see the sympathy between the skin and the other organs of life, nor the causes of suppressed perspiration, (an action which brings on the most of our disorders,) nor the connection between the skin and the nervous system. Being ignorant of this vital organ, he abuses and neglects it. He gives no attention to suitable clothing, to ventilation, nor to washing and bathing; for he has no information on these subjects.

"He has learned nothing of the structure and action of the muscles, nor of the degree and kind of exercise which they require to give them strength, elasticity and health. He has no acquaintance whatever with anatomy, and knows not that the bones are composed of animal and earthy matter, and that they are essential to motion and to the security of the vital organs: he does not study the growth and decay of the bones, nor perceive the advantages of their vitality and insensibility, and their adaptation to contained parts.

"Of the nature and use of respiration, the structure of the lungs, the necessity of pure air, and the healthy condition of the digestive organs, the common school pupils never hear or read a word. They grow up and live entirely ignorant of the nervous system, knowing nothing of its functions and education—nothing of these great inlets of knowledge and instruments of pleasure and pain.

"They are not taught even the causes of good or bad health, nor the physical consequences of immoral conduct. Not one truth of this science, which shows that man is 'fearfully and wonderfully made,' is taught in our district schools. This need not be so; for there are no truths more simple or pleasing than some of the most important facts of physiology. There should be a text-book on this subject for our common schools.

"Although there are 'sermons in stones,' they are not 'delivered' to the common school student. Neither his teacher nor his books speak even of the first principles of geology or mineralogy. The earth, our common mother—the womb and the grave of every living object—the great companion and benefactor of the farmer, has, in the country, scarcely a teacher to make known her nature, her elements and her energies. That which the agriculturist has to labor with, and from which he obtains his 'blessings and his bread,' forms no part of the farmer's education.

"Does not the neglect of even one department of natural history show a great deficiency in our common school education? But the vegetable kingdom is as little attended to. Plants, flowers and trees find no teacher in district schools. The places they enliven with their freshness, sweeten with their fragrance and cool with their shade, never speak of their bounty or their beauty, their wisdom or their Author.. Many of those who spend their lives in nursing flowers and cultivating plants know nothing of their structure or their organs, nor even their artificial or natural classification. What additional interest would the farmer feel, amidst the freedom and the freshness of his labor, if he could be enlightened with even a faint ray from the science of botany! But it would be a lonely and wandering ray that would enter the room of the district school."

The Bible as a school-book and moral instructor is made a part of every day's education in every good school both in the Old World and in the New. A few years have accomplished a truly marvellous revolution in public opinion on this subject. Ever since the French Revolution —that era of terror, that age of atheism and infidelity, that triumph of lawless despotism and licentious majorities—enlightened minds have looked to the Bible with more intense interest and assurance than before, as the palladium of all human rights—as the only strong and safe guarantee of our social immunities and privileges, whether political, moral or religious. The true philosopher, the patriot, the statesman and the philanthropist, equally with the Christian, say that intellectual without moral culture is a curse to each and every community. To educate the head, and neglect the heart, is only giving teeth to the lion, claws to the tiger, and talons to the eagle to seize and devour their prey. The ablest politicians and the most profound philosophers of France, England and America now affirm that education in universities, in high schools and common schools, without the Bible and moral training, is a national calamity rather than a public benefaction. Hence, in Prussia, and in most of the German States, in France, England and America, there is but one voice to be heard on this subject. All concur, sectarianism with all her brood and all her rival fears to the contrary notwithstanding, all unite, in recommending the Bible as a universal school-book, from the first lesson in the reading-class to the last recitation in the college course.

I had the pleasure to see even the Catholic Bishop of Cincinnati, with all the clergy of all denominations—Episcopal, Presbyterian, Baptist and Methodist—then present at a meeting of the College of Teachers in that city, voting in favor of my amendment of a resolution to give the Bible to every school in the country, without one sectarian or denominational note or comment; and that, too, within one year after a debate on Romanism, growing out of that cardinal tenet of Protestantism, viz. the Bible, the whole Bible, and nothing but the Bible, as the rule of Christian faith and manners. It is now a settled point, proclaimed from the thrones of the Old World, and from the heads of all departments in the New, that education without the Bible, and without moral training, is not to be tolerated by any civilized community.

It is also becoming more and more evident that, notwithstanding all our sectarian differences, we yet have something called a *common* Christianity;—that there are certain great fundamental matters—indeed, every thing elementary in what is properly called piety and morality—in which all good men of all denominations are agreed; and that these great common principles and views form a common ground on which all Christian people can unite, harmonize and co-operate in one great system of moral and Christian education.

If names truly great were needed to illustrate and confirm these views, we could give them in superabundance. I will at present select but one, from one of the highest places in the Old World, and from a nation that has a more ample experience of the neglect of Bible-instruction than any other in the civilized world—Italy, the land of saints and pilgrims, only excepted. From the minister of public instruction—from the great philosopher and statesman, Monsieur *Victor Cousin*—whose titles are, Peer of France, Councillor of State, Professor of Philosophy, Member of the Institute and of the Royal Council of Instruction—we quote a few words out of very many which he has fitly spoken on religious and moral culture:—

"We have abundant proof that the well-being of an individual, like that of a people, is nowise secured by extraordinary intellectual powers or very refined civilization. The true happiness of an individual, as of a people, is founded on strict morality, self-government, humility and moderation; on the willing performance of all duties to God, his superiors and his neighbors.

"A religious and moral education is consequently the first want of a people. Without this, every other education is not only without real utility, but in some respects dangerous. If, on the contrary, religious education has taken firm root, intellectual education will have complete success, and ought on no account to be withheld from the people, since God has endowed them with all the faculties for acquiring it, and since the cultivation of all the powers of man secures to him the means of reaching perfection, and, through that, supreme happiness. . . .

"We must lay the foundations of moral life in the souls of our young masters, and therefore we must place religious instruction—that is, to speak distinctly, Christian instruction—in the first rank in the education of our normal schools. We must teach our children that religion which civilized our fathers—that religion whose liberal spirit prepared, and can alone sustain, all the great institutions of modern times. . . .

"The less we desire our schools to be ecclesiastical, the more ought they to be Christian. It necessarily follows, that there must be a course of special religious instruction in our normal schools. Religion is, in my eyes, the best—perhaps the only—basis of popular education. I know something of Europe; and never have I seen good schools where the spirit of Christian charity was wanting. Primary instruction flourishes in three countries—Holland, Scotland and Germany; in all it is profoundly religious. . . .

"No more than grapes can be gathered from thorns, or figs from thistles, can any thing good be hoped from school-masters who are regardless of religion and of morality. For this reason religious instruction is placed at the head of all other parts of education: its object is to implant in the normal schools such a moral and religious spirit as ought to pervade the popular schools. . . .

"I must confess, that in religious instruction I do not confine myself to any particular method; I try by meditation to bring the thing clearly before my own mind, and then to expound it intelligibly, in fitting language, with gravity and calmness, with unction and earnestness, because I am convinced that a clear exposition obliges the pupils to meditate, and excites interest and animation. Christianity ought to be the basis of the instruction of the people; we must not flinch from the open profession of this maxim; it is no less politic than it is honest. . . .

"I am not ignorant, sir, that this advice will grate on the ears of many persons, and that I shall be thought extremely *dévot* at Paris. Yet it is not from Rome, but from Berlin, I address you. The man who holds this language to you is a philosopher, formerly disliked and even persecuted by the priesthood; but this philosopher has a mind too little affected by the recollection of his own insults, and is too well acquainted with human nature and with history, not to regard religion as an indestructible power; genuine Christianity as a means of civilization for the people, and a necessary support for those on whom society imposes irksome and humble duties without the slightest prospect of fortune, without the least gratification of self-love."

The second item of our address demands at least an equal share of your attention. The question, the great question, before this Convention, and in the wishes of very many in Eastern and Western Virginia, is yet to be discussed. Having sketched a rude outline of the essential elements of a proper system of primary and common school education, the next and all-absorbing question is, *How shall such a system be established and made commensurate with the wants of the whole community?* We are not, indeed, left wholly to imagine how such a system might be introduced and consummated, nor to argue from *a priori* and abstract reasonings its practicability. Other states and nations have gone before us, and not only taught us the golden theory that *the great end of all human government is to teach men to govern themselves,* and that therefore it is the duty of the Government to provide a system of national education, and to place it under a very strict and rigid supervision,—we say, they have not only expounded to us the sage theory, but have actually exemplified it by a variety of successful experiments.

Saxony, the cradle of liberty, because the cradle of Protestantism, first conceived the theory, but Prussia first developed and put it in full operation. It was under that rather paternal than monarchical Government that the world first saw the entire youth of a whole nation at school—three millions of children well educated during eight years—the whole expense being paid by about five millions of adults. Prussia will soon exhibit to the world a grand but rare spectacle—a whole nation of fifteen millions strong, every individual comparatively well educated. For half a century she has been trying many experiments, maturing and perfecting a grand scheme of popular education. Advancing from one improvement to another, in a long series of experiments, she has now arrived at such an enviable eminence as to attract the attention and command the veneration of the civilized world.

She, however, had her feeble infancy and childhood in these benevolent and patriotic efforts before she reached her manhood prime. We also must have ours. When, however, we begin profiting at her expense and by her experience, and by that of other nations, especially by the enterprise of our sister States, we may expect to advance more rapidly than any of them.

It must be frankly admitted that we have some difficulties peculiarly our own—difficulties unknown to those States and nations that have led the way in public instruction. We have a large territory, much of it mountainous, a sparse population, farms large, roads bad, streams unbridged, no districts, without any metes or boundaries or divisions other than those irregular, disproportionate and misshapen things called *counties*, of all sizes and figures, varying from twenty freeholds to territories equal in size to ancient Greece and sundry other renowned kingdoms of former times.

Other nations and States have various subdivisions of territory favorable to a district or common school system. Prussia has her Gemeinden, her Kreis, her Regierungen and her Provinz; France has her Communes, Cantons, Arrondissements and Departements; England has her Parishes, Townships, Counties; but Virginia knows nothing less than a county.

In order to any system of common schools worthy of public patronage, a survey and distribution of counties into some sort of districts, either according to territory or population, or a mixture of both, would be an indispensable preliminary. We take the world in some respects as we find it; but, really, I have long thought that a new survey of all the Southern and some of the Middle States, after the manner of Ohio, Michigan and certain other new States, would be the shorter and cheaper way of placing school and other public matters on a rational, convenient and economical basis. We would save more in one single census than would pay the whole expense, and would thus lay a permanent foundation for various important improvements.

But another difficulty in Virginia, it is alleged, is found in the fact that the aristocracy are more disposed to patronize colleges and one great Eastern university, than to extend education throughout the length and breadth of the land. Perhaps, indeed, there may be some foundation for this imputation of this exclusiveness of feeling. Well, as two wrongs cannot make one right, we must be cautious that we do not set up a rival monopoly of common schools against colleges. In the sacred and benevolent cause of education we are not allowed to have any castes or parties; we are neither aristocrats nor democrats; we do not plead for the rich or for the poor, but for the people, the whole people, and nothing but the people. Such is my theory. I am for rendering to all their dues. I would not rob the poor for the rich, nor would I filch from the rich to benefit the poor. We must have common schools, normal schools and colleges. The whole wants of society must be met.

All persons have not exactly the same physical or the same intellectual appetites and tastes. Nature suits them all. So must we have common schools suited to the common wants of all; but should there be some who have larger appetites and peculiar varieties of tastes, we must have high schools and colleges for them, as well as common schools for the others.

But, my fellow-citizens, it is a great mistake to imagine that we want colleges for the rich and common schools for the poor. Political demagogues may say so, and perhaps they may have no more sense than to think so. But we neither think nor say so. We want colleges for those who by nature's moulding and formation have more appetite, taste and capacity than the common standard; and we want common schools for all. We must satisfy the common wants of all, and the peculiar wants of the few. But this commonalty and this minority are not the rich nor the poor. The rich are not the monopolists of genius, talent or capacity; nor are the poor necessarily the monopolists of sterile minds and humble capacity. Let us not, then, act as though God had given all mind, genius and wealth to one class and withheld them from the other. We plead for an ample supply for *all*.

There are many of us in the West who will be satisfied with nothing short of a wise and just provision for all. We will not allow that it is either just or honorable that Eastern Virginia should have all the university and college powers, and that Western Virginia should have only common schools. Shall we of the West be satisfied that the Legislature of Virginia shall bestow four hundred and fifty thousand dollars on one Eastern university and put us off with an annual pittance for common schools? Let it only do half as much for two or three Western colleges as it has done for an Eastern one, and then we of the West will begin to think that we are not regarded as step-children. Let it give us our full share of the literary fund, and, with some hope of success, we shall endeavor to provide for our own wants, and repay our Eastern brethren not with empty thanks only, but with a class of citizens more worthy of their brotherhood and esteem.

We ask for colleges, not because the rich want them—not because a few only have taste, inclination or means of possessing themselves of their advantages—but because all the community need them as much as they need common schools; for without them no country has ever had, and no country can ever have, qualified teachers. We can have no good common schools without good teachers; for it is now a canonical maxim in France and Prussia, almost as evident and current as the golden rule, that, "*as is the master, so is the school.*" An ill-educated and immoral teacher is a pest rather than a blessing to any community. I wonder not, then, that Prussia and other States which have paid much attention to common schools have found it indispensable to establish *normal schools* or colleges for the education of school-teachers.

The system requires it. If the whole State were divided into school-districts, and had school-houses erected and public libraries in them all, without a proper supply of accomplished teachers it were comparatively labor and expense in vain. We must have colleges or normal schools to supply teachers; and, therefore, in pleading the cause of universal education, we must not oppose colleges and universities—the only means now extant of supplying ourselves with teachers.

New York now wants one thousand teachers every year. Ten thousand is her present supply. Of these, some thousand annually leave the business by death, emigration and change of profession. She requires ten colleges to supply her institutions. How shall we supply ours?

We must have a supply of teachers in view, whatever plan we may adopt. The more respectable the qualifications we require in our teachers, and the greater the remuneration we give them, the greater the benefit to the whole community. Colleges and common schools are reciprocally advantageous to each other. True, we want hundreds of common schools for every college. There ought to be, however, no rivalry, no exclusiveness, no monopoly in the views, feelings or actions of our fellow-citizens on this subject. Universities and colleges are to common schools what oceans and seas are to lakes, rivers, pools and springs of water. If there were no oceans and seas, we should have no lesser collections of water. The sun and the winds carry from our oceans a constant supply to all the lakes, rivers and fountains of the country.

We blame not the aristocracy of the East nor the memory of Thomas Jefferson for erecting and liberally endowing one great Eastern university, nor for founding other colleges in that quarter: we only blame them for not granting similar favors to the West, and good common schools to the whole country.

We have a fund, indeed, annually accumulating, which, under a proper and wise administration, together with some other aids in the way of legislation, and perhaps some additional taxation, might be made available to the introduction of at least an incipient system of common schools. But there is a singular apathy—to use no harsher name—on this whole subject. I know not why it is, that the convention which revised and amended the Constitution of Virginia refused to admit into it a single provision expressive of the necessity of any legislative action on the subject of education. I had, indeed, the honor of offering the only resolution on that subject, which appears on the Journal of that distinguished body. In anticipation of the demands of this community, and believing it would be an additional impulse to future legislation on the subject, if not a formal demand for it, I anxiously desired to have it recognised as a national object in the supreme law of the land. I therefore offered the following resolution, as reported on said Journal, page 181:—

"Whereas republican institutions and the blessings of free government originated in, and must always depend upon, the intelligence, virtue and patriotism of the community; and whereas neither intelligence nor virtue can be maintained or promoted in any community without education, it shall always be the duty of the Legislature of this Commonwealth to patronize and encourage such a system of education, or such common schools and seminaries of learning, as will, in their wisdom, be deemed to be most conducive to secure to the youth of this Commonwealth such an education as may most promote the public good."

Judge, fellow-citizens, of my disappointment and mortification to see a resolution, every way honorable (as I supposed) to the Old Dominion, and replete with blessings to the State, nailed to the table by a mere parliamentary manœuvre—by those, too, who had not courage to vote against it or formally to oppose it. In this way, however, it was virtually negatived; and so it came to pass that Virginia, once distinguished for her profound and eminent statesmen and eloquent orators, has sent her *Magna Charta* to the world without the recognition of education at all—without one word upon the subject, as though it were no concern of the State.

In providing against the difficulties in the way of a great and successful effort on the part of this convention and its friends, it is essential to our success that we have all the difficulties in our eye. This apathy on the part of legislators is supported by a more fatal apathy on the part of a multitude of the people. Since the days of common schools till now—since the project of getting them up was first named—this apathy on the part of the great mass of the uneducated (not wholly confined to them either) has generally, even after a system was provided by law, necessitated compulsory measures to require some parents even to send their children to school.

In examining the old statutes on the subject of public education in the European families, we find in some of the German States statutes enforcing what in our vernacular is called "*school obligation*,"—*i.e.* the obligation of sending children to school. In the Hanoverian dominions, provisions were made on this subject so long ago as 1681; in Saxe-Gotha, as far back as 1642; in Prussia, in 1769; in New England, early in the last century; and by acts of the Scotch Parliament, they are found as far back as the middle of the fifteenth century—at least fifty years before the Protestant Reformation. These facts are very pertinently arrayed by Mrs. Austin, of New York, in her translation of Monsieur Cousin's Report on the State of Public Instruction in Prussia, in proof that the legal obligation to educate children is no modern invention, and not peculiar to what some call the military and despotic Government of Prussia.

But it is obvious to all that we want common schools for the common wants; and the question is, How shall we get them? We do not want poor schools for poor scholars, or gratuitous instruction for paupers; we want schools for all at the expense of all. Theory might have taught what experience has everywhere proved—that few of the worthy poor, who most deserve education, will accept it under such humiliating conditions as it must be tendered on any plan hitherto attempted of having two classes of pupils in the same school—one class educated at the public expense, and another at their own. Some, indeed, who are sufficiently able to educate their own children, will, from innate meanness, accept of the poor-fund; but the really indigent and honorable poor will, in very many cases, do without education altogether rather than acknowledge their abject poverty, or afterwards lie under what they consider the opprobrium of having been charity-scholars.

To avoid all this is one of the objects of common schools; and that common schools can be introduced in Western Virginia without any or or at least with very little additional expense to the richer classes, or to the whole community, I am confident can be made apparent to all. But, in order to this, we must go to work not only energetically, but systematically. We must not wait till all the East and the West agree on one system. This would be equivalent to postponing indefinitely the matter altogether.

Our brethren of the East have difficulties—great difficulties—that lie not in our way. They have two sorts of population, of great political disparity. We are not so unfortunate. Common schools and aristocracy are not homogeneous. A patrician will not have a plebeian system of education. It would humiliate his son to learn out of the same grammar, under the same teacher and in the same school-room with the son of a plebeian! We of the West are generally too poor—that is, too democratical—for such notions. Poverty and humility have some little homogeneity between them, though we find them occasionally divorced. Were we richer, we might perhaps be a little more aristocratical than we are; for, after all, there is no political aristocracy but that which, first, middle or last, stands upon gold. This is the real sovereign of America; and the nobility are those who have most of it. Hence the easy transition from democracy to aristocracy. I have known a lottery-ticket, luckily bought, or a good trip to New Orleans or to Cuba, convert a flaming democrat into a spruce, well-starched, decent little aristocrat of full five feet stature. It is, however, problematical whether aristocracy ever did thrive in a region so high and rough as ours. It is rather indigenous to extended plains, great cities and level countries; and, being an exotic on our calcareous hills, grows slowly, and is, upon the whole, of a sickly appearance. We, therefore, in the great aggregate of our population, would be glad to send our children to the same good common school, and would have no patrician scrupulosity of conscience in permitting them to read the same primer or Greek Testament with those of mere plebeian honors, whose good fortune it might be, perchance, to be placed under the same teacher.

Again, our plebeian farms are smaller, and therefore our sons and daughters would not have to walk from the centre of a thousand-acre parallelogram to see the domicile of a near neighbor, or to explore a school-house situate in the middle of three or four such plantations, with not more than a dozen elect pupils assembled in the sunniest days of the year. The propinquity of less patrician inheritances is our happier lot; and, therefore, not merely equality of fortune but propinquity of residence are signs in our zodiac favorable to a cordial co-operation in the introduction of a common school system. A simultaneous, well-concerted, vigorous and persevering effort on our part is all that is necessary to the success of this great enterprise.

Still the question recurs, How is the system to be introduced? Without further delay, I shall then frankly suggest, with great deference to the opinions of others, my views of the ways and means by which common schools may be established in Western Virginia.

1st. Public lecturers could be obtained, who would, at several points in each county, lecture at full length upon the whole subject of common schools and primary instruction, pointing out clearly the intellectual and moral wants of the community, the nature and objects of a system of common education, developing its numerous advantages to society, political, moral and economical, and urging its claims upon all humane and benevolent persons. This, together with the labors of the periodical press, would enlighten the people on their great interests in such a system.

2d. In the second place, petitions can be got up, and addresses to the legislature, praying for a fair distribution of the annual avails of the Literary Fund to all Western Virginia, or to such ranges of counties and districts in it as may agree in one system of operations, after having done proportionally as much for the colleges of Western Virginia as for those of the East.

3d. Power also may be obtained from the Assembly for every county in a given district, or even for a single county by itself, by and with the consent of a majority of the voters in such county, or district of counties, to levy an *ad valorem* property-tax, to be added to the annual dividend of the Literary Fund from the State, for the purpose of creating a common school fund for the aforesaid district; to which also voluntary subscriptions from the more wealthy and benevolent may be added.

4th. The counties can and should be surveyed into school districts five or six miles square, or of such other dimensions as will be most equitable and convenient for all the population. In the centre of each of these districts one good school-house should be erected, and one good teacher engaged at the public expense. These districts ought to be arranged with regard to the sparseness or density of the population, including not less than fifty nor more than one hundred families in one district. In this district school all the pupils should be placed on an equal footing, so far as equal rights are involved. There should be neither rich nor poor scholar known in the district school. They should be all district pupils, in a district school and under a district teacher. This should be the sum of all the distinctions, titles and honors in their charter.

5th. School committees and a treasurer, men of probity and responsibility, should be elected or otherwise appointed in each district, who should obtain competent instructors and strictly and faithfully supervise the schools.

Here are five practicable means, which, whenever any county or number of counties in Virginia pleases, can be adopted and made very efficient, to establish and sustain common schools in a county or in a large district.

I am a practical man, and advocate practical schemes. When we cannot accomplish all we want at once, we must do what we can. We must begin and persevere, and we shall not fail to consummate our wishes. That this will cost us little or nothing more than the present invidious, selfish and impotent system, can be easily demonstrated. For example, suppose that there are only fifty families in one school district, the least we have contemplated, none of them probably more than from one and a half to two and a half miles from a centre school-house. Suppose that these fifty freeholds should have a school-tax levied upon them, averaging five or six dollars each: can not any one see that this sum, with the addition of only fifty dollars from the Literary Fund, would constitute an annuity equal to the necessary expenditures of that district for a good common school? Here would be an annuity of from three hundred to three hundred and fifty dollars per annum, a sum adequate to secure a respectable teacher in most districts in Western Virginia. And although this be a less average sum than any head of a family, with a freehold of fifty acres, should ordinarily pay for the education of his own children, under such a system as we have projected it would be amply sufficient to educate all the children, rich and poor, within said district, for as many years as may be necessary to the attainment of a good common school education.

Fellow-citizens, I have doubtless exhausted your patience,—unless you have an unusual share of that article; still I feel as though I had hardly touched the subject, and regretting, as I do, the adverse circumstances which have forbidden me the pleasure of participating in your counsels, I could not do less than give a general sketch of my views on the whole premises which I supposed were directly to come before you.

The subject of common schools and common education has long been regarded by me as one of paramount importance to the patriot, the philanthropist and the Christian. When we consider that at least *nineteen-twentieths* of the whole population obtain from common schools all the scholastic education they ever obtain, and that most of our public functionaries—our legislators, judges, magistrates and leading men—there receive the first elements of thought, their rudimental views and conceptions of men and things, of how much importance it is to the world that we have not only a sufficient number of them, but that we have them under the best possible intellectual and moral discipline!

What a melancholy thought that, in the great, ancient, venerable and opulent Commonwealth of Virginia, there is one county possessing more than twenty-one hundred adults that cannot read!* What a waste—what a dreary waste—of uncultivated intellect! What a loss to the present and to future times! What a loss of intellectual and moral pleasure to those unfortunate, untaught and uneducated men and

* Shenandoah county, as the last census indicates.

women! What sort of mothers and fathers for another generation? How much superior to the four hundred thousand uneducated negroes east of the Blue Ridge? Tell it not at Mecca, publish it not among the wild men of the forest, that in the civilized and Christianized State of Virginia there are in a single county twenty-one hundred persons of mature age and reason who can neither read nor write! Yet they must vote, and their illiterate vote would, in our government, outweigh the vote of two thousand and ninety-nine Solomons, could they be found. Is this rational? Is this right? Is this an oracle of wisdom or of folly? If we must have universal suffrage, let us have universal education. I would limit the one by the other. Till I shall have another sort of head, and until we have another sort of world than this, I cannot consent to think that it is good, or reasonable, or fair, or honorable that the vote of a Franklin, a Jefferson, a Madison, or a Washington, should be neutralized by that of one who never knew the letters that compose his own name, or read one verse of the Bible in any language spoken by the many-tongued tribes of men! The right of suffrage in the hands of such voters, uneducated in morals and literature, is like a razor in an infant's hand, or a flambeau in the hands of a drunkard in a magazine of gunpowder. I care not for measuring or counting votes by cash, whether in the form of land, or gold, or bank-notes, or sheep, or cattle, or asses. The poor man's vote may be as good as that of Monsieur Girard or that of Baron Rothschild; but that ignorance should neutralize intelligence, or that two thousand uneducated persons should decide the election of a State or the fate of a nation, is, to my mind, no less preposterous than the custom of naturalizing certain foreigners who swear to support a Constitution not one word of which they have ever heard or ever read.

On whose heads, may I ask, rest the shame and the guilt of those untaught thousands of adults in Western Virginia, who cannot read the Saviour's name, nor one line of the gospel of eternal life! Some must be to blame. "Their parents," you say. But perhaps they were left orphans, or their parents had not such a legacy to transmit to them: for I contend that a moral and virtuous parent will always in our country either teach his children, or have them taught, to read, provided always he can read himself. The State, then, is to blame; that is, the community is to blame. But that community consists of individuals; and hence the blame is to be distributed amongst them. Well, then, fellow-citizens, let us endeavor to clear ourselves of this manifold evil. Let us all discharge our relative duties to the State, and we shall soon have an intelligent, virtuous and happy community.

The scheme I propose is practicable, and you can make it popular. In other countries, the few that opposed have often been among the first to partake of its blessings and to sound the praises of the system. Let us enter upon the labor, persuaded that it is a good and necessary one; let us commence, in the assurance that it is perfectly practicable; let us put forth our energies in the confidence of ultimate success; let us take "a long pull, a strong pull and a pull all together," and we shall gain for ourselves, our country and posterity, richer blessings, political and religious, than ever followed the blood-earned victories of the Alexanders, the Cæsars or the Napoleons of the earth. Their reward was the wild huzzas of maddened multitudes—ours will be the approval of conscience, the smiles of Heaven, and the thanks of a grateful, virtuous and happy posterity.

ADDRESS.

THE PHILOSOPHY OF MEMORY AND OF COMMEMORATIVE INSTITUTIONS.

TO THE

UNION LITERARY SOCIETY, WASHINGTON COLLEGE, 1841.

MR. PRESIDENT,

And Gentlemen, members of the Union Literary Society:—

An incident occurred on the 10th of November in the year of our Lord 1808, which has occasioned our meeting together this evening. That incident is of some interest both to you and me, else we had not assembled in commemoration of it. It was the day of the nativity of your literary institution—a day in which the founders of your association resolved to prepare themselves more thoroughly for the enjoyment of the social state, by placing themselves in a new relation to one another, and solemnly agreeing to discharge to one another certain social duties and obligations with a special reference to their mutual improvement. They very naturally imagined that they could create a miniature world, in which, on a limited scale, they would have the great world of mankind represented in all those points affecting their literary and moral improvement. They discovered in themselves certain common wants and desires, as well as certain individual aptitudes and powers of supplying those wants and of gratifying those desires; and, in order to this, they agreed to meet on a certain day in every week, and to come with all the available means of improving one another, and of being improved—by comparing their respective views, and calling forth their individual energies in discussing such questions as naturally tended to the development and cultivation of their intellectual and moral powers, and thus fitting themselves for advantageously acting their part on the great theatre of the world.

You, their successors, approving of these objects of their association, and of the principles and motives which influenced them thus to act, have incorporated yourselves with them as component members of the same institution, and, in pursuance of the very laudable objects of your association, have met this evening to receive an anniversary address from one who cannot but feel himself both honored and happy in being invited to further the wise and benevolent ends of your institution.

To me, gentlemen, it is frequently no easy task to select a subject pertinent to the occasion. During the last three months—the busiest in my life—the subject of *commemorative institutions* has occurred to my mind as one of some importance; and presuming it to be as apposite to the present occasion as any I could think of, I decided to offer you a few practical thoughts on THE PHILOSOPHY OF MEMORY AND OF COMMEMORATIVE INSTITUTIONS.

Preparatory to this, however, it is expedient that we very briefly glance at the faculty of memory itself, as a prerequisite to the comprehension of the philosophy of commemorative institutions. But, gentlemen, what can we say of memory that has not been already said, and better said than we can say it, by some of the great masters of mental philosophy, such as Bacon, Locke, Reid, Watts, Stewart, Brown, or Combe? We shall not attempt to say what they have said, in the way of developing the abstract nature or peculiar attributes of any faculty, instinctive or acquired, denominated Memory. With us, memory is contemplated merely as a monumental tablet, not as an organ nor as an active power. Recollection, indeed, is a faculty, an active power of reading what has been written and inscribed on the tablet of memory. Memory is as passive as the marble tables on which the finger of God inscribed the ten everlasting precepts, while recollection is as active as the pulse of life in reading the inscriptions on those mysterious and incomprehensible tables.

It is, indeed, agreed by the ancients and the moderns that, of all the faculties or capacities of improvement bestowed on man, either associated with, or supplementary to, reason, memory is first in rank, if not in development. The powers usually styled perception, memory, reflection—or, if any one prefer the new nomenclature to the old, the perceptive and reflective powers—are the eyes, and ears, and hands of the soul; without which its very existence were unknown to itself.

Instead, then, of descanting upon themes so trite as the usual disquisitions upon this noblest of our intellectual powers, permit me to invite your attention to it as one of the most sensible and incontrovertible demonstrations of the immateriality, if not immortality, of the human soul.

To locate this power is nowadays regarded as wholly impossible. The new philosophy avers that, though it has a name, it is without a habitation. Gall, Spurzheim, and Combe, the illustrious trio of the new school, can find for it no organ at all; and the metaphysicians of the old school could never find a single cavern for it within all the enclosures of head or heart. In their sublimated and ethereal science, it is a faculty of the soul—an abstract essence, which the most exquisite *forceps* ever invented by imagination could not seize or hold up to the eye of the mind for the millionth part of a second.

If material it be, it is matter borrowed from another sphere. It is some of the mould or clay of heaven—of a peculiar unearthy type and temper. It is spiritual matter—a substratum so ethereal and divine as to elude the intellectual grasp and comprehension of a new Aristotle—seventy times more ideal and refined than the celebrated author of the Ten Predicaments.

Upon its tablet it is, however, agreed there can be written not only all the words of a living or a dead language, but those of many living and dead languages, together with as many volumes of science and images of persons, places, events, facts and documents of individual experience as would busily occupy the oldest antediluvian sage during his whole life of a thousand years to read or recall. Gentlemen, can any of you deny the fact, or, affirming it, can you explain it? Can you show from any earthly material, analogy or fact, how it is possible to engrave or write over a billion or a quadrillion of times the same substance and still preserve the distinct clear legibility of every letter and point? Take the phrenological sinuosities, folds and convolutions of any organ of the brain, each having its own book-keeper with his celestial patent for short-hand abbreviations, and ask how he can write a million of pages upon them, or upon the ends and points of those intellectual horns, blunted only by the bony case which envelops them. Or take the fine fluids of a Voltaire or an Epicurus, so subtle and imperceptible that the very nerves of sensation along which they roll their gentle current of animal life cannot detect them; and suppose the soul to embark upon these tides of spiritual life all its discoveries: how could such a navy bear within its bosom the immense accumulation stowed away for years in the warehouses of Memory? Would not the smallest of Memory's craft, so often stranded on the numerous bars of such a river, be likely to fail of performing their regular trips at the call of other powers constantly waiting upon their arrival to put themselves in motion! Ridiculous and preposterous though such visions and hallucinations be, there have not been wanting men of such a peculiar organization as not only to cherish within their own bosoms such idealities, but to seek to propagate them in the world.

It has, indeed, also been affirmed that memory is not exclusively an attribute of mind; because creatures destitute of mind possess it, and, in reference to sensible objects, in some cases in a degree superior to man.

It is admitted that as respects ideas and impressions received through sensation and perception, as well as in matters of instinctive knowledge, some animals, such as the elephant, horse, dog, &c., possess the faculty of memory in a very liberal degree. But what does the fact of animal memory prove? Does it prove that terrestrial matter thinks, remembers, feels, or that irrational animals have that peculiar faculty called *mind* in man? Or does it only prove a proposition which all nature attests?—viz. that wherever there is organization there is life, either animal or vegetable; and wherever there is animal organization and animation there is a portion, or at least some of the properties, of the great Universal Mind. This is demonstrably a true proposition. Mind is printed on paper, as well as possessed by him that writes; mind is impressed on all the works of the Creator, animate or inanimate; but in some of its modifications it is *in*, as well as *upon*, the animated creation of God. There is just such a portion of intelligence communicated to every creature, according to its organization, such a measure of instinctive knowledge, wisdom and memory, as fits it for its exact position in creation, that it may fulfil the benevolent designs of the Creator. With one of our best-reasoning poets we may say:—

> "Far as creation's ample range extends,
> The scale of sensual, mental power ascends.
> Mark how it mounts to man's imperial race
> From the green myriads in the peopled grass:
> What modes of sight betwixt each wide extreme—
> The mole's dim curtain, and the lynx's beam.
> Of smell, the headlong lioness between,
> And hound, sagacious on the tainted green.
> Of hearing, from the life that fills the flood,
> To that which warbles through the vernal wood.
> The spider's touch, how exquisitely fine,
> Feels at each thread, and lives along the line!
> To the nice bee what sense so subtly true
> From poisonous herbs extracts the healing dew?
> How instinct varies in the grovelling swine,
> Compared, half-reasoning elephant, with thine!

'Twixt that and reason, what a nice barrier,
Forever separate, yet forever near !
Remembrance and reflection, how allied !
What thin partitions sense from thought divide !
And middle natures, how they long to join,
Yet never pass the insuperable line !
Without this just gradation, could they be
Subjected these to those, or all to thee ?
The powers of all subdued to thee alone,
Is not thy reason all these powers in One ?"

Thus, the memory of man, compared with that of the most gifted of the merely instinctive tribes, is as the solar beam of nature's noonday-sun compared with the feeble ray of evening's glow-worm.

They are, indeed, essentially different powers—as different as instinct and reason—as the phosphorescent light of rotten wood and the bright glow of the most radiant gem that beams upon a monarch's crown.

Let us not, however, gentlemen, lose ourselves or our subject in the curious labyrinth of fanciful speculations. The palpable fact is before us. The tablet of human memory is neither a tablet of brass, of stone or of flesh; it has neither length, breadth nor thickness; it has neither soildity nor gravity: yet are inscribed on it not only the words of many languages, but the history of nations, their origin, progress and fall. The actions of their kings and their princes, their heroes and their statesmen, their philosophers and their sages, their orators and their poets — with all their arts of war and of peace—are recorded not only on the same mysterious and unearthy substratum, but are repeated many quadrillions of times, and yet are clearly legible and unambiguous.

The art of reading these monuments and inscriptions of the past is as mysterious and inexplicable as the art of writing upon the same substance and upon the same lines, already written over so unspeakably often, the scenes and the transactions, the thoughts and the emotions, of the present. Who of the prosing materialists, so profoundly read in the secret operations of nature, can explain to us, on their own philosophy, that imponderable, intactable, immeasurable, invisible point, or line, or substance, on which can be written, and from which can be read, so many millions of ideas and impressions? With what curious magnifying microscope shall its dimensions or its location be ascertained? If it be a lonely pilgrim, wandering from organ to organ—having neither sympathy, homopathy nor antipathy in common with flesh, blood or bones—who can describe its most peculiar personality, or draw out the lineaments of its singular physiognomy, that we may distinguish and honor it with appropriate regards?

It is found in the heart, and yet is no part of it. Its presence or its absence affects not in the least its dimensions or its gravity. What a new and sublime chapter in intellectual chemistry will the development of this singular fact afford!—the exposition of the reason why one head in the balance, without a single idea, and destitute of life, will weigh just as much as one of the same dimensions, density and solidity, having within it life, and, in legible characters, imprinted a hundred or a thousand volumes. Who can survey that curious point, or line, or surface on which may be engraven the history of a world and the experiences of an eternity—itself, too, subject to impressions from every sense and from every thing, real and imaginary, commanded by something called *attention*, and controlled by something called *volition?*

Where now the materialist, the skeptic, the atheist? Let them expatiate on matter, solid, fluid, gaseous, aeriform; let them bring their intactable crucibles, their hypothetical laboratories, their imponderable agencies, and distil the quintessence of that substratum on which are legibly inscribed all that is written upon the tomes of an Alexandrian Library; let them demonstrate the peculiar attributes, essential and accidental, that belong to that nameless substance, more durable than marble or brass, and yet of so delicate a texture and so fine a surface as to receive the most gentle touch of the softest pencil in Fancy's pallet when portraying upon it the phantoms of some imaginative scene.

I presume not to speculate on a subject so incomprehensible. I only affirm the conviction that a more instructive exemplification of the infinite superiority of mind to all earthly matter, and a more soul-subduing demonstration of the fact that there is a spirit in man composed of no earthly elements, cannot, in my humble opinion, be afforded, than are deducible from the philosophy of memory, and the art of recollecting or reading off whatever may have been fairly inscribed upon it.

But when the whole philosophy of memory and of commemorative institutions becomes the theme of contemplation, we are obliged to inquire after the *cui bono?* the benevolent designs of the Great Author of all good in those manifestations of his bountifulness to man. And, in the first place, our attention is called to the use of memory itself, before we consider the character and object of her commemorative rites.

It requires but a slight power of abstraction to perceive that man, though possessing every other attribute and capacity that belongs to his nature, wanting only the single power we call *memory*, must have continued as he was born—a perfect infant in knowledge—a speechless, idealess, thoughtless biped, deriving neither intelligence, impulse nor motive from a single incident, sensation or reflection in his whole antecedent existence. The universe, in all its developments of wisdom, power and goodness, in all its demonstrations of riches, beauty and magnificence, as well as the soul within him, would be to him one universal and perpetual *carte blanche*—an indistinguishable mass of being, without a single manifestation of design indicative of its great and glorious Author. Destitute, as the animal man is, of that measure of instinct belonging to inferior creatures, without memory, we may safely affirm, he could not live at all. Eating and drinking would be to him as great a mystery every hour as it was when first he appeared upon the stage of life. It is, then, an essential attribute of the human soul—of the being designated *man*—without which, neither the past, the present nor the future would be known, appreciated or enjoyed.

But to delineate even the outlines of its designs in the development of the human soul and in the formation of human character, it is requisite that we briefly advert to one or two of its primary functions.

It as certainly causes the soul, or mind, to grow in stature, in all its dimensions, as the atmosphere we inhale and the food we eat contribute to the growth of the body. There is as certainly a spiritual system with which the human soul is homogeneous, as there is a material system with which the body sympathizes. Each element in man seeks its kindred system, and as naturally tends to it as the atoms of material nature seek their kindred and common centres. It is requisite, therefore, that the mind have powers of assimilation and accretion as well as the body. The body is destined to grow, and for this purpose it has its apparatus of separating from external and surrounding elements whatever is congenial with its peculiar organization. It has the power of gradually assimilating such elements, and finally of incorporating them with itself. Just so the inward man, and the spiritual system with which it is kindred. It communes with mind and all its manifestations in sensible nature; and for this purpose it needs and is provided with an appropriate apparatus for secerning from inert matter the indications of reason, adaptation and design—of assimilating these and of incorporating them with itself, and thus of increasing its stature, its capacities and its vigor.

Who does not perceive, when the question is presented to him, that if the body, by its Creator, has been endowed with that marvellous power of abstracting from all the elements around it such particles as it can assimilate to itself and incorporate with the different departments of its own organization, to its great enlargement and corroboration, there can be no reason why the soul should not have the same powers and capacities of assimilating to itself whatever is homogeneous in the mental and moral elements, in the midst of which it has its being, and of so incorporating them with itself as to promote its own growth and vigor. This is the first and main use of reason and recollection. By means of this species of rumination with which the mind is furnished, under the names of memory and reflection, the human soul secerns and detaches from material nature all its earthly feculency and gross ingredients, and attaches to itself the reason, argument and design with which the great unseen and eternal Spirit holds an unobtrusive and perpetual communion with its kindred offspring within us. Memory and reflection are measurably to the soul what the powers of digestion are to the body. That portion of both the corporeal and the mental repast, which does not amalgamate with the system, is, by a wise and benevolent provision of nature, carried out of it. The analogy is more exact than at first thought would have been presumed. The fact is, the soul grows in stature and in vigor, by the provisions which perception, through sensation, acquires, and memory retains; and which reflection, aided by imagination, and those powers of abstracting and generalizing, converts into the very pabulum and stimulus of its healthful and vigorous advancement. By the harmonious and combined action of perception, memory, reason and reflection, the mind acquires, treasures up and separates to its own use so much of every kindred principle as is favorable to its growth and enlargement; and when, disencumbered from the imperfect machinery of its terrestrial tenement, its growth will be eternally cumulative and progressive.

When we see the amateur touch with exquisite sensibility and almost instinctive sagacity the strings of the harp, and "*wake to ecstasy the living lyre*," when we hear an accomplished reader perform fifteen hundred enunciations in a minute, without the consciousness of an effort, and when we enumerate the ten thousand acts that conspire in the movements of a single habit, what striking demonstrations have we of the avails of memory in the development and growth of the human soul!

These indications of the influence and power of memory on the acts and habits of the outward man are but a mere exponent of its more mysterious and wonderful power over the whole intellectual and moral man, in the development and perfection of all its powers. They are all as dependent upon it for maturity and perfection as are the members of the human body upon the organs of digestion and accretion.

But there is another and a still more important function which memory performs to the whole man—body, soul and spirit. By it we not only commune with the present and the past, but by its instrumentality we acquire both impulse and motive for future action. It holds up to our feet the torches of past observation and experience, and throws upon our path the concentrated light of bygone years; thereby furnishing us from its rich and varied treasures those arguments and motives which constitute the very elements of wisdom and prudence. Without the faculty of memory, how barren the incidents of the past to afford either counsel or comfort to man! Without it, the age of a Methuselah were lived in vain, so far as intellectual or moral improvement is concerned. It is a gift which rescues from oblivion the experience of the past, and which converts into the currency of every moment the wealth acquired through years of labor and sorrow.

It also furnishes us with the experience of others for our still further improvement. The illustrious dead, whose talents and whose virtues afford so much instruction and encouragement to the living—our beloved ancestors and relatives that have left our world—are entombed in memory's sacred urn, over which is inscribed all that endeared them to the living. Though dead, they yet live in our admiration and affection, and often exert a salutary influence upon our conduct. They have, too, a sort of indefinite immortality in the esteem and affections of the living in virtue of that power which memory sways over the desolations of the grave. It is just at this point that the philosophy of commemorative institutions rises above our horizon.

To aid memory in her pious and benevolent efforts to profit from the example of the great and the good who have honored our nature and blessed our world, man has erected other monuments, and inscribed on other tablets than those of the head or the heart, the names, the deeds and the excellencies of those who deserve an immortality in the recollections of the living. Nowhere heaves the grassy turf or rises the lettered stone, indicative of departed worth, that an appeal is not made to the passing stranger to pause and inquire after the humble tenant that lies beneath. It is an appeal to the living to remember the dead. It is a device and an effort to snatch from oblivion those whose names or whose deeds can contribute any thing to the happiness of the world.

The great and the noble have had recourse to monuments of costlier construction and of a more enduring architecture. From the family vault up to the proud pyramids of Egyptian kings, through all the intermediate mausoleums of human pride and human folly, we read the same lesson and learn the same moral. All wish to live in the affection and admiration of posterity. True, indeed, is it that often those magnificent tombs owe their origin and their melancholy splendors more to the pride and ambition of the living than to the virtues or the wishes of the dead. Still, it is a petition on the part of the humble tenant within, or of the constructors of the monumental pile, for a place in memory's faithful register—a desire to extort from every visitant a tribute of respect for something supposed to be worthy of the regard, if not of the admiration, of mankind. Some, indeed, of these proud and stately cenotaphs have inscribed upon them, or associate in our recollections, the memory of deeds of tyranny, misrule and cruelty, that awaken in our souls a just contempt for those whose ashes are enshrined within. These, indeed, are not without an advantage to the living. As beacons over the rocks which mariners are taught to shun, these marble biographies in epitome indicate to the living the rocks and shoals on which the lofty sons of earth have shipwrecked their fortunes and engulfed themselves in ruin.

But, when we stand before the monumental pillar which a nation's gratitude or a people's admiration has erected in commemoration of departed philanthropy and great public worth, and when the mind reverts to those generous and noble deeds which embalm in kindred hearts the memory of the illustrious dead, what deep emotions and melancholy pleasures arise within us and struggle for utterance! Could the sons of science, of poetry and philosophy find the grave of Homer, of Socrates, of Plato or Archimedes, or stand at the tomb of Bacon, of Locke, of Newton, of Shakspeare or of Milton—those "plenipotentiaries of intellect and giants of the soul"—what awe and reverence for intellectual greatness would possess their minds in the remembrance of the mighty triumphs and splendid trophies of their illustrious and wonderful genius!

Or, could the saint who spends his years in Bible studies find the cave of Machpelah, where repose the ashes of the more illustrious Abraham, Isaac and Jacob, or, in traversing the plains of Moab, discover the tomb of Moses, or find along the banks of the Tiber where rests the head of Paul, or, in visiting Jerusalem, ascertain with certainty the sepulchre of David, the tombs of departed prophets, saints and martyrs, what unspeakably solemn and sublime thoughts would spring up within him, and bewail the impotence and imperfection of human language!

It is when we stand within the precincts of those sacred spots of earth where repose in her fond embrace the mortal remains of those we dearly love or greatly admire, that the philosophy of commemorative institutions arises most clearly to our view and opens its sacred treasures to our consideration.

But, as the sons of the inductive philosophy always begin with history, advance to classification and end with deduction, we are obliged to glance for a moment at the history of commemorative institutions in order to a mere glimpse of their true philosophy.

Suffice it, then, to say that nature, religion and society have each their commemorative rites—in the form of eras, anniversaries, or symbolic institutions. To say nothing of the developments of astronomy in the kindred worlds and systems around us, the animal, vegetable and mineral kingdoms of our own globe present an irrefragable host of witnesses in attestation of the truth that nature herself leads the way in originating both the fact and the meaning of commemorative institutions. Not to appeal to the eras or the facts of the first and second dentition in the infancy and childhood of man, the distinct and well-marked periods of infancy, puberty and old age, with all their peculiar phenomena; not to appeal to the teeth of the horse or the horns of the ox—those intelligible witnesses of the number of their years; not to enumerate the growths of the trees marked in the circles of their wood—we may at once appeal to mother earth herself and her ten thousand hills and mountains, diluvial and volcanic, her deep, alluvial valleys, her mineral and fossil proofs, stereotyped in her innumerable petrifactions, by means of which she teaches us of former generations, and registers the genera and species of animal and vegetable creations, with the various epocha of their past existence. Thus nature perpetuates the memory of her wonderful achievements, and erects the monuments of the great eras, incidents and cycles of her wonderful history. On the tops of her loftiest mountains she records the fact of at least one universal deluge, and in her volcanic excavations develops not only the wondrous power of those hidden and mysterious fires that are continually excavating channels for receding oceans, and thus still more enlarging and enriching the earth for the increasing wants of man, but also affords us specimens of the untold treasures which God has concealed in the bowels of the earth for the comforts and conveniences of generations yet unborn.

But from the monumental and commemorative rites of dame Nature we turn to those of religion. These naturally classify themselves under three heads—the Patriarchal, Jewish and Christian. As persons and events multiplied in the world, commemorative institutions kept pace with them. But we can only select one or two of these, as a fair specimen of this class of monumental records.

And to begin with the first:—The oldest commemorative institution in the world is that which records the voluminous fact that nature—that familiar, indefinable and inappreciable something, admired by all and worshipped by a few—is herself an *effect*, and not a primary cause. It is in this sublime and philosophic way that the man of true science views that primeval solemnization of time called "*the Sabbath*," the first and one of the most significant and important of all patriarchal institutions. Most modern philosophers, though Baconians in every thing else, are Platonists and Aristoteleians here. They assume, because their philosophic wand is too short to reach up to the first Sabbath—they assume, I say, that nature is an *effect;* and then gravely ask in their *a posteriori* arguments, "*Can there be an effect without a cause?*" Prior to the era of facts and deductions, in the age of hypotheses and speculation, before men had learned the true art of reasoning, this was an astounding question, which brought every deist and theist to his knees.

That nature is an effect, is not to be gathered from analogy, from abstract reasonings, or from any data in all the premises over which philosophy has legitimate sway. The transcendent fact that nature has a Creator—that matter is the offspring of a spirit—a fact which is yet doubted by multitudes, and denied by many called philosophers—(rather philosophists)— is a fact, however, which is the corner-stone of the very temple of reason, of piety and morality—a fact which, to be clearly perceived and realized, seizes the soul with the grasp of Omnipotence, inspires it with the sentiment of the sublime, and causes it to thrill with the elementary emotions of every principle of piety and humanity that elevates, adorns and glorifies man.

Heaven left not this fact, the basis of a thousand volumes, to be gathered from abstract reasonings, vitiated traditions, ingenious analogies or plausible conjectures, but from a monumental institution, which was as universal as the annals of time, as the birth of nations, and as the languages spoken by mortals. An institution, too, which notwithstanding its demand not only of the seventh part of all time, but of the seventh day in uninterrupted succession, was celebrated from the creation to the deluge, during the deluge, and after the deluge till the giving of the law; and which, when transcribed by the finger of God from the tablets of memory to the tables of marble, begins with the very word "*remember*," the only word which is legitimately inscribed in every land and language upon every sort of monumental record, natural, religious, moral or political. The humblest pillar that rises in honor of the dead has either "*in memory of*" inscribed in fact or by circumstances upon its front; and so reads the fourth precept of the everlasting ten—"*Remember* that in six days God created the heavens and the earth, the sea, and all that in them is, and rested on the seventh: wherefore, *remember* the seventh day, to sanctify and hallow it."

The inductive philosopher, finding the civilized world from time immemorial observing the Sabbath and counting time by *sevens*, sets himself to inquire into the cause of this mysterious division of time. He first looks to nature, then to art, and finally to history, to find for it a reasonable cause. Nature has divided time into days, months and years, but she proceeds no further. Art has divided it into hours and minutes and moments, but there she stops. Modern history refers him to the ancient. He finds in Homer, in Hesiod, in Callimachus and others, traces of the weekly observance and consecration of time. He hears Josephus say, "There is no city, Grecian or barbarian—there is no nation—which does not rest on the Sabbath." He shuts all the volumes of human history; he presumes not to explain the fact upon hypothesis or by abstract reasonings. He opens the Bible, he turns his ears to the Sabbath and hears a supernal voice from the remotest age proclaiming that nature is not self-existent and eternal—that time began—that there was a *first* day and a *seventh* day—that nature is a work, the work of an almighty, supernatural hand—that the awful stillness of eternity was first broken by an almighty *fiat* that impregnated dark inanity with all the primeval elements of light and life and beauty.

Here he finds a sufficient reason for the universality and solemnity of the Sabbath, and also for the sacred and mystic import of the number *seven*, which is found in all antiquity, in all the rudimental nations of the earth. Here first, and here alone, he ascertains the momentous fact that nature is an effect, the work of an almighty hand; and from that moment he improves his style by forever repudiating from his speech the silly, infidel and preposterous phrase, "*the works of nature.*"

Now, as we are acting the part of the inductive philosopher, we shall select two or three more commemorative institutions, from which to deduce the philosophy of this much-neglected, though most interesting and important, department of divine and human science. We shall take a second from religion and from the highest antiquity.

Sacrifice is also as old as the Fall, and as universal as the human race. It consists in putting to death an unoffending victim in expiation of the sin of him who offers it to an offended Divinity. What, then, does it commemorate? *That man through sin became subject to death.* It commemorates this fact in all its ten thousand smoking altars and in all their numberless bleeding victims. Such was its retrospective and prospective character; for, like the Sabbath and all other religious and symbolic institutions, sacrifice had a prospective as well as a retrospective aspect; and therefore intimated the momentous and soul-subduing fact, that if man lives again in another and a better world, he shall live there in virtue of the substituted death of an innocent and unoffending victim.

But the whole ground of commemorative institutions requires that we have a specimen of a mixed character between the religious and political; and such a one may be found in the phenomena of language itself, oral and written.

If sacrifice be commemorative of the fall of man, oral language, in its most simple form, may be regarded as commemorative of the fact of a previous state of primeval innocence, when God and man held society together and communed face to face. The existence of human language is as inexplicable as it is inconceivable on any other hypothesis.

All things begin in miracle and end in nature: in other words, all things are supernatural and divine in their origin; and that which we call *nature* indicates only their mode of continuous existence. Thus, not only did the Christian religion, the Jewish and the Patriarchal, begin in miracle, but nature and society also began in miracle.

The first man, in every point of view, was a miracle. He never was an infant. Unlike every other child, *compos comporis*, he never learned his mother-tongue. Unfortunately, his mother was dumb; she was, made without a tongue. Every son of man speaks whatever *lingo* was first spoken to him; but, mother-earth having no tongue, Adam was compelled to learn his Father's tongue. He had no other language than that of God; and, therefore, as every human being speaks the language first spoken to him, Adam spoke a dialect pronounced by God himself. In this summary, direct and incontrovertible way, we establish the fact that *oral language is of divine origin;* and thus it is a monumental pledge that God spoke to the first man before he spoke to God or to any kindred being. When any one finds a human being that speaks a language he never heard, then, but not till then, he may set out to prove that human language is of human origin.

But, while the commemorative institution—human language—is in our horizon, we may find inscribed on this monument an argument for the divinity of the Bible and a further illustration of the genius of commemorative institutions.

That argument is found in the dislocated languages and dialects of earth. These all proclaim to the discriminating ear that some preternatural circumstance or calamity has happened to man that has fallen on no other creature. So far as the language of the passions and the appetites is common to man with the inferior animals, he ought to resemble them in this, that as every species has one uniform language, in whatever clime or latitude it is found, so should he have but one. The horse, the cow, the sheep, the goat, with every thing that moves upon the earth or wings its way in the midst of heaven, has each but one language and but one speech. Assemble them from the remotest islands and continents, and they perfectly understand one another; but man, "the lord of the fowl and the brute," ferried over a river or carried over a mountain, finds not so much communion often with his own species as with the horse on which he rides or with the dog that waits upon his steps. On account of this, and sometimes for no better reason,

> "Lands intersected by a narrow frith abhor each other;
> Mountains interposed make enemies of nations
> Who had else, like kindred drops, been mingled into one."

This is a monument of that melancholy fact that mankind, soon after the deluge, again rebelled against God, and, in contravention of his governmental arrangements for the settlement of the whole earth and its equitable distribution, resolved on building a city and a tower as the centre of one great empire.

The many-tongued nations of the earth, with their three thousand dialects, constitute an awful monument of the fact that our fathers at Babel united in one great rebellious effort against the Divine government; for, until then, "the earth was all of one language and of one speech."

But for this, gentlemen, your heads had never ached with the gibberish of Greece or Rome; you had never consumed the midnight oil in making sense out of the *Barbara celarent, Darii ferioque prioris,* or wasted the bloom of youth in learning the interminable idioms and jargons of nations dead and alive. Instead of this rough discipline of the soul, you had found the discoveries of all ages and the experience of all mankind—the genius of poetry, oratory, eloquence, science, and of all arts, useful and ornamental—in your own vernacular, enriched with all the varied improvements and beautiful embellishments of near six thousand years. What a finished medium of converse—what a perfect instrument of thought—what a translucent envelope of the soul—what an exquisitely-refined vehicle of the passions and feelings of the heart—would human speech have been, if all the labors of all the mighty spirits—the Mercuries, the Demosthenes, the Ciceros and the Apollos of Chaldea, Egypt, Arabia, Greece, Rome, Germany, France and England—had been spent on one language and on one universal medium of thought and feeling! But, alas! the bankrupt fortunes of our parents' follies are the inevitable portion of the meagre inheritance of fallen man.

The Jewish passover and the anniversary of our national birth are the only two political commemorative institutions which we shall add to the induction of monumental rites. The passover has been annually celebrated by one nation for the long period of three thousand three hundred and thirty-two years, commemorative of a great national deliverance from an oppressive and cruel bondage. It always reminds the Jew that his ancestors were once enslaved by Egyptian masters, and ground down to the dust under a most unrighteous and relentless tyranny, divested of every right dear to the human heart—even of the right of petition. God, however, in due time, heard the voice of their affliction. The cry of their suffering, the groanings of their oppression, entered the ears of the Lord of hosts. The era of his vengeance arrived: he arose in the majesty of his wrath, and poured out the fierce vials of his indignation upon the blood-stained throne and the wicked administration of the Pharaohs. He slew the first-born of man and beast throughout all the land of Egypt.

The blood of a lamb, sprinkled upon the doors of the Israelites by the commandment of Abraham's God, was the means of redemption, the signal of deliverance, while the angel of destruction was executing vengeance on the doomed people. That messenger of death *passed over* every house besprinkled with blood; and thus the whole nation was saved without the loss of a man, and emancipated from a long and ruthless despotism. The Jews, by an oracle of God, set apart the fourteenth day of the first month of their new era as the day for eating a lamb, with peculiar rites, indicative of this great national deliverance. Not a single year has passed in the history of that people without a solemn domestic commemoration of that most memorable event.

We too, residents of this New World, and citizens of these United States, have, as we imagine, been delivered from a very hard colonial bondage to English tax-masters. After years of unavailing remonstrance with and humble petitioning to the mother-country and its then illiberal and churlish Government for a redress of their wrongs, our patriotic and venerable forefathers felt themselves justified before heaven and earth in making a grand appeal to the whole family of man, and in declaring themselves independent of the mother-country and claiming rank as a nation amongst the nations of the earth. This event happened on the ever-memorable fourth day of July, 1776.

That was the birthday of our nation—the era of our existence as a sovereign and independent people. In conformity to this law of society, or this commemorative principle in our constitution, we have voluntarily set apart this most interesting of all the days of the year to every lover of his country and Government, as sacred to the memory of that event. The annual return of that day does, therefore, necessarily recall to our remembrance the incidents of this memorable epoch, and opens afresh in our hearts those sympathies and antipathies which prompted and animated our fathers to achieve for us so rich an inheritance, and for themselves a fame and a glory commensurate with all the days of our national existence and prosperity.

May we not now perceive the true philosophy of commemorative institutions? Are they not designed to recall past events in their most lively forms, for the sake of producing or reproducing those states of mind and modes of feeling homogeneous with the events which they record? They are a device for raising from the dead and for giving an immortality to persons, facts and events which have in them a character and a design intimately and strongly affecting some deep and pleasurable emotion of our nature—some vital interest or affection of the heart.

They are therefore an irresistible evidence of the truth and supposed importance of the events which they commemorate—a species of historic evidence of the highest character, and as far removed from the imputation of fraud or fiction as is any species of evidence extrinsic of that of the five senses. The history of the world, ancient and modern, as far back as all authentic tradition reaches, furnishes not, I fearlessly assert, one instance of a monumental institution established in commemoration of a fiction. There have ever been, as there now are, certain principles and passions in the human constitution and in human society that peremptorily forbid the accomplishment of such an effort to impose on the faith or credulity of mankind.

We judge of human nature from the samples which we have seen. We make the present race always represent the past, and sometimes the future. Think you, gentlemen, that ten thousand dollars, or their value in labor, could be now raised in any city, county, state or nation in the civilized world, to build a column, raise a pyramid or erect a triumphal arch in honor of a person who never lived, or of a military or any other triumph which was never achieved? It is impossible: the constitution of human society, the passions and principles of human action, conspire with every man's experience and observation to preclude such an assumption.

Nay, even of events that have transpired at a given time, not so much as the date of their occurrence can be pushed back or forward a single day or month. As the American people could not now be induced to change the anniversary of their national birth to the 4th of June or the 14th of July, or you, gentlemen, the anniversary of the organization of your literary society from the 10th of November to the 10th of May, so the Jew could not change his passover from the 14th of Nisan to the 14th of Tizri, or his Pentecost from the 5th of the third month to the 5th of the seventh, or the Christian his *Anno Domini* to the Mohammedan Hegira, or his Lord's day to the Sabbath of the Jew. If, then, the refined ingenuity or the polished fraud of the present day could not change even the time of observance of any commemorative institution, literary, political or religious, I ask, How could they introduce a new observance in pretended confirmation of that which never happened? Such a thing is now, always was and evermore shall be impossible to any man or set of men whatever. Nay, all history gives no instance of the kind. The history of all nations, languages and of all antiquity may be challenged for an instance of any commemorative institution got up at the time or near the time of any alleged sensible fact or event that has been proved or can be proved not to have happened. On the contrary, they are all incontrovertibly certain and demonstrable. Commemorative institutions are, therefore, a species of historical evidence of incorruptible integrity, of the highest certainty and authority, and wholly beyond the imputation of fraud or fiction.

Now, although the true and proper design of commemorative rites, as has been alleged, is the revival of those ideas and impressions, the reproduction of those feelings and emotions, which were the native offspring of those facts and events at the moment of their occurrence in the minds of those who understandingly witnessed and attended them, —I say, although this be their true philosophy, the reason and cause of their existence, still, as this design is dependent upon the truth and certainty of the events attested in those rites, they must be regarded as affording incontestable evidence of the truth of the facts themselves; and therefore the testimony which they afford in proof of the certainty of great and interesting occurrences is equally important to mankind with the design or philosophy which gave them birth. The resurrection, for example, of the Founder of the Christian faith on the first day of the week, is first made certain by the existence of its commemorative rite, and then a corresponding class of grateful and joyful emotions spontaneously arise in the mind of every one who fully apprehends and believes the fact attested by the consecration of a day to its memory.

Thus, gentlemen, as the Jews spent forty years in the wilderness while making a three or four days' journey from Egypt to Palestine, I have by a very circuitous route arrived at a point which might have been attained in a very few sentences. But, as we do not in excursions for pleasure always choose the shortest route, nor in making canals for the irrigation of a country or for the transportation of its produce prefer the most direct course, so have I led you in a very circuitous path to a point which might have been approached in a much more direct and immediate way.

In conclusion, permit me, gentlemen, to express the desire that your society may continue to make the date of its organization still more and more worthy of remembrance; and that by the high and useful attainments of its members, the wide and extended sphere of public usefulness to which they aspire, and to which you shall attain, its anniversaries for many years to come may be celebrated, not only with such honors as these, but with the heartfelt assurance of the many great and enduring advantages your association shall have conferred upon its members, and upon that community in which you design to employ your cultivated powers, in prosecuting the high ends of your existence, and in promoting the intelligence and virtue, the prosperity and happiness, of your country and the human race.

ADDRESS ON COLLEGES.

WHEELING, VA., 1854.

LADIES AND GENTLEMEN:—

We have selected for this occasion, connected, as it is, with the erection of a temple for Christian worship, the subject of Colleges. Colleges and churches go hand in hand in the progress of Christian civilization. Indeed, the number of colleges and churches in any community is the index and exponent of its Christian civilization and advancement. There is, it appears, designedly or undesignedly, some sort of a connection or relationship between them. The oldest college found in the annals of the world is thus associated. Seven hundred years before the Christian era there was a college in Jerusalem, intimately associated with religion. A prophetess made it her abode, in connection with other eminent personages. But we presume not to say what were its peculiarities or distinguishing characteristics. "Schools for the Prophets" there were in the days of the kings of Israel. Indeed, in the latitude of this word *prophets*, nothing is specific, save that they were teachers of the people, and, in some way, connected with the teaching of religion.

But, as we can learn little from these colleges, we shall say little of them, and request your attention to those institutions called colleges amongst ourselves, and in the history, progress and philosophy of which we and our contemporaries are better informed and incomparably more interested.

Colleges and schools of every rank are, or ought to be, founded on some great principle in human nature and in human society. They are presumed to have been, and of right ought to be, founded on a sound philosophy of man, in all his relations to society and the universe. Hence, the first question to be satisfactorily settled is, *What is man?* Lord, what is man? The greatest mystery to man is often man himself. It is yet with myriads of our race a litigated question, Is he a mere animated particle of this earth—a purely physical and animal being? If he be so, then his education or development should be purely physical, differing little from that of a horse, a dog or an ox. These are gregarious animals, and, therefore, social in their nature. And, having been created for the use of man, they are only susceptible of such an education as fits them for his use and service. Apart from their relation to man, they need no education for themselves. They, indeed, according to those who deny the inspiration of the Bible, are superior to man in this respect,—that they have in themselves an instinctive and infallible law, that safely conducts them through life, and with reference to their whole destiny. The gross materialists and skeptics, of all schools, degrade themselves below these animals, in denying the Bible. Man has not instinct sufficient to choose or to refuse food or medicine. But the brute creation have an infallible instinct, adequate to all that is necessary to their whole destiny. They are, moreover, as we have just remarked, susceptible of receiving such an education and training as amply fits them for the service of man. We have schools and teachers for them. The graduates in the schools of dogs, oxen and horses are much more valuable than uneducated and untrained dogs, oxen or horses. A well-educated ox, ass, horse or dog will command a much greater price, because much more valuable to man. If man, then, were a mere animal, his education, of course, should differ little from that of the dog, the horse or the ox. And, indeed, with shame be it spoken, we occasionally find some in human form not even so well educated as their dogs, oxen and horses.

But is man himself a mere case of well-assorted instruments, with locomotive power? A mere beast of burden? A purely carnal machine? If so, in what consists his superiority to the beasts that perish? Is it that he is a biped, and more sagacious than the beasts of the field—more imitative than a monkey or an ape? Then, indeed, his education is a very simple affair, and soon consummated. But who so contemplates man? Shall we admit such a fallen creature into the circles of humanity? We need not argue such a question in the nineteenth century and in the presence of American citizens.

We venture to assume, in your presence, that man was not originally a sensitive-plant, detached from its stem by the balmy Zephyrus, breathing on Flora, metamorphosing its roots into limbs and its branches into arms, and then sending him adrift in quest of new adventures.

Nor shall we poetically imagine that blind dame Nature tried her youthful hand on the crustacea of old ocean and Terra, produced a lobster and graduated it up to man. We will rather acquiesce with Moses, in his record of the six days' operations of the Self-Existent Jehovah, whose omnipotent volition spread out the heavens like a curtain, and founded the earth upon nothing extraneous of his own fiat; guided by nothing but his own wisdom and benevolence; radiating from himself countless systems of suns and planets moving in the boundless fields of space, and in the infinite harmonies of his own unbounded goodness. Such an origin is infinitely more honorable to man than would be all the fictions of all the poets of six thousand years. Here, then, we fix our Jacob-staff, in commencing the survey of the grand plantation of our common humanity.

Lord, what is man? Thine own offspring, reared out of the dust of earth, inspired with a portion of thine own spirit, and endowed with an intellectual and a moral as well as with an animal nature. Man, then, is, in one sense, a triune personality. In his constitution, like that of the Temple, there is an outer court, a holy place and a most holy. Such is his specific and essential constitution and embodiment. In the more plain and less figurative style of an apostle, he has a *body*, a *soul* and a *spirit*. No two of these are identical. His body is an animal body of the most admirable structure and the most exquisite finish and adornings. It is a splendid edifice, a beautiful building of God, an exquisite habitation for an ethereal guest called the soul, or animal life, which is itself but the envelope of a spirit that communes with the finite and the infinite in the universe.

Greeks, Romans, Anglicans and Americans, have three distinct names for the three constituents of the triune man. The Greeks had their *soma*, their *pseuchee* and their *pneuma*. The Romans had their *corpus*, their *anima* and their *spiritus*. The English have their *body*, their *soul* and their *spirit*. No two of these three are identical, or equivalent, either in Greek, Roman or English. In the freedom or licentiousness of our language, we often confound the soul and the spirit. But this is as ungrammatical as it is unphilosophical. In the New Testament the word *pneuma* occurs some three hundred and eighty times, and is never once translated *soul*—always *spirit* or ghost. The word *pseuchee* occurs one hundred and fifty times, and is never once translated *spirit*, but always *soul* or *life*. The horse and the dog—indeed, every creature possessing life, from the mammoth to the veriest animalcule—has an *anima*, a soul or a life, but not one of these has a *pneuma*, a spirit or a guest. This word is always used when speaking of the Holy Spirit—sometimes Holy Guest or Ghost. Physicology and pneumatology are, and ought to be, distinct sciences.

From these data we ascend gradatim to the conception of the dignity and glory of man. Man is not a mere vegetable, a mere animal, nor even a mere intellectual being. In his present condition he is truly an animal, an intellectual and a moral being, and, consequently, he is a microcosm, an epitome of the universe, having within himself the elements of the earth and of the heavens—something in common with God, with angels, and with the brutes that perish. There is therefore a divinity stirring within him; for as humanity and divinity were united, not mixed, but embodied in one personality, in the person of Adam the second, so by the Divine Spirit shall our ransomed humanity be changed into the image and likeness of the glorified Adam, who is equally the son of Adam and the Son of God, and constituted an heir of the whole empire of creation.

Such being the true data of man, we have made some progress in eliminating the true theory of his education or development. We have neither amplified the field nor exaggerated the nature of the soil to be cultivated by all the sciences of the schools, and by all the arts of the highest Christian civilization.

Man is not merely his own body, his own soul, or his own spirit. These three comprehend neither more nor less than the legitimate meaning of the great pronominal *I*, myself. The pronoun *I* is purely a *personal* pronoun, indicative of all that constitutes the thinking, feeling, willing, acting personality, and not any one portion of it. True, indeed, grammarians give it gender, number and case. But in this they philosophically err. *I* has no gender, number or case. Other words, such as *me* and *mine*, have been associated with it, and substituted for it, in certain relations, after the example of the Greeks and the Romans. But *I*, as well as *ego*, and all its ancient and venerable ancestry, only indicate the perplexity of grammarians in attempting to subject this singular-plural and plural-singular to grammatical and philosophical proprieties. All our august personages betake themselves for refuge to the plural *we*. Hence kings, potentates and all sovereigns shelter their majesties under a singular-plural, and say, *we* enact, ordain and establish.

The grandeur of the fact is this, that God, after whose image man was created, is singular and plural; singular in one ineffable nature, and plural in three personalities—all of which is adumbrated in man's three natures in one personality. His spirit, soul and body are, therefore, three distinct entities, constituting one thinking, willing, acting, sublime personality, the brightest image of that Divinity whose awful *fiat* gave birth and being to this stupendous universe.

Grammar and philosophy have no greater difficulty to compromise than in this case. The reason is obvious: grammar is arbitrary and tyrannical, while philosophy is rational and consistent. *I* is, therefore, in our language, a mere representative of one personality—of one body, soul and spirit, acting in one corporation, constituting one *substantive* pronoun and one human person.

This human person, this pronominal *I*, may live, and move, and have its proper being and individuality in ten bodies during seventy years. Still, it is the same *person* inhabiting ten different houses. It may in some of these houses lose a room and some of its furniture—an arm or a limb, for example, or both arms and limbs—and yet the personal identity, and the consciousness of this thinking, willing, acting I myself, remain immutably the same.

But there is, most happily, another fact. This spirit, or inner man, while residing in one house of two stories, is not necessarily one immutable *character*. It is impressible and transformable by intellectual, moral and spiritual considerations, arguments or motives. Hence a *new spirit*, or tenant, is conceivable and possible in an old house.

It is, indeed, propounded as a scriptural fact. But it is new only in its character, not in its essence. The spirit of a man is a positive entity, and not a mere mode of being—a new temper or a new feeling; more or less, indeed, depending upon, and affording impressions *ab extra*—by its associations with other persons and their respective characters. Thus, even in one and the same body, a pure, holy and happy spirit may become a very monster in all that defiles and degrades human nature. And hence the value and importance of a rational and moral education, and of proper teachers and associates, "since as the twig is bent the tree's inclined."

Thus we are led to conceive of the proper elements that enter into the constituency of a philosophical, rational and moral education.

A school is well defined to be "any establishment in which *persons* are instructed in arts, science, languages, or in any species of learning; and occasionally it merely indicates the pupils assembled for instruction." It may be a family school, an infant school, a common school, an academy, a college, or a university. But, of whatever character its subjects or its objects, its aim should be the physical, the intellectual, the moral and the religious development and culture of the pupils that compose it. Such are the views now generally entertained by all writers of reputation, in the Old World and in the New. Such, certainly, are our views, long since reported, frequently repeated, and now reiterated in the full assurance of understanding, as truly in harmony with the wants of human nature and of human society.

There are in this view of the subject two capital ideas. The first is *development*, the second is *culture*. The first supposes that in a human being there are certain organs, powers or capacities, that may be expanded, developed and corroborated to a certain maximum or extent, which will give to the subject the entire use of himself in respect to himself and to his species.

1. Physical education takes under its special surveillance and instruction the physical constitution, in all its characteristics, and sets about the scientific development and corroboration of all its organs, especially its head, heart, lungs, stomach and viscera, essential to vital action, good health and growth. It directs the character and the extent of the self-denial and physical exercise essential to these ends, with the necessary attention to food and raiment.

2. Intellectual education, after giving an analysis of the intellectual powers—perception, memory, reflection, reason, imagination, abstraction—proceeds to the exercise and employment of them in the acquisition and communication of knowledge, including grammar, logic, rhetoric, oratory, taste, discussion and debate.

3. Moral culture is not the mere study of moral science. It begins with an analysis of the moral powers—the conscience, the affections, the passions, and the continual exercise of them in all the relations of life—in truthfulness, justice, honor, benevolence, humanity and mercy.

4. Religious development. Man being the subject of religious and moral obligations, he must be made to perceive, realize and acknowledge these obligations in every step of his progress in all the relations of life. The only text-book for this study and science is the Bible. It is, therefore, and ought of right to be, more or less the study of every day in every seminary of learning. It is the only proper text-book for these most essential and important of all the sciences and studies of life. Its Author is also the Author of man. He who formed the human eye formed it for the light of the sun, or formed the light of the sun with a reference to it. He who formed the sun and the human eye for each other, so far as vision is concerned, formed, in like manner, both the Bible and man. But the Bible came into being after man lost Paradise and had fallen into a *preternatural* state, and therefore it is as admirably adapted to man, *as he now is*, as the laws of nature were to man *as he was* at the beginning.

The Bible is, therefore, the only infallible text-book of the true science of man. No mere man, nor all humanity, could have been the author of it. None but the Author and Creator of man could furnish the text-book of man in all his relations to matter and spirit; to things past, present and to come. Without it no man ever was, is now, or will hereafter be educated. Mankind in all ages, and under all circumstances, have felt and acknowledged, in word and deed, the indispensable need of religion in order both to education and to nationality. Hence the mythologies of the barbarous tribes of earth in all the eras of humanity. Gods, altars, priests, sacrifices and worship, are both as ancient and universal as human kind.* There cannot be found in universal history a people without something called religion. A man without reason is not a *man*, though he may wear the outward form and livery of man; and reason without religion is both halt and blind, although it may be, by the simpleton, presumed to be perfect and complete.

In all nations, as well as in our own, there is a by law established religion. "What?" say some American citizens: "have *we* a *by law* established religion?" Yes, fellow-citizens, we have a by law established religion. I do not affirm that we have a *by law established* Jewish, Christian or Pagan religion, in the specific terms of a Jewish, a Christian, a Roman or an English hierarchy. Still, we have a *by law established religion;* not, indeed, in any specific form of worship, but in the rights of conscience, in the administration of oaths, or appeals to God, on the part of all the organs of civil government; from the President of the United States down to a common magistrate, and in the administration of oaths to all witnesses, according to the conscience. In these we have a solemn recognition of the being and perfections of God, of a day of judgment, of future and eternal rewards and punishments. We have, moreover, a still more specific recognition, though not an exclusive recognition, of the Christian religion, in the observance of the ordinances of Christian worship, in the cessation of all secular and legal business on the "Christian Sabbath," or Lord's day, in the recognition of every citizen's right to exemption from all civil interference on that day, and in a perfect freedom to worship God according to the dictates of every citizen's own conscience.

Indeed, we might go further, and affirm that *the Christian religion*, but no sectarian form of it, is by law established and recognized in the institution of marriage, in the inhibitions of bigamy, adultery, fornication and incest. The Jew and the Gentile are alike protected in the practice and enjoyment of all the religious dictates of their consciences towards God, without any interference or infraction of these rights and dictates of conscience on the part of their fellow-citizens. This is a very broad and rational provision in behalf of religion—of all religious faith and worship. No Jew nor Greek, no Romanist nor Protestant, can in reason or in justice demur at our *national religious ordinances* and *constitutional provisions* on the subject of religion in general, or of any special form of religion in particular.

Religion, in its essence and spirit, can never be compulsory, as in the Papal States and territories; but it can, and of political right and immunity ought to, be left to the free choice and spontaneous action of every human being. And such is its exact position in these United States; and it is as it ought to be, the pre-eminent source and fountain of all our national prosperity, dignity, honor and happiness. And may it ever be the boast and the glory of our common country that every citizen, and even every alien, may freely worship Almighty God according to the last and the best dictate of his reason, his conscience and his affections! We regard this not as an act of mercy, but as an act of justice, not to ourselves only, but to our species—to our common humanity.

As Cowper sung of England's mercy, so say we of American justice—

> "Spread it, then, and let it circulate
> Through every vein of all your empire,
> That where" *American* "power is felt,
> Mankind shall feel" her *justice*, too.

The genius and spirit of our national institutions, it is fairly presumed, and as all our experience demonstrates, must more or less pervade, indeed, permeate, all the institutions of our country, whether religious, moral or educational. We need in this case no legislative act of conformity. It is a law of our species—an order, a decree of Heaven. A theology necessarily terminates in a theocracy; a christology, in a christocracy; an oligarchy, in an absolute monarchy; a universal freedom of speech and action, in a fierce or in a tame democracy. There is a centre in every circle, and a central idea in every system in heaven and on earth. All the rest are either chemical or philosophical, intellectual or moral, religious or political, conglomeration. The central idea gives character, form and spirit to every system, whether ontological or deontological, material or spiritual.

Absolutism pervading the state, it will pervade the church, the synagogue, the school and the family. Democracy pervading the state, it will pervade every human, and sometimes every Divine, institution in it. Hence a political despotism terminates in Paganism or Popery. Is there a Jupiter Tonans in the state? There will be a Pope—a spiritual Jupiter Tonans—in the church. Is there an aristocracy in the state? There will be an aristocracy in the church. Is there democracy in the state? There will be democracy in the church. Is there anarchy in the state? There will be anarchy in the church. Hence Protestantism and Liberty are like the Siamese twins—united in life and united in death.

A papacy is an exotic in a land of Protestantism, and can never thrive in such a soil. It, therefore, largely imports guano.

Protestantism, under an absolute despotism, if permitted to live at all, lives only in a hot-bed. Thus, in America, we have, as yet, common schools; but how long we shall have them, is already a question mooted by foreign Romanists. Odious they, indeed, are, and always have been, to the taste of the whole Roman See; yet every true American citizen regards them as the palladium of our free government and the true nurse and cradle of both civil and ecclesiastic liberty. Without them, indeed, we would have either a tyrannical oligarchy, an absolute autocracy, or a fierce democracy, in both church and state.

All the centres in the universe, like our sun, are both attractive and radiating. Moons are only reflectors. In all Papal countries, the Pope is symbolically the sun; the king is only the moon. There was, indeed, one Joshua, a Hebrew, who bade both sun and moon to stand still, and they immediately obeyed him. We once had an American Joshua, who bade the politico-ecclesiastic sun and moon to stand still, and they, too, obeyed him. But our Joshua sleeps in Mount Vernon, and all the thunders of earth cannot wake him. He has, indeed, no successor,—because God creates nothing in vain. We shall, therefore, cherish the hope that we may never need another. But should we, by neglect of duty, apostatize from our religious and political faith, and superinduce a second reign of darkness, ignorance and terror, we might then need another Joshua. I fear that in that case our prayers would not be heard. For should we, or our children, for so many benefits received, crouch to such arrogance, and meanly and ungratefully sacrifice these principles and birthrights for a mess of pottage, at the shrine of ignorance, superstition and despotism—

> "And, for so many benefits received,
> Turn recreant to God, ingrate, and false,"

our country might expect from heaven a second Alaric rather than a second Washington.

Would we, then, have our posterity to escape such a calamity and mortification, let us ever plead the cause, and be the efficient aiders and abettors, not only of universal education, but of a universal education founded on the Bible, the charter of all earthly blessings, as well as of eternal life to man.

No man ever saw himself, ever knew himself, who has not stood before this mirror. It is as much a revelation of man to himself, as of God to man. A man who has never heard God speak to his soul is not only ignorant of his proper self, but also of his own species. He alone can be a true philanthropist who contemplates himself in all his relations to the universe, as developed in the Holy Bible. He must listen to the angelic anthem sung when Adam rose out of dust at the bidding of the Almighty. He must hear the morning stars sing the song of creation, when, in one grand concert, all the sons of God shouted for joy, especially when light from darkness issued, and man from earth arose, the diapason of earth's first anthem pealing through heaven's imperial dome. With these seraphic echoes and emotions in our souls, let us listen to the wail of suffering humanity, under the heartless, remorseless tyranny of ignorance and superstition which would debar even the Book of Life from the schools of childhood, youth and manhood, as if it designed to make man the tame and easy prey of a foul and mercenary man-worship.

But while we hold in superlative importance to our country and the church the common school, the Sunday-school, the infant-school—and, after these, the academies and colleges of our country—the grave question rises, *How are these schools to be supplied with teachers?* We at once answer, just as the little springs and rivulets in our fields and gardens, the creeks, the rivers, the lakes and the seas, are supplied with water. They are, one and all, supplied by the great oceans of earth.

The sun, that great fountain of all heaven's temporal blessings to man, plays off his artillery of calorific rays upon the waves of the wide-spread ocean of earth, giving life, activity and wings to its invisible particles, uplifting them towards heaven, and placing them in the swaddling-bands of the atmosphere. They are nursed into fog; then, misting along the mountain-tops, they launch into the bosom of some congenial realm of air, and, coalescing, form large companies or schools of clouds. Soon a war of elements begins. The electric spark gleams into life, coruscating amidst these vapors, until, condensed by a change of temperature, in the strife of elements, they fall upon the fields and gardens, pouring their contents into the veins and arteries of earth. Hence the springs, the brooks and the rivers of earth are supplied; thus replenishing all nature with its water of life, which makes the hills and valleys glad, Carmel and Sharon to rejoice, the wilderness and the solitary place to rejoice and blossom in the fulness of their joy. And all this in answer to the cries of earth, parched and dry, invoking in poetic strains—

> "Come, gentle Spring! Ethereal mildness, come!
> And from the bosom of yon dropping cloud,
> While music wakes around, veil'd in a shower
> Of shadowing roses, on our plains descend!"

Thus the oceans and seas furnish every drop that irrigates our fields and gardens, cools the air, and warms our hearts with food and gladness. Such, analogically, are our colleges—our great seminaries and fountains of learning. They are the sources whence issue the science and the literature, the professors and the teachers, that create the academies, the schools and the seminaries of every grade, furnishing teachers for all the schools in Christendom.

But A, B and C respond, We are teachers, male and female teachers, and we never were within the walls of a college. True; often, alas! too true.

And whence derived you your learning and science? From books. And whence the books? Originally, doubtless, from those who were nurtured and cherished in colleges. Colleges furnish the garniture and the means by which you, male and female teachers, were yourselves furnished and fitted for the work. As well assume that the early and the latter rain, "the green-growing showers" that fall on your fields, and the diamond dew-drops that bespangle the flower-buds of your gardens, originated not in the ocean, but in the balmy breezes that bear them from the lakes or rivers or seas of the earth. Or as well assume that the calorific rays that create the heat of summer originate not in the sun, but are radiated from the earth.

Men, and not brick and mortar, make colleges, and these colleges make men. These men make books, and these books make the living world in which we individually live, and move, and have our being. How all-important, then, that our colleges should understand and teach the true philosophy of man! They create the men that furnish the teachers of men—the men that fill the pulpit, the legislative halls, the senators, the judges and the governors of the earth. Do we expect to fill these high stations by merely voting or praying for men? Or shall we choose empirics, charlatans, mountebanks, and every pretender to eminent claims upon the suffrages of the people? Forbid it, reason, conscience, and Heaven!

But, as radical and most fundamental of all, we must have the true theory of education—a theory grounded in the true philosophy of man—before we can devise any system of public or private education in harmony with the genius of humanity and the wants of society. And here, again, we call attention to the importance of having the true science or theory of man before we can devise a system of instruction in accordance with the wants of the individual and of society. It has become a trite saying, that the whole man—body, soul and spirit—must be developed and educated up to the entire capacity of his nature, and with especial reference to his present, future and eternal destiny.

And at this stand-point we must congratulate ourselves that we live not merely in an age of progress, but that we have progressed so far as to ascertain, from the analytic and synthetic science of the past and the present age, that man has a purely physical, a purely intellectual and a purely moral nature, in his own proper personality. And also that these three are of necessity to be subjects of man's education from the cradle to the grave. Of these now conceded points, we shall not speak particularly. Nor need we dilate upon the physical department of our constitution, nor, indeed, upon the intellectual. Light, no doubt, has greatly increased, even beyond our practice, upon these two departments of human culture and of the human constitution. The third, usually called the *moral*, is, by some, made to include the religious nature and constitution of man. We cannot dissect the inward as we do the outward man. The inner man is not made of materials separable and distributable, as are the bones, the muscles, the arteries and the veins of the outer man. Nor can we separate the constituents of the intellectual man. We can, indeed, learnedly speak of perception, reason, judgment, memory, imagination; but we cannot separate and discriminate the lines within which they operate and co-operate. And still more subtle the moral man, and too remote from all personal analysis. Indeed, the phrase or term "*moral constitution*" is more current and popular than appreciable by most thinkers and speakers—two classes of men very dissimilar in certain attributes of character.

Moral, moral action, moral evidence, moral sense, &c., show how vague and indefinite the term has become. We have, in our dictionaries, columns of definitions of this term and all its family, derived from the Roman *mos*, *moris*,—a custom. Morals, with the Romans, formerly indicated the *customs,* or the established usages, of society, good and bad. But we choose to define it more legally and evangelically, from the second table, or what has, in Christendom, been called "*the moral law*"—the ten commandments.

But this is somewhat indefinite, because the ten precepts contain alike the elements of religion and morality. The last six are, however, scripturally, philosophically and formally, *the moral law.* Hence our duties to man, to each and every individual, is the true, the legal and the evangelical import of the term. The moral sense or conscience is that power which, when properly educated, dictates and appreciates the character of actions, as they affect and bear upon the persons, the property and the character of our neighbors and fellow-citizens. Religion sanctions these, but religion properly indicates our duties to God. Hence the law of the ten commandments is the summary outline of all our duties to God and to our fellow-man.

We, therefore, prefer to use the word *moral*, in reference to our proper theme, as indicative of our relations to God and man, merely because the term in *reference to education* is so used; and especially as the authority that sanctions the purely moral code must be regarded as alike sanctioning all the principles of religion and morality.

By moral culture or education, we, therefore, include the proper development and direction of our moral constitution, both as respects our duties to God and to man. Both are not only within the legitimate precincts of moral education, but indispensable elements of it; for all that sanctions the six precepts of the moral code is contained and found in the four precepts of the religious code, and of these the first precept is the only one in its nature and relation *absolutely* religious. Hence, the greatest philosopher that ever lived said that all religion and all morality are contained in two precepts—purely, abstractly and philosophically sublime and explicit. The authority that sanctions both is asserted and clearly stated in the sublime preamble, "I AM THE LORD THY GOD:" "*therefore*." This is a nonesuch *therefore*. It has no parallel in all the tomes of earth. Without the recognition of its preamble or premises, neither religion nor morality can be studied, taught or learned. Hence our grand corollary—that moral culture, or *moral education*, cannot be communicated or received except upon and after the admission and acknowledgment of this superlatively sublime and ineffably grand oracle. Without it, you may create a popular gentleman, or a fashionable philosopher, at the meridian of London, Paris or Washington. But without it, you cannot create a *man*, in all the nobility, moral grandeur and sublimity of his origin, relations and destiny in God's universe. A college or a school, therefore, adapted to the genius of human nature—to man as he is, and as he must hereafter be—cannot be found in Christendom, in the absence of a moral education founded upon the Bible, and the Bible alone, without the admixture of human speculations, or of science falsely so called.

But, essential as religion is, both to the school and to the state, the preternatural and unfortunate condition of Christendom is such as to inhibit the introduction of any form of Christianity into colleges and seminaries of learning. And the masses of religionists of every school are so sensitive on this subject as to prefer a college or a school wholly disconnected with any form of religious instruction, unless it should happen to be of their own peculiar type. Many prefer to banish the Bible from the college or the school, rather than to jeopard the spiritual fortunes of a child or a ward through the gloss or the theory of a teacher, that might possibly conflict with that class of opinions which they have already pronounced to be orthodox and Divine. The consequence is, that we must either have no college with the Bible in it as a text-book, or as many colleges as there are sects in any given state or territory. Either of these is a misfortune not easily to be exaggerated. The question of this age is, How is this difficulty to be met and overcome?

That it should be met and overcome, no reflecting mind can reasonably doubt. A bald infidelity or a gross polytheism must be the necessary consequence, in the absence of Bible studies. The Greek and Roman classics, and the Pantheon, are essential constituents of a college education. Not only the infidel Gibbon and Hume, but the Westminster Review, and many similar infidel works, are placed on the shelves of college libraries, and largely read by many of the students of every institution. And what antidote have we for all this poison, made pleasant and agreeable by all the associations of a brilliant style and a luxuriant imagery? None whatever, in college studies, if the Bible and its evidences are excluded.

To substitute for it the cold and lifeless formulæ of a metaphysical creed, the shade of departed truth, or the cut-and-dry question and answer of some quaint spectacle-bestridden orthodoxy, is not Peter robbing Paul, nor Paul Peter, but some cynical Diogenes torturing both. What a compliment to the towering genius of our American youth, to put into their hands the yet litigated opinions of the hoary rabbis of far-distant centuries, compelling them, ferule in hand, to take sides with those holding the dogmata of one school against those holding the dogmata of another! Such is, indeed, the fact in Romandom, and in some portions too of our American Protestantdom. And shall we of the second half of the nineteenth century, citizens of these United States, countenance, aid and comfort such an irrational, discourteous and intolerant despotism over the minds of our own offspring?

There is but one sovereign remedy for these educational difficulties and embarrassments. We Protestants have a Bible, as well as a literature; and that Bible, as well as the Greek and Roman Bible, states certain prominent Christian facts, precepts and promises, so plainly, so perspicuously and so fully that all Christendom admits them. These facts, so fundamental, are, in the judgment of all, the capital items of the whole Christian institution. They, moreover, contain all in them that enters into the remedial system, and are the foundation of all Christian faith, hope and love. They are not only catholic in fact, but in import. All Christian ordinances are founded on them, and ordained to perpetuate them. These, with the moral evidences which sustain them, are so evident that no Christian denomination doubts or denies them. They, therefore, are common property, and, without any factitious aid, are competent to man's redemption. They are—1st. That Christ died for our sins; 2d. That he was buried; and, 3d. That he rose again from the dead and ascended into heaven. Some make of the last two distinct facts. But whether ascension is to be regarded as distinct from his resurrection, or as only exegetical of it, it matters not, so far as faith, hope and charity are concerned. Every man that believes that Christ died for our sins and rose again for our justification, so far as his faith is concerned, is said by the Holy Spirit to be saved.

Since, then, these facts are admitted by every denomination of Christians, they may, with great propriety, in all their evidence and moral grandeur, be taught in every school and college in Christendom; and that, too, without any censure or exception taken by any Christian denomination, Greek, Roman or Protestant. That this can be done, is demonstrated by actual experiment on our part, and with the consent and concurrence of every denomination in our country. Further than this, public instruction, *ex cathedra*, in Christianity, is neither desirable nor expedient during a collegiate course of learning.

The evidences of natural and revealed religion, by Paley and others, being already in use in almost every college in the Union, form a happy succedaneum in all respects but one; and this is, the daily reading of the inspired writings themselves, in the audience of the whole institution, with appropriate thanksgivings and invocations.

Even our legislative assemblies, and both houses of Congress, in their united wisdom, deem it expedient to have some form of religious worship daily dispensed. True, it degenerates into a form, and, too often, into an unmeaning ceremony. Were I a member of any one of these branches of our Government, I would certainly urge the great propriety of prefacing these prayers by the reading of at least one chapter previous to these intercessions and thanksgivings. It would, I conceive, greatly tend to smooth the troubled waters of legislative strife, could our lawmakers hear God speak to them before their orator addresses him.

But there are other reasons why the Holy Scriptures should be read, daily and publicly read, in every school, from the nursery up to the university. The literature of the Bible is the most sublime literature in all the libraries of earth. Its history, too, is the only authentic history in the world of almost half its existence. The Jewish people and institutions antedate all the literature of Greece and Rome, those two great fountains of European and American literature. More than half the years of the world had passed into eternity before Hesiod or Homer sung, or Plato, Socrates or Aristotle reasoned on the works and ways of God or man. The Jewish Scriptures were finished before Aristotle, Socrates or Plato was born; and David sung in Hebrew verse before Hesiod or Homer saw the light of day.

The biography and the autobiography of Bible saints—the achievements of its heroes—the wisdom of its sages—the sublimity of its bards—the eloquence of its orators—and the rational and heaven-inspired purity of its saints and martyrs, have commanded, and will, to the last generation of men, command, the admiration and the homage of the world. The Book of God spans the whole arch of time, emblazoned with its momentous deeds; and, leaning on an eternity past, it reposes upon an eternity to come. It is the only book of life, and the only charter of an immortality to come. And shall man, whose grand *epic* it is, withhold it from his fellow-man, or exclude it from the nurseries, the schools and the colleges in which are educated the generation most dear to us of all the generations of men—our sons and daughters, for whom we wish to live, and for whom we would dare to die? Forbid it, reason, conscience, and every tender sympathy of our hearts!

We make no apology to any Christian people, and still less to those at whose instigation and at whose behest we now appear before you, for thus uniting the Bible and the college. We only wish to wed the college and the Bible in the holy bands of a more indissoluble matrimony than any ever celebrated by priest or 'squire on the waters of the Mississippi. It is the charter of all our charters, the school of all our wisdom, the alpha and the omega of all the sciences and the knowledges of man as he was, as he is and as he shall hereafter and forever be.

The learned professions of all civilized communities are the benefactions of our colleges. For their endowment and support, we receive in return, as items of profit, all the wisdom and eloquence that fill the legislative halls, the courts of justice, the synagogues and temples of religion and virtue; all who learnedly minister to our wants and wishes in literature, in science, in physics and metaphysics, in the elegant and useful arts of our age and country. They furnish us not only with lawyers, physicians, ministers of religion, teachers of all the sciences and arts of the living age, but, directly or indirectly, they are the fountains of all the discoveries and improvements in our country and in the present civilized world.

I know no earthly subject, no political question, so full of eloquence, so prolific in argument, and so powerful in its claims upon the patronage, the support, the liberality, of the age and of a civilized people, as these great fountains of civilization and blessings to ourselves, to our children and to the human race. All that lies between barbarism and the highest civilization, all that distinguishes the rude American Indian and the most polished citizen, the barbarian and the Christian, has been achieved by the learning, the science, the arts, the religion and the morals which colleges have nourished, cherished and imparted to the world.

And yet, how strange it is, that of *one hundred and twenty colleges* in these United States, but one has a chair for Sacred History and Bible Literature! Of these one hundred and twenty, one has been in existence two hundred and eighteen years. Yes: Harvard University, in Massachusetts, was erected two hundred and eighteen years ago; William and Mary, in Virginia, and Yale College, in Connecticut, before the close of the seventeenth century.

The clergy, too, were the prime movers in getting up these institutions. The thirteen colleges of New England annually graduate some five hundred students; not one of whom, during his whole collegiate course, ever heard, in college, a series of lectures on Bible history, Bible facts and Bible institutions.

The Congregationalists and Presbyterians have been most active, most liberal and most enterprising in erecting colleges as well as theological schools. These denominations have, less or more, the control of full one-half the colleges in America. Methodists and Baptists have each but thirteen colleges. Episcopalians have only eight, and Romanists eleven. Yet, I repeat it, in all these there has never been delivered a course of lectures on the Pentateuch or the four Gospels. The acts of the Greeks and of the Romans are read and expounded with much learning and eloquence; but the acts of Jehovah, the acts of Jesus Christ and the *acts of prophets and apostles* have not been publicly read or developed in any one of them.

The Pantheon, the hero gods and goddesses—their amours and intrigues, their lusts and passions, their broils and battles—have been read, studied, lectured upon to satiety in most of these hundred and twenty colleges, as though they had been consecrated to Jupiter Tonans, to Mars, to Bacchus, to Venus and the harlotry of Pagan worship and Pagan lusts and passions.

Yet we are a *Christian* people, of professedly noble, humane and philanthropic impulses—glorying in our Christian civilization, our exquisite taste, our good morals, our sound discretion and our benevolent impulses. Why is it, then, that the Bible is, if not by statute, yet, in fact, thus proscribed the halls of literature and science?

The only apology is, that we fear the misdirection of the judgment, the conscience and the destiny of our children, by what is called sectarian or partisan influences; and, therefore, we must have sectarian institutions of learning, a catechism of doctrines ready made, or made to order, for the conscience and the affections of our sons and wards. Yet, strange to tell, in all the annals of conversion reported in the current century, I have not had the good fortune to find in any journal or record that one single person was either converted or sanctified by memorizing any catechism, heterodox or orthodox, throughout all the states and territories in our modern Christendom, European and American.

But we assume that if these formulas of speculative theology do not convert any one, they may save some from being entangled in the meshes of a false faith, a false doctrine or a false philosophy. This is a very questionable assumption; but, when granted, what does it mean? That mere ecclesiastic or magisterial authority alone, and not reason or investigation, is of any value or importance in giving direction to the understanding, the conscience and the heart of saint or sinner.

In physics or in metaphysics, in philosophy or in science, there was no progress—no perceptible or valuable progress—for many centuries; during, indeed, the entire reign of the Aristoteleian philosophy and the tyranny of the mere logical and catechetical learning. Answers printed or written, for stereotyped questions, propounded in seminaries of learning—I care not what the subject or the science—never made a thinker, a scholar, a philosopher, or a great man, much less a saint or an heir of immortality.

It is observation, comparison and deduction that make the man, the philosopher, the Christian. It is faith in the mysterious and sublime facts attested by prophets and apostles, obedience to supernatural and divine precepts, well authenticated, and a rational and well-grounded hope in promises guaranteed and sustained by the divine veracity, that constitute a Christian.

And do we need such auxiliaries to secure the special rights of our creeds and our denominations? So think the Romanists. We may not, indeed, go the length of the Cenobites and the Sarabites. We may not have the Benedictines, the Bernardines and Franciscans; but we may have the same mystic personages, under names quite as sacred and quite as superstitious, too, and not less offensive to humanity and good taste than the Jesuits or the Dominicans, with their Inquisition and its *auto da fe.*

But we are Republicans and Protestants. Then let us act in harmony with the oracle of the great Chancellor Chillingworth—"The Bible, and the Bible alone, is the religion of Protestants." Let it be venerated as it superlatively merits, in every school, from the nursery to the university. Let its history of the past and its history of the future be daily studied and taught. Let its stupendous facts, its sublime precepts and its rich and ineffably transcendent promises command a daily portion of our time and of our studies. Let its deep and lofty philosophy and divine science imbue the minds of all our youth that receive instruction and garniture for our social system, and the high offices in the schools, the churches, the courts, the legislative-halls and great councils of our august Republic. Let no sectarian dogmata, no ready-made and finished creed or formula of faith, be introduced into any school or into any literary or philosophic institution. Let the Lord himself teach in all our seminaries in his own words and in his own arguments, and let us fear not that he may impinge upon our shibboleths or weaken our earth-born sanctions of heaven-descended truths. Bribe not the infant mind with the honeyed arguments and paltry tinsellings of your favorite dogmata, which neither their authors nor their advocates can demonstrate or make intelligible to any discreet and inquiring mind.

He that made the eye of man, can he not see? He that made the ear, can he not hear? He that made the heart, does he not know how to awaken all its sympathies, to open all its fountains of feeling, to allure it to himself, that he may beatify and gladden it forever? Patronize, then, ladies and gentlemen, no church, no school, no seminary, that does not honor God's own Book, by giving it to all the people as God gave it to the human race.

When God himself, by plenary inspiration, educated the Bible philosophers, orators and scribes, shall we embargo their tongues by imprisoning them in papal cells and inquisitorial dungeons, or by inhibiting their being read in any or in every vernacular of the many-tongued earth? Let us rather elevate them to the highest schools and chairs in all our colleges, and risk all the consequences of permitting them to speak to us the Divine Oracles, under the plenary inspiration and guidance of the Spirit of wisdom and of utterance.

Proscribe every creed and manual, every catechism and formula of sound doctrine, from all the theatres of education of every name and of every party, rather than the Bible; and fear not to permit God himself to be heard, in his own wisdom and eloquence, by every pupil and every student in the land, and leave the consequences to God.

If ignorance be a reproach to any people, and if intelligence and righteousness exalt a nation to the highest rank and dignity amongst the nations of the earth, then, under such auspices, we, as a nation and people, shall stand among the nations of the earth great and happy and powerful—fair as a morning without clouds, "bright as the sun, and terrible as an army with banners."

ESSAY.

IS CAPITAL PUNISHMENT SANCTIONED BY DIVINE AUTHORITY?

THE true philosophy of man, even amongst philosophers themselves, is yet a desideratum. We are all agreed that neither the Egyptians nor the Chaldeans, neither the Medes nor the Persians, neither the Greeks nor the Romans, had attained to the true science of man. They had their astrologers, soothsayers and magicians. They had their sages, philosophers and poets, as they had their great generals, heroes and conquerors. They had their sciences and arts, both useful and ornamental; but they had not the knowledge of themselves; they had not the Bible. Hence their proper origin, relations, obligations and destiny, were to them alike unknown and unknowable. The profound Socrates, the learned and acute Aristotle, the splendid and erudite Plato, the still more enlightened and eloquent Cicero, were as profoundly ignorant of their own moral constitution and moral relations to the great unknown and eternal God, as they were of the grand discoveries and inventions of the present century.

We may, indeed, have as exaggerated views of our own attainments in this our "age of reason," "march of mind," and brilliant advances into the mysteries of nature, as they had of themselves and their attainments. Posterity, too, may look back upon our age as we are wont to contemplate ages long since passed away, and wish, as "duteous sons, their fathers had been more wise." Certain it is, that we are not satisfied with ourselves, and that a spirit of inquiry, revolution and change is now abroad in the land, which no man can limit or restrain.

We live in the midst of a great moral revolution. Opinions held sacred by our fathers, usages consecrated by the devotion of ages, institutions venerated by the most venerable of mankind are now subjected to the same cold, rigid analysis, and made to pass through the same unsparing ordeal, to which the most antiquated errors and the most baseless hypotheses of the most reckless innovators are now so unmercifully doomed. Few, indeed, of the most popular theories of the Pagan schools on the great subject of man's social and moral relations, have, when cast into this fiery furnace, like Shadrach, Meshach and Abed-nego, come out unscathed.

Times of revolution are, however, more or less, dangerous times. For, as in the tumultuous rage of passions long pent up, and in the fitful frenzy of an inflamed multitude long down-trodden, the innocent with the guilty are sometimes immolated on the same altar, reared to the presiding genius of revolt; so truths rightfully enthroned in the judgment of the intelligent, and deeply cherished in the hearts of the faithful, are, in times of great excitement, and in the reign of skepticism, repudiated as reprobate silver, and sacrificed at the shrine of a licentious and indiscriminating spirit of innovation.

Ours, however, is an age of invention, rather than of discovery: the arts, more than the sciences, are cultivated and improved. The invention of printing, the discovery of America, and the Protestant reformation, have imparted to the human mind an impulse so vigorous and so enduring, that neither time nor space seem able to impair it. Stimulated by former conquests over error, and the new discoveries since made, the human mind seems intent on carrying on war against false assumptions and unwarranted conclusions—as if determined to advance from victory to victory over every species of error and delusion: so that we may not unreasonably anticipate a day when the last error shall be exploded, and the last baseless assumption shall be entombed in the same unfathomable abyss with the vortices of Descartes, or in the nethermost hollow sphere of the speculative and hypothetical, though ingenious, Captain Symmes.

But there are many things already established. The human mind is not wholly at sea without pilot or compass. The mariner's compass has been invented. And many truths are immovably fixed and certain in every well-cultivated and intelligent mind.

Physical nature is, indeed, still open to investigation in some of her most interesting and sublime departments. Astronomy is yet in progress of development. Geology is a new science, still incomplete and imperfect. The physical constitution of man has yet numerous mysteries sealed from the most discriminating eye. Not only several of its most sublime and delicate tissues are unexplored, but the design as well as the peculiar structure of some of its organs are unappreciated and unknown. The human head has only recently been explored and developed by the mighty genius and indefatigable toils of a Gall and a Spurzheim. That men have souls as well as bodies, and spirits as well as souls, seems likely soon to be satisfactorily proved, not by metaphysical reasoning, but by ocular and sensible demonstrations. Nor is the day far distant when it is presumed that all parties will agree that, as God has made the world, he should govern it.

There are, indeed, two sciences, and but two, wholly unsusceptible of improvement. These, the Author of the Universe, by a patent which no man can invade but at the peril of his eternal destiny, has both wisely and kindly reserved to himself. I need not say that these are the sciences of religion and morality. No angelic being, unable to survey the universe in its infinite and eternal dimensions, nor man, in all his mysterious and sublime organization and capacities, could possibly project or develop these. They are sciences which, by an insuperable and stern necessity, are not merely superhuman, but supernatural and divine. There is a world above us and a world within us for which no man or angel could legislate. There is a moral code beyond the capacity and supervision of man—extending, too, in its requisition into a kingdom over which no human tribunal can find any jurisdiction, and which is as necessary to moral government as oxygen to combustion, or caloric to human life. There is an empire in the human heart over which no man or angel can preside, and a throne in the midst of it on which no king can sit but the King of Eternity. For this one reason alone, which is as good as a thousand, and to which the addition of a thousand could give no weight, religion and morals are sciences wholly supernatural and divine.

Civil government is itself a divine appendix to the volumes of religion and morality. Though neither Cæsar nor Napoleon, Nicholas nor Victoria, were, "*by the grace of God,*" king, emperor or queen; still the civil throne, the civil magistrate, and, therefore, civil government, are, *by the grace of God*, bestowed upon the world. Neither the church nor the world could exist without it. God himself has, therefore, benevolently ordained magistrates and judges. Men may call them kings, emperors or presidents, (for much of politics, like much of speculative theology, is but a mere logomachy—a war of ill-assorted words,) but they are God's ministers, executors of his will and of his vengeance, ordained to wait upon him and to execute his mandates. They are a sort of viceroys—vicegerents under law to God, and to govern according to his revealed will. The Bible is of right, and it ought to be, just as much a law to kings and governors and presidents, as it is to masters and servants, to husbands and wives, to parents and children. Those magistrates, therefore, who will not be governed and guided by it in the faithful execution of God's laws, God himself, in his own proper person, will judge and punish.

Since the days of Plato, men have conceived republics. They have invented new orders of society, new theories of socialism, and new names for things. But these are mere demonstrations of human weakness and of human skepticism. The Bible has sanctioned republics, and commonwealths and kingdoms, without affixing any peculiar name to them. It prescribes no form of human government, because no one form of government would suit all the countries, climes and people of the earth. But the Bible, in the name and by the authority of its Author, demands of all persons in authority that they protect the innocent, that they punish the guilty, and that they dispense justice to all. It also demands of the governed that they submit to "THE POWERS THAT BE," however denominated, as an ordinance of God; not through the fear of the sword, but for the sake of conscience. It inhibits them also from treason, insubordination and rebellion.

In the freedom of debate, and in harmony with that spirit of innovation of which we have just spoken, a question has been mooted, and is now before the American public a matter of very grave discussion. A question, too, than which, in my humble judgment, no one pertaining to this life is worthy of a more profound deliberation, nor whose decision is fraught with more fearful and important results, affecting the whole community, involving the foundation of civil government, all the fixtures of society, the extent of all earthly sovereignty, and all the principles of international law, commerce and responsibility. That question is propounded in the solemn interrogatory, IS CAPITAL PUNISHMENT SANCTIONED BY DIVINE AUTHORITY? or, in other words, *Has man a right to take away the life of man on any account whatever?*

If he have not a divine right, I frankly admit that he has no human right—no warrant or authority derived from man—that will authorize such a solemn and fearful act. Though we should not, in the first instance, take into account the consequences of any decision, as having direct authority in influencing our reasonings upon the question, still it is important that we have some respect for them as arguments and incentives to a calm, discreet and patient investigation of the premises from which are to be adduced conclusions so deeply involving the interests of the world.

And what, let me inquire, would be the consequences should it be decided that man has no right to take away the life of man on any account whatever? Is not the right to inflict upon him any penal pain whatever involved in this question? A single stripe may kill; nay, a single stripe, inflicted by an officer of justice, and that no very violent one, has sometimes killed. A man has no right to punish at all in any way, if he may not in that punishment lawfully take away the life of him that is subjected to it. He has not even the right to imprison or confine a person in a jail, workhouse or penitentiary, if he have not, in any case whatever, the right to kill. How many die in jails, workhouses and penitentiaries, from causes to which they would not have been exposed but in those places of punishment!

But, further, if man has not the right to kill, nations have no right to go to war in any case, or for any purpose whatever. We argue that whatever power a Government has is first found in the people; that men cannot innocently or rightfully do that conventionally, or in states, which they cannot do in their individual capacities. True, when a Government is organized, the citizens or subjects of it cannot use or exercise the powers to legislate, to judge, to punish, which, by the social compact, they have, for wise purposes, surrendered or transferred to the Government. Still, the fundamental fact must not be lost sight of—that *nations have the right to do those things only which every individual man had a right to do anterior to the national form of society.* If, then, man had not originally a right to kill him who killed his brother, society never could, but from a special law of the Creator, have such a right. And such, we may hereafter show, was originally the divine law. The natural reason of man, or a divine law, enacted that the blood of the murdered should be avenged by the blood of the murderer, and that the brother of the murdered was pre-eminently the person to whom belonged the right of avenging his blood.

Wars are either defensive or aggressive. But, in either point of view, they are originated and conducted on the assumption that man has a right, for just cause, to take away the life of man. For it needs no argument to convince any one, however obtuse, that man cannot rightfully kill a thousand or a million of persons, if he cannot lawfully kill one! I wonder not, then, that peace-men are generally, if not universally, in favor of the total abolition of capital punishment.

What an immense train of consequences hang upon the final and correct decision of this question! Wars would, from an insuperable necessity, cease. We should then, indeed, "beat our swords into ploughshares and our spears into pruning-hooks." We would hang the war-trumpet in the halls of peace, and study war no more. Cannon, military establishments, standing armies, mighty navies, extensive arsenals, and all the other munitions of war, would no longer be the *ultima ratio regum*. No longer would Governments rely upon the arm of flesh for self-defence or for redress of wrongs. What millions of gold would be saved, and what oceans of blood would be prevented!

It is true, however, that wars might cease and universal peace spread its halcyon wings over the earth, and still the murderer be rightfully, and by the supreme authority of the state, put to death. There is no incompatibility whatever in the argument of settling national controversies by another way than by war. We may settle them as we pacifically settle individual and corporate misunderstandings, and still argue against the abolition of capital punishment. But our argument is, that there would be an end of all wars, offensive and defensive, in the national mind, if men have no right to kill those who have killed their neighbors. Certainly, no one would place himself in the absurd attitude of defending wars for territory—for mere depredations on trade and commerce—in defence of chartered rights or violated treaties, if it can be shown that we ought not to wage war against the most savage tribes and barbarous nations for having butchered our wives and children.

Again, if nations may not rightfully go to war—if man cannot, in any case, lawfully take away the life of man, in how dishonorable an attitude stand the patriots of all Christian lands—the Hampdens, the La Fayettes, the Washingtons! And where stand the men of faith, the men of sacred fame—the Joshuas, the Samsons, the Baraks, the Gideons, the Davids?

And what shall we say of the morality of those who do honor to their memory? Of those who are always approbating, applauding and eulogizing our own Revolutionary heroes and those who distinguished themselves in the Indian wars—in wars against untutored savages, desirous to retain and to defend their patrimonial inheritance from European invasion and aggression—of those, a very numerous host of patriotic contemporaries, who have no civil honors to bestow, no civic wreath prepared, but to adorn the brows of military chieftains whose garments have been rolled in the blood of vanquished enemies—and especially of those who desire new wars for manufacturing new generals and new heroes, the idols of a nation's worship, to fill the empty niches in the temple of our heroic fancies!

Such are a few of the consequences that must follow the decision of the question before us in the negative. Still, as before said, we only use these as arguments for a calm, dispassionate and thorough investigation of the subject. It must be tried by some law and before some tribunal having supreme authority in the case. But what shall be that law, and where shall that tribunal be found? It is not the law of phrenology—of expediency—of tradition—of our common statute-books—of even public opinion. None of these have legitimate jurisdiction over a question that has so much of the temporal and eternal fortunes of human kind at stake.

We may, indeed, listen, either for instruction or amusement, to the pleasing fancies of poets—to the visions of enthusiastic philanthropists—to the decisions of various sects of philosophers, or to the codes and enactments of olden times and of fallen empires; but from their speculations or their decisions we can derive neither argument nor authority.

Some of the most dogmatical of the new schools of philosophy assume that the sole end of punishment is the reformation of the offender; that the murderer must be sent to a school of repentance and be better educated, and, when properly instructed and honorably graduated, he shall have his passport into the confidence of society, and be permitted to develop himself in the midst of more favorable circumstances. Such is one of the most popular substitutes for capital punishment. Plato's favorite dogmas—that man was made for philosophy, and not philosophy for man—that a perfect civil code would make a nation virtuous—and that offenders could be reformed by wise and benevolent exhortations—are not more whimsical and ridiculous than the theories of such abolitionists of capital punishment. They are, indeed, but an ingenious preface to the Elysian hell of some Universalian philanthropists, who imagine that place of punishment to be but a portico to heaven—a sort of purgatorial ante-chamber, in which men are to be purified by gentle flames for an induction into the innermost sanctuary of the universe.

We agree with those who affirm that punishments ought, in all cases, to be enacted and enforced with a special regard to the reformation of transgressors; but we cannot say with an *exclusive* regard. Emphatic and special, but not *exclusive*, regard, should be shown to the reformation of the criminal. There must also be a special and a supreme regard to the safety of the state, and the protection of the innocent and unoffending. The laws of every civilized community should unite as far as possible the reformation of the offender with the safety of the state.

But how these two may be best secured, is a matter not yet agreed. A sentence of perpetual imprisonment is no guarantee of protection or safety to the state. The sentence, in the first place, may not be executed. It seldom is, in the case of persons holding high places in society. Governors sometimes reprieve. Political demagogues, too, will not very conscientiously demur at the offer of many suffrages for a gubernatorial chair, on a private understanding that certain persons of influential connections sentenced to perpetual imprisonment shall on their election be pardoned. But, further, it is no guarantee that the monster who has been guilty of one murder may not murder some of his attendants or fellow-prisoners in hope of escape, or that he may not fire his prison or in some way elope. He may be confined for life, and yet may again perpetrate the same foul crime. Are there not numerous instances of this kind on record? And has not the professedly reformed and pardoned criminal at times been guilty of a second, and sometimes of a third, murder? Such instances have been known in our own country and in our own memory. A sentence of perpetual confinement is not an adequate security against a murderer, in any view that can be taken of it. Society demands a higher pledge of safety—a more satisfactory guarantee. It demands the life of the murderer.

And, strange as it may seem, we affirm the conviction that the certainty of death is, upon all the premises, the most efficient means of reformation. When—I do not say the *unfortunate,* (a name too full of sophistry, though unfortunate he may be,) but—the *malignant and wicked murderer* has been tried, convicted and sentenced to die after the lapse of so many days or weeks, when all hope of pardon is forever gone, then evangelical instruction is incomparably more likely to effect a change than are the chances of a long or short life within the walls of a penitentiary. It is, therefore, I must think, more rational and humane, whether we consider the safety of the state or the happiness of the individual, to insist that the sentence of death be promptly and firmly executed.

So we reason against the assumptions of those who would abolish capital punishment, on the ground that all punishment should be for the salvation of the transgressor, and that his imprisonment for life, or till evident reformation, is an ample pledge for the safety and security of the state.

They reason as illogically against capital punishment who assume that imprisonment for life is a greater punishment than death. Satan, more than three thousand years ago, reasoned more logically than they. He then argued in the face of high authority, on the trial of a very distinguished person, that a man would give the world for his life.

"Skin for skin, all that a man hath," said the devil, "will he give for his life."

I am reminded of one of the fables of Æsop in the only speech I ever read in favor of capital punishment, so far as my memory bears witness. The writer, in disproof of the assumption that imprisonment for life is a greater punishment than death, adduces the following fable:—"Æsop has finely satirized the prevalent disposition to complain of life as a burden when we are oppressed by the ills to which humanity is heir. We are all familiar with the fable of the poor man who was groaning under the weight of the fagots which he was carrying to his home. Weary and exhausted, he threw his load from his shoulders, sat down by the wayside, and loudly invoked Death to come and relieve him from his misery. Instantly the greedy tyrant stood before him, and, with uplifted dart, inquired, 'What wouldst thou have with me?' 'Good Death,' exclaimed the poor man, in terrified amazement, 'I want thee to help me get this bundle of sticks upon my back.' The fable needs no interpreter. Its moral is obvious."* Were imprisonment for life a severer punishment than death, it would not be lawful to exact it, so far as the divine law indicates what is just and equal. Neither the *lex talionis*, nor the Bible, nor right reason, so far as I can judge, would authorize any punishment severer than death.

But we can very sincerely sympathize with many good men in their aversion to capital punishment for any other crime than murder. Indeed, much of the excitement and indignation against capital punishment arises from two sources:—the many crimes that have been judged worthy of death; and the fact that the innocent sometimes suffer while the guilty escape. In noticing the various topics from which men reason against the justice of demanding life for life, our design is to show how doubtful and inconclusive all mere human reasonings and statutes on this subject must be, rather than to enter into a full investigation of all that may be alleged from these sources of reason and argumentation.

We cheerfully admit that our criminal code is not in unison with the spirit of the age, nor with the presiding genius of European and American civilization. Christian justice, humanity and mercy have, indeed, in some countries, and in none more than in our own, greatly modified and improved political law and political justice.

---

* Rev. Dr. Berg, as reported in the Philadelphia "Saturday American" for December 12, 1845.

Public opinion has for more than a century been vacillating between two extreme systems of punishment—one of which punishes more than a hundred varieties of offence with death, while the other inflicts death on no transgressor for any crime whatever. During the reign of sanguinary law in England, as Blackstone very correctly observes, "It is a melancholy truth, that among the variety of actions which men are daily liable to commit, no less than a hundred and sixty have been declared, by act of Parliament, to be felonies without benefit of clergy; or, in other words, to be worthy of instant death. So dreadful a list," adds the learned jurist, "instead of diminishing, increases the number of offenders."

Such a criminal code was, indeed, very likely to lead to another extreme. It has, therefore, been yielding in severity to the more humane genius of modern civilization. The human mind, ocean-like, has its ebbings and its flowings, its high tides and its low tides, on all exciting subjects. Time was when an Englishman forfeited his life for a very paltry theft—for the mere purloining of twelvepence sterling. That there ought to be a correspondence between offences and their punishment, is an oracle of reason and justice, so obvious to all, that it may be regarded in the light of a primary truth—a sort of self-evident proposition, that needs only to be stated to any person of reflection to secure his immediate assent.

We advocate a discriminating tariff of penalties and punishments, not for the sake of revenue alone, but for the sake of protecting innocence and virtue. We have no faith either in the justice or expediency of a horizontal tariff, awarding one and the same punishment to each and to every one of a hundred crimes. We would not hang one man for stealing a shilling, and inflict the same punishment for treason sacrilege, rape or murder. We believe in the scriptural phrases, "worthy of stripes," "worthy of a sorer punishment," and "worthy of death." These forms of speech occur in both Testaments, but more frequently in the New than in the Old. They are phrases from which a sound and irrefutable argument in support of capital punishment may be deduced, and which no one opposed to it will dare on any occasion to employ.

With the profound Montesquieu, I argue that "the severity of laws prevents their execution; and, therefore, whenever punishment transcends reasonable limits, the public will not unfrequently prefer impunity to inhumanity or to excessive punishment." Nay, with a greater than Montesquieu, I believe that an eye should not be taken for a tooth, nor a few years' imprisonment for a man's whole life.

The penal code of every community should be an index of its moral sense and of its moral character. It ought to be regarded as a licensed exposition of its views upon the comparative criminality and malignity of every action affecting the life, the liberty, the character or the prosperity of its citizens,—a polished mirror from which may be reflected upon its own citizens and upon the world at large a nation's intelligence, moral taste and moral excellency. Should it affix the same punishment to various and numerous offences, irrespective of their grade in criminality, it will confound and bewilder the moral perceptions of the people, and exhibit to the world a very fallacious test of the comparative atrocity and malignity of human actions.

It may, indeed, be assumed that all sins are equally violations of the law of God—equally dishonorable to his majesty—equally obnoxious to his displeasure—and, therefore, equally to be punished. But be this view abstractly right or wrong, it is alien to our subject; for it is only with sin as it *respects man* in its injurious tendency that human legislation and human punishment have to do. The Lord has reserved to himself the right to punish sin as committed against himself, and has delegated to man the authority to punish sin only in so far as it is fraught with evils to the human race. In this view alone are sins to be estimated more or less atrocious, and more or less severely to be punished. The doctrine of sound reason, as well as that of revelation, is, "that every transgression and disobedience of the divine law should receive a just and adequate recompense of reward."

From such considerations and reasonings as these, we would advocate a scale of punishments in harmony with the most correct views of the criminality and wickedness of human actions, rising up to capital punishment only in the case of wilful and deliberate murder, not to be extenuated in any case by passion, intemperance, or any temptation whatsoever. To obviate the exception not unfrequently taken to capital punishment on the ground that sometimes the innocent may suffer while the guilty escape, might there not be such legal provisions as would prevent the possibility of any one being convicted without such strength of testimony and proof of guilt as would not leave the shadow of a doubt? We doubt not the practicability of such a provision.

Thus we reason with those who reason from their conceptions of the congruity, expediency and rational propriety of human theories and codes as respects penal statutes in general, and capital punishment in particular. Should we, then, claim no more authority for our reasonings than those who differ from us claim for theirs, (though, of course, we suppose we have the stronger and the better reasons,) we have gained this point, that, in demurring to our conclusions, we must both appeal to a higher court, and await the decision of the Supreme Lawgiver and Judge of the universe. This is all we have sought in these preliminary views and reasonings; and certainly it will be conceded to us by those who may dissent from the positions we have already assumed.

In this present erratic world there are two ultra schools of philosophy:—the one takes nothing, the other takes almost every thing, on credit. With the one, the fathers are wiser than their sons; with the other, the sons are wiser than their fathers. The antiquity of an opinion is a passport to the favor of one; the novelty of an opinion secures for it a favorable introduction to the confidence of the other. The tendency of the one school is to a blind devotion; that of the other to an absolute skepticism. We will not abide by the decision of either school. We prefer to carry this question up to a higher court—to a Judge who perfectly comprehends the whole constitution of man as an animal, intellectual and moral being—by whom the fundamental laws of the moral universe, and man in all his mysterious and sublime relations to that universe, are contemplated—not in the dim light of time, but in the clear and bright effulgence of a glorious and awful eternity. We, therefore, appeal, from all human reasonings and from all human codes to the infallible decisions of that court as registered in the faithful records of the Old and New Testaments. The question before us is, *What punishment does the Supreme Lawgiver and Judge award to the murderer?* This is a mere question of fact, and not of a philosophic theory. We must, then, decide it by testimony. We shall, therefore, make a direct appeal to the Divine Record, and endeavor to find an answer for it from an induction of the cases and statutes therein recorded; or, at least, so many of them as will satisfactorily indicate the Divine will on the subject.

The first case in the annals of time brought before this court was that of Cain, indicted for the murder of his brother Abel. Abel's blood, thus shed, in the judgment of God called for vengeance on him that shed it. His words are, "The voice of thy brother's blood crieth unto me from the ground." He immediately added, "Thou art cursed from the earth," dooming him to become "a fugitive and a vagabond."

This excommunication beyond the pale of the Divine protection, Cain understood to be a license given to any person to kill him. His language clearly indicates this:—"It shall come to pass," said he, "that every one who findeth me shall kill me." A single question on this case, it seems, might decide the matter: viz. Was this the voice of reason, the voice of conscience, or the voice of God? Rather, was it not the voice of them all? If so, then, is not the crime of murder, on its first appearance, judged worthy of death?

Does any one doubt it? Let him place the matter before his own mind in the form of a trilemma. Either Cain's own natural reason and conscience, or an antecedent law, or the sentence God pronounced upon him, decreed his death for that crime. Can any one assign any other reason than some one of these three as extorting from Cain the declaration that "every one who findeth me will kill me"? The whole three may, indeed, have conspired to produce the conviction; but certainly some one of them did; and this is enough to prove that, in the sight of God, his crime was worthy of death: for none of the three could exist without a revelation from God. Such was the decision of the first case. God, indeed, for reasons growing out of the condition of the world at that period, was pleased to reprieve him for the time-being, and gave him a pledge that no one should kill him.

Some may ask, Why did not God himself immediately kill Cain, seeing that his brother's blood called for vengeance? To which several answers may be given; such as—God, who knows the hearts of all men, and whose prerogative it is to show mercy, may have known that Cain did not intend to kill his brother, but only to humble him; or he may have judged it expedient to give proof of his mercy in the exercise of his sovereignty in the beginning of the world, waiting till further developments of the violence of human passion would justify him before the universe in inflicting adequate penalties upon transgressors; and also in demonstration of another truth, viz. that a government all mercy would not promote the safety or happiness of man; for this experiment resulted in the earth's being so filled with violence that God was finally constrained to punish the antediluvians by one common death inflicted by his own hand. This was capital punishment in the superlative degree.

What numerous and various acts of violence characterized the antediluvian world we are not informed. What laws were promulged by Divine authority we are not told. But the silence of antiquity is no proof that such laws were not enacted. For, although we have no published code of antediluvian laws, we have allusions to existing institutions which could not have been introduced without laws. A priesthood, altars, victims and sacrifices could not have existed without positive law. The distribution of animals into clean and unclean with regard not to food, but to sacrifice, presupposes very clear and positive enactments. Neither Abel, nor Seth, nor Enoch, could have pleased God, or walked with God, without law. The light of nature could not have originated altars, victims and priests. Indeed, the fact that the earth was filled with violence, is no inconsiderable argument that the will of God had been revealed; for where no law is, there is no transgression.

But, besides what is affirmed of vengeance in the case of Cain, we have, so late as the time of his great-great-grandson, Lamech, another very direct reference to the punishment of murder. Lamech, of the family of Cain, was the first of polygamists known to history. His wives, Adah and Zillah, being apprehensive of the vengeance threatened, called forth from him the oldest poem in the world. It may be translated as follows:—

"Adah and Zillah, hear my voice;
Wives of Lamech, hearken to my speech;—
For I have slain a man for wounding me,
A young man for having beaten me.
If Cain be avenged sevenfold,
Surely Lamech seventy-and-seven."

This, being written in hemistichs in the original, is generally, by the learned, regarded as the oldest poetry in the literature of the world. There is, to my mind, but one ambiguity in the passage. It respects the punctuation of the third line. It may be read interrogatively or indicatively:—either,

"I have slain a man for wounding me,"

or,

"Have I slain a man for wounding me,
A young man for having bruised me?"

Read indicatively, it intimates that Lamech killed a man in self-defence. Read interrogatively, it denies that he killed any person. In either case, he rebukes the evil forebodings of his wives; for if any one killed him, not being guilty of murder, sevenfold vengeance would be inflicted upon him more than on Cain,—than which we know of nothing more terrible. On the above version I may say I have the Jewish Targums, Adam Clarke, and other rabbis of distinction with me. The whole case, taken complexly, indicates that death for murder was the penalty affixed by the justice of the antediluvian world.

From this fragment of antediluvian history, we shall turn to the more copious details of the postdiluvian. It is worthy of special consideration that the first act of legislation in the new world, while the whole human race was in Noah's family, was *an act against murder*. This was a law not for Jew or Gentile—not for Egyptian, Chaldean, Greek or Roman—but, being enacted before any of them existed, for the whole human race. It was not an act against any particular kind of murder—such as parricide or fratricide—but an act against murder simply on its own account.

The occasions and circumstances accompanying the enactment of many laws are explanatory of them. These are worthy of special attention. The whole world, one household excepted, had been destroyed by the immediate hand of God. This destruction was made necessary because of the unparalleled violence that filled the earth. One family was wholly destroyed. This family was that of Cain, to which all cases of murder, or of punishment for it, named in the old world, belonged. The earth being thus depopulated, the family of Cain and of Lamech being wholly destroyed—to prevent the increase of crime and the necessity of a similar catastrophe, God gave to man, by a positive and express precept, the power, the authority and the injunction to cut off all murderers.

The occasion of this act of legislation, and the positive and peremptory terms in which it is expressed, alike commend it to our consideration and regard. It is expressed in the following words:—"*At the hand of every man's brother will I require the life of man. Whoso sheddeth man's blood, by man shall his blood be shed: for in the image of God made he man.*" No statute was ever more free from ambiguity, or more intelligible, than this one. I never have met with one who misunderstood it. Why, then, is its Divine obligation not universally felt and acknowledged?

To one unacquainted with the power of sympathy, especially when its victim is seized with a morbid philanthropy or charmed with the fascinations of a new theory, it will appear somewhat mysterious how a precept so express, so authoritative and peremptory could be disposed of or evaded. It is done by the magic of a single assumption:—"Christianity is more mild and generous and philanthropic than the law of Moses." But that this is a provision of the law of Moses, is an assumption which rests on the simple ground that Moses the lawgiver wrote the book of Genesis. One might as justly assume that Noah's ark or Melchizedek's pontificate was a part of the law of Moses, because Moses is the only person who wrote their history. From the age of spiritual Quakerism until now, the abolitionists of capital punishment generally occupy this ground. As there is no dispute about the meaning of the precept, the only way to dispose of it is to locate it amongst the Jewish rites and usages which have been abolished. But the simple fact that this precept was promulged in the year of the world 1658, and that Moses gave not the law till the year 2513—that is, full eight hundred and fifty-five years after—is a fact so prominent and so indisputable as to render any other refutation of the assumption a work of the most gratuitous supererogation. I wonder why the same romantic genius that embodied with the Jewish code a precept given to the whole human family almost a thousand years before there was a Jewish nation, did not also embody with the same code, and appropriate to the same people, the right to eat animal food, then for the first time given to man—the covenant of day and night, of summer and winter, of seed-time and harvest, indicated and confirmed by the celestial arch which God erected upon the bosom of a cloud in token of his "covenant with all flesh." The constitution that guarantees the continuance of day and night and the seasons of the year also secures and protects the life of man from the violence of man, by a statute simultaneously promulged and committed to the father of the new world for the benefit of the whole human race. Why not also represent this, too, as done away, and thus place the world without the precincts of the covenanted mercies given to Noah for his family and recorded by Moses the man of God? There is not, then, the shadow of a reason for the assumption that the present human family is not obliged to enforce the statute above named. The right to eat animal food, to expect the uninterrupted succession of seasons, and the obligation to put the murderer to death, are of equal antiquity and of the same Divine authority. Every one claiming any interest in the world, because of his relation to Noah, and God's charter of privileges granted to him, must either show, by some authority equally express and incontrovertible, that God has abolished one part of it and perpetuated the remainder, or advocate capital punishment upon Divine authority.

But still more convincing and decisive is the reason assigned by the divine Author of the statute commanding capital punishment. It is in these words:—"FOR IN THE IMAGE OF GOD MADE HE MAN." A reason, indeed, for the statute, worthy of God to propound and worthy of man to honor and regard. Why a reason so forcible and so full of eloquence and authority could be so frequently disparaged by an intelligent and Christian community, is, to my mind, indicative not merely of the want of piety, but of that of humanity and self-respect. The reason here assigned for this precept places the crime of murder in an entirely new attitude before the mind. Much, indeed, has been said of this crime—of its enormous dimensions—of its moral turpitude—its appalling guilt—its diabolical malignity; but here it is presented to us as the greatest insult which man can offer to his Creator—to the Supreme Majesty of the universe, apart from all its bearings upon human society and its unfortunate victim.

On one occasion the Messiah said of Satan that he "was a liar and a murderer from the beginning." It is impossible, then, that we can exaggerate the wickedness and malignancy of murder. No one has yet been able to do it justice. It desecrates in effigy, and, as far as the impotent arm of flesh has power, destroys, the once brightest image of the invisible and eternal God that adorns any province of his vast and glorious universe. Man is still great in his ruins. Once the most exact and beautiful similitude of the Great Original of universal being, he is still to be reverenced; and, when renewed in the moral image of his Maker, he is to be loved and admired not only as the noblest work of almighty power, but as the special and exclusive object of redeeming grace and mercy. But it is enough for our present purpose to know that in making it the duty of society to avenge this crime, God makes its dishonor to his own image the paramount reason why the life of the murderer should be taken from him. The Most High does not give many reasons for his precepts; but, when he gives one, it is worthy of himself and of the occasion, and claims the profound respect of every discerning and moral man.

Before we dismiss this divine statute, which has never been repealed, which never can be abolished, we must add one other remark, in the form of an argument against the possibility of its abrogation. The reason given for slaying the murderer is one of perpetual validity. If it was ever good and obligatory, it must always be so. So long as it stands true that man was created in the image of God, so long it will bind every religious and moral people to take away the life of the murderer. It is, therefore, of immutable and perpetual obligation.

We shall now briefly glance at the criminal code of the Jewish nation, merely to see whether it harmonizes with the prominent statutes of the postdiluvian, if not of the antediluvian, age. It is often very properly observed that the Jewish nation was placed under a theocracy. Punishment by death was, under it, somewhat extended beyond the single crime of murder. Various crimes affecting human life, endangering or implying murder, were, under the special government of God, amongst a people whose ecclesiastic and political constitutions were one and the same, punishable by death. According to the latest and one of the most respectable treatises yet written on the "Elements of Moral Science," by one of the living ornaments of Trinity College, Cambridge, the Jewish code took a proper view of polity. For, as Mr. Whewell very profoundly observes,* "It is to be recollected that one requisite for our advancing towards a state of society so generally satisfactory, is the establishment of moral rules as realities; and to this, at present, *there appears to be no way except by making ignominious death the climax of our scale of punishments.*" It is, indeed, the climax of several categories in the Jewish code. Not only he that *mortally* smote a fellow-citizen, but he that smote his father or his mother, whether mortally or not; he that stole a man and sold him; he that cursed his parents; the reckless owner of an animal that killed, when through his neglect life was lost; all that practised witchcraft, blasphemy, incest, sodomy, bestiality, &c. were deemed worthy of death. Both the letter and the spirit of the Jewish code on the subject of murder, and the reasons given for exacting life for life, demand our special attention: we shall therefore copy a few of the more prominent statutes of that institution.

The fullest summary of the ordinances concerning manslaughter and murder, enjoined upon the Jews, is found in the book of Numbers, with some of the reasons annexed, indicative of the philosophy of the Divine requisitions. We shall read the whole passage:—

9. And the Lord spake unto Moses, saying,

10. Speak unto the children of Israel, and say unto them, When ye be come over Jordan into the land of Canaan,

11. Then ye shall appoint you cities to be cities of refuge for you; that the slayer may flee thither which killeth any person at unawares.

12. And they shall be unto you cities for refuge from the avenger; that the manslayer die not until he stand before the congregation in judgment.

13. And of these cities which ye shall give, six cities shall ye have for refuge.

14. Ye shall give three cities on this side Jordan, and three cities shall ye give in the land of Canaan, which shall be cities of refuge.

15. These six cities shall be a refuge both for the children of Israel, and for the stranger, and for the sojourner among them; that every one that killeth any person unawares may flee thither.

16. And if he smite him with an instrument of iron so that he die, he is a murderer: the murderer shall surely be put to death.

* Vol. ii. p. 329, sect. 1058.

17. And if he smite him with throwing a stone, wherewith he may die, and he die, he is a murderer: the murderer shall surely be put to death.
18. Or if he smite him with an hand-weapon of wood, wherewith he may die, and he die, he is a murderer: the murderer shall surely be put to death.
19. The revenger of blood himself shall slay the murderer: when he meeteth him he shall slay him.
20. But if he thrust him of hatred, or hurl at him by laying of wait, that he die;
21. Or in enmity smite him with his hand, that he die; he that smote him shall surely be put to death; for he is a murderer: the revenger of blood shall slay the murderer when he meeteth him.
22. But if he thrust him suddenly without enmity, or have cast upon him any thing without laying of wait,
23. Or with any stone, wherewith a man may die, seeing him not, and cast it upon him, that he die, and was not his enemy, neither sought his harm;
24. Then the congregation shall judge between the slayer and the revenger of blood, according to these judgments:
25. And the congregation shall deliver the slayer out of the hand of the revenger of blood, and the congregation shall restore him to the city of his refuge, whither he was fled; and he shall abide in it unto the death of the high-priest, which was anointed with the holy oil.
26. But if the slayer shall at any time come without the border of the city of his refuge, whither he was fled;
27. And the revenger of blood find him without the borders of the city of his refuge, and the revenger of blood kill the slayer; he shall not be guilty of blood;
28. Because he should have remained in the city of his refuge until the death of the high-priest; but after the death of the high-priest the slayer shall return into the land of his possession.
29. So these things shall be for a statute of judgment unto you, throughout your generations, in all your dwellings.
30. Whoso killeth any person, the murderer shall be put to death by the mouth of witnesses: but one witness shall not testify against any person to cause him to die.
31. Moreover, ye shall take no satisfaction for the life of a murderer which is guilty of death; but he shall be surely put to death.
32. And ye shall take no satisfaction for him that is fled to the city of his refuge, that he should come again to dwell in the land, until the death of the high-priest.
33. So ye shall not pollute the land wherein ye are; for blood it defileth the land: and the land cannot be cleansed of the blood that is shed therein, but by the blood of him that shed it. (Num. ch. xxxv.)

The ordinance for erecting the cities of refuge and the police under which they were placed, like every other part of the Mosaic institution, commend the wisdom, justice and benevolence of the Lawgiver and King of Israel. Two great objects were contemplated and secured by that institution—a refuge for the innocent, and a *caveat* against manslaughter.

When any one killed another by mere accident, without any malice or evil intent on the part of him that did it, he was, when admitted into any one of these cities, legally secure against the avenger of blood. The right of avenging blood, from Adam to Moses, during the whole patriarchal age, seems to have been, with the Divine approbation, conferred upon the nearest kinsman of the deceased. It is very evident, not merely from the silence of the law, but from the retention of the ancient official name, that the erection of these cities created no officer in the land other than he to whom, from the beginning, the duty had belonged. The next in blood still retained the right to avenge his murdered relative. These cities were, therefore, intended to protect the innocent from rash and unjust executions. Before that time, the altar, it appears, (Ex. xxi. 14,) had been the sanctuary of refuge for the unfortunate manslayer.

But, in the second place, the cities of refuge were not unlike penitentiaries, to which even an innocent manslayer was required, at the peril of his life, to be confined until the death of that high-priest under whose administration the event had taken place. This sometimes happened to be for life. If at any time during the pontificate of the high-priest he presumed to go out of the city, it was at the hazard of his life. This was placing a new guard around human life. A wise provision, truly, against manslaughter! He that was so unfortunate as to kill any person by the veriest accident, incurred two imminent risks—that of being killed, before he got into the city of refuge, by the avenger of blood; and, if not killed, that of being confined for years—perhaps all his life—within its walls, away from his family and home.

But in case of murder, whether premeditated or from the rage of passion, the cities of refuge afforded no asylum whatever. On trial and conviction the criminal was, in all cases, taken from them and put to death. For the guilty murderer there was no asylum. If he escaped the hand of the avenger of blood while fleeing to the city, if, perchance, he fled there for trial, he always expiated the blood that he had shed by his own.

It is scarcely necessary to remark how often and with what clearness and authority it is promulged—"The murderer shall surely be put to death;" and again, "The avenger of blood himself shall kill him when he meeteth him." No one will, I presume, after a single reading of this statute, require any other evidence that capital punishment was divinely ordained during the whole period of Old Testament history—that it was an essential part of the Jewish institution, and during its continuance extended much beyond the patriarchal requisition.

But there is a reason connected with these ordinances that demands our special consideration. Like that given to Noah, it has no respect to time, place or circumstance. It belongs exclusively to no age, to no nation or people. It is a reason, too, why murder shall not be pardoned, and why the Lord so solemnly and so positively said, "You shall take no satisfaction for the life of a murderer"—he must not be ransomed at any price. Does any one ask why there should be no ransom, no commutation, no pardon? The answer, the reason, is one of fearful import. It is this:—"*The land cannot be cleansed of the blood that is shed therein* BUT BY THE BLOOD OF HIM THAT SHED IT." So God Almighty has ordained in his infinite wisdom, justice and benevolence. It is enough. *He* has said it. No tears of repentance, no contrition of heart, no agony of soul, can expiate the sin of murder. Lebanon is not sufficient, nor all the beasts thereof, to afford one burnt-offering to cleanse from defilement a land polluted with the blood of one unexpiated murder. As soon could the breath of a mortal melt the polar mountains of ice, dissolve the Siberian snows and fill the dreary wastes with the verdure, the beauty and the fragrance of ancient Eden, as soon would the sigh of remorse quicken into life the ashes of the murdered dead, or a single penitential tear extinguish the fires of hell, as any expiation or ablution of mortal hand, other than the blood of the murderer, atone to God's violated law, do honor to his insulted majesty and purify the land from the dark defilement of unavenged blood.

I cannot but tremble for our country, if this be the decision of the Governor of nations, when I reflect upon the multitude that have in single combat sacrificed each other, in purpose or in fact, at the shrine of a false and factitious honor; and upon those who, in the sullen rage and malice of the dastardly assassin, avenged their imaginary wrongs by the blood of their fellow-citizens; and upon those who sought to conceal their infamous crimes of lust and passion—of burglary, arson and rapine—with the blood of those who might have been witnesses against them; I say, when I reflect upon the hundreds and the thousands thus murdered, whose blood yet unexpiated still pollutes our soil, and through the vagueness and ambiguity of our laws, the venality, corruption or incompetency of our tribunals, or the servility or selfwilledness of our chief magistrates, yet cries to heaven for vengeance, not merely upon the head of those that shed it, but upon the Government and the people that still suffer them to live, methinks I see a most portentous cloud, dark, swollen and lowering, surcharged with the fires of divine indignation, ready to burst in accumulated vengeance upon our blood-polluted land.

But, in extenuation of our apathy or as an apology for our indifference, it is sometimes assumed that the Messiah has forever abolished the bloody code of Moses and the patriarchs, and has preached a larger benevolence and forgiveness to the nations. What a baseless assumption! What an outrage upon the character of the Messiah! True, indeed, he came not to judge the world, to act the civil magistrate, the civil lawgiver, or to assume regal authority over any nation or people of this world. His kingdom was spiritual and heavenly. In it, he would not have an eye for an eye, a tooth for a tooth, or stripe for stripe. He would not have his followers go to law for any violence, fraud or wrong inflicted on them on his account. They might, indeed, sue those out of his kingdom for civil wrongs in civil courts, or they might consent to be sued for unjust demands upon them in their political and civil relations; but any wrong, violence or compulsion inflicted on them for their religion, their conscientious allegiance to him, they were to endure cheerfully, and rejoice that they were counted worthy to suffer wrong or even shame for his name's sake. But he that hence argues for the abolition of civil government, of civil penalties, or for the abrogation of the statutes given to mankind by God himself, founded on his own perfections and the immutable relations of things, not merely typical and adumbrative in their nature, but jurisprudential and for the safety of society, shocks all common sense. As well might we say that morality and the moral character of God are mutable things. The New Testament abolished nothing that was not in its own nature temporal, local and prospective of better things. It enacts no civil statutes. It does not even designate the persons between whom the institution of marriage may be consummated. It abrogates nothing in the Old Testament that was not substantiated in Christ, or that was not peculiar to the twelve tribes. But we have shown that the precept in discussion belonged not to any institution, Patriarchal, Jewish or Christian, but to the whole family of man.

Does not an apostle say that "the law is good if a man use it lawfully"? Does he not say that "the law was not made for a righteous man, but for the lawless and disobedient: for murderers, man-slayers, man-stealers, thieves, liars, perjured persons," &c.? And surely for all these evil-doers it has, or ought to have, its penalties. In executing these on their proper subjects the law is used lawfully.

Again, does not Paul teach that the "powers that be are ordained of God"?—that the magistrate "is his minister," and that he rightfully wears a sword not his own, but God's? And, in the name of reason, why have a sword in the state, and worn by the civil magistrate, if it be unlawful or unchristian to put any one to death on any account whatever? That would, indeed, be to "bear the sword in vain;" a thing which the apostles themselves would have reprobated. Christians, then, must remember that the magistrate is God's armed minister, and that he must be obeyed by every Christian man, not merely through the fear of his wrath, or of his avenging sword, but for the sake of a conscientious regard to God's authority, whose minister of justice he is. The civil magistrate is now the civil avenger of blood. Paul calls him "*a messenger of wrath* upon him that doeth evil."

There is not, then, a word in the Old Testament or the New inhibiting capital punishment, nor a single intimation that it should be abolished. On the contrary, reasons are given as the basis of the requisition of life for life, which never can be set aside—which are as forcible at this hour as they were in the days of Cain, Noah, Moses and Jesus Christ. We reiterate the statute with clearer conviction of its obligation and utility on every consideration of the broad, deep, solid and enduring premises on which it is founded:—"Thou shalt take (no ransom) no satisfaction for the life of the murderer."—"He that sheddeth man's blood, by man shall his blood be shed; for in the image of God made he man."—"The land cannot be cleansed from blood but by the blood of him that shed it." For this purpose the magistrate is "God's minister, an avenger, to execute wrath upon him that doeth evil."

The necessity, utility and importance of capital punishment, we must regard, on the premises already considered, as unequivocally and irrefragably established, so far as divine authority can require or establish any thing. And although the most plain and striking passages, found in the Patriarchal, Jewish and Christian institutions, have been adduced and partially considered, the half has not been told, nor the argument fully developed. A single address on such an occasion as the present is not sufficient for a subject so comprehensive and important. It would, indeed, require a volume rather than one short lecture. Conscious of our inability fully to discuss such a question on such an occasion, we shall therefore add but a few remarks further.

It has been said, not by those of old time, but by those of our time, that the sixth precept of the Decalogue, "*Thou shalt not kill,*" inhibits all taking away of human life. A sect of extreme pietists on Long Island, it is reported, gave to the precept a broader interpretation, and forbade the killing of any living creature for food. They are as consistent as he who says the precept "*thou shalt not kill*" prohibits capital punishment. It is the very precept which calls for the blood of him that violates it.

Moses did not himself so interpret this precept; for on the very day he descended from the mount with the autograph in his hand, he commanded the sons of Levi to gird on their swords and kill the idolaters who had eaten and drunk and danced to an idol—of whom no less than three thousand fell that day.

I introduce this case for another purpose—to repudiate an objection urged against capital punishment. It is asked, What Christian man, or what man of delicate moral sensibility, could execute such a sentence—could despatch to the judgment-seat a criminal crimsoned with the blood of his fellow-man?

It is not the sheriff's hand—it is not the sword of the executioner. It is the hand of God—it is the sword of his justice that takes away that life which he himself gave, because the criminal has murderously taken away a life which he could not give.

Is the hand of a man purer than the hand of an angel? And who was it that, in one memorable night, passing through the land of Egypt, by a single stroke smote to death the first-born of all the realms of Pharaoh, from the royal palace down to the cottage of the meanest serf that breathed upon his soil! And who was it that, on another fatal night, while passing through the camp of the insolent Assyrian chief, killed one hundred and eighty-five thousand of his most valiant men? *Was it not an angel of the Lord?* Nay, rather, who was it that in the days of Noah inflicted with his own hand capital and condign punishment upon a world filled with violence and with blood? Who was it that rained down fire and brimstone from the heavens on the devoted cities of the Plain, saving, as in the former case, but a single family? Was it not the Lord himself in person?

And what shall we say of the father of the faithful, returning from the slaughter of the confederate kings?—of Moses, as the messenger of God, slaying not merely a single Egyptian, but smiting with his rod, in the depths of the Red Sea, the strength, the pride and the glory of

Egypt?—of Joshua, the son of Nun, destroying seven idolatrous nations?—of Samuel, the pure and pious Samuel, hewing to pieces with his own hand the king of Amalek?—of David and his hundred battles? Time would fail me to name all the instances in which God has made the purest, the holiest and the best of men, as well as angels, the executioners of his justice. I shall mention another case—the case of Joab—one that, before I understood the statutes of the Lord on the subject of murder, often perplexed me. There lay king David, the beloved of his God, on the bed of death; and while making his last will and testament, he remembered Joab—the brave, the valorous, the mighty Joab—than whom no king could boast of a truer friend or a greater or more successful general—his own kinsman, too—his own sister's son. He names him to his son Solomon, his successor of the sceptre of Israel. And what is his will concerning Joab? What honors or rewards has he in store for him? Hearken to his words:—"Solomon, my son—thou knowest also what Joab, the son of Zeruiah, did to me, and what he did to the two captains of the hosts of Israel: to Abner, the son of Ner, and to Amasa, the son of Jether, whom he slew, and shed the blood of war in peace, and put the blood of war upon his girdle that was about his loins, and in the shoes that were upon his feet. Do, therefore, according to thy wisdom, and let not his hoary head go down to the grave in peace." So willed the dying David. And what did Solomon his son? There was no city of refuge for Joab, but, flying into the tabernacle and taking hold of the horns of the altar, Joab said, "Here will I die." And what said the king? "Go, Benaiah, do as he hath said. Fall upon him and bury him, that," adds the king, "thou mayest take away the innocent blood which Joab shed from me and from the house of my father." Was there ever such a comment on such a text as the following?—"The land cannot be cleansed of the blood that is shed therein, but by the blood of him that shed it."

But we have yet a stronger case—the case of David's son and David's Lord. His words are oracles from which there is no appeal; his example is an argument to which there is no response. Is he, or is he not, on the side of capital punishment? While on earth he was a *saviour*. In heaven he is now a *king*. Hereafter he will appear in the character of a *judge* and an avenger. We ask not what he will do then in finally and eternally punishing the impenitent. We ask not what he did while on earth as a Saviour; for then "he came to save men's lives, and not to destroy." But we ask, What did he do when he became king, when exalted to be the prince and the governor of the universe? He intimated the leading principles of his government before he was crowned Lord of all, to those Jews who were intent on his destruction. "I will," said he, "send you prophets, wise men and scribes. Some of them you will kill and crucify, others you will scourge in your synagogues and persecute from city to city, that upon you may come all the righteous blood shed upon the earth, from the blood of Abel to the blood of Barachias, whom ye slew between the temple and the altar. Verily, I say to you, all these things shall come on this generation." Did he when king execute this threat? Ask Josephus, Tacitus and a hundred other witnesses. As governor of the world, he despatched Titus with a Roman army, and laid siege to Jerusalem and other cities in Judea. In the whole of these various wars and sieges—in the destruction of the city and the temple, he killed more than one million of the rebellious Jews, and sent the remainder into exile. But this is not the only case. It is but the first one of notoriety in his reign of justice. Ever since he ascended the throne his promise is, "All that take the sword shall perish with the sword." As king of nations and governor of the world, he executes wrath by his "ministers of justice" upon wicked men and nations, in the temporal punishments which he awards. According to king David, in the second Psalm, when the Messiah should be placed as king on Mount Zion, he was to "rule the nations with a rod of iron, and to break them in pieces like a potter's vessel." This he has already done in more than one instance, and will yet do in many more. But he does it not in person, but by his "ministers." Still, he does it.

It being evident, as we suppose, that capital punishment is not only countenanced by innumerable Biblical precedents, but that it is also most positively enjoined upon all persons to whom God has revealed his will, who are intrusted with the government of the world, we shall henceforth regard it as a divine precept and requisition, to which we are bound to yield our cordial assent; not because it chances to fall in with our theories of what is expedient, useful or consonant to the genius of our age and government, but because of the supreme authority that enacts it—because it is a decree of the King of the universe, the ultimate Judge of the living and the dead, and because he himself has practised it, and still continues to practise it, as moral governor of the world.

Though not disposed to appear paradoxical, I hesitate not to avow the conviction that the divine ordinance is as merciful as it is just—that, for example, it was most humane and merciful on the part of David to command his son Solomon to take away the life of Joab. I cite this case and avow this conviction, for the sake of those opposers of capital punishment, who, under the pretence of a more refined and enlarged philanthropy, are, nowadays, declaiming both eloquently and impassionedly against capital punishment because of its alleged cruelty and inhumanity. That those who thus inveigh against it are philanthropic in purpose and feeling, I doubt not. But that they are so in fact, is not quite so evident.

In seeking to abolish capital punishment, do they not divest human life of one of its main pillars of defence? In all countries, and, I believe, in all ages, murders increase and diminish in the ratio of the certainty or uncertainty of the exaction of life for life. It must, in the nature of things, be so. Every thing is safe or unsafe as it is guarded or not guarded by education—by law—by the magnitude and certainty or uncertainty of rewards and punishments. In abolishing capital punishment, the main bulwark against the perpetration of murder falls to the ground. The broad shield of a nation's safety and defence from violence and blood is broken to pieces, and the honorable and virtuous citizen, naked and defenceless, left exposed to the murderous assaults of malice and envy. Of what avail is the bare possibility of a punishment infinitely less than the injury inflicted on the individual and the state,—enfeebled, too, as it must be, by a hundred chances of escape against one of apprehension and conviction? Who could feel himself safe under a government where there is no protection of his life against the furious passions which not unfrequently display themselves in the most appalling forms, in some of those terrific monsters with which human society more or less abounds? Exile, confinement in prisons or workhouses, are to such demons as an act of Congress to a South American tiger, or as the stubble to Job's Leviathan.

In saving a murderer from death, through a morbid compassion, society acts with more indiscretion than the fabled husbandman who, in commiseration, carried home to his hearth a congealed serpent, which, when warmed into life, fatally struck the children of its benefactor. In saving from the penalty of God's law a single murderer, society sins against itself, as well as against God, and occasions, or may occasion, the destruction of one or more of its citizens. If every one convicted of murder in any of its various forms was infallibly put to death, can any intelligent citizen imagine that crimes of this sort would not rather diminish than increase? The strong probability of escape disarms every legal punishment of its terror to evil-doers.

It has been observed that murder and robbery more frequently accompany each other in all states that punish the robber as well as the murderer by death, than in those that never visit theft or highway-robbery with capital punishment. As true it is that in those states where murder is very seldom punished with death, the crime, so far as my reading and observation go, is more frequently perpetrated than in those states in which its proper punishment is much more certain. We cannot, therefore, but think that the court of Judge Lynch would not have held its sessions so frequently in late years, had it not been that other courts so often failed to hold their sessions, with that certainty of capital punishment for capital offences which right reason, human prudence and God's holy law so clearly and authoritatively demand. We cannot but trace the present appalling increase of murders in our country to those morbid philanthropists who, in the form of judges, juries and chief magistrates, in these days of new theories, experiments, and irreverence for God's law and authority, are ever and anon making void our laws, lame though they be, by suffering the convicted murderer to live.

The master-spirits of France, now, and at former times, have been much addicted to theorize against capital punishment. Robespierre in early life published a treatise against capital punishment, but when he rose to power, he became the presiding genius of the guillotine. Strange that such a theory should have been popular in France before the reign of terror began! France, however, is not the only country that has theorized against the Bible and its justice. Nor is it the only one that suffers for it. Indeed, all states that have more or less theorized against capital punishment have been signally punished by an increase of the crime. In truth, it is as some poet says—

"**Mercy murders in pardoning him that kills.**"

The protection and safety of human life is the first and paramount concern of every intelligent and moral community on earth. The first statute ever enacted by the heavenly Father in the present world, as before observed, was a statute *for preserving life.* I am not singular, I hope, in judging of the civilization of every community by the care it takes of human life. May not the religious and moral character of a community be very fairly estimated by the value it puts upon human life, and the care it takes of it, as indicated in its statute-books, its courts of justice, its general police, and its numerous and various means of defence against the accidents and dangers which may imperil it? And may not these be learned from its public highways, its public conveyances, its public buildings, and from the character and capacities of the officers to whose fidelity these great interests are committed, as well as from the various exactions of service, and the extent of the penalties inflicted upon them for delinquency or malfeasance in the discharge of their duties?

In countries long settled, do we see the public highways bordered with dead trees, whose ponderous and decaying branches are bending over our heads? Are the streams that cross them unbridged, or, if bridged, are these bridges, decayed and dilapidating under the wasting hand of time, permitted to betray the unwary traveller into danger? Are their dread precipices unwalled, their deep ravines uncovered, their miry sloughs unpaved? Are their public conveyances by land and sea, by lake and river, uncomfortable or unsafe, as far as science or art can promote either safety or comfort? If so, must we not regard such a people as imperfectly educated—as but partially civilized—as essentially defective in the pure and excellent morality of the Christian religion?

If the Lawgiver of the Universe, when acting as King of Israel, found that man guilty of blood on the roof of whose house there was no defence against falling over, when it became necessary to walk upon it—if he said to every subject of his kingdom, "When thou buildest a house, then shalt thou make a battlement for thy roof, that thou bring not blood upon thy house, should any man fall from thence,"—and if he held every man liable for the damage accruing from a pit which he had digged and left uncovered, what should we think of those Christian philanthropists that pay so little regard to the life of man as not only to subject him to all the dangers of bad roads, bad bridges, bad coaches, bad boats, and bad officers, but, when his life is taken by the hand of a duellist or an assassin, extenuate the offence, and abolish the proper punishment, and allow this wretch again to go at large and hazard other deeds of violence and blood?

In conclusion, we would only ask, who can form a just estimate of the value of the life of one man, either to himself or to society? No one lives or dies to himself alone. The unhappy victim of a murderer's fear or hate has not only lost his life, but the world has lost it too. And what is life? Ay, what is life, to its possessor, to his relatives, to his country and to the world? How much would he himself take for it? Ask not the princes and the nobles of the earth in the morning of life—in the enjoyment of all the honors, pleasures and possessions of earth that imagination can body forth, or passion can desire. Ask not the men of genius, who dwell in enchanted palaces, who drink the pleasures of imagination from the purest and the loftiest fountains of creation. Ask not poets, orators and philosophers, who find a heaven in the admiration of their contemporaries, and an eternal reward in the worship and envy of posterity. Ask not the military chieftain, returning from the field of blood, flushed with the victories he has won, and crowned with the laurels of a hundred battles. But ask that poor, old, decrepit galley-slave, who has seen his fourscore years, what posthumous fame he would accept, what sum of money would satisfy him, for the pittance of days that might yet be allotted to him. One's life might be safely staked on it, that neither the wealth of a Crœsus nor the fame of a Napoleon would be accepted by him for his chances of another year.

Again, what immense stakes has society in the lives of some men! What great interests are often wrapped up in the life of a single individual! It is not the interest of one city, one state, or one empire; it is not the interest of one age or of one generation of men; but the interests of a world, and of ages yet to come, that sometimes providentially hang upon the life of a single individual. Let any one conversant with the history of the last three or four centuries consider how much interest had the world in a few individuals—in such men as Christopher Columbus, Martin Luther, Sir Francis Bacon, Sir Isaac Newton, Benjamin Franklin, Robert Fulton, and George Washington. Suppose that each of these had met with some Aaron Burr, as did Alexander Hamilton, (a name of no inferior fame—whose death, as a national misfortune, no living man can estimate:) what would have been the present condition of the world? Can any man form a proper estimate? Can any one subtract from science, and art, and society, the exact amount of our indebtedness to any one of them, much less to them all? It is from such a sacrifice as this, laid upon the altar of the implacable demon of a false honor, immolated at the promptings of malice and envy, that we learn the demerit of the murderer—what the world may lose by permitting him to live, and why the fiercest thunderbolts of Almighty wrath are treasured up for him.

From this view of the subject, (and who that venerates the authority of the Bible can reasonably dissent from it?) may we not entreat every patriot, philanthropist and Christian in our country to use his best endeavors to create a sound public opinion on the obligations resting on every State government to exterminate the crime of murder by a firm, persevering and uniform execution of the murderer according to the Divine precept? Every one can aid in this cause, more or less.

And now is a most important crisis. While so many are for taking away the greatest restraint and for substituting a less one, under the preposterous assumption that man is wiser than God, and that a minor punishment will be more effectual than a greater one, it is high time that the real friends of man should speak out.

And should I not more especially address myself to the softer, more sensitive and humane portion of my audience—to that sex to whose soul-subduing counsels and fostering hands the God of nature and of society has so wisely and kindly assigned the formation of human character, and to whose influence, direct and indirect, he has almost entirely consigned the destiny of man under the most endearing and fascinating of all titles and associations—those of *Mother*, *Wife* and *Sister?*

If the ladies in this our age of civilization will only concur with us in opinion, and lend their mighty aid in propagating right views on this subject—if they will combine their irresistible energies in this cause of genuine humanity, and frown from their presence not only the reckless duellist, but every one who pleads his cause or countenances in any way his factitious code of ignoble honor—if they will forever discard from their admiration and esteem every candidate for their favor who is known to wear upon his person any weapon whatever, fabricated with a view to violence against the life of man—the mighty work is done. Then may be averted the vials of Divine indignation which must be poured out on every government and country deaf to the demands of God's righteous law and regardless of the true safety and happiness of society.

I can only add my earnest prayer that a timely repentance may dissipate that dark and portentous cloud that yet lowers over our beloved country; that by a just consideration of the dignity of man as created in the image of God, the value of human life as respects the eternal destiny of its possessor, the interest which the state has in all its citizens, the solemn requisitions of the Divine law, exacting in all cases the life of the murderer—those having it in their power to form, direct and govern society may perceive that it is alike an oracle of reason, of justice and of mercy that "whosoever sheddeth man's blood, by man shall his blood be shed," and that, therefore, no ransom or substitute shall be taken for the life of the murderer, inasmuch as, by the eternal and immutable law of God, "the land cannot be cleansed of the blood that is shed therein but by the blood of him that shed it."

ADDRESS ON WAR.

WHEELING, VA., 1848.

Ladies and Gentlemen:—

Has one Christian nation a right to wage war against another Christian nation?

On propounding to myself, and much more to you, my respected auditors, this momentous question, so affecting the reputation and involving the destiny of our own country and that of the Christian world, I confess that I rather shrink from its investigation than approach it with full confidence in my ability to examine it with that intelligence and composure so indispensable to a satisfactory decision. With your indulgence, however, I will attempt, if not to decide the question, at least to assist those who, like myself, have often, and with intense interest, reflected on the desolations and horrors of war, as indicated in the sacrifice of human life, the agonies of surviving relatives, the immense expenditures of a people's wealth, and the inevitable deterioration of public morals, invariably attendant on its existence and career. If, with Dr. Dick, of Scotland, we should put down its slain victims to the minimum of 14,000,000,000, or, with Burke, of Ireland, at the maximum of 35,000,000,000, or take the mean of 24,500,000,000, what imagination could picture all the miseries and agonies inflicted upon the slain and upon their surviving relatives and friends? And who could compute the wealth expended in the support of those immense armies whose butchered millions can never be exactly computed? If Great Britain alone, from the revolution in 1688 to the overthrow of Napoleon in 1815—during her seven years' wars, occupying sixty-five years of one hundred and twenty-seven—expended the sum of £2,023,000,000 sterling—more than $10,100,000,000—a sum much more easily expressed than comprehended by even the most accomplished financier—how can we compute the aggregate expenditures of all the battles fought and wars carried on during a period of some five thousand years? Yet these millions slain and these millions expended are the least items in its desolations, to the mind of an enlightened Christian philanthropist. When we attempt to reflect upon one human being in the amplitude and magnitude of his whole destiny, in a world that has no limit, and also survey the capacities and susceptibilities of his nature according to the Christian revelation, how insignificant are the temporal and passing results of any course of action, compared with those which know neither measure nor end! How important, then, it is that, in investigating a subject whose bearings on society arithmetic cannot compute nor language express, we approach it with a candid and unprejudiced temper, and examine it with a profound and concentrated devotion of our minds to all that history records, philosophy teaches and religion enjoins!

But, before entering upon the proper examination of this question, it may be of much importance to a satisfactory issue that we examine the terms in which it is expressed. More than half the discussions and controversies of every age are mere logomachies, verbose wranglings about the terminology of the respective combatants; and more than half the remainder might be compressed into a very diminutive size, if, in the beginning, the parties would agree on the real issue, on the proper terms to express and define them.

As public faith or commercial credit, founded upon an equivocal currency, on its exposure suddenly shrinks into ruinous dimensions, at once blighting the hopes and annihilating the fortune of many a bold adventurer, so many a false and dangerous position, couched in ambiguous terms, when pruned of its luxuriant verbiage, divested of its captivating but delusive elocution, and presented in an intelligible, definite and familiar attitude, is at once reprobated as unworthy of our reception and regard.

On comparing the literature and science of the current age with those of former times, we readily discover how much we owe to a more rigid analysis and a more scrupulous adoption of the technical terms and phrases of the old schools, to which the whole world at one time looked up as the only fountains of wisdom and learning. When submitted to the test of a more enlightened criticism, many of their most popular and somewhat cabalistic terms and phrases have been demonstrated to be words without just or appropriate ideas, and have been "nailed to the counter" as spurious coin; others, however, like pure metal in antique forms, have been sent to the mint, recast and made to receive the impress of a more enlightened and accomplished age.

The rapid progress and advancement of modern science is, I presume, owing to a more rational and philosophical nomenclature and to the more general use of the inductive system of reasoning, rather than to any superior talent or more aspiring genius possessed either by our contemporaries or our immediate predecessors.

Politics, morals and religion—the most deservedly engrossing themes of every age—are, in this respect, unfortunately behind the other sciences and arts cultivated at the present day. We are, however, pleased to see a growing conviction of the necessity of a more apposite, perspicuous and philosophical verbal apparatus in several departments of science, and especially to witness some recent efforts to introduce a more improved terminology in the sciences of government, morality and religion.

To apply these preliminary remarks to the question of this evening, it is important to note with particular attention the popular terms in which we have expressed it,—viz.:—

"*Has one Christian nation a right to wage war against another Christian nation?*"

We have prefixed no epithet to *war* or to *right,* while we have to the word *nation.* We have not defined the *war* as *offensive* or *defensive.* We have not defined the *right* as *human* or *divine.* But we have chosen, from the custom of the age, to prefix *Christian* to *nation.* The reasons for this selection and arrangement of terms shall appear as we proceed.

First, then, had we prefixed the word *offensive* to the word *war*, we would, on proving that a Christian nation had no right to wage an offensive war, be obliged to institute another question, and to ask, Can a Christian nation wage a defensive war against another Christian nation?—thereby implying that one Christian nation might be the aggressor and another the aggrieved. But we cannot without great difficulty imagine such a thing as a Christian nation carrying on an aggressive war. We, therefore, simplify the discussion by placing in the proposition the naked term *war.* Nor shall we spend our time in discussing the political right of one nation to wage war against another nation, and then ask whether they have a divine right. Indeed, the latter generally implies the former; for, if a nation have a divine right, it either has or may have a political or moral right to do so.

But we must inquire into the appropriateness of the term *Christian* prefixed to *nation*—for popular use has so arranged these terms; and the controversy, either expressly or impliedly, as now-a-days occasionally conducted in this country, is, Has one *Christian* nation a right to wage war against another *Christian* nation? But, as we assume nothing, we must ask the grave and somewhat startling question—Is there a *Christian* nation in the world? or have we a definite idea of a *Christian* nation? We have, indeed, had, for many centuries past, many nations called *Christian* nations; but we must fearlessly ask, At what font were they baptized? Who were their godfathers? In what record are their sponsors registered? Ay, these, indeed, are preliminary questions that demand a grave and profound consideration. That there are many nations that have Christian communities in them is a proposition which we most cheerfully and thankfully admit. By a common figure of speech, we also give to that which contains any thing the name of the thing contained in it. Thus, rhetorically, we call one edifice a college; another, a bank; a third, a church; not because the brick and mortar, the plank and nails, constitute a college, a bank, a church, but because these buildings contain these institutions. So we have—if any one contend for the name—as many Christian nations as we have Christian communities in different nations, and as many Jewish nations as we have nations with Jewish synagogues in them, and as many Mohammedan nations as we have nations containing mosques in them. But, according to this rhetorical figure, we may have a Christian and a Jewish nation, or a Christian and a Mohammedan nation, in one and the same nation, as we sometimes find both a Jewish and a Christian synagogue in the same nation. But a rhetorical Christian nation and a proper and unfigurative Christian nation are very different entities. A proper literal Christian nation is not found in any country under the whole heavens. There is, indeed, *one* Christian nation, composed of all the Christian communities and individuals in the whole earth. The Apostle Peter, in one letter addressed to all the Christians scattered throughout Pontus, Galatia, Cappadocia, Asia and Bithynia—though "*strangers*" or *aliens* in these respective nations—calls them, collectively, "*a holy nation, a royal priesthood, a peculiar people.*" In strict logical and grammatical truth, there is not, of all the nations of the earth, one properly called a Christian nation. Therefore, we have never had, as yet, one Christian nation waging war against another Christian nation. Before any one, then—no matter what his learning or talents may be—can answer the great interrogatory now in discussion, he must form a clear and well-defined conception of what constitutes a *nation* and what constitutes a *Christian*.

We have very high Roman authority for defining a *nation*—from *nascor*. Pardon me for quoting it:—*Genus hominum qui non aliunde venerunt, sed ibi nati sunt;* which, in our vernacular, means, *a race or tribe of men who have not come from abroad, but live where they were born.* Being a Roman word, derived from natural birth, a Roman author has the best right to define it. Now, a Christian is not one born where he lives: he is born from above, as all Christians of all parties admit. Therefore, no nation, *as such,* as respects either its natural birth or its constitution, can with any show of truth or reason be called a Christian nation. When any one produces the annals of a nation whose constitution was given by Jesus Christ, and whose citizens are all born of God spiritually, as well as of man physically, I will at once call it, in good faith, without a figure, a true, proper and literal Christian nation.

Now, although we have this advantage, which no one can take from us, and conceded, too, by all the literary and Christian authorities in Christendom, we will not build on it alone—nor at all. We will not have it said that we carry our definition by a grammatical or rhetorical decision of the great question. We appeal to all our public documents, without regard to party. We appeal to all our elementary and most profound writers on the subject of nationality. Nay, we appeal to the common views of this whole community. Have we not a church and a state in every State in the Union, and in every European nation? Do not all belong to the state or nation, and a part only, and that often a small part, to the church? Is not the bond of political union *blood,* or *naturalization?* Is not the bond of union in the Christian kingdom faith, or the new birth? What nation is there whose citizens, or a majority of them, are Christians? Not one—even in profession.

But there is a reflex light of Christianity—a moralizing and a civilizing influence as well as a direct and soul-redeeming radiance, which imparts to those nations that have the oracles of God a higher standard of moral excellence, a more discriminating conscientiousness and a more elevated national character; which, in contrast with Pagan nations, obtains for them the honorary distinction of *Christian* nation. Still, as nations, or states, the spirit and character of the nation are *anti-Christian.* A community of Jews in New York or New Orleans, even were they naturalized citizens of the United States, would not impart to those cities an American or Gentile spirit, nor would they impart to our nation a Jewish spirit or character. They would still be Jews and we Americans.

The American nation, *as a nation,* is no more in spirit Christian than were Greece and Rome when the apostle planted churches in Corinth, Athens, or in the metropolis of the empire, with Cæsar's household in it. Roman policy, valor, bravery, gallantry, chivalry, are of as much praise, admiration and glory, in Washington and London, as they were in the very centre of the Pagan world in the days of Julius or Augustus Cæsar. We worship our heroes because of their martial and Roman virtue. *Virtue*, in the Roman language, was only a name for bravery or courage. Such was its literal meaning. With a Roman it was queen of all the graces and of all moral excellencies. It raised from plebeian to patrician rank, and created military tribunes, decemvirs, triumvirs, dictators, consuls, kings, emperors. With us it cannot make a king, but may, perhaps, a third time make for us a President. If, indeed, it does not yet make for us a king, we shall blame the soil, not the culture. Kings cannot grow in America. But under our free and liberal institutions we can impart more than kingly power under a less offensive name.

But a Christian community is, by the highest authority, called a *kingdom*. He, however, who gave it this name said to Cæsar's representative, "*My kingdom is not of this world.* Had my kingdom been of this world, my servants would have fought, and I should not have been delivered to the Jews. *But now is my kingdom not from hence.*" It is, then, decided—first, that we have no Christian nation or kingdom in the world, but that Christ has one grand kingdom, composed of all the Christian communities in the world, of which he is himself the proper sovereign, lawgiver and king.

Having, then, no Christian nation to wage war against another Christian nation, the question is reduced to a more rational and simple form, and I trust it will be still more intelligible and acceptable in this form —viz. *Can Christ's kingdom or church in one nation wage war against his kingdom or church in another nation?* With this simple view of the subject, where is the man so ignorant of the letter and spirit of Christianity as to answer this question in the affirmative? Is there a man of ordinary Bible education in this city or commonwealth, who will affirm that Christ's church in England may of *right* wage war against Christ's church in America?

But I will be told that this form of the question does not meet the exact state of the case, as now impinging the conscience of very many good men. While they will, with an emphatic *No*, negative the question as thus stated, they will in another form propound their peculiar difficulty:—"Suppose," say they, "England proclaims war against our nation, or that our nation proclaims war against England: have we a *right, as Christian men,* to volunteer, or enlist, or, if drafted, to fight against England? Ought our motto to be, 'Our country, right or wrong'? Or has our Government a *right* to compel us to take up arms?"

This form of the question makes it important that we should have as clear and definite conceptions of the word *right* as of any other word in the question before us. We must, then, have a little more definition. For the doctrine of right and wrong, so frequently spoken of by elementary political writers, I cannot say that I entertain a very high regard. Men without religious faith, being without an infallible guide, are peculiarly fond of abstractions. Led by imagination more than by reason, authority or experience, they pride themselves in striking out for themselves and others a new path, rather than to walk in the old and long-frequented ways. They have a theory of man in society with political rights, and of man out of society with natural rights; but as they cannot agree as to the word *natural* prefixed to *right*—whether nature be a divinity or the cause of things—I will not now debate with them the question of *natural* rights, but will take the surer and well-established ground of a divine warrant, or a right founded on a *divine* annunciation.

Much, in all cases of any importance, depends on beginning right; and in a question upon *right* itself, every thing depends upon that ultimate tribunal to which we make our appeal. In all questions involving the moral destinies of the world, we require more than hypothetical or abstract reasoning from principles merely assumed or conceded. We need demonstration, or, what in this case of moral reasoning is the only substitute for it, *oracular authority*. All questions on morals and religion, all questions on the origin, relations, obligations and destiny of man, can be satisfactorily decided only by an appeal to an infallible standard. I need not say that we all, I mean the civilized world, the great, the wise, the good of human kind, concede to the Bible this oracular authority; and, therefore, constitute it the ultimate reason and authority for each and every question of this sort? *What, then, says the Bible on the subject of war?*

It certainly commanded and authorized war amongst the Jews. God had given to man, ever since the flood, the right of taking away the life of man for one specified cause. Hence murderers, ever since the flood, were put to death by express Divine authority. "He that sheds man's blood, by man shall his blood be shed." He gave authority only, however, to one family or nation, whose God and King he assumed to be. As soon as that family was developed into a nation, he placed it under his own special direction and authority. Its government has been properly called by Josephus, a distinguished Jew, a THEOCRACY. It was not a republican, an aristocratical or monarchical, but a *theocratical* government, and that, indeed, of the most absolute character, for certain high ends and purposes in the destinies of mankind—temporal, spiritual and eternal. God was, therefore, in person the King, Lawgiver and Judge of the Jewish nation.

It was not simply for desiring a king that God was at one time displeased with them. It was for asking a king *like those of other nations*, and thereby refusing God himself and God alone as their king. Still, he never made their kings any more than viceroys. He, for many centuries, down to the end of Old Testament history, held in his own hand the sovereignty of the nation. Hence the kings ruled *for him*, and the high-priest, or some special prophet, was the Lord's mouth to them. Their kings were, therefore, unlike other kings. They truly, and only they, of all the kings on earth, were "THE LORD'S ANOINTED." The Jewish kingdom was emphatically a typical institution, prospective of a kingdom not of this world, to be instituted in future times and to be placed under the special government of his only Son and Heir. Hence it came to pass that the enemies of Israel became typical of the enemies of Jesus Christ; and hence the temporal judgments inflicted on them were but shadows through which to set forth the spiritual and eternal judgments to be inflicted on the enemies of the Messiah's reign and kingdom. Whether, therefore, the enemies of the Jews fell in battle, or by any of the angels of death, it was God that slew them. Hence their kings and God's angels were but mere sheriffs, executing, as it were, the mandates of high heaven.

It is, however, important to reiterate that God gave to Noah, and through him to all his sons and successors in government, a right to take away, in civil justice, the life of a murderer. As the world of the ungodly, antecedent to the deluge, during the first five hundred years of Noah's life, was given to violence and outrage against each other, it became expedient to prevent the same violence and bloodshed after the flood; and for this purpose God gave to man, or the human race in Noah's family, the right to exact blood for blood from him who had deliberately and maliciously taken away the life of his fellow. Had not this been first ordained, no war, without a special divine commission, could have been sanctioned as lawful and right even under the Old Testament institution. Hence we may say that wars were first allowed by God against those who had first waged war against their fellows, and consequently, as viewed by God himself, they were murderers.* The first and second wars reported in the annals of the world were begun by the enemies of God and his people, and hence the reprisals made by Abraham and Moses are distinctly stated to have been occasioned by the enemies of God and his people.

But what is most important here and apposite to the occasion, is, that these wars waged by God's people in their typical character were waged under and in pursuance of a special divine commission. They were, therefore, right. For a divine precept authorizing any thing to be done, makes it right absolutely and forever. The Judge of all the earth can do only that, or command that to be done, which is right. Let those, then, who now plead a *jus divinum*, a special divine warrant or right for carrying on war by the authority of the Lord Jesus Christ, produce a warrant from the present Monarch of the universe. What the God of Abraham did by Abraham, by Jacob, or by any of his sons, as the moral governor of the world, before he gave up the sceptre and the crown to his Son Jesus Christ, is of no binding authority now. This is a point of much more importance than we can at present develop, and one which has been, so far as known to me, wholly slurred over in this great investigation. The very basis of the Christian religion is that Jesus Christ is now the Lord and King of both earth and heaven, and that his Father and our God no longer assumes to be either the Lawgiver, Judge or King of the world. It is positively declared by him that all legislative, judiciary and executive power is now committed into the hands of one who is both our kinsman and God's only-begotten Son. Two grand declarations that ought to revolutionize our whole views of civil government as respects its ultimate authority, and change some of our forms of legal justice, are wholly overlooked so far as they are of any practical value and importance. The first was announced by the Messiah immediately before his ascension into heaven; the other was publicly propounded by an embassy from heaven immediately after his ascension. The former declares that "all *authority*," (*exousia*,) all legislative, judiciary and regal authority in heaven and earth, is given to Jesus Christ; the other affirms that God has made Jesus, Lord and Christ, or anointed him Sovereign of the universe. Kings of the earth and courts of high judicature are all under him, but they do not really acknowledge it; few of them, perhaps, know or believe the fact, that Jesus Christ has been on the throne of the universe for more than eighteen hundred years. Hence, the courts of England and America, the two most enlightened nations in the world, are yet deistical in form, rather than Christian. In every place where they have the phrase "*In the name of God*," they ought to have *In the name of the Lord*. This is the gist of the whole controversy between the friends and the enemies of war, on the part of the subjects of Christ's kingdom. The coronation of Jesus Christ in heaven as LORD OF ALL, his investiture with *all authority* in heaven and earth, legislative, judiciary and executive, is the annunciation, on the belief and public acknowledgment of which the first Christian church was founded in Jerusalem, where the throne of David was, in the month of June, eighteen hundred and fourteen years ago, Anno Domini 34.

God the Father, *in propria persona,* now neither judges nor punishes any person or nation, but has committed all judgment to his Son, now constituted Head of the universe and Judge of the living and the dead. This simplifies the question and levels it to the judgment of all. It is this :—Has the Author and Founder of the Christian religion enacted war, or has he made it lawful and right for the subjects of his government to go to war against one another? Or, has he made it right for them to go to war against any nation, or for any national object, at the bidding of the present existent political authorities of any nation in Christendom?

The question is not, Whether, under the new administration of the universe, Christian communities have a right to wage war, in its common technical sense, against other communities—as the house of Judah against the house of Israel, both of the same religion, language and blood. This is already, by almost universal consent, decided in the negative, probably only one society of professed Christians excepted. But the question is, May a Christian community, or the members of it, in their individual capacities, take up arms at all, whether aggressively or defensively, in any national conflict? We might, as before alleged, dispense with the words *aggressive* and *defensive;* for a mere grammatical, logical or legal quibble will make any war either aggressive or defensive, just as the whim, caprice or interest of an individual pleases. Napoleon, on his death-bed, declared that he had never engaged, during his whole career, in an aggressive war—that all his wars were defensive. Yet all Europe regarded him as the most aggressive warrior of any age.

But the great question is, *Can an individual, not a public functionary, morally do that in obedience to his Government which he cannot do in his own case?* Suppose the master of apprenticed youth, or the master of a number of hired or even bond servants, should fall out with one of his neighbors about one of the lines of his plantation, because, as he imagined, his neighbor had trespassed upon his freehold in clearing or cultivating his lands. His neighbor refuses to retire within the precincts insisted on by the complainant; in consequence of which the master calls together his servants, and proceeds to avenge himself, or, as he alleges, to defend his property. As the controversy waxes hot, he commands his servants not only to burn and destroy the improvements made on the disputed territory, but to fire upon his neighbor, his sons and servants. They obey orders, and kill several of them. They are, however, finally taken into custody and brought to trial. An attorney for the servants pleads that these servants were bound to obey their master, and quotes these words from the Good Book:—"Servants, obey in all things your masters according to the flesh." But, on the other side, it is shown that the "*all things*" enjoined are only "all things lawful." For this obedience is to be rendered "as to Christ;" and again, "as the servants of Christ, doing the will of God from the heart." No judge or jury could do otherwise than condemn as guilty of murder servants thus acting. Now, as we all, in our political relations to the government of our country, occupy positions at least inferior to that which a bond-servant holds towards his master, we cannot of right, as Christian men, obey the POWERS THAT BE in any thing not in itself justifiable by the written law of the Great King—our liege Lord and Master, Jesus Christ. Indeed, we may advance in all safety one step further, if it were necessary, and affirm that a Christian man can never, of right, be compelled to do that for the state, in defence of state rights, which he cannot of right do for himself in defence of his personal rights. No Christian man is commanded to love or serve his neighbor, his king or sovereign more than he loves or serves himself. If this is conceded, unless a Christian man can go to war for himself, he cannot for the state.

We have already observed that the Jews were placed under a theocracy, that their kings were only vicegerents, and that they were a symbolic or typical nation adumbrative of a new relation and institution to be set up in "the fulness of time" under an administration of grace. In consequence of this arrangement, God was first revealed as the GOD OF ABRAHAM; and afterwards, when he was about to make himself known in all the earth, in contrast with the idols of the nations, he chose, by Moses, to call himself THE GOD OF THE HEBREWS. As the custom then was, all nations had their gods, and by their wars judged and decided the claims and pretensions of their respective divinities. Esteeming the reputation and pretensions of their gods according to their success in war, that nation's god was the greatest and most to be venerated whose people were most successful and triumphant in battle. God, therefore, chose this method to reveal himself as the God of the Hebrews. Hence he first poured out ten plagues upon the *gods* of Egypt. The Egyptians worshipped every thing, from the Nile and its tenantry to the meanest insect in the land. He first, then, plagued their gods. Afterwards, by causing the Jews to fight and destroy many nations, in a miraculous manner, from the victory over Amalek to the fall of the cities and kings of ancient Palestine, he established his claims as supreme over all. Proceeding in this way, he fully manifested the folly of their idolatries, and the omnipotence, greatness and majesty of the God of the Jews.

The wars of Pagan nations were, indeed, much more rational than those of our miscalled Christian nations. No two of these nations acknowledged the same dynasties of gods; and, therefore, having different gods, they could with much propriety test their claims by invoking them in battle. But two Christian nations both pray to one and the same God to decide their respective quarrels, and yet will not abide by the decision; for success in war is not by any of them regarded as an end of all strife as to the right or justice of the demands of the victorious party. Did our present belligerent nations regard victory and triumph as a proof of the justice of their respective claims, they would in the manner of carrying on their wars prove themselves to be very great simpletons indeed; for why sacrifice their hundred millions of dollars and their fifty thousand lives in one or two years, when they could save these millions of men and money, by selecting, each, one of their genuine Simon Pure *patriots* and *heroes*, and having them voluntarily to meet in single combat, before a competent number of witnesses, and encounter each other till one of them triumphed—and thus award, from Heaven's own court of infallible rectitude, to the nation of the survivor, the glory of a great national triumph, both in heroism and justice? But this they dare not do; for these Christian nations are quite skeptical so far as faith in the justice of their own cause, or in the right decision of their claims in the providence and moral government of God, is concerned. To what purpose, we therefore ask, do they both appeal to the same God, when neither of them feels any obligation to abide his decision?

But as we are neither under a Jewish nor a Pagan government, but professedly, at least, under a Christian dispensation, we ought to hear what the present King of the universe has enacted on this subject. The maxims of the Great Teacher and Supreme Philanthropist are, one would think, to be final and decisive on this great question. The Great Lawgiver addresses his followers in two very distinct respects: first, in reference to their duties to him and their own profession, and then in reference to their civil rights, duties and obligations.

So far as any indignity was offered to them or any punishment inflicted upon them as his followers, or for his *name's sake*, they were in no way to resent it. But in their civil rights he allows them the advantages of the protection of civil law, and for this cause enjoins upon them the payment of all their political dues, and to be subject to every ordinance of man of a purely civil nature, not interfering with their obligations to him.

"If a heathen man, or persecutor, smite you on one cheek, turn to him the other also. If he compel you to go with him one mile, go two. If he sue thee at the law, and take away thy coat, let him have thy mantle also," &c. &c. These and whatever else of evil treatment they might receive, as *disciples* of Christ, they must, for his sake, endure without resistance or resentment. But if in their *citizen* character or civil relations they are defrauded, maligned or prosecuted, they might, and they did, appeal to Cæsar. They paid *tribute* to civil magistrates that they might protect them; and therefore they might rightfully claim their protection. In this view of the matter, civil magistrates were God's ministers to the Christian "FOR GOOD." And also as God's ministers they were revengers to *execute wrath* on those who did evil. Therefore, Christians are in duty bound to render to Cæsar what is Cæsar's, and to God what is God's—to reverence, honor and support the civil magistrate, and, when necessary, to claim his protection.

But as respects the life peculiar to a soldier, or the prosecution of a political war, they had no commandment. On the contrary, they were to live peaceably with all men to the full extent of their power. Their sovereign Lord, the King of nations, is called "THE PRINCE OF PEACE." How, then, could a Christian soldier, whose "*shield*" was faith, whose "*helmet*" was the hope of salvation, whose "*breastplate*" was righteousness, whose "*girdle*" was truth, whose "*feet were shod* with the preparation of the gospel of peace," and whose "*sword*" was that fabricated by the Holy Spirit, even "*the Word of God*,"—I say, how could such a one enlist to fight the battles of a Cæsar, a Hannibal, a Tamerlane, a Napoleon, or even a Victoria?

Jesus said, "All that take the sword shall perish by the sword." An awful warning! All that take it to support religion, it is confessed, have fallen by it; but it may be feared that it is not simply confined to that; for may I not ask the pages of universal history, have not all the nations created by the sword finally fallen by it? Should any one say, "Some few of them yet stand," we respond, All that have fallen also stood for a time; and are not those that now stand tottering just at this moment to their overthrow? We have no doubt, it will prove in the end that nations and states founded by the sword shall fall by the sword.

When the Saviour, in his sententious and figurative style, indicating the trials just coming upon his friends, said, "You had better sell your outside garments and buy a sword," one present, understanding him literally, as some of the friends of war still do, immediately responded, "Lord, here are two swords." What did he say? "It is enough." Two swords for twelve apostles! Truly, they are dull scholars who thence infer that he meant they should literally use two swords to fight with! When asked by Pilate whether he was a king, he responded that he was born to be a king, but not a king of worldly type or character. Had he been such a king, his servants would, indeed, have used the sword. But his kingdom neither came nor stands by the sword. When first announced as a king by the Jewish prophets, more than seven centuries before he was born, the Spirit said of his reign, "He shall judge among the nations, and decide among many people. And they shall beat their swords into ploughshares, and their spears into pruning-hooks: nation shall not lift up sword against nation, neither shall they learn war any more." (Isa. ii. 2–4.) Two prophets describe it in almost the same words. Micah, as well as Isaiah, says—

> "Out of Zion shall go forth the law,
> And the word of Jehovah from Jerusalem;
> And he shall judge among many people,
> And decide among strong nations afar off;
> And they shall beat their swords into ploughshares,
> And their spears into pruning-hooks;
> Neither shall they any longer learn war:
> But they shall sit every man under his vine
> And under his fig-tree, and none shall make him afraid;
> For the mouth of Jehovah of hosts hath spoken it."

Such was, according to prophecy, such is, according to fact, the native influence and tendency of the Christian institution. The spirit of Christianity, then, is essentially pacific.

There is often a multiplication of testimony for display rather than for effect. And, indeed, the accumulation of evidence does not always increase its moral momentum. Nor is it very expedient on other considerations to labor a point which is generally, if not universally, admitted. That the genius and spirit of Christianity, as well as the letter of it, are admitted, on all hands, to be decidedly "peace on earth, and good will among men," needs no proof to any one that has ever read the volume that contains it.

But if any one desires to place in contrast the gospel of Christ and the genius of war, let him suppose the chaplain of an army addressing the soldiers on the eve of a great battle, on performing faithfully their duty, from such passages as the following:—"Love your enemies; bless them that curse you; do good to them that hate you, and pray for them that despitefully use you and persecute you: that you may be the children of your Father in heaven, who makes his sun to rise upon the evil and the good, and sends his rain upon the just and the unjust." Again, in our civil relations:—"Recompense to no man evil for evil." "As much as lieth in you, live peaceably with all men." "Dearly beloved, avenge not yourselves; but rather give place to wrath." "If thine enemy hunger, feed him; if he thirst, give him drink." "Be not overcome of evil; but overcome evil with good." Would any one suppose that he had selected a text suitable to the occasion? How would the commander-in-chief have listened to him? With what spirit would his audience have immediately entered upon an engagement? These are questions which every man must answer for himself, and which every one can feel much better than express.

But a Christian man cannot conscientiously enter upon any business, nor lend his energies to any cause, which he does not approve; and, in order to approve, he must understand the nature and object of the undertaking. Now, how does this dictate of discretion, religion and morality bear upon the case before us?

Nothing, it is alleged, more tends to weaken the courage of a conscientious soldier than to reflect upon the originating causes of wars and the objects for which they are prosecuted. These, indeed, are not always easily comprehended. Many wars have been prosecuted, and some have been terminated after long and protracted efforts, before the great majority of the soldiers themselves, on either side, distinctly understood what they were fighting for. Even in our country, a case of this sort has, it is alleged, very recently occurred. If, it is presumed, the true and proper causes of most wars were clearly understood, and the real design for which they are prosecuted could be clearly and distinctly apprehended, they would, in most instances, miscarry for the want of efficient means of a successful prosecution.

A conviction of this sort, some years ago, occasioned an elaborate investigation of the real causes for which the wars of Christendom had been undertaken from the time of Constantine the Great down to the present century. From the results furnished the Peace Society of Massachusetts, it appeared, that, after subtracting a number of petty wars, long since carried on, and those waged by Christian nations with tribes of savages, the wars of real magnitude amounted in all to two hundred and eighty-six. The origin of these wars, on a severe analysis, appeared to have been as follows:—Twenty-two for plunder and tribute; forty-four for the extension of territory; twenty-four for revenge or retaliation; six for disputed boundaries; eight respecting points of honor, or prerogative; six for the protection or extension of commerce; fifty-five civil wars; forty-one about contested titles to crowns; thirty under pretence of assisting allies; twenty-three for mere jealousy of rival greatness; twenty-eight religious wars, including the Crusades—*not one for defence alone;* and certainly not one that an enlightened Christian man could have given one cent for, in a voluntary way, much less have volunteered his services or enlisted into its ranks.

If the end alone justifies the means, what shall we think of the wisdom or the justice of war, or of the authors and prominent actors of these scenes? A conscientious mind will ask, Did these two hundred and eighty-six wars redress the wrongs, real or feigned, complained of? Did they in all cases, in a majority of the cases, or in a single case, necessarily determine the right side of the controversy? Did they punish the guilty, or the more guilty, in the ratio of their respective demerits? No one can, indeed, no one will, contend that the decision or termination of these wars naturally, necessarily, or even probably, decided the controversy so justly, so rationally, so satisfactorily as it could have been settled in any one case of the two hundred and eighty-six, by a third or neutral party.

War is not now, nor was it ever, a process of justice. It never was a test of truth—a criterion of right. It is either a mere game of chance, or a violent outrage of the strong upon the weak. Need we any other proof that a Christian people can in no way whatever countenance a war as a proper means of redressing wrongs, of deciding justice, or of settling controversies among nations? On the common conception of the most superficial thinkers on this subject, not one of the two hundred and eighty-six wars which have been carried on among the "Christian nations" during fifteen hundred years was such as that an enlightened Christian man could have taken any part in it—because, as admitted, not one of them was for defence alone: in other words, they were all aggressive wars.

But to the common mind, as it seems to me, the most convincing argument against a Christian becoming a soldier may be drawn from the fact that he fights against an innocent person—I say an innocent person, so far as the cause of the war is contemplated. The men that fight are not the men that make the war. Politicians, merchants, knaves and princes cause or make the war, declare the war, and hire men to kill for them those that may be hired on the other side to thwart their schemes of personal and family aggrandizement. The soldiers on either side have no enmity against the soldiers on the other side, because with them they have no quarrel. Had they met in any other field, in their citizen dress, other than in battle-array, they would, most probably, have not only inquired after the welfare of each other, but would have tendered to each other their assistance if called for. But a red coat or a blue coat, a tri-colored or a two-colored cockade, is their only introduction to each other, and the signal that they must kill or be killed! If they think at all, they must feel that there is no personal alienation, or wrong, or variance between them. But they are paid so much for the job; and they go to work, as the day-laborer to earn his shilling. Need I ask, how could a Christian man thus volunteer his services, or hire himself out for so paltry a sum, or for any sum, to kill to order his brother man who never offended him in word or deed? What infatuation! What consummate folly and wickedness! Well did Napoleon say, "War is the trade of barbarians;" and his conqueror, Wellington, "Men of nice scruples about religion have no business in the army or navy." The horrors of war only enhance the guilt of it; and these, alas! no one can depict in all their hideous forms.

By the "horrors of war" I do not mean the lightning and the thunder of the battle-field—the blackness and darkness of those dismal clouds of smoke which, like death's own pall, shroud the encounter; it is not the continual roar of its cannon, nor the agonizing shrieks and groans of fallen battalions—of wounded and dying legions; nor is it, at the close of the day, the battle-field itself, covered with the gore and scattered limbs of butchered myriads, with here and there a pile, a mountain heap of slain heroes in the fatal pass, mingled with the wreck of broken arms, lances, helmets, swords, and shattered firearms, amidst the pavement of fallen balls that have completed the work of destruction, numerous as hailstones after the fury of the storm; nor, amidst these, the sight of the wounded lying upon one another, weltering in their blood, imploring assistance, importuning an end of their woes by the hand of a surviving soldier, invoking death as the only respite from excruciating torments. But this is not all; for the tidings are at length carried to their respective homes. Then come the bitter wail of widows and orphans—the screams and the anguish of mothers and sisters deprived forever of the consolations and hopes that clustered round the anticipated return of those so dear to them, that have perished in the conflict.

But even these are not the most fearful desolations of war. Where now are the two hundred thousand lost by England in our Revolutionary War?—the seventy thousand who fell at Waterloo and Quatre-Bras?—the eighty thousand at Borodino?—the three hundred thousand at Arbela?—or where the fifteen million Goths destroyed by Justinian in twenty years?—the thirty-two millions by Jenghis Khan in forty-one years?—the sixty millions slain by the Turks?—the eighty millions by the Tartars, hurried away to judgment in a paroxysm of wrath, amid the fury of the passions? What can we think of their eternal destiny?* Besides all these, how many have died in captivity! How many an unfortunate exile or captive might, with a French prisoner, sing of woes like these, or even greater!—

"I dwelt upon the willowy banks of Loire;
I married one who from my boyish days
Had been my playmate. One morn,—I'll ne'er forget,—
While choosing out the fairest twigs
To warp a cradle for our child unborn,
We heard the tidings that the conscript-lot
Had fallen on me. It came like a death-knell!
The mother perish'd; but the babe survived;
And, ere my parting day, his rocking couch
I made complete, and saw him, sleeping, smile,—
The smile that play'd erst on the cheek of her
Who lay clay-cold. Alas! the hour soon came
That forced my fetter'd arms to quit my child!
And whether now he lives to deck with flowers
The sod upon his mother's grave, or lies
Beneath it by her side, I ne'er could learn.
I think he's gone, and now I only wish
For liberty and home, that I may see,
And stretch myself and die upon, their grave!"

But these, multiplied by myriads, are but specimens of the countless millions slain, the solitary exiles, the lonely captives. They tell the least portion of the miseries of war. Yet even these say to the Christian, How can you become a soldier? How countenance and aid this horrible work of death?

For my own part, and I am not alone in this opinion, I think that the moral desolations of war surpass even its horrors. And amongst these, I do not assign the highest place to the vulgar profanity, brutality and debauchery of the mere soldier, the professional and licensed butcher of mankind, who, for his eight dollars a month, or his ten

---

* "War a Destroyer of Souls,"—(a tract of the Peace Society.)

sous per day, hires himself to lay waste a country, to pillage, burn and destroy the peaceful hamlet, the cheerful village or the magnificent city, and to harass, wound and destroy his fellow-man, for no other consideration than his paltry wages, his daily rations, and the infernal pleasure of doing it, anticipating hereafter "the stupid stares and loud huzzas" of monsters as inhuman and heartless as himself. And were it not for the infatuation of public opinion and popular applause, I would place him, as no less to be condemned, beside the vain and pompous volunteer, who for his country, "right or wrong," hastens to the theatre of war for the mere plaudits of admiring multitudes, ready to cover himself with glory, because he has aided an aspirant to a throne or paved the way to his own election to reign over an humbled and degraded people.

I make great allowance for false education, for bad taste, for the contagion of vicious example: still, I cannot view those deluded by such sophistry, however good their motives, as deserving any thing from contemporaries or posterity except compassion and forgiveness. Yet behold its influence on mothers, sisters, and relatives: note its contagion, its corruption of public taste. See the softer sex allured, fascinated by the halo of false glory thrown around these worshipped heroes! See them gazing with admiration on the "tinselled trappings," the "embroidered ensigns," of him whose profession it is to make widows and orphans by wholesale! Sometimes their hands are withdrawn from works of charity to decorate the warrior's banners and to cater to these false notions of human glory! Behold, too, the young mother arraying her proud boy "with cap and feather, toyed with a drum and sword, training him for the admired profession of a man-killer!"

This is not all. It is not only at home, in the nursery and infant-school, that this false spirit is inspired. Our schools, our academies, our colleges, echo and re-echo with the fame of an Alexander, a Cæsar, a Napoleon, a Wellington. Forensic eloquence is full of the fame of great heroes, of military chieftains, of patriotic deliverers, whose memory must be kept forever verdant in the affections of a grateful posterity, redeemed by their patriotism, or rescued from oppression by their valor.

The pulpit, too, must lend its aid in cherishing the delusion. There is not unfrequently heard a eulogium on some fallen hero—some church-service for the mighty dead; thus desecrating the religion of the Prince of Peace, by causing it to minister as the handmaid of war. Not only are prayers offered up by pensioned chaplains on both sides of the field, even amid the din of arms, but, Sabbath after Sabbath, for years and years, have the pulpits on one side of a sea or river, and those on the other side, resounded with prayers for the success of rival armies, as if God could hear them both, and make each triumphant over the other, guiding and commissioning swords and bullets to the heads and hearts of their respective enemies!

And not only this, but even the churches in the Old World, and sometimes in the New, are ornamented with the sculptured representations of more military heroes than of saints—generals, admirals and captains, who "gallantly fought" and "gloriously fell" in the service of their country. It is not only in Westminster Abbey or in St. Paul's that we read their eulogiums and see their statues, but even in some of our own cities we find St. Paul driven out of the church to make room for generals and commodores renowned in fight. And last of all, in consummation of the moral desolation of war, we sometimes have an illumination—even a thanksgiving—rejoicing that God has caused ten or twenty thousand of our enemies to be sent down to Tartarus, and has permitted myriads of widows and orphans to be made at the bidding of some chieftain or of some aspirant to a throne!

But it would exhaust too much time to speak of the inconsistencies of the Christian world on this single subject of war, or to trace to their proper fountains the general misconceptions of the people on their political duties and that of their Governments. This would be the work of volumes—not of a single address. The most enlightened of our ecclesiastic leaders seem to think that Jesus Christ governs the nations as God governed the Jews. They cannot separate, even in this land, the church and state. They still ask for a Christian national code.

If the world were under a politico-ecclesiastic king or president, it would, indeed, be hard to find a model for him in the New Testament. Suffice it to say that the church, and the church only, is under the special government and guardianship of our Christian King. The nations, not owning Jesus Christ, are disowned by him; he leaves them to themselves, to make their own institutions, as God anciently did all nations but the Jews. He holds them in abeyance, and as in providence, so in government, he makes all things work together for the good of his people, restrains the wrath of their enemies, turns the counsels and wishes of kings as he turns the rivers, but never condescends to legislate for the bodies of men, or their goods or chattels, who withhold from him their consciences and their hearts. He announces the fact that it is by his permission, not always with his approbation, that kings reign and that princes decree justice, and commands his people politically to obey their rulers and to respect the ordinances of kings, that "they may lead quiet and peaceable lives, in all godliness and honesty." And where the gospel of Christ comes to kings and rulers, it addresses them as men in common with other men, commanding them to repent of their sins, to submit to his government, and to discharge their relative duties according to the morality and piety inculcated in his code. If they do this, they are a blessing to his people as well as an honor to themselves. If they do not, he will hold them to a reckoning, as other men, from which there is neither escape nor appeal. What Shakspeare says is as true of kings as of their subjects:—

> "War is a game that, were their subjects wise,
> Kings would not play at."

For, were both kings and people wise, wars would cease, and nations would learn war no more.

But how are all national disputes to be settled? Philosophy, history, the Bible, teach that all disputes, misunderstandings, alienations are to be settled, heard, tried, adjudicated by impartial, that is, by disinterested, umpires. No man is admitted to be a proper judge in his own case. Wars never make amicable settlements, and seldom, if ever, just decisions of points at issue. We are obliged to offer preliminaries of peace at last. Nations must meet by their representatives, stipulate and restipulate, hear and answer, compare and decide.

In modern times we terminate hostilities by a treaty of peace. We do not make peace with powder and lead. It is done by reason, reflection and negotiation. Why not employ these at first? But it is alleged that war has long been, and must always be, the *ultima ratio regum*—the last argument of those in power. For ages a father Inquisitor was the strong argument for orthodoxy; but light has gone abroad, and he has lost his power. Illuminate the human mind on this subject also, create a more rational and humane public opinion, and wars will cease.

But, it is alleged, all will not yield to reason or justice. There must be compulsion. Is war, then, the only compulsory measure? Is there no legal compulsion? Must all personal misunderstandings be settled by the sword?

Why not have a *by-law-established umpire?* Could not a united national court be made as feasible and as practicable as a United States court? Why not, as often proposed, and as eloquently, ably and humanely argued, by the advocates of peace, have a congress of nations and a high court of nations for adjudicating and terminating all international misunderstandings and complaints, redressing and remedying all wrongs and grievances?

There is not, it appears to me, a physical or a rational difficulty in the way. But I do not now argue the case: I merely suggest this expedient, and will always vote correspondingly, for reasons as good and as relevant as I conceive them to be humane and beneficial.

To sum up the whole, we argue—

1. The right to take away the life of the murderer does not of itself warrant war, inasmuch as in that case none but the guilty suffer, whereas in war the innocent suffer not only with, but often without, the guilty. The guilty generally make war, and the innocent suffer from its consequences.

2. The right given to the Jews to wage war is not vouchsafed to any other nation, for they were under a theocracy, and were God's sheriff to punish nations: consequently no Christian can argue from the wars of the Jews in justification or in extenuation of the wars of Christendom. The Jews had a Divine precept and authority: no existing nation can produce such a warrant.

3. The prophecies clearly indicate that the Messiah himself would be "THE PRINCE OF PEACE," and that under his reign "wars should cease," and "nations study it no more."

4. The gospel, as first announced by the angels, is a message which results in producing "peace on earth and good will among men."

5. The precepts of Christianity positively inhibit war—by showing that "wars and fightings come from men's lusts" and evil passions, and by commanding Christians to "follow peace with all men."

6. The beatitudes of Christ are not pronounced on patriots, heroes and conquerors, but on "peace-makers," on whom is conferred the highest rank and title in the universe:—"Blessed are the PEACE-MAKERS, for they shall be called THE SONS OF GOD."

7. The folly of war is manifest in the following particulars:—

1st. It can never be the criterion of justice or a proof of right.

2d. It can never be a satisfactory end of the controversy.

3d. Peace is always the result of negotiation, and treaties are its guarantee and pledge.

8. The wickedness of war is demonstrated in the following particulars:—

1st. Those who are engaged in killing their brethren, for the most part, have no personal cause of provocation whatever.

2d. They seldom, or never, comprehend the right or the wrong of the war. They, therefore, act without the approbation of conscience.

3d. In all wars the innocent are punished with the guilty.

4th. They constrain the soldier to do for the state that which, were he to do it for himself, would, by the law of the state, involve forfeiture of his life.

5th. They are the pioneers of all other evils to society, both moral and physical. In the language of Lord Brougham, "Peace, *peace*, PEACE! I abominate war as unchristian. I hold it the greatest of human curses. I deem it to include all others—violence, blood, rapine, fraud, every thing that can deform the character, alter the nature and debase the name of man." Or with Joseph Bonaparte, "War is but organized barbarism—an inheritance of the savage state." With Franklin I, therefore, conclude, "There never was a *good* war, or a *bad* peace."

No wonder, then, that for two or three centuries after Christ all Christians refused to bear arms. So depose Justin Martyr, Tatian, Clement of Alexandria, Tertullian, Origen, &c.

In addition to all these considerations, I further say, were I not a Christian, as a political economist, even, I would plead this cause. Apart from the mere claims of humanity, I would urge it on the ground of sound national policy.

Give me the money that has been spent in wars, and I will clear up every acre of land in the world that ought to be cleared—drain every marsh—subdue every desert—fertilize every mountain and hill—and convert the whole earth into a continuous series of fruitful fields, verdant meadows, beautiful villas, hamlets, towns, cities, standing along smooth and comfortable highways and canals, or in the midst of luxuriant and fruitful orchards, vineyards and gardens, full of fruits and flowers, redolent with all that pleases the eye and regales the senses of man. I would found, furnish and endow as many schools, academies and colleges, as would educate the whole human race,—would build meeting-houses, public halls, lyceums, and furnish them with libraries adequate to the wants of a thousand millions of human beings.

Beat your swords into ploughshares, your spears into pruning-hooks; convert your war-ships into missionary packets, your arsenals and munitions of war into Bibles, school-books, and all the appliances of literature, science and art; and then ask, What would be wanting on the part of man to "make the wilderness and solitary place glad;" to cause "the desert to rejoice and blossom as the rose;" to make our hills "like Carmel and Sharon," and our valleys as "the garden of God"? All this being done, I would doubtless have a surplus for some new enterprise.

On reviewing the subject in the few points only that I have made and with the comparatively few facts I have collected, I must confess that I both wonder at myself and am ashamed to think that I have never before spoken out my views, nor even written an essay on this subject. True, I had, indeed, no apprehension of ever again seeing or even hearing of a war in the United States. It came upon me so suddenly, and it so soon became a party question, that, preserving, as I do, a strict neutrality between party politics, both in my oral and written addresses on all subjects, I could not for a time decide whether to speak out or be silent. I finally determined not to touch the subject till the war was over. Presuming that time to have arrived, and having resolved that my first essay from my regular course, at any foreign point, should be on this subject, I feel that I need offer no excuse, ladies and gentlemen, *for* having called your attention to the matter in hand. I am sorry to think—very sorry indeed to be only of the opinion—that probably even this much published by me some three years or even two years ago, might have saved some lives that have since been thrown away in the desert—some hot-brained youths

> **"Whose limbs, unburied on the shore,**
> **Devouring dogs or hungry vultures tore."**

We have all a deep interest in the question; we can all do something to solve it; and it is every one's duty to do all the good he can. We must create a public opinion on this subject. We should inspire a pacific spirit, and urge on all proper occasions the chief objections to war. In the language of the eloquent Grimké, we must show that "the great objection to war is not so much the number of lives and the amount of property it destroys, as its moral influence on nations and individuals. It creates and perpetuates national jealousy, fear, hatred and envy. It arrogates to itself the prerogative of the Creator alone, to involve the innocent multitude in the punishment of the guilty few. It corrupts the moral taste and hardens the heart; cherishes and strengthens the base and violent passions; destroys the distinguishing features of Christian charity—its *universality* and its *love of enemies;* turns into mockery and contempt the best virtue of Christians—*humility;* weakens the sense of moral obligation; banishes the spirit of improvement, usefulness and benevolence; and inculcates the horrible maxim that murder and robbery are matters of state expediency."

Let every one, then, who fears God and loves man, put his hand to the work; and the time will not be far distant when

> "No longer hosts encountering hosts
> Shall crowds of slain deplore:
> They'll hang the trumpet in the hall,
> And study war no more."

AN ORATION

IN HONOR OF THE FOURTH OF JULY, 1830.*

CHRISTIAN CITIZENS:—

Omnipotent is the word of God. He spake, and a world was made. "*Let there be light*," he said, "*and there was light.*" He uttered his voice, and from darkness light was born, from chaos order sprang, and from an inert mass of lifeless matter animated beings of ten thousand ranks and orders stood forth in life triumphant.

* A number of disciples, principally members of the Church of Christ, in Pittsburg, agreed to have a *love-feast* on Monday, the 5th of July, 1830. They chose that day *in honor of the fourth of July*, 1776. Grateful to Heaven for the blessings which that day vouchsafed the citizens of this country, they thought that Christians participating in them ought *religiously* to call to mind the goodness of God in granting that deliverance. While the children of *this* world, with voluptuous joys and noisy mirth, are regarding the day because of the *political* privileges which they inherit, we know of no good reason why Christians may not, if they please, consecrate the day to the Lord as a *free-will offering*, and convert the occasion into one of joy and rejoicing in the Rock of their salvation, giving glory to the Governor of the nations of the earth that they are made *free* citizens, not only of a free Government on *earth*, but of the kingdom of *heaven*.

More than a hundred and twenty disciples, with sundry visitants and many children, dined together in an arbor about two miles from the city. The day was spent in joy and gladness of heart, singing the praises of the Lord, and in conversing about the good things of the heavenly country. I had the pleasure of pronouncing the following oration immediately before dinner. After the oration, the following song was sung:—

Behold, the mountain of the Lord
In latter days shall rise
On mountain-tops, above the hills,
And draw the wondering eyes.

To this the joyful nations round,
All tribes and tongues shall flow;
"Up to the hill of God," they'll say,
"And to his house we'll go."

The beam that shines from Zion's hill
Shall lighten every land;
The King who reigns in Salem's towers
Shall all the world command.

Among the nations he shall judge;
His judgments truth shall guide;
His sceptre shall protect the just,
And quell the sinner's pride.

No strife shall rage, nor hostile feuds
Disturb those peaceful years;
To ploughshares men shall beat their swords,
To pruning-hooks their spears.

No longer host encountering host
Shall crowds of slain deplore:
They'll hang the trumpet in the hall,
And study war no more.

Come, then, O house of Jacob, come
To worship at his shrine;
And, walking in the light of God,
With holy beauties shine.

Thus came the universe from the command of God. But how gradual and progressive was the development of the wisdom, power and goodness of the Almighty Maker! Light was the first born; next, the aerial expanse called heaven; then the water heard his voice, and of the terraqueous globe this element first felt the impulse of the all-creating energy. It was congregated into its aerial and terrestrial chambers. Naked from the womb of waters the earth appeared. The new-born earth God clothed with verdure—with all the charms of vegetable beauty—and gave to its apparel a conservative principle, a reproducing power.

Light was itself chaotic until the fourth day. No luminaries garnished the firmament until the week of creation was more than half expired. It was then that the sun, moon and stars were lighted up by the great Father of Lights. Until the earth was born of water, no sun beamed in heaven, no ray of celestial light shone upon its face. No life was in the earth until the sun beamed upon it: then were the waters peopled, and from them came forth the inhabitants of the air. In the domain of this wonderful element life was first conceived and exhibited.

The race of earth-borns, creatures of a grosser habit, did not hear the voice of God until the sixth day. On that day they obeyed the command of God, and stepped forth into life. Then the Almighty changed his style. Till then his commands were all addressed in the third person. "*Let there be*" was the preamble, "*and there was*" was the conclusion. But now, "*Let us make man;*" and let us make him after a model. The only being made after a model was man. All other creatures were originals. If any creature approached him, in any one similitude, it was in anticipation. Man steps forth into life in the image of his Maker, and finds himself the youngest child of the universe, but the darling of his Father and his God. Here the chapter of creation closes, and man has the last period.

Such was the value stamped on man by his Creator. A world is made and peopled for him; a palace reared and furnished and deco-

---

After dinner, Brother Walter Scott delivered a very interesting discourse on *the great and notable day of the Lord* which is to introduce the millennium. Many citizens assembled to hear the discourse; after which, we proceeded to the river, where five persons were immersed into the ancient faith. Thus closed one of the most joyful anniversaries of our national independence which we ever witnessed. Every incident of the day was pleasing and agreeable, and the whole celebration was well adapted to promote the edification and comfort of every disciple of the Prince of Peace. All was conducted in the simplicity, decency and good order which become the Christian profession.

rated for his abode; the great Architect plans and executes the edifice, and then introduces to its richest apartment the favorite of the universe. It is here we are taught the science—it is here we learn the numbers which, when combined with wisdom, tell of how much account we are.

On man, thus valued, dignified and honored by his Maker, a lordship is conferred. Over all that swims, that flies or that walks upon the earth, his dominion extends. The crown placed upon his head had attractions which angels saw, and charms which angels felt. Man thus placed in Eden, with his Eve *from* and *by* his side—having all its fruits and flowers and sweets and charms under his control, with the smallest reservation in favor of the absolute Sovereign of the universe; having, too, the whole earth, from Eden's flowery banks to both the poles, subject to his will—becomes the most enviable object in all the great empire of the universe. His fortune was not to *make*—it was only to *keep*. But, alas! to one destitute of experience, however exalted, how hard to guard, how difficult to retain, possessions gratuitously acquired!

Man, the last, best work of God, environed with the riches and glory of a world built and furnished for him, is envied, and his ruin meditated, by the prince of apostates. He falls through his machinations. From God and Eden he falls at once, and involves with him the fortunes of a world.

For his recovery, a remedial system is set on foot by his Creator; and such a system it is as was worthy of its author and of the admiration of an intelligent universe. To turn from the catastrophe of man to this recuperative system, is, of all transitions, the most grateful to the human mind. This is "*a theme which never, never old shall grow.*" Eternity itself, vast and unbounded as it is, can never do more than develop it. Time furnishes but the scaffolding for rearing this temple of science. It is in a temple yet to be built that this science is to be perfected, to be taught and to be learned.

The knowledge of God is all the bliss which rational beings can propose to themselves. This knowledge, indeed, requires an acquaintance with all his works; for, as we learn men only by their works, we learn our Creator only by his works. But *here* we are only in the alphabet, and *here* we can never rise above it; and few, indeed, in this life acquire an accurate knowledge of the art of reading God. The *primer* which God has put into the hands of man in this primary school is divided into three chapters. The heads of these are *creation, providence* and *redemption.* It is God alone who, to the initiated, is seen in every character, word and sentence in this elementary volume; and he who sees not God in every sentence of this *primer*, knows neither himself nor any thing else in the universe.

This memorable occasion, fellow-citizens of the kingdom of God, calls for a few remarks on the past, the present and the future providence of God. Aided by the lights of the living oracles, we can look back to the birth of time, and forward to the funeral of nature, time and death. Looking back through the long vista of past ages, beyond the birth of the empires of antiquity, beyond the birth of kings and emperors and governments, we find a world without *civil* government. This is farther back than human records and chronology extend, but not farther than the records and chronology to which God has vouchsafed us access. In a world without civil government, the earth was filled with violence, and crime multiplied, until, in the judgment of God, the destruction of the whole race, with a single exception, became indispensable. As water first felt the creative energy of God, by its agency the first general judgment was inflicted. The anarchists were drowned; and in their death and burial the earth was washed from the pollutions of one thousand six hundred and fifty-six years.

In the New World an avenger of crime, and especially of blood, is the first institution. The second chapter of the history of the Divine government over men begins with the establishment of civil government. The inhabitants of the new world were filed off into small groups, called *tribes,* and the first effort to resist this arrangement was avenged by the confusion of human speech, which made dispersion unavoidable. Patriarchs and princes over these small detachments of human beings, called *nations,* wielded the sceptre for nearly a thousand years without any remarkable incident. Cities and towns and palaces were reared and ruined during the interval from the deluge till the erection of a religious nation. At that time tribes had grown up into nations, and nations began to form alliances, and thus empires began to be developed. As these increased, idolatry began to increase. The larger the groups of human beings, either in cities or empires, the more idolatrous they became. They refined in crime, until idolatry became the desolating sin of the second world, as violence was the damning sin of the antediluvian world.

To save the second world from one general ruin, a religious nation was erected, upon all the institutions of which the Divinity was inscribed, and in such a way that nothing but the annihilation of that nation could annihilate the knowledge of the one only living and true God. This nation began in miracle, progressed in miracle, was governed specially, or by miracle, and, though exiled from its possessions because of its crimes, miraculously exists still, a monument of the favor of God, and carrying with it everywhere a proof of the Divinity which no ingenuity, however perverse, can obliterate or deface. It held its possessions in the land allotted to it for nearly fifteen hundred years.

Then opens a new era. A celestial King is born, and born to reign over the human race forever. The principles of his government, in their grand essentials, are new principles. This new institution, new once, and still new in contrast with the past and with the reigning earthly systems, is called, significantly, *the Reign of Heaven.* The King is heaven-born and divine. Heavenly and divine are the principles of his government; and though his subjects live a while on earth, his government is designed to give them a taste of, and a taste for, heavenly things.

His government began in conquest, by conquest still increases, and will by conquests ultimately subdue all things to himself. On a white horse, with a single crown upon his head, with a bow and a full quiver, in the book of symbols he appears as going forth to war. But at the end of the long campaign he appears again, with many crowns upon his head, with all the kingdoms of the world in his train, and with the trophies of many battles, worshipped as the King of kings and the Lord of lords.

The cardinal principle in his government is love. He subdues by no other sword than that of the Spirit. Other kings subdue men's persons and hold a sovereignty over their estates, but he seizes the hearts of men. To conquer enemies is his grand enterprise. Philosophy as well as religion teaches us that to conquer enemies is not the work of swords, or lances, or bows of steel. It is not to bind men's persons to a triumphal car, to incarcerate them in strongholds, or to make them surrender to superior bravery, prowess and strength. *To conquer an enemy is to convert him into a friend.* This is the noble, benevolent and heaven-conceived enterprise of God's only-begotten Son. To do this all arms and modes of warfare are impotent, save the arms and munitions of everlasting love. By vivid displays of God's philanthropy he approaches his enemies, and by the arguments with which this eloquence is fraught he addresses a rebel world. Such is his mode of warfare; a system devised in heaven, and, like all of God's means, perfectly adapted to the high ends proposed.

But, not to lose sight of the great outline of things begun, let us pause and survey the chapters we have scanned. In the first we saw society without civil government; in the second, society with civil government without religious associations; in the third, society under a politico-religious government; and in the fourth chapter, a scheme begun which contemplates the government of men by religion without politics, by the efficacy of one principle alone. This is the chapter of chapters now in progress and full of the greatest and most astonishing incidents. We saw the rise, progress and issue of three states of society; but as yet we cannot distinctly see the issue of the present. Its progress we may survey and its tendency we may appreciate, but its full development and glorious issue are, perhaps, too far removed from our optics and from our experience to be clearly and distinctly apprehended.

But, to aid us in looking *forward,* let us again look *back.* Christianity, or the New Institution, was set up under a Jewish government. Under that government it existed for a time; thence it passed under a Pagan government; next under a Papal government; and now, in this portion of the earth, it has come under a *political* government.

Under a circumscribed Jewish government it began. With this it did not, could not, coalesce. Over that government it ultimately triumphed. The principles of that government and of the government of Jesus Christ were at variance, and therefore one or the other must be destroyed. The Jewish government fell, and fell chiefly through its opposition to Christianity.

It next passed under a Pagan government. The conflict soon began, and the Pagan government fell. Christianity triumphed. But let it be distinctly marked that Christianity set itself in no other way against either the Jewish or Pagan government, than as its principles tended to bestow upon mankind a happiness from which that government debarred them; and therefore the religion of Jesus—though passive in that conflict, and though imperial Rome, armed with all political power, and allied with all the superstitions of past ages, was active in opposing it—prevailed and broke in pieces the Pagan power which resisted it.

Papal Rome rises out of the ruins of Pagan Rome. Christianity is then subjected to a more insidious and a more unconquerable government. This government, by its largesses to Christianity, and by its paganized Christian institutes, held its dominion longer over the institution of Jesus than ever did, or than ever can, any government openly opposed to its principles. But even over this Christianity is triumphing, and so far has triumphed that the New World has set up twenty-four governments, and is setting up others, upon principles at variance with those of all the Papal and Pagan governments of the Old World. So far, then, Christianity has triumphed and is triumphing over Papal Rome.

Citizens of the reign of heaven, let us for a moment turn our eyes to that government under which Christianity exists in this most favored of all lands, in this wide and capacious and still-extending empire. Tired and jaded with the conflicts of Papal Rome, grieved and incensed at the infractions of the rights of conscience and the rights of men and at all the tyrannies of conflicting sectarian institutions, our ancestors sought a city of refuge, a hiding-place from the storm, in this newly-discovered section of the patrimony of Japheth. God, more than four thousand years ago, promised to Japheth an enlargement of his territory, when he gave him the broken and indented patrimony of Europe. Here he found it; and our fathers, taught in the schools of Papal and sectarian proscription, imagined that a government without any religion, a government purely deistical, skeptical or political, was the *summum bonum*—the very maximum of social bliss. They went as far as mortals, stung by the fiery dragon, could go, to devise a government without a single religious institution. They succeeded not only in *declaring* but in *sustaining* their independence in the eyes of all the sons of pride, and in rearing for themselves and their children political institutions which have hitherto secured, and will, we hope, continue, to secure, till Christianity conquers the world, the greatest amount of political and temporal happiness hitherto enjoyed by any people. This government proposes only to guard the temporal and worldly rights of men. It regards this world as the only appropriate object of its supervision and protection. It permits every man to be of no religion, or of any religion he pleases. It has no partialities for the Jew, the Christian, the Turk or the Indian. Such is its creed. Here the affairs of another world are left to themselves. The government says to all the rival sectarian interests, "FAIR PLAY AND THE RIGHTS OF MEN!" It will not help by its statutes, nor retard by its proscriptions, any religion, or sect of religionists, now on the theatre. This is all that Christianity asks, or can ask, until she conquers the world. Whenever a sect calls for the governmental arm to help her—to hold her up—she proclaims herself overmatched by her competitors, and declares her consciousness that on the ground of *reason* and *evidence* she is unable to stand.

The present government aims at being *purely political*, and therefore can secure only man's political rights and promote his political happiness. This is all that worldly men wish; and it is all that a sectarian profession of religion can reasonably or justly require. He is a tyrant in principle, and would be one in practice, who asks for *exclusive privileges.* None but tyrants and knaves have ever sought pre-eminence by law or by force.

But still we are far from considering that a political government can ever fill up the measure of human, of social, of rational enjoyment. And all confess that were men truly religious political government would be unnecessary. So far this is a concession in favor of our grand position, *that Jesus Christ will yet govern the world by religion only, and that by the operation of one single principle.* Then shall they literally "beat their swords into ploughshares and their spears into pruning-hooks, and learn war no more." Christianity rightly understood, cordially embraced and fully carried out in practice, will as certainly subvert all political government, the very best as well as the very worst, as did the Jewish institution and people subvert and supplant the seven nations which once occupied the land of Canaan.

The admirers of American liberty and American institutions have no cause to regret such an event, no cause to fear it. It will be but the removing of a tent to build a temple—the falling of a cottage after the family are removed into a castle. Not by might, nor by sword, but by the Spirit of the Lord will the political institutions of our government be laid aside. The sun itself and the systems of worlds which revolve round it we can well dispense with when we arrive in the palace of the universe, where God is the Sun, the Light and the Glory. So our best political institutions we can part with without a tear or a sigh, when Jesus reigns on earth, and has placed a throne in every heart and built a temple in every family.

The *fourth of July,* 1776, was a memorable day, a day to be remembered as was the Jewish Passover—a day to be regarded with grateful acknowledgments by every American citizen, by every philanthropist in all the nations of the world. The light which shines from our political institutions will penetrate even the dungeons of European despots, *for the genius of our Government is the genius of universal emancipation!* Nothing can resist the political influence of a great nation, enjoying great political advantages, if she walk worthy of them. The example which our Government gives is necessarily terrible to the crowned heads of Europe, and exhilarating to all who look for the redemption of man from political degradation.

But there is the superlative as well as the comparative degree. A more illustrious day is yet in prospect—a day when it shall be said, "Rejoice over her, you holy apostles and prophets, for God has avenged you on her!"—a day on which an angel shall proclaim, "The kingdoms of this world have become the kingdoms of our Lord!"—a day on which it shall be sung, "The kingdom, and dominion, and the greatness of the kingdoms under the whole heaven, is given to the people of the Most High, and all people shall serve and obey him!" This will be a day of gladness only to be surpassed by the joys of the resurrection.

The American Revolution is but the precursor of a revolution of infinitely more importance to mankind. It was a great, a happy and a triumphant revolution. But time and space limit and circumscribe all its blessings to mankind. It will long, perhaps always, be accounted an illustrious and happy era in the history of man. Many thanksgivings and praises have reached unto heaven because of this great deliverance. The incense of gratitude, perfumed with the praises of saints, has long risen from myriads of hearts, and will continue to rise until the cloud shall cover the whole earth, and the glory of the Lord be reflected upon all the nations of the earth.

The praises of a Washington, a Franklin and a Jefferson will long resound through the hills and valleys of this spacious country, and will, in proportion as men are prepared to taste the blessings to result from the next revolution, continually increase. Posterity will only mingle their regrets that, like Moses, all their political leaders died short of the promised land—that, while they guided the tribes almost to Canaan, they fell in the wilderness, without tasting the sweets of the good inheritance.

A more glorious work is reserved for this generation—a work of as much greater moment, compared with the Revolution of '76, as immortality is to the present span of human life—the emancipation of the human mind from the shackles of superstition, and the introduction of human beings into the full fruition of the reign of heaven. To liberate the minds of men from sectarian tyrannies—to deliver them from the melancholy thraldom of relentless systems, is a work fraught with greater blessings, a work of a nobler daring and loftier enterprise, than the substitution of a representative democracy for an absolute or limited monarchy. This revolution, taken in all its influences, will make men free indeed. A political revolution can only make men politically free to task themselves, and to exact from themselves a service which few of the despots of more barbarous climes inflict upon their veriest slaves.

Talk not of a liberty which only makes men greater slaves. Under the monarchies of the Old World men are more free from themselves than under the free government of these United States. The reason is, under this free government the citizens have the opportunity and the liberty of improving and bettering their circumstances to such an extent as to engross all their energies, to call forth all their powers: hence, upon themselves they impose such tasks and inflict such toils and privations as few of the monarchs of the East would be so cruel as to impose upon their subjects. Here in this land of liberty we see all men striving for power. The accomplishment of one or more projects does not diminish their labor or their enterprise. Quite the reverse: the more successful, the more eager to commence again. And how often, how very often, do we see men dying under the whip of their own cupidity, in full harness pulling up the hill of their own ambition, when death kindly interposes, takes the burden off their galled shoulders, and strips them for the shroud! Yet they boast of being free! Free!—yes, to make slaves of themselves! If the Son of God had made them free, they would not thus toil till the last pulsation of their hearts.

Men love independence; and of this we boast. Yet there is not a perfect consistency in our assumptions upon this subject. We have heard men boast of their independence, when the tailor, the cordwainer, the merchant and the physician were continually called upon for their services. We have heard our citizens boast of their national independence, when almost every article of their apparel, even to the buttons on their wrists, was of foreign growth and manufacture. And, what is still more inconsistent, we have heard our fellow-citizens boast of political independence, and seen them content to import their creed from Scotland, to yield to a system manufactured in Geneva, and at the same time slavishly serving divers lusts, and living under the dominion of the fiercest passions and most grovelling propensities of human nature.

Conscience makes slaves as well as cowards of multitudes who boast of being free. No person who is under the fear of death ever can be free. They who are afraid of the consequences of death are all their lifetime in bondage. To escape from this vassalage is worthy of the greatest struggle which man could make. This, however, is the first boon which Christianity tenders to all who put themselves under its influence. It proclaims a jubilee to the soul—it opens the prison-doors, and sets the captives free. The King of Saints holds not one of his voluntary subjects under a vassalage so cruel. The corruptions of antichristian systems are admirably adapted to increase and cherish this fear, which tends to bondage; but to those who embrace and bow to the real gospel, there is bestowed a full deliverance, and a gracious exemption from this most grievous bondage of the soul.

But when I name the true gospel, the proclamation of God's philanthropy, the declaration of the independence of the kingdom of Jesus, I am constrained to remind you, my fellow-citizens of the Christian kingdom, that this is the mighty instrument by which this world is to be revolutionized—this is the sword of the Eternal Spirit—this is that weapon which is mighty, through God, to the demolition of all the strongholds of the man of sin, as well as of that strong one that rules and reigns in the hearts of the children of disobedience. By it alone, proclaimed and proved and sustained in the lives of its advocates, were the Jewish and Pagan institutions of former ages supplanted by the Christian, and that great change in society effected which is still blessing the earth with the influences of peace and good will. By its influences the leopard and the kid, the lion and the lamb, have in innumerable instances been made most friendly associates and companions. It imparts courage to the timid, strength to the infirm, hearing to the deaf, and speech to the dumb. It gives peace to the conscience, rest to the soul, ardor to the affections, and animation to the hopes of men. It is God's wisdom and his power, because it is his philanthropy drawn to the life, and exhibited by the strongest argument in the universe —the death of his only Son.

To introduce the last and most beneficial change in society, it is only necessary to let the gospel, in its own plainness, simplicity and force, speak to men. Divest it of all the appendages of human philosophy, falsely so called, and of all the traditions and dogmas of men; and in its power it will pass from heart to heart, from house to house, from city to city, until it bless the whole earth. See how fraternal it is. Since it began to be proclaimed, and sustained by the ancient order of things, see what changes it has made, and what effects it has produced, and with what rapidity it has spread over the country. More new churches have been formed within twelve months, where the primitive gospel has been proclaimed with clearness and power, than the twelve preceding years can count under the humanized gospel of the sects.

While the mere politicians of the land and the children of the flesh are rejoicing together around their festive boards, and in toasts and songs boasting of their heroes and themselves, we ought to glory in the Lord, rejoice in the God of our salvation, and sing a loftier song and of purer joy than they. And while with them we remember with gratitude the achievements of the patriots of the land, we ought to rejoice with joy unspeakable and full of glory in recollecting the Christian Chief, and his holy apostles, who has made us free indeed, and given us the rank and dignity, not of citizens of earthly states, but of heaven. Yes: he is worthy of all gratitude, and of all adoration, who has made all the citizens of his kingdom not citizens only, but citizen-kings and priests to God.

While they extol the bloody battles of the warrior, as "every battle of the warrior is with confused noise and garments rolled in blood," let us not forget the victories of Him who did not lift up his voice in the streets—who did not use so much as a broken reed, nor consume a single torch, until he made his laws victorious. In that spirit of mildness, meekness and unostentatious heroism, let us fight the good fight of faith, and, as good soldiers of Jesus Christ, let us all be found faithful at our posts.

We may not rejoice once, but always. We may have our feasts of gratitude and love, and with the saints of olden times we may shout for joy. We may say, with Isaiah, "Sing, O heavens! and be joyful, O earth! and break forth into singing, O mountains! for the Lord has comforted his people, and will have mercy upon his afflicted. Sing unto the Lord, for he has done excellent things! Cry out and shout, O inhabitant of Zion! for great is the Holy One of Israel in the midst of thee." And with Habakkuk let us say, "Although the fig-tree shall not blossom, neither shall fruit be on the vine; though the labor of the olive shall fail, and the fields shall yield no food; though the flocks shall be cut off from the fold, and there shall be no herd in the stalls: yet we will rejoice in the Lord, and joy in the God of our salvation." "Let the heavens rejoice; let the earth be glad; let the sea roar; let the fields be joyful; let all the trees of the forest rejoice; let the hills be joyful together before the Lord, because he comes to bless his people. Bless the Lord, all his works, in all places of his dominions: bless the Lord, O my soul!"

ADDRESS ON DEMONOLOGY.

DELIVERED BEFORE THE POPULAR LECTURE CLUB, NASHVILLE, TENNESSEE, MARCH 10, 1841.

MR. PRESIDENT,

And Gentlemen, members of the Popular Lecture Club:—

While the antiquary is gathering up the mouldering ruins of ancient temples, palaces and cities, or poring over the coins, medals and statues of other ages, seeking to prove or to embellish some theory of the olden times; while the astronomer is directing his largest telescope to some remote ethereal field, far beyond the Milky Way, in search of new nebulæ unseen hitherto, in hope to find the nucleus of some incipient solar system; while the speculative geologist is delving down to the foundations of the eternal mountains, in quest of new evidences of his doctrine of successive and long-protracted formations of the massy strata of mother earth, "rock-ribbed and ancient as the sun;" while the skeptic is exultingly scanning the metaphysical dream of some imaginary system of nature, or seeking in the desolations of the ancient mythologies arguments against the mighty facts and overwhelming demonstrations of the Christian faith—may I be allowed, gentlemen, to invite you into the precincts of Demonology, to accompany me in a brief excursion into the land of demons, whence, dark and mysterious though it be, we may perhaps, guided by some friendly star, elicit some useful light on that grand and awful world of spirits which, as we descend the hill of life, rises higher and higher in its demands upon our time and thoughts, as embracing the all-absorbing interests of human kind?

Think not, however, that I intend to visit the fairy realms and enchanting scenes of wild romance, or that I wish to indulge in the fascinating fictions of poets, ancient or modern; think not that I am about to ascend with old Hesiod into his curious theogony of gods and demigods, or to descend with the late Sir Walter Scott to the phantasmatic realms of Celtic and Scottish ghosts and demons. I aim at more substantial entertainment, at more sober and grave realities, than the splendid fancies of those gifted and fortunate votaries of popular applause.

The subject of demons, as forming a portion of the real antiquities of the world—as connected with Pagan, Jewish and Christian theology —the subject of demons, sometimes called devils, not in their fictitious, but in their true character, is that which I propose to discuss; for even here, as in every thing else, there are the fact and the fable, the true and the false, the real and the imaginary. The extravagant fancies of the poets, the ghosts and spectres of the dark ages, have spread their sable mantles upon this subject, and involved it either in philosophical dubiety or in a blind indiscriminate infidelity.

The Christian philosopher in this department, as in most others, finds truth and fable blended in the same tradition; and therefore, neither awed by authority, nor allured by the fascinations of novelty, he institutes an examination into the merits of this subject, which, if true, cannot but deeply interest the thoughtful, and if false, should be banished from the minds of all.

That a class of beings designated *demons* has been an element of the faith, an object of the dread and veneration, of all ages and nations, as far back as memory reaches, no one who believes in a spiritual system —no one who regards the volumes of divine inspiration, or who is even only partially acquainted with Pagan and Jewish antiquity, can reasonably doubt. But concerning these demons, of what order of intelligences, of what character and destiny, of what powers intellectual and moral, there has been much debate, and there is need of further and more satisfactory examination.

Before entering either philosophically or practically into this investigation, it is necessary that we define the true and proper meaning of the term *demon.* This word, it is said, is of Grecian origin and character—of which, however, we have not full assurance. In that language it is written and pronounced *daimoon,* and, according to some etymologists, is legitimately descended from a very ancient verb, pronounced *daioo,* which means *to discriminate, to know. Daimoon,* or *demon,* therefore, simply indicates a person of intelligence—*a knowing one.* Thus, before the age of philosophy, or the invention of the name, those were called demons, as a title of honor, who afterwards assumed the more modest title of philosophers. Aristotle, for his great learning, was called a *demon,* as was the celebrated Thucydides: hence among the Platonists it was for some time a title of honor. But this, it must be observed, was a special appropriation, like our use of the words *divine* and *reverend*. When we apply these titles to sinful men, who, because of their calling, ought to be not only intelligent, but of a divine and celestial temper and morality, we use them by a special indulgence from that sovereign pontiff with whom is the *jus et norma loquendi*.

But as some of the Platonists elevated the spirits of departed heroes, public benefactors and distinguished men into a species of demigods or mediators between them and the Supreme Divinity, as some of our forefathers were accustomed to regard the souls of departed saints, this term began to be used in a more general sense. Among some philosophers it became the title of an object of worship; while, on the other hand, it degenerated into the genii of poetry and imagination.

In tracing the popular transitions of words, permit me, gentlemen, to say that we are not to imagine that they ceremoniously advance, like our naval and military officers, from one rank to another, by some systematic or conventional agreement. On the contrary, the transitions are exceedingly anomalous, and sometimes inverted. In this instance the term *demon*, from simply indicating *a knowing one*, became the title of a human spirit when divested of its clay tenement, because of its supposed initiation into the secrets of another world. Thus a separated spirit became a genius, a demigod, a mediator, a divinity of the ancient superstition, according to its acquirements in this state of probation.

But we shall better understand the force and import of this mysterious word from its earliest acceptation among the elder Pagans, Jews and Christians, than from the speculations of etymologists and lexicographers. Historical facts, then, and not etymological speculations, shall decide not only its meaning, but the character and rank of those beings on whom, by common consent, this significant title was conferred.

To whom, then, among Pagan writers shall we make our first appeal? Shall we not at once carry up the question to the most venerable Hesiod, the oldest of Grecian bards, whose style even antedates that of Homer himself almost one hundred years? Shall we not appeal to the genealogist of all the gods, the great theogonist of Grecian mythology? Who more likely than he to be acquainted with the ancient traditions of demons? And what is the sum of his testimony in the case? Hear him speak in the words of Plutarch:—"The spirits of mortals become demons when separated from their earthly bodies." The Grecian biographist not only quotes with approbation the views of Hesiod, but corroborates them by the result of his own researches, avowing his conviction that "the demons of the Greeks were the ghosts and genii of departed men; and that they go up and down the earth as observers, and even rewarders, of men; and although not actors themselves, they encourage others to act in harmony with their views and characters." Zenocrates, too, as quoted by Aristotle, extends the term to the souls of men before death, and calls them demons while in the body. To the good demons and the spirits of deceased heroes they allotted the office of mediators between gods and men.* In this light Zoroaster, Thales, Pythagoras, Plato, Plutarch, Celsus, Apuleius, and many others regarded the demons of their times.

Whoever, indeed, will be at pains to examine the Pagan mythologies, one and all, will discover that some doctrine of demons, as respects their nature, abodes, characters or employments, is the ultimate foundation of their whole superstructure; and that the radical idea of all the dogmata of their priests, and the fancies and fables of their poets, is found in that most ancient and veritable tradition—that the spirits of men survive their fallen tabernacles, and live in a disembodied state from death to the dissolution of material nature. To these spirits, in the character of genii, gods or demigods, they assigned the fates and fortunes of men and countries. With them a hero on earth became a demon in hades, and a demigod, a numen, a divinity, in the skies. It is not without some reason that the witty and ingenious Lucian makes his dialogist, in the orthodoxy of his age, ask and answer the following questions:—*What is man? A mortal god. And what is God? An immortal man.* In one sentence, all Pagan antiquity affirms that from Titan and Saturn, the poetic progeny of Cœlusm and Terra, down to Æsculapius, Proteus and Minos, all their divinities were the ghosts of dead men, and were so regarded by the most erudite of the Pagans themselves.

Think not, gentlemen, that because we summon the Pagan witnesses first, we regard them as the first either in point of age or character. Far from it. They were a set of plagiarists, from Hesiod to Lucian. The Greeks were the greatest literary thieves and robbers that ever lived; and they had the most consummate art of concealing the theft. From these Pagans, whether Greeks or Romans, we ascend to the Jews and to the Patriarchs, whose annals transcend those of the most ancient Pagans many centuries.

---

* Hence the saint-worship and saint mediators of the dark ages, and of the less favored portions of the Anglo-Saxon race.

In the times of the Patriarchs, in the infancy of the Abrahamic family, long before the time of their own Moses, we learn that in the land of Canaan, almost coeval with the promise of it to Abraham, demons were recognized and worshipped. The consultation of the spirits of the dead, the art and mystery of necromancy, familiar spirits, and wizards, are older than Moses, and are spoken of by him as matters of ancient faith and veneration. Statutes, indeed, are ordained, and laws are promulged from Mount Sinai in Arabia, by the Eternal King, against the worship of demons, the consultation of familiar spirits, the practice of necromancy, and all the arts of divination; of which we may speak more particularly in the sequel. Hence we affirm that the doctrine of a separate state—of disembodied ghosts, or demons—of necromancy and divination, is a thousand years older than Homer or Hesiod, than any Pagan historian, philosopher or poet whomsoever. And so deeply rooted in the land of Canaan, so early and so long cherished and taught by the seven nations, was this doctrine in all its branches, that, notwithstanding the severe statutes against it, traces of it are found among the Jews for almost a thousand years after Moses. Of the wicked Jeroboam it is said, "He ordained priests for the high places, and for the demons."* Even David admits that his nation "learned the works of the heathen, served their idols, and sacrificed their sons and daughters to demons;" and he adds, "they ate the sacrifices of *the dead;*" a clear intimation that worshipping demons was worshipping the dead. Isaiah, too, lamenting their idolatry, asks the mortifying question, "Shall a people seek the living to the dead?"

But there is a peculiarity in the acceptation of this term among Jews and Pagans which demands special attention. With them the term *demon* generally, if not universally, denoted an unclean, malign or wicked spirit; whereas amongst the Pagans it as often represented a good as an evil spirit. Who has not heard of the good demon of Socrates, and of the evil genius of Brutus? while among Jews and Christians so commonly are found the *akatharta pneumata* or the *ponera pneumata*—the unclean and malign spirits—that our translators have almost uniformly translated them *devils.*

In the Christian Scriptures, we meet the term *demon,* in one form or other, seventy-five times, and in such circumstances as, with but one or two exceptions, constrain us to regard it as the representative of a wicked and unclean spirit. So general is this fact, that Beelze-

* **Deuteronomy xviii. 10; Leviticus xvii. 7, &c.; 2 Chron. xi. 15; Psalm cvi. 37.**

bub is dignified *"the prince of the demons"*—unfortunately rendered *devils.* This association of the idea of wickedness with the word *daimoon* may have induced our translators to give us so many *devils* in their authorized version. But this misapprehension is now universally admitted and regretted; for, while the Bible teaches many demons, it nowhere intimates a plurality of devils or Satans. There is but one devil or Satan in the universe, whose legions of angels and demons give him a sort of omnipresence, by acting out his will in all their intercourse with mortals. This evil spirit, whose official titles are the serpent, the devil and Satan, is always found in the singular number in both the Hebrew and Greek Scriptures; while *demon* is found in both numbers, indicating sometimes one, and sometimes a legion.

But, not to be tedious in this work of definition, and that we may enter at once upon the subject with a zeal and spirit worthy of a topic which lays the axe at the root of the tree of modern Sadducism, materialism and skepticism, we shall proceed to sum up the evidence in proof of the proposition which we shall state as the peculiar theme of this great literary adventure. That proposition is—*The demons of Paganism, Judaism and Christianity were the ghosts of dead men.*

But some of you may say, You have proposed to dismiss this work of definition too soon; for here is the horrible word *ghost.* Of what is that term the sign in your style? Well, we must explain ourselves.

Our Saxon forefathers, of whom we have no good reason to be ashamed, were wont to call the spirits of men, especially when separated from their bodies, *ghosts.* This, however, they did, not with the associations which arise in our minds on every pronunciation of that startling term. *Guest* and *ghost,* with them, if not synonyms, were, at least, cousins-german. They regarded the body as the *house,* and, therefore, called the spirit the *guest;* for guest and ghost are two branches from the same root. William Tyndale, the martyr, of excellent memory, in his version of the New Testament—the prototype of that of King James—very judiciously makes the Holy Spirit of the Old Testament the Holy Ghost of the New; because, in his judgment, it was the promised guest of the Christian temple.

Still, it is difficult, I own, to hear the word *ghost* or *demon* without the recollection of the nursery tales and fictions of our irrational systems of early education. We suffer little children to hear so much of

> "apparitions tall and ghastly,
> That take their stand o'er some new-open'd grave,
> And, strange to tell, evanish at the crowing of the cock,"

that they become, not only in youth, but often in riper years, the prey and sport of idle fears and terrors "which scarce the firm philosopher can scorn." Not only the graveyard,

> "but the lonely tower
> Is also shunn'd, whose mournful cloisters hold—
> So night-struck fancy dreams—the yelling ghost."

Imagination once startled,

> "In grim array the nightly spectres rise:
> Oft have we seen the school-boy, satchel in hand,
> When passing by some haunted spot, at lonely even,
> Whistling aloud to bear his courage up. Suddenly he hears,
> Or thinks he hears, the sound of something purring at his heels;
> Full fast he flies, nor does he look behind him,
> Till, out of breath, he overtake his fellows,
> Who gather round and wonder at the tale."

Parents are greatly in fault for permitting such tales to disturb the fancies of their infant offspring. The love of the marvellous and of the supernatural is so deeply planted in human nature, that it needs but little cultivation to make it fruitful in all manner of fairy-tales, of ghosts and spectres. But there is an opposite extreme—the denial of spirits, angels, demons, whether good or bad. Here, too, *media ibis tutissima*—"the middle path the safer is."

But to our proposition. We have, from a careful survey of the history of the term *demon*, concluded that *the demons of Paganism, Judaism and Christianity were the ghosts of dead men.* But we build not merely upon the definition of the term or on its philological history, but upon the following seven pillars:—

1. All Pagan authors of note, whose works have survived the wreck of ages, affirm the opinion that demons were the spirits or ghosts of dead men. From Hesiod down to the more polished Celsus, historians, poets and philosophers occasionally express this opinion.

2. The Jewish historians, Josephus and Philo, also avow this conviction. Josephus says, "Demons are the spirits of wicked men, who enter into living men and destroy them, unless they are so happy as to meet with speedy relief."* Philo says, "The souls of dead men are called demons."

---

* De Bello Jud., cap. viii. 25; cap. vi. sect. 3.

3. The Christian fathers, Justin Martyr, Irenæus, Origen, &c. depose to the same effect. Justin, when arguing for a future state, says, "Those who are seized and tormented by the souls of the dead, whom all call *demons* and madmen."* Lardner, after examining with the utmost care the works of these and all the other fathers of the first two centuries, says, "The notion of demons, or the souls of dead men, having power over living men, was *universally* prevalent among the heathen of these times, and believed by many Christians."†

4. The evangelists and apostles of Jesus Christ so understood the matter. As this is a very important, and, of itself, a sufficient, pillar on which to rest our edifice, we shall be at more pains to illustrate and enforce it. We shall first state the philological law or canon of criticism, on the generality and truth of which all our dictionaries, grammars and translations are formed. *Every word not specially explained or defined in a particular sense, by any standard writer of any particular age and country, is to be taken and applied in the current or commonly-received signification of that country and age in which the writer lived and wrote.* If this canon of translation and of criticism be denied, then we affirm there is no value in dictionaries, nor in the acquisition of ancient languages in which any book may be written, nor is there any confidence to be placed in any translation of any ancient work, sacred or profane; for they are all made upon the assumption of the truth of this law.

We have, then, only to ask, first, for the current signification of this term *demon* in Judea at the Christian era; and, in the second place, Did the inspired writers ever give any special definition of it? We have already found an answer to the first in the Greeks and Jews of the apostolic age, and of the preceding and subsequent ages. We have heard Josephus, Philo, Lucian, Justin and Lardner, from whose writings and affirmations we are expressly told what the universal acceptation of the term was in Judea and in those times. In the second place, the apostles and our Lord, as already said, use this word in various forms seventy-five times, and on no occasion give any hint of a special, private or peculiar interpretation of it; which was not their method when they used a term either not generally understood, or understood in a special sense. Does any one ask the meaning of the words Messiah, prophet, priest, elder, deacon, presbytery, altar, sacrifice, sabbath, circumcision, &c.? We refer him to the current signification of these words among the Jews and Greeks of that age. Why, then, should

---

* Jus. Apology, b. i. p. 65, par. 12, p. 54.

† Vol. viii. p. 368.

any one except the term *demon* from the universal law? Are we not, therefore, sustained by the highest and most authoritative decision of that literary tribunal by whose rules and decrees all works sacred and profane are translated from a dead to a living tongue? We are, then, fully authorized to say that the demons of the New Testament were the spirits of dead men.

5. But as a distinct historic evidence, and as confirmatory rather of our views than of the authority of the inspired authors, I adduce a very explicit and decisive passage from the epistle to the Smyrneans, written by the celebrated Ignatius, the disciple of the Apostle John. He quotes the words of the Lord to Peter when Peter supposed he saw a spirit or a ghost. But he quotes him thus:—"Handle me and see, for I am not—*daimoon asomaton*—a disembodied demon;"—a spirit without a body. This places the matter above all doubt that with those of that day demon and ghost were equivalent terms.

6. But we also deduce an argument from the word *angel*. This word is of Bible origin, and confined to those countries in which that volume is found. It is not found in any of the Greek poets, orators or historians, so far as known to me. Of that rank of beings to whom Jews and Christians have applied this official title, the Pagan nations seem never to have had the first conception. It is therefore certain that they could not use the term *demon* interchangeably with the word *angel*, as indicative of an order of intelligent beings above men and intermediate between them and the Divinity. They had neither the name nor the idea of an angel in their mythology. Philo the Jew has, indeed, said that amongst the Jews the word *demon* and the word *angel* were sometimes used interchangeably; and some have thence inferred that lapsed angels were called demons. But this is not a logical inference; for the Jews called the winds, the pestilence, the lightnings of heaven, &c., *angels*, as indicative of their agency in accomplishing the will of God. In this sense, indeed, a demon might be officially called an angel. But in this sense demon is to angel as the species to the genus: we can call a demon an angel, but we cannot call an angel a demon—just as we can call every man an animal, but we cannot call every animal a man.

Others, indeed, have imagined that the old *giants* and *heroes*, said to have been the fruit of the intermarriage of the sons of God with the daughters of men before the flood, were the demons of all the world—Pagans, Jews and Christians. Their most plausible argument is, that the word *hero* and the word *love* are identical; and that the *loves* of the angels for the daughters of men was the reason that their gigantic offspring were called *heroes;* whence the term was afterwards appropriated to persons of great courage as well as of great stature. This is simply ridiculous.

But to return to the word *angel.* It is a Bible term, and not being found in all classic, in all mythologic, antiquity, could not have entered into the Pagan ideas of a demon. Now, that it is not so used in the Christian Scriptures is evident from the following reasons:—

1st. Angels were never said to enter into any one.

2d. Angels have no affection for bodies of any sort, either as habitations or vehicles of action.

3d. Angels have no predilection for tombs and monuments of the dead.

In these three particulars angels and demons stand in full contrast, and are contradistinguished by essentially different characteristics: for—

1st. Demons have entered into human bodies and into the bodies of inferior creatures.

2d. Demons evince a peculiar affection for human bodies, and seem to desire them both as vehicles of action and as places of habitation.

3d. Demons also evince a peculiar fondness for their former mortal tenements: hence we so often read of their carrying the possessed into the graveyards, the tombs and sepulchres, where, perchance, their old mortalities lay in ruins. From which we argue, as well as from the fact that the Pagans knew nothing of a devil, nor an angel, nor Satan, before the Christian era, that when they, or the Christians or Jews, spoke of *demons,* they could not mean any intermediate rank of spirits apart from the spirits of dead men. Hence in no instance in Holy Writ do we find *demon* and *angel* used as convertible terms. Is it not certain, then, that they are the ghosts of dead men? But there yet remains another pillar.

7. Among the evidences of the Papal defection intimated by Paul, he associates the *doctrine concerning demons* with celibacy and abstinence from certain meats, as chief among the signs of that fearful apostasy. He warrants the conclusion that the purgatorial prisons for ghosts and the ghostly mediators of departed saints, which, equally with the command to abstain from lawful meats and the prohibition of marriage to the clergy, characterize the times of which he spoke, are attributes of the same system, and indicative of the fact that *demons* and *ghosts* are two names for the same things. To this we add the testimony of James, who says *the demons believe and tremble* for their doom. Now, all eminent critics concur that the spirits of wicked men

are here intended; and need I add that oft-repeated affirmation of the demoniacs?—"We know thee, Jesus of Nazareth: art thou come to torment us before the time?" Thus, all the scriptural allusions to this subject authorize the conclusion that demons are wicked and unclean spirits of dead men. A single saying in the Apocalypse makes this most obvious. When Babylon is razed to its foundation, it is said to be made the habitation of demons—of the ghosts of its sepulchred inhabitants. From these seven sources of evidence—viz. the Pagan authors, the Jewish historians, the Christian fathers, the four Evangelists, the epistle of Ignatius, the acceptation of the term *angel* in its contrast with *demon*, and the whole of the New Testament—we conclude that the demons of the New Testament were the ghosts of wicked men. May we not henceforth reason from this point with all assurance as a fixed and fundamental principle?

It ought, however, to be candidly stated that there have been in later times a few intellectual dyspeptics, on whose nervous system the idea of being really possessed by an evil spirit produces a frenzied excitement. Terrified at the thought of an incarnate demon, they have resolutely undertaken to prove that every demon named in Holy Writ is but a bold Eastern metaphor, placing in high relief dumbness, deafness, madness, palsy, epilepsy, &c.; and hence that demoniacs then and now were and are a class of unfortunates laboring under certain physical maladies called unclean spirits. *Credat Judæus Apella, non ego.*

On the principle that every demon is an Eastern metaphor, how incomparably more eloquent than Demosthenes or Cicero, was he that had at one time within him a legion of Eastern metaphors struggling for utterance! No wonder, then, that the swineherds of Gadara were overwhelmed by the moving eloquence of their herds as they rushed with such pathos into the deep waters of the dark Galilee!

Great men are not always wise. The seer of Mesopotamia was not only admonished, but reformed, by the eloquence of an ass; and I am sure that the Gadarene speculators were cured of their belief in Eastern metaphors when they saw their hopes of gain forever buried in the Lake of Gennesareth. It requires a degree of gravity bordering on the superlative, to speculate on an hypothesis so singularly fanciful and baseless as that which converts reason and eloquence, deafness and dumbness, into one and the same metaphor.

Without impairing in the least the strength of the arguments in favor of actual possession by the spirits of dead men, it may be conceded, that because of the similarity of some of the effects of demoniacal possession with those of maladies of the paralytic and epileptic character, it may have happened on some occasions that persons simply afflicted with these diseases, because of the difficulty of always discriminating the remote causes of these maladies, were by the common people regarded as demoniacs, and so reported in the New Testament. Still, the fact that the Great Teacher himself distinguishes between demons and all human maladies, in commanding the apostles not only to "heal all manner of diseases—to cleanse the lepers, and raise the dead," but also to "cast out demons;"—and the fact, still more palpable, that in number and power these demons are represented as transcending all physical maladies, preclude the possibility of contemplating them as corporeal diseases.

"When I read of the number of demons in particular persons," says a very distinguished Biblical critic, "and see their actions expressly distinguished from those of the man possessed; conversations held by the demons about their disposal after their expulsion, and accounts given how they were actually disposed of; when I find desires and passions ascribed peculiarly to them, and similitudes taken from their manners and customs, it is impossible for me to deny their existence, without admitting that the sacred historians were themselves deceived in regard to them, or intended to deceive their readers."

Were it not in appearance like killing those that are dead, I should quote at length sundry passages which speak of "unclean spirits *crying with loud voices*" as they came out of many that were possessed, which represent unclean spirits falling down before Jesus, and crying, "Thou art the Son of God," and of Jesus "charging them not to make him known;" but I will only cite a single parable framed upon the case of a demoniac. It is reported by Matthew and Luke, and almost in the same words. "When the unclean spirit," says Jesus, "is gone out of a man, he walketh through dry places, seeking rest and finding none. Then he saith, I will return into my house from whence I came out; and when he is come, he findeth it empty, swept and garnished. Then he goeth and taketh with him seven other spirits more wicked than himself, and they enter in and dwell there; and the last state of that man is worse than the first. Even so shall it be also to this wicked generation." On this observe, that "unclean spirits" is another name for demons—that is, a metaphor of a metaphor; for, if demons are metaphors for diseases, the unclean spirits are metaphors of metaphors, or shadows of shades. Again, the Great Teacher is found not only for once departing from himself, but also from all human teachers of renown, in basing a parable upon a parable, or a shadow upon a shade, in drawing a similitude from a simile. His object was to illustrate the last state of the Jews. This he attempts by the adventures of a demon—first being dispossessed, finding no rest, and returning, with others more wicked than himself, to the man from whom he was driven. Now, if this was all a figure to illustrate a figure, the Saviour has done that which he never before attempted, inasmuch as his parables are all founded not upon fictions, but upon facts—upon the actual manners and customs, the incidents and usages, of society.

That must be a desperate position to sustain which degrades the Saviour as a teacher below the rank of the most ordinary instructors of any age. The last state of the Jews compared to a metaphor!—compared to a nonentity!—compared to a fiction! This is even worse than representing a trope coming out of a man's mouth, "crying with a loud voice," "wandering through dry places"—unfigurative language, I presume—seeking a period, and finding a comma—and at length, tired and fatigued, returning with seven fiercer metaphors more wickedly eloquent than himself, repossessing the orator, and making him internally more eloquent than before. It will not help the matter to say that when a disease leaves a man it wanders through dry or wet places, through marshes and fens, through deserts and prairies, and, finding no rest for its foot, takes with it seven other more violent diseases, seeks for the unfortunate man from whom the doctors expelled it, and, re-entering his improved constitution, makes that its eternal abode.

In one sentence, then, we conclude that there is neither reason nor fact—there is no canon of criticism, no law of interpretation—there is nothing in human experience or observation—there is nothing in all antiquity, sacred or profane—that, in our judgment, weighs against the evidence already adduced in support of the position that *the demons of Pagans, Jews and Christians were the ghosts of dead men, and, as such, have taken possession of men's living bodies, and have moved, influenced and impelled them to certain courses of action.*

Permit me, gentlemen, to demonstrate that this is no abstract and idle speculation, by stating a few of the practical aspects and bearings of this doctrine of demonology:—

1st. It relieves the Bible from the imputation of promulging laws against non-entities in its legislation against necromancers, diviners, soothsayers, wizards, fortune-tellers, &c. When Jehovah gave this law to Israel, he legislated not against mere pretences:—"You shall not permit to live among you any one that useth divination, an enchanter, a witch, a consulter of familiar spirits, a wizard or a necromancer; for all that do these things are an abomination to the Lord: and because of these abominations the Lord thy God doth drive these nations out before thee." A Divine law demanding capital punishment because of a mere pretence! The most incredible thing in the world! The existence of such a statute, as before intimated, implies not merely the antiquity of the fact of demoniacal influence, but supposes it so palpable that it could be proved by at least two witnesses, and so satisfactorily as to authorize the taking away of human life without the risk of shedding innocent blood.

That there have been pretenders to such mysterious arts, impostors and hypocrites in necromancy, witchcraft and divination, as well as in every thing else, I doubt not; but if the pretence to work a miracle or to utter a prediction be a proof that there were true miracles and true prophets, the pretence of necromancy, witchcraft and divination is also a proof that there were once true necromancers, wizards and diviners. The fame of the Egyptian Jannes and Jambres who withstood Moses in the presence of Pharaoh—the fame of the woman of Endor, who evoked Samuel, or some one that personated him—and of the Pythonic damsel who followed Paul and Barnabas, and who enriched her master by her divination, stand on the pages of eternal truth as imperishable monuments not merely of the antiquity of the pretence, but of the reality of demoniacal power and possession.

May I be permitted further to observe, on this mysterious subject, that necromancy was the principal parent of all the arts of divination ever practised in the world, and was directly and avowedly founded on the fact not only of demoniacal influence, but that demons are the spirits of dead men, with whom living men could, and did, form intimacies? This the very word *necromancy* intimates. The necromancer predicted the future by means of demoniacal inspiration. He was a prophet inspired by the dead. His art lay in making or finding a familiar spirit, in evoking a demon from whom he obtained superhuman knowledge. So the Greek term imports and all antiquity confirms.

There are two subjects on which God is silent, and man most solicitous to know—the world of spirits, and his own future destiny. On these two subjects, ghosts who have visited the unseen world, and whose horizon is so much enlarged, are supposed to be peculiarly intelligent, and on this account were originally called *demons*, or *knowing ones*. But, this knowledge being forbidden—kindly forbidden—man to seek it at all, and especially by unlawful means, has always been obnoxious to the anathema of Heaven. Hence the popularity of the profession of evoking familiar spirits, and hence also the indignation of Heaven against those who consulted them.

Still, we will be asked, Has any spirit of man, dead or alive, power to foresee and foretell the future? Does any one know the future but God? To which we cheerfully respond, The living and inspired prophets knew only a part of the future. God alone knows all the future. But angels or demons may know much more of it than man. How this is, analogy itself will suggest. Suppose, for example, that one man, possessed of the discriminating powers of a Bacon, a Newton or a Locke, only of a more capacious and retentive memory, had been coeval with Cain, Noah or Abraham, and, with a deathless vigor of constitution, had lived with all the generations of men from their day till now: how great would be his comparative power of calculating chances and contingencies—the laws of cause and effect—and of thence anticipating the future! Still, compared with one who had passed that mysterious bourn of time, he would be but the infant of a day, knowing comparatively nothing of human destiny. Indeed, the powers of knowing peculiar to disembodied spirits are to us as inscrutable as the elements of their being. But that they know more of a spiritual system and more of human destiny than we do, all antiquity, sacred and profane, fully reveals and confirms.

2. But a second practical aspect of this theory of demons demands our attention. *It is a palpable and irrefragable proof of a spiritual system.* The gross materialists of the French school, when atheism triumphed over reason and faith, proclaimed from their own metropolis, and cut it deep in marble, that death was an eternal sleep of body, soul and spirit. Since their day, the species has been refined and sublimated into an intermediate sleep of only some six or seven thousand years between our earthly exit and the resurrection-morn. These more speculative materialists convert demons into metaphors, lapsed angels, or devils—into any thing, rather than the living spirits of dead men.

Our premises being admittted, they see that there must be a renunciation not only of the grosser but of the more ethereal forms of materialism, as held by those who lull the spirit to repose in the same sepulchre with its kindred mortality. They gain but little who assume that demons are lapsed angels rather than human ghosts; for who will not admit that it may be more easy for a demon, than for an angel who has a spiritual body of his own, to work by the machinery of a human body, and to excite the human passions to any favorite course of action? Were not this the fact, they must have tenanted the human house to little purpose, if a perfect stranger to all its rooms and doors could, on its first introduction, move through them as readily as they.

"If weak thy faith, why choose the harder side?"

To allegorize demoniacal influences, or to metamorphose them into rhetorical imagery, is the shortest and the most desperate escape from all spiritual embarrassment in the case. But the harder you press the skeptical philosopher on the subject of his peculiar dogmas, the more bold his denial of all spiritual influences, celestial or infernal; and the more violently he affirms that demoniacal possessions were physical diseases; that necromancy, familiar spirits and divination, though older than Moses and the seven nations of Canaan, were mere pretences and an imposition on the credulity of man, as idle as the legends of Salem witchcraft, or the fairy tales of the mother-land of sprites and apparition. But this, let me tell you, skeptical philosopher, relieves not the hard destiny of your case. Whether necromancy in all its forms was real or pretended, true or false, affects not the real merits of the question before us.

In this branch of the argument, it is perfectly indifferent to me whether it was a pretence or a reality; for, had there not been a senior and more venerated belief in the existence of a spiritual system—a general persuasion that the spirits of the dead lived in another world while their bodies lay in this, and that disembodied spirits were demons or knowing ones on those peculiar points so interesting and so unapproachable to man—who would ever have thought of consulting them, of evoking them by any art, or of pretending to have had any familiarity with them? I gain strength either by the denial or by the admission of the thing, so long as its high antiquity is conceded. I contend that a belief in demons, in a separate existence of the spirits of the dead, is more ancient than necromancy, and that it is a belief and a tradition older than the Pagan, the Jewish, or the Christian systems—older than Moses and his law—older than any earthly record whatever.

Not a few of our modern sages ascribe to a Pagan origin that which antedates Paganism itself. They must have a Grecian, Roman or Egyptian origin for ideas, usages and institutions existent ages before the founders of those states or the inventors of their superstitions were born. No earthly record, the Bible alone excepted, reaches within hundreds of years of the origin of the idea of demons, necromancy, and of infernal as well as of supernal agency.

Others there are who have more faith in what is modern than in what is ancient. They would rather believe their children than their fathers. The moderns, indeed, in most of the physical sciences, and in some of the arts, greatly excel the ancients, as they excelled us in architecture, sculpture, painting, poetry, &c. But though we excel them so much in many new discoveries and arts, in traditionary and spiritual knowledge they greatly excelled us; excepting always that portion of the moderns fully initiated into the mysteries of the Bible. Some seem to reason as if they thought that the farther from the fountain the more pure are the waters—the longer the channel the freer from pollution. With me the reverse is the fact. Man was more intelligent at his creation and his fall, respecting his own being and destiny, than he has ever been since, except so far as he has been the subject of a new revelation. Would it not appear waste of time to attempt to prove that our national Government is purer now than it was while its founders were all living amongst us? Equally futile the attempt to prove that the Patriarchal, Jewish and Christian institutions were purer five hundred or a thousand years after than at their commencement. With Tertullian, I assert that in faith, religion and morality, whatever is most ancient is most true. Therefore the Patriarchs knew more of man living and dead, and of the ancient order of things in nature, society and art, than we, their remote posterity.

The age of philosophy was the era of hypotheses and doubts. Man never began to form hypotheses till he lost his way. Having then traced the belief in demons and necromancy beyond the age of conjecture and speculative reasoning, and located it amongst the oldest traditions in the world, we are compelled by the dicta of our inductive philosophy to admit its claims to an experience, observation and testimony properly authenticated and documented amongst the earliest fathers of mankind. One of the oracles of true science is, that *all our ideas are the result of sensation and reflection, or of experience and observation;* that the archetypes of all our natural impressions and views are found in material nature; and therefore man could as easily create a world as a ghost, either by imagination, volition or reason. Supernatural ideas must therefore have a supernatural origin. So speaks the Baconian system; and therefore its author believed in demons, spirits and necromancy, as much as your humble servant, or any other living Baconian.

When any man proves he can have faith without hearing and testimony—the idea of color without sight, or of hardness and softness, of heat and cold, without feeling, and understand all the properties of material nature without any of his five senses—then, *but not till then,* he may explain how, without supernatural influence, he may form either the idea or the name of a spirit, a ghost, or a demon—of a spiritual, invisible and eternal system of intelligences of a supernatural mould and temper. He who can create the idea of an abstract spirit, or of a spiritual system of any sort, may create matter by volition, and a universe out of nothing.

Dispose of the matter as she may, we affirm it as our conviction that Philosophy herself is compelled to admit the existence of demons, familiar spirits, and the arts of necromancy and divination, which all ancient literature and ancient tradition, all Patriarchal, Jewish and Christian records, assert. In this instance, as in many others, faith is easier than unbelief; and Reason voluntarily places herself by the side of Faith as her handmaid and coadjutor in sustaining a spiritual system, of which demons in their proper nature and character are an irrefragable proof.

3. A third practical tendency of this view of demoniacal influence is to exalt in our esteem the character of the Supreme Philanthropist.

We will be asked, Whence have all the demons fled? What region do they now inhabit? Have they not power to possess mankind as formerly? Are necromancy, divination and witchcraft forever exiled from the abodes of men?

Many such questions may be propounded, which neither philosophy, experience nor religion can infallibly determine. But we may say in general and in truthful terms, that the heralds of salvation, from the day of their first mission to the end of their evangelical labors, cast out demons, restrained Satanic influence, and made inroads upon the power and empire of Beelzebub, the prince of the demons. The mighty chieftain of this holy war had a personal rencounter with the malignant chief of all unclean spirits, angelic and human, and so defeated his counsels and repelled his assaults, divesting him of much of his sway, and thus gave an earnest of his ultimate triumph over all the powers of darkness. His success and that of his ambassadors called from his lips two oracles of much consolation to all his friends: "I saw," said he, "Satan fall like lightning from heaven." This he spake when they told him, "The demons are subject to us through thy word." "Behold," he adds, "I give you power to tread on serpents and scorpions, and on all the power of the enemy, and nothing shall by any means hurt you." The partial dethronement of Satan, prince of the demons, is here fully indicated. The Roman orator uses this style when speaking of Pompey's overthrow. His words are, "He has fallen from the stars." And again, of the fall of the colleague of Antonius, "Thou hast pulled him down from heaven." So spake the Messiah:—"I beheld Satan as lightning fall from heaven." His empire over men from that day began to fall. And on another occasion he says, "Now is the prince of this world cast out." These, together with similar indications, allow the conclusion that the power of demons is wholly destroyed as far as Christians are concerned, and, if not wholly, greatly restrained in all lands where the gospel has found its way. With an old prophet or diviner who tried his hand against God's people once, we may say, "There is no enchantment against Jacob; there is no divination against Israel." Some arrogate to human science what has been the prerogative of the gospel alone. They say the light of science has driven ghosts and witches from the minds of men; whereas they ought to have said the gospel and power of its Author have driven demons out of the hearts and dispossessed them of their power over the bodies of men.

The error of these admirers of human science does not differ much from that of some European theologists concerning Mary Magdalene. They think her to have been an infamous rather than an unfortunate woman out of whom were driven seven devils. They have disgraced her memory by erecting "Magdalene Hospitals" for infamous, rather than for unfortunate, females; not knowing that it was the misfortune rather than the crime of Mary of Magdala, that seven demons had been permitted to assault her person.

As to the abodes of the demons, we are taught in the Bible what the most ancient dogmatists have said concerning their residence in the air: I say we are taught that they dwell *pro tempore* in the ethereal regions. Satan, their prince, is called "the prince of the power of the air." The great Apostle to the Gentiles taught believers to wrestle against "wicked spirits that reside in the air;" "for," says he, "you fight not against flesh and blood, but against principalities and powers, against the rulers of the darkness of this world; against spiritual wickedness in high places"—properly rendered "*against wicked spirits in the regions of the air.*" Paul's shipwreck at Malta by the Euroclydon, and Job's misfortunes by an Arabian tempest, demonstrate the aerial power of this great antagonist when permitted to exert it against those whom he envies and calumniates.

Evident it is, then, from such testimonies, facts and allusions, that the atmosphere, or rather the regions above it, the ethereal or empyreal, and not heaven, nor earth, nor hell, is the proper residence of the ghosts of wicked men. They have repeatedly declared their perfect punishment or torment as yet future, to be after the coming of the Lord, when he shall send the devil and his emissaries into an eternal fire. How often did they say to Jesus, "Art thou come to torment us *before the time?*" That they are miserable, wretchedly miserable, is inferrible from the abhorrence of their nudity and their awful forebodings of the future. They vehemently desire to be embodied again. They seek rest, but find none, and would rather possess any corporeity, even that of the swine, than continue naked and dispossessed. Their prison is called by the Messiah "outer darkness;" by Paul it is called *epourania, high places, aerial regions.* This is the Hebrew-Greek name of that region in which there is neither atmosphere nor light; for, strange as it may appear, the limits of our atmosphere are the limits of all terrestrial light. These intervals between the atmospheres of the planets are what we would call "*outer darkness.*" Could a person ascend some fifty miles above the earth, he would find himself surrounded by everlasting night—no ray from sun, or moon, or stars could find him where there is no medium of reflection.

That demons may still give oracles, as they were wont to do before the Christian era, and possess living men in heathen lands, or in places where Christianity has made little progress, is not altogether improbable. Of this, indeed, we have not satisfactory evidence, and therefore ought not to speak dogmatically. Many affect to regard the whole subject as a piece of childish superstition, as did our two great poets Scott and Byron, who, nevertheless, like them, are under the influence of that same childish superstition. One thing is abundantly evident, that although the number of such spirits is vast and overwhelming, and their hatred to the living intense and enduring, the man of God, the true Christian, has a guardian angel, or a host of sentinels around him that never sleep; and, therefore, against him the fiery darts of Satan are employed in vain. For this we erect in our hearts a monument of thanks to Him who has been, and still is, the Supreme Philanthropist and Redeemer of our race.

This view of demonology not only vindicates the law of Moses from the imputation of catering to the superstitious prejudices of mankind, and justifies Paul in placing witchcraft amongst the works of the flesh; it not only affords to weak and doubting minds new and striking evidences of a spiritual system, and shows our great indebtedness to the Author of the Christian faith for rescuing man from the tyranny of the arch-apostate, the prince of demons; but it also inducts us into more grand and sublime views of the magnitude, variety and extent of the world of spirits—of our relations to them—and of our present liability to impressions, suggestions and influences from classes of agents wholly invisible and inappreciable by any of those senses which connect us with external and sensible existence. That we are thus susceptible it were foolish and infidel to deny. How many well-authenticated facts are found in the volumes of human experience of singular, anomalous and inexplicable impulses and impressions wholly beyond all human associations of ideas, yet leading to actions evidently connected with the salvation of the subjects of them, or of those under their care! And how many have, by some malign agency, been suddenly and unexpectedly led into the most fatal positions and precipitated to ruin, when such exigencies prove to be exceptions to all the known laws of cause and effect, and contrary to all their wonted courses of action! To assign to these any other than a spiritual cause, it seems to me, were to assign a *non causa pro causa;* for on no theory of mind or body can they be so satisfactorily explained, and so much in harmony with the Bible method of representing such incidents. Thus the angel of the Lord smote Herod that he died, and in dreams has he admonished the faithful of the ways and means of escaping impending evils.

Will it not be perceived and admitted that if evil demons can enter into men's bodies and take away their reason and excite them to various preternatural actions, and if in legions they may crowd their influences upon one unhappy victim, spirits, either good or bad, may make milder and more delicate approaches to the fountains of human action, and stir men up to efforts and enterprises for weal or woe, according to their respective characters and ruling passions?

Certain it is that angels have not only demonstrated their ability to assume the human form, but to exert such influence upon the outward man as to prompt him to immediate action—as in the case of Peter, who was suddenly stricken on the side by the hand of an angel when fast asleep between a Roman guard, and roused to action. The gates and bars of the prison open at his approach and shut on his escape, touched by the same hand; and thus the apostle is rescued from the malice of his foes.

What an extended view of the intellectual and moral universe opens to our contemplation from this point! We see an outward, visible universe, studded with constellations of suns and their attendant systems, circling in unmeasured orbits around one invisible and omnipotent centre which controls them all. Amazed and overwhelmed at these stupendous displays of creative power, wisdom and goodness, in adoring ecstasy we inquire into the uses of these mighty orbs, which, in such untold millions, diversify and adorn those undefined fields of ethereal beauty that limit our ideas of an unbounded and inconceivable space. Reasoning from all our native analogies, and from the scattering rays of supernal light that have from suns unseen reached our world, we must infer that all these orbs are the mansions of social beings, of every conceivable variety of intelligence, capacity and employment, and that in organized hierarchies, thrones, principalities and lordships, they constitute each within itself an independent world—of which societies we are allowed to conclude that there are as many varieties as there are planets for their residence.

In all these intellectual assemblages, spread over the area of universal being, there are but two distinct and essentially diverse confederations—one under the rightful sovereignty of Messiah, the Lord of all, the other under the usurped dominion of that spirit who has spread over our planet all the anarchy and misrule, all the darkness and gloom, all the sorrow and death, which have embittered life, and made countless millions groan in spirit and sigh for a discharge from a conflict between good and evil, pleasure and pain, so unequal and oppressive.

This rebel angel, of such mysterious character, is always found in the singular number—as *the Satan, the Devil* and *the Apollyon* of our race. With him are confederate all disloyal spirits that have conspired against Heaven's own will in adoration of their own. In reference to this usurper and his angelic allies against the Lord's Anointed, we are obliged to consider those unhappy spirits who during their incarnation took sides with him in his mad rebellion against the Eternal King. The number of angels that took part with him in his original conspiracy remains amongst the secrets of eternity, and will not be divulged till the devil and his angels, for whom Tophet was of old prepared, shall be separated from the social systems of the universe and publicly sentenced to the bottomless gulf of irremediable ruin.

The whole human race, at one time or another, have been involved in this war against Heaven. Many have, indeed, deserted the dark banners of Beelzebub, and have become sons of light. Hitherto, alas! the great majority have perished in the field of rebellion and gone down to the pit with all their armor on. These spirits, shown to be the demons of all antiquity, sacred and profane, are now a component part of the empire of Satan, and as much under his control as the conspirators that took part with him in his primeval defection and rebellion.

How numerous they are, and how concentrated are their efforts, may be gleaned from sundry allusions in the inspired writings, especially from the melancholy history of the unfortunate Gadarene who dwelt among the tombs, tortured by a legion of them—not, perhaps, by six thousand demons, according to the full standard of a Roman legion, but by an indefinite and immense multitude. How innumerable, then, the agents, demoniac and angelic, on Satan's side!

What hosts of fallen men and angels have conspired against the happiness of God's moral empire! No wonder that Satan is sometimes spoken of as omnipresent! If Napoleon, in the day of his power, while in the palace of the Tuileries, was said to be at work in Spain, in Portugal, in Belgium and in France at the same moment, with how much less of the figurative may Satan, whose agents are incomparably more numerous and diversified, as well as of vastly superior agility and power, be represented as wielding a sort of omnipresent power in all parts of our terraqueous habitation! And how malignant, too! The fabled Furies were not more fierce than those unclean and mischievous spirits whose pleasure it was to torture with the direst agonies the unhappy victims whom they chose to mark out for themselves.

But here we must pause; and, with this awful group of exasperated and malicious demons in our horizon, it is some relief to remember that there are many good spirits of our race, allied with ten thousand times ten thousand, and thousands of thousands, of angels of light, all of whom are angels of mercy and sentinels of defence around the dwellings of the righteous, the true *élite* of our race. These, we learn from high authority, are ministering spirits waiting on the heirs of salvation. These attending spirits know our spiritual foes and are able to cope with them; for when Satan and Michael fought for the body of Moses, the fallen seraph was driven to the wall and lost the day. For how many services rendered, for how many deliverances from evil spirits and from physical disasters, we are indebted to the good and benevolent, though invisible, agents around us, will never be known, and therefore never told, on earth; but it may nevertheless be known hereafter.

With what unspeakable pleasure may some happy being in this assembly yet sit down, side by side, with his own guardian spirit under the eternally verdant boughs of the life-restoring tree in the paradise of God, and listen to the ten thousand deliverances effected for him by the kind ministrations of that generous and beneficent minister of grace, that watched his path, numbered his steps, and encamped around his bed from the first to the last moment of his terrestrial day! With what grateful emotions will the ransomed spirit listen to the bold adventures and the triumphant rencounters with belligerent foes of his deliverer! and while in the midst of such social raptures he throws his immortal arms around his kind benefactor, he will lift his bright and beaming eye of grateful piety to Him who gave him such a friend and deliverer in the time of peril and of need, and who, through such a scene of trials and of conflicts, brought him safely to the city of eternal rest!*

---

* The preceding essay is an almost extemporaneous effusion on a subject requiring much and profound thought. The invitation to address THE POPULAR LECTURE CLUB of the city of Nashville was received but a few evenings before it was spoken. Meanwhile, having almost daily lectures on portions of the Christian system, I had leisure only to sketch, with much rapidity, at various intervals, the preceding remarks. True, indeed, the subject had been often on my mind, especially since the time of my writing a few essays on that skeptical and abstract something called *Materialism*. The facts and observations crowded together in this popular lecture are matters of grave and serious import, and not hasty or crude imaginations, occurring at the impulse of the moment. I would rather have given them under a more logical and philosophical form; but this is not the most popular nor, to the great mass, the most intelligible form. At the request of some who heard them, and of many who heard of them, I am induced to publish the identical draft which I read to the audience, with only a very few verbal alterations.

I think the subject of *demons* is one that fairly comes in the path of every student of the New Testament, and ought to be well understood; and as the reader will doubtless have observed, I regard it as constituting an irrefragable proof of a spiritual system, a full refutation of that phantasm called Materialism, to those who admit the authority of Jesus Christ and the twelve apostles. To such it is more than a mere refutation of materialism: it is a demonstration of a separate existence of the spirits of the dead—an unequivocal evidence of a spiritual system, and of a future state of rewards and punishments.

A. C.

ESSAY.

LIFE AND DEATH.

ANY theory of a future state founded upon human wisdom and science, however elevated the rank and standing of its author and its adherents, wanting the sanction of Divine authority and scriptural demonstration, can afford neither confidence nor comfort to any reflecting mind. If, indeed, it be a truth worthy of the assertion of an apostle, that "the world by wisdom knew not God," equally true and worthy of the same authority is the declaration that Jesus Christ "hath abolished death and brought life and immortality to light by the gospel." Philosophy, in her wisdom and modesty, has at length confessed that the soul of man, as to its origin, nature and destiny, is wholly beyond the precincts of her jurisdiction; and therefore she utterly refuses to dogmatize or reason on the subject. We are, therefore, thrown upon the Bible and faith for all that we can know or learn of this most mysterious and absorbing subject. Till we have "shuffled off this mortal coil," and have learned the first lessons of that "great teacher, DEATH," we must be content with what the Bible teaches on the spiritual nature of man, and on the future destiny of the righteous and the wicked.

But that volume must be subjected to the same laws of interpretation by which we ascertain the meaning of the words of other works addressing us from ancient times and in languages long since dead. Regardless of that rule, we are, to all intents and purposes, without a revelation in human language, and, still worse, we never can have one. It is absolutely essential to the very idea of a Divine communication in the form of a revelation, that its words and sentences be understood according to their usual sense at the time when that communication was made, and amongst the people to whom it was addressed and to whose care it was committed. Since the apparel of thought changes as the apparel of our persons, and words in the lapse of time vary from their original and primitive meaning, a very strict regard must always be had to their received acceptation and sense in the age and country in which they were employed as the vehicle of a Divine revelation.

Through ignorance of these facts or a disregard of them, it has come to pass that we now have very dissimilar and contradictory theories of the future state amongst those who profess to believe in and teach from the Bible. Take, for example, the future state of the disobedient and unjust, and how dissimilar are the representations of it given by the Universalist, the Restorationist, the Destructionist, the Romanist, and the Christian,*—all professing to hold the same book as a Divine revelation!

The Universalist proper teaches that a full retribution of sin takes place in this life, and hence, after death, the wicked are as holy and as happy as the righteous. With him, the scriptures that speak of future punishment speak in metaphors, inasmuch as there can be no future punishment either according to his theory of the Divine attribute or according to the gospel. Hence the words of Jesus, "He that shall have believed and shall have been baptized shall be saved, and he that believeth not shall be condemned," mean "he that believeth, &c. and he that believeth not shall be saved."

The Universal Restorationist teaches that there will be punishment of a *disciplinary character* after death, which shall, in all cases, issue in perfect reformation, holiness and happiness. Hence there will be, hereafter, a continual egress from hell to heaven, until the latter shall have received the entire population of the former.

The Destructionist teaches that, ultimately, the souls and the bodies of all the wicked shall be destroyed; that is, reduced to perfect non-entity. Some of them (for there is less unanimity among them than among the theorists above mentioned) teach that the soul and body die together, and are never again conscious, any more than a vulture or a dove, a horse or a lamb. Others teach that the souls of the wicked sleep from death to the final resurrection, and that then, with their bodies, they shall revive and undergo a second death, proportioned to their former sins. Some will suffer more, others less, both in duration and in intensity, but finally they shall all be annihilated. This, with them, is "the second death."

These three theories agree in one great point—viz. that the wicked shall all be destroyed out of the universe, not one left. The Universalist and Restorationist destroy their *character*, and make them saints,

* I use the word *Christian* in its sectarian sense, and not in its general sense.

while the Destructionist reduces them to nothing—giving them neither sense nor reason, neither person nor name, neither habitation nor existence—thus making them absolute *nonentities.*

The Romanist has, for some of the dead, an intermediate state of purgatorial purification. All men die under certain liabilities to punishment because of venal offences which disqualify them for heaven. They must, therefore, pass through purgatory—an imaginary place, concerning which an infant knows just as much as Gregory XVI. with all his ecclesiastic conclaves. Their residence and sufferings in purgatory are to be commensurate with the number and character of their various offences; for which, indeed, they must make expiation. Still, their passage through that imaginary region will be much shortened and alleviated by reason of the masses said for the dead, which are always repeated in number and efficiency according to the contributions given to the priests. Hence, the rich pass through on steam-cars, while the poor trudge along on crutches. Ultimately, indeed, all its inmates get through; the irremediably wicked passing directly into punishment.

The *Christian* believes that the wicked suffer an "*everlasting punishment,*" and that, therefore, they never cease to exist. He believes that the wicked are cast into hell and there suffer "an everlasting destruction from the presence of the Lord and from the glory of his power;" that in that state "the worm dieth not, and the fire is not quenched."

Now, as the Universalist, the Restorationist, the Destructionist, the Romanist and the Christian equally profess to believe the Bible, and, therefore, equally profess to build their respective theories on Divine revelation, follows it not that they have adopted different methods of interpreting and applying the words of that sacred record? The difference is not in the standard to which they all appeal, (for they all have the same Bible,) but in the mode of interpreting it. Can any fact more convincingly demonstrate the necessity and importance of having some fixed canons or rules of interpretation?

Now, as it frequently happens that words have different significations, as literal and as figurative, and are consequently used in diverse acceptations, sometimes meaning this and sometimes that, the first and most necessary inquiry must always be, *How shall we, in any particular case, ascertain whether the literal or the figurative use of any given term shall be regarded as its proper signification?* To which important inquiry we give this answer:—The particular writer or speaker, or the particular subject on which he writes or speaks, or the particular context or the particular adjuncts or words in construction with it, will generally, if not universally, ascertain and limit the meaning beyond any reasonable doubt.

There are four words, in this controversy, of cardinal importance. These are *destruction*, *life*, *death* and *punishment*. To ascertain their grammatical or historical and their tropical or figurative meaning, is indispensable to any correct knowledge of the passages in which they occur. The most palpable error of those whose views of the future state of wicked and impenitent men we are now about to review and examine is that they generally commence the proof by assuming or taking for granted the very question in debate. For example, the destructionists, in arguing for the entire and eternal extinction of the unconverted, assume that the term *destruction* means the *absolute extinction of personal being and existence.* Now, if the term *destruction* always means, in the sacred usage, *the absolute extinction of personal existence*, or, in other words, personal annihilation, then, indeed, there might be some excuse for such a palpable and daring assumption; but if such be not the fact, or if the word *destruction* has other meanings than absolute extinction of personal existence, then we need scarcely show that their foundation is a mere assumption, or a mere begging of the question.

We shall, then, institute a scriptural induction and examination of the words *destruction* and *destroy* as found in the New Testament. And, first, of the noun, *destruction:* it occurs in the English Concordance *twelve* times. These are—Matt. vii. 13; Rom. iii. 16, ix. 22; 1 Cor. v. 5; 2 Cor. x. 8, xiii. 10; Phil. iii. 19; 1 Thess. v. 3; 2 Thess. i. 9; 1 Tim. vi. 9; 2 Peter ii. 1, iii. 16. In these places in which we have *destruction* in the common version, we have in the original Greek four terms—viz. *apooleia*, *olethros*, *kathairesis* and *suntrimma*. The first is found in Matt. vii. 13; Rom. ix. 22; Phil. iii. 19; 2 Peter ii. 1, iii. 16: in all, five times. *Olethros* is found in 1 Cor. v. 5; 1 Thess. v. 3; 2 Thess. i. 9; 1 Tim. vi. 9: in all, four times. *Kathairesis* is found in 2 Cor. x. 8, xiii. 10. *Suntrimma* in Rom. iii. 16. There are, then, four varieties of *destruction* in the Greek original, all represented by one and the same word in the common version. This is a startling fact to those who assume that the term *destruction* uniformly represents the same thing.

How dangerous those guides who assume, as the basis of their theory, that destruction means only absolute extinction of personal existence, or personal annihilation! And yet such men have we amongst us, pretending to be learned men! Even Dr. Watts and Dr. Priestley were among the number. But neither poets nor philosophers are safe guides in theology.

Now, our method is, in the second place, to examine each of these four terms, translated *destruction*, by considering them in every passage in which they occur, and by observing how they are translated in the common version. To begin with the first and chief of these—viz. *apooleia*—we discover that this word is found in the New Testament in this form, as a noun-substantive, only twenty times. In these, it is translated eight times *perdition*, five times *destruction*, twice *waste*, and once by each of the following words:—*die*, *perish*, *damnation*, *damnable*, *pernicious ways*. Here are, then, in our common version, eight versions of the noun-substantive *apooleia* in only twenty occurrences of the word; of these, the most common are *perdition* and *destruction*.

But we have the verb *apollumi*, ("to destroy,") from which the noun is derived, occurring in the New Testament no less than *ninety-two* times. From these ninety-two cases we cannot fail to arrive at a radical conception of the meaning of this word. We shall, then, classify and enumerate its various significations. Of these, the most common is *perish*, and sometimes *perished*. In this sense it is found no less than *thirty-two* times. It is also found *thirty-one* times translated *lose* and *lost*, and *twenty-seven* times *destroy* and *destroyed*. It is only once translated *marred*, and once *die*.

Now, as this is the term most frequently used indicative of the destiny of wicked men, it is all-important that its various acceptations be very strictly observed and considered. Its derivative, *aioonios olethros*, is found (2 Thess. i. 9) translated "*everlasting destruction*." We have also, (1 Thess. v. 3,) "Then sudden destruction (*olethros*) cometh;" 1 Cor. v. 5, "for the destruction of the flesh;" and 1 Tim. vi. 9, "drown men in destruction."*

Kathairesis is found only three times:—2 Cor. x. 4, translated "pulling down of strong holds;" 2 Cor. x. 8, "not for your *destruction*;" and 2 Cor. xiii. 10, "edification, and not destruction." This word etymologically indicates "pulling down," and, figuratively, it indicates "destruction." In the latter sense it is found but twice in the New Testament.

* To those who can appreciate it, we would state that from *ollumi*, or, anciently, *olluoo*, (whereof *oleso*,) come also *apollumi*, *apooleia* and *olethros*. The radical meaning of them all is, *to lose*; in Latin, *perdo*. Hence, *perdition* is the first meaning of *olethros*—four times found in the New Testament; and in classic use it denotes death, or any thing pernicious or damnable.

Suntrimma is found but once, and literally indicates destruction by attrition or breaking down.

We have now exhibited every passage in the Christian Scriptures in which the English words "destroy" and "destruction" are found, and also all the words in the Greek New Testament which are supposed either grammatically or rhetorically to authorize such a translation. It will next be important to notice some other versions of the same words found in the common version.

First, then, *apooleia* is applied to a *waste* of ointment, Matt. xxvi. 8; Mark xiv. 4: "To what purpose is this waste (or destruction) of the ointment?" It is also translated *perdition* in immediate contrast with (*olethros*) destruction, showing that *olethros* denotes a still higher punishment than *apooleia*. It is also applied to "pernicious ways," and to "damnable sects," 2 Peter ii. 2; also to destruction (Phil. iii. 19) in the abstract.

The verb *apollumi*, in the original, whose New Testament history we have given, is applied both to persons and things, as well as its derivatives *olethros* and *apooleia*. It is applied to persons, members of the body, bottles, sheep, soul and body, life, reward, those who take the sword, money, nation, and even to JESUS, the Messiah, himself.

Bottles, by one evangelist, are, in the common version, said "to be destroyed," and "to perish," and by another evangelist the same bottles are said to "be marred." In these cases *apollumi* is found in the original: A sheep that was destroyed or lost is said to live and to be brought back to the fold; a man is said to destroy his life, and again to find it; "I am sent," says the Messiah, "to the destroyed sheep of the house of Israel." This resembles a passage in the Old Testament, viz. "O Israel, thou hast destroyed thyself, but in me is thy help found!" "I have come to seek and to save," says Jesus, "that which was destroyed;" "Ask Barabbas, and destroy Jesus;" "This my son was destroyed, but is now found;" "Our gospel is hid to them that are destroyed."

Such are a few, and but a few, of the cases in which this word is so used as to demonstrate to the most undiscriminating that it cannot mean, either primarily or generally, the absolute extinction or annihilation of persons and animals at one time said to be destroyed, and afterwards represented as living and happy. "This my son was dead, and is now alive, was lost, and is found." Such applications of the words *dead, lost, destroyed,* &c. are of frequent occurrence in the judgment of those acquainted with the *usus loquendi* of the Jewish and Christian Scriptures.

Should any one demur at an appeal to the original text in explanation of the force of words in the Christian records, we will refer him to Cruden's Concordance, in which he may examine from three to four hundred passages of Scripture in which some branch of this numerous family of words will be found. In these he will find abundant proof of the facts already offered; or, in other words, he will discover how exceedingly hazardous and reckless are those innovators who, from the mere force of the phrase *destruction of ungodly men*, confidently affirm their absolute and utter personal extinction or annihilation.

To conclude our dissertation on this family of words, we must remark that the words *destroy* and *destruction* have, like many other words, besides a grammatical or literal definition, a figurative one, and are sometimes used in a relative and subordinate as well as in an absolute and unqualified sense. For example: Jesus is said to have assumed our nature "that he might *destroy* him that had the power of death, that is, *the devil*," and to have been "manifested that he might *destroy* the works of the devil." Has he yet accomplished either? Does not Satan yet live? do not his works still exist? His power has truly been crippled, but not annihilated. But it may be asked, Will he not finally annihilate Satan and destroy his works? If so, we will respond by asking, Would it not have been better to have absolutely and forever destroyed the arch-apostate at the moment of his rebellion, than after he had done all the evil that he could—after he had, at least relatively, destroyed millions of millions of our tempted and beguiled race? Into what singular predicaments will some persons precipitate themselves by the infatuation of some new theory, under the captivating spell of some brilliant novelty!

The assumption that when this word is applied to the future state of the wicked, it always means absolute destruction, or the entire and eternal extinction of the subject, will be reprobated by every well-educated man, nay, by every sane, uncommitted man, in the world. If such had been the current and common use of the term, then we might, indeed, listen with approbation to the disquisitions of the critic who, from its current signification, would seek to show that when it applies to the future state of the wicked it must be taken in its common meaning, and must then, also, denote the absolute cessation of their being. But a position directly contrary to this is selected by those now called destructionists. They do not pretend to argue that such is the common meaning of the word, but that such must be its meaning in this particular case, for no other reason than that it comports more agreeably with their notions of expediency and consistency. They are so clearly and profoundly penetrated with the singularity of their position, that few of them will allow themselves to be designated annihilationists, because, say they, nothing can be said to be annihilated; every thing continues to exist in some mode or form of being. But when pressed with argument, they do admit that the wicked man ceases forever—that he is no more a man. Of course, then, he is a nonentity. The wicked are to all eternity what Adam was before God made him. The elements of his being were in the earth and in the universe, but *he was not.* So these destroyed wicked men exist not in any sense, only in the elements of their constitution as those are dispersed throughout the universe. *They exist no more;* and this is all that we mean by annihilation.

Our first objection, therefore, to the destructionism now being taught, is, *that its teachers take for granted what they neither have proved nor can prove—viz. That the phrase "everlasting destruction" necessarily means the everlasting extinction of the person of an ungodly man.*

Our second objection to this new-vamped old theory, is, *that it assumes that eternal life and eternal death mean eternal being and eternal not-being.* Or, in other words, that simple existence is *life,* and simple non-existence *death.*

We shall, then, bestow some attention on the Biblical use of these all-important words, *life* and *death.*

But who can define life? It is neither a person nor a thing, yet it may be affirmed of both. We have a living man and a living tree. Logicians, however, say we cannot have a dead man, nor yet a dead tree; because when life is extinct, of the man we have but a corpse, and of the tree but wood. This is just as good sense as good logic; for in a corpse there is not a man, nor in wood a tree: they are but remainders of both; the tree or the man is not where life is not. Life, then, we may venture to say, is a connection with God through the system called nature, and death is a disseverance from that system. Union with nature, or *union with God, is life, separation from nature or from God is death.* If this be not a definition of life, it will be at least an essential element of a true definition, whenever that definition shall have been completed.

A man lives while he inhales the atmosphere, or while the air is in his lungs. This is the connecting link between him and external nature. He dies when that connection is broken up: this is, however, but animal life. A tree lives while its leaves or bark absorb from the atmosphere so many of its elements as are in harmony with its nature. This is vegetable life. A spirit lives while in connection with the Spirit of God: its death consists in the withdrawal of that Spirit. But as the Spirit of God produces all sorts of life—animal, vegetable and spiritual—it must communicate of itself various gifts and powers, adapted to any one of these living organizations. So that connection with the Spirit of God is essential to all sorts of life, animal, vegetable or spiritual. There is no life but in God. He alone "hath life in himself." Now, the withdrawal of any specific influence eventuates in a death analogous to the influence withheld. Hence, we have three sorts of life, and, of course, as many sorts of death. We have vegetable, animal and spiritual life and death.

But a spirit may live in one sense and be dead in another; or, in other words, a spirit may have connection or communion with God in one sense, and not in another. Thus, a tree has connection with God, but not as an animal has; and an animal has connection with God, but not as a spirit has; and a spirit has connection with God, but not as an animal has; and spirits have connection with God in a twofold sense—merely as beings, and then as holy or moral beings. Hence, the connection of a spirit with the natural perfections of God gives men intellectual life, such as that possessed by Satan and evil spirits; and connection with the moral attributes of God gives moral or spiritual life, such as that which good angels and good men possess. Wherever, then, there is organization and union with God there is life—according to the nature of that organization and union; and where there is neither organization nor union of any kind, there is no sort of life whatever.

In Scripture style, a man is living in one sense and dead in another, or dead in one sense and living in another, at the same time. Of men in the flesh, yet living, John said, "He that hath the Son hath life, and he that hath not the Son hath not life." Here, then, is the case fairly made out—viz. a dead living man, and a living dead man; alive in one sense and dead in another, at one and the same moment.

"He that hath the Son" not only retains the life which he had before he had the Son, but, superadded, he has the life spiritual and divine; and what is this but the incipiency of eternal life or immortality? There is a life more than human, possessed by every Christian, so that the Christian man has at the same time the human and the divine life. A few specimens of the proof of this fundamental view, fundamental, indeed, as respects the entire superstructure of the arguments between us and all annihilationists or destructionists, shall now be given. We shall begin with the words of the Great Teacher:—

1st. "Verily, verily, I say unto you, he who heareth my word, and believeth on him who sent me, hath everlasting life, and cometh not into condemnation, *but hath passed from death to life,*" (John v. 24.) Such a one was dead and is now alive; and yet he possessed human life while dead in that sense in which he is now made alive. He has now a new and divine life superadded to his former merely human life. There is, then, a merely human life, and there is a spiritual and divine life, resident in the same person at the same time. But there must also be two sorts of death as well as two sorts of life: the one unavoidably implies the other. Hence we have, according to the Messiah, a living man *passing from death to life.* So that he who possesses human life may at the same time be dead in some sense. Such is the antithesis which he places before us. He exhibits a man both alive and dead, passing from death into life. The transition is effected by obeying his word and confiding in Him that sent him; or, to quote his own words, "He that heareth my word and believeth on him that sent me . . . hath passed from death to life."

Our second proof is from the same source. Jesus said to one who sought leave of absence from his work for the purpose of interring his father, "Let the dead bury their own dead, and follow me," (Matt. viii. 22; Luke ix. 60.) How could a dead man bury a dead man, unless he can be alive in one sense while dead in another? Is it not as clear as demonstration that one may possess human life, and at the same time be as dead to God as a man void of human life is dead to the world?

The words of Jesus to a rich young man in the prime and vigor of life, "This do, and thou shalt live," together with many other sayings of his, confirm this important view of the subject. But we must hear his apostles, also, in proof that this is no peculiar nor idiomatic expression of his.

The Apostle John says, "We know that we have passed from death unto life, because we love the brethren. He that loveth not his brother abideth in death." Here, certainly, is indisputable evidence that John understood this matter as we are now contemplating it. Here is a person living who has passed from death spiritual to life spiritual, while possessing, before and since, human life.

To these we may add a definition of spiritual life and spiritual death drawn from the writings of Paul, (Rom. viii. 6.) This great apostle says, "The minding of the flesh is death, the minding of the spirit is life;" or, according to the common version, "For to be carnally minded is death, but to be spiritually minded is life and peace." This is a definition in fact, and not a merely verbal definition. Again, (Rom. vi. 21,) "The end of those things is death," and "the end or fruit of holiness is everlasting life." Still more strongly affirms this same apostle that one may be dead and alive at the same time, though not in the same sense, in the following words, (1 Tim. vi. 6:)—"She that lives in pleasure *is dead while she lives.*" It is unnecessary to array the whole host of evidence which the Bible furnishes in proof of these facts. Much more evidence of the same kind may be found by consulting parallel passages. We shall, then, regard it as established by the highest authority, that life and existence are not the same thing—that a man may have human life or existence without spiritual life—that he may be alive and dead at the same time, in different but proper meanings of the words "death" and "life"—and that intellectual life and spiritual life are as much realities as animal life or animal death.

In this sense only could Adam die the day he violated the Divine precept, "In the day on which thou eatest of it, thou shalt surely die." That day he did die, though afterwards he may have lived nine hundred years. The "angels that kept not their first estate" have all died in the sense in which Adam died when he departed from his first estate; though they still live in another sense. Death, indeed, as the original word intimates, signifies *separation* from God: this is its true and divinely-authenticated meaning. A tree, a man, an angel, can, therefore, die in just as many senses as they can be separated from God, or from any system of communication with him. A tree has but a physical connection with God, through the system of material nature, consequently it is susceptible of but one death; a man has connection with God through physical and spiritual nature, and therefore he may die physically or spiritually.

We, therefore, legitimately come to the conclusion, that as life and death are necessarily contrasted with each other, as indicative of contrary states, we can have just as many varieties of death as there are varieties of life. Have we physical, intellectual and spiritual or moral life? then have we physical, intellectual and spiritual or moral death. Have we temporal and eternal life? then have we temporal and eternal death.

But some of these terms indicate the essential and some the accidental attributes of life and death. Thus, physical, intellectual and spiritual denote the nature or essential characteristics of life and death; while temporal and eternal denote, not the nature, but the accidental attributes, of life and death. The former denotes the *kind* of life, while the latter denotes merely the *continuance* of it. Whether a person have a landed estate for a term of years, or "forever," as our deeds run, affects not the character or nature of the estate, but the mere continuance of the possession. Hence, "*eternal*," prefixed to life or death, intimates not the nature of either, but their mere continuance.

It is, however, with some, a question of uncertain decision whether eternal life be not a different sort of life from spiritual life, or from any life enjoyed on earth, or by man as he now exists. With some, mere existence is life; and such persons are wont to speak, not of eternal existence, but of eternal life, in misery!

But, while mere animal existence or vegetable existence is life animal or vegetable, such is not spiritual life. It is not mere existence, but spiritual existence, enjoyed; it is a perennial communication between an angelic or a human spirit, and the eternal Spirit of God, "in whose presence there is fulness of joy and at whose right hand are pleasures for evermore." Hence, in New Testament language we have the phrase "*eternal life*" forty-four times, and *forty-four times only*, and never used to indicate mere eternal existence, but the eternal enjoyment of life and of the God of life.

An analysis of these several passages in their proper contextual circumstances certainly indicates that eternal life is only another name for eternal happiness. When the Messiah says to his faithful disciples that in this world they shall receive a hundredfold more than they lose, and in the world to come eternal life, can any one be so simple as to imagine that he means mere eternal existence? What an anticlimax do they put into the mouth of the Messiah on such a view. (Mark x. 29, 30.)—"There is no one who hath left house, or brethren, or sisters, or father, or mother, or wife, or children, or lands, for my sake and the gospel's, but shall receive a hundredfold more in this world; houses, and brethren, and sisters, and mothers, and children, and lands, with persecutions, and in the world to come something greatly less—eternal life—mere eternal existence!" Can any one think the Messiah was ever guilty of such a deception under pretence of holding out something greater in the world to come, truly, and in fact, holding out something greatly less? He does not promise his followers mere existence in this world, but a hundredfold more enjoyments than they have lost for his sake. But there are some amongst us who, in their self-esteem, imagine that they have discovered that eternal life is mere eternal existence, and who present the Great Teacher in the singular attitude of saying to his followers, "My friends, in this world you shall have a hundredfold more than mere existence, and, in the world to come, eternal existence only."

Having shown that eternal life is not eternal existence, (and if that be not shown, then nothing can be ascertained from the lips of the Messiah,) follows it not that *the second death,* in contrast with eternal life, cannot possibly intimate second non-existence? Indeed, is not the very definition absurd? The first death, first non-existence; the second death, second non-existence! Did any human writer ever speak greater nonsense! And yet we have amongst us some men so full of the conceit of superior wisdom as to make the inspired writers utter such nonsense.

Are not eternal life and eternal punishment placed in contrast by our Saviour? "These," says he, "shall go away into eternal punishment, and the righteous into eternal life." That is, according to the new school of destructionism, the wicked shall go away into eternal non-existence, and the righteous shall enter into eternal existence. And yet they had entered into eternal existence when they were first born! From such doctors may the Lord preserve his Church! But hearken to Paul. "To them," says he, "who seek for glory, honor and immortality, he will bestow eternal life." Simple existence? mere being? Nay, verily, eternal life is here made the sum of glory, honor and immortality. These are the three grand items that make up the aggregate called eternal life. God, says Paul, will grant them then what they now seek. They, by a "patient continuance in doing well, are seeking for glory, honor and immortality:" therefore God will bestow upon them ETERNAL LIFE.

We shall henceforth regard it as an established fact, that eternal life is not existence, but eternal happiness, and that consequently the second death, or everlasting punishment, is not merely second non-existence. Meantime, we shall only add a fact in confirmation of our definitions—viz. there are two classes of angels as well as two classes of men. There are the holy and happy angels, and there are the unholy and unhappy angels. There are Michael and his angels, and Satan and his angels. There are angels that kept their first estate, and "angels who have sinned." Now, seeing both classes yet exist, do they exist in one state? Does not one class exist in happiness, while the other exists in misery? Satan and his angels have lived six thousand years in rebellion, and consequently in comparative misery, waiting condemnation at the judgment of the great day. How instructive the language of the demons, those wicked spirits of fallen men, when beseeching the Lord not to torment them before the time! They are said to be reserved in chains of darkness until the judgment of the great day. We have, then, angels existing and suffering misery, and angels existing and enjoying eternal life. Simple existence and non-existence are, therefore, not the ultimate conditions of human nature. The possibility of existence in misery we have in fallen angels, and the possibility of existence in happiness we have in the angels that sinned not. There is a fire prepared for the devil and his angels, as well as a heaven for the Messiah and his angels. The former constitutes "everlasting punishment," and is, therefore, called *"the eternal fire;"* the other is called "eternal life" and "the salvation to be revealed when the Lord comes."

We presume it to be unnecessary to multiply evidences in this portion of our essay on the mere meaning of the phrases *eternal life* or *eternal punishment*, designing at this time only to demonstrate that in the sacred style simple existence is not life, nor continued existence eternal life.

But we have said that eternal life is only the consummation of *spiritual life*—that it is only the full development of the life we now have, in having union and communion with the Lord Jesus. The life of an adult man is not different from the life of the embryo or the infant man. So eternal life is but the full development and perfect enjoyment of that new life which we have begun in us by the Spirit of God when united to Christ. For "we are dead, and our life is hid in Christ by God." And, therefore, "when Christ our *life* shall appear, we also shall appear with him in glory."

We are not, however, in speaking of spiritual or eternal life, to imagine that either of these is any distinct substantive life superadded to human life, like the addition of one substance or principle to another; for life is not any substance, but merely a sensitive intellectual or moral enjoyment of ourselves and of God. It is a state or condition of existence, and not existence itself. It is the state of the soul or of mind as capable of receiving and using Divine communications. Hence the same mind may at one time be in one state, and at another time in another state, as respects any person or thing. The same body is susceptible of various conditions or states of existence; and why should not the same mind be susceptible of similar changes and modes of existence? How often are we disposed and indisposed to one and the same thing! We hate and love, and love and hate, the same person under different views of his character or of his actions towards us. The mind loving is not really one life, nor the mind hating another life. It is the same mind in different states.

Very analogous are the various lives of which we have been speaking. It is one and the same living spirit that is the subject of them all. The same angelic spirit may be at one time a seraph, and at another a devil. Paul was at one time the enemy, at another the friend, of the Lord. The same mind in one state constitutes a friend, and in another state an enemy. In these states he may be said to be alive or dead to the same person, as he feels towards him.

But it must be emphatically stated that this is not the whole mystery, but only a part of the mystery, of the new life. The sunflower turns its face to the sun; while the sun in return pours his genial rays of light and life into its bosom. In this case, then, there is more than a single change of position. The sunflower opens its bosom as well as turns its face to the sun; and the sun not only lifts its full-orbed face and looks upon it, but it also sheds abroad within its bosom its vital power. Thus, when a sinner turns to the Lord, attracted to him, as the sunflower is to the sun, by an emanation from him, then the Sun of Righteousness and of Mercy, by his good spirit, pours out into his soul the love of God; and then, indeed, he begins to live to God and to enjoy him, not only through nature and providence, but through his spiritual favor and love. This is my conception of spiritual life, and this is the embryo blossom of eternal life in the immediate presence of God for ever and ever.

This spiritual connection is very appositely and beautifully set forth by the Saviour himself under the similitude of a vine and its branches. Addressing his disciples, he said, "I am the vine; you are the branches. He that abideth in me, and I in him, the same bringeth forth much fruit: for without me you can do nothing." The vital fluid that is in the root and in the stem circulates through all the branches. To this they owe their verdure, their odor and their fruitfulness. The life that is in the root is in the branches. Dissevered from that, they wither and perish. Connection with the vine is life, if life be in the vine; separation from it is death. Thus reasoned the Great Teacher.

On another occasion he said, "I am the bread that came down from heaven. If any man eat of this bread, he shall live forever; and the bread that I will give him is my flesh, which I will give for the life of the world." Of this bread he said, "Except you eat the flesh of the Son of man, and drink his blood, you have no life in you. Whoso eateth my flesh and drinketh my blood hath eternal life, and I will raise him up at the last day." On another occasion he said, "I pray . . . for them who shall believe on me, that *they all may be one;* as thou, Father, art in me and I in thee; that *they also may be one in us.*" This is that union and communion with the Divine Father and his beloved Son which constitutes spiritual and eternal life. And to him that is alive to God there is no eternal life, no eternal glory, no immortality greater, more desirable, more blissful, than this. How truly, then, may it be said that "Christ is *our life*"—that he is the way, the truth and THE LIFE—that we are dead, and that our life is *laid up in him by God!*

Still, the new constitution, in all its sublime developments, exhibits the Holy Spirit of God as the immediate source and fountain of all spiritual life in us. God alone "*has life in himself*," underived, unoriginated, uncreated. He is life's fountain, its eternal spring, its unwasting fulness. He imparted it to the Messiah. He was the earthen vessel in which this treasure was deposited. Without measure or limit THE SPIRIT was communicated to him; and ultimately, on his ascension, he received the HOLY SPIRIT as its administrator to and for the human race. He is now sole "LORD OF THE SPIRIT."

As the life that is in all mankind was once in Adam, and is derived from him, and as the life that is in the human body is in its head, as its primitive source, so is our spiritual life in the second Adam, the living head of the mystic body, animated by the Holy Spirit with impartations of a Divine and eternal life. By faith, then, we are united to him, and instantly that life Divine is imparted to us by which we are prepared for the enjoyments of heaven and immortality. With the greatest propriety, then, he said, "I AM THE RESURRECTION AND THE LIFE." He quickens the dead, reanimates their bodies, and is to them the fountain of eternal blessedness. Such is the life we have in him. With Paul, we may individually say, "I am crucified with Christ, nevertheless I live; yet not I, but Christ liveth in me."

Now, as before shown, death is just the contrary of life: hence there is a species of death for every species of life. The Gentile, dead in trespasses and sins, is merely a son of Adam; while he that is in Christ is a new creature and a son of God through Adam the second. Connection with Adam the first is but human life and spiritual death; while connection with Adam the second is divine life and eternal blessedness.

But in this age and country, and especially amongst those whose minds have been carried away with the new theories of the world's age and end, and with new schemes of apocalyptic interpretation, a new theory of Divine judgment has become very rife, and has found favor amongst some excellent persons who have been much enamored with the splendors of a celestial paradise during a terrestrial millennium—not, indeed, well defined by its most learned and eloquent advocates; for it seems no one can tell much about it, save that the living wicked shall be destroyed at its commencement, and in the second resurrection all that shall be accounted worthy of it shall be punished with a very painful and extended dissolution, or with a mysterious and ignominious transition into nothing. These are, now-a-days, generally called Destructionists. A more special and methodical examination and exposition of this common speculation is imperiously called for, and shall now be attempted with all possible brevity and perspicuity.

In the first place, then, the extinction of the unjust is alleged to be a Bible doctrine, because in the New Testament the term *destruction* is applied in direct reference to the ultimate destiny of the wicked. But we have already shown that the Christian Scriptures authorize various acceptations of this word, and that, indeed, no case can be adduced in which it must signify an absolute extinction, or annihilation of a human person.

There is, moreover, in fact, both a *relative* and an absolute *destruction.* A leather bottle, for example, is said to be destroyed when only *rent* by new wine; a thoughtless prodigal is said to have been destroyed when he had squandered his fortune in riotous living; and a box of precious ointment is said to be destroyed when *wasted,* &c. Now, in none of these examples can it be said that the subject is absolutely destroyed,—it is only wasted, lost or abused; and this is but relative destruction, and by no means the utter and eternal extinction of the person or thing so destroyed.

In the second place, the foundation of the theory of destructionism, when closely analyzed, is found to consist in an imaginative expediency. Some very benevolent and humane persons think that it would be much more expedient that the universe were rid of all sin and misery, and that eternal existence in misery would be an eternal annoyance to all the friends of the unfortunate sufferers. Who, says the pious Destructionist, could feel happy in heaven, if he knew that the once beloved wife of his bosom, and the dear objects of his paternal love and tenderness, were suffering the vengeance of an eternal fire? To get rid of this apprehension, the Universalist annihilates hell, and the Destructionist the wicked. These benevolent enthusiasts, in their respective notions of expediency, remove both eternal misery and the irreclaimably wicked from the creation of God. They imagine there is no necessity whatever for eternal punishment, but, on the contrary, that a universe wholly occupied and enjoyed by pure and righteous persons would be just such a universe as would be both expedient and suited to the character of an all-wise, all-powerful and all-merciful Creator. The only difficulties they have to encounter are those scriptures that speak of the future destinies of the wicked, and these can, by a new code of laws of interpretation recently enacted by themselves, very satisfactorily (at least to themselves) be disposed of.

It is hard to reason with those who feel themselves competent to build a new universe, or, at least, to arrange and improve one already in being. Some of our modern world-makers amuse us with very splendid imaginations of what ought to be, and then gravely proceed to teach us what will and must hereafter be. Even in the incipiency of their endeavors, they object to our own terraqueous habitation as encumbered with so much sea, so many large deserts, so many bleak mountains, and subjected to the dread extremes of frigid and torrid zones. They would have made an earth whose surface should have been, at worst, but a series of inclined planes, widely extended and gently sloping in all directions. These would have been interspersed with a few small lakes and rivers, occasionally variegated with a pyramidal peak or a beautifully grotesque little mountain, forming Elysian landscapes. No rocky deserts, no Libyan sands, no dismal swamps, would have disfigured their rich and beautiful earth, fanned with balmy breezes mild as Eden, and refreshed with delicious odors emanating from the garden of God.

No burning mountains, no volcanic fires, no desolating earthquakes, would have frightened any inhabitant of their blest earth. No mighty cataracts, no fierce tempests, no appalling thunders, would have terrified the most flagrant transgressor. Nay, they would have prevented transgression by absolute fate, and enacted virtue by an invincible necessity. Their heavens would have been studded with alternating suns of magnificent dimensions; while planets of every variety, and comets of orbits the most eccentric, would have perpetually sported in fields of ether for the amusement of its laughing inhabitants. And as for hell—the dread "*elsewhere*," no such ungracious lake of boiling sulphur, no such fathomless gulf of pitchy darkness, would have disturbed the imagination of the sons of pleasure. And should sin or folly, by any unforeseen casualty, have appeared in their system of nature, it would have been instantly annihilated, and thus prevented from spreading its dire contagion through the unaffected regions of rational intelligence.

Amongst the stricter sort of religionists, such speculators are not, indeed, of much reputation. But instead of this bold and presumptuous class of real skeptics, we have, under the banner of the Christian Bible, a few rare philosophers of much intellectual pride, who can so manage both prophets and apostles as to oblige them to depose in favor of any assumption they may choose to commend to public patronage. These subject the testimonies of saints and martyrs to the torture of an illogical and ungrammatical criticism, much to the annoyance of less pretending and more modest professors. But before we examine any of their learned labors, we must hastily glance at the philosophic scheme which has given rise to all these efforts.

It is assumed that in a future life men will have their present animal affections and feelings, at least the same personal attachments to relatives and friends, that they now have, and also the same reluctance to acquiesce in the will of God and in the results of the final judgment. The Sadducean puzzle, that in the resurrection we shall have the old relations of husbands and wives, parents and children, and attachments corresponding with them, is at the bottom of all these speculations. Our Saviour, to such persons, in vain teaches that then we shall be like the angels, without sex, without animal attachments, as without mortality. But to those who think with him, there can be no difficulty on this view of the subject. The fact that God himself is infinitely more merciful than man, and that the whole human race is nearer and dearer to him than ever were to each other husband and wife, parent or child, is now, and ever will be, to every intelligent being, an omnipotent argument to reconcile all God's children to his judgment in every particular case. No human being ever loved another as much as God once loved the devil and his angels; and yet he has not only expelled them from heaven, but bound them fast in chains of darkness, to the judgment of the great day, and has prepared for them an unquenchable fire, a punishment everlasting. So the Messiah himself unequivocally declares.

The relation of Creator and creature is a relation we cannot comprehend. It is incomparably nearer than that of parent and child. And as affection and love are measured by the nearness of relation, we have reason to presume that for all those creatures to whom our Father Creator has imparted so much of himself as intelligence and moral susceptibility, he has a love inconceivable and ineffable. From all such premises, as well as from express scriptural declarations, we have reason to infer that there will be such a perfect acquiescence in his final adjudication of the whole intellectual and moral universe as to fill every pure heart with joy unspeakable and full of glory; even when that judgment may condemn to eternal anguish a relation now dear to us as that seraph once was to God whose name and character have been changed to Satan. And yet this view of the subject is by no means irreconcilable with the persuasion that, as Paul anticipated an eternal joy and an unfading crown from the relation subsisting between him and those by him converted to God, so we shall have a peculiar pleasure and felicity in those of our kindred who have been by our instrumentality, or by that of others, redeemed to God. From which considerations and reflections we may readily perceive how little philosophy or reason there is in the assumption of those who plead for absolute destruction on the ground that it will contribute more to the eternal happiness of the saved, than a belief of the eternal existence of sinners in torment!

In the third place:—It is assumed by some of the advocates of destructionism that an annihilation of personal existence is a greater punishment than eternal existence in misery. This is an assumption so ultra as to require but little reflection. To me it has always appeared that were immediate annihilation or eternal fire presented to any human being as objects of choice, no one, *compos mentis*, could for a moment hesitate which to prefer. Nay, indeed, an escape from a lake of fire, or from any punishment set forth under that imagery, into a gulf of personal extinction, would appear rather as happiness than as torment. It may, indeed, with much propriety, be inquired whether annihilation, or a literal destruction of consciousness and of personal existence, could be called punishment for sin, or *whether sin could be punished by annihilation*. If so, the reptiles and beasts of every class that were burnt in Sodom and Gomorrah, or that were drowned in the deluge, were as much punished as the wicked men and women who perished in the flood or in the fire. In the universal conflagration, will not the pigeon and the dove, the calf and the lamb, suffer as much as the wicked—if, indeed, both are then finally and forever deprived of consciousness and personality? If, then, the threatenings of the Bible addressed to wicked men involving their eternal destiny amount to no more than the fate of the most innocent and harmless animals, what shall we think of the sincerity of the author of Christianity, who, in holding up "*the terrors of the Lord*" as a caveat against sin, as an inducement to "*flee from the wrath to come,*" representing them as proportioned to the number, magnitude and malignity of transgressions, only, in unexaggerated fact, meant that they should have the same fate as the most innocent birds, beasts and fishes—suffer an hour or a minute, and then pass into eternal unconsciousness! I have certainly misconceived the whole Bible and the character of its author, if, like a weak nurse, he has been terrifying us by ghosts and spectres of horrible stature, himself well knowing that they are but mere phantoms, innocent frauds practised for our good! In this attitude do those place the great Messiah who, with all the awful judgments denounced against the wicked by himself and his apostles before their minds, represent these judgments and denunciations terminating in, and amounting to, no more than the annihilation of a kid or a lamb—a moment's pain and eternal unconsciousness.

But, in the fourth place, I argue against this assumption from the fact that it amounts to an annihilation of the sanctions of the gospel, and directly contradicts the positive declarations of the Saviour concerning eternal punishment. *With destructionists there can be no eternal punishment; for with them there is no eternal fire.*

This is truly a very grave charge against any system of doctrine, and requires to be well sustained. What, then, let me inquire, is indicated by the term *punishment?* It is not mere animal suffering; for then the lamb would be punished for its innocence, and the dove for its meekness. Both these frequently endure great animal sufferings. There must, then, be some other pain than animal sufferings to constitute punishment. There is mental pain as well as physical pain. But mental pain presupposes guilt or crime; for in the absence of crime there can be no mental pain. The martyr at the stake, though enduring much animal pain, suffers no mental agony. There must always be consciousness of guilt, or a sense of crime committed, in order to punishment.

Punishment, it appears, begins and ends with the feeling of pain inflicted for the commission of crime. If, then, at any time consciousness of guilt, or the feeling of pain, mental or physical, because of sin, should cease, that moment punishment ceases. *Punishment begins and ends with the consciousness of pain inflicted because of guilt contracted through the violation of law or the neglect of duty.* Now, as the destructionists assign an end to the endurance of pain because of sin, they of course incontrovertibly deny "*everlasting punishment.*" But Jesus Christ says, "The wicked," at the final judgment, "shall go away into everlasting punishment," and the righteous "into life eternal." The same word—*aiooinos, everlasting*—determines the continuance of the punishment and of the life. Can any thing, then, be more evident than that the destructionists have formed a direct issue with Jesus Christ on the subject of eternal punishment? The Messiah says it is everlasting; the destructionist says it will come to an end at the second death.

For the sake of a few mere pretenders to sound argumentative discrimination and great logical acumen, I shall give this argument the regular form, that any one disposed to attack it may immediately perceive what he has to encounter. Logically expressed, it stands thus:—

No one dispossessed of conscious guilt can be punished. But persons annihilated are dispossessed of conscious guilt: therefore, no one annihilated can be punished.

Annihilation or personal extinction may, indeed, be an end of punishment, but never the beginning of it. This single argument, unless fairly met and refuted, annihilates the whole theory of destructionism. We build this argument upon no ambiguous premises. We have the word of the Saviour and Judge of the world for it. In giving an account of the final judgment, he says that all on his left hand shall depart "into everlasting punishment." He uses the word *kolasis* to indicate what sort of punishment he means. The word occurs but twice in the New Testament. In 1 John iv. 18, it is translated "*torment.*" They shall go into everlasting torment. How weak or how vicious the head which thence infers that torments are to end in a second death!

It is worthy of remark that eternal life, as the reward of the righteous, is contrasted with eternal punishment, as the reward of the wicked; and that this is infinitely greater than death, we learn from another passage, which we ought to regard as a distinct argument for or evidence of the doctrine of everlasting punishment.

Argument 5.—Paul says to the Hebrews, "He that despised Moses' law died without mercy at the mouth of two or three witnesses: of how much sorer punishment [than death without mercy] shall he be thought worthy who has trodden under foot the Son of God," &c. The doctrine of the New Testament is, that men shall be rewarded according to their works. Hence there are diverse honors and diverse punishments awaiting both the righteous and the wicked. Now, death is but a separation from life, or from God; and, whatever may precede it or succeed it, it is neither more nor less than such a separation. But Paul intimates a vengeance greatly surpassing a death without mercy—a "sorer punishment" by far than mere separation from life. Hence the sentence inflicted upon sinners at the ultimate judgment is not a mere extinction of life or of physical identity, but an everlasting punishment, set forth under the imagery of "eternal fire."

This suggests a sixth argument, furnished by our Lord himself, in evidence that something much worse than death awaits the finally impenitent:—"Fear not them that kill the body, and after that can do no more; but fear Him who, when he hath killed the body, has power to destroy both soul and body in hell. Yea, I say unto you, fear him." The destruction of the soul is not annihilation, as before shown; for simple annihilation could be effected as easily without hell as with it. An eternal destruction calls for an everlasting fire. Hence our Lord, more than any other speaker in the Bible, dwells upon the "fire unquenchable," the undying worm, and the destruction of the whole person by being cast into hell.

This view of hell as the ultimate prison of wicked men, in which they are to be "tormented day and night forever," is corroborated by another saying of our Lord, which we must place as a seventh argument in confirmation of everlasting punishment. He says to those on his left hand, "Depart, ye cursed, into the eternal fire *prepared for the devil and his angels.*" The eternal vengeance into which wicked men are driven from the presence of the Lord was originally, it seems, a *place* prepared for fallen angels. Now, as angels "*cannot* die," according to the words of the Messiah, and as wicked men are doomed to the same punishment with them, follows it not that the continuance of their torment is the same? The punishment of those who reject the gospel is set down as equal to the punishment of apostate angels who would not have God to reign over them. Will any materialist, destructionist or soul-sleeper affirm that angels will die—will cease to live? If he presume so to affirm, we then ask, in what portion of revelation does he read of the death of angels? And if he can find no such passage, we ask, *how then can he affirm that evil spirits die, while their punishment is commensurate with that of immortal angels?* This is, I presume, an insuperable difficulty lying in the way of the whole scheme of substituting a *temporal* for an *everlasting* punishment: at least, I must regard it as unanswerable till some one furnish something in the form of a reply.

But here is a pamphlet of no less than *four* small pages, purporting to prove that man is all soul! The first sentence is, "What, in the language of the Bible, constitutes the living soul?" Answer: "*The man.*" The next, "Is not the soul distinct from the man as the jewel from the casket? And does it not reside in the body as a bird in a cage? No; for the Lord God formed man of the dust of the ground, and breathed into his nostrils the breath of life, and MAN *became a* LIVING SOUL. (Gen. ii. 7; 1 Cor. xv. 44, 45.)" "This," he adds, "is God's definition." So publishes to the world a very sincere Adventist of the Miller school, baptized into Elder Storrs's newly-improved system of spiritual mortality, enlarged and improved by one of our most gifted "investigators" of the school of Dr. Priestley. It is, then, the quintessence of what was formerly called "*materialism,*" refined and condensed into a single tract of four small pages, from the pen of Elder J. B. Cook, a good and excellent man, for whom I entertain a very high regard.

But our friend Cook, in the warmth of his feelings, assures us that he gives us "God's definition" of the soul. It is neither Storrs's, nor

Priestley's, nor the more profound Thomas's, but "God's own definition." Of course, in that view of it, it is scarcely a proper subject of examination. I must, then, powerful though it be, respectfully say that God has never given us a definition of the human soul, much less such a one as defines man to be the soul, and then the soul to be the man. I am obliged to take this ground before I dare to object to a definition purporting to be of such awful authority. It is, then, but Elder Cook's definition—unless we may suppose that every definition is God's own definition to which any one may choose to append a passage of scripture.

We shall, therefore, presume to show that it is Elder Cook's, or Elder Storrs's, or Dr. Priestley's definition. God has *not* said that the living soul is man; but he has said that "man *became* a living soul." Now, when any one says, "Mary became his wife," does it not mean that Mary existed before she became a wife? As this expression intimates that *Mary* and *wife* are not convertible terms, or that the one is the meaning of the other, why should we conclude that *man* and *living soul* are convertible terms, or that the one is the meaning of the other? Such, however, is the license which this school of Biblical expositors assume to themselves—a license which no literary tribunal can possibly concede to them. If, therefore, the constitution of man is to be inferred from the words cited, we must, according to every law of interpretation, consider that *man* existed *before* he was possessed of a living soul, or before God breathed into his nostrils the breath of lives. These words, then, are to be qualified by some other explanations. And, as much capital has been sought to be manufactured out of these, I may perhaps be indulged in a somewhat extended examination of their current acceptation.

The phrase *breath of life* occurs but four times in the Bible. These are, Gen. ii. 7, vi. 17, and vii. 15, 22. In the Hebrew Bible we find uniformly the same phrase, *Ruach Chaiyim,* in the plural form—viz. "*breath of lives.*"

Dr. Adam Clarke, Bishop Patrick, Matthew Henry, and other commentators, infer, from Gen. ii. 7, that God did inspire Adam with vegetative, animal and spiritual life at one and the same moment, because we are told that "God formed man out of the dust of the ground, and breathed into his nostrils the breath of *lives,*" (as the Hebrew word *Chaiyim,* in the plural number, might import,) and he became a *living soul.* This very superficial view of *Ruach Chaiyim* has arrested the critical attention of those mathematical Christians who suppose that words on moral subjects must have the same fixedness and precision of signification as the technical terms of necessary or mathematical truth. Hence, with them, the words *soul, life, death,* like triangle, square and circle, are exactly and immutably the representatives of one and the same idea.

This new class of destructionists are very adroit in this mode of assault upon the citadel of truth. But their logic is as frail as their tenets are discreditable to human nature. They presume that the human constitution is wholly revealed and developed in these words:— "The Lord God formed man of the dust of the ground, and breathed into his nostrils the breath of lives, and man became a living soul." This "living soul" is immediately placed before their inquisition, and tried by scourging. It is clearly proved that this living soul is a mortal soul and a mortal body. That the whole man is but one living soul is again reiterated, and a text summoned that convicts it of a sin worthy of death. Then come the words, "The soul that sinneth, IT shall die." Thus the human soul is easily decomposed, dissipated and annihilated by the sheer force of one or two philological criticisms.

A little Hebrew would have much facilitated the operation. The gloss put upon *Ruach Chaiyim* by the aforesaid commentators could be shown off to great advantage by citing three passages—indeed, the only three other passages found in the Bible—in which this word *Chaiyim,* in construction with *Ruach,* is found. And in these three (Gen. vi. 17; Gen. vii. 15 and 22) it is applied to the animals destroyed by the flood. "I will," says God, "destroy all flesh wherein is the breath of life (*Ruach Chaiyim,* breath of lives) from under heaven." Again, (chap. ix.:)—"And they went into the ark, two and two, of all flesh wherein was the breath of life," (*Ruach Chaiyim,* breath of lives.) One more, (chap. vii. 22:)—"All in whose nostrils was the breath of life, (*Ruach Chaiyim,*) of all that was on the dry land, died." Might not a shrewd destructionist here say, with an air of triumph, "Now, if breath of LIVES indicate intellectual and immortal spirits, then were they imparted to dumb brutes, *then did they perish in the flood!*'

But we must help them a little further on the words, "*man became a living soul.*" Here the word *nepesh* is found generally, and correctly, translated *soul.* But, unfortunately, it is found, for the first time in the world, in the twentieth verse of the first chapter of Genesis; and, again, in the thirtieth verse of the same chapter, descriptive of the souls of fish, birds and reptiles. "God said," (Gen. i. 20,) "Let the waters bring forth abundantly, the moving creatures that have life," (a soul, *nepesh.*) Again, verse 30, "I have given every green herb for food to every beast of the earth, to every bird, and to every reptile that hath a soul," (*nepesh* here rendered *life.*) We could give many instances in which *nepesh*, so often translated soul, denotes the blood,* the animal body, alive or dead. In these respects it exactly resembles its Greek representative *psuchee*, and its Latin converse *anima*.

It often denotes any creature that lives by breathing. Parkhurst judiciously observes that this word does not, "certainly, in any other passage, (than Gen. ii. and vii., if there!) signify the spiritual part of man, usually called his soul." From all which, and much more to the same effect, we may logically conclude, that so soon as God breathed into the nostrils of Adam the breath of lives, he became a *living creature*. But yet, in fact, all this makes nothing for those who will have Adam a mere biped animal with a superior organization, but as susceptible of death, in his entire constitution, as any other creature. For this reason:—It is not a definition of body, soul or spirit, in their technical meaning. It presumes not to define man either as respects body or soul, but simply states the singular manner of his creation, as different from all God's other works. God speaks on this occasion in a language wholly different from that employed in any other creation.

When all this, and much to the same effect, is stated and conceded, nothing is gained by the whole class of destructionists—by all who plead for the soul's materiality and mortality. Man has a *spirit*. And Moses gives no direct account how he obtained it. He tells of the formation of his body, and of the impartation of animal life, but says not one word upon the subject of his spirit. True, the word *soul* is, by many, supposed to be synonymous with the word *spirit*. This is, indeed, assumed by all materialists and destructionists, ancient and modern. They build upon a false assumption. They are not synonymous. Sometimes, indeed, the word *soul* is substituted for the words *spirit* and *mind*. Hence, the soul is immortal in one sense, and mortal in another. The word *nepesh* in Hebrew, *psuchee* in Greek, and *soul* in English, as often signify life, mere animal life, as any thing else.

Of one hundred and five times in which the word *psuchee* is found in the New Testament, it is *forty-one times translated life*, and might have been much oftener. It is twice translated *mind*, and once *heart*, while at other times it is distinguished from them, thus:—"With all thy heart, and with all thy soul, and with all thy mind." (Matt. xxii. 37; Mark xii. 30.) Again, "To love him with all the heart, and with all the understanding, and with all the soul," &c. (Mark xii. 33.) In

* Virgil, Æneid, ix. l. 349. Purpuream vomit ille animam: His purple soul he vomits forth.

these instances, and such like, there is, virtually, a contrasted difference between the mind, the understanding and the soul.

Soul, and *souls*, frequently stand for *persons*. For example:—"Fear fell upon every soul;" "There were added three thousand souls;" "Every soul that shall not hear will be destroyed;" "Threescore and fifteen souls," &c. Substituting such instances as these, we have a majority of cases in which it does not mean the spirit, or understanding, or mind of man. True, it is sometimes used as equivalent to the word spirit; *though never translated spirit in the New Testament.* When the Saviour spake in the Jewish idiom, he said, "Fear not them that can kill the body, but who *cannot kill* the soul." Here some immortal part of man is called soul; which, upon the whole, is a Jewish idiom. It is evident that in this case it cannot mean the animal soul or life; for man can kill that. A few instances occur, however, in which it clearly indicates the spirit of a man; such as, "I saw under the altar the souls of them that were slain for the word of God," (Rev. vi. 9.) Again, (Rev. xx. 4,) "I saw the souls of them that were beheaded." These are disembodied souls, or spirits. These, of course, are immortal souls. Still, in the same book we have this word used in the same sense as in the first chapter of Genesis. When speaking of the fish of the sea, John said, "Every living soul that was in the sea died."

But, to have all the premises before us, we must have a short dissertation upon the word *spirit;* for, as before observed, certainly man has a spirit as well as a soul—using the word *soul* in its primary and unfigurative sense. Of the creation of this spirit Moses gives no account further than that God made man in his own image and likeness. Now, as God is spirit, and as man was made in his image, he too must have a spirit. But that he has a spirit is distinctly and frequently averred by the Holy Spirit speaking to us in the living oracles. The spirit of a man is wholly intellectual. "Who knoweth the things of a man, but the spirit of man that is in him? And who knoweth the things of God, but the spirit of God?" Here the spirit of man and the spirit of God are introduced as *intelligent* spirits, each knowing, and alone knowing, the things of the person to whom he belongs. This is the reason why *mortality*, or death, or destruction, is never once alleged of a spirit—any spirit, good or bad. *Spirits belong not to the precincts of mortality.* No expression could be more incongruous or revolting than that "a *spirit died*, or *can die*." Indeed, it is said, "*they cannot die*," when it is said that angels cannot die. For the reason that angels cannot die is not because they are *angels*, or messengers, (for this is an *official* name,) but because they are *spirits*. Perhaps this is the reason why these two words, *soul* and *spirit*, are never interchanged or substituted the one for the other in any version of their originals.

In the Sacred Scriptures of the New Testament we find PNEUMA, *spirit*, nearly *four hundred times*. We have before said that we find PSUCHEE *one hundred and five times*. Now, PNEUMA is never translated *soul*, nor PSUCHEE *spirit*, in any version of the New Testament that I have seen—*certainly not once in our common version*. Does not this fact speak a volume to those who confound the animal soul with the human spirit, in their speculations upon the mortality of the soul, and who thence infer the mortality of the whole man?

Of the whole number of three hundred and ninety-three occurrences of *pneuma*, in the apostolic writings, it is applied to the *spirit of God* some two hundred and eighty-eight times; to *evil spirits* some thirty times; to the *human spirit* forty times; and figuratively, to indicate *temper* or *disposition*, some seventeen times. From an analysis of the numerous occurrences of the word *spirit*, and its different acceptations, we have ascertained one very important fact, of much significance in this controversy with modern destructionists. It is this:—*When any one in dying gives up or commends himself to the Lord, or to the Father, in such words as, "He gave up the ghost," or, "Lord Jesus, receive my spirit," or, "Father, into thy hands I commit my spirit,"* PSUCHEE *or* soul *is never used, but always* PNEUMA. This, more than any other fact, shows the marked difference, the essential difference, between *soul* and *spirit*. The literal soul dies, the literal spirit lives, at the dissolution of man. The body returns to the dust with its animal life, or soul; "the spirit returns to God who gave it." Ought we not, then, as Paul says the word of God does, "divide asunder," or separate between the soul and spirit, as well as "between the joints and marrow of the spine"? The word of God is truly "sharper than any two-edged sword," when thus separating matters so much alike in so many particulars. The same discriminating word of the Lord taught Paul to pray for the Thessalonians that God would preserve their "whole spirit, soul and body, blameless, to the coming of the Lord." What God thus hath separated, let not man confound.

There is a clear and well-defined difference between these three, in the strict interpretation of them, indicated in this summary of our persons by this great apostle. With him it is spirit, and soul, and body, and not spirit, or soul, and body. True, indeed, inasmuch as *soul* and *body* are equally expressive of one idea, so far as mere life is contemplated, it has come to pass that *soul* is sometimes used to comprehend all that is set forth under the term *spirit;* though, as before declared, they are never used in the original as convertible terms. When any one of sense and reflection speaks of the immortality of the *soul,* he employs the word as equivalent to *spirit,* and not as it is employed in Genesis, first and second chapters, to indicate animal life or a living creature.

The sophistry of the materialists and the destructionists of every school who acknowledge the Bible, so far as they seek to prove their doctrine from Gen. ii. 7, i. 20, 30, vi. 17, vii. 15, 22, and 1 Cor. xv. 44, 45, consists in this:—*They select one meaning of the word* SOUL *as its universal and immutable meaning;* and because in certain passages it denotes animal life, which is essentially mortal, they infer that all souls are mortal. And because the words *soul* and *spirit* are sometimes used as, in their opinion, synonymous, spirits also die. Hence wicked men will be wholly and forever annihilated in body, soul and spirit; so far, at least, as is essential to their personal extinction and perpetual unconsciousness. All of which they confirm by the same illegal process of reasoning on the terms *destroy* and *destruction* —assuming that these words must be taken in a special sense in this case, though by no means in accordance with their current and popular acceptation.

The passage in 1 Cor. xv. 44, 45, deserves a special remark. It thus reads, (the human body being the subject of development:)—"It is sown an animal body; it is raised a spiritual body. There is an animal body, and there is a spiritual body; and so it is written, the first man Adam was made a living (animal) soul; the last Adam, a quickening spirit."

The position of PSUCHIKOS, *natural,* in contrast with PNEUMATIKOS, *spiritual,* justifies Macknight and others in rendering it *animal.* There is no contrast between *natural* and *spiritual,* inasmuch as, in the proper sense of the word *natural,* the spirit is just as natural as either body or soul. It must, therefore, in this place mean *animal* as the proper contrast with *spiritual.* This common meaning of the word being preferred, there is no further mystery or difficulty in the passage. It means that man in two conditions may have one of two bodies—an animal or a spiritual. The one he has now in possession; the other, in hope. It is also indicated that the difference between these two bodies is analogous to the difference between the two Adams in their origin: the one was of the earth, earthy; the other is of the heaven, heavenly. The animal body of the first Adam was animated by an animal soul; the spiritual body of the saints, after the resurrection, will be animated by rational spirits. So far only are we authorized to extend the contrast, inasmuch as BODIES, and neither *souls* nor *spirits*, are the subject of comparison.

There is, then, no more foundation in 1 Cor. xv. 44, 45, than in Gen. ii. 7, for the destruction or for the mortality of the spirit of man. Paul nowhere teaches that a spirit dies, or that a soul, as a name for the rational spirit or mind of man, will ever be destroyed or annihilated. These are but the figments of ill-balanced and erratic minds, or over-heated imaginations. Nothing dies that is not wholly of the earth. Angels, human spirits, Satan and demons cannot die.

From this brief dissertation on *soul* and *spirit*, we may draw at least one or two arguments against destructionists, or in proof of the eternal punishment of the wicked. The first of these constitutes our *eighth* argument against destructionists. It is founded on the fact that there is a radical and essential difference between the words *soul* and *spirit* in the original tongue—so great as to preclude the employment of the word *soul*, in any case, as a fair representation of the word PNEUMA, *spirit*, or the employment of the word *spirit* as a correct version of the word PSUCHEE, *soul*. The radical difference seems to consist in this:—that "soul" is a more *general* and "spirit" a more *specific* term. *Nepesh* in the Hebrew and *psuchee* in the Greek, *anima* in Latin and *soul* in English, represent *animal life, a person, blood*, and sometimes the *human spirit*, while *ruach* in Hebrew, and *pneuma* in Greek, *spiritus* and *animus* in Latin, and *spirit* in English, represent only the *rational and moral nature* of man. Hence, *the Holy Spirit, the spirits of the just, angelic spirits, are never represented by* PSUCHEE, *soul;* WHILE THE TERM "SPIRIT" IN NOT ONE CASE IS EVER SAID TO BE DESTROYED, TO DIE, OR TO CEASE TO EXIST. In one word, death is nowhere in the inspired volume predicated of a spirit. Mortality, therefore, is no predicate of spirit.

A *ninth* argument is deducible from another prominent fact developed in the history of dying saints. Not one of them ever commended his *psuchee*, or soul, into the hand of the Lord. But many a dying saint has committed his spirit, or *pneuma*, to the care of his Redeemer. There is nothing, then, in *psuchee*, soul, necessarily intimating a separate and future existence; while there is nothing in *pneuma* indicating mortality.

It is assumed, by those who plead for a final extinction of all evil spirits and wicked men, that there is nothing in spiritual nature necessarily implying eternal continuance. Hence the effort to demonstrate that man is not necessarily immortal. A very gratuitous undertaking, truly. We concede, without argument, that God has never created any thing which he cannot destroy. "He can create, and he destroy." But the question is not one of omnipotent or of limited power. It is rather, *What doth God will?* or, *What has he said?* The whole argument upon the immortality of the soul, as a *necessary* immortality, because an emanation from the Divinity, is Platonic, speculative and curious, rather than learned or important. It is, indeed, wholly foreign to this subject; inasmuch as the inquiry is not, What saith Philosophy? but, *What saith the Scriptures?* And where have they said that a spirit or that a ghost dies or is extinguished? Such an idea is never expressed in the books of apostles or prophets. That animals die, whether human or brutal, is as certain as that they live. And that animal souls, with all their passions, appetites and desires, die, is, so far as I know, admitted by all well-informed persons. There are some persons peculiarly fond of assailing the weaker points in an argument without noticing the strong; and where there are no weak points, their ingenuity must manifest itself in assuming for those whom they assail certain weak points, merely for the sake of displaying their controversial tact and logical acumen in refuting them.

Of the same character is the special logic of that class of reasoners who assail the doctrine of a separate state of existence, as indicated by the word *hades*. What and where is hades? Is it heaven, or hell, or the grave? Dives and Lazarus were, according to the parallel, both in Hades; and yet the one was comforted and the other tormented. Hence, they perplex the subject by inquiring, Are these two places the same, or so proximate that the inhabitants of both can hold conversations similar to Lazarus and Abraham? Some intelligent persons are not a little embarrassed when attempting to comprehend all that is said of *sheol* in the Old Testament, and of *hades* in the New; and no less embarrassed when told that *hades* means both the *grave* and the separate state of the dead. In the New Testament, *hades* occurs but eleven times, and is ten times translated *hell*, once *grave*. Yet we have the term *hell* in the English Testament *twenty-two times*. Of these, however, twelve are the English representatives of the word *gehenna*, found just twelve times in the Greek Testament. Our Lord is the only person who uses this word with a reference to future punishment. James uses it metaphorically, of the tongue, but once. Of that member he says it is sometimes "set on fire of hell." *Gehenna* and *hades* do not represent the same idea. The former is the receptacle of the wicked only, the latter is the receptacle of the spirits or bodies (as the case may be) of all mankind, good and bad. Certain it is, then, that two words so dissimilar ought not to be represented by one and the same English word. It would have greatly startled an English Christian to have read the words of Jacob to his sons thus:—"You shall bring down my gray hairs with sorrow to *hell.*" And yet the word *Sheol,* the Hebrew representative of *hades,* is there found. They have, judiciously enough, in this case, translated it *grave,* as they have in 1 Cor. xv. 58: "O *grave,* (not O *hell,*) where now thy victory?" Doubtless they ought in other cases to have so translated it. The spirit or soul of Jesus did not descend into *hell,* as the Church of Rome and our English Testaments read it:—"Thou wilt not leave my soul in hell, nor wilt thou suffer thy holy one to see corruption."

Again, it would seem no less confounding to say of the rich man that in hell he lifted up his eyes in torment, if it meant no more than the grave, or that in the grave he saw Lazarus in Abraham's bosom. To say, also, that Capernaum or its inhabitants, and other wicked places, should be brought down to the *grave,* if it means only the receptacle of human bodies, would be equally inapposite and confounding to our reason. We are, therefore, obliged to contemplate the word as it was used by the Jews in the times of the Messiah as indicative of the state of departed spirits, whether they were good or bad—thus representing the state of the dead rather than the place of spirits.

For example: should we represent the matrimonial state by the word *Hymenia,* and say of all persons when married that they entered into *Hymenia,* and that in Hymenia some enjoyed happiness and others misery, might not many persons, ignorant of the meaning of Hymenia, be not a little embarrassed to comprehend what sort of a *place* Hymenia was, in which some persons might be happy and others miserable? *Place* and *state* in things terrestrial are more easily distinguished than in things not terrestrial. In the same terrestrial place, persons in different states may meet, without any confusion of ideas. Still, in such cases there is no resemblance between the state and the place. Where there is, however, a very striking resemblance between the state and the place, as between a jail or a palace and their respective inmates, we are more apt to associate the one with the other, and are more perplexed in reconciling to the same place persons in states essentially diverse from each other.

But as soon as we leave terrestrial objects and the abodes of sense, our reasonings from place and state rather perplex than aid us in any effort to understand Heaven, Hell and Hades. These are sometimes considered as places—distinct from each other as sun, moon and earth. At other times they are considered as mere states. *Place* and *state*, beyond the confines of earth, may, therefore, in some sense, be regarded as one and the same. But that *hades*, always improperly translated *hell*, and sometimes improperly translated *grave*, the common representative of the Hebrew *sheol*, sometimes indicated both place and state, may be inferred with certainty, as I conceive, from several occurrences in both Testaments.

The Hebrews, Greeks and Romans located the souls of all the dead under the ground. Among the Romans, *Infernus* contained both Elysium and Tartarus, repositories for all souls—good and bad. *Inferi*, in the Latin tongue, comprehends all the dead.*

Among the Jews it sometimes indicates the *grave*, and is, therefore, equivalent to *keber*, in their tongue, sepulchre. Still, it more frequently means something deeper than the grave, the profound abyss where souls abide. Numerous examples may be found in Jewish writings. From the Jewish prophets we can find ample proof. God, according to Moses, said, "A fire is kindled in mine anger, which shall burn to the lowest hell." Grave! That were an anticlimax indeed! Here it is *sheol*—in the Septuagint, *hades*. Job, too, or one of his contemporaries older than Moses, said, "The knowledge of God is higher than heaven, deeper than hell." *Sheol, Hades*. The grave!! No. The mansion of departed spirits. David, also, "If I ascend up into heaven, thou art there; if I make my bed in hell, behold, thou art there," (Septuagint, *eis ton haden*.) Amos represents God as saying, "Though they dig (*eis haden*) into hell, thence shall my hand take them; though they climb up to heaven, thence will I bring them down; and though they hide themselves on the top of Carmel, I will search and take them out thence; and though they be hid from my sight in the bottom of the sea, thence will I command a serpent, and he shall bite them." The contrasts here are most sublimely beautiful. In this place, certainly, hades descends below the grave.

In the same style the Messiah said, "Thou, Capernaum, that art exalted to heaven, shalt be brought down to hell;" *hades*—certainly lower than the grave. This Hebrew and Greek view of the mansions of the dead, seems, also, to have been in the mind of our apostle when

---

* A passage in the 8th Æneid of Virgil intimates this:—

Non secus, ac si qua penitus vi terra dehiscens
Infernas reseret sedes, et regna recludat
Pallida, diis invisa, superque immane barathrum
Cernatur, trepidentque immisso lumine manes.

he said, "At the name of Jesus every knee in heaven, in earth and *under the earth* shall bow;" and in the mind of John when he said, "No man in heaven, nor in the earth, nor *under the earth*, was able to open the book, neither to look into it."

That souls separated from their bodies (not merely animal souls—and dead bodies—sometimes in Hebrew called *nepesh*) are the proper inhabitants of *hades*, may be learned from other passages—such as, "Thou wilt not leave my soul in hades; nor wilt thou suffer thy holy one to see corruption." Here, in all propriety of contrast, the body is not to be doomed to *corruption*, nor the soul to *hades*. The same usage obtains under the word *abussos*, (Rom. x.)—"Say not in thy heart, Who shall ascend into heaven, to bring Christ down from above? nor, Who shall descend into the deep, [a grave six feet deep!] to bring him up from the dead?" The dead are then in the deep; the *abussos*, the *hades*, the *sheol*. No one ever called the grave the abyss, or the unfathomable gulf.

Were it either desirable or necessary to demonstrate that the receptacle of human spirits was understood by the ancient nations, Egyptians, Jews and Pagans, of all superstitions, to be deeper than the ground, a very long induction of authorities could be here introduced. Beginning with the necromancy of the Seven Nations, the provisions of the Mosaic law against consulting the spirits of the dead, the case of the witch of Endor, &c., we might fill a volume with documentary evidence, incontrovertibly clear and definite. But the occasion demands no such offering at our hand.

I will only add that this word *hades*, like all other words of much importance, has a figurative meaning as well as a grammatical or historical meaning. In contrast with heaven, it indicates something very low:—Exalted to *heaven*, thou shalt be brought down to *hades*. Here heaven indicates great height, and hades great depression. I shall go, said Hezekiah, to the *pulas hadou*, "the gates of hell," the gates of death. Thus, the Messiah says, concerning his church, "The *pulai hadou*, the gates of hades or death shall not prevail against it." My church, said he, shall be immortal.

But one passage in the Book of God would seem to favor the assumption that it sometimes signifies *hell*, properly so called, or the place of future punishment. In HELL, *hades*, the rich man "lifted up his eyes, being in torment." In this single passage it would seem to be equivalent to *gehenna*. But the fact before stated, that it merely represents the state of the dead—or the place of departed spirits—comprehending, as separated from their bodies, all spirits, good and bad, those in Abraham's bosom or in paradise, and those in

Tartarus or in prison, forbids the idea that even in this place it is used as synonymous with *gehenna*, or the state of ultimate punishment. The four questions propounded and before noted, and all similar questions, may, I think, be most satisfactorily answered by observing that *state*, *mode* or *condition of existence* is the radical and important idea in *hades*. And, as in the illustration from *Hymenia*, persons entering it may be contemplated as happy or miserable, in Paradise or Tartarus, in Abraham's bosom or in torment, *without any regard to local position* but as respects their capacity, individual character and associations. Thus, the rich man and Lazarus were both in *hades*, as Queen Victoria and the slave Matilda are both in *matrimony;* but the former lives in a palace and enjoys the smiles of a prince, while the latter endures the peltings of the storm and the squalid poverty of a cheerless hut. In this view of the matter, Jesus could say to the dying penitent, "To-day shalt thou be with me in paradise," and the risen Samuel could say to the distracted Saul, "To-morrow shalt thou and thy sons be with me."*

While, then, location belongs to heaven and hell, in their proper

---

* It is an old adage, that "a child may ask questions which a wise man cannot answer;" and so it has happened in the case of *Virtuoso* and *Biblicus* at the last church meeting for discussion, held in the Harbinger. *Virtuoso* asks the following questions in substance:—

1. Do the souls of the righteous go into *hades* at death? and if so, are they present with the Lord?

2. Does the word *hades* signify a place or a state? If a state, why translate it hell, grave, or unseen world?

3. From what part of the Bible do we learn that Abraham's bosom is a part or parcel of *hades?*

4. Will any that are Christ's be found in *hades?* and if so, will they not be subject to the second death?

In neither of these queries is there a word said about the separate existence of soul and body; and why did Biblicus contend for such separation in his answer?

Biblicus goes on to say that "*hades* means whatever it meant among the Jews of that age." Very well; and what did the Jews of that age mean by the word?

Josephus speaks of *hades* as a place located somewhere in or under the earth; and Paul says, "Now this . . . having ascended, and what is it, unless indeed he had also descended into the lower parts of the earth?"

Both Paul and Josephus were Jews of that age; and they locate *hades* in the lower parts of the earth, and not in the atmosphere, nor in ether beyond the atmosphere.

Now, if David meant by *hades* what Paul and Josephus meant, then it is evident that Jesus is not there, but has ascended from thence: consequently the souls of the righteous, when separated from their bodies, do not go into *hades*, else they are not present with the Lord.

Present and *absent* always have reference to locality or place. So I think, and so I reason. VIRTUOSO.

import and current signification, it enters not into the idea of hades, as now contemplated by intelligent Christians. That there was such a state currently believed in by all the world down to the Christian age, we can have no rational doubt. The ancients, we have shown, located it in the earth—they added the idea of place to it. This only goes to show how firmly, as well as universally, they believed it. We may dissent from their notion of place and other circumstances without at all impairing the weight of the evidence in favor of such a state as was indicated by the word *hades*.

The term is strikingly descriptive of the condition. It is drawn from the darkness and ignorance of its inmates as respects what is transpiring in this world. "The dead," said Solomon, "know not any thing." They see not, they know not aught of the affairs of earth. The etymology of the word fully indicates this. It is compounded of *a*, negative, and *eidoo*, I see. *I see not*. The state is mysterious, obscure, invisible; and those in it are void of the light and the knowledge of this life. The grave itself is called "the house of darkness," and the environs of it "the region and shadow of death."

We have amongst us those who argue that the spirits of the dead are wholly unconscious, from such sayings as, "Their thoughts perish," "The dead know not any thing," "Abraham is ignorant of us," &c., and hence "the soul sleepeth," or is dead with the body. Admirable critics! Sage interpreters! Sublime philosophers! Truly, they prove how dangerous a little learning is! The first phrase indicates that when a man dies his purposes die with him. His schemes fall to the ground. He can no further accomplish his designs. The second phrase intimates their ignorance of what transpires amongst the living. "Their sons come to honor" or dishonor, "and they know it not." The affairs of earth are to them as though they were not. But does this prove that they are ignorant or unconscious of every thing else? When a person migrates from England to America, he personally knows nothing that transpires there from the moment he quits its coasts. Are we thence to infer that he never after knows any thing of America or any other place, because he knows nothing of England? Just such philosophers have we amongst us—preaching soul-sleeping and eternal unconsciousness from their profound knowledge of language!.

That there is some analogy between a dead man and one asleep, is very obvious to the least attentive observer. But that analogy is only in that which is outward and visible. For even when men are literally asleep in body, the mind is oft employed in the most active enterprises, pains and pleasures—so much, indeed, as to arouse the body from the lethargy of repose. The sophism on the part of such reasoners consists in their assuming that a resemblance in one or more respects is always proof of universal resemblance. If it be not always proof of universal resemblance, why infer it is so in this case? Do not those who deny that souls can sleep themselves say of the dead that "they have fallen asleep," merely because of the resemblance between the body of a living man in sleep and that of a man dead? Strange logic, indeed, it would be, should every figure we use be taken as proof that we are always to be understood according to the letter. Then any one may prove from all the philosophers in Christendom that not one of them believes the Copernican or Newtonian system of astronomy, or even the sphericity or diurnal rotation of the earth, because they all say, in common with the most ignorant child, "The sun rises, and the sun sets;" while yet they teach that the sun is the immutable centre of the solar system and that all the planets move round it. As learned and as discriminating they who infer, from Paul's words, "Them that sleep in Jesus God will bring with him," that Paul believed and taught that all the saints slept from death to the resurrection.

The ashes of the dead sleep no more than do the ashes of a tree. If the dead sleep, it is, therefore, not their ashes, but their spirits, that sleep. Why, then, should the dying saints so often commend their spirits, and never their bodies, to the Lord? Why should the dying Stephen say, "Lord Jesus, receive my spirit," if his spirit slept in the grave with his body till the resurrection?

But we do not remonstrate against the delusion of this system only from such passages as the Lord's address to the penitent thief, "To-day shalt thou be with me in Paradise;" or from the parabolic representation of Lazarus borne by angels to Abraham's bosom, (while yet the rich man's brothers lived on earth and his soul "in torment," all solicitous about their condition;) or from the words of the dying Stephen, or those of the dying Messiah, commending their spirits to God when their animal life was expiring; but also from the clear, definite and positive declaration of the apostle that the saints immediately after death are present with the Lord, not in their bodies, but in their spirits.

Immediate though not complete blessedness, and immediate though not complete torment, after death, is the doctrine of the Messiah and his apostles. Lazarus died, and was instantly carried to Abraham's bosom. Dives died, and immediately lifted up his eyes in torment. So taught the Messiah; and certainly he would not introduce a false and deceptious imagery, to bewilder and perplex the world. Paul also affirms that as soon as "absent from the body we are present with the Lord," and "while in the body we are absent from the Lord." May I not ask, What language could more clearly and certainly indicate a continued and uninterrupted consciousness than this, or the fact of a separate state—a state in which the soul lives out of the body? What language could any one choose more definitely expressive of such a state than that above quoted, if he desired to inform us of the fact?

Again, Paul contrasts the pleasures which as a Christian man he could enjoy while in the body, with those he could enjoy out of the body, and from his inspired knowledge of the whole premises concludes it would be better for him immediately to die than to live, so far as his own happiness is concerned. "To me to live is Christ, and to die is gain." What could he gain by death but sleep, according to the theory of destructionism? Can any of the soul-sleeping or soul-dying school state what Paul would have gained by death on their philosophy of man? We should like to have a clear estimate of the gain from immediate death to those who sleep, or are unconscious, from death to the resurrection. Can any one, or will any one, enlighten us on the items of gain?

Paul further declares that to *depart* from earth, or from the tabernacle of flesh, is *far better* than to continue in the flesh. Strange language, to the ears of those who cannot distinguish between the flesh and the spirit—between *continuing in the flesh* and *departing from it*. To interpret the words "continuing" and "departing," without some place to continue in, and some place to depart from, as well as *something* to depart, and *something* to continue, distinct from that in which it abides and from which it departs, will require some person of more discrimination and learning than I possess. May I ask some one skilled in this new philosophy of language to favor us with an explanation of the mode of continuing in and departing from the flesh, when the whole man is all flesh or all soul, according to the theory which we oppugn?

We shall also solicit another favor from some of the adepts in this new theory. Paul affirms that it is FAR BETTER for him to leave the flesh than to continue in it. If, then, Paul's spirit slept in his body for eighteen centuries, that is, down to the present time, of what number and variety of items of gain does this *far better* consist? To make death far better than life, demands certain specifications. Can any one denying an immediate return of his spirit to the Lord make such an exhibit as will sustain his declaration? We wait for a response.

The only attempt to reconcile Paul's language to the facts of the case supposed by all who advocate soul-sleeping is a metaphysical speculation upon the difference between real and apparent or absolute and relative time. They are aware that, if Paul meant real time, their position is wholly untenable. But they assume that Paul meant *apparent* time; and, therefore, sleeping so soundly as do the saints, to them there is no time between death and the resurrection. According to them, the interval between death and the resurrection is, to the dead, annihilated. Paul, knowing this, spoke of departing from the flesh and being immediately present with the Lord, giving no intimation of any reserved or private sense, and, therefore, has virtually passed upon the Philippians, and all other readers, a cheat—substituting apparent for real time! A meritorious solution, truly, and highly creditable to the moral honesty of the apostle!

But this policy wholly fails in disposing of the phraseology of being at home in the body and absent from the body. For, according to common sense, no man could speak of *being absent from the body* if he can *live only in the body*. It would require a greater genius than any of our new theorists, to convince us that a man of sound sense and common honesty—an apostle, too—could speak of being absent from the body and present with the Lord, at any time, soon or late, if, indeed, he were all body, or all soul, or if the soul cannot live without the body.

May we not, then, conclude that we have irrefragable evidence of a separate state of existence, a *hades*, or that human spirits can exist either within or without bodies, and that when the spirits of the just are absent from the bodies they are not asleep, but positively happy in the presence of the Lord?

This argument in proof of HADES as distinct from heaven and hell—as the condition of all human spirits from death to the final resurrection—is itself, our tenth argument against the doctrine of destructionism. For if spirits live in a state separate from their bodies for thousands of years after their bodies are destroyed, so far, at least, as to be converted into dust, and if their bodies be considered merely—as Peter represents his—a *tabernacle* to be put off at death, there is no instance of the extinction of a soul; there is, moreover, no axiomatic evidence of such an event, and no one has ever presumed to demonstrate the extinction or destruction of a soul, from any data, human or divine; nor has any one been able to find a single text of Scripture that intimates the extinction, annihilation or absolute destruction of a human spirit.

But, so much depending upon a clear scriptural indication of the existence of hades as distinct from heaven and hell—or the fact of the separate existence of human spirits without their bodies—we shall sum up the arguments on which we principally rely for its development and confirmation:—

1. The promise made to the penitent thief by the dying Saviour:—"To-day shalt thou be with me in Paradise"—both of them that same day expiring together.

2. The dying words of the Messiah:—"Father, into thy hands I commend my spirit."

3. These are the last words of Stephen:—"Lord Jesus, receive my spirit."

4. "I knew a man in Christ, some fourteen years ago, caught away to paradise: *whether in the body or out of the body*, I cannot tell, God knoweth." Had it been impossible for a man to live out of the body, or for a spirit to exist in a separate state, I presume all, but those intoxicated with a new theory of man, will agree with me that Paul could not, as a man of truth, much less as an apostle of Christ, say that he could not tell whether he "was in the body or out of the body."

5. There is no intimation that human spirits dwell in human bodies after death, or that they are interred with them in their graves. To this agree the words of Matt. xxvi. 52, 53:—After our Lord's resurrection, when the graves were opened, "many *bodies* of the saints arose, went into Jerusalem and appeared unto many." Now, had the spirits of these saints been sleeping in their bodies, would it not have been said, many of the "saints arose, went into Jerusalem and appeared unto many"? The fact that *bodies* only came out of these graves, will be regarded as proof that bodies only were deposited in them.

6. An argument may be deduced from the restoration to life of the son of the widow of Sarepta by Elisha the Tishbite. The story is told, 1 Kings xvii. The prophet prayed for its restoration in the following words:—"O Lord my God, let the child's soul come into him again." The Lord heard the voice of Elisha, and the *soul* of the child came into him again, and he revived.

7. From the names given to the body by the Apostles Peter and Paul. They both call the body a *tabernacle;* they both regard the soul as dwelling in a house, a temple, or a tabernacle. Hence the soul is a *guest* or a *ghost*. Thus said Peter:—"I must soon lay aside or put off this tabernacle." There was some person that put off this tabernacle. This is corroborated by Solomon, who said, "The body returns to the dust, and the spirit to God who gave it."

8. From demons, evil spirits, and the whole doctrine of familiar

spirits and necromancy—their possession and dispossession—it is shown at great length that the spirits of wicked men perish not in their bodies, and that spirits are so diverse from bodies as to go into them and come out from them, &c. No materialist or destructionist can in any plausible way whatever dispose of this argument. They can only say that demons and familiar spirits, and all spirits, are phantoms. They are phantoms, however, the belief of which has always been as universal as any sentiment, or view, or tradition ever expressed in language.

9. From the parable of the rich man and Lazarus. This comparison, founded upon facts, as all the Lord's parables are, clearly indicates that while the body is in the grave the spirit is in conscious existence, susceptible of pleasure or pain. It was before the resurrection, and while the rich man's brothers were still living, that Abraham told the rich man that while Lazarus was comforted he was tormented.

10. From the developments on opening the fifth apocalyptic seal. John "saw under the altar *the souls* of those who had been slain on account of the word of God and the testimony which they held;" and they cried with great earnestness, soliciting information on the subject of the continuance of God's forbearance to punish those who had shed the blood of saints and martyrs. Now, had there been no separate state, no souls distinct and separate from their bodies, how could such a case have been introduced as representing God's schemes of providence towards the living and the dead?

11. Our next argument is deduced from a passage in John xi.:—"*Whosoever liveth and believeth on me shall never die.*" Martha's faith only went so far as to repudiate a pre-millennial resurrection of the saints. She, simple woman, only believed that her good brother Lazarus should "at the resurrection rise on the LAST DAY," *not a thousand years before the last day;* for she was technically a post-millennial adventist; but this point of never dying had not yet become familiar. Still, she believed it when the Lord said it.

My eleventh argument, then, is, that if he that believes in Christ shall never die, and as Christians actually die so far as their bodies are contemplated, their souls must certainly survive their bodies, else the Lord has deceived us.

I hold this to be as evident as any proposition can be—an argument, I humbly think, irrefragable. It bears equally against soul-*sleeping* as against soul-*dying*. For if death is compared to a sleep, as some contend, in all respects, then the sleep of death, or unconscious existence after death, is wholly repudiated in the words *"he shall never die,"* that is, he shall never pass into a state of unconscious existence.

12. My twelfth argument shall be deduced from an argument offered to the Sadducees by the Messiah in person, as reported by Luke, in the following words, to wit:—"Then came to him certain of the Sadducees, which deny that there is any resurrection, and they asked him, saying, Master, Moses wrote unto us, If any man's brother die, having a wife, and he die without children, that his brother should take his wife, and raise up seed unto his brother. There were, therefore, seven brethren: and the first took a wife, and died without children. And the second took her to wife, and he died childless. And the third took her, and in like manner the seven also; and they left no children, and died. Last of all the woman died also. Therefore in the resurrection whose wife of them is she? for seven had her to wife. And Jesus answering said unto them, The children of this world marry, and are given in marriage; but they which shall be accounted worthy to obtain that world, and the resurrection from the dead, neither marry, nor are given in marriage; neither can they die any more: for they are equal unto the angels; and are the children of God, being the children of the resurrection. Now that the dead are raised, even Moses showed at the bush, when he calleth the Lord the God of Abraham, and the God of Isaac, and the God of Jacob. For he is not a God of the dead, but of the living: for all live unto him." (Luke xx.) To understand this most important passage, we must quote another from Luke's Acts of the Apostles, xxiii. 6–8:—"But when Paul perceived that the one part were Sadducees, and the other part Pharisees, he cried out in the council; Men and brethren, I am a Pharisee, the son of a Pharisee: of the hope and resurrection of the dead I am called in question. And when he had so said, there arose a dissension between the Pharisees and the Sadducees: and the multitude was divided. For the Sadducees say that there is no resurrection, neither angel nor spirit; but the Pharisees confess both." "The Pharisees acknowledge BOTH"—*two tenets, not one.* Angels and spirits are the one tenet—the resurrection of the body, the other. The Sadducees deny spirits and a future state, consequently, the resurrection of the body. The non-resurrection of the body was, therefore, a mere consequence of their doctrine. Now, the Messiah always aims a blow at the root, the tap-root, of the system of error. He proves that *spirits are*—that the spirits of the dead ARE. The Sadducees say they *are* NOT. Jesus affirms not that they *were*, but that they ARE. Abraham is dead, and Isaac is dead, and Jacob is dead, said the Sadducees, wholly dead; "spirits are not, bodies only

are; and as their bodies once were, but are not, the resurrection is absurd." But Jesus affirmed that spirits *are;* and his proof is, that *God is the God of Abraham*—of some existing person—not the God of what *was*, but the God of what *is*. Therefore, as he is not the God of the dead, but of the living, Abraham, Isaac, Jacob, now live—*always live*. For, adds he, "All live to God"—"*If dead to us, they are alive to him*." "But their bodies are yet in Palestine; their sepulchres are yet with us. For neither David nor Abraham is yet ascended to heaven; their sepulchres and their ashes are still with us, but their spirits live with God."

13. Paul said he was a Pharisee, in the midst of an assembly of Pharisees and Sadducees. He intended to save his life by it. Did he lie? He was, in the sectarian sense, a Pharisee, and not a Sadducee. This was solemnly affirming for them in all the points designating their peculiarity on the Sadduceean hypothesis. I offer it now in confidence as a conclusive argument against Destructionism, against Sadducism, against Materialism in every form of it. The resurrection of the dead, the existence of angels and spirits, and the everlasting existence of man, either in happiness or misery, were the whole constituents of a Pharisee. Paul affirmed these to be true when he solemnly declared that he was, in opposition to the skepticism of the Sadducees, Pharisee in faith and by descent, not merely the son of a Pharisee, but a Pharisee himself.*

14. A *fourteenth* argument may very naturally be deduced from our Lord's words to Thomas when he convinced him that he was not a spirit. He defines a spirit in comparison with a body, as essentially unlike it in its materiality. "A spirit," says he, "has not flesh and bones, as you see me have." This cannot be plausibly denied to be a clear proof of the existence of spirits without bodies. When, indeed, the Sadducees say that there is neither angel nor spirit, do they not mean *human spirit?* For of what other spirit than angelic, save the human spirit, do the Scriptures speak? And did the Sadducees ever deny that there was a spirit in man while he lived? Never: they only denied departed spirits, or human spirits existing after or without their bodies. Now, as the Pharisees confessed both angelic and human disembodied spirits, and the Sadducees neither, and as our Lord and his apostles agreed with the Pharisees and not with the Sadducees in their peculiarity, follows it not that we have in this argument a clear

---

* These arguments have been stated in my essays on the Tyranny of Opinionism, but are here presented in connection.

and irrefragable evidence of the existence of human spirits without bodies, and consequently of *hades*, as before propounded? May we not now regard these fourteen arguments in proof of the existence of human spirits in a state called *hades*, separate and distinct from their bodies, as amply sufficient to confirm its certainty, and to explode a theory which reduces man to a simple *animal* possessed of a *vital principle* called *soul*, whose existence is not only identical with the body but inseparably coexistent, with it?

The last evidence we shall here offer of an intermediate or separate state of existence, is the fact that Moses appeared on earth about fourteen hundred and eighty years after his death. That great lawgiver died on Mount Pisgah, in the land of Moab, in the one hundred and twentieth year of his age, in the year of the world 2553. The Lord buried him in a sepulchre in the valley opposite Beth-peor, where his ashes repose unto this day. We are, however, distinctly informed that shortly before the crucifixion, in the thirty-third year of Christ, he appeared on Mount Tabor, in company with Elijah, whose body had been translated into heaven five hundred and fifty years after Moses died and eight hundred and ninety-six before the birth of the Messiah.

This is a fact so incontrovertible that the most reckless and presumptuous of the opponents of a separate and intermediate conscious existence of human spirits presume not to deny it. The only disposition of it which they can make is to assume that the Lord raised him from the dead for this purpose. But against this assumption there is one fact which they seem not to have noticed,—viz. that Jesus Christ, and not Moses, was "*the first-born from the dead*," "*the first-fruits of them that slept*," that in all things he might have the pre-eminence and be regarded as the RESURRECTION and the LIFE. And might we not with great propriety object to this assumption that no hint of this sort, by way of explanation of the marvellous fact, is given by any inspired writer, and that to have remanded Moses to the vale of Pisgah, and Elijah to heaven, would have seemed so arbitrary a disposition of them as to call for some explanation from some one of the three Evangelists that record the transfiguration? They do, indeed, inform us that their destiny was the same. One and the same bright cloud overshadowed them both, in which the Father Almighty was present, and from which, for the last time, he spoke aloud, commending his Son, then on the mount, as his ORACLE to the human race.

I should not have dwelt so long on this memorable incident, but for the sake of developing the presumption of those daring innovators who for some reason are seeking to overthrow the glorious sanctions of our religion, expressed in the words "eternal punishment" and "everlasting life," delivered by the Lord himself. A modern philosopher has recently enlightened the world by two treatises—one on "The Philosophy of Man," another on "The Philosophy of the Intermediate State." He yet proposes a third treatise, to be denominated "The Philosophy of a Future Life." In his generosity, he has only taxed us with a single sheet of developments on the whole philosophy of man; and, with equal kindness, he has contracted his philosophy of the intermediate state within equally restricted dimensions. I have but two faults to find with his treatise on the intermediate state. The first of these might by some utilitarians be regarded as its greatest perfection. It is a valuable exemplification of the fallacy technically called *petitio principii*, or, vulgarly, "the begging of the question." Any one who desires to see how far a man may wander from reason and common sense, without seeming to notice it, will be edified by reading this extended assumption. He disposes of the strongest passages in proof of hades, or the separate state, by this admirable argument:—

A state of conscious existence between death and the resurrection is nowhere taught in the Scriptures: therefore it is not taught in this passage nor in that: therefore it is not taught in this parable nor in that: therefore it is not taught by Jesus nor by any of the apostles.

Another exception which I record against it is its striking irreverence for the authority of the Bible. I do not recollect to have read any treatise less respectful of the authority of apostles and prophets, from any one pretending to believe the Bible to have come from God. It is only a reiteration of obsolete glosses in a more daring and presumptuous style. For example, "To-day shalt thou be with me in Paradise," means, "This day or that day, when I come to the possession of my kingdom, some two or three thousand years hence, then shalt thou be with me in Paradise"! As for Moses in the Mount of Transfiguration, that is all explained, according to this philosopher, by a single assumption—viz. God raised Moses from the dead, and, after he had shown him on the mount, caused him to die a second time; after which the Lord himself buried him in some unknown sepulchre! And, not to weary my readers with such displays of the waywardness of self-opinionated theorists, when Paul tells us of his not knowing "whether he was in or out of the body," it only meant that he was in a dream, somewhat confounded at the time, and had no distinct apprehensions of himself! Seriously to respond to such irreverence is, I presume, as unnecessary as it would be irksome to any one who trembles at the word of the Lord.

On the arguments and facts already offered we rest our cause, so far as the ascertainment of the proper import of the terms *life, death, destruction, punishment, hades* and *gehenna* is concerned.

Of the term *gehenna,* translated *hell,* we have said but little. It is defined by our Lord to be a place of "eternal punishment"—a place of "eternal fire," where soul and body, or the whole wicked man, is to be tormented for ever and ever. Against this view destructionists and Universalists argue from the fact that "*the Vale of Hinnom,*" (whence is derived the word *hell,*) in the environs of Jerusalem, was the place of consuming the carcasses of dead animals, and therefore wholly earthly, temporal and inapposite to represent any thing that did not come to an end. How short-sighted, or how diseased, the vision of such doctors! Were not Jerusalem, Mount Zion and the City of David places as earthly and temporal as the Vale of Hinnom in their environs? And in reason's ear is it not as good an argument against the perpetuity, spirituality and felicity of heaven that it is so often represented under the imagery of earth—of that same Jerusalem, Mount Zion and City of the Great King? When Paul says, "You Christians are the children of the Jerusalem which is above, the mother of us all," or when he says, "You are not come to the tangible mountain, but to Mount Zion, the city of the living God, the heavenly Jerusalem," does he not use imagery of earth as inapposite to set forth the eternal state of the righteous as gehenna is to set forth the eternal destiny of the wicked? As learnedly and as rationally, therefore, might the new theorists object to the *heaven* as to the *hell* of the New Testament, inasmuch as the imagery of both comes from the same vicinity—from Judea, Jerusalem and the environs thereof. And, indeed, the same mad philosophy and philology might, and sometimes does, object, with as much reason, to the existence of angels or spirits and their correlates; for they, too, are terms of earth, as is every other term appreciable by mortal man. I once knew a crazy literalist who affirmed that wind and spirit were the same—that a man's breath was his soul, because both were represented by the same word. Nor did he stop at these absurdities, but persisted in the maintenance of a literal river of life, jasper walls, pearly gates and golden streets in the heavenly Jerusalem.

That a lake of fire and brimstone, the flames of Tophet, and the perpetual burnings of the Vale of Hinnom, should become emblems and representations of the fearful doom of wicked and ungodly men, is certainly as rational and consistent as that a garden of delights, a golden city, spacious and splendid mansions, crowns of glory, and kingly thrones, should constitute the imagery of the eternal honors and blessedness of the children of God. No man of good sense and scriptural information understands these representations to be exact literal delineations of the future condition of saints and sinners. Pleasure or pain corresponding with these figurative representations is all that persons of sound sense and accurate discrimination understand by them.

In conclusion of this already too prolix dissertation on terms and definitions, we must say, in regard to destruction as *involving the sanctions of the Christian religion*, that salvation and damnation are its sublime, awful and tremendous sanctions. He that diminishes either of these in its character, extent or duration, detracts just so much from the claims of the whole institution upon the attention and acceptance of every man. If the life to be enjoyed is not to be everlasting, or if the *condemnation to hell* (for so our Lord denominates it) is to terminate in a year, a century or a millennium, then neither the salvation is of infinite importance, nor the condemnation of infinite dread. A pain, however intense, which continues but a day, a year or an age, is nothing compared to a pain that is everlasting. Whatever reasons, then, justified our Saviour in holding forth a "fire unquenchable," a "worm undying," a "punishment everlasting," will justify every other preacher in arraying the same awful issues before the mind of every impenitent sinner.

Again, the motives that induce some persons to broach the doctrine of soul-sleeping, and to impose it upon others, have neither reason nor philosophy to commend them to any man's acceptance, nor to justify any conflicts concerning them in the Christian community. For, suppose a human spirit sleeps for a thousand years and awakes in felicity, unconscious of a moment's interval, or in one moment departs and is with the Lord: there is nothing fatal to either party's comfort in whatever theory he may adopt. Consequently, to introduce such a question, and to seek partisans to it, is voluntary schism for its own sake, without the slightest hope of advantage or interest to any.

It is only in their bearings upon other parts of the Christian system, and in the tendencies of such idle speculations to minister strife rather than godly edifying, that we deem them worthy of Christian reprobation. Neither soul-sleeping, then, nor destructionism, has one argument in its favor; while the latter is in direct opposition to the sanctions of the gospel and the definite and clear signification of a hundred scriptures.

The authors of all false theories of religion and morality are persons who assume to be philosophers, so far, at least, as to be able to construct a universe and a Divinity, in their judgment, more rational and worthy of all acceptation than those which they oppose. Such, most certainly, are the Universalist, the Restorationist, the Destructionist and the drowsy, dreaming inventors of spirit-sleeping—with the microscopic doctors of infant and Pagan annihilation. To one, universal salvation—to another, the partial annihilation of mankind—is the beau-ideal of a wise and just and benevolent system. To all such spirits the Bible is but an encyclopedia of proof-texts to confirm their theory. The rational, healthy and practical Christian forms no theory of things incomprehensible. He only seeks to know and understand what the Bible teaches. He feels himself inadequate to comprehend the history of sin and of punishment in the amplitude of their bearings upon a universe, upon the character of its Author and the destinies of his liege and loyal subjects. He wisely concludes that whatever reasons may justify God in inflicting temporal and partial evil upon any human or angelic being may justify the infliction of eternal punishment upon such portions of intelligent creatures as have been placed under special dispensations of divine mercy and love. With all such the true philosophy is, What say the oracles of God?

God is said to be THE FATHER OF THE SPIRITS—not of the *bodies*, nor of the *dispositions*, nor of the *breath*—but of THE SPIRITS of all flesh. And as such he will judge and retribute all. He has solemnly said that *all that are in their graves* shall hear his voice and come forth—they that have done good and they that have done evil; the one shall rise to salvation, the other to condemnation. He does not say in any passage of Scripture, that there is only a portion of mankind that will come out of their graves. Nay, he has said that "the sea gave up the dead that were in it, and that death and hades gave up the dead that were in them, and that they were all rewarded according to their works."

The Christian believes that a future state is neither clearly nor fully set forth in the law of Moses, nor in the Jewish prophets. His faith is, that "life and immortality have been brought to light in the gospel," and that the solution of all questions concerning the state of the dead, a future judgment and the world to come, must be learned from Jesus and his apostles. He is THE RESURRECTION and THE LIFE. And to his chosen witnesses he committed the secrets of the future state, to be divulged just so far as the true interests of mankind should require. He and they have taught us that he will raise *all the dead*, judge *all mankind*, separate the righteous from the wicked, and consign the latter to such an *everlasting punishment* as he has prepared for the devil and his angels; while the righteous only shall inherit an *everlasting life,* an eternal blessedness; that salvation consists in being forever with the Lord, and condemnation in "an everlasting destruction from the presence of the Lord and the glory of his power."

Aware that beyond the Bible there are no *data,* no facts, from which to reason, a prudent man—one that fears God and loves mankind—will not presume to affirm any thing concerning man, adult or infant, not clearly indicated in that book; he will introduce no idle speculation; he will affirm nothing for which he cannot produce a "*thus saith the Lord.*" His wisdom and honor alike consist in preaching Christ, as the wisdom of God and the power of God to salvation. He will make known nothing—introduce nothing—but Christ and him crucified, under the title of Christian doctrine and Christian preaching.

Does the Bible indicate that a man has a body, a soul and a spirit, as clearly as that he has a head, a heart and a hand, he presumes not to deny it. Does it teach that the intellectual and moral something called "spirit" is not that animal something called "soul" or "animal life," he will not affirm that the soul is the spirit, or that the spirit is the soul, and that both are breath. Does the Messiah say that a spirit, a human spirit, has neither flesh nor bones, he will not deny that there is any such thing as spirit. He will not make his own dulness, indocility or incapacity an argument against the facts and dictations of the holy oracles. Nay, he will, in all matters, bow to the authority of the Bible. He will not proceed to annihilate infants, Pagans and wicked men, because he cannot comprehend the principles of the Divine administration. He will not assign to Pontius Pilate, Judas Iscariot, Annas and Caiaphas, Nero, Domitian and Mohammed, the eternal punishment of a humming-bird, a turtle-dove or a pigeon, because of his want of intellectual and moral discrimination. He will not fraternize with the Sadducee in denying angels or human spirits, because he never saw either himself, or because he doubts whether he himself has any thing in him but stomach and breath. He will not make the sterility of his own soul an infallible criterion of all souls in the universe. He will not first teach that the human spirit is mortal, and then set about refuting the Messiah's affirmation that *spirits cannot die,* or that man cannot kill the soul. Because of his defects in the science of interpretation, he will not assume that the word *destroy,* when applied to man, always means absolute annihilation or complete extinction; well knowing that such a one would be essentially wanting in consciousness, and most unfit to be a leader or a guide to the ignorant and unlearned inquirers after the will and ways of the Lord.

I have by no means exhausted this subject. A mere miniature view of its prominent points and aspects is all for which we have had either room or leisure. I suggest these views and considerations to those whose minds have been unsettled by presumptuous and wayward dogmatists, rather as a help to their own investigations than as a full and perfect treatise on the subject. Believing, as I do, that there is but a very narrow isthmus between absolute skepticism and the affirmations of those views of the new philosophy of man, and of the intermediate state—the denial of a universal resurrection and of the eternal punishment of unbelieving and ungodly men—I cannot but observe with great solicitude every attempt made to weaken the sanctions of the gospel and to reduce man to a mere two-legged animal, whose soul is blood, whose spirit is breath, and whose destiny in sin is but the punishment of an insect—the decomposition of an organized atom. From such philosophists and prosing dreamers, such conceited dogmatists and reckless schismatics, may the Lord save his cause and people!

ADDRESS.

ON THE

IMPORTANCE OF UNITING THE MORAL WITH THE INTELLECTUAL CULTURE OF THE MIND.

DELIVERED TO THE COLLEGE OF TEACHERS, CINCINNATI, 1836.

IF, in accordance with the philosophy of things, we could trace effects from their immediate to their remote causes, it is presumed that we would find the momentous changes already accomplished in English society, whether in the Old World or in the New, to be the legitimate consequences of a single maxim, consecrated into a rule of action, both by the precept and the example of the master-spirit of the Protestant Reformation. That maxim is, "Man by nature is, and of right ought to be, a *thinking* being." Hence it is decreed that, as a matter of policy, of morality and of religion, he ought not only to think, but *to think for himself*. This, as the paramount duty, was most successfully inculcated by that illustrious Saxon to whom, more than to any other mortal being, the sons of Japhet in Europe and America owe their best literary, moral and political institutions. To the inculcation of this obligation, more than to any other precept in the religious or moral code, was Martin Luther indebted for that eminent success which elevated him to the highest niche in the temple consecrated to the memory of European and American benefactors. Nor is the day far distant, in our anticipations of the approaching future, when the philosophic historian, in his attempts to trace to its proper cause the general superiority of that portion of our race which speaks the English tongue, in whatever land, under whatever sky, it may happen to have its being, will find it supremely, if not exclusively, in the single fact that the English nation first adopted the Lutheran creed of thinking, speaking and writing without restraint on every subject of importance to the individual and to society.

But to set the mind abroach, to take off every restraint but that of moral law, to encourage free inquiry, especially in an age of comparative ignorance and superstition both in things political, religious and literary, is always a hazardous experiment. In such a revolution as must necessarily ensue, not only the institutions of false philosophy, unequal policy and arbitrary legislation, but also the altars, the temples, and the ordinances of reason and truth and justice, may be blended together in one promiscuous ruin. Who can arrest the progress of free inquiry? What human spirit can ride upon this whirlwind and direct this storm? What philosopher or sage can, with effect, say, "Hitherto shalt thou come, and no farther," and here shall your investigations cease? Experience says it is much easier to communicate the spark than to arrest the flame. Still, however, we have this consolation that truth is in its own nature indestructible, and that however for a time it may be hid among the rubbish of human tradition, or buried in the wreck of revolutions and counter-revolutions in human affairs, it will ultimately gain the ascendant and command not only the admiration but the homage of all mankind.

To those of the most enlarged conceptions of human affairs and of the natural tendencies of things, we imagine it will appear most evident that it is safer and happier for society that the mind should be permitted to rest with full assurance only upon its own investigations, and that perfect freedom of inquiry should be guaranteed to every man to reason, to examine and judge for himself on all subjects in the least involving his own present or future destiny or that of society.

Happy is it, then, for the general interests of all science and of all society, that when men begin to think and reason and decide for themselves on any one subject, unrestrained by the proscriptions and unawed by the authority of past ages, it is not within their own power, nor within the grasp of any extrinsic authority on earth, to restrain their speculations, or to confine them to that one subject, whatever it may be, which happened first to arouse their minds from the repose of unthinking acquiescence and to break the spell of implicit resignation to the supposed superior wisdom of the reputed sages of ancient times. Hence, the impetus given to the human mind by the Protestant Reformation extends into every science, into every art, into all the business of life, and continues, with increased and increasing energy, to consume and waste the influence of every existing institution, law and custom not founded upon eternal truth and the immutable and invincible nature of things.

This spirit of free inquiry first seized the church, then the state, then the colleges, then the schools; and now, even now, in the second quarter of the nineteenth century, it has invaded not only the *penetralia* of every temple, but even the inmost recesses of the nursery, the infant head, the infant brain; and, in full harmony with the divining spirit of the age, are we now in solemn conclave assembled to inquire if aught of error yet remains unscathed, or of truth undiscovered, in the most useful among sciences and arts—that of educating man.

The philosopher, the politician, the moralist and the Christian regard the subject of education as of transcendent importance to the individual and social well-being of man. If in other matters they differ, in this they agree—that nothing connected with time or sense so supremely deserves the best thoughts and most concentrated efforts of the human mind as the proper method of training and developing the physical, intellectual and moral powers of man. For, whatever may be, in the eye of the philanthropist, the chief *desideratum* in the future earthly destiny of man—whatever may be the measures of temporal bliss or temporal glory to which he would exalt his species, as the *ultimatum* of all his aspirations—he contemplates and designs to effect it all by a system of education in perfect unison with the whole nature of man. The Christian himself, in seeking the eternal happiness and glory of his own offspring and of society at large, forms no scheme, can conceive of no means in human power, to further his wishes and to secure his object, other than an education in perfect harmony with human nature as it now is under the remedial administration of Heaven.

One of the most exhilarating and promising signs of a better era in human destiny is the increased and increasing interest displayed on this very subject. Happy are we to find that not only in the East and in the West, in the North and in the South, in the length and breadth of our own happy land, but in the land of our forefathers and in all the regions of English and American commerce, wherever the Protestant religion is known, men are awaking to the examination of how much has been done and how much remains to be done, not only in extending the means of education of some sort, but in adapting that education, according to the lights of true science, to the whole constitution and circumstances of mankind.

Much, very much, indeed, remains to be accomplished to meet the exigencies of the times and to dispel the clouds and darkness yet resting upon various questions either intimately connected with a rational system of education or forming a part of it. This is true not only of our own country, but of the most enlightened portions of the Old World. Among the resolutions of the British and Foreign School Society, of March, 1831, it is repeatedly acknowledged that "ENGLAND IS YET UNEDUCATED." Lord Brougham, in 1833, in his speech at the Wilberforce meeting at York, strongly affirms that in England "IGNORANCE PREVAILS TO A HORRIBLE EXTENT"—ignorance, too, of a proper system of education. And certainly this is true of large portions of our own country.

Creditable it is in the highest degree to our country that, in the estimation of all mankind, she stands foremost in the work of education; and to the honor of the founders of the College of Teachers, in the Valley of the Mississippi, it may yet be said that this institution has been the commencement of a new era in the literary annals of the West.

But the subject before us demands, at least as preliminary, a definition not merely of the term *education*, but of that which is to be educated. And yet, plain and hackneyed as the subject is, it is not altogether without its difficulties. Education, as usually defined, imports no more than "the formation of manners in youth," or the cultivation of the intellectual powers. But, in its true and philosophic signification, it takes a wider range, and denotes the full development and proper training of all the human powers. These are generally called physical, intellectual and moral. But, as our physical powers are held in common with inferior animals, they are not regarded as strictly human; and, therefore, with the most accomplished thinkers the human powers are purely intellectual and moral. Still, it will be conceded that even man's animal powers are susceptible of improvement under a scientific education; that even his external senses, with all his physical organization, by proper exercise and discipline, can be greatly improved.

But who has accurately defined the intellectual and moral powers? Agreed it is on all hands that the human mind is composed of various innate and primitive powers, however they may be enumerated or defined, and that these are the proper subject of education. But because they have never yet been defined with authority—because no two philosophers, from the days of Plato to the beginning of the present century, have agreed in any one theory of the intellectual and moral powers—every system of education hitherto patronized is, in some respects, inadequate or imperfect. The words "intellect," "moral powers" and "affections" are of universal currency, and appear on many a learned and eloquent page as the well-established representatives of the most precise ideas in mental philosophy. It has been our misfortune, however, never to have met with an author of standard value, in any of the schools of English or American literature, who could make us understand what are the intellectual and moral powers—"the understanding, will and affections"—which constitute that *something* called the human mind or soul, and concerning the education of which so many hundred authors have written to so little purpose.

The mental and moral philosophy of the schools—especially the latter—in spite of all our efforts and predilections, yet appears to us a science about words rather than things—a science without a solid basis. Fine discourses have been written and eloquent speeches have been pronounced about the passions and affections, the intellectual and moral powers; but whose definition of these is canonical or of general credit? Such being the fact, who can affirm that the science of mind is perfect, or that a perfect system of education can exist, while no two philosophers or teachers of note agree about what it is that is to be educated?

In the schools of the highest reputation there appears little certainty in the department of the intellectual powers. Operations of the mind in one school are regarded as primitive powers; while in another the primitive powers are ranked amongst mere operations of the mind. Thus, we read of the faculty or primitive power of perception, of attention, of reflection, of memory, of consciousness, &c.; while, according to other authorities, these are but mere "*modes of mental action*"—mere operations of certain energies or powers innate, which are known and designated under other names.

Need we a single argument to show that a system of education which sets about improving operations, mistaking them for the operating powers, must fail—wholly fail—of any practical utility? And such—unless we are greatly mistaken—is one of the most injurious errors in *all* the systems that have reigned from Aristotle to Dr. Watts.

It is to be hoped that the present century, already distinguished for many useful discoveries, inventions and improvements, if it have not already, in the new science of phrenology, ascertained a solid basis for a truly inductive system of mental philosophy and literary and moral education, will add to its renown the glory of substituting psychological fact for hypothesis, and of discarding from our schools and colleges the imaginative conjectures and metaphysical theories of ages more speculative and romantic than the present. Then we are disposed to imagine that it will be universally conceded that the excellence of education will consist in three things—in teaching and training man to *think*, to *feel* and to *act* in perfect harmony with his own constitution and with the constitution of nature and society around him; not merely to think, not merely to feel, not merely to act right, but to think, to feel and to act rationally, morally and religiously, or in harmony with the whole universe and with his relations to each and every part thereof.

If we might be indulged in another preliminary and introductory observation, we would hasten to suggest that as there is but one way of learning mind—viz. by its own manifestations—so there cannot be a proper or philosophical system of education that is not founded upon the manifestations of mind. In the universe there is nothing to be seen but the manifestations of mind; for it is all the effect of mind, and under the dominion of one Supreme and Omnipotent Intelligence. If there be sublimity, grandeur or beauty in the height and depth, in the length and breadth, of creation—in the extent, number and variety of organic and inorganic existences—it is in the manifestations of mind that all this beauty and magnificence consist. Hence, the most refined and exquisite pleasures of which we are now or ever shall be susceptible, are the pleasures of mental communion with that Infinite Intelligence which will be manifesting itself to us in an infinite series of creations through an endless succession of ages. If there were no mind displayed in the universe, to human eye there would be no beauty, grandeur or magnificence in it; and exactly in the ratio of mind possessed by each individual will be the sources of enjoyment opened in all the works and ways of the Infinite Intelligence. He that has most mind will see and enjoy most mind in creation; and in this will be found the philosophy of that oracle which says, "The fool hath said in his heart, There is no God."

But neither the divine nor the human mind can be manifested to human reason but by an organized system. If we are too sanguine, and if it be not yet discovered, in this truth will be found the immovable basis of the true philosophy of mind and of education. The created universe is not God; but God is manifested in and by the universe. The human mind, so far an image of the divine, is not the human head nor heart nor body; but in and by these it is manifested. God, however, is not more distinct from the universe which manifests him, than the human mind from the brain and heart and body, by which it manifests itself.

As, then, we learn God by and through his works and words, or through the universe, so we learn the human mind through that organic mass through which it operates and by which it is operated upon. Now, it is obvious that all our organs, whether called the brain or the muscles or the external senses, are the means or energies by which our spirit operates, and by which, so far at least as mundane things are concerned, it is operated upon. Consequently, no philosopher can overlook the organs by which the mind acts and by which it is acted upon in adopting a system of education suited to the culture and development of our intellectual and moral powers.

To illustrate this view of ascertaining and educating mind, let it be supposed that we have a thousand or any definite number of concentric circles the common centre of which is a radiating point: it will then be apparent that all the light in these thousand circles is in fullest splendor in the innermost circle. The manifestations of light will improve in every circle from the one-thousandth to the first. The most brilliant manifestations will, of course, be found immediately around the radiating centre. So of the supreme and human intelligence. The manifestations of the Deity are found in ten thousand concentric spheres. But it is in the innermost circle—in the palace of the universe—the *sanctum sanctorum* of creation—that he is seen and known in his glory.

The human mind is manifested in all the works of man, as the architect is seen in the castles he has reared, or the author in the volumes he has written. Still, we approach nearer to the human spirit when we approach the human body, and to the head of that body in which it is located. The cranium is the innermost circle which the spirit, the radiating point, fills with the most splendid manifestations of itself. Hence, the "mind-illumined face," with the five senses most ingeniously situated around the head and in it, with all the displays of the organs of thought, moral feeling and passion which adorn its outside, manifest all that is to be educated, whether we call it mind or spirit—the animal, the intellectual, or the moral man. The activity of the human spirit—that great intellectual and moral radiating centre in the human system—must necessarily first appear in the walls of that apartment in which it first begins to operate. We ought not, then, to wonder that at this *punctum saliens* its strength should be equal to manifesting itself by indenting and depicting its activities on the bony circumference which encloses all those organs by which it *first* acts in all its animal, intellectual and moral operations.

Thus have we very circuitously arrived at the solid basis of mental philosophy and rational education—if, indeed, there be yet any such basis found. It is indeed already fully ascertained that the mind acts, and that, as a matter of course, it will have power and variety of action according to the variety, strength and activity of its organs. Again, it is ascertained that as the mind sees by an eye, hears by an ear, strikes by a hand and thinks and reasons and feels by a brain, and as the strength of every organ is in the ratio of its size and firmness, so the mind's energies or faculties will be improved as these organs are enlarged, strengthened or made active by well-directed exercise.

If now we may be pardoned for this circular approach to our subject, it would be presumption to expect remission should we further delay by an attempt to detail either the organs or faculties, intellectual and moral, to be improved by education. This, indeed, we are not able to do; for these all are not yet to us individually and fully ascertained. It is, however, generally agreed that we have intellectual and moral powers, and that both are innate and primitive and susceptible of improvement; and this is all that our subject, strictly regarded, demands. Moreover, there is, perhaps, a more general concurrence in the number and distinct character of our moral than of our intellectual powers; and these are they whose culture is the burden of the present essay.

What the metaphysician or the moral philosopher calls the active powers or affections, and the phrenologist the moral impulses or instincts, are much nearer allied than their theories of the perceptive and reflective powers. All men of sense of all philosophic creeds agree that benevolence, veneration, hope, self-love, love of approbation, a sense of justice, conscientiousness, firmness, &c. are essential elements in the formation of moral character, and that they are positive, primitive and independent powers of mind, susceptible of culture, and that they ought to be educated.

True science affirms that all that is in man, and only what is in him, is to be educated; that every organ and sense and power, whether animal, intellectual, moral or religious, can be improved, and ought to be improved by education. The accomplished teacher aims not, indeed, at working miracles, by creating new powers or faculties of any sort: he regards only what is innate in man as the proper subject of education. He has two objects supremely in view —the improvement of the faculties, and the communication of knowledge. As respects the improvement of the faculties, his theory is very simple. With him, every faculty has some organ or organs susceptible of improvement. These organs are improvable only by exercise. His whole creed contains but *seven articles*, and these are rather definitions of terms than abstract speculations. They are the following:—

1. The human soul incarnate operates only through organs, and through organs only can it be operated upon.

2. An organ is a natural instrument—such as the brain, the eye, the ear, the tongue, the hand. The human soul thinks and feels by the brain, sees by the eye, hears by the ear, speaks by the tongue and operates by the hand.

3. A faculty, contradistinguished from its organ, is the power of the organ. The eye is an organ; but seeing is its faculty or power. The ear is an organ; but hearing is its faculty.

4. Organs and faculties are simple and compound. The eye and the ear are simple organs; the brains and the hand are compound organs. Each and every subdivision of the brain, as every finger on the hand, is a single organ and has a single faculty. But there are faculties which require a plurality of organs: thus, while the faculty of apprehending requires but a finger, the faculty of comprehending a substance requires the whole hand. The faculty of perceiving a single object requires but one organ of the brain; while the faculty of remembering an event requires various organs. The faculty of perceiving requires the organs of perception; the faculty of reflecting requires the organs of reflection; the faculty of remembering requires all the organs originally employed in perceiving the object and in reflecting upon it.

5. Operations are to be distinguished from the organs and the faculties. Organ is the instrument; faculty, the power of the instrument; operation, the act of the faculty or of the organ. Thus, the eye is an organ; seeing, the faculty of that organ; and a particular look, sight or seeing, the operation of that organ. Again, there is one organ of the brain by which we perceive color—this is the organ of color: perceiving color is the faculty of that organ, and the observance of any particular color is the operation of that organ.

6. The strength of an organ is its size and firmness. It is a law of the animal economy that exercise directed by reason enlarges and confirms every organ; hence, every fibre of the human system is improved by exercise. To improve a faculty is to enlarge and confirm its organ or organs. By strengthening and making more active an organ, we not only improve its faculty, but also every particular operation of that organ. Education, if rational, will, therefore, seek to improve the mind by improving its organs: it will seek to improve the organs by improving the faculties, and the faculties by improving their operations. The natural order of education, in seeking to improve the

intellectual and moral powers, is first the operation, then the faculty, then the organ, then the mind. It is by this course the painter, the sculptor, the musician, the orator and the practical moralist attain to perfection. Single acts precede habits and strengthen faculties, and these faculties strengthen the organs, and then the organs in turn strengthen the faculties, and the faculties strengthen their particular acts and operations. Thus, we strengthen the muscles in the arm by acts or operations; these operations strengthen the faculty of the whole arm or increase its muscular power, and that strength increased redounds to the improvement of those very acts by which it was itself improved. Hence, if the natural organs did not decay by age, the mind would, like the rotation of a wheel on an infinite declivity, be perpetually increasing its activity and its momentum in a series of infinite progression; which, no doubt, after it has "shuffled off this mortal coil," will be its eternal destiny.

7. It must be laid down with all the formality of a positive precept that *the exercise of any one organ only improves itself.* That we cannot improve the eye or the ear without exercise is not more incontrovertible than that we cannot improve the eye by improving the ear, or the faculty of tasting by the faculty of smelling. No person will, therefore, seek to improve the memory by improving the imagination, nor the organs of perception by the organs of reflection; neither will a wise man seek to improve the moral powers by exercising only the intellectual.

This synopsis or summary of definitions, constituting the essential articles of the skilful teacher's creed, leads us directly to the very point of the specific task assigned us—viz. "*the importance of uniting the moral with the intellectual culture of the mind.*"

In the proposition that it is important that the culture of the moral powers should be united with the culture of the intellectual powers, it is implied that both are susceptible of cultivation and that both are to be cultivated. It is only affirmed that both are to be cultivated at one and the same time. But the point to be elaborated is, that *the moral powers are especially to be educated,* or that moral culture is the chief end of education.

Three good reasons are, in our judgment, sufficient to enforce the superlative importance of moral culture.

Of these, the first is, that man has received from the hand of his Creator certain innate moral powers, and that these are, without education, not more perfect than his physical and intellectual powers. Now, as the five senses—the perceptive and reflective faculties—

require the special attention of those intrusted with the formation of the human constitution and human character, certainly the moral affections and feelings, simply as an essential ingredient in man, as one of the gifts and endowments bestowed on him by his Creator, are deserving of improvement. But this argument is not yet set forth in all its strength; for it is agreed that the moral powers, because of the peculiar and ever-changing character of the objects on which they are to be employed and of the actions to which they impel, are more imperfect by nature, or, what is the same thing, differently expressed, naturally more unfit for discrimination and guidance than are our physical and intellectual powers; therefore their cultivation is the more necessary.

But, in the second place, the paramount necessity of moral culture is argued from higher considerations than can be offered in favor of the development and proper training of our physical and intellectual powers. It is argued from the fact that moral nature is superior to intellectual and to animal nature, as the means are superior to the end; for, in man, animal organization is but the means to intellectual organization, and intellect itself is but the means to moral endowment. A proof of this is experienced by all the cultivated, in the fact that animal pleasure is but the positive degree, intellectual pleasure the comparative, while moral pleasure is the superlative of human bliss: just as man's animal organization is the positive, his intellectual the comparative, and his moral the superlative, of his excellence and glory, graduated on the scale of all earthly existence. True, indeed, we cannot view these as simple elements and compare them as so many ingredients in the human composition; still, we have no difficulty in forming a comparative estimate of their respective value in human nature and in human character. Our second argument, therefore, is, that as three superlatives—viz. that of moral nature, that of moral pleasure and that of moral glory—constitute the superlative of human excellence, moral culture above the physical, above the intellectual, deserves to occupy the superlative place in the education of youth.

The evidence of this position, and consequently the conviction of its truth, are susceptible of much augmentation as we improve in the knowledge of man as a social being—as related to other intelligent and moral agents. It is for society, and for society alone, that man possesses a moral nature; and, therefore, it is only in society that man can fully enjoy himself. Need we ask of what use were benevolence, justice, generosity, compassion, love of approbation, any more than the power of communicating intelligence, were there no kindred beings as objects of the exercise of these endowments? And certain it is, that without benevolence, a sense of justice, the love of approbation and the power of communicating information, man would be unfit for society and incapable of enjoying any pleasure from it. Hence the conclusion that the animal passions are not more necessary to the preservation of our own existence, or to the continuance of our species, than our moral nature is to the enjoyment of society. And hence, says the moralist, oxygen is not more essential to combustion, nor respiration to human life, than morality to the well-being of society. The Christian philosopher ascends only one step further, and alleges that, as without a material constitution a material universe could not be enjoyed, as without a moral nature society could not be appreciated, so without that religious affection called veneration—a sublime part of man's moral constitution—God himself could not be known or enjoyed.

But, to reinforce this topic, we shall only add that it is not the simple possession of any capacity or power, but the *exercise* of it, that affords either utility or pleasure to ourselves or others. Hence, it is not the possession of a moral nature any more than the possession of an animal organization, but the employment and exercise of that nature in society, in all religious and moral feeling, according to enlightened intellect, that promotes our own felicity or that of others: so important is it, then, that our moral nature should be properly educated.

Our third argument is, that "*nature itself, or the universe, is constituted in harmony with the supremacy of the moral powers guided by intellect.*" Our most profound moralists and our most accomplished teachers have been constrained to announce it as the result of their most studious and deep researches into the physical constitution of the world, that "*it is actually arranged on the principle of favoring virtue and punishing vice,*" just as evidently as it is "*adapted to all the faculties of man as an intelligent, moral and religious being.*" "Whenever"—says one of our best writers on the constitution of man—"whenever the dictates of the moral sentiments, properly illuminated by the knowledge of science and of moral and religious duty, are opposed by the solicitations of the animal propensities, the latter must yield; otherwise, by the constitution of external nature, evil will inevitably ensue." This is what we mean by alleging that nature is constituted in harmony with the supremacy of the moral feelings, guided by intellect. Hence, the happiness not merely of the individual himself, but of the whole human race, by the insuperable arrangements of the Creator, are made consequent upon the obedience of a cultivated and enlightened moral nature to a moral code. This being conceded—as, indeed, it must be by every philosopher enlightened in the studies of nature—it authorizes the conclusion that the voice of the Creator is heard in all his works and by all his laws, bearing testimony in favor of bestowing superlative attention on the moral culture of youth. May we add, that if this be apparent to the philosopher, who sees the bearings of physical nature upon the physical and moral constitution of man, much more evident is it to the student of the Bible, that the violation of moral principle, not only in consequence of the constitution of the realms of nature, but also and more especially in pursuance of every divine law and institution, must be accompanied with pain. So important is it, then, that the moral culture should not only occupy a place, but the most prominent place, in the education of youth.

Although we have in these three arguments, as we judge, evidence enough of the sovereign importance of moral culture, still, to illustrate and enforce the importance of the subject, we shall confirm our reasonings by the testimony of two or three distinguished names in the commonwealth of letters.

Lord Kames says, "It appears unaccountable that our teachers generally have directed their instructions to the head, with very little attention to the heart. From Aristotle down to Locke, books without number have been composed for cultivating and improving the understanding; few in proportion for cultivating and improving the affections. Yet surely, as man is intended to be more an active than a contemplative being, the educating of a young man to behave properly in society is of still greater importance than the making him even a Solomon for knowledge."

Locke says, "It is virtue—direct virtue—which is the hard and valuable part to be aimed at in education, and not a forward pertness or any little arts of shifting. All other considerations and accomplishments should give way and be postponed to this. This is the solid and substantial good, which tutors should not only read lectures and talk of, but the labor and art of education should furnish the mind with and fasten there, and never cease till the young man had a true relish of it, and placed his strength, his glory and his pleasure in it.

"Learning must be had, but in the second place, as subservient only to greater qualities. Seek out somebody (as your son's tutor) that may know how discreetly to form his manners; place him in hands where you may as much as possible secure his innocence, cherish and nurse up the good, and gently correct and weed out any bad inclinations and settle him in good habits. This is the main point; and, this being provided for, learning may be had into the bargain.

30

"But, under whose care soever a child is put to be taught, during the tender and flexible years of his life, this is certain—it should be one who thinks *Latin and language the least part of education;* one who, knowing how much virtue and a well-tempered soul is to be preferred to any sort of learning or language, makes it his chief business to form the mind of his scholars and give that a right direction; which, if once got, though all the rest should be neglected, would, in due time, produce all the rest; and which, if it be not got and settled so as to keep out ill and vicious habits, languages and sciences and all the other accomplishments of education will be to no purpose but to make the worse or more dangerous man."

Milton says, "The end of learning is to repair the ruin of our first parents by the knowledge of God aright, and out of that knowledge to love him, to imitate him, to be like him, as we may the nearest, by possessing our souls of true virtue, which, being united to the heavenly grace of faith, make up the highest perfection."

And St. Pierre, in his "Studies of Nature," often enjoins that religion and morality should be the first lessons communicated to children, because this education more than any other fits them for society, for usefulness and happiness.*

Unpopular and unpleasant as the task may be, it is necessary, to the accomplishment of the object contemplated in the discussion of this question, that we not only state the fact that *moral culture is an essential part of national and popular education almost wholly neglected,* but also examine the reasons why it is so. That it is neglected to an alarming degree is, alas! too easily proved from the fact that the great majority of the best-educated portion of our youth are decidedly immoral, at least in the Christian acceptation of that word.

It is to be regretted that we have not regular and authentic statistics of the educated classes of society as respects the influence which they exert in society for or against religion and morality. Had we correct reports of the amount of moral and immoral influence exerted upon the whole community through only the graduates of English and American colleges and universities, we should feel ourselves much more able to understand and set forth their actual value in forming the character and in deciding the destiny of a people. In the absence of such definite information, we have to depend too much on gross estimates, founded upon our own observation and the conjectural calculations of others.

---

* Fourteenth Study.

Something very like what we want, yet not exactly in kind, has been attempted in the reports of the Minister of Public Instruction in France. From a recent report on the state of education in that country, by M. Carle, it appears that, in that country at least, there is no apparent connection between education and morality, but, upon the whole, that education is extremely prejudicial to both religion and morality. And certainly from every document to which we have access, it would appear that in Germany, Spain, Italy, and, indeed, on the European continent generally, the educated classes, taken as a whole, exert a very immoral influence upon the whole community. It were, indeed, well for our own and the mother country that the evidence were less decisive than it is that such, at present, is the actual tendency of the established modes of education in both communities.

Were I to make my own personal observation and acquaintance the exclusive data of my estimates of the moral tendencies of the grammar-school, college and university course of education—judging from hundreds, if not from thousands, of individual cases that have come under my inspection both in Europe and America—I must say that the tendencies are decidedly immoral, and that I remember no instance of distinguished moral worth that owed not its existence to the influence of parental piety, which at an early period had so deeply imbued the mind with moral sentiment, or so fully developed the moral powers, as to place the virtuous youth beyond the contaminating influence of the polluted fountains of Grecian and Roman literature or the vitiated and impure atmosphere of licentious classmates, who happened to be less favored with a pious parentage than himself.

It is remarkable how much more men are wont to admire intellectual than moral worth. Parents are usually far more delighted to perceive in their children the dawnings of talent and of genius than of benevolence and philanthropy; and history dwells with peculiar complacency upon the names of those who have rendered themselves illustrious for depth of learning or for genius and ambition—of sages and philosophers—of chiefs and warriors: while most of the true benefactors of the human family are scarcely noticed, and their superior merits are undiscovered and forgotten. This disposition to enhance mental endowments above moral excellence is manifested in the admiration bestowed upon those to whom belong a precocious development. Thus, men are filled with astonishment when they read of a Henderson, who taught Latin, at eight years of age, in Kingswood School, and Greek at fourteen, at Lady Huntingdon's College, in Wales—of a Candiac, who could translate Latin at five years, and at six read Greek and Hebrew to the admiration of the learned, being at the same time well versed in arithmetic, geography, history, geometry and antiquities—of a Baratier, who, at the age of four, could converse with his mother in French, with his father in Latin and with the servants in German; who was perfectly acquainted with Greek at six, with Hebrew at eight, and in his eleventh year translated from the Hebrew into French the travels of the Rabbi Benjamin of Tudela, which he enriched with valuable annotations; and who, when, upon visiting the University of Halle, he was offered the degree of Master of Arts in his thirteenth year, drew up fourteen theses, upon which he disputed next morning with such ability and precision that he delighted and surprised a crowded audience—or of a Mirandola, who, when a boy, was one of the best poets and orators of the age; who commenced the study of the canon law at fourteen, and at sixteen comprised the "Essentials of the Decretals" (contained in three volumes, folio) in an abridgment which won the applause of the most learned canonists; who, at eighteen, knew a great number of languages, and, at twenty-three, published at Rome nine hundred propositions in logic, mathemathics, physic, divinity, magic and cabalistic learning, drawn from Latin, Greek, Jewish and Arabian writers, upon which he challenged the learned in all the schools of Italy to dispute with him.

Hence a Crichton has been surnamed "The Admirable," and excited the wonder of the age in which he lived. Before he was twenty, he spoke and wrote ten different languages, and was master of all the sciences, of riding, singing and dancing, and played upon almost all sorts of musical instruments. At Paris, he challenged all who were skilled in any art or science to dispute with him in any of them—in Hebrew, Syriac, Arabic, Latin, Greek, Sclavonian, French, Spanish, Italian, English, Dutch and Flemish, in prose or verse—at the end of six weeks; during which time he regarded nothing but his amusements, while his learned competitors were preparing for the contest. He acquitted himself beyond all expectation. At Rome, also, he displayed astonishing powers and knowledge, and sustained for three days a scholastic conflict against all opposers, in any form they chose.

Hence, too, a Dousa, who was conspicuous as a translator and a poet, was called by Joseph Scaliger "the ornament of the world;" and we are called upon to admire a Marcilia Euphrosyne, who at ten years of age had made extracts from the most famous historians and orators, and could write Latin and Greek correctly, and at thirteen was conspicuous for her knowledge and taste in architecture; or the self-taught Constantia Grierson, of Kilkenny, who was mistress of French,

Latin, Greek and Hebrew at nineteen, besides having a good knowledge of mathematics and other branches of learning; or a Dermody, who was an eminent linguist and poet at ten years of age.

And hence Juliette d'Aulincourt—who, at the age of eleven, was perfectly acquainted with ancient and modern history and possessed of great powers of mind and memory—was cited by French mothers as a model for their daughters; while those of Italy pointed to a Lilia Fundana, who, though she died in her fifteenth year, was celebrated beyond the Roman territory for her learning and accomplishments.

Yet, after all the applause and admiration which men are accustomed to bestow upon mere intellectual superiority, it is no more to be compared with moral virtue than is the transient splendor of the meteor to the life-giving radiance of the orb of day. Some of the illustrious persons just enumerated died in childhood or in youth from the delicacy of their organization; while the gifted Dermody perished through intemperance, and "the Admirable Crichton" lost his life in a quarrel about a mistress in the streets of Mantua. None of them can be said to have benefited humanity, and the world is nothing the better for their having lived in it.

Far different, indeed, are the merits of those honored spirits, and their conduct far more worthy of imitation, who have devoted their intellectual powers to the service of morality and their lives to the happiness of mankind, and who, if they have not been crowned with bays, have been embalmed in the tears of the orphan, the widow or the oppressed, and by their example have so illustrated the beauty and dignity of virtue that generations yet unborn will feel its influence. The names of Penn and Wilberforce will deserve to be remembered while men have rights and human nature has a friend; while to the remotest ages the victims of misfortune will be cheered by the name of Howard, who, in the language of Burke, "visited all Europe, not to survey the sumptuousness of palaces or the stateliness of temples, not to make accurate admeasurements of the remains of ancient grandeur nor to form a scale of the curiosities of modern art, not to collect medals or to collate manuscripts, but to dive into the depths of dungeons, to plunge into the infection of hospitals, to survey the mansions of sorrow and pain, to take the gauge and dimensions of human misery, depression and contempt, to remember the forgotten, to attend to the neglected, to visit the forsaken and compare and collate the distresses of all men in all countries. His plan was original, and as full of genius as it was of philanthropy: it was a voyage of discovery—a circumnavigation of humanity."

It is a misfortune that parents not a few often speak in the presence of their children as if they would rather see them great than good, talented than moral, cunning than candid, selfish than generous, knavish than honorable. They would seem as if at all pains to cherish in their infant bosoms contempt for the poor, pride, arrogance, deceit, ambition, selfishness, rather than to have them admire goodness for its own sake, whether associated with wealth or poverty, beauty or deformity. And yet they are sometimes heard to complain that their children are what they have taught them to be, and are not what they never inculcated by precept or example.

So commonly have all the rank vices of the age been found most conspicuous among the educated classes, that philosophers for the last century have been often employed in inquiries into the causes of this sad discrepancy. They have generally agreed that it is owing, in a great measure, to the devotion to Pagan literature, mythology, and morality necessary to collegiate honors. There is so much more of Grecian and Roman ambition, cruelty, perfidy, murder, rapine, injustice, selfishness, debauchery, general licentiousness and lewdness in an academic course, than of the Christian virtues and morality, that most theorists on the moral condition of the learned would ascribe to this the delinquencies of the age. "I do not hesitate a single moment," says that moral and beautiful writer, St. Pierre, "to ascribe to our modern education the restless, ambitious, spiteful, pragmatical and intolerant spirit of most Europeans. The effects of it are visible in the miseries of the nations. It is remarkable that those which have been most agitated internally and externally are precisely the nations among which our boasted style of education has flourished the most. The truth of this may be ascertained by stepping from country to country, from age to age. Politicians have imagined that they could discern the cause of public misfortunes in the different forms of government. But Turkey is quiet, and England is frequently in a state of agitation. All political forms are indifferent to the happiness of a state, as has been said, provided the people are happy: we might have added, and provided the children are so likewise.

"The philosopher Laloubere, envoy from Louis XIV. to Siam, says, in the account which he gives of his mission, that the Asiatics laugh us to scorn when we boast to them of the excellence of the Christian religion as contributing to the happiness of states. They ask, on reading our histories, how is it possible that our religion should be so humane while we wage war ten times more frequently than they do. What would they say, then, did they see among us perpetual lawsuits, the malicious censoriousness and calumny of our societies, the jealousy of courts, the quarrels of the populace, the duels of the better sort and our animosities of every kind, nothing similar to which is to be seen in Asia, in Africa, among the Tartars or among savages, on the testimony of missionaries themselves? For my own part, I discern the cause of all these particular and general disorders in our ambitious education. When a man has drunk, from infancy upward, into the cup of ambition, the thirst of it cleaves to him all his life long, and it degenerates into a burning fever at the very feet of the altars." Here we have the fact and one of its chief causes clearly and forcibly set before us. To this we would add a second cause—viz.:—

Intellectual greatness is estimated far above moral excellencies. Intellectual splendor is as the ruby and the diamond, while moral goodness, however eminent, is as the pavement in the street. The eulogies on splendid talent, great eloquence, diplomatic skill, forensic tact and clever management are long and loud and numerous; while the praises of virtuous deeds, in gentle whispers, short and far between, in private corners, fall upon our ears as matters of inferior moment.

But a third reason of the neglect of moral culture is found in a very common error—viz. in the supposition *that in cultivating the intellect we are cultivating the moral sentiments and feelings*—that in enlightening the head we are improving the heart.

Were it not a matter of fact, forcing itself upon our daily observation, that there is a possibility of intellectual culture without moral culture, one might be induced, from speculative reasonings, to conclude that in cultivating the mind he was cultivating the morals of youth. To the philosophic Christian it is impossible to study nature without seeing God in every law and in every arrangement of nature. The Christian philosopher will therefore be apt to conclude that the knowledge of nature and the knowledge of God are not only intimately, but, in some degree, inseparably, connected; yet society, as it now exists, presents to him the phenomenon of an avowed atheistic philosopher—of one who not only studies nature without seeing God the Supreme Architect and Lawgiver of nature, but of one who, while he boasts of the knowledge of nature, denies the existence of the God of nature. This being possible, it must not be thought incredible that we may have a system of intellectual culture without any moral influence, or that the intellectual powers of youth may in some degree be highly cultivated, while the moral powers are in no respect improved.

True, indeed, philosophically and religiously regarded, every man is uncultivated, uneducated and impolite who is immoral or profane. With the man of true science, every person is uneducated who cannot or who does not discern moral excellence, who cannot or does not appreciate it. And, if we except pure mathematics, we find it difficult to conceive how a person can understand any one science without discerning and appreciating the nature and value of moral and religious truth; for vapors do not more naturally ascend to the tops of the mountains, nor rivers more uniformly descend to the valleys, than do all the facts and truths of genuine science lead to religion or morality. Yet, by some unpropitious management, intellectual and moral culture have been divorced, and we have got up systems of education and schools for youth, the unnatural and unscientific object of which is to cultivate the perceptive and intellectual powers without the moral, and to give a fashionable, a popular and a scientific education without any knowledge of religious or moral truth. The consequence has been that amongst the most highly educated there is often less religion and less morality than amongst the uneducated community. So generally has the notion obtained that religion and morality are neither sciences nor arts, neither useful nor elegant accomplishments, that it has become expedient to prove that moral culture is an essential part of a good education.

The innumerable instances of moral degradation and ruin found in the ranks of the most talented and best educated in popular esteem, are beginning to excite a laudable interest on the subject of education. The fact that thousands of the flower of the community are forever ruined by receiving a college education, and that thousands of the wisest and best fathers, who have sons full of promise and ample means of giving them a liberal education, are deterred by the countless bankruptcies in fame and fortune amongst the educated, imperiously demands a change in the whole system, or at least furnishes an unanswerable argument in favor of uniting a rational system of moral training with the intellectual in the education of youth.

Not only the absolute ruin of many of the educated, but the widespread mischief entailed upon society by the powerful influence of educated talent, shows that there is no necessary union between talent, education and morality, and also admonishes us of the necessity of a more infallible moral culture than is at present in existence. All the world acknowledge that education gives power—that it enables its possessor to be greatly advantageous or greatly injurious to society. A few educated persons in society are like an armed band well practised in all the tactics of war amongst an unarmed and undisciplined community. They may be its best friends or its worst enemies, according to circumstances and as they employ themselves. We all know what talent and some learning could achieve in the life and labors of Voltaire, Diderot, D'Alembert, Rousseau, and in the other profane and licentious wits who introduced the "reign of terror" and the horrid scenes of the French Revolution, and whose writings to this hour, sustained by Hobbes, Volney, Chesterfield, Hume, Paine, Taylor and others of minor fame, are flooding society with profanity, impiety, debauchery, rapine, duelling, assassination, and every species of sensuality, fraud and injustice. The influence on society of such men, contrasted with that of Bacon, Locke, Newton, Boyle, Euler, Addison, Milton, Grotius, Butler, and a thousand kindred spirits who have bestowed science, religion and morality on millions of our race, fully proves that talent and learning, with religion and morality, are the choicest blessings. Without these, they are the most grievous curses to the individual and society.

A fourth reason we shall now offer for the general neglect of moral culture in popular systems of education is, that "religion and morality are matters of private and individual concern, and that it belongs to parents and ministers of religion, rather than to the preceptors of literature or to schools and colleges, to take charge of such concerns."

And what shall become of those who have irreligious and immoral parents and no ministers of religion? This view of the matter appears to us exceedingly erroneous and in the highest degree detrimental to the whole community. I am aware, indeed, that, like the Berlin and Milan Decrees, it is a special arrangement authorized only in preternatural circumstances by the great belligerent and antagonist powers, in contravention of the common and supreme decisions of the international code in times of general amity and peace. It is, indeed, a melancholy fact that we have no common religion even amongst Protestants, and that in a distracted, divided and alienated community, to secure party interests and to prevent rival ascendencies, we make a decree that it shall be unfair, ungenerous, impolitic and even immoral, if not irreligious, in any teacher, guardian or other person having in ward any infants or minors, to make a single suggestion on the whole subject of religion, lest in so doing his party should gain some advantage or its rival some loss by the operation. Therefore it is decreed that the subject of religious instruction shall belong exclusively to parents and ministers of religion, and, by consequence, all the grand, vital impulses to morality are taken away from schools and teachers; for, in spite of skepticism, deism, atheism or pantheism, there is an inseparable connection between true morality and true religion. It is religion—the religion of the Bible, as we all agree—that suggests the master-motives and controlling impulses to morality. It is the belief of the Self-Existent, of the Eternal Majesty, whose omniscient eye pierces night and day, earth and sky, time and eternity; whose ear tries every sound, hears every whisper, and whose memory records every thought and word and action for a day of trial; that prompts, impels and guides the heart, the tongue, the hand, the foot, in the paths of virtue and morality. Apart from this belief, morality is mere policy or public utility, or the hypocrisy of a polite education.

And can we not have a common religion, and free ourselves from this incubus that paralyzes every vital effort to introduce a purer, a brighter and a happier day on our country and the world? Protestants will all say, We may—we can—we ought. Let them say, We will—we shall; and it is done. Meanwhile, let the simple facts, without the theories of religious belief—let the belief of God, of Christ, of immortality, of eternal life and eternal death, without any partisan theory—let temperance, righteousness, benevolence, and judgment to come, without metaphysics, be inculcated on one, on all, by every parent, guardian, teacher, and in every school and college and university in our land—and we may have—nay, we shall have—quite another and a better state of things. The evidences, the absolute certainty and divine authority, of the Christian religion, of the Old and New Testaments, ought to be taught and inculcated, as an essential part of a good and liberal and polite education, in every high-school in Christendom.

But there are some who, in their ultra-republicanism, say we ought to keep our children from any religious bias, creed or sentiment till they are of mature age and reason, and then leave it to themselves to choose what religious or moral system they may, in their independent judgment and full maturity of intellect, judge most suitable and profitable. This is the superlative of ultraism. Such a being as that described, free from religious or moral bias, educated, too, in the principles of literature and general science, marching forth in manhood's prime in quest of a religious creed, in search of religious and moral principles, never yet appeared amongst the children of men. It is full as rational and as probable as the late theory of making man immortal. Some French physiologist recently discovered that all the diseases that infect the human family are swallowed down into the stomach in the form of aliments of nature, and, therefore, logically argues that men would never be sick, and, consequently, would never die, if they could live without eating, and very philosophically recommends a new art of living by absorption, as a salutary substitute for the dangerous and alarming process of eating and drinking.

Some principles of religion and morality, or of irreligion and immorality, must be imbibed in society as it does now, or as it ever did, exist, by every child before it can reason or judge for itself; and the only alternative left is to decide whether parents and teachers shall leave it to accident what these principles shall be, or whether they shall attempt, in obedience to philosophy, to Solomon and to Paul, (for, in this, these three are one,) to "train up the infant in the way he should go," in the persuasion that "when he is grown he will not depart from it."

The soil of the human understanding and heart must receive some seed before we arrive at boyhood, much more before we arrive at manhood. The question then is, whether we ourselves, the parents and the teachers of our youth, ought to plant the seeds of piety and humanity in their understandings and hearts, or whether we ought to let the soil bring forth the thorn, the thistle, the brier, or the other rank weeds of vice and immorality whose seeds may happen to be borne upon every polluted breath which at this hour infests the city and the country, the public and the private walks of life. It is not, methinks, the part of reason to prove a self-evident proposition: we, therefore, proceed to the last point of our discussion, without which it would seem to be without any interesting point and without much profit. That point is embraced in the question—

How shall moral culture best accompany intellectual in the education of youth?

If at any time we might indulge in a solecism, or in a paradox, or in something not exactly represented by either of these words, we would here ask the privilege to say that *moral culture must always accompany intellectual culture, by always preceding and always following it.* But how can it precede it and at the same time accompany it? It can precede it in the work of training or improving the moral faculties themselves, by exercising them before we artificially exercise the intellectual faculties. By presenting an object worthy of sympathy or of benevolence, and by exercising the mind, or the faculty of benevolence, upon this subject, we may improve the special organ by which the mind operates, if there be any, and certainly the faculty of benevolence; and, while the object is presented and the faculty exercised, we may direct the perceptive and perhaps employ the reflective powers upon this object. In some such way would we explain ourselves when asked to unriddle this rather enigmatic representation. One thing we know, that all the feelings have appropriate objects in nature, and that the objects must be present before the senses or the mental vision or the feelings can be moved. Now, it happens that the feelings in infancy are much more easily moved and directed than the intellectual powers; and this is one reason—and the best reason—why they should be first exercised, in order not merely to give them a proper direction, but to strengthen and improve them. There are few who have not observed how soon an infant can feel the expressions of anguish or distress, and sympathize with them. Now, if any one wish to give a strong bias this way to the mind of a child, on the principle that frequent and healthy exercise always strengthens or makes more active and easy of operation every organ and faculty of man, all that is necessary to secure this distinctive attribute of character is to accustom the infant to many such scenes, accompanying and following them up with suitable instructions addressed to the intellectual powers. And so of every other affection and feeling in its constitution; for all are under the same law, and what is true of one is true of all.

Another reason why the moral feelings ought to be first cultivated is found in the fact that if not cultivated soon they can never be so fully and successfully cultivated afterwards. This nature points out by giving them the greatest susceptibilities at first. Indeed, the excellency of the human constitution requires this; for if at more advanced developments of the mind and at riper years the moral nature of man could easily take on a new color or immediately assume another hue, then stability—the very basis of character, without which every thing in morals is modish and freakish—would be unattainable. It is, therefore, necessary to human excellence that only in early youth should the moral nature of man be susceptible of being moulded into any form. It is, then, true in philosophy, because true in fact, that moral culture must be attended to in perfect infancy and childhood, if we would have our pupils attain to high degrees of moral excellency.

In harmony with this, we believe, are all human experience and observation; so that in the inductive science of mind and morals, it has become a law, or rather it is ascertained to be a law, of human nature, that *early impressions are always the strongest.* Therefore, sings the poet,—

> "Just as the twig is bent the tree's inclined."

And it is a maxim fast passing into popular use; and Heaven speed its progress through all nations and languages! "There is but one moral seedtime in human life"—one time for moral training with certain effect, and that one period is that of infancy. The perceptive and reflective powers are susceptible of improvement, and have been improved almost to the end of life; whether the moral feelings become too rigid or have not room for expansion, it may not be the province of philosophy to decide; but the fact is certain that they are not greatly to be improved by education after the periods of infancy and early childhood have passed away. Hence, always excepting the omnipotent power of truth and love divine when interposed, we find the cunning, knavish and covetous lad a dishonest, secretive and roguish man; while we have in the benevolent, noble, generous youth the liberal, magnanimous and philanthropic citizen.

The Bible offers no theories of astronomy, geology, chemistry or mental philosophy. It fears nothing, however, from the developments of the sciences of matter or of mind. Ignorance of nature, of the Bible and of true science led the Pope and his ecclesiastics to denounce all the leading scientific innovations upon ancient opinions, on the ground that they were unfriendly to religion and would finally destroy the credibility of the Bible. But a better knowledge of nature and of the Bible has shown that there is no discord or contradiction in their testimonies. Hence, without theorizing, the Bible says, "Train up a child in the way he should go, and when he is old he will not depart from it." The most improved science of mental philosophy says the same. Phrenology, rightly understood, demonstrates it.

The philosopher of human nature, to illustrate the formative influence of early education, will tell us that if we habituate an infant to acts of cruelty towards animals or to his associates—if we early familiarize him with blood and carnage, though it be only with the destruction of innocent birds and innoxious insects—if with this we accustom him to deceit, debate, contention—it will require no spirit of prophecy to foretell that such a child will become a cruel, resentful and savage tyrant, fit for wars and stratagems and spoils. The Bible, without speculating on the force of habit, prohibits the use of blood as an article of food; forbids cruelty to animals; enjoins benevolence to all; and affirms that the sable Ethiopian and the spotted leopard can as easily change their color as those who have been habituated to doing evil can cease from it and change their course of action.

Every monster in crime, when he tells the truth, tells such a story as Murrel the famous land-pirate of the West, now in the Nashville penitentiary, has told. "My mother," says he, "was of the pure grit: she learned me and all her children to steal as soon as we could walk, and would hide for us whenever she could. At ten years old I was not a bad hand." We have not the history of any one who has come to an infamous end whose story does not begin with some early depravity that was fostered, or, if not fostered, that was not restrained by the hand of discipline of those whose office it was to be the guide and the guardian of his youth.

That there is the *bona indoles* of the Romans—a good natural disposition, a better and a best, though sometimes this may be owing to an early and unperceived bias, and that in such cases less labor will be requisite to form a strong moral inclination—will be admitted; and that there is also the *prava indoles*—a bad, a worse and a worst disposition, though this is not unfrequently the creature of bad nursing, and that in such instances much more attention will be necessary even at the beginning—will not be denied; yet still it will be contended that both the good and the bad disposition will be overcome by education, and that by the early appliances of a rational moral culture the worst natural disposition may be completely subdued, and the best greatly improved.

In proof of this innate and incorrigible *prava indoles* and of the natural bias to a certain course of action, it is said that Alexander the Great, when asked in his youth to contend for a prize in the Olympic games, answered, "he would if he had kings to run against him." And Cassius, who conspired against Cæsar for the good of Rome, is said, when a lad, to have struck the son of Sylla because he said his father was master of the Roman people. Now, of these and many such instances it may be affirmed with all certainty, and proved by many incidents, that a proper education might have changed their character—might have turned the ambition of Alexander into another direction, and the patriotism of Cassius into the love of human kind.

In illustration, if not in proof, of this also, this same Alexander may be again summoned from the repose of many centuries. On the authority of his most credible biographers, it is said that he was naturally and decidedly of a generous and even of a merciful disposition; yet he was guilty of some very barbarous actions—such as dragging at the wheels of his triumphal chariot the conquered governors of vanquished cities. Plutarch, says the "Spectator," explains this by informing us that "Alexander, in his youth, had a teacher named Lysimachus, who, though he was a man destitute of all politeness, ingratiated himself both with Philip and his pupil, and became the second man at court, by calling the king Peleus, the prince Achilles, and himself Phœnix. It is no wonder if Alexander, having been thus used not only to admire Achilles, but to personate him, should think it glorious to imitate him in this piece of cruelty and extravagance."

There are none so good or so bad by nature as not to be greatly improved by moral culture. I know that Seneca, in his own pretty style, has somewhere said, "As the immortal gods never learned any virtue, though they are endued with all that is good, so there are some men who have so natural a propensity to what they should follow, that they learn it almost as soon as they hear it." Still, let it be remembered that it is conceded by this distinguished philosopher that they must *hear* it and *learn* it. There is nothing that lives, animal or vegetable, that is not susceptible of improvement by proper training. Plants and flowers and fruits of every sort are improved by the science and art of man. But even here the hand of cultivation must be timeously applied.

If any thing further on the *power* of early education were necessary, we would remind our hearers that it is to be found in Spartan history. The care of the Spartans, and their ingenuity in the early training of their children, have become proverbial; and history amply testifies that "Sparta became the mistress of Greece, and famous throughout the earth for her civil and military discipline, as the fruit of her system of infant education." The Spartan boy who suffered the fox he had stolen and concealed under his garment to eat into his bowels rather than be detected in a theft—which, according to his education, was the most shameful of all things imaginable—speaks volumes to those who are intrusted with the education of children.

But enough, and more than enough, for the intelligent, has been said on the necessity, importance and power of early moral culture; and that moral training must, and, of right, ought, if possible, to precede, to accompany and to succeed every other kind of education, from the very dawnings of mind to the valedictory oration of the university, is, we presume, satisfactorily decided in the judgment of all.

But yet, in answer to the question, How shall moral culture be most successfully promoted as the most important branch of early education? we would presume to suggest that, in addition to all that intelligent and virtuous parents and nurses can accomplish at home, infant schools, *exclusively for moral culture*, should be patronized in every city, village and hamlet in the land. These schools, having *behavior* alone for their object, could be made most interesting and pleasing to children. It would not be easy to describe any thing more interesting than a class of infants from two to six years old, formed into a little commonwealth, for the sake of learning, practising and displaying all the social virtues. Under an accomplished male or female teacher or teachers, by oral instruction, by precept, by example, by the early and healthy exercise of the moral powers, every thing that is pious, just, true, good, kind, merciful, benevolent, honorable, dignified—by a thousand incidents, amusements, recreations, adapted to health, pleasure, and the development and control of passion, feeling and propensity in perfect unison with nature and age—could be most happily and successfully inculcated and deeply impressed upon the juvenile constitution.

The only thing we recollect to have met with in our reading similar to this project is the *Persian school of equity*, of which Xenophon, in his life of the great Cyrus, gives some account. It would appear from those brief notices that the Persian children went to this school to learn justice, sobriety, temperance and the social virtues useful to the state, as children in other countries went to the schools of literature to learn the arts and sciences of a liberal education. We are told that the governors of these schools spent much of the day in adjusting differences and in teaching their pupils to give judgment against their companions convicted of the crime of violence, cheating, slander or ingratitude.

We would be far from proposing these Persian schools as a model to a Christian community; yet, so far as they bear witness to the supremacy of morality, they deserve our admiration, and suggest to us the utility and practicability of having schools for the cultivation of the social virtues.

Perhaps the present infant-school institutions might be converted into seminaries of moral excellence, or have appended to their literary and scientific character a moral regimen, which would for the first years be their principal rather than their secondary concern, and thus make the simple rudiments of knowledge an interlude between the different scenes of moral culture.

To the domestic and infant-school system of moral training—which only gives a bias to virtue and sows the seeds of moral excellence in the human constitution—must be added the influence of every school and every seminary through which the pupil advances in his literary career. Every teacher must himself be moral; and whatever truth or fact or event he teaches or communicates to his pupils—if moral meaning or moral bearing it have, he must either point it out himself or induce the students to point it out to one another. They must be made to perceive and to feel that in man's physical endowments and in his intellectual powers there is neither virtue nor vice, good nor evil, honor nor dishonor, except as they are or are not guided by the moral sentiments. It must be placed before them in the strongest colors and enforced by the brightest example, that the most beautiful person and the most splendid intellect render not their possessor respectable or amiable unless he be adorned with the graces and excellencies of virtuous character. To them the idea must be made most pleasing and acceptable that honor comes not from country, family, place, or fortune, but from good behavior; and that not a renowned or titled ancestry, but virtue itself, is the true and the sole nobility; that, in one word and in the true sense of that one word,

"AN HONEST MAN'S THE NOBLEST WORK OF GOD."

Gentlemen of the College of Professional Teachers:—

Permit one who for several years has experienced your toils, who has felt your responsibilities and shared in the pleasure of your calling, both in Europe and America, to remind you that you are engaged in an object of superlative importance, not only to the present generation, but that, in a good measure, is intrusted to you the destiny of the future. The youth of this generation are the hope of the next; and, consequently, in forming the intellectual and moral character of this germ of future generations, you cannot but in some good degree shape their destiny. But, further than this, gentlemen, your influence extends beyond the mere temporal conditions of our being. On the bias which you may give in favor of truth and moral principle, may depend the eternal destiny of many generations. Next to the parents of your pupils, you possess a power over human character paramount to any officers in the whole community—I would say, if I had time to qualify it, beyond even the ministers of religion. It is only sometimes that we can trace to the conscientiousness and benevolence of an individual benefactor the happiness and prosperity of a whole community; but this has been occasionally done, as in the case of Roger Williams and William Penn. And, were we more observant of the concatenation of things in the way of cause and effect, we would more frequently find that to the nursery and to the school we are indebted for that first impulse which has turned the current of human action into a new channel and materially changed the complexion of society for many generations. May it not, then, be in your power—co-operating, as you do, in your efforts to introduce a more philosophical and moral system of education in harmony with the human constitution—to stamp a character upon future times alike honorable to yourselves and beneficial to the world?

Give me leave, then, gentlemen, to say to you, and, through you, to all intrusted with the formation of a better character, for the next and future generations, than that which the present has attained, that this cause can never flourish as it ought till the public mind is so imbued with its importance and practicability as to make it the paramount duty of the whole government of every State to take into its most grave and deliberate consideration the whole chapter of the ways and means by which it will be impossible for ignorant and vicious parents to exist, or, if existing, to corrupt their offspring; and by which a solid, substantial, literary and moral education shall be made accessible to every child born upon its territory, and not only accessible, but unavoidable in all cases where nature has not withheld the powers and susceptibilities necessary to its attainment.

It is only, indeed, when the maxim that intelligence and virtue are the essential pillars of the state shall have deeply penetrated the public mind and indelibly engraven itself upon the apprehension of all, that it will become entirely obvious that it is incomparably more rational and commendable to legislate for the training of children than for the punishment of vicious men; that it is much more economical and philanthropic to raise funds to educate and discipline youth in the paths of true science and moral excellence than to erect houses of correction or to provide ways and means of preventing rapine, violence and murder, or of suppressing tumults and insurrections among the people; that the rational education of youth is the highest object to the whole community—to the patriot, the philanthropist and the Christian; and that those who will improve and elevate its character and facilitate its operations are to be honored and ranked amongst the most useful citizens and the best benefactors of mankind.

You have the honor, gentlemen, of having begun at the right place, of having selected the best subject in existence on which to concentrate your powers of doing good. While other friends of human kind—the patriot, the politician and the economist—have taken the country—its convenience, its trade, its commerce, its resources—under their kind auspices, you have wisely selected the human species—the human soul itself—on which to exercise all your powers of doing good. If, then, he who, by his science and devotion to his country's interest, has made two blades of grass grow where formerly nature produced but one, is worthy to be ranked amongst a nation's benefactors, how large the dimensions of his fame, how wide the circumference of that Christian's glory, who shall have doubled, trebled, and perhaps more than quadrupled, the powers and capacities of his race for knowing, for doing and for enjoying good!

NOTE.

It was this address that occasioned the debate between A. Campbell and Bishop Purcell.

In the month of May, 1836, I read a printed letter from the Executive Committee, requesting my attendance in October last, and proposing to me a subject on which to furnish a lecture to the college at the then approaching session. This letter came to hand a few days before my departure on my Eastern tour; to which I replied that, all things concurring, I would attend and deliver said lecture.

I did not return from my Eastern tour till September, and the college was to meet in Cincinnati the 3d day of October. In the numerous and pressing obligations which crowd upon one standing in so many relations to society, on returning from an absence of more than three months, I could not find that leisure and abstraction of mind necessary to a satisfactory discussion of so important a question as that on which my views were solicited. I sketched a few thoughts, as expressed in the foregoing essay; and, rather in token of my good will to the institution than in hopes of rendering it any essential service, I hastened to the city at the time appointed. I had not the least expectation of meeting with any Roman Catholics in such a college; for, of all their sins, that of being exceedingly zealous in diffusing information among all classes of society and in supporting free institutions is neither the most common nor the most mortal. But yet, until in the pulpit, reading my lecture, I did not imagine that there was in it a single allusion to that superstition which could provoke any controversy with any American Roman Catholic. And certainly I did not intend it; nor, in my judgment, was it either necessary or expedient for any of that priesthood to take exceptions at a single reference to the Protestant Reformation in its literary bearings and influences.

Nevertheless, Bishop Purcell, of the Roman Catholic community, took exceptions against that allusion, and made it the occasion of the most serious allegations against the Protestant *religion*, not merely in a *literary* point of view, but as deeply affecting the best interests of society, in being the cause of infinite contention and infidelity. It was by the most dexterous management and great forbearance on the part of all the Protestants present that this occurrence was so overruled as not seriously to mar the operations of the college. It has, however, occasioned a discussion of the claims and pretensions of that religion, which, we trust, may be of some value to the whole community.

It is devoutly to be wished that Bishop Purcell, or the Bishop of Bardstown, Kentucky, or of St. Louis, or that Mr. Hughes, of Philadelphia, or some other competent prelate of the Roman persuasion, will be on the ground in January next, to sustain the lofty and bold pretensions of that ancient sect.

It will not satisfy this community to be told of what has been achieved in Rome, in

Philadelphia, in New York, by the defenders of that religion. We all wish to hear what they can say for themselves in the Valley of the Mississippi; for we are fully persuaded that this is the place to which they look with most earnestness as the seat of their American empire; and therefore it behooves them to be ready to sustain themselves, if they feel that assurance and infallibility which they profess. And surely amongst the vigilant and able shepherds of that orthodox flock, some one will be prompt to defend from Protestant wolves their feeble sheep now scattered in this vast wilderness. Our confidence in the Protestant principles is such as to banish all fear of the issue of meeting any prelate of the East or West on any of the propositions which have already been most respectfully submitted.

A. C.

ADDRESS.

THE CORNER-STONE OF BETHANY COLLEGE.

DELIVERED MAY 31, 1858.

Circles have their centres, squares their rectangles, and all terrestrial edifices their corner-stones. These should always rest upon the solid earth. The solid earth itself rests upon the heavens, and the heavens rest upon the omnipotent *will* of God. Such is the splendid architecture of the present domicile of man. A practical recognition of these facts is honorable to man, to educated reason, and to the wisdom, power and goodness of God—himself the supreme projector and architect of the universe. He "weighed the mountains in scales, he placed the hills in a balance." He measured the waters of oceans and of seas, of lakes and of rivers, in the hollow of his hand. He gave to these oceans and seas, to these lakes and rivers, limits and boundaries which they cannot pass:—a decree that their waters shall not cover the earth.

A man of good sense, of well-developed mind, who is always a Christian, recognizes the hand of God, the power, wisdom and goodness of God, in every work of his hand. He recognizes the Bible as the book of Divine wisdom, the oracle of God, the volume of human redemption, the charter of a future and an eternal life to man.

He, therefore, delights to honor it, to build all his hopes of an eternal future upon it, and to regard and venerate it as the star of his own eternal destiny in this magnificent creation.

While a rock is the only reliable basis of terrestrial edifices, the Rock of Ages is the sub-basis of the entire empire of the universe. All that we truthfully and satisfactorily know of our origin, our destiny and our eternal relations to the whole creation is contained in the Holy Bible. It is, indeed, the true philosophy of Divinity and the true science of humanity.

Bethany College—not the edifice so called, but the institution of which it is the domicile—was the first college in the Union, and the first known to any history accessible to us, that was founded upon the Holy Bible, as an *every-day* lecture and an *every-day study*—as the only safe and authoritative text-book of humanity, theology and christology—of all true science upon the problems of Divinity and humanity—of the world or worlds that preceded this, or that shall succeed it.

From the origin of Bethany College, on the first Monday of November, 1841, till this day, a period of over sixteen years, there has been a Bible study and a Bible lecture for every college day in the college year. The Bible is read, as it was written, in chronological order, and a lecture on every reading is delivered, exegetical of its *facts and documents*—historical, chronological, geographical; whether they be *natural, moral* or *religious*, in reference to the past, the present and the future of man. Theories, speculations, sometimes called *doctrines, faith, orthodoxy, heterodoxy*, come not within the legitimate area of collegiate, literary, moral or Christian education.

In *Natural Science* we have the *facts* of nature as its appropriate area of observation, comparison and deduction.

In *Intellectual Science* we have the powers, facts and acts of the human understanding—the powers of perception, reflection, comparison, deduction, abstraction, imagination, ratiocination and generalization.

In *Moral Science* we have *conscience*, or the *moral sense* of personal and social right and wrong; moral law, moral obligation, rewards and punishments, &c.

In religion—or in Christianity—we have a Divine remedial interposition; a mediatorial institution—a prophet, priest and king, invested with all Divinity and humanity in one personality—*himself* the altar, the sacrifice and the priest; all forms of majesty, honor and glory culminating in him, "the Alpha and the Omega" of all legislation and interpretation, of all judicial and executive authority.

Such is Christianity, *scientifically* conceived and exhibited, in the Christian or remedial institution. But Christianity, if actually enjoyed, is a new and a spiritual life; a life of communion and fellowship with God through Christ—in our hearts the hope of glory.

Such, therefore, being the premises of all social institutions connected with the social system called the state, the nation, the empire, the world, unless based on these premises and conducted in harmony with them, no system of education is rational, scientific, philanthropic, or adequately adapted to the real condition and cravings of our common humanity.

Education is, therefore, a theme of the first importance, possessing paramount claims on the patriot, the philanthropist, the philosopher and the Christian. It comprehends in its premises the development of Creator and creature, heaven and earth, time and eternity, in full and perfect adaptation to the wants and capabilities of man.

Lamentably true it is that few—comparatively very few—have the capacity, the patience, the perseverance, the taste and the means adequate to its acquisition and consummation; and equally to be regretted is the fact, that larger and more liberal provisions are not made for its extension and perfection, both by the state and the church, as to both it is the greatest known or conceivable auxiliary.

There are no people in the civilized world, known to us, who have indicated a higher estimation of the value and importance of education, in its fullest latitude and longitude—in its height and in its depth, in its length and its breadth—than the citizens of these United States of North America. *We* have more schools and academies male and female, more colleges and universities of all growths and varieties, than are possessed and sustained by the same amount of population under any one Government, whether national or imperial, aristocratical or monarchical. *We* have more graduates in languages, sciences, arts and professions, annually issuing from our numerous literary and scientific institutions, our medical, theological and legal schools and colleges, than can be shown by any people on the civilized globe, of the same number, means and facilities.

We have, indeed, too many colleges and universities, too many institutions so *called*, in all the religious denominations of our country. And we, as a *Christian* people, have, in one sense, already outgrown ourselves, as well as outgrown other denominations of religionists in the *penchant* for colleges and universities. We have the Missouri Canton University, the Indiana Indianapolis University, and the Kentucky Harrodsburg University, on paper and in print—in stones and in brick, as well as in men, women and children. We have also in Illinois no less than three stripling colleges, Abingdon, Eureka and Jacksonville—one in Arkansas, one in the environs of Nashville, and I know not how many more in inception.

England has had her two great universities for hundreds of years; to these she has added two of more recent origin.

Scotland's glory, in this particular, for centuries flourished in the Edinburgh, Glasgow and Aberdeen universities — Ireland in her Dublin, Maynooth and Belfast universities.

Pennsylvania has sundry such institutions—two of them within twenty miles of Bethany College, in the bosom of the Presbyterian Church. Ohio has one, twenty miles west of us. So that we at Bethany are living in a constellation of colleges. This speaks loftily for Young America, however it may speak for the cause of literature, science and religion. But a college, well endowed, well furnished with buildings, with libraries, with apparatus and with a well-educated corps of professors, is not quite so easily reared and consummated as Young America dreams or imagines. We have had some little experience on this subject in the colleges of the Old World and the New. We have some volumes of theory and a few chapters of experience, which have been read and studied with care; and the impression is deep and abiding that it is *men*, and not *stone*, nor *brick*, nor *mortar*, nor a *charter*, nor a good *code of by-laws*, nor a few *ten thousands of dollars*, safely invested in good banks, or loaned on mortgaged real estates, nor even a board of annual or semi-annual curators in attendance on any emergency, that constitute the essentials of a college, or endow it with claims on the patronage of a discriminating population, much less make it a fountain of blessings to society—to the church or to the state.

It is mind alone that works on mind. It is educated mind that educates mind. It is living men and living books that quicken, inspire, develop, energize and polish mind. It is not theory nor a dead letter that animates and actuates the faculties of man. It is the animation of the teacher that animates the student. Hence it was Paul that made Timothy and Titus, and neither Moses nor Aaron. Paul owed much to Dr. Gamaliel. Had there not been a Demosthenes amongst the Greeks, there might never have been a Marcus Tullius Cicero amongst the Romans. It is the present living generation that gives character and spirit to the next. Hence the paramount importance of accomplished and energetic teachers in forming the taste, the manners and the character of the coming age.

Man never lives for a past generation. He lives for the present and for the future. Colleges, too, are for the present and the coming generations. The good or the evil that men do is not always interred with their bones. Both the good and the evil that we may do not unfrequently survive us for several generations.

Colleges are, in every point of view, the most important and useful institutions on earth, second only to the church of Christ in their inherent claims upon Christian liberality and Christian patronage. If they be not worthy of the smiles, the prayers and the contributions of a Christian community, I know not, beyond the church, what is, or ought to be, an appropriate and an approved object of Christian patronage and Christian liberality. We must have educated mind in order to the prosperity and progress of society.

And can there be a question or a doubt, whether the educated mind shall be Christian or Infidel? And can there be in any seminary of learning a Christian education without the Christian oracles? But, unfortunately, we have a patented orthodoxy and an unpatented heterodoxy, altogether, in most cases, factitious and accidental. How, then, shall we dispose of these? Abjure them both! Proscribe them both! Substitute for them the five historical books of Moses, and the five historical books of the Evangelists and Apostles of Jesus Christ! The wisdom of God was and is displayed in presenting neither a theory nor an abstract formula of doctrine or mere learning, but *facts, documents, precepts* and *promises*. These are the only appropriate themes of faith, hope and love. And these three, says Paul, shall ever abide in the Church.

On these views and premises, Bethany College was first conceived, matured and founded. We have had an ample and a most satisfactory experience and proof of the perfect practicability of the views long cherished upon the whole premises of mental development and moral culture. There is an energy of spirit and a moral polish of character which this system has demonstrated as perfectly practicable, and exhibited as a natural, necessary and rational result.

The calamity which has befallen Bethany College* will, we hope, soon be turned to good advantage, through the liberality already developed, and still being developed, to raise its towers and bulwarks, and to furnish its libraries and laboratories with all that is essential to the increasing demands of the age—to place it in the front rank of beneficent and potent institutions, literary, scientific and moral.

With these aims and objects, and through the encouragement already vouchsafed by a generous public—the friends and patrons of Bethany College, and especially by the alumni of this institution, we now proceed, this thirty-first day of May, to lay the corner-stone of the edifice of the second edition of Bethany College, enlarged and improved. *Hic jacet non lapis terminalis, sed lapis angularis, Collegii Bethaniensis, literaturæ, scientiæ et religioni sacri; hoc die trigressimo primo Mai, Anno Domini unum mille, octingenti quinquaginta octo.*

In this corner-stone we deposit a copy of the Holy Bible, not to bury it in the earth, but as a monumental symbol of the fact that this book,

---

* It was recently destroyed by fire, and is now upon a magnificent scale being rebuilt.

this everlasting document, ought to be the true and proper foundation of every literary, scientific, moral and religious institution—that it is of right Divine entitled to be, and ought to be, the basis, the sub-basis, of every public and benevolent institution—essential to the perfect and complete development of man in his whole constitution—as a citizen of the commonwealth, a citizen of the kingdom of heaven, an heir of the universe through all the cycles of an eternal future. To God, who is its author, be all glory and honor, now, henceforth and forever!

This is in harmony with the all-suggestive and eloquent fact that the whole universe was founded and continues to rest securely upon the *Word of God*—the everlasting Word. John, the beloved apostle, the most philosophic and elevated in his conceptions among the original twelve, thus speaks:—"In the beginning was THE WORD, and the WORD was with God, and THE WORD was God." All things were made *for* him, as well as *by* him. Hence he is "the ALPHA and the OMEGA" of universal being and blessedness.

It is, in our esteem, apposite to the occasion—this solemn and sublime occasion—that of erecting a monument in honor of the paramount claims of literature, science, religion and the arts, both the useful and the ornamental, to call upon all true patriots, philanthropists and Christians, irrespective of local or partisan feelings, *pro or con.*, to co-operate with us on the broad basis of a common humanity—a common country—a common political destiny and a common Christianity.

We, therefore, desire it to be known and realized, that we do not selfishly refuse the generous and liberal contributions of our fellow-citizens, of every creed and of every name, to re-erect, furnish and garnish Bethany College; which, we doubt not, will be an investment on their part, as profitable to themselves, their heirs and representatives, as it will be acceptable and gratifying to us. We have taken pleasure in assisting our fellow-citizens in similar benevolent enterprises. And may it not be proper to extend to them such opportunities as they have been pleased to vouchsafe to us?

But to conclude: The legitimate position, end and aim of all colleges, properly so called, is, or ought to be, the education or development of the whole man—*body*, *soul* and *spirit;* and this, too, in harmony with the attributes and laws of God, exhibited and developed in the five cardinal dramas of the universe—creation, legislation, providence, moral government and redemption.

The analytic and synthetic methods of investigation and development, already canonized, with the consent and concurrence of the great masters of science, truly so called, are those we have judged supreme in the conduct and career of all schools adapted to the wants and cravings of man in the world that now is, and also in reference to that which is to come. Years of experience in schools and colleges have fully satisfied us that this is the true philosophy of education, and that it has the approval of every well-informed man, indeed, of all who are capable of understanding the subject.

We, therefore, have no new positions to assume or defend on the premises. We consequently do no more than to pledge ourselves to prosecute the same course which at the commencement we adopted and have prosecuted till now. It is simply that which *educationally* meets and satisfies all the wants of man, in reference to the present and to the eternal future, of his being, relations, obligations and destiny.

BACCALAUREATE ADDRESS.

TO THE GRADUATES OF BETHANY COLLEGE.

READ BY THE VICE-PRESIDENT, JULY 3, 1847.*

YOUNG GENTLEMEN:—

Venerating as we all do the president of our institution, we cannot but regret his absence on this interesting occasion. The fields of his usefulness, however, are too varied for any one interest exclusively to claim his attention, and therefore, whilst our feelings would have him here, our better judgment must make us content that he is away. It will be gratifying to you to know that even amidst the solitudes of the sea, floating on its boundless bosom and wrapt in the spell of its sublimity, his heart is still turned towards this scene of his labors, and, as the prophet of old, when a captive among strangers, opened his windows towards Jerusalem and prayed before God, so he looks back to this our loved institution, and sends up his petition for its welfare and growth. He neither forgets you, gentlemen, nor would be forgotten by you, but both as an evidence of his affectionate remembrance, and as a further claim upon your gratitude, has sent you, from the midst of the Atlantic, a testimonial of his regard, which I shall now read you.

ATLANTIC OCEAN, EAST OF THE BANKS OF NEWFOUNDLAND,
Longitude 38° 10′ *W.*; *Latitude* 41° 20′ *N.*

Young Gentlemen:—Though absent from you in person, and now gently moving under as bright a sky and on as smooth an ocean as you can well imagine, I feel myself, in spirit, present with you on the auspicious day which, while it records the birth of the greatest nation and the happiest community on the earth, terminates your collegiate years, and awards to you the honors due to those who have success-

* Written by President A. Campbell at sea.

fully pursued their way through the academic paths of literature and science. Having not only directed your studies, but participated in your education, watched over your morals and tested your attainments at the stated examinations, I cannot but regret that I have not the pleasure of hearing your last performances, of taking you personally by the hand, and of giving you severally the parting benediction. Still, I have the pleasure, though in the midst of the vast Atlantic, and far removed from the halls in which we have so often met, of communicating to you a few suggestions of practical importance, which, indeed, as the occasion demands, must be few, and which, I assure you, are dictated not merely by a sense of duty, nor simply in conformity with ancient usage, but which flow from attachments already formed, and from desires, long cherished, that your future years may be full of usefulness and happiness, the only rational and practicable preparation for a blissful immortality.

In order to this, it is expedient that you clearly and fully understand your exact position in the great family of man, and the claims which your country, the church of God, and the human race have upon you. A general knowledge of the past and present condition of the world, of its bearings on the future, and of your interests in it, is highly important to your judicious choice of a profession, and to the filling up the proper measure of your duties to yourselves, to your fellow-men, and to God.

You have long since subscribed to the adage that "knowledge is power," not merely to govern others, but also to govern ourselves. Equally evident to you I presume it is, that, in the intention of your parents to impart to you an education, as well as in your own efforts to obtain it, you both regarded it, not merely as conferring upon him who possesses it a power to promote his own interest and happiness, but also the interests and happiness of his contemporaries and posterity. The preparation which it affords its possessor to accomplish these ends, you are aware, consists not only in the amount of information which he obtains, but in the habits of thinking which he forms, and in the strength and vigor of mind which he acquires, in pursuing it, to make his acquisitions available to his own advantage and to that of others. Hence, it invariably comes to pass, in the struggle and business of life, that an educated mind excels an uneducated mind in every conflict in which the parties enter the lists on equal terms; that is, all things except education being equal. The victory gained, too, in such competition is great in the direct ratio of the difference in the education possessed by the aspirants. Now, as educated mind governs the universe by a law not of human but of Divine legislation, it ought to be remembered by every young man that he may and ought to possess a *moral power* in the full ratio of his talents and education, in any sphere in which his lot may be cast.

Having on several occasions called your attention to these subjects, I intend not now to generalize or moralize upon them; but, assuming them as matters no longer debatable, I wish on the present occasion to advert to a momentous conflict which not myself only, but very many truly intelligent and well-informed men in both Europe and America, anticipate as inevitably to occur in our own country, and that, too, in all probability, before your days shall be numbered.

In order to this, we must first glance at our country, at its immense resources, its population, its institutions as compared with those of the Old World, and its destiny. These are the materials for a volume or a series of volumes yet to be written. Having now but a few moments to devote to them, I shall merely name the topics, or state a few facts from which these are yet to be developed; and this with special reference to two or three suggestions which I desire to make to you on the present occasion.

Time was when thirteen English colonies became THE THIRTEEN FREE, SOVEREIGN AND INDEPENDENT STATES OF NORTH AMERICA. Their territory extended from a line passing through the great North-western lakes to the thirty-first degree of north latitude, and from the Atlantic Ocean on the east to the Mississippi on the west. But, in less than the life of one man, to this domain we have added Louisiana, and the territories beyond, extending westward to the Pacific Ocean. On the south we have thrown our arms around the Floridas and Texas, stretching to the Mexican Gulf, while on the north we have secured possession on Oregon extending to "latitude forty-nine." This immense territory, reaching from the Atlantic to the Pacific, from the mouth of the Rio Grande to the forty-ninth of Oregon, is now owned by only twenty millions of people, exclusive of the wandering tribes of Indians continually wasting away under the baleful influence of the stern vices of a portion of our Christian civilization.

But it is not alone the amplitude of our country that demands either our admiration or our gratitude. I would not compare America with Asia, but I would advantageously compare our portion of it—our own national domain—with that of any one people or nation now existing on the face of the earth, in all the elements that impart interest, grandeur, beauty, prosperity and happiness to a country.

In what other country are fruitful mountains and luxuriant plains, navigable lakes and rivers, fertile hills and valleys, projected on a scale of such varied, grand and magnificent dimensions? What immense defiles of stupendous mountains, decorated with variegated forests and towering cliffs, storehouses of the richest minerals, as well as of the fuel to refine them and of the streams to convey them to market, are seen lifting their proud eminences to the clouds, both in the east and west, the north and south, of our immense territory! In what other land are seen such inland seas, in the form of lakes, and such rivers, measured by thousands of miles, on whose broad bosoms is yet destined to float the wealth of nations? Where else shall we find, connected with such highways of commerce, unmeasured prairies of the richest soils, whose luxuriant grasses and fields of corn wave to the winds of heaven like inland seas of verdure and beauty? And where such myriads of hills and valleys, covered with rich harvests or crowned with green pastures, teeming with flocks and herds that can neither be told nor numbered?

But, leaving this field of admiration, which I cannot survey any more than I can fathom this mighty ocean, on whose fair bosom I move so majestically along, let us for a moment look at the increasing number, the gigantic strides, the mighty commerce and the unparalleled enterprise of our people.

In 1755 our entire population was twenty thousand less than one million. Now, in 1847, it cannot be less than twenty millions. In 1855, one century after its first census, it will have advanced from *one million to twenty-five!* England, the prodigy of Europe and of the world, in a little more than half a century has doubled its population. In less than a quarter of a century the United States have doubled theirs. On this ratio of increase, which cannot be expected to diminish during the present century, the next century will commence with a population of *seventy-five millions!* Young gentlemen, there are some of you standing here to-day who may live to see the day, not quite fifty-three years hence, when the American *family shall number its seventy-five millions of citizens!*

The commerce of our country is still more wonderful than its increase of population. It now amounts to two millions and a half of tonnage—twelve times greater than it was half a century ago. During this period, Great Britain, the greatest maritime Power in the world, has only increased her tonnage by about one-half of what it was some fifty years ago. Having lake-shores with their tributaries extending almost five thousand miles, draining an immense territory, the city of New York already receives, of all the products of our soil, more than the city of New Orleans; although on our Western waters there ply some eight hundred steamboats, carrying but a portion of the produce that grows on the banks of the Father of Waters with his unnumbered tributaries, draining over one million three hundred thousand square miles, and bearing to New Orleans the gleanings of shores twelve thousand miles in extent!

Next to these immense rivers and lakes, another element of our national greatness is our inland means of communication and transport. Of these I shall only say that they are no less wonderful and unexampled than those already mentioned. In 1790, only *fifty-seven years ago*, in all the United States we had but *seventy-five post-offices*, and the whole mail-routes were short of two thousand miles. Now we have thirteen thousand four hundred and eighty-eight post-offices, and mail-routes more than *one hundred and fifty thousand miles* in extent! Already we travel on canals more than four thousand miles, and on railroads over five thousand!

With another element we shall complete our allusions to the more impressive indications of our national greatness. It is the all-absorbing subject of education—with me the *alpha* and the *omega* of a people's greatness, usefulness and happiness. While Prussia, in the number of her schools and in the mode of conducting them, may excel us, as well as in the number of children that attend them, it is presumed that we excel her and all the world beside in the character of the education imparted to our youth. There is, indeed, one class of natives in our country most imprudently, most unphilosophically, and in a manner the most unchristian-like, debarred from scholastic education. This every Christian and every philanthropist in the country sincerely deplores. But taking our *white* population into view, in all the Union there was, in 1840, *one child in every seven* at school. Should we divide the Union into districts, and place the free States in one district, there was *one in every five;* or should we take all New England and New York only, there was *more than one in four.* Compared with England, Scotland and Wales, our country is, indeed, very considerably in advance. In Wales, but one in twenty, in England, but one in twelve, in Scotland, but one in ten were attending school in 1840. Of England and Wales I lately saw it somewhere stated that not more than one-half of the whole adult population can write their own names. I will not speak of churches, for in these it is known that, as respects the number of them in our old settlements, we excel all the world.

When, then, gentlemen, we look into the elements of a nation's greatness—territory, soil, climate, population, commerce, post-offices, public highways, education, schools and colleges—in all of which it is, I believe, conceded that we excel all the world beside; and when it is remembered that we are but in our infancy, while other nations with whom we compare are in more than their manhood prime, what reasons of thankfulness have we for our happy lot! What bright anticipations of future greatness! What a glorious destiny seems to await us! But we must also ask ourselves, What obligations are laid upon us to act a part in the great drama of life worthy of ourselves, harmonious with our national birthrights? And how shall we most certainly transmit to posterity the rich inheritance which God has put into our hands for them?

Still, the main cause of our true greatness as a people is the result of a happy combination of those several causes co-operating in the production of a new order of society, which has been developed in our free institutions, both religious and political. I do not say *political* and religious, but *religious* and political; because, however startling to some ears, it is nevertheless true, that the political institutions of every nation and people on earth are but the legitimate offspring of their religion, whatever it may be.

Whence came that peculiar, distinguishing freedom of thought, of speech and of action, which is the quickening spirit of our social system, and the supreme characteristic of our political institutions? Believe me, gentlemen, it is but a portion of the emancipating, enlarging and soul-redeeming spirit of the Christian religion, as developed in part through the Protestant Reformation, carried to this continent by our stern, uncompromising Puritan ancestors. Could you, or any one else, accustomed to seek for adequate causes for important events, imagine that the intolerant hierarchal spirit, whether it exist in the form or under the name of an English or a Roman despotism, which compelled the founders of our free institutions to seek for a refuge and a home in a North American wilderness, could have originated and developed such a social system as that which we, through their instrumentality, now enjoy? As the stream cannot rise above its fountain, so free institutions cannot possibly spring out of absolute despotisms, whether religious or political.

We find in the ancient Pagan idolatries the *beau-ideal* of an absolute monarchy, just as we find in the Jewish institution the reasons of a pure theocracy, and in the gospel the proper and justifiable elements of a christocracy. So in every form and theory of religion we can find the outlines and the elements of the political institutions of the people that receive them. Had there never been the idea of a

Roman emperor, there never would have been either a Pagan or a Papal supreme pontiff claiming political authority over the persons and the estates of men. The spirit of the supremacy of the Messiah, as *Lord of all,* which we properly denominate THE CHRISTOCRACY, is essentially the spirit of liberty, justice and love; because, having himself absolute control of the affections of the human heart, he sets us free from every allegiance to man which he himself has not by a clear and express warrant instituted. In the christocracy, therefore, we find the never-failing spring of that aversion to ecclesiastic dogmatism which has given to pure Protestantism its noble characteristics of mental independence, sense of equal rights, and love of perfect freedom. If the Son of God emancipate a man, he is free indeed. This, also, was the proper and immediate cause of that peculiar energy of character which has done so much for us as a people, which gave rise to our political organization, our general education and our ecclesiastic independence.

Opposed to the christocracy, there are yet three grand powers in the field. They are most familiarly known under the designations of Idolatry, Mohammedanism and Popery. Light and darkness, good and evil, do not present a more evident contrast than these severally do to the spirit and tendency of the Christian religion. Before the christocracy, therefore, can be fully developed in all its redeeming and transforming excellency, these three great rivals of the Messiah must be driven from the field.

The head of idolatrous Rome was *Cæsar imperator et pontifex maximus.* That form of idolatry has faded from Europe. The mitre and the cross distinguish his Papal successor, while the crescent and the sword are the proper symbols of the Arabian impostor. The religion of the false prophet of Mecca totters to its fall, while that of Rome, according to prophecy, must remain yet a little longer. Its doom, however, is written, and we need no new prophet to reveal its final catastrophe. The theatre of the Koran and that of the ancient idolatries are very far distant from us, and, therefore, we cannot be expected to be directly or personally implicated in their overthrow, its precursors or its concomitants. But the last great conflict of the Papacy, and that in which we are most likely to be interested, seems to be reserved for a theatre somewhere in the New World: most probably it will be found in the great valley of the Mississippi. We fight against the idolatries of Asia and Africa through our Missionary and Bible Society operations; but we must personally act a part in that conflict which must necessarily precede the long-predicted triumph of the Christian church over all her enemies.

That you may properly apprehend the nature of this conflict, and what is rightfully expected from you, you must know that there is one man in Europe, of whom you have often heard, whom we have to fear more than any other man in the world. He calls himself "the *vicar* of Christ," "the *prince of the apostles*," "the *pontifex maximus*" of the whole Christian empire. As vicegerent of God Almighty, he sits on the throne of St. Peter, as chief of the hierarchs of earth. From his girdle hang the keys of the kingdom of heaven. He opens and shuts the gates of mercy according to his own will. Myriads of ecclesiastic aspirants burn incense at his shrine, and worship at his feet. Legions of hungry monks and begging friars proclaim his intercessory power, while pious matrons and vestal nuns present his claims to every infant ear to which they can find access. One hundred millions of admiring worshippers recognize his spiritual jurisdiction, and through their bishops swear eternal allegiance to his will. His power is, indeed, spiritual, unearthly, transcendent, immortal.

Through his arrogant abuse of power, a portion of the Old World has been partially alienated from him; on which account his spiritual despotism has not its wonted admiration. He is, however, seeking to regain it in the Old World and to establish it in the New. Since his European fortunes have begun to wane, because of the development of his spiritual despotism in the miseries of his most faithful worshippers—the plundered and down-trodden millions that are crying for bread—he looks to America, and especially to the vast and fruitful valley of the Mississippi, with a peculiar intensity of affection, and yearnings of paternal commiseration, to impart to us the holy consolations which he alone has power to administer, and from which he regards us as most unfortunately debarred, through our obstinate and uncompromising Protestantism.

Possessing, as he does, undivided empire over South America, the devoted allegiance of Mexico, with the majority of Canadian professors, he only wants the valley of the Mississippi to secure the spiritual monarchy of the New World. He already boasts of two millions of true sons of the church in the United States of America. For these few sheep in the wilderness he has created bishops and ecclesiastic helps for them with unprecedented liberality. With the zeal of Peter the Hermit, his missionary Jesuits peregrinate our country from New York to New Orleans, and leave no valley in all the West unexplored, up to the summit of every tributary stream. Already Papal gold has filled our Western cities and towns with Gothic cathedrals of enormous dimensions. Everywhere are magnificent altars being reared on which new sacrifices are to be offered. Through the sacerdotal power of her priesthood the bread and wine of our country is to be converted into the flesh and blood of a new-made Christ, to be both eaten and worshipped on the banks of our rivers and in the great radiating centres of our literature, wealth, commerce and civilization. From the Vatican, from the throne of St. Peter on the banks of the Tiber, the decree has already gone forth that our Protestant American liberties shall be new-modelled and rebaptized at the sacred font of the "prince of the apostles," and made to minister to the dictates of a confessor, according to the interests and honors of "Holy Mother Church."

Now, then, young gentlemen, you may comprehend the nature of that anticipated conflict to which we call your attention. It is no ordinary struggle, I assure you, which presents itself to our vision. Popery has passed its zenith in Europe. Indeed, the metes and boundaries of Roman and Protestant states in the Old World have been stereotyped centuries ago. In the midst of both a third power has arisen. I allude to the infidel power, that revolutionized France, and kindled a flame of war all over Europe which is yet scarcely extinguished. The infidel power is yet of fearful stature. On its banners are direful omens and portents of woe to all potentates and powers, spiritual and temporal. Proselytes from Romanism to Protestantism, and from Protestantism to Romanism, combined, do not, probably, equal in numbers those who renounce the pretensions of both and unite their fortunes with the infidel power. It does not, indeed, always organize itself, and publicly assume the attitude of a separate and distinct power. But on that account it is the more dangerous and the more to be feared, because the more pervading and the less vulnerable. It aspires after the liberty to hate religion without shame, and to inveigh against it without reproach. It seeks to create a new public opinion, that it may annihilate respect for the Bible and those who delight to honor it. While Romanists luxuriate on the outbreaks, heresies and divisions of Protestants, and while Protestants make reprisals from the hundred abominations of Romanism, infidels seize the vices and blemishes of both, and eloquently declaim in favor of universal skepticism. They have no creed, no principle, no bond of union, other than a common hatred of religion, and a mere negation of every thing believed by Jew or Gentile, Romanist or Protestant. This party, I fear, already holds the balance of power, if not a majority, both in Europe and America. Its policy is always to take sides with what it deems the weaker party. Unfortunately, too, for itself, as well as for us, it seems to regard Protestantism and Romanism as alike tyrannical, proscriptive and intolerant. It gives no preference. On any emergency, it will coalesce with either party, so far as thereby it may promote its own ends. It will help the weaker party, on the assumption that the strong either is a tyrant or will become one if successful. Hence the sympathy now displayed by infidels for the Romanist party in the United States. This, gentlemen, is one of the chief sources of my fears for the destiny of our country. The influx of Romanists, though somewhat alarming, is not so much to be deprecated as the still greater influx of infidels, because these together are certainly more than two-thirds of all the immigrants into our country. Now, from the junction of infidels and Romanists, I contend, our country has much to fear, if not with regard to the ultimate triumph of the christocracy, with regard to the ordeal and tribulation through which it must pass. Let us not dream of perpetual prosperity, of indefinite ages of tranquillity, of an unbroken series of splendid triumphs. Depend upon it, a conflict will as certainly come, in this valley of the Mississippi, between the friends of one Mediator and the friends of many, as it must come in the plains of India between the worshippers of one God and the worshippers of many.*

Allow me, in conclusion, to tender you a suggestion or two on the premises, with regard to your duties in such an issue. First, then, you ought to inform yourselves on all the premises now laid before you. Make yourselves familiar with the history of both Protestantism and Popery. You owe it to yourselves, your country and the human race,

---

* The Newtons in philosophy and theology have anticipated and predicted a mighty struggle between Popery and Protestantism before the final triumph. Tillotson, almost two centuries ago, interpreted the barbarous verses of Herbert on the translation of Protestantism to America from England in this way. Herbert says,—

"Religion stands on tiptoe in our land,
Ready to pass to the American strand.
When Seine shall swallow Tiber, and the Thames,
By letting in them both, pollute her streams,
Then shall religion to America flee;
They have their time of gospel as we."

The archbishop, who flourished in 1660, remarked on these verses, "When the vices of Italy shall pass into France, and the vices of both shall overspread England, then the gospel will leave them both, and pass into America to visit those dark regions." (Vol. iii. p. 587.) This has come to pass; and recent events make it quite as evident that, as American Protestantism is now the purest in the world, the great struggle for the empire of the world between Protestantism and Popery may be expected in the centre of this New World.

to understand the genius and character of your own age, and its bearings upon the future, as far as you can. The history of Romanism and the dark ages you must thoroughly digest. I will commend but two books at present—Dowling's History of Romanism, and, for both sides of the controversy, a Discussion with Bishop Purcell, in Cincinnati, in 1837, endorsed by the parties. With regard to infidelity I will also name two—Simpson's Plea for Religion, and a Discussion with Robert Owen, Esq., in Cincinnati, 1829, endorsed by the parties. These works will suggest to your own minds others.

But I especially entreat you to be always prepared to lift up your voices for the free circulation of the Bible without note or comment, both at home and abroad, and to plead the cause of universal education. These are the main pillars of all our valued institutions. Intelligence and virtue are the foundations of a free, representative and popular government. They are the unfailing sources of a nation's greatness, prosperity and happiness. Be, then, the constant, fearless and zealous champions of universal education, without which writing, printing and speaking are of comparatively little value to the world. For these works of benevolence and humanity, gentlemen, you must qualify yourselves. You must read, think, write and talk much on these great, soul-redeeming topics. Your own destiny and that of your country, more or less, depend upon the faithful and able discharge of these duties. Assail Romanism and infidelity with the Bible in every man's family, and with a good common school for every man's children in the land. A well-educated, Bible-reading nation has nothing to fear from Popery, prelacy or infidelity; but without the Bible and the common school no nation can be free, virtuous and happy.

With these premises before you, my young friends, with your advantages of mental discipline, and with your acquirements in the various branches of a liberal education, most of you also professors of religion, you may form a proper estimate of your possible influence for good or for evil on human destiny. Possessing, in common with your contemporary friends and fellow-citizens, the largest and the richest patrimony kind Heaven now bestows on any people; speaking a language the most copious, rich and forcible of any living tongue; enjoying, too, the advantages of the most improved literature, science and civilization; inferior to no nation or people in the arts of war or in the arts of peace; living in an age in which we print by light, converse by lightning and travel by steam, by means of which we have almost annihilated both time and space, communing with one another across oceans and continents with more certainty and despatch than our fathers did with neighboring towns and counties a century ago; having in our hands the Bible so cheap and so abundant that a man can buy the New Testament for sixpence, and the whole Bible for three shillings; with a Government the least expensive and with civil institutions the most rational, equitable and free ever vouchsafed to man: what, I ask, are your responsibilities and duties to God, your country and the human race?

Consider well, I beseech you, what you can do, for what you *can* you *ought* to do, in preparation for the business and conflicts of life. You must take some side in the great controversies of the age. Survey the battle-ground before you. On the one side are ranged antiquated error, superstition, despotism and misanthropy; on the other, truth, intelligence, liberty, religion and humanity. In such a war no good man can be neutral. Are you not ardent for the encounter? May I not say for you all, that you will go heart and hand into the work of man's redemption from ignorance, error and sin? Certainly you will espouse the cause of the Bible, education and human liberty.

I call not upon you, young gentlemen, to furnish yourselves with swords and spears, with the weapons of desolation and death, for the impending conflict. This is not the work of scholars, or philosophers, or Christians. Your profession is not to kill and to destroy, but to redeem and to rescue man from evil. Camps, not colleges, are the seminaries for warriors, heroes and conquerors. The weapons of this our warfare are not swords and spears, but reason, truth, persuasion. Under the broad banners of peace, righteousness and love, with the sharp two-edged sword of reason, argument and truth, approach the lines of the enemy, saying, with one of old, *Nil desperandum, te duce Christe*, and the victory is yours!

BACCALAUREATE ADDRESS.

TO THE GRADUATES OF BETHANY COLLEGE.

DELIVERED JULY 4, 1846.

YOUNG GENTLEMEN:—

A DISTINGUISHED poet has said, "The world's a stage, and all the men and women players." On such a stage, covered with so many actors, one might expect a splendid drama. And such indeed is the momentous drama of human life.

Its acts are numerous and eventful. Its scenes are infinitely diversified and interesting. Its principal characters are few. They are the thunderbolts of war and the angels of peace. Its master-spirits are a fallen seraph and a risen Lord.

On the proper performance of our respective parts eternal issues hang. Not empires nor worlds only, but the universe itself, is the prize for which we play. All ranks and orders of intelligence, celestial and terrestrial, are interested in the grand result. The galleries above and around us are filled with an assembly of spectators and auditors as immense as it is grand and imposing; while the pit beneath is crowded with classes of a very different character, but equally interested in the whole performance—in the development of the plot and in the awfully sublime and glorious catastrophe.

The players are grouped in generations, making their respective debuts and exits in good keeping with the immense area of the stage, the length of the performance, the infinite number of actors engaged and the eternal hazards in debate. The antagonistic genii of the stage have so conducted the plot as to have every human being acting a part in subordination to their conflicting views, characters and designs. The drama is divided into seven nights of a thousand years each. Almost six of them are already past, and, as the consummation advances, the scenes become more interesting and the struggle more impetuous and absorbing.

Few, very few, indeed, of the actors comprehend the part they assume, because they do not apprehend the master-spirits nor their designs. The points at issue between them, the plot and the catastrophe, are not understood nor appreciated by one in a thousand of either the actors or the spectators. The multitude are not informed that some six thousand years ago a seraph, the most puissant of the peers of heaven, rebelled against God and formed a party against his government. This caused their expulsion from the court and palace of the King of Eternity, and secured their banishment to the desolate regions of unending night.

Man, not long after, made his appearance in Eden, sitting under the shade of the Tree of Life, hard by a crystal stream of living water issuing from a hidden fountain near the throne of God. No sooner seen than envied, he became the object of the implacable hate of the lapsed archangel. His ruin was instantly plotted, undertaken, and as far accomplished as was possible under the first constitution of humanity. The Divine Father of man had, however, anticipated the prince of demons, bearing in his bosom deep concealed a counterplot of mercy and judgment. Soon after the first act of the mighty drama, the scheme was darkly intimated to man and put into the hands of the heir of the universe for its consummation. This illustrious person, during a succession of full forty centuries, conducted *incog.* this scheme of redemption in the persons of prophets, priests and kings, till in the fulness of time he appears in person upon the stage and commences the work of illumination, setting on foot schemes of remedial mercy profoundly wise yet divinely simple and intelligible. He associates with him all the liege angels of heaven, and enlists into his service all the truly noble of earth. He institutes a new form of government, and presents a splendid scheme of bringing light out of darkness, good out of evil, beauty from deformity, and immortality from the grave. The fallen seraph, under the name of Satan, the antagonist of the Great Philanthropist, brings upon the battle-ground of earth his confederate angels of darkness and revolt, and makes a strong party of worshippers. He embodies all the passions of men in the form of "gods many and lords many," and in their worship fills the earth with ignorance and idolatry, with lust and violence. Meanwhile his career is suddenly and unexpectedly arrested for a time by the catastrophe of a watery deluge, then by the confusion of human language and the abbreviation of human life.

Numerous and various acts and scenes of this complicated and mysterious drama are made to pass before us, during a succession of many generations of actors. Many prominent characters, of much conspicuity and a long-enduring fame, appear upon the stage. After Noah and

Shem, Ham and Japheth, we see the great actors Abraham, Isaac, Jacob, Joseph, Moses, Joshua, Samuel, David, with illustrious lines of Jewish prophets, priests and kings. Finally, the Incarnate *Word* and *Oracle* of Jehovah is solemnly announced by his harbinger as "the Light of the world," the High-Priest of the human race, and the Founder and King of a new order of society.

He associates around him a school of evangelists and apostles, selects a host of prime ministers of light and sends them to the world on missions of mercy. He voluntarily falls into the hands of his enemies, who, as wickedly as foolishly, murder him, and thus seek to extirpate his party. But while among the dead, and in the dungeon of the grave, he grapples with the monster Death and gives him a fatal wound. He revives again, unbolts the mighty gates of the grave, and, like Samson of old imprisoned in Gaza, he carries upon his shoulders the gates and bars and pillars of the city of death, and upon Mount Olivet breaks them to atoms.

Soon after he leaves the battle-ground and ascends to heaven. Being there received with great honor, he sends to earth a new and omnipotent agent, who, in the person of apostles, evangelists and teachers, takes the field, becomes the advocate of his cause, the true *esprit du corps* of his party, and more than copes with all the unseen agents that animate and inspire the opposition. He plants his standard in a hundred cities in less than one generation, and soon constrains the homage of his enemies, who, after a few acts of the drama, instigated by the evil spirit, make for him a Vicar Christ and a politico-ecclesiastic sanctuary. The "sable goddess from her ebon throne," in "rayless majesty," again extends her "leaden sceptre o'er a slumbering world," and ignorance, superstition and error regain much of their former ascendency. Under the mask of an humble sanctity, the stage is filled with new hosts of actors. From a cardinal down to a begging friar, the world is filled with spiritual wretches, seeking, Satan-like, whom they might devour. Meantime, skepticism, in the person of Leo X., perches itself on the altar of St. Peter. Literature revives. Luther is born. The Elector of Saxony espouses his cause. Princes smile upon him, kings wink at him, emperors do him homage. Many were willing to patronize the bright star of a new destiny, and the school-master rose in rank next to the priest.

From that time to the present, Christian society has advanced in intelligence and civilization. And the nations that most revere the Bible and patronize the school-master have greatly transcended, in literature and science, in the arts of war and the arts of peace, in all the elements of national greatness and national glory, those who, disparaging the school-master and the Bible, have done obeisance at the shrine of a Papal supremacy or offered incense to the genius of atheism or universal skepticism. Still, the work of illumination and human exaltation is but advancing to a higher standard. The conflicts between a true and false philosophy of God and man, of nature and society, of literature and science, have not yet wholly ceased. We are, indeed, but partially convinced (for the conviction is not yet deep and universal) that man is susceptible of a better education than he has hitherto enjoyed, and that it is the interest of the whole community that it be universal.

What education is, and who should participate in it—whether it should be universal or partial—are indeed the peculiar themes of the present century. And, young gentleman, this leads me to address you specially on the part you should act in the pending controversy on the two great questions, *What is education, and who should enjoy it?*

I need not now intimate to you *what education is*, nor need I even say to you that, in some reasonable portion, it ought to be secured to every child born within the confines of what we call our country. My present purpose is to call your attention to the obligations resting upon you to advocate this cause, and to suggest to you how you may do it most effectually.

1. As to your obligation to plead this cause, be it observed that our obligations are sometimes both common and special. Every man is under obligation, so far as talent, opportunity and means are possessed, to use his influence to promote the happiness of the human race, and especially in that way most important to them and to him most ready and available.

2. But especially are you under obligation to advocate just views of education, and to plead for its universal diffusion throughout society. You are to consider yourselves as charged with this duty from the special call given you in this dispensation of Divine Providence. You enter the drama of life under peculiar advantages—Americans by birth, citizens of the United States, the gifted sons of a gifted ancestry, a majority of you Christians, and all of you ought to be. You have yourselves laboriously passed through the whole course of a liberal education. You have read Grecian and Roman history, philosophy, poetry and eloquence, in the language of Greece and Rome. You have made the grand tour of the sciences, physical, intellectual and moral. You are well read in mathematics, pure and mixed, and in the mysteries of number and magnitude. Few of your juvenile contemporaries will enter the arena of public life with more advantages than you possess.

You ought, then, to occupy a large space in the pending conflicts, in the passing acts of the grand drama now in progress in this department. You may be captains not of hundreds only, but of thousands and of ten thousands; provided you can only comprehend your abilities and opportunities, and the virtue of making preparations to plead this cause ably and persuasively.

But I must speak to you more definitely, and perhaps more perspicuously. I do not say, then, that you should all become authors of treatises on these subjects. Alas! this is an age too prolific of authors—of mushroom authors—of books with one idea, and of books without one idea, original or useful. We have many writers of very expansive minds, who can convert one drop of water into many gallons of vapor; who can from one grain of sense manufacture pounds of nonsense; who can transform some of the primers of our fathers into ponderous tomes of huge dimensions, in which a man may read a hundred pages without knowing what the author means. Gentlemen, I do not mean that you should punish the world or afflict your country with new books—short methods to be wise, easy ways to be learned, the art of making a fortune out of nothing, or of being great or good by wishing. Leave this task to the authors of panaceas, catholicons and specifics for all maladies—to the herbalists, the vaporists, the mineralists, who profess to heal all diseases and to remove all obstructions by one sovereign remedy. No, gentlemen: we mean nothing so superlatively ridiculous and absurd.

Nor do we mean that you should all become professional teachers and school-masters; though I know of no calling in which you could act a more useful or honorable part, if a sense of duty or if your taste or inclination should incline you to it. Some of the greatest philosophers, statesmen, authors and public benefactors have been teachers of schools. Nor do I say that you are to study any particular profession or calling with a reference to the performance of this duty. But, whatever be your calling or profession or position in life, you are, one and all, to prepare yourselves to advocate this cause, to seek an influence and a power to promote this great object. You are to make yourselves able to expose the abuses of the word "education." You must show what is not education, and what is education—that it is not the art of reading, writing, and ciphering as far as Vulgar Fractions; that it is not the acquisition of languages, living or dead; that it is not the cultivation of the head, nor the activity of the hand, nor the improvement of any fraction or part of a human being. You are to show that the intellect, the conscience and the heart are to be educated, first at home, then in the primary school, in the academy and in the college. On the development, training and corroboration of the physical, intellectual and moral constitution of man you must learn to speak clearly, forcibly, learnedly and convincingly.

But, gentlemen, the great point to which I would now specially call your attention, and for which I have introduced this subject, is to show some reasons and to offer some suggestions why you ought to become advocates of universal common-school education. It is not to plead the cause of education in general terms, nor to plead for a liberal collegiate education. It is not to lift either your pen or your voice in favor of grand schemes of education for the aristocracy of the community, to induce them to patronize and build up great universities for the benefit of their sons and wards, the future patricians and nobles of our country. "Capital," as the saying is, "can take care of itself," and the patricians can take care of themselves and their families. Should they prefer wealth to education, and seek to build up banks rather than schools or colleges—if they prefer to make deposites of their superabundant wealth in lands and tenements and mortgages, rather than in the minds of their sons and daughters, permitting them to continue a dreary, uncultivated desert, to grow up a moral waste—you cannot help it, and you need not grieve for it. But there are the plebeians in all communities, and these are the great majority. Besides these, there is a third caste: these are the improvident, thriftless, dissipated tatterdemalions, whose wealth consists in an open cabin, that needs neither light nor ventilation, well filled with a numerous retinue of ragged, squalid, ill-fed and untaught children. These also furnish a respectable class—if not in rank, at least in number—in some of our States and Territories. Have these no claims upon our benevolence nor upon our selfishness? These are to be your neighbors—possibly your servants, the inmates of your families. To prevent the increase of such a caste, of such poverty and wretchedness, of such vice and misery, is an object worthy of every patriot, philanthropist and Christian in the land. Common-school education is an essential element of every scheme of human improvement, of social enjoyment, of true national prosperity, without which all other means will fall short of that great desideratum.

Do you ask me how you are to contribute to such a consummation? I will make a few suggestions, and leave the subject to your own reflections.

You are, first, to make yourselves well acquainted with the subject of common-school education—what it means, what it comprehends, and what stakes and interests the state has in it, the church has in it, what interest yourselves have in it. When these subjects are well understood, you will not lack arguments to convince every thinking and intelligent man that it is the paramount interest and duty of every government and community to provide by law for the education of its entire population,—nay, that it is the first duty of every government to make provision for the practical literary and moral education of its youth, by levying and collecting imposts for this purpose, by setting on foot and supporting a vigorous and efficient system of common schools, commensurate with the means, the wants, the interests, of the whole community.

To make such a system popular, you must make it appear that it is not only the public interest, but the individual interest of every man, that such an education be universal. You must show that it costs more to have an ignorant, immoral, thriftless and wretched state or community than to have such a one as that of Massachusetts, Connecticut, or Rhode Island. This you can do only by opening to the mind of the community the sources of national wealth, national greatness and national prosperity. You must be able to charge upon ignorance and vice all the poverty, wretchedness and misery in any country possessed of a soil and climate worthy of human residence.

The statistics of every well-read political economist will furnish you with the data for such a development. You need only to assume that the natural wealth of a community is found in its territory, in its soil, its climate, its mineral, vegetable and animal products, and in its industry, skill and economy in discovering and applying these, or in importing them from other countries and manufacturing them for themselves and for others. You must prove—because it can be proved —and you must be able to prove it to the conviction of every man of good common sense, that the *wealth* of a community—its entire wealth, personal and real—is but the embodiment of its science, industry and virtue.

The materials of all human wealth are in the earth and upon it, in the form of minerals, vegetables and animals. These three kingdoms contain it all. Science directs and art converts it all to human health, wealth and happiness. Of what use the metals without the smelter, the furnace, the crucible and the smith? Of what use the most precious gems without the lapidary?—the Egyptian and the Parian marble without the polisher, the mason and the sculptor? Of what use the forests of Lebanon, the cypress, the shittim, the olive and the mahogany, without the carpenter and his tools of art? Of what mercantile value are oceans without ships, the earth without the plough, the spade, the scythe and the sickle? What avail the cotton, the wool, the flax and the silk without the machinist, his spindle and his loom?

I speak not of the great achievements of science and learning, that have circumnavigated the earth and measured the heavens. I speak not of that science that foretells for ages the phenomena of suns, and comets, and stars. I speak not of that science that directs and manages the lightnings of heaven, that inscribes upon them, as they pass along, the events of the day, and that makes them angels of intelligence from city to city and from nation to nation. I speak not of those developments of science and art that have almost annihilated distance, that have converted nations into neighborhoods and placed us on terms of intimacy and daily intercommunication with those who a few years since were regarded as aliens and foreigners, never to be seen and seldom to be heard from. But I speak of those familiar sciences and arts of social life that make the wilderness and the solitary place glad and that cause deserts to rejoice and to blossom as the rose. I speak of that education and science that make the man, that clothe and feed him—that education and science that furnish him with a house, a table, a chair and a bed—and those arts that minister to his daily comforts by supplying him with all the implements and instruments essential to the maintenance of the social state and the fruition of social life. And these, I affirm, he can neither possess nor enjoy without schools and colleges and the provisions necessary to their establishment and continuance.

But this is only one reason why common schools and colleges should be publicly and liberally supported. Another reason is, the *safety* of the state. Education, in its proper import, not only enlightens the understanding, but forms the conscience and humanizes the heart of man. Some philanthropist has said, and very properly said, "The education required by the people is that which will give them the full command of every faculty, both of mind and body, which will call out their powers of observation and reflection, which will change mere creatures of impulse, prejudice and passion to thinking, living and reasoning men; an education that will lead to objects of pursuit and habits of conduct favorable to the happiness of each individual and of the community; an education that will multiply the means of moral enjoyment and diminish the temptations to vice and sensuality." Such an education is a better defence to a state than standing armies and puissant navies. "To govern men," said some writer, "there must be either soldiers or school-masters, camps and campaigns or schools and churches, the cartridge-box or the ballot-box." "Education," said Edmund Burke, "is the cheap defence of nations." There is no defence, indeed, from vice, but in education. Neither wars nor prison-ships, neither jails nor workhouses, neither laws nor civil magistrates, can secure the person, the family or the fortune of a good man from the assaults of the malignant and the wicked. This is the province of education.

A Bostonian plebeian said to a Bostonian patrician, who had but one son, and who was very rich, whose annual tax for the common school in his own district was some one hundred and fifty-six dollars per annum, and who was complaining that, having but one son, and educating him at his own expense, he should be compelled by law to pay one hundred and fifty-six dollars per annum to educate his neighbors' children, "You must not complain, sir: you are as much bound to educate your neighbors' sons as you are to educate your own; for," continued he, "your son inherits a large fortune, and his estate will be amongst our poor children: if then our sons are not educated, but immoral and wicked men, what guarantee can your son have for his life or property, living among them? None whatever. Your love for your son, then, had you no love for our sons, demands of you that our sons be morally and religiously trained as well as yours, that he may enjoy the fortune and the life that he has derived from you." This speaks volumes; and, gentlemen, I hope you will make volumes out of it. No insurance of life or property will compare with that insurance of both from wicked men which a rational and moral education, universally dispensed, confers on every citizen. As a means of self-defence, then, it is the paramount duty of every community that taxes and imposts be laid upon the whole community to secure a good and an efficient system of common-school education. "Taxes," said a sensible gentleman to a rich old bachelor, "for the support of schools are like vapors which rise only to descend again, to beautify and fertilize the earth. Education is the great insurance-company which insures all other insurance-companies. No one is so high as not to need the education of the people as a *safeguard.* No one is so low as to be beneath its uplifting power. The safety of life and the security of property lie in the virtue and intelligence of the people; for what *force* has law, unless there is *intelligence* to perceive its justice, and *virtue* to which that law can appeal?"

There yet remains a third topic of argument, which must not be omitted in every efficient appeal in favor of universal common-school education. Religion is founded upon learning so far as it is founded upon truth and the knowledge of truth. The Bible is a *written* communication from Heaven to man, and must be *read* in order to be understood, believed and obeyed. Of what use is the art of writing or the art of printing without the art of reading? Why translate the Scriptures of truth into various languages, unless those amongst whom they are distributed are taught to read them? While it is possible—barely possible—to communicate a saving portion of religious knowledge to those who cannot read, certain it is that it is impossible to make any one, however gifted, master of any book, human or divine, which he cannot read. To withhold from myriads the means of reading and understanding the Book of God—the volume of human destiny—is the greatest sin of omission of duty to God and man that any community, acknowledging the Divine authority of that volume, can be guilty of. How it will answer for it, I presume not to say. But such is the melancholy fact.

If, then, the *wealth*, the *safety* and the *eternal happiness* of a people depend upon education—and education depends upon schools, as we are all constrained to admit—is it not the paramount duty of every individual member of the community to advocate and, as efficiently as possible, to plead the cause of universal education? And is it not the first duty of a civilized Government to provide for and to carry out an adequate and an efficient system of common-school education at the public expense?

I shall institute no investigation of matters which you, as political economists, can easily demonstrate—such as that it will, in the long run, cost very little more, to those who do educate their children, to have the blessing universally diffused, than it now does to educate their own families under the present system. I affirm the position, and will leave you to prove it hereafter. One of the darkest clouds that lowers over our good Old Dominion of Virginia is the melancholy fact that she has at this moment some one hundred and twenty thousand adults, male and female, and these not slaves, but white men and women, who, if their eternal destiny were staked on it, could not read one verse of Holy Writ.

Gentlemen, it is with peculiar earnestness and solicitude that I now press this matter upon your consideration, because of the part you are soon to assume in the grand drama of human life as respects yourselves, and because of the bearings of the part you are to act upon the destinies of your country and the world. No man lives for himself alone. If we have some claims upon the world and something at stake in it, the world has its claims upon us and some interest in us. We can all in some degree make the world the better or the worse for our having lived in it. It is all-important, then, that we enter upon the stage on the right side of every question affecting or involving the moral destinies of the world.

If God began the creation by first creating light, we also should resemble him so far as to begin our career in life by diffusing light ourselves or by making some effort to have it diffused throughout society. The illuminators of the world are its greatest benefactors. The Great Philanthropist himself was THE LIGHT OF THE WORLD and *the life of man*, and those next to him were the prime ministers of light to the nations of the earth.

Of all the trees in the forest, the olive is the most verdant, because its product is the oil that once illuminated the sanctuary of the Lord. They, too, are the most verdant in virtue and the most productive of good to the human race whose good fortune it is to resemble the sun in scattering light upon society, or who, if they cannot become radiating centres themselves, at least resemble the moon in reflecting upon others the light which they have themselves received from others.

But, gentlemen, the sands of our hour-glass are almost exhausted, and I am admonished to remind you once more that the acts of the drama and the scenes in which you are to take a part are but of momentary continuance. More than the one-third of the average of your lives has already passed into eternity, and what portion of the remaining two-thirds may yet be yours is involved in impenetrable obscurity. The young generally calculate on long years of pleasure yet to come; but their extended visions of those happy years are often unexpectedly cut short by some sudden stroke of death. It has often been observed that parents have more frequently to weep over their children's tomb than their children have to carry them to that place where "lies the mouldering heap" of generations already gone, and that the land of silence is more densely peopled by the young than by the old.

Of ten of your fellow-students who graduated where you now stand, but one short year ago, two have already passed into

> "that undiscover'd country
> From whose bourn no traveller returns."

And who of you now less expects such an event than they did then? I am sure you will all agree with me that if moral excellency and real worth of character and preparation for extensive usefulness could have secured to them a long and happy life, that life would have been theirs. But, alas! there is in this mysterious world of ours no guarantee of a single hour to youth, to beauty or to virtue, not even to the most athletic frame. Man's life is forfeited as soon as he is born; and whether the respite allotted to him shall be one year or one hundred, is hidden in the deep counsels and sovereign will of Him to whom the issues of life and death belong. But, gentlemen, your incumbent duty it is to be prepared to live many years and to die at any hour. A life of usefulness is a life of wisdom, a life of happiness and the best preparation for a triumphant exit. While on the stage, then,

"Act well your part: there all the honor lies."

But, in acting that part which wisdom prompts and taste prefers, remember that your Alma Mater, your country and the world expect from you that on every proper occasion you will lift up your voice and give your support in favor of universal common-school education as the only solid basis of a nation's wealth, the only invincible palladium of its safety and the only enduring charter of its independence, prosperity and happiness.

ADDRESS

TO THE

CHRISTIAN MISSIONARY SOCIETY.

CINCINNATI, 1853.

Beloved Brethren in the Cause of Christian Missions :—

Missions and angels are coeval, inasmuch as message and messenger are correlates: the one implies the other. As message implies a messenger, so both imply two parties—one that sends and one that receives the message.

Christianity itself is a message from God to man; not to man as he was at first, but to man as he now is. It was conceived in eternity, executed and revealed in time, and, in the wisdom and grace of God, it is the only sovereign specific for all the diseases and maladies of our fallen and degenerate race.

The Messiah, the Prince of Peace, was himself the great ambassador of God. The apostles were his ambassadors to the world. Hence, Christianity itself is a message of peace, and, "by the commandment of the everlasting God, is made known to all nations for the obedience of faith."

So essentially diffusive and missionary is the spirit of Christianity, that all forms of it have acknowledged the duty and obligation to extend its empire and to propagate it in all lands and amongst all people. Hence, Romanists themselves, and Protestants of every name, have instituted and sustained missions, domestic and foreign, and sacrificed both property and life, to a large amount, in their endeavors to evangelize the world, by bringing it under the sceptre and the sway of the Prince of Life and Peace.

It was not, indeed, till the sixteenth century that the Papal See was engaged to any extent in establishing missions beyond its own limits.

Then it was that Dominicans, Franciscans and Jesuits took part in a missionary field as broad as Asia, Africa and America. Their missionary St. Xavier penetrated the Portuguese settlements not only in the East Indies, but in the Indian Continent, in Ceylon and Japan. Chili and Peru were visited by Papal missionaries, and Greeks, Nestorians and the Egyptian Copts came in for a share of their labors.

Early in the seventeenth century, the Pope was induced to establish a congregation of cardinals, with large revenues, called *De Propaganda Fide.* They penetrated through the wilds of America and those of Siam, Tonquin and Cochin-China. Even the Chinese Empire was penetrated, and Japan, for a while, permitted their efforts. They endured numerous and various hardships amongst these Pagans, but were finally expelled from their territories.

Protestants followed their example early in the seventeenth century. Formosa, Java and Malabar heard them gladly. It seems that the great Indian apostle, Eliot, of Old England, visited New England as early as 1631, and spent fifty-nine years of his long life in this new missionary field, now the territory of the New-England colonies. He even translated some of the Christian books into the Indian dialects. The Mayhews followed him. Father Mayhew, his son and grandson, were, for almost a century, pastors of an Indian church, gathered and nurtured by their untiring exertions. But the Moravians transcended all others in their free gospel and in their free labors. Historians have assigned to them the conversion of some twenty-three thousand Indians.

Nine islands of the ocean were more or less evangelized and civilized by these bold heralds of the cross. Not only the islands of St. Thomas, St. Juan and St. Croix, under Danish rule, but also the English islands of Antigua, Jamaica, Barbadoes and St. Kitts, yielded, more or less, to the claims of Messiah the Prince, through their benevolent operations. Negroes of Surinam and Berbice, Indians of Arrowack, Canadians and citizens of these United States, have loudly attested their work of faith and their labors of love in many a mission-field. Not content with these fields of labor, they have penetrated the realms of the Hottentots, the Cape of Good Hope, the coasts of Coromandel, Abyssinia, Persia and Egypt, and have even scaled the mountains of Caucasus. They have gained the palm of all Christendom for sacrifices and labor in the cause of missions.

So late as 1795, the London Missionary Society was formed, and, four years after, a Particular Baptist Society, for propagating the gospel among the heathen, under whose benignant auspices missionaries were sent to India, and by their instrumentality the Holy Scriptures were translated into sundry Indian dialects of speech.

In the year 1700, a society was formed in Scotland for promoting Christian knowledge; and, just one hundred years after, in England, the Church Missionary Society was instituted. It has now no less than sixty stations. This is one of the most affluent institutions in Protestant Christendom. More than twenty years ago, almost two millions of dollars, in one year, were paid into its treasury, for propagating Christian knowledge.

It is to the honor of our own country that its citizens are generally more or less imbued with the missionary spirit. An unequivocal proof of this statement lies found in the fact that the missionaries of our country are now found laboring in the Sandwich Islands, in Africa, Palestine, Armenia, India, Burmah, Siam, the Greek Islands and China.

Do we not, then, safely argue, *a posteriori* as well as *a priori*, that the spirit of Christianity is naturally and necessarily a *missionary spirit?* Hence, I take the ground that every man's spirituality and humanity are to be estimated according to his zeal, industry and liberality in the cause of missions, or, in other words, in endeavoring to convert the world. Need we argue this as a doubtful question? Does any one hesitate to concede this assumption? It is scarcely a supposable case. But, for the sake of developing the fact, we shall assume that it is questionable.

It is said by some that the two forms of true religion—the patriarchal and the Jewish—which preceded ours were both true and divine, but that neither of them was proselyting or missionary in its character. In the nature of things, the Adamic and the Noahic institutions were purely family institutions, and necessarily knew nothing beyond themselves. There was no family beyond Adam's, none beyond Noah's, at the commencement of the two sections of the patriarchal age. Besides, the head of every new household was constituted prophet, priest and king of his own immediate family; and, if he discharged his paternal or parental duties faithfully, there was nothing wanting to the perfection of that economy. There were no communities, no public assemblies, no preachers, no meeting-houses, from Adam to Moses. Every father or godfather or patriarch had his true and proper family altar and family worship. They had neither Bible, law nor gospel other than the traditional institutions. Every thing was oral, visible, sensible, that affected the religion and moral character of families and tribes from Adam to Moses.

Of Abraham—the beau-ideal of a good and venerable patriarch—

God said, "I know Abraham, that he will command his children and his household after him, and that they will keep the way of the Lord, to do justice and judgment, that the Lord may bring upon Abraham that which he has spoken of him."

To the abuse of the family institution polygamy was chargeable; and for a licentious intermarriage of saint and sinner the old world was drowned and the Noahic institution of family worship reinstated. This continued to the exodus of Israel from Egypt, and then commenced a national religion. This, indeed, made provision for proselytes and additions from other nations and peoples. But there went abroad no missionaries; for the special mission of the Jews was accomplished in holding up the golden candlestick to all the nations contemporary with them. It had its peculiar spirit, which was essentially that of *one blood,* for the sake of the public blessing that was in it.

Neither the prophets, nor John, the harbinger of the Messiah, nor his apostles, were constituted missionaries beyond the twelve tribes. Neither our Lord himself—the glorious Founder of the Christian kingdom—nor any one of his apostles during his lifetime, was a missionary beyond the "lost sheep of the house of Israel." But when his work, prophetic and legislative, was accomplished, and after he had tasted death for all mankind, then, indeed, this sublime Philanthropist established a grand missionary scheme, in the persons and mission of the twelve apostles. That commission embraced Jew and Greek, barbarian, Scythian, bond and free, all nations and peoples and tongues and languages of earth. The whole world—all the nations of the earth—became one great missionary field. "Go into all the world, announce the gospel to the whole creation," was the new commission.

The missionary institution is, therefore, the genuine product of the philanthropy of God our Saviour. It is the natural offspring of Almighty love shed abroad in the human heart; and, therefore, *in the direct ratio of every Christian's love he is possessed of a missionary spirit.*

That "God is love" is the most transforming, soul-subduing proposition ever propounded to a fallen world. This granted, it follows that every one begotten of God loves God and his brother also. And this love of the brotherhood, superadded to the native philanthropy of Christianity, gives to its possessor an ardent zeal for the conversion of mankind, which cannot be dormant, but must find a vent for itself in such efforts as those which a true-hearted Christian missionary institution delights to honor and to institute for the renovation and beatification of man.

We do not theorize in uttering these views; we only give utterance to the sentiments and emotions of every renewed heart, of every one who has ever tasted that the Lord is gracious. Of all the rewards ever conferred upon man, that of receiving souls for his hire is the richest and the best. The thought, the assurance, the sight of one sinner transformed into a saint, refulgent in eternal glory and blessedness, through our individual enterprise and effort, would seem to be a prize, an honor, a blessedness, that would repay the labors of a life like that of Methuselah.

Myriads of men in the flesh will labor, in body, soul and spirit, for a lifetime, to secure temporal honors and rewards. They will imperil all that is dear to the human heart, for some imaginary gain, which, when possessed, fails to satisfy an ardent, immortal mind. But the Christian herald or missionary who, with a true heart, an enlightened zeal and untiring labor, engages in the service of the wisest, richest, noblest and most exalted Potentate in the universe, and for the honor, the blessedness and the glory of his own degenerate race, to raise them from poverty, wretchedness, infamy and ruin, to glory, honor and immortality, is the noblest spectacle that earth affords or that angels have seen on this side the gates of the heavenly Jerusalem.

And does not this object owe all its allurements and attractions to the discovery of the estimate that the great God places on man, in that sublime, mysterious, ineffable love which he cherishes in his heart for sanctified humanity; which he always cherished, even when, in the purposes of an eternity past, he held sublime counsel with himself, in the ineffable fulness of the Godhead; when, before the world was, "THE WORD that was in the beginning with God, and that was God"—"by whom, and for whom, all things were created and made"—was set up, appointed, foreordained to become the author of an eternal deliverance to all that obey him; and, in the fulness of time, became the antitypical offering of every lamb slain from the foundation of the world?

To the eye that descries this—to the eye anointed with the true eye-salve that can see objects of celestial beauty and grandeur, and to the heart that throbs and palpitates with the vigorous impulses of Almighty love, what object of time or sense, what employment of the human faculties, what use of all literary, scientific and artistic attainments, can be compared with the effort to renovate man in all moral beauty and loveliness, and to raise him from his state of ruin to the dignity of a peer of the celestial realm, and to an inheritance incorruptible, undefiled and unfading? When elevated to the conception of such visions of real grandeur, beauty and loveliness—to adequate views of the infinite, eternal and immutable love of Jehovah—our spirits are roused to vigorous impulses, purposes and activities, to become co-workers with the crowned and glorified Immanuel in the work of the Christian ministry—the most dignified and honorable which God could vouchsafe to fallen man.

Such is the stand-point and bearing of the truly enlightened and consecrated Christian missionary. And such are his inspirations, drawn from a right conception of the love of God displayed in the person, mission and work of the Divine Redeemer.

This Christian Missionary Society, my beloved brethren, we trust, originated in such conceptions as these, and from having tasted that the Lord has been gracious to us, in giving to us a part in his own church, a name and a place in that Divine institution which, in his mind, far excels and outweighs all the callings, pursuits and enterprises of this our fallen and bewildered world.

The great capitals of earth—the centres of nations and empires—with all their thrones, their halls legislative, judiciary and executive, are but for the present scaffolding of humanity, while the Christian temple—that building of God's own Son—is in progress of erection, and which is designed to hold in abeyance the impulses, the passions and the follies of the children of the flesh, till the cap-stone of this glorious fabric of grace shall be laid amidst such shoutings of joy and glory as man or angel never heard before.

The commission given to the apostles embraced, as a mission-field, the whole world. "Go ye," said the great Apostle of God, "*into all the world*, and preach the gospel to every creature." Wide as humanity and enduring as time, or till every son of Adam hears the message of salvation, extends this commission in its letter, spirit and obligation. The apostles, indeed, are yet upon the earth, in their writings. Though dead, they still are preaching.

When Jesus our Lord ascended to heaven, "he gave gifts to men." He gave apostles, prophets, evangelists, pastors and teachers. "Preach the word," was the apostolic charge to Timothy; and so long as there is an unbelieving Jew or Gentile in the world, the gospel is to be preached to him just as it was in the beginning.

There are yet nations, great and mighty and populous, without the revelation of the gospel, as much under the dominion of Satan, in all the forms of living Paganism, as were the nations of the earth when the commission was first given to the apostles. These have just as many and as strong claims on the Christians of the present day as Rome, Athens, Corinth or Ephesus had on the apostles and evangelists seven years after the ascension of our Lord to heaven. In the ears of sanctified humanity the cry is still heard, "Come over and help us." The harvest is yet great, very great, and, alas! the reapers are still few, very few. Shall we, then, only *pray* to the Lord of the harvest to send forth reapers to gather it? Shall we not rather send and also sustain those who are sent by the Lord, or disposed by his grace to consecrate themselves to this great work?

The solemn and awful fact that, "where no vision is, the people perish," should, in all that believe it, awaken every sentiment of humanity, every feeling of benevolence, every principle of true philanthropy, to take a lively and active interest in the conversion of the world, and in sending out heralds to announce the glad tidings to those perishing through lack of Christian knowledge, ignorant of the only name given under the heavens by which they can be saved.

If it be a good work—a work of Christian benevolence—to feed the starving poor with the bread of this life, to clothe the naked, to take benevolent care of widows and orphans in their afflictions, as all Christians admit, need I ask, is it not a better work, a more enduring work, a work of greater importance, to send the word of life, and the living ministers of that word, to nations sitting in darkness—in the region and shadow of death; to translate them from darkness to light, from the power and tyranny of Satan to God, that they may receive the forgiveness of their sins and "an inheritance amongst them that are sanctified"? Shall we weep with them that weep, in sympathy with the afflictions and sorrows of this transitory life, and have no tears of commiseration, no bowels of mercies, no agony of soul, for those who are perishing in their sins—aliens from the commonwealth of Israel, strangers to the covenants of promise—living without God, without Christ, and without hope in the world? Does not every feeling of our hearts, does not every sentiment of piety within us, conspire to urge us to take a paramount interest in this glorious enterprise of enlightening, converting and saving our fellow-men—participants of our common humanity, who at present are in Pagan darkness, invoking gods formed by their own hands or created by their own fears, that can neither hear nor see, that can neither succor nor save any who trust in them?

This missionary enterprise is, by universal concession, as well as by the oracles of God, the grand work of the age—the grand duty, privilege and honor of the church of the nineteenth century. God has by his providence opened up the way for us. He has given us learning, science, wealth, and knowledge of the condition of the living world—of the Pagan nations, their languages, customs, rites and usages. He has given to us the earth, with all its seas, lakes, rivers and harbors. He has, in the arts and improvements of the age, almost annihilated distance and time, and by our trade and commerce we have, in his providence, arrested the attention and commanded the respect of all heathen lands, of all creeds and of all customs. Our national flag floats in every breeze; our nation and our language command the respect, almost the homage, of all the nations and the peoples on earth. God has opened the way for us—a door which no man or nation can shut. Have we not, then, as a people, a special call, a loud call, a Divine call, to harness ourselves for the work, the great work—the greatest work of man—the preaching of the gospel of eternal life to a world dead, spiritually dead, in trespasses and sins? And shall we lend to it a cold, a careless, an indifferent ear?

We have but one foreign mission-station—a station, indeed, of all others the most apposite to our profession—the ancient city of the Great King, the city of David, on the summit of the "holy hill," once the royal residence of Melchezidek, priest of the most high God—the sacred Solyma—the abode of peace. There stood the tabernacle, when its peregrinations ended. There stood the temple, the golden palace which Solomon built. It rested upon a hallowed foundation—Mount Moriah. To that place the tribes of God went up to worship. There was the Ark of the Covenant, with its tables engraven by the hand of God. The Shekinah was there, Calvary was there, and there our Lord was crucified, buried and rose again. There clusters every hallowed association that binds the heart of man to man. There Christ died, and there he revived. There the Holy Spirit, as the messenger of Christ, first appeared. There the gospel was first preached. There the first Christian baptism was administered. There the first Christian temple was reared, and thence the gospel was borne through Judea, Samaria and to all the nations which have ever heard it. Jerusalem, the city of the Great King, is the centre of all Divine radiations, the centre of all spiritual attractions, and, in its ruins, it is an eternal monument of the justice, faithfulness and truth of God.

But, most instructive of all, it was decreed and predicted by the Jewish prophets, ages before Jesus the Messiah was born, that out of Zion should go forth the law, and the word of the Lord from Jerusalem.*

One of the capital points of this Reformation is the location, in time and place, of the commencement of the reign of grace, or the kingdom of heaven. The Christian *era*, and the commencement of *Christ's*

---

* Isaiah ii. 3; Micah iv.

Church, have long been confounded by every sect in Christendom. The materials of Solomon's temple and of Christ's church were chiefly provided for at least one generation before either of these was erected. The grand elements of Christianity, or of the kingdom of Christ, are his life, death, burial, resurrection, ascension, and glorification in heaven. This last event occurred more than thirty-three years after his nativity. So that the Christian era, and the commencement of Christ's reign or kingdom, are one generation—thirty-four years—apart. The Holy Spirit, who is the life, the bliss and the glory of Christianity, was not given till Jesus Christ was glorified. *Hence, John the Harbinger, and Jesus the Messiah, both lived and died under the Jewish theocracy*—a fact that has much moral and evangelical bearing on the Christian profession, as exhibited by both Baptists and Pedobaptists. This alone should give direction to all our efforts in all missions, domestic or foreign. It is the only legitimate stand-point at which to place our Jacob-staff when we commence a survey of the kingdom of heaven or propose to build a tent for the God of Jacob—the Holy One of Israel, our King. Had we no other object than to give publicity and emphasis to this capital item, it is worthy of the cause we plead, whatever the success may be, to erect and establish our first foreign mission in the identical city where our Lord was crucified; where the Holy Spirit first descended as the missionary of the Father and the Son; where the gospel of Christ was first preached, and the first Christian church was erected. As a simple monument of our regard and reverence for these events, it is worthy of all that it has cost, and more than it will ever cost us, to have made our first foreign mission-station near the cross, the mount of ascension of the Saviour, and of the descension of the Holy Spirit as the sacred guest of the house which Jesus founded.

But this alone, worthy though it be of all the honor we can give it, is not by any means our whole argument for the continuance of this station, and its liberal patronage on the part of all the holy brotherhood. It is not contemplated, at least by me, that any mission or missionary in Jerusalem is to convert that city, or even raise in it a flourishing church, in a few years. Still, it is to me a theatre no less inviting or important in this view of it.

Jerusalem is a great centre of attraction in the eyes of all Christendom, in the esteem and admiration of all Jews and Gentiles. It will long continue to be so. The crowds of tourists—Jews, Turks, Infidels, Romanists and Protestants—that visit, sojourn and take interest in it, give it a paramount interest and claim to locate therein a herald of the original gospel and of the apostolic order of things, free from the false philosophies of an apostate Christendom. An accomplished missionary in Jerusalem, even in the private walks of life, in his daily intercourse with strangers and sojourners, may sow the precious seed in many a heart, that may spring up in many a clime, and bring forth a large harvest of glory to God and happiness to man, when those who originated the mission and have sustained it shall repose with their fathers in the bosom of Abraham.

If there were but a single church in that city of the true type of a Christian family, exhibiting, in word and deed, in faith, in piety, in humanity, the beauty of holiness and the graces of the Christian life, it would justify all the costs of our missionary station.

But we have reaped, as well as sown, in Palestine. Some, of different languages and creeds, have been baptized into Christ in Jerusalem, through the labors of the beloved Barclay. And had he, as have some missionaries of the Anglican and other communities represented in Jerusalem, the means of supporting the converts, or had he the disposition to cater to worldly interests and to use such arguments as savor of worldly policy, he might already have numbered more than an Anglican Episcopal mission has there enrolled as the fruit of some thirty years' labor.

But the personal labors of a missionary in Jerusalem, and the immediate visible fruits, are not to be regarded as the sum-total of the avails of his services. He personally distributes Bibles, in all the languages spoken in the East, to those visiting that great centre of Asiatic and African attraction. Bibles in Arabic, Syriac, Syro-Chaldaic, Judeo-Arabic, Armenian, Turkish, modern Greek, German, Spanish, Italian, may be almost daily distributed, by those residing in Jerusalem, to the foreigners who daily crowd its streets and explore its solemn ruins and revolutions. Moslem intolerance, too, is annually waning, and the dupes of the grand impostor are now more accessible than at any former period.

But, as it is a settled point with us that Jerusalem is, and ought to be, our first choice, we presume not to argue her special claims upon our Christian benevolence. When we speak of "the rapidly waning Crescent," of the "drying up of the Euphrates," of Jerusalem as "one of the foci of Mohammedanism," anciently "the city of the Great King" and long destined to be "the joy of all the earth," "a city not forsaken," "of the year of recompenses for the controversy of Zion," "the Mount Zion which God loves for his servants' sake," we do not argue these glorious and sublime indications of her destiny as though any of us doubted our premises, her influence or her destiny. Jerusalem's fall is already written, and her future rise and glory occupy a large space in the visions of the future. Towards the end of the Babylonish Captivity, in the prophetic visions of that day, as presented in the 102d Psalm, we have some joyful indications of the rise of Jerusalem :—

> "Thou, Jehovah, wilt yet arise and have mercy on Zion;
> For the appointed time to favor her is come.
> For thy servants take pleasure in her stones,
> And show tender regard to her very dust;
> Then shall the Gentiles fear thy name, Jehovah,
> And all the kings of the earth thy glory.
> When Jehovah hath rebuilded Zion,
> He will appear in his own glory.
>
> Let this be written for a future generation,
> That a people to be born may praise Jehovah,
> Because he looked from his high sanctuary,
> From the heavens Jehovah beheld the earth,
> To attend to the groaning of the prisoners,
> To release those that were doomed to death;
> That Jehovah's name may be declared in Zion,
> And his praise again resounded in Jerusalem."

It is good to love Jerusalem, and to seek her peace and prosperity. So sang and prayed the Jews in their songs of degrees—Psalm cxxii. :—

> "Pray for the peace of Jerusalem:
> They shall prosper who love thee.
> Peace be within thy walls,
> And prosperity within thy palaces!
> For my brethren and companions' sakes,
> I will now say, Peace be within thee.
> Because of the house of Jehovah, our God,
> I will ever seek thy prosperity."—Ps. cxxii. (Boothroyd's Ver.)

Jerusalem, indeed, has long been given up to desolation, and it is to continue, according to Daniel, "till the consummation determined," or until the purposes of God respecting it are accomplished. Our Lord, by Luke, speaks still more plainly:—"Jerusalem shall be trodden down by the Gentiles, till the times of the Gentiles be fulfilled." This is our index to the prophecies concerning the Jewish reign. "The times of the Gentiles" yet continue. God permitted them to destroy Jerusalem, and thereby to crush its persecuting power. Its fall contributed much to the spread of the gospel throughout the world. Hence Paul reasons, "If the casting off of the Jews" from their relation to God "became the reconciling of the world, [the Gentiles,] what will the resumption of them be but life from the dead?"

The fall of the Jews became the rise of the Gentiles. The Gentiles have yet their times. And "blindness," not total, but "in part, has happened to the Jews," and will continue "till the fulness of the Gentiles" be come in. Then will come the fulness of the Jews; "for the Redeemer shall come out of Zion," the city of David, "and shall turn away ungodliness from Jacob."

This mystery is now revealed. It was, in the Hebrew style, *mystery*, a thing hidden or concealed. It is no longer so. The Jews, as a people, are still beloved, because of their fathers, though long punished, as was threatened; for, said Jehovah, by his prophet, "Thee, O Jerusalem, have I acknowledged" more than the Gentiles; "therefore will I punish you for all your iniquities." But the time "to favor her" is not far distant.

> **"For thy servants take pleasure in her ruins,**
> **And show a tender regard for her very dust."**

Hence David sings—

> **"Then shall the Gentiles fear thy name, Jehovah,**
> **And all the kings of the earth thy glory."**

With Paul, we rejoice in the prophetic drama, and, therefore, anticipate a glorious triumph of grace in the redemption of ancient Israel according to the flesh.

Our duty on all the premises is plain. During these times of the Gentiles, we have a dispensation of the gospel committed to us. We have, therefore, established a mission in Palestine, in the literal city of David. It is not designed merely for the Jews residing in their own hallowed metropolis or visiting it, but also for the Gentiles now sojourning in this great centre of mingled attractions.

We have, also, happily found a brother and his family who not only fully meet our anticipations, but, in fact, transcend them. Their qualifications for the station are acknowledged not only by all our whole brotherhood, but also by those of other denominations who visit the Monumental City. A Presbyterian minister of our own country, who not long since returned from Jerusalem, having made his acquaintance in Jerusalem, candidly avowed his conviction that "a more accomplished missionary than Dr. Barclay he had not seen, and one better adapted to Jerusalem he could scarcely imagine."

What, then, need I ask, is our duty, our privilege, our honor, in relation to our Jerusalem mission and our missionary there? I need not argue this question with any one present on this occasion. It is cordially conceded that he shall not only be continued there, but sustained with ample means to devote his whole energies to the great work. If, then, the means are not sufficiently ample, let those who have the matter confided to them report what is wanting to invest him with every facility to consecrate all his powers to this grand and sublime undertaking. Our prayers for his success, our counsels and our means, are all justly due to him, and certainly will not be withheld by any one of us. Who that loves the Lord—the grand missionary of Jehovah, who laid down his life, and expiated our sins by the voluntary sacrifice of himself; who that loves Abraham, the father of us all, if not in the flesh, certainly in the faith; who that desires that the blessing of Abraham might come upon the Gentiles, at home or abroad—can withhold his aid from a cause so noble, so rich in promise, so full of blessing to ourselves, our children, and the great family of man? Surely there is not one of us present who would not, according to his ability, contribute his equal part. It would be uncharitable to imagine that there is one Christian present who does not freely and fully consent to this. I shall not, therefore, further press this matter upon your attention.

But this is not the exclusive object of our zeal, ability and liberality. Jerusalem and Judea do not constitute the world, nor is our Jerusalem mission exclusively the longitude and the latitude of our missionary obligation, enterprise or benevolence. Has Africa, debased, degraded and down-trodden at home and abroad, no part in our Christian humanity and sympathy? Are we under no obligation to Africa? Have we forgotten that Ham, though degraded, is our great-granduncle, the brother of our great-grandfather Japheth, and the brother, too, of our more illustrious great-granduncle Shem? Or do we not believe that God has made of one blood all nations of men to dwell on all the face of the earth, and that he marked out, ages since, the limits of their patrimonial inheritance, as well as the different eras of the world? Shall one of our great-granduncle's sons engross and exhaust all our humanity and all our Christian benevolence, leaving the others unpitied, unaided and unprayed for, to perish in their idolatries and to die in their sins? Forbid it reason, conscience, humanity and mercy!

But these are foreign missions, and located on another continent. Have we no home mission-stations? Have we no fields to cultivate beyond the precincts of our American Zion? We *have* home missions, as well as foreign missions, and these have claims upon us. Have we made, or can we make, no provision for these? These are questions that call for our consideration; and ought we not as a brotherhood, if not as a missionary society, to give them some attention?

"Glorious things are spoken of thee, O Zion, city of our God. Thy foundations are on the holy mountains. Jehovah loveth the gates of Zion more than any of the dwellings of Jacob. Shall I mention Rahab and Babylon among those that acknowledge thee—Philistia and Tyre? and last, though not least, shall I mention Ethiopia as stretching out her hand to God? Yes: they shall say of Zion, This man and that man of Egypt, of Babylon, of Philistia, of Tyre, and of Ethiopia, was born in her and to her. For the Most High shall himself establish Zion." In the records of peoples born unto God, Jehovah shall relate, This man and that man were born in her. They shall sing as those leading the dance—"all my springs of joy are in thee."

We are encouraged, then, to raise an ensign, to establish a mission, and to invite to our Zion "the frozen Icelander and the sunburned Moor," the Indian and the negro, the Patagonian, and the natives of all the isles of the ocean.

It is not for me or for any one to choose, but for us all to unite, to select, to contribute and to co-operate in the large field of our fallen humanity. Let us open our hearts, our hands and our treasure-houses to the Lord, his cause and his people, and heaven will open its windows and pour out a blessing more than we can receive.

Let no one say he is straitened in God, in his providence, or in his own means. God loves a cheerful giver, and he will multiply his blessings upon his seed sown; for God is able to make every blessing abound toward us, that, having always all sufficiency in all things, we may abound in every good work. As it is written, "he hath dispersed abroad, he hath given to the poor, his righteousness remaineth forever."

That we should have an African mission as well as an Asiatic mission—a station in Liberia as well as in Jerusalem—missionaries peregrinating accessible portions of the land of Ham as well as of the land of Shem, appears to me alike a duty, a privilege and an honor. We have an abundance of means, and are wanting, if wanting at all, only in will, in purpose or in liberality.

Through the benevolence of brethren in Kentucky, there has been emancipated from slavery a colored brother, a gifted preacher of the gospel—a workman, we are informed, well qualified for such a field of labor. Bro. Ephraim A. Smith, whose praise is in all the churches, has, of his own accord and at his own expense, volunteered to visit Africa, to survey the premises in Liberia, and to return and report the condition of things there. He asks nothing from this Society in the form of pecuniary aid, nor has he ever suggested—to me, at least—a desire to be specially noticed on this occasion. Still, knowing him so well and so long as I do, I conceive it my duty, before sitting down, to offer the following resolution, viz. *That Bro. Ephraim A. Smith be requested to report, at proper intervals, to the Corresponding Secretary of this Board, whatever he may deem important on the condition and prospects of Liberia in particular and of Africa in general, with special reference to the location of a missionary station in Africa, and that the prayers of the brethren, not only of this organization, but of all the brethren everywhere, be offered to the throne of grace for his safe-keeping and protection, and for the Divine blessing upon his work of faith and his labor of love in this philanthropic and noble enterprise, and also for the brother who is to accompany him in his labors.*

"Now, may he that supplieth seed to the sower and bread for food, supply and multiply your seed sown, and increase the fruits of your righteousness and humanity—being enriched in every thing to all bountifulness," which will yield a rich harvest of glory to God and blessedness to man.

ADDRESS

AT THE

ANNUAL MEETING OF THE CHRISTIAN MISSIONARY SOCIETY.

A.D. 1857.

MEN AND BRETHREN:—

Missions are essential and rudimental elements of creation and of the universe. They are older than our earth. The angels of God are one and all *messengers* or ministers of God. The "chariots of God," said the sweet Psalmist of Israel, "are *thousands of angels*"—each of whom is a missionary acting under a Divine commission. By missionary agencies God intercommunicated with the primitive fathers of mankind. Through them, as his functionaries, he held converse with men and women in the primitive conditions of human society. Through these missionaries he communed with Abraham, Isaac and Jacob, Hagar, Lot and Moses, and others, down to the beloved John, the last amanuensis of the Holy Spirit.

Besides these missionary spirits, he also employed and constituted *men* as his missionaries to the world and to his ancient servants and people.

The first missionary in the Christian Scriptures was John the Baptist, who was sent by God to *prepare a people* to receive and welcome the Lord Jesus on his entrance upon his grand mission. Angels ministered to him during his whole life, and occasionally waited upon the apostles and evangelists in the execution of their respective missions.

Missions and missionaries are comparatively of modern date in our nomenclature. But they are older than creation—certainly older than the creation of our earth.

Jehovah said to Job, "Where wast thou when I founded the earth?

> "Declare, if thou hast attained such knowledge,
> Who fixed its proportions; for thou knowest.
> On what are its foundations fixed?
> Or who laid its corner-stone—
> *When the morning stars sang together,*
> *And all the sons of God shouted for joy?"*

This antedates all the missions and missionary operations in the annals of nations—in the annals of time. It is the beau-ideal of the grandeur of the missionary institution of the Christian age and dispensation. John the Harbinger was the pioneer missionary to prepare a people to give an honorable reception to the Prince of missions and missionaries. His superlative oracle was, "*Behold the Lamb of God, who bears away the sin of the world!*"

Jesus, after the manner of the Peripatetics, immediately opened his missionary school, and in person taught twelve missionaries during his public ministry. Thus commenced the Christian ministry and the Christian mission.

It may be expedient emphatically to note, in the opening of this subject, that missions and missionaries are the natural, the necessary and the immediate results of the appreciation of the dignity, grandeur and eternal importance of the gospel of Christ, and its soul-engrossing and soul-captivating end and aim.

A silent Christian is an anomaly in creation. The blessed are ever blessing. A full heart makes an eloquent tongue. A heaven-magnetized soul magnetizes all within its periphery. The Christian's gospel is a theme as lofty as the throne of God, and as deep as the mansions of the dead. It imparts true light to them that are in darkness—hope to the disconsolate, joy to those that mourn, and life eternal to those dead in trespasses and in sins. There is, in truth, no theme imprinted on the tables of time that compares with it, in its attractions, in its soul-reviving, soul-subduing, soul-transforming power and virtue. It is, indeed, incomparably worthy of universal acceptance.

It is, too, as wisely as it is philanthropically adapted to the actualities of our condition. As light is to the eye, as music to the ear, as bread to the hungry, as water to the thirsty soul, so does the gospel adapt itself to all the native longings, cravings and aspirations of that inner man, awakened to an adequate conception of himself in the light of God's own book, as he was, as he is, and as he must forever be in Christ or out of him.

One of the first impulses of the new-born soul is to desire the sincere milk of the word, that he may grow thereby; and, next to this, that he may have it in his power to bless others, as he himself is blessed of

God, in having them united with himself in the same Lord, in the same hope, in the same joy, in the same peace and in the same inheritance, incorruptible, undefiled and unfading, in the heavens. His soul is all alive to the gospel *facts*—the birth of Christ, the life of Christ, the character of Christ, his miracles, his sayings, his doings, his sufferings, his death, his burial, his resurrection, his ascension, his glorification in heaven, his exaltation, the honors paid him there. He joyfully anticipates his second coming, his descent to our horizon, his appearance on the throne of his glory arching the whole heavens, surrounded by all the hosts of heaven, with all the sons of men on his right and on his left, and the books of all human history opened before him, and in their midst THE BOOK OF LIFE. He distinctly hears him say, "Come, ye blessed," to those on his right; and, "Depart, ye cursed," to those on his left hand.

Such is the faith, such is the hope and such is the joy of every true and faithful disciple and follower of the Lord Jesus—the Christ of God.

Now, by these visions, realizations and hopes is every true missionary of the cross influenced, moved, excited, animated, strengthened and encouraged to go forth into the world, and to battle against all its lusts and passions; against its frivolities and trifles; against its errors, illusions and delusions; against its sordid and demoniacal passions, and every lust and temptation that wars against man's true interests, honor, usefulness and happiness in the present world, and in that which is to come.

But let us trace out the footprints of the missionary spirit and character, as developed in the providence of God, from the fall of our father Adam to the consummation of the fulness of the times of the Jewish age.

The ministry of angels was instituted immediately after the apostasy and fall of our father Adam. God drove him out of Paradise, and on the east of the garden he located cherubs with *flame brandishing swords* to guard the way to the tree of life. The first *angel* or *missionary* named in the Sacred History is he who appeared to Abraham, (Gen. xxii. 11,) in the year of the world *two thousand one hundred and thirty-two*—eighteen hundred and seventy-two years after the first FIAT, and on a most interesting occasion—that of the voluntary sacrifice of his dearly-beloved son Isaac, in whom was deposited the promise of the blessing of all nations. This, too, occurred on Mount Moriah, most probably on the identical spot on which David built his altar, the threshing-floor of Araunah, where the Temple was afterwards built. Some, indeed, suppose it to have been on Mount Calvary. On one or the other of these, most probably, Isaac was voluntarily offered up by Abraham, in obedience to a Divine command. "Here the *angel Jehovah*" called to him from the heavens and said, "Abraham, Abraham! Stretch not forth thy hand against thy son, nor do him any harm." A ram was caught by his own horns in a thicket, and that was substituted for Isaac. Hence to the end of the Jewish history the place was called JEHOVAH-JIREH, (JEHOVAH WILL PROVIDE.)

Two promises followed this splendid scene. God said to Abraham, "*Thy seed shall possess the gates of their enemies.*" "*And in thy* SEED *shall all the nations of the earth be blessed.*" In the Jewish Scriptures, after this, angels of God, or of the Lord, are frequently named in their missions and employments.

The Jewish *prophets* were, in the full import of their calling and work, *missionaries*. Such, too, was John the Baptist, the immediate harbinger of Jesus the Son of Mary. Such were *the seventy* whom the Lord appointed and sent, *two and two*, "into every city and place whither he intended to come.'

This mission of the Seventy is replete with wisdom and instruction to the church in all ages down to this our day and generation. Let us state it more fully.

"Afterwards, the Lord appointed seventy others, also, and sent them, two and two, before him, into every city and place whither he intended to go. And he said to them, The harvest is plentiful, but the reapers are few: pray, therefore, the Lord of the harvest, that he should send laborers to reap it. Go, then; behold, I send you forth as lambs amongst wolves. Carry no purse, nor bag, nor shoes; and salute no person by the way. Whatever house you enter, say first, Peace be to this house. And if a son of peace be there, your peace shall rest upon him; if not, it shall return upon yourselves. But remain in the same house, eating and drinking such things as it affords; for the workman is worthy of his wages: go not from house to house. And whatever city you enter, if they receive you, eat such things as are set before you; cure the sick, and say to them, The reign of God comes upon you. But whatever city you enter, if they do not receive you, go out into the streets, and say, The very dirt of your streets which cleaves to us, we wipe off against you; know, however, that the reign of God draws nigh to you. I assure you that the condition of Sodom shall be more tolerable on that day, than the condition of that city." Luke x. 1–2, (Campbell's Ver.)

These missionaries, the instructions given them, and their faithfulness in the discharge of the duties of their mission, are, in our opinion, most suggestive models to all missionaries how they should be instructed, how they should be initiated, how they should attend upon the work and duties assigned to them; how they should mind their own business, not naming politics—monarchy, aristocracy or democracy, *pro-slavery* or *anti-slavery politics*—whether monarchists or oligarchists, Whigs or Democrats, or of any other school, ancient or modern; and, with Paul, say, "God forbid that we should know, or make known, any thing amongst you, save Jesus the Christ, crucified in weakness, but raised in power;" and especially dwell upon the momentous fact that he is LORD OF ALL; that it is by him that all kings do reign and that all princes decree justice; that he is ordained by God the Father to be the judge, the final judge, of angels, men and demons, and that he will without partiality "reward every man according to his works."

While the missionary spirit and the missionary work are essentially the same, the condition of the missionaries, and the condition of the field, or the area of their missions, are, or may be, greatly diversified. The mission of the Harbinger John, of the Messiah himself, as a prophet and as a preacher of his own mission and work, the mission of the *seventy* heralds, the mission of the *twelve* apostles, the mission of *special churches*, such as that of the seven churches in Asia Minor, were not identically the same. They were, indeed, in certain points the same. They were one and all to preach and teach Jesus as the Christ. His person, offices, mission and work were to be announced and developed in all their attitudes and bearings upon heaven and earth, upon time and eternity—the world that now is, and that which is to come. But not simultaneously; not in each and every address. In this, as in every other work, there is a time and a place, there are conditions and circumstances, which call for special attention, special development and special application. No two discourses in the four Gospels or in the Acts of the Apostles are identically the same. True it is that the *person* and *mission*, the *character* and *work*, of the Lord Jesus Christ, in all the inspired evangelists and proclaimers of the glad tidings of great joy unto all people reported to us in the Christian Scriptures, were, in their facts and documents, one and all, the same in sense and purport, though diversified in style and manner, in general and special details.

There were, indeed, but a few facts, however diversified in style and manner of exhibition, continually pressed upon the attention and cordial reception of those to whom the glad tidings were announced. These were propounded not in identical terms and phrases, not in stereotyped formulas of speech, but in all the varieties of terms and phrases best adapted to the diversified education and training, to the peculiar modes of thinking and speaking, of the persons addressed. Still, the materials that constitute the gospel, with their evidences and claims upon the understanding, the conscience and the affections, were fully presented in such forms and imagery as were most appreciated by the parties addressed.

The difference between *preaching* and *teaching* Christ, so palpable in the apostolic age, though now confounded in the theoretic theologies of our day, must be well defined and clearly distinguished in the mind, in the style and utterances of an evangelist or missionary who would be a workman that needs not to blush, a workman covetous of the best gifts and of the richest rewards.

Facts *versus* theories have revolutionized the scientific world. Facts *versus* human traditions have protestantized much of the Papal world. Facts *versus* natural *religion** have christianized many theists, deists and atheists; while between *nature* and *theology, properly so called*, there is not one discordant note, in heaven, earth or hades. Nature may create theists and annihilate atheists; but she cannot create a Christian nor bestow the hope of immortality. Christianity is, therefore, super-sensuous, supernatural, super-intellectual and superlatively Divine.

Hence the indispensable necessity of spiritual regeneration in order to the appreciation of the reality, the beauty, the glory, the paramount excellency, of that life and immortality brought within our vision through the condescension and affiliation with us on the part of Him who hath brought life and immortality to light by his own triumph over death and the grave.

The *didachee*, or the *doctrine*, that is, the *teaching*, of Christianity, is the exposition of its own peculiar developments—of its history, its facts, its precepts, its promises, its rewards or retributions. The missionary—the would-be-successful missionary—must be well versed, fully indoctrinated, in these. They are his directory or guide in successfully executing the great work of his mission. He must be able to contemplate the parts in the whole, and the whole in its parts. He must not only have a large and rich treasury well assorted, but he must have it at command. He must be able to bring out of it, on demand, things new and old. He must, therefore, have in his evangelical treasury a place for every thing, and every thing in its place.

---

* By *natural religion* we do not mean natural *theology*. These are frequently, and rather unceremoniously, used as verbal equivalents.

Still, in the discharge of the duties of this work he must properly and fully understand the whole oracles of God, and clearly distinguish the difference between *preaching* and *teaching* Jesus Christ.

This is no mere speculative distinction. It was appreciated, fully understood and acted upon, or carried out, in the apostolic ministry. Hence we read, in Acts v. 42, that, after thousands of Jews had been converted to Christ, the apostles "daily in the temple, and from house to house, ceased not to *teach*, and to *preach* (or to announce the glad tidings) that Jesus was the Christ." *Keerux*, the *preacher*, *keerussoo*, I *preach*, and *keerugma*, the speech, or the *preaching*—and also *euanggelistees*, the evangelist, *euaggelion*, the gospel, and *euaggelizoo*, I preach the gospel—frequently occur in the Greek Christian Scriptures, and are of nearly equal circulation, but are always distinguished from *didaskoo*, I *teach*, *didaskalia* and *didachee*, a doctrine, and *didaskalos*, a teacher. No two such families of words of so many branches and of so large a currency are more distinguishable or more frequently distinguished in the whole nomenclature of the Christian Scriptures. An evangelist or preacher, or missionary, in our present ecclesiastic currency, may have both these works committed to his hands. This, however, does not make them one and the same, any more than preaching and baptizing are one and the same act because performed by one and the same person or functionary. For the sake of accurate and intelligible language and a clear appreciation of the Christian Scriptures and the Lord's will concerning us, these words and works should be clearly understood and employed by every evangelist or missionary of the church sent out and patronized by the church; and more especially by our brotherhood, who unite on the apostolic platform of church union, communion and co-operation.

A *doctrine*, a *theory* or a *science* is always in the eye and aim and effort of the *teacher*. A person his office, work and character are always in the heart and aim and effort of the evangelist, preacher or missionary. Indeed, these three words in ecclesiastic or religious currency are interchangeably used as indicative of one and the same functionary. We are aware that we find the word *evangelist* but three times in the apostolic writings—Acts xxi. 8, "Philip the evangelist," Ephesians iv. 11, "He gave some evangelists, and some prophets, and teachers," and 2 Timothy iv. 5, "The *work* of an evangelist." There being two Philips, one was called *the evangelist*, in contradistinction from Philip the Apostle. See Matthew x. 2; Mark iii. 18; Acts i. 13; but especially Acts xxi. 8.

Every selected and ordained preacher of the gospel is, *ex officio*, an evangelist. Every missionary selected, sent and ordained to act out the duties of a missionary, domestic or foreign, is, *ex officio*, an evangelist. And may we not ask, Why should any one be selected, ordained and sent to preach the gospel, beyond the precincts of any church—to convert pagans, infidels or sinners of any category—and not be invested with the requisite power to collect his converts into societies, called *congregations*, or churches, and not have the power to unite, set in order, or constitute such converts into communities, called churches, and leave them in the hands and under the supervision of such officers, usually called *elders*, or *overseers*, and *deacons*, or *servants*, as may be selected by such communities to be ordained to such services? This is not only the order, the suggestion, but the oracle, of reason, of prudence, of propriety, as well as consentaneous with apostolic order and precedent.

But this is not our present theme. It is only an allusion to the great object and the grand subject before us as a missionary society. We have all, we trust, learned that Christianity is neither more nor less than *Divine philanthropy*.

It is Divine philanthropy in harmony, too, with every other attribute of God; in harmony with his rectoral government of the whole universe; in harmony with all that is known of God in heaven, appreciated, loved and revered by all the principalities and powers and lordships in all the celestial realms of this grand and awful and glorious universe. Angels of all ranks and orders desire to contemplate it; because they delight to study, to admire and to adore the perfections, the grandeur, the glory and the majesty of Jehovah in the lofty and profound study and admiration of the infinite perfections and the adorable attributes of the Father of the whole family of natural, moral, worshipful, adoring spirits, whether known as angels or spirits, cherubim or seraphim.

We are satisfactorily informed that all the spiritual and angelic hosts desire more and more profoundly to contemplate the mysterious, divine and wonderful revelation of God, exhibited, developed, aggrandized, in and by the incarnation, substitution, humiliation unto death, the resurrection, the ascension, and the coronation of humanity and Divinity in the union of the finite and the infinite, of the earthy and the heavenly, of the temporal and the eternal, in the person of the Son of man and the Son of God.

The thought of securing an eternal weight of glory purposed, promised and guaranteed to every true, sincere, honest, enlightened and obedient Christian, man, woman or child, is, or ought to be, the all-absorbing aim, object, desire, effort and endeavor of every disciple of the Lord Jesus Christ. In open vision of the glory and grandeur of this great salvation—*the inheritance of God himself and of all his creatures*—what manner of persons ought we to be in zeal, in diligence, in effort, in self-government, self-sacrifice, liberality, generosity, beneficence, magnanimity! No mean, penurious, selfish, penny-wise and pound-foolish professor or nominal Christian can rise to such a conception of future glory and blessedness as that which warms, animates, enlarges, beatifies, the believing, confiding, hoping, longing soul that has tasted the rich grace of God in the delightful antepast and soul-cheering foretaste of the glory to be revealed when the Lord Jesus shall come in all his glory and majesty, with ten thousand times ten thousand, even thousands of thousands, of angels.

No living man, no living tongue of man, can estimate or express that exceeding and eternal weight of glory. Pauls himself labors (2 Cor. iv. 17) with the aid of two *hyperboles* as prefixes to his *αιώνιον βάρυς δοξης*, his *exceeding and eternal burden* of glory. No such phrase as this is found in any lexicon or dictionary, of any language living or dead, ever consulted by me; and we have the largest number of them that I have ever seen in any private library.

Christianity—*the gospel*—cannot be fully appreciated by any living man, in any language living or dead. It is well said, and it is truthfully said, that "eye hath not seen, nor ear heard, nor has it entered the heart of man to conceive, the things which God has prepared for them that love him." We know, too, that Dr. A. Clarke, Dr. MacKnight, and some others regard these words as applying to Greek and Roman philosophers not having been able to conceive of a Christian's birth-rights. This may be conceded, though of doubtful propriety; and could we call them all by name—like the names and titles of God the Father and of the Lord Jesus—it were then true that we have no conception, no adequate conception, of the eternal glory of ransomed humanity in that inheritance which is imperishable, unpolluted, and everlasting as the throne of God. Still, we have in the Christian's charter an inheritance incorruptible, unpolluted and unfading, rich as the price paid for it by the second Adam, the Lord from heaven—an exceeding weight of glory. We know that we shall see our Lord in all his grandeur, and we know that he will be our elder brother, and that we shall be heirs in common with him of all the glories of God's own heaven.

Now, I propound the question—and may I not put it with all earnestness and propriety on the premises submitted?—*What are we doing for the Lord Jesus—his cause and people? What are we doing to enlarge his dominion, to extend his empire, to bless the church, to convert the world?* I put this question, not to a people enslaved to or by a dominant, avaricious, worldly, selfish, grasping priesthood. You, my Christian, my beloved brethren, greatly appreciate your political birthrights, your Christian birthrights, which in prospect present to us a crown of glory that fadeth not away. We are permitted, we are invited, we are most cordially pressed by the tender mercies of our God, by the importunities of Him who made himself poor, houseless, homeless, penniless, that he might inaugurate us citizens of heaven and make us joint heirs with himself—I say, he has permitted us to aspire to great honor, by leaving something for us to do, not engrossing to himself the exclusive honor and glory of the conversion and salvation of our families, our relations, our kinsmen according to the flesh, our fellow-citizens, our neighbors, our down-trodden and oppressed fellow-men, at home and abroad. We have always with us not the poor only in this world's goods and chattels, but the ignorant, priest-ridden, slaves of lying fables and fanatical imaginations. He has spread out before us a large area of ignorant, uneducated—almost uncivilized—heathen at home—in our cities, our villages, our hamlets—even living in our houses and on our farms.

What humane and Christian interest take we in them, in approaching them, in addressing them, in preaching to them the words of eternal life? Do we go out to the lanes, the squalid huts, of cheerless poverty—the filthy cellars that germinate our epidemics and our endemics? Do we gather their children to our Sunday-schools? Do we send our evangelists, our young preachers, to them? Do we approach them ourselves? *What do we for them?* What do we for our fellow-citizens scattered over the West, the Southwest, the Northwest? What do we across the seas? What for Pagandom, abroad or at home? What for Jerusalem? We have done some good, probably much good, there. Why not carry on the work? The door is open—quite open. And what shall we do for Jerusalem?—the city of David and Solomon, in whose environs the work of redemption was consummated? "They shall prosper that love thee." Oh, Jerusalem! Jerusalem! "I can feel both wrath and pity when I think of thee!" "Unto that city the tribes of God went up—the tribes of God went thither." I am far from hopeless as to that field. Let us not abandon it. It is a great centre of attraction. It is also a city of radiation. Let our prayers and our means go hand in hand in behalf of Jerusalem and the venerated Mount Zion, and will not the Lord pour out a blessing upon them and upon us? Let us do our duty, and the Lord will not withhold his blessing. We cannot sow and reap the same day, the same month, sometimes not even the same year. Have we no tears for Jerusalem? What said the songs of degrees—in the days of the captivity of ancient Israel? Hearken to these words:—

> "When Jehovah reversed the captivity of Zion,
> We were like those that dream.
> Then were our mouths filled with laughter,
> And our tongues with rejoicing;
> Then said they among the nations,
> Jehovah hath done great things for them.
> Jehovah hath done great things for us;
> And therefore we are glad.
> They who sow with tears shall reap with joy,
> For he who goeth forth weeping to sow the seed
> Shall assuredly come again with joy,
> Bringing his sheaves with him."—Psalm cxxvi.

So reads the seventh of the fifteen degrees, or of the *psalms of degrees*, sung, most probably, by the Jews on the event of their deliverance from the captivity of Babylon.

My Christian brethren, my fellow-citizens of every ecclesiastic platform, can we not unite and harmonize and sympathize with old Jerusalem, and co-operate in behalf of the ancient city of the Great King—the city of David—the city of Solomon—the city of the Temple—the city over which the Lord Messiah wept in anticipation of her long, long years of moral and religious desolation? Oh, Jerusalem! Jerusalem! We have had for years a missionary there. And if of the inhabitants of that city few, very few, were benefited, so far as reported on earth, others have been, and the blessing of having labored there has redounded to our honor and beatified ourselves.

We have still on the premises there a sister,* of strong faith and large hope, toiling every day in her school of Jewish and Gentile children—a matter-of-fact, missionary-school. It appears from a late letter from her, received at Bethany, that Christian Jews are building a mission-house in Jerusalem, and that Mr. Cohen, a missionary Jew, with his son, are teaching over fifty Jewish children in his school. Mr. Coleman, also, a Russian Jew, late superintendent of the hospital there—now a Christian—addressed a congregation assembled at the laying of the foundation of their first dwelling-house, from the 127th Psalm:—

> "Except the Lord do build the house,
> The builders lose their pain;
> Except the Lord the city keep,
> The watchmen wake in vain."

* Mrs. Mary Williams, (since dead.)

The very interesting theme of Mr. Coleman's address was the dawning day of mercy to Israel. Mr. Graham, also, late Secretary of the Jewish Society in Jerusalem—greatly devoted to the promotion of their best efforts—in his prayer on the above occasion, while importuning the Divine blessing, commended them to His keeping who said, "As you have been a curse, O house of Judah and house of Israel, so will I bless you, and you shall be a blessing."

There is, from these indications, much to encourage our efforts even in Jerusalem—not for the sake of the Jews only, but also for the sake of all kindreds and tongues and people, who from all nations meet there in their respect for that monumental city, hallowed in the memories of all who appreciate the great work of human redemption consummated there.

But this is not the only cry in our ears. "Come over and help us," echoes from every point of the compass. Myriads are yearly perishing in ignorance and unbelief—living and dying without God, without Christ and without hope! If we cannot evangelize the whole world perishing in Pagan and Papal darkness, superstition and error, let us select our fields of labor, domestic and foreign, and send out our missionary evangelists to such fields as promise the most fruit, whether at home or abroad. Unless we do this, I ask, what evidence have we of the sincerity of our faith in that commission which was given to the apostles, and through them to the Christian church and ministry, till the curtain shall fall upon the stage of earth and time? Is not the whole unconverted world within the area of the missionary field, and within the commission given to the apostles and through them to the people? —"Go ye into all the world, and preach the gospel to every creature." Upon the church, the united church, founded on the apostles' doctrine and faith, rests this solemn and authoritative oracle.

"Charity," it is said, "begins at home." True, very true, if there be objects at home. But it is no proverb in our Israel that charity tarries at home. Like nature's brightest type of God, our sun, it shines not upon our country and our homes alone, but also spreads its vivifying beams upon all the nations and tribes of our humanity. So shines the Sun of righteousness and of mercy. If the East witnesses his earliest dawn, the West rejoices in his last lingering ray. Indeed, he is rising and setting every moment of the four-and-twenty hours upon myriads of our race.

Shall we not, then, as far as in us lies, as far as God has vouchsafed to us any instrumentality—shall we not send the light of life everlasting to all the world, if God vouchsafes to us the honorable opportunity and instrumentality? At all events, shall we not avail ourselves of every opportunity, and create, as far as we can, opportunities to send the word—the gospel of life everlasting—to a perishing world—embracing in the arms of a common humanity, a common paternity, a common fraternity, the whole family of man? Christianity in another point resembles our sun. In its own system it is both radiating and attractive. Hence said our Lord, "If the Son of man be lifted up, he will draw all men to him." We are not straitened in God; we are straitened in ourselves. He commanded the gospel to be preached not only *in*, but *to*, the whole world. "The fields," as Jesus once said, "are already white to harvest." And why is not the harvest reaped? Because the reapers have fallen out by the way, and have thrust their sickles into one another. This is enrolled in heaven as the curse of God upon all the sectarists and sectarisms. "A house" or an army "divided against itself cannot stand." So said the highest authority in the world.

For almost three centuries—at least two and a half centuries—Greek, Roman and Protestant Christendom have had their troops and commanders, captains, majors and generals, engaged in ecclesiastic wars, stratagems and spoils. Church politics, church philosophies, church doctrines, church ordinances, have been the apples of discord, the bitter fruits of an apostasy from primitive, original, apostolic Christianity. We charge the existing Mohammedanism, Patriarchism, Papalism, Protestantism and its four forms of church politics—Episcopacy, Presbyterianism, Independency and Methodism—I say we charge these, one and all, to the substitution of human prudence, human policy and human philosophy for the plain and truthful oracles of the Lord Messiah and for the teachings of his inspired apostles.

Associated with these have been the lusts of the flesh, the lusts of the eye and the pride of life. And to this last category we must assign much of all the strifes, discords and schisms which now superabound and constitute what is appropriately called "*modern Christendom*."

We would not if we could, and we could not if we would, exaggerate the fearful paralysis superinduced upon the body of Christ, his *mystical body*—the church, of which he is the head, and of which the Holy Spirit, or Holy Guest, is the heart—by this fearful apostasy, now existing more or less in all communities, paralyzing every heart and every arm engaged in the great work of harmonizing Christians upon the *seven pillars* erected by the great Apostle to the Gentiles, viz. one Lord, one faith, one immersion, one God and Father of all, one body, one Spirit and one hope. And must we not fear that while this paralysis continues the great field of the world, in its Jewish infidelity, its Mohammedan delusions, its Pagan idolatries and its Papal despotisms, will not be, cannot be, successfully approached by any ordinary missionary enterprise, however evangelically originated, constituted and conducted? Suppose this were more or less in any degree to be the case: would that, should that, could that, justify cessation from all endeavors? Certainly not. Has not the Lord commanded the gospel to be preached to all the world, and constantly preached, till he personally appear on the field himself and call the world to judgment? This is the identical mission of the church; this is her duty, her privilege, her honor, as it is now and will ever be her chief glory and her highest happiness.

At this stand-point we most profoundly regret the jars and schisms, so rife, so antagonistic and so antagonizing, within the area of what we call Protestant Christendom. We spend more in keeping up these rival distinctions, differences and animosities than we spend in all our missionary fields and stations from the rising to the setting sun. Could we have the sum-total expended first in erecting, then in adorning, our splendid churches—our stone and lime *churches*—with their splendid pulpits, galleries, ornaments, organs, paintings, &c., our rival theological seminaries, professors, libraries, and all other contributions to the denominational pride and ambition consecrated to Christian missions, we might have Asia and Africa, with the outposts of America, more civilized, humanized and evangelized in one century than any State in our confederation. We can tax ourselves to hundreds and thousands to secure the pride of life—and cast our weekly dimes into the Lord's treasury, to bless our souls and to convert the world! I say *we*, not *denominationally*, but we, of the living fashionable world of hebdomadal Christians, and high-church and low-church conformists; we can adorn our persons, our churches and our pews, our horses and our carriages, if not our livery-servants, at the expense of thousands, and then give twenty, or fifty, or a hundred dollars a year to convert the Jews and the paganized Gentiles of the whole world! Is this a fancy sketch, a freak of imagination; or a positive, substantial reality? Is it an Indian pagoda, a Papal palace, a Mohammedan mosque? Such was not a Jewish synagogue. Such is not a *Christian* meeting-house.

The Christian church is, indeed, a much more expensive institution. It cost the sacrifice of prophets and apostles, of saints and martyrs. It cost the blood of that precious Lamb of God foreordained and symbolized from the foundation of the world. It cost the confiscation of goods unpriced, the banishment, the imprisonment and the cruel slaughter of myriads of the purest, the most just and generous and magnanimous men and women that ever adorned the annals of the world. And what does it propose? Ay! This is the question that places all our powers of reason and imagination under tribute to prophets and apostles, to saints and martyrs who sealed their testimony by the voluntary sacrifice of themselves. They loved not their lives as they loved their Lord. They joyfully imperilled their all on earth, their all in time. They took joyfully the plundering, the spoiling of all their earthly goods and chattels, that they might glorify their Lord and obtain for themselves a crown of martyrdom, "a crown of glory that fadeth not away." They, indeed, counted all things but loss that they might gain Christ. But the inventory given of some of their estates in reversion proves them to have been the most rational and *far-seeing* of human kind. They had a guarantee to the following effect:—"All things are yours, whether Paul, or Apollos, or Cephas, or the world, or life, or death, or things present, or things to come; all are yours, and you are Christ's, and Christ is God's," and all this for an eternal future.

I ask you, my fellow-citizens, in your cool, deliberate reason and foresight, *were they not the most rational persons of whom you have ever read?* There is no wild enthusiasm in all this. Who would not give a *cent* for a thousand millions? a day, a year, or a century, for all the millions, billions, trillions, quadrillions, or quintillions of ages of any number within the precints of earth's largest figures?

Who would not, of earth's richest bankers, give all the treasures of the natural universe for the riches, honors, glories and beatitudes of an *heir of God* and *all his riches* and glories guaranteed to him irrevocably, to the utmost capacities of creature enjoyment? And let me ask, emphatically ask, are not all these within the precincts of "ALL THINGS"? Assuredly, then, "eye has not seen, nor ear heard, nor human mind conceived," the riches, the grandeur, the honor, of an heir of God through Christ Jesus our Lord and Redeemer.

And here I must pause and pray, *O Lord, increase our faith!* Every cent you spend on earth for yourself, for things of earth and time, is lost to you forever!

Jesus Christ our Lord made himself so poor that he might make many rich forever, that, he said, on earth he had not a spot whereon to repose his wearied head! And all this to enrich his friends forever! Was there ever love like this? We must, my Christian friends and brethren, stop and think, before we further go.

All the gold of Ophir could not ease an aching heart, nor soothe a disconsolate spirit. To give freely, cheerfully, liberally, as the Lord has blessed and prospered us, to every great work, is not only our duty, but our highest honor, our greatest happiness. It was long since decided in the highest court of law and equity in this universe that it is "*more blessed to give than to receive.*"

To *lend* is more felicitous than to *borrow:* for "the borrower is always servant to the lender." And to *give* to feed the hungry, to clothe the naked, is not so felicitous, though even this is, in heaven's own grace, called "*lending* to the Lord," as it is to dispense "the bread and the water of life," to convert sinners from the error of their ways, to hide a multitude of sins, and to constitute them *heirs of God* through Jesus Christ our Lord! Hence, of all the causes most interesting to man the cause of missions is supreme. It is the cause of eternal redemption, of everlasting life, honor, glory and blessedness. It is, too, of all the sacrifices of man the most acceptable to God; because most in unison with his own philanthropy in expending more to redeem man than he gave to furnish and garnish the whole universe.

We now reason, only *reason,* with you, my Christian brethren, on the missionary cause. There is no enthusiasm in this. It is a cool and deliberate act of the highest reason, as the most profound reasoner could demonstrate, to give freely, cheerfully, liberally, to the cause of human salvation, in the form of instituting, sustaining and conducting missionary enterprises. We need missionaries, well-educated missionaries, at home and abroad, in the centres of our highest civilization and on our most remote and savage frontiers. Let us, then, awaken from our speculations and day-dreams of earth's fantastic visions of political honor, of worldly affluence, of large fortunes and rich estates for our heirs to send them comfortably to eternal perdition, to everlasting bankruptcy and ruin.

And let me not ask you what you would *take* for any earthly property or estate which the Lord has given you as a steward, but how much you would *give* to save one soul from everlasting perdition, bankruptcy and ruin? In order to this, I ask you the value of one soul! How much would you—speaking commercially—take or ask for your soul? You, doubtless, remember the unanswered and unanswerable question propounded by the wisest, the most intelligent and most benevolent personage that was ever clothed in humanity. It bankrupts all the powers of language, human or angelic, to express. "*What is a man profited should he gain the whole world and lose his life, his soul or himself?*" Any one of these three words is of equal value as an exponent of *psuchee* in its one hundred and fifteen occurrences in the

Christian Scriptures. We may be peculiar in entertaining the opinion, but we cannot divest ourself of it, that this was a common saying, current in that day, "*What advantage in gaining the whole world at the loss of one's life?*" "*What gain in gaining the whole world and losing one's life?*"—or losing one's self. This, if we could conceive of such a thing, is *a moral absurdity* No gain whatever; but an utter, an infinite and an eternal loss!

To be the means of saving one *soul*, or one person, in the course of the longest life and by the most arduous struggles, is quite enough of honor and of happiness to satisfy any sensible, any rational man of Christian aspirations. This is a fact we do not argue. Its simple statement, to any one familiar with its terms, is sufficient to produce a cordial acquiescence. Even to correct and reclaim one erratic brother who has wandered out of the fold is a greater work than any work achieved by Cæsar, Napoleon or our own Washington. They fought and they conquered for themselves, their offspring and their country. They obtained for them an exemption from involuntary taxation and the despotic encroachments of a tyrannic and absolute monarchy.

For this statement we have the sanction of the venerated Apostle James. He says, in plain English, "Brethren, if any of you do err from the truth, and one turn him back to it, let him know that he who turns a sinner back from the error of his way will save a soul from death, and cover his multitude of sins." (James v. 20.) So thought and so wrote the venerated James to the twelve tribes dispersed through Mesopotamia, Media and Babylon, A.D. 61.

Any one and every one of the converted Jews in that day, it seems, had an invitation to convert sinners in the church as well as sinners out of the church. And have not we still need to preach and teach Jesus Christ often out of the church and sometimes in the church? Missionaries and evangelists may in their journeyings occasionally find it expedient in some churches to *declare* the gospel, as Paul did to the Corinthians, and as James did to the brethren in the dispersion.

What is every man's business is said, with much propriety, to be no man's business. Hence, *home missions* as well as *foreign missions* are still expedient. Paul and Barnabas found it expedient to visit and *revisit* the churches which they had planted and watered. (See Acts xv. 36.) Paul, who made this motion, said, *Let us survey, supervise* their condition—see how they do. In all this work of faith, in all this labor of love, they were building up and establishing the churches, as well as increasing their numbers and augmenting their strength in the Lord and in his cause. This is, and ever should be, a prominent portion of the missionary operations of all those consecrated and devoted to this work.

For this reason, they ought to be freed from all necessity of providing for themselves and families. It is quite as much the Christian duty of the churches to support, and *comfortably sustain*, their evangelists or missionaries, as it is the duty of those ordained to this office "*to do the work of an evangelist*" and to make "full proof" of their mission and ministry. *So Paul commanded Timothy*, (2 Tim. iv. 5,) and so he commanded the churches in their fields of labor not to forget those who labored for them; and that, too, by their own request. "The soul of the liberal" Christian "waxeth fat," and "he that waters others shall be watered again." There is justice lying at the basis of every Divine institution. For "justice and judgment" are celebrated by the sweet bard of Israel as the *basis* or the "foundation of the throne of God." See Psalm lxxxix. 14.

Have we not now, Christian brethren, sufficient premises before us as to our duties, privileges, honors and rewards in this great and glorious work? First, then, we ask, *What Christian, worthy of the name, can be found who cherishes not in his heart a missionary spirit?* Who does not pray that the Lord's work may progress in usefulness and in honor to all co-operants in it? Where shall we find a Christian, a genuine Christian, who is not willing, cheerful, joyful and happy in being thus a joint laborer with God and Christ and the Holy Spirit, with the angels of God, the ministering spirits of his loving kindness and of his tender mercies to the sons and daughters of men, who love, honor and adore Him who is the Alpha and the Omega, the *Beginning* and the *End, the First and the Last* of the most august drama ever acted on the broad and splendid theatre of the material universe?

There lives not the man, worthy of the name, who has ever seen himself mirrored in the unveiled face of Immanuel—who from Pisgah, Nebo's loftiest peak, has gazed upon the promised land on Jordan's farther side—who does not earnestly, ardently and joyfully anticipate the riches, the honors, the glories, the felicities, of that inheritance incorruptible, undefiled and that fadeth not away, secured and guaranteed to him through the immaculate life and the sacrificial death of the Lamb of God promised and adumbrated in all the sacrifices from the death of the righteous Abel to that of Immanuel on the accursed tree.

Every such ransomed man feels himself constrained to vow eternal allegiance to his will and to consecrate himself, and all the talents he possesses, to his honor and glory. He studies both Divinity and humanity in his person and character—in what he said, in what he did, in what he suffered in behalf of fallen man. He supremely desires to be like him in spirit, in temper, in word and in deed. His person, his office, his character, his works of love and of mercy, his obedience unto death to the will of his Father and for the ransom of man, seizes his heart, animates his soul, energizes his character, and prompts him to imitate his example—to consecrate his heart, his person, his life, his influence, his all, to his honor and glory.

Now, as *philanthropy*—a word of heaven's own dialect and inspiration—supremely distinguished the Hero of our emancipation in his whole sojourn on earth, and was the efficient reason of his manifestation from the manger to the cross, every Christian participates more or less abundantly of that same self-sacrificing missionary spirit. As Jesus the Christ, the fruit of this philanthropy of God our Father, became a prophet, a missionary, an evangelist, so every Christian, every one born from above, is, in his new heart and spirit, disposed to be a missionary in some field, in some circle of humanity, great or small, either in his own person or in that of some kindred spirit, better gifted, better qualified, better fitted for the work than himself. Hence every true Christian will unite and co-operate in and by such better-qualified herald, and hold up his hands, cheer his heart, spirit him on and sustain him in his work of faith, his labors of love and patience of hope, and thereby become a partaker with him in full copartnery in all the avails of his mission, in all the conquests and triumphs of the gospel dispensed by him. In the book of God's remembrance every such co-operant is unquestionably enrolled. For illustration, suppose that one hundred persons, all citizens of Christ's kingdom, all heirs and joint partners of the grace of eternal life, should select a man of God, possessed of a missionary spirit, possessed of all the essential endowments for such an office and calling, and send him out into a certain field and sustain him in the work, agreeing with him that he will and shall consecrate his whole time, every day of the year, and exclusively consecrate every hour and every opportunity, to the duties of his mission; and suppose in said field in one year he should be the instrument of bringing into Christ's kingdom any definite number of genuine converts—for illustration say any number, fifty if you please; then conceive of their annual influence for any definite number of years, in the same ratios, and add to these the influence of these new converts in their respective spheres during life, and the influence of all their converts for one generation, and here pause. What a revenue of glory and honor and felicity! But this is a lame and imperfect view even in its brightest attitude before our minds. For, through the influence of these, in a century or two, what a multitude may enter the everlasting mansions! And these, too, all in a primary sense are the trophies of Him who gave birth to this institution. In this way the twelve apostles have credited to their labors and toils all the Christian family of God, past, present and future. But there is this never-to-be-forgotten fact, that while the glories of the apostles surround them forever, they interfere not with, they diminish not from, the glories and the honors of all who have, like them, in spirit, in labors, in toils and in sufferings, acted, suffered, toiled in their respective ages, generations and contemporaries. God can, in the riches of his grace, beautify, beatify and glorify them all, as if each and every one had been both the originator, the author and finisher of his own work! This, and this only, is the proper, the rational and the religious conception of that remedial institution, and of the grace of the Lord Jesus Christ. "He will give grace, and he will give glory;" and he is rich enough, and kind enough, and generous enough to give both grace and glory on a scale transcendentally sublime, surpassing all that eye has ever seen, ear ever heard, or heart ever conceived.

Who would not, then, that has ever in truth tasted that the Lord is gracious, that believes he will give grace to do his will and reward those that have done it, as though, without his aid or grace, they had done it—we ask who, with such a faith, would not, on such well-established premises, firm as the throne of God, enduring as the ages of eternity, give, devote and consecrate his whole personality—body, soul and spirit—to his service, honor and glory? Who would not bring his offerings into Christ's treasury? Who would not labor and toil for means to invest in such a cause, under such a leader, and for ends and consummations of glory, honor and immortality beyond all conception, and consequently beyond all expression.

And now, brethren beloved in the Lord, I ask you, in his name and for his sake—I importune and beseech you—that you act worthily of your faith and hope in God, worthily of your relations to him, worthily of your indebtedness to him, and most worthily of that rich grace bestowed upon you, and of that high hope cherished in your hearts, that, when he comes in all his glory, he may not be ashamed of you, nor you ashamed of yourselves in his presence. And to Him who redeemed us by the voluntary sacrifice of himself, be all glory and honor, all blessing and praise, now, henceforth and forever. Amen!

ADDRESS.

THE MISSIONARY CAUSE.

DELIVERED TO THE AMERICAN CHRISTIAN MISSIONARY SOCIETY,

CINCINNATI, OCTOBER, 1860.

"He that winneth souls is wise."—PROV. xi. 30.

THE missionary cause is older than the material universe. It was celebrated by Job—the oldest poet on the pages of time.

Jehovah challenges Job to answer him a few questions on the institutions of the universe. "Gird up now thy loins," said he; "and I will demand of thee a few responses. Where wast thou when I laid the foundations of the earth? Declare, if thou hast understanding. Who has fixed the measure thereof. Or who has stretched the line upon it? What are the foundations thereof? Who has laid the corner-stone thereof? When the morning stars sang together, and all the sons of God shouted for joy. Who shut up the sea with doors when it burst forth issuing from the womb of eternity?—when I made a cloud its garment, and thick darkness its swaddling band? I appointed its limits, saying, Thus far shalt thou come, but no farther; and here shall the pride of thy waves be stayed.

"Has the rain a father? Who has begotten the drops of the dew? Who was the mother of the ice? And the hoar-frost of heaven, who has begotten it? Can mortal man bind the bands of the Seven Stars, or loose the cords of Orion? Can he bring forth and commission the twelve signs of the Zodiac, or bind Arcturus with his seven sons?

"Knowest thou, O man, the missionaries of the starry heavens? Canst thou lift up thy voice to the clouds, that abundance of waters may cover thee? Canst thou command the lightnings, so that they may say to thee, Here we are? Who can number the clouds in wisdom? Or who can pour out the bottles of heaven upon the thirsty fields?"

If such be a single page in the volume of God's physical missionaries, what must be its contents could we, by the telescope of an angel, survey one single province of the universe of universes which occupy topless, bottomless, boundless space!

We have data in the Bible, and in the phenomena of the material universe, sufficient to authorize the assumption that *the missionary idea circumscribes and permeates the entire area of creation.*

Need we inquire into the meaning of a celestial title given to the tenantries of the heaven of heavens? But you all, my Christian brethren, know it. You anticipate me. The sweet poet of Israel told you long since, in his sixty-eighth ode, that the chariots of God are twenty thousand thousands of angels.*

And what is an angel but a *messenger*, a *missionary?* Hence the seven angels of the seven churches in Asia were seven missionaries, or messengers, *sent to* John in his exile; and *by these* John wrote letters to the seven congregations in Asia.

Figuratively, God makes the winds and lightnings his angels, his messengers of wrath or of mercy; as the case may be.

But we are a missionary society—a society assembled from all points of the compass—assembled, too, we hope, in the true missionary spirit, which is the spirit of Christianity in its primordial conception. God himself instituted it. Moses is the oldest missionary whose name is inscribed on the rolls of time. He was born in Egypt, three thousand four hundred and ninety-five years ago. His name is monumental. He was in his infancy lodged in a cradle of bulrushes. His sister, under God, was his guardian angel. Pharaoh's daughter heard his wailings as she enjoyed her sunny bath in the river Nile. He was then three months old. By a special providence, he was nourished in his own mother's bosom, in the very palace of his intended destroyer—"instructed, too, in all the wisdom of the Egyptians," as the heir-apparent of the royalty of Egypt.

When forty years old, moved by a Divine intimation, he undertook the emancipation of his own people. He married Zipporah, the daughter of Jethro, or Ruel, a prince and a priest of Midian, then residing in Arabia Petra. He became a shepherd, and kept his flocks in the

---

* This is an exact literal version of *Rebotayim alphey shenan.* The Targum says, "The chariots of God are two myriads—and two thousand angels draw them." A myriad is 10,000—two myriads 20,000. "To know this," Adam Clarke says, "we must die."

vicinity of Mount Horeb, or Sinai, for forty years more. On Mount Sinai the Lord was pleased to make him the redeemer of Israel from the yoke of Pharaoh. He retained his mental vigor for another forty years, and died, the most memorable, the most honorable and the most famous man in the world, at the age of one hundred and twenty years. His name and character will continue as long as the sun, as the purest of men and the greatest of lawgivers and princes inscribed on the rolls of time.

He was the first Divine missionary, and, if we except John the Baptist, he was the second in rank and character to the Lord Messiah himself.

Angels and missionaries are rudimentally but two names for the same officers. But of the Incarnate Word, God's only-begotten Son, he says, "Thou art my son, the beloved, in whom I delight." And he commands the world of humanity to hearken to him. He was, indeed, God's own special ambassador, invested with all power in heaven and on earth—a true, a real, an everlasting plenipotentiary, having vested in him all the rights of God and all the rights of man. And were not all the angels of heaven placed under him as his missionaries, sent forth to minister to the heirs of salvation?

His commission, given to the twelve apostles, is a splendid and glorious commission. Its preamble is wholly unprecedented—"*All authority in heaven and on earth* is given to me." In pursuance thereof, he gave commission to his apostles, saying, "Go, convert all the nations, immersing them into the name of the Father, and of the Son, and of the Holy Spirit; teaching them to observe all things whatever I have commanded you: and, lo, I am with you always, even to the end of the world." Angels, apostles and evangelists were placed under his command, and by him commissioned as his ambassadors to the world.

The missionary institution, we repeat, is older than Adam—older than our earth. It is coeval with the origin of angels.

Satan had been expelled from heaven before Adam was created. His assault upon our mother Eve, by an incarnation in the most subtle animal in Paradise, is positive proof of the intensity of his malignity to God and to man. He, too, has his missionaries in the whole area of humanity. Michael and his angels, or missionaries, are, and long have been, in conflict against the devil and his missionaries. The battle, in this our planet, is yet in progress, and therefore missionaries are in perpetual demand. Hence the necessity incumbent on us to carry on this warfare as loyal subjects of the Hero of our redemption.

The Christian armory is well supplied with all the weapons essential to the conflict. We need them all. "We wrestle not against flesh and blood, but against principalities, against powers, against the rulers of the darkness of this world, against wicked spirits in the regions of the air." Hence the need of having our "loins girded with the truth;" having on the breast-plate of righteousness, our feet shod with the preparation to publish the gospel of peace; taking the shield of faith, the helmet of salvation, and the sword of the Spirit, the word of God, always praying and making supplication for our fellow-missionaries and for all saints.

The missionary-fields are numerous and various. They are both domestic and foreign. The harvest is great in both. The laborers are still few, comparatively very few, in either of them.

Bethany College and Church are annually sending out laborers. But the supply is not a tithe of the demand. The Macedonians cry, "Come over and help us;" "Send us an evangelist;" "Send us missionaries;" "The fields are large, the people are desirous, anxious, to hear the original gospel. What can you do for us?" Nothing! Nothing! My brethren, ought this so to be?

Schools for the prophets are wanting. But there is a too general apathy or indifference on the subject. *We pray* to the Lord of the Harvest to send out reapers to gather it into his garner. But what *do we*, besides praying for it? Do we work for it? Suppose a farmer should pray to the Lord for an abundant harvest next year, and should never, in seed-time, turn over one furrow or scatter one handful of seed: what would we think of him? Would not his neighbors regard him as a monomaniac or a simpleton? And wherein does he excel such a one in wisdom or in prudence who prays to the Lord to send out reapers—missionaries, or evangelists—to gather a harvest of souls, when he himself never gives a dollar to a missionary, or the value of it, to enable him to go into the field? Can such a person be in earnest, or have one sincere desire in his heart to effect such an object or purpose? We must confess that we could have no faith either in his head or in his heart.

The heavenly missionaries require neither gold nor silver, neither food nor raiment. Not so the earthly missionaries. They themselves, their wives and children, demand both food and clothing, to say nothing of houses and furniture. Their present home is not

> "The gorgeous city, garnish'd like a bride,
> Where Christ for spouse expected is to pass,
> With walls of jasper compass'd on each side,
> And streets all paved with gold, more bright than glass."

If such were the missionary's home on earth, he might, indeed, labor gratuitously all the days of his life. In an humble cottage—rather an unsightly cabin—we sometimes see the wife of his youth, in garments quite as unsightly as those of her children, impatiently "waiting their sire's return, to climb his knees the envied kiss to share." But, when the supper-table is spread, what a beggarly account of almost empty plates and dishes! Whose soul would not sicken at such a sight? I have twice, if not thrice, in days gone by, when travelling on my early missionary tours—over not the poorest lands nor the poorest settlements, either—witnessed some such cases, and heard of more.

I was then my own missionary, with the consent, however, of one church. I desired to mingle with all classes of religious society, that I might personally and truthfully know, not the theories, but the facts and the actualities, of the Christian ministry and the so-called Christian public. I spent a considerable portion of my time during the years 1812, '13, '14, '15, '16, travelling throughout Western Virginia, Pennsylvania and Ohio.

I then spent seven years in reviewing my past studies, and in teaching the languages and the sciences—after which I extended my evangelical labors into other States and communities, that I might still more satisfactorily apprehend and appreciate the *status*, or the actual condition, of the nominally and professed religious or Christian world.

Having shortly after my baptism connected myself with the Baptist people, and attending their associations as often as I could, I became more and more penetrated with the conviction that theory had usurped the place of faith, and that, consequently, human institutions had been, more or less, substituted for the apostolic and the Divine.

During this period of investigation I had the pleasure of forming an intimate acquaintance with sundry Baptist ministers, East and West, as well as with the ministry of other denominations. Flattering prospects of usefulness on all sides began to expand before me and to inspire me with the hope of achieving a long-cherished object—doing some good in the advocacy of the primitive and apostolic gospel—having in the year 1820 a discussion on the subject of the first positive institution enacted by the Lord Messiah, and in A.D. 1823 another on the same subject—the former more especially on the *subject* and *action* of Christian baptism, the latter more emphatically on the *design* of that institution, though including the former two.

These discussions, more or less, embraced the rudimental elements of the Christian institution, and gave to the public a bold relief outline of the whole genius, spirit, letter and doctrine of the gospel.

Its missionary spirit, though not formally propounded, was yet indicated, in these discussions; because this institution was the terminus of the missionary work. It was a component element of the gospel, as clearly seen in the commission of the enthroned Messiah. Its preamble is the superlative fact of the whole Bible. We regret, indeed, that this most sublime preamble has been so much lost sight of even by the present living generation. If we ask when the church of Jesus Christ began, or when the reign of the Heavens commenced, the answer, in what is usually called Christendom, will make it either to be contemporaneous with the ministry of John the Harbinger, or with the birth of the Lord Jesus Christ. We will find one of these two opinions almost universally entertained. The Baptists are generally much attached to John the Baptist; the Pedobaptists, to the commencement of Christ's public ministry. John the Baptist was the first Christian missionary with a very considerable class of living Baptists; the birth of Christ is the most popular and orthodox theory at the respective meridians of Lutheranism, Calvinism, and Arminianism.

But, by the more intelligent, the resurrection, or the ascension of the Lord Jesus Christ, is generally regarded as the definite commencement of the Christian age or institution.

Give us Paul's or Peter's testimony, against that of all theologians, living or dead. Let us look at the facts.

Did not the Saviour teach his personal pupils, or disciples, to pray, "*Thy kingdom*"—more truthfully, "thy REIGN—*come*"*?* Does any king's reign or kingdom commence with his birth? still less with his death? Did not our Saviour himself, in person, decline the honors of a worldly or temporal prince? Did he not declare that his kingdom "is not of this world"? Did he not say that he was going hence, or leaving this world, to *receive* or to obtain a kingdom? And were not *the keys of the kingdom* first given to Peter to open, to announce it? And did he not, when in Jerusalem, on the first Pentecost, after the ascension of the Lord Jesus, make a public proclamation, saying, "*Let all the house of Israel know assuredly that God has made* (or constituted) the identical Jesus of Nazareth, the son of Mary, both the *Lord* and the *Christ*, or the *anointed Lord*"*?*

Do kings reign before they are crowned? before they are anointed? There was not a *Christian* church on earth, or any man called a *Christian*, until after the consecration and coronation of Jesus of Nazareth as *the Christ* of God.

The era of a son's birth was never, since the world began, the era of his reign or of the commencement of it. It is a strange fact, to me a wonderful fact, and, considering the age in which we live, an overwhelming fact, that we, as a community, are the only people on the checkered map of all Christendom, Greek, Roman, Anglican or Amecan, that preach and teach that the commonly called Christian era is not the era or the commencement of the Christian church or kingdom of the Lord Jesus *the Christ.*

The kingdom of the Christ could not antedate his coronation. Hence Peter, in announcing his coronation, after his ascension, proclaimed, saying, "Let all the house of Israel know assuredly that God *has made—touton ton Ieesoun*—the same, *the identical Jesus* whom you have crucified, *both Lord and Christ;*" or, in other words, has crowned him the legitimate *Lord of all.* Then indeed his reign began. Then was verified the oracle uttered by the royal bard of Israel, "*Jehovah said to my Jehovah*"—or, "the Lord said to my Lord,"—"Sit thou on my right hand till I make thy foes thy footstool."

Hence he could say, and did say, to his apostles, "All authority in the heavens and on the earth is given to me." In pursuance thereof, "Go you into all the world, proclaim the gospel to the whole creation; assuring them that every one who believes this proclamation and is immersed into the name of the Father, and of the Son, and of the Holy Spirit, shall be saved."

Here, then, the missionary field is declared to be the *whole world*—the *broad earth.* They were, as we are afterwards informed, to begin at the first capital in the land of Judea, then to proceed to Samaria, the capital of the ten tribes, and thence to the last domicile of man on earth.

There was, and there is still, in all this arrangement, a gracious and a glorious propriety.

The Jews had murdered the Messiah under the false charge of an impostor. Was it not, then, divinely grand and supremely glorious to make this awfully blood-stained capital the beginning, the fountain, of the gospel age and mission? Hence it was decreed that all the earth should be the parish, and all the nations and languages of earth the objects, and millions of them the subjects, of the redeeming grace and tender mercies of our Saviour and our God.

What an extended and still extending area is the missionary field! There are the four mighty realms of Pagandom, of Papaldom, of Mohammedandom and of ecclesiastic Sectariandom. These are, one and all, essentially and constitutionally, more or less, not of the apostolic Christiandom.

The divinely-inspired constitution of the church contains only *seven* articles. These are the seven hills, not of Rome, but of the true Zion of Israel's God. Paul's summary of them is found in the following words:—"*One body, one spirit, one hope, one Lord, one faith, one baptism, and one God and Father of all.*"

The clear perception, the grateful reception, the cordial entertainment of these seven divinely constructed and instituted pillars, are the alone sufficient, and the all-sufficient, foundation—the indestructible basis—of Christ's kingdom on this earth, and of man's spiritual and eternal salvation in the full enjoyment of himself, his Creator, his Redeemer, and the whole universe of spiritual intelligence through all the circles and the cycles of an infinite, an everlasting future of being and of blessedness. May we not say—

> "A hope so great and so divine
> May trials well endure,
> And purify our souls from sin,
> As Christ himself is pure"?

The missionary spirit is, indeed, an emanation of the whole Godhead. God the Father sent his Son, his only-begotten Son, into our world. The Son sent the Holy Spirit to bear witness through his twelve missionaries, the consecrated and Heaven-inspired apostles. They proclaimed the glad tidings of great joy to all people—to the Jews, to the Samaritans, to the Gentiles, of all nations, kindreds and tongues. They gave in solemn charge to others to sound out and to proclaim the glad tidings of great joy to all people. And need we ask, is not the Christian church itself, in its own institution and constitution, virtually and essentially a *missionary institution?* Does not Paul formally state to the Thessalonians in his first epistle that from them sounded out the word of the Lord not only in Macedonia and in Achaia, but in every place?

No man can really or truthfully enjoy the spiritual, the soul-stirring, the heart-reviving honors and felicities of the Christian institution and kingdom, who does not intelligently, cordially and efficiently espouse the missionary cause.

In other words, he must feel, he must have compassion *for* his fellow-man; and, still further, he must practically sympathize *with* him in communicating to his spiritual necessities as well as to his physical wants and infirmities. The true ideal of all perfection—our blessed and blissful Redeemer—went about continually doing good—to both the souls and the bodies of his fellow-men; healing all that were, in body, soul or spirit, oppressed by Satan, the enemy of God and of man.

To follow his example is the grand climax of humanity. It is not necessary to this end that he should occupy the pulpit. There are, as we conceive, myriads of Christian men in the private walks of life, who never aspired to the "sacred desk," that will far outshine, in eternal glory and blessedness, hosts of the reverend, the boasted and the boastful right reverend occupants of the sacred desks of this our day and generation.

But Solomon has furnished our motto:—"*He that winneth*" or *taketh* "*souls is wise.*" (Prov. xi. 30.) Was he not the wisest of men, the most potent and the richest of kings, that ever lived? He had, therefore, all the means and facilities of acquiring what we call *knowledge*—the knowledge of men and things; and, consequently, the *value* of men and things was legitimately within the *area* of his understanding; or, in this case, we might prefer to say, with all propriety, within the area of his comprehension.

Need I say that comprehension incomparably transcends apprehension? Simpletons may apprehend, but only wise men can comprehend any thing. Solomon's rare gift was, that both his apprehension and his comprehension transcended those of all other men, and gave him a perspicacity and promptitude of decision never before or since possessed by any man. His oracles, indeed, were the oracles of God. But God especially gave to him a power and opportunity of making one grand experiment and development for the benefit of his living contemporaries, and of all posterity, to whom God presents his biography, his Proverbs and his Ecclesiastes.

"The *winning of souls*" is, therefore, the richest and best business, trade or calling, according to Solomon, ever undertaken or prosecuted by mortal man. Paul was fully aware of this, and therefore had always in his eye a "triple crown"—"a crown of righteousness," a "crown of life," a "crown of glory." And even in this life he had "a crown of rejoicing," in prospect of an exceeding and eternal weight of glory, imperishable in the heavens. May it not, on such premises, be well and truthfully said, "Godliness is profitable in all respects, having promise of the life that now is, and also of that which is to come"?

There is, too, a present reward, a present pleasure, a present joy and peace which the wisdom, and the riches, and the dignity, and the glory, and the honors of this world never did, never can, and consequently never will, confer on its most devoted and persevering votaries.

There is, indeed, a lawful and an honorable covetousness, which any and every Christian, man and woman, may cultivate and cherish. Dr. Young had a very just conception of it. He said,—

> "Thou shalt not covet, is a wise command,
> But bounded by the wealth the sun surveys;
> Look further, that command stands quite reversed,
> And avarice is a virtue most divine."

Paul himself justifies the poetic license, when he says, "Covet earnestly the best gifts."

The best gifts in his horizon, however, were those which, when duly cultivated and employed, confer the greatest amount of profit and felicity upon others. We should, indeed, desire, even covet, the means and the opportunities of beatifying and aggrandizing one another with the true riches, the honors and the dignities that appertain to the spiritual, the heavenly and the eternal inheritance.

But we need not propound to your consideration or inquiry the claims—the paramount, the transcendent claims—which our enjoyment of the gospel and its soul-cheering, soul-animating, soul-enrapturing influences present to us as arguments and motives to extend and to animate its proclamation by every instrumentality and means which we can legitimately employ, to present it in all its attractions and claims upon the understanding, the conscience and the affections of our contemporaries, in our own country and in all others, as far as our most gracious and bountiful Benefactor affords the means and the opportunities of co-operating with him, in the rescue and recovery of our fellow-men, who, without such means and efforts, must forever perish, as aliens and enemies, in heart and in life, to God and to his divinely-commissioned ambassador, the glorious Messiah.

Brethren, we have another argument for you, of great moral and evangelical power. It is, indeed, rather invidious in the esteem of many of our contemporaries. It is, with some of them at least, a species of arrogance on our part to assert it, and still more to urge it on their attention. But, nevertheless, it is upon us a paramount duty. We plead for the original apostolic gospel and its positive institutions. If the great apostles Peter and Paul—the former to the Jews and the latter to the Gentiles—announced the true gospel of the grace of God, shall we hesitate a moment on the propriety and the necessity, divinely imposed upon us, of preaching the same gospel which they preached, and in advocating the same institutions which they established, under the plenary inspiration and direction of the Holy Spirit? Can we improve upon their institutions and enactments? What means that singular imperative enunciated by the evangelical prophet Isaiah,

(Isa. viii.,) "*Bind up the testimony, seal the law among my disciples*"? What were its antecedents? Hearken! The prophet had just foretold. He, the subject of this oracle, viz. "THE DESIRE OF ALL NATIONS," was coming to be a sanctuary; but not a sanctuary alone, but for a stone of stumbling and a rock of offence [as at this day] to both the houses of Israel—for a gin and for a snare to the inhabitants of Jerusalem.

He adds, "And many among them shall stumble and fall, and be broken, and be snared, and be taken;" and then immediately adds, "Bind up the testimony, and seal the law among my disciples;" and still further, to command the testimony and to guard it, he adds, "If they speak not according to this word, it is because there is no light in them."

It is the glory, the honor and the felicity of the Christian church to be the light of the world, the salt of the earth, and the life everlasting to multitudes "dead in trespasses and in sins." The church is the bride, her Saviour is the bridegroom, and, therefore, their offspring is of God.

The church, therefore, of right is, and ought to be, a great missionary society. Her parish is the whole earth, from sea to sea, and from the Euphrates to the last domicile of man.

But the crowning and consummating argument of the missionary cause has not been fully presented. There is but one word, in the languages of earth, that fully indicates it. And that word indicates neither less nor more than what is represented—literally, exactly, perspicuously represented—by the word *philanthropy*. But this being a Greek word needs, perhaps, in some cases, an exact definition. And to make it memorable we will preface it with the statement of the fact that this word is found but *twice* in the Greek original New Testament, (Acts xxviii. 2, and Titus iii. 4.) In the first passage this word is, in the common version, translated "*kindness*," and in the second, "*love toward man*." Literally and exactly, it signifies *the love of man*, objectively; but, more fully expressed, *the love of one to another*.

The love of God to man is one form of philanthropy; *the love of angels to man* is another form of philanthropy; and *the love of man to man*, as such, is the true philanthropy of the law. It is not the love of one man to another man, because of favors received from him: this is only gratitude. It is not the love of one man to another man, because of a common country: this is mere patriotism. It is not the love of man to man, because of a common ancestry: this is mere natural affection. But it is the love of man to man, merely because he is *a man*. This is pure philanthropy. Such was the love of God to man as exhibited in the gift of his dearly beloved Son as a sin-offering for him. This is the name which the inspired writers of the New Testament give it. So Paul uses it, Titus iii. and iv. It should have been translated, "After that the kindness and *philanthropy of God our Saviour* appeared." Again, Acts xxviii. 2, "The barbarous people of the Island of Melita showed us no little philanthropy."* "They kindled a fire for us on their island, because of the impending rain and the cold."

There are, indeed, many forms and demonstrations of philanthropy. For one good man another good man might presume to die. But the philanthropy of God to man incomparably transcends all other forms of philanthropy known on earth or reported from heaven.

While we were sinners, in positive and actual rebellion against our Father and our God, he freely gave up his only begotten and dearly beloved Son as a sin-offering for us, and laid upon him, or placed to his account, the sin, the aggregate sin, of the world. He became in the hand of his Father and our Father a sin-offering for us. He took upon himself, and his Father "laid upon him, the iniquity of us all." Was ever love like this? Angels of all ranks, spirits of all capacities, still contemplate it with increasing wonder and delight.

This, the gospel message, is to be announced to all the world, to men of every nation under heaven. And this, too, with the promise of the forgiveness of sins and of a life everlasting in the heavens, to every one who will cordially accept and obey it.

This is, in brief, the gospel message. The mission and commission of the Lord Jesus Christ gave birth and being to all evangelical missionary institutions. Not based on this, they are wholly worthless. But based on this, they are under the shield and auspices of the Lord God Almighty.

In this age of partyism, we have denominational theories, feelings, sympathies, operations, and co-operations. All these are, more or less, refined forms of selfishness. And, pray, what is selfishness? The insulation or the isolation of our views, feelings, motives, interests, actions,—having as the chief end and object of life our own individual ease, honor, dignity, glory, happiness. This is a highly civilized, aggrandized, glorified selfishness. But there is in it not one element of magnanimity, nobility, or philanthropy. In the sight of God it is sheer selfishness, without the semblance of either piety or humanity, in their legitimate currency and import.

* So we have always translated this term, in this passage.

The truth is, if love blinds the eyes of its subject, self-love, more than any other passion, effectually blinds the eyes of the mere worldling. He never sees himself at the true and proper angle of vision. Without piety and humanity, there is, in fact, no true, real magnanimity.

We are met here, not as the Episcopal, the Presbyterian, the Congregational, the Methodist or the Baptist Missionary Society, but the *Christian* Missionary Society. The Lord's prime missionaries were properly called *apostles*. They were educated, trained and commissioned by himself in person. They had seven points differential from all other functionaries. These were:—

1st. They should have seen and heard and known the Lord Jesus Christ himself in person.

2d. They should have been immediately called and chosen to that office by himself.

3d. Infallible inspiration was an essential requisite to the exercise of that office.

4th. The power of working miracles was an indispensable qualification to the full discharge of the duties of that office.

5th. To them was specially given the power of imparting spiritual gifts and miraculous powers to others.

6th. Their mission was universal: the whole world was the field of their operations.

7th. They exercised, while they lived, a superintendence over all the churches planted by their instrumentality; and their authority was paramount to that of all other functionaries.

They were, to speak in modern style, ambassadors of the Lord Jesus Christ; and received their commission from himself in person.

They could not, therefore, themselves, by any possibility, impart or transfer their office to others.

We have now, therefore, but three official personages in the Christian church. These are evangelists, pastors or bishops, and deacons.

The missions of this universe incomparably transcend all human conception; and still more incomprehensible are the missionaries requisite to the completion and perfection of these missions.

A Christian community without missions and missionaries would, indeed, be a solecism in creation, and a gross deviation from the order, the economy and the government of the universe.

And when we gravely ponder upon the magnificence of the empire of the author and founder of the Christian kingdom and its august sovereign, the Lord our King, and his resources as monarch of all creation—Lord of all instrumentalities, possessing all authority in the heavens above us, under us and around us; and in the still small voice of his claims asking our aid and co-operation with him, honoring us with a copartnery with himself in the riches and the glories and the honors of his august position, and his boundless empire of true riches, true honors, true dignities, true grandeur and magnificence—in sitting down with him on his throne and participating with him in the glory, the honor and the immortality of his everlasting empire—I ask, shall we, will we, dare we, withhold from him our cordial aid, our liberal contributions, out of the abundance of all good things which he has, in his liberality, conferred upon us? Let your response, my beloved brethren, be to him, and not to me, your humble brother.

ADDRESS

TO THE

BIBLE UNION CONVENTION.

HELD AT MEMPHIS, TENNESSEE, APRIL 2, 1852.

"God said, Let there be light, and light was."—GEN. i. 3.

MEN, BRETHREN AND FATHERS:—

This was the first speech ever made within our universe. It is, indeed, the most sublime and potent speech ever made. It is, however, but the expression of an intelligent omnipotent volition. It was pregnant with all the elements of a material creation. It was a beautiful portraiture of its author, prospective of all the developments of creation, providence and redemption. It was a Bible in miniature, and future glory in embryo. We, therefore, place it as the motto of an address upon the greatest question and work of our age—*Shall we have the light of life as God created it?*

All was chaos before God uttered this oracle. All was order, beauty and life when he ended this discourse. Creation was but a sermon—a speech. Its exordium was light, and its peroration man. Redemption, too, was, in perspective, shown in the first utterance that broke the silence of eternity. Hence its author is called "THE WORD OF GOD"—"*the light and the life of man.*" Hence, too, in its first enunciation we are carried back to this primordial oracle, "In the beginning was the *Word*, and the *Word* was with God, and *the Word was God.* The same was in the beginning with God. All things were created by him, and without him was not any thing made that was made. In him was life, and the life was the light of men." True, "this light" yet "shines in darkness, and the darkness comprehendeth it not." Under the same Divine imagery, at the end of the volume, he is called "The Alpha and the Omega, the Beginning and the End, the First and the Last." "All things were created by him, and for him; and he is before all things, and by him all things subsist." The "Word became incarnate, and dwelt" amongst men, and men "beheld his glory"—the Divine image of the invisible Jehovah—"the glory as of an only-begotten of the Father, full of grace and truth."

The volume emphatically called THE BIBLE spans the arch of time. In its commencement it rests upon an eternity to us past, and in its termination upon an eternity to us future. But God himself in Hebrew is called "*The Eternities* of Israel," and time is but a continued creation of the spiritual tenantry of the Eternities of Israel, commencing in the first and terminating in the last. This heaven-descended volume is, therefore, the chart of the interval that lies between the heaven that is past and the heaven that is to come. It delineates the path of life, and, in harmony with "the divinity that stirs within us," it points out an hereafter and intimates an eternity to man. How important, then, that we have it in our own language, as they had who first received it from the hand of God! As the golden cherubim that overshadowed the propitiatory, while guarding the written word of God with one eye directed to the throne of glory and with one immovably fixed on the printed tablets of the Divine constitution, so ought we to guard the sacred oracles committed to the church of Christ, and preserve them in their primeval purity and integrity.

In full conviction and assurance of these preliminary statements, and of the eternal truth and value of the Divine oracles, and of the obligations therein contained and resting upon the church of Christ to translate them into all languages and to give them to the human race, I would very respectfully submit to your consideration and for your adoption the following resolution—

Resolved, That it is a paramount duty of the Christian Church of the nineteenth century to give to the present age, in our own vernacular, a perspicuous, exact and faithful version of the living oracles of God, as we find them in the Hebrew and Greek originals of inspired prophets, apostles and evangelists.

In submitting to your consideration and for your adoption this resolution, it is assumed that we have not now extant, in our own language, publicly accredited, such a version as that proposed in the resolution which I have at present the honor to submit to your most grave consideration. And is not this a generally, nay, a universally conceded fact, throughout the length and breadth of Protestant Christendom? Is there a single sect, party or denomination, known to history or to any one of us, which in its aggregate, or even in a respectable minority of its most intelligent communion, is fully satisfied that it has in its possession such a translation of either the Jewish or Christian Scriptures? Nay, is there a learned rabbi, doctor or minister of any denomination that can or would, *ex animo*, affirm the conviction that we have such a version in public use? If any one doubt it, let him assume the task—the herculean task—of examining the popular commentaries and versions, from those of Luther, Beza, Erasmus, or that of Rheims, A.D. 1582, down to that of Dr. Boothroyd, of 1836, patronized, or occasionally used, by our religious denominations, Romanists and Protestants; and if he does not find objections to, and emendations of, each and every one of them, proposed by hundreds and by thousands, I will concede the position assumed.

Dr. George Campbell suggests some four hundred and fifty emendations in the single testimony or gospel of the Apostle Matthew, and Dr. MacKnight nearly as many in his translation of two of Paul's Epistles—viz. that to the Romans and that to the Hebrews. And what shall we say of Drs. Whitby, Benson, Doddridge, D'Oyly and Mant, Gill, Pierce, Thomas Scott, Taylor of Norwich, Philosopher Locke, Dr. Boothroyd, Professor M. Stuart and Secretary Thompson? From all these, and others besides, we have imported from *Pater-Noster Row*, London, the Holy Bible with its *twenty thousand emendations!* In the United States, these, and many others not named, are found, not only in our public libraries, but in many of our private libraries. Indeed, these all stand on my own shelves, with several others not named, of equal value and importance.

In this country we are happy to find no by-law-established version of Old Testament or New. We voluntarily use that which was introduced by King James, merely because it is in fashion, and by law of Protestant Britain appointed to be read in all the churches of its establishment. We have, indeed, been favored with one volume from the British press, called the English Hexapla, exhibiting six important versions of the New Testament Scriptures—viz. that of Wickliffe, of A.D. 1380; Tindal's, of 1534; Cranmer's, (falsely so called,) of 1539; the Geneva, of 1557; the Rheims, or the English College of Rheims, 1582; and that of James, of 1611. These, with one exception, were made within seventy-seven years—the lifetime of one man.

We have also the Polyglot *Biblia Sacra*, containing the Greek and Hebrew originals, with the Latin Vulgate, German, English, French, Spanish and Italian versions, under the supervision of Dr. Samuel Lee, Professor of the Hebrew Language at Cambridge, England, Doctor of Divinity, and honorary member of all the great literary societies in

Britain and on the Continent of Europe. This is the greatest and best offering of the press of the nineteenth century—indeed, of any century since the first of the Christian age. We are, therefore, better furnished with the aids and materials for an improved and correct version than at any former period in the history of Christianity.

If, in the judgment of Paul, the greatest honor and advantage bestowed upon the Jews was that "to them were committed the oracles of God," is it not our greatest privilege and honor to have the oracles of God, just as he spoke them, committed to us, not only for ourselves, but for our children and our contemporaries in all the earth?

The Jews' religion possessed no proselyting spirit or precept. "He showed his statutes unto Jacob, and his testimonies to Israel: he has not dealt so with any other nation; and as for his judgments, they have not known them."

The Jews sent no missionaries abroad. There was no missionary spirit infused into their religion. There was no commission given to the patriarchs or the Jews, none to Judah or to Levi, "to go into all the world" and preach and teach to other nations the statutes and the judgments, the precepts and the promises, that God gave to them.

They needed no translators, no verbal expositors, for themselves. Their dispensation was circumscribed by the flesh, and the language of Abraham had no spirit of extension in it; and therefore Levi was commissioned "to teach Jacob God's judgments; to make Israel know his laws; to place incense before God, and holocausts, or whole burnt-offerings, upon his altar." Beyond this they had no obligation or mission.

But God has been to us much more gracious than to Israel, according to the flesh. He has given to us a better constitution of grace—a better covenant, established upon better promises. He has called us to a noble work, and given to us a large mission. He has committed to us the Christian oracles, with authority to announce them to the whole human race.

But they have come to us in a translation, and in an imperfect translation, by no means equal, in clearness and force, to the original. He has, however, also given to us the originals; but only a few can read them, and of that few all read them after having been taught the vernacular Scriptures. They read the originals through the spectacles of their vernacular versions, and, superadded to this, through a ready-made theology, imparted to them by early education and high authority—parental or ministerial, or both. It has become part and parcel of their individuality. Few can ever divest themselves of it. It is harder, far, to unlearn than to learn—to divest ourselves of old errors than to acquire new truths. Still, it is our duty, as it is our safety and our honor, to take the living oracles, and, with an unveiled face, an unblenching eye and an honest heart, to learn and study what God has spoken to us.

To the Christian church are committed the oracles of Christ, as to the Jewish church were formerly committed the oracles of God. The original Scriptures were given in solemn charge to the Jewish people, that nothing was to be added to them or subtracted from them. They were to preserve and teach them to their children through all generations.

A similar ordinance in the New Testament, with the most solemn sanctions, gives to the Christian church the keeping of the Christian Scriptures. If any one add to them, God will inflict upon him all the maledictions found in the holy volume. If any one subtract from them, God will take away from him all the Christian birthrights promised in them, and consign him to perdition.

But they were committed to both people in their own native language, directly from those persons to whom God had given them in charge. Were they, then, to translate them into other languages? This question, though not propounded in the very words of the book, and, consequently, not formally answered, is, nevertheless, clearly intimated, and most satisfactorily disposed of, in the Christian Scriptures. To its consideration and disposal we are now, in the providence of God, especially called; and it is our special duty on the present occasion to investigate the subject and ascertain our duties and privileges on all the premises exhibited in the Christian records.

On such questions and occasions as the present, it is essential to success that we entertain and cherish clear, enlarged and lofty conceptions of the whole subject and object of Divine revelation, and that we duly appreciate the times and circumstances in the midst of which our lot has been cast.

The Bible, in its vast and glorious amplitude and object, is the book of life—the charter of immortality to man. It is, in its manifold developments and details, most worthy of God to be both the author and the subject of it, and of man to be both its theme and its object, in the awful grandeur of his origin, relations and destiny. Every thing superlatively interesting to man, with respect to the past, the present and the future of his being and of his well-being, constitutes the all-engrossing theme and intention of the volume. It follows, therefore, that its faithful preservation and transmission from age to age, and from nation to nation, is, and ought to be, the paramount duty and concern of every one who believes its Divine authenticity and realizes its transcendent value. We shall, therefore, endeavor to ascertain our immediate duty with regard to an improved translation of it in our own language and country at the present time.

To this end, it is also essential that we appreciate and comprehend the character and the spirit of our own age, and the actual condition of the Christian profession in our own country, and, indeed, in our own language, wherever spoken, at home or abroad. It is almost as difficult to appreciate our own times—the spirit and the progress of our own age—as it is to see ourselves, either as others see us, or as we really are.

And what is the actual condition of the present church militant? I mean of the whole Christian profession—not within the Popedom nor in the Patriarchdom, but in the European and American Protestantdom. Is it not emphatically in a politico-heretico belligerent state? There is, indeed, much said in praise of a *catholic* spirit, and much said against a narrow, contracted, sectarian, bigoted spirit. But, alas! how many praise the life which they never dare to lead! If all who praise truth, virtue, temperance, charity, practised those virtues, what a happy world—what a triumphant church—we should have! Too much credit, as well as too much credulity, has ruined many a man. It has, alas! too often bankrupted and ruined church and state.

There cannot be an honest league between truth and error. A smiling face over a frowning heart is an abomination to earth and heaven. True charity "rejoices not in iniquity, but rejoices in the truth." There can be no compromise between God's truth and man's error. "Let God be true," as Paul said, "though it should make every man a liar"—no matter on whom the falsehood lies. We never can heal the wounds of sectarianism but by the healing unction of heaven-descended truth. But the truth must ever be spoken in its own spirit, which is the spirit of love and of a sound mind.

But what are the bearings of these aphorisms upon the subject of a faithful translation of the Christian Scriptures? Much, very much; as we hope the sequel may show. We desire—*I mean the true church of Christ desires*—to know the whole truth—the mind and will of God.

An apostate church never did, never can, never will, desire such a version. The most apostate church on earth often prays in Latin, and glories in a Roman service. I would to God that she sinned only in Latin! But she glories in the *Roman* tongue, and in the *Roman* city, because of her *Roman* spirit, her *Roman* head and her *Roman* hierarchy. Like the Roman Cæsar, she has her *pontifex maximus*, her *imperator universus*, and her *Jupiter tonans*.

That all men who love truth, and especially Bible truth, desire to come to the light, or to have the light brought to them, is as clearly an historical as it is a philosophical fact. It is well established in the history of translations. Were I to assert dogmatically that truth and light are cognate, I would stake my reputation on the fact that every lover of truth loves light. The Saviour himself suggests to us this idea, in saying, "He that doeth truth cometh to the light, that his deeds may be made manifest that they are wrought in God." Error or falsehood, and darkness, are also akin. They are of cognate pedigree. Hence said the Great Teacher, "He that does evil hates the light;" and men whose deeds are evil "come not to the light, lest their deeds should be reproved," or made manifest.

But I have said that this is an historical fact, and amply demonstrated and sustained by a reference to the history of Bible-translations. From the era of Protestantism till now, Protestants, in the ratio of their Protestant sincerity, or true Protestantism, have been active, zealous and forward in the great work of translating the Hebrew and Greek Scriptures into the vulgar tongues.

The Roman church has been equally distinguished for her opposition to popular versions, or to translations made in the language of the common people. So have those Protestants that have borrowed freely from Papal Rome. If Protestant Reformers have been well sustained in alleging that there is but a paper wall between certain Protestant denominations and the Papal institutions, then are we sustained in affirming that those most opposed to popular versions are more akin to the Popedom than those who advocate them. In proof of these views and facts I appeal to the history of all the versions into the English language from the Reformation down to the present time.

I will not limit my proofs to the English language. I will challenge an investigation of the facts of history from the dark ages of Papal absolutism down to the present day. Of course, we begin with Luther and the era of Protestantism, A.D. 1534. His version, printed A.D. 1530, made directly from the Hebrew and Greek, gave rise to ten other Protestant versions—viz. the Lower Saxon, in 1533; the Pomeranian, in 1588; the Danish, in 1550; the Icelandic, in 1584; the Swedish, in 1541; the Dutch, in 1560; the Finnish, in 1644; the Livonian, in 1689, (sometimes called the Lettish version;) the Sorabic or Wendish, in 1728; and the Lithuanian, in 1735. During the period in which these eleven Protestant versions appeared, the Romanists, to quiet their population, were obliged to issue three versions, not one of which was made from the original tongues. They were rather translations of the Vulgate than of the Hebrew or Greek originals. The German laity of the Roman community read them with considerable avidity, "notwithstanding the fulminations of the Papal See against them."

From Germany and the Continent we pass over the Channel into the British Isles. A few partial versions into the Saxon language were made before the first English version, which appeared in 1290. Of course, none of these were printed.

Wickliffe's, from the Vulgate, appeared in 1380. But in 1408 the Archbishop Arundel, in a convocation held at Oxford, decreed "that no one thereafter should translate any text of Holy Scripture into English by way of a book or tract; and that no book of this kind should be read that was composed in the time of Wickliffe or since his death." Some, however, read, and were put to death.

The immortal Tindal about this time fled to Antwerp, in Flanders, and in 1526 printed his English version of the New Testament, from the Greek original. Sundry editions of it were, in a few years, printed and scattered over the Continent, and not a few of them found their way even into England.

But, strange to tell, an edition of Tindal's version, under the direction and supervision of his convert, John Rogers, printed abroad, was introduced into England in 1537, and that, too, with the consent of King Henry VIII., and that of his vicegerent Cromwell, and that, too, of his archbishop Thomas Cranmer—all of whom had a short time before most violently opposed it. The history of this change is too long to tell; but it has never ceased to be a wonder to all who know it, and to be regarded as a very singular and special providence.

Banished from his native land fourteen years before, and finally murdered, too, for his translation, yet, by royal authority, that same version is introduced into England under the auspices of the crown and the mitre of the realm!

Next year, Grafton, who had published the first edition of Tindal's Bible imported into England, sets about another edition in Paris, and, to correct the press, takes with him Coverdale—under the protection, too, of Henry VIII. But an order from the Inquisition, dated December 17, 1538, under the auspices of the Pope and the French King Francis, seizes a portion of the edition, almost out of the press, which compelled the publisher to flee to England, where, under the protection of Henry VIII., it was completed, and issued in April, 1539. Next year (1540) another edition, under the auspices of Cranmer, was issued from the English press. Thus the first English version of Tindal's Bible was wholly imported into England in 1537. A second, redeemed from the Inquisition, mostly printed in Paris and finished in London, in 1539, succeeded it. The third edition was wholly printed in England; and after this the editions of 1540 and 1541 were issued under the auspices of Cranmer himself. From that time England became the land of Bibles.

History is philosophy teaching by example. And here we must date the true commencement of England's glory amongst the nations of the earth. She, of all the nations of Europe, thus becomes emphatically the land of Bibles and of freedom. So true it is that where the Spirit of the Lord is there is liberty, and where the Bible, in the vernacular of any people, is much read and much pondered upon, there the Spirit of the Lord exerts a mighty influence. "Where no vision is, the people perish," and are the easy prey of aspiring demagogues and haughty pontiffs.

From a careful review of the history of new versions, in all past time, we are compelled to the conclusion that their authors, friends and advocates have generally been the lovers of truth and of the God of truth; whereas their opponents have as uniformly been mere temporizers, carnal and secular, lovers of place, of person and office more than lovers of God. I have said "generally," but was about to say "universally." In this view I am sustained by the judgment and the practice of those we now call orthodox. What are generally now called orthodox versions were, without an exception known to me, got up in despite of more popular, more worldly and more secular establishments. This is a very instructive fact. We may, indeed, concede that some vain, secular errorist or demagogue may have, from sinister motives, attempted to carry some favorite dogma by an effort at a new version of some passage or book, or even of the whole volume; but how soon have these fallen still-born from the pen or the press and vanished from the world! This, or some such concession, is essential to a general law: otherwise we might be in danger of affirming it universal, and thereby endanger the cause of truth.

I am glad, however, to assert, with a strong emphasis, that I have the concessions of all our would-be recognized orthodox partisan contemporaries in favor of my position. They have recently become unusually eloquent in their laudations of the present approved version of King James. I wonder if they have read the whole history of that version. Some seem to think that King James himself, or his Government, or his bishops, have made it, out and out. So far from this, it fought its way, every inch, from the head and heart and conscience of Wickliffe, Tindal, Luther, Beza, Frythe, Barnes, Poyntz, and even Erasmus, &c., and scores of co-operants in contributions of learning, books, money, protection and prayer, before it attracted the smiles and approval of bishops, courtiers and princes. Printers, paper-manufacturers and bookbinders are as much entitled to our thanks for King James's version as many of those worshipful persons who are said and believed, "by the grace of God," to have given to us our English Bible. Instruments they were, willing or unwilling, meritorious or unmeritorious, in this great work. But it originated not with, and proceeded not from, them. *It was individual piety, learning, zeal, enterprise, that gave to us our present English Bible.* There is scarcely amongst us a living man who can tell how this sacred volume, the King James's Bible, revised and re-revised, has come down to us. The best-read living man on this subject, Christopher Anderson, of Edinburgh, in his two octavos on the English Bible, has not told, because he could not tell, the whole story. And yet his history of it is by far the best ever printed. He was conscientiously constrained to affirm the melancholy fact, "That a mighty phalanx of talent, policy and power has been firmly arrayed against the introduction of Divine truth in our native tongue." (Vol. i. p. 7.) There are now one hundred and fifty versions of the Bible extant in the living tongues of earth; and yet, strange and wonderful to relate, more copies in the English language are called for than in the languages of all other nations put together! This is the glory, the chief glory, of England. She has colonized America, Africa, Asia, New Holland, New Zealand, and the bosom of the Pacific. While I speak these words, the English Bible is being read from the rising to the setting sun. "Not one hour of the twenty-four, not one round of the minute-hand of the dial, is allowed to pass, in which, on some portion of the surface of the globe, the air is not filled *with accents that are ours.* Every English Christian, in this one grand fact, may rejoice that his Bible, at this moment, is the only version in existence on which *the sun never sets.*"

This caps the climax of English glory. Her English version is every moment being read, from the banks of the Thames to the banks of the Ottawa and the St. Lawrence, and thence to the banks of the Ganges, to Sidney, Port Philip and Hobarttown. It girdles the whole earth, and is destined to be the enduring bond of its nations. How important, then, that the English Bible should be a pure, perspicuous, precise and faithful expression of every idea, of every precept, of every promise, of every institution, of the inspired originals! It is inevitable, from the signs of the times, from the openings of Divine Providence—to say nothing of the prophecies fulfilled, fulfilling, and yet to be fulfilled—that the English Protestant Bible is to mould, form, and, more or less, to characterize all the new versions in all the missionary-fields on the already-tenanted earth. This is far more probable than some of the events that have actually occurred in the present day—incomparably more probable than that an improved version of the New Testament, got up and published by your humble speaker, should in the short period of twenty-five years have passed through six editions, and be now read by even a few individuals residing in Asia, Africa, Europe and America. This is the Lord's doing, and wondrous in our eyes!

The language of a people is not only an index of their intellectual calibre, but also an exponent of their moral and political power amongst their contemporaries. It is, indeed, the vehicle of all their attainments in those arts and sciences which have given them a standing and an influence amongst their contemporaries at home and abroad, and an elevation in the scale of civilization. Judging from this acknowledged fact, it must be admitted that, as the English people stand at the top of the ladder of modern civilization, their mind, their language and their religion must have a paramount influence upon all the nations and people of the globe. Need I ask, then, at this stand-point in the centre of this immense horizon, who can compute the influence of our best efforts to exhibit the true sense and meaning of the Hebrew and Greek oracles of God, in that pervading and continually extending language to which God, in his providence and moral government, has already vouchsafed such a preponderating influence in the world?

But it may be asked, *What can the "Bible Union" accomplish in this work?* So ask our contemporary Baptist and Pedobaptist brethren. However uncongenial to their taste or to our own, I cannot but associate their attitude and port and bearing with those of the too orthodox Jews in the days of Ezra and Nehemiah, which, together, give us the history of one century of their nation. In those days they had no priest, with "*Urim and Thummim.*" We have one who has passed into the heavens, and who has the "*Urim and the Thummim*" in all their Divine potency. They had also with them only Zerubbabel and Joshua, as commanders-in-chief. But we have the Lord of hosts. The adversaries of Judah and Benjamin proposed to co-operate with them in rebuilding the Temple and in restoring the ancient order of things. But the paternal chiefs, along with Joshua and Zerubbabel, refused their proffered aid. The consequence was, they became the enemies of Israel and their cause. So the work was abandoned for some sixteen years, till the second year of Darius, King of Persia.

The prophets Haggai and Zachariah were then sent to encourage and aid this remnant of Israel. Darius, on searching the records of the government, gave a decree in their favor, and they went to work. Every thing then went on prosperously, and the house of the Lord was finished. But the walls and palaces of Jerusalem were still in ruins.

Nehemiah obtains a commission from Artaxerxes, and, with zeal and courage, commences their erection and repair.

But he is opposed and resisted by Sanballat, and Tobiah the Ammonite, who, in mockery, said, "How feeble this band, and how weak their efforts! Were a jackal to run against their stone walls, he would break them down." Thus were the rebuilders of Jerusalem insulted and hindered in their work.

Nehemiah, however, and his party, went on with the work of the Lord. Their enemies, becoming still more chagrined at their success, formed new alliances, and brought to their aid Arabians and Ashdodites, and "conspired to fight against Jerusalem, and to hinder the work." But Nehemiah exhorted them "to fight for their brethren, their sons, their daughters, their wives and their homes." Thus they prayed, and wrought, and fought, and conquered.

Ezra, meantime, got a copy of the Jewish oracles. He opened the book in the sight of all the people, and the priests and the Levites caused the people *to understand the law*. "So they continued to read in the book of the law distinctly, and gave the sense, *and caused them to understand the reading*." Thus the Divine law and institutions were restored to Israel, and thus were their Temple and city rebuilt.

"Now, the things," says Paul, "that happened to them, occurred to them as types, or examples, and are written for our admonition, upon whom the end of the world, or the consummation of the Jewish age, has come." Let us, then, profit from their example and success, and we will achieve all that we desire. We will cause the people to understand the law of our God, by the reading of his oracles.

But we have more than the encouragement of example to inspire us with zeal and energy in this great work. Other men have labored in this fruitful field, to our unspeakable interest and honor. We have the Christian oracles committed to us, with an injunction to *interpret*, that is, to *translate*, them, with fidelity and perspicuity. The apostles possessed not only a commission to convert the nations, but to teach the converts to observe and practise whatsoever the Lord had commanded. To qualify them for this work, the Lord gave them a splendid education. They had wisdom, knowledge and eloquence bestowed upon them. They had the immediate inspiration of the Holy Spirit, to give them a perfect revelation. They had the gift of foreign tongues, and the gift of interpreting them. The power of translating their own conceptions into the languages of their auditors was gratuitously vouchsafed, not only to the apostles, but to other members and teachers in the churches which they planted and which they nourished with the pure milk of the word. It was, on two accounts, necessary for the apostles to receive this power of knowledge and of utterance by immediate inspiration. The mission was extraordinary, and needed a seal to authenticate it. The gift of tongues itself was one of the most useful seals of apostleship.

Time, also, was to them most precious. Their work was great. Their lives were short, and the hand of the Lord was necessarily the pledge of their mission to the nations of the world, and his inspiration of ideas, and of words to express them, was essential to their success.

A necessity of the same kind, but not of the same degree, still exists. The revelations of the Spirit are complete, but the languages in which they were originally given have become obsolete.

The Hebrew of Moses and of the prophets, and the Greek of the apostles, after the consummation of the revelations of God committed to them, soon began to change, and virtually died. Still, their bodies were embalmed, and the means of recognizing them were preserved and transmitted to us, by their immediate legal representatives. Indeed, the living tongues of earth, like living men, are continually changing. Dictionaries, like histories, transmit the past to the future. Hence both the necessity and the means of substituting correct words and phrases for those that have, from the attrition and waste of time, lost their original value, become uncurrent, and passed out of use. Even Shakspeare and his contemporary poets, orators and authors now require glossaries, or the substitution of modern terms for those which they have used that are now become obsolete and unintelligible. The common version of the Scriptures was made and completed six years before the death of the great English poet. It, therefore, has also acquired the rust of the Elizabethan age, although occasionally since polished by hands we know not of.

The great science of interpretation, strange to tell, like good wine, improves from age to age. Not, indeed, the scriptural gift of interpretation; but the literary and acquired gift of exposition and elucidation is matured and perfected from the better means and better learning now possessed—the product and growth of a revived and reviving literature.

A remarkable revival of literature preceded the Protestant Reformation. That revival is now regarded by every philosophic historian and student—indeed, by every reader who thinks profoundly upon principles and their tendencies, who weighs the remote and proximate causes of things, or who fathoms their legitimate and immediate tendencies—I say the revival of literature in Italy and in Western Europe, which occurred in the fourteenth century, is now regarded by every informed mind as the harbinger, or cause, of the Protestant Reformation; and that reformation may be regarded as the pioneer and patron of Bible-translation.

No living man can realize the midnight darkness with which the Papal See, in its appalling triumph over the Bible, human reason and conscience, had paralyzed and enfeebled the human understanding.

In the thirteenth century, as soon as the English barons had wrested from the feeble-minded King John the Magna Charta, the Pope, who regarded England as "his garden of delight," on John's appeal annulled that charter, boasting that he received three times as much per annum, from England alone, for his throne of St. Peter, as King John received for his political throne. But, be it noted, there was not then a Bible in any vernacular tongue within the Popedom. In the fourteenth century it was not much better. But in that century the revival of literature began. The Italians discovered, as it were, anew the ancient world. "They discovered and felt an affinity of thought, of hopes and of taste with the best of the old Latin writers, which inspired them with the highest admiration."

"Petrarch and Boccaccio passed from this study to that of Grecian antiquity, and, at the solicitation of the latter, the Republic of Florence, in 1360, founded a chair of Grecian literature—*the first in the Western Roman Empire.* The highest glory was attached to Grecian literature and learning, and these two mighty pioneers attained a degree of celebrity, credit and power unequalled by any other men in the Middle Ages. They became the pontiffs and interpreters of antiquity. Italy, in the fifteenth century, became the garden of literature and the arts—the wonder and the delightful resort of the learned throughout Europe. Indeed, it became the well-spring of all the less civilized nations of the West. Dante and Petrarch, Boccaccio and Poggio Bracciolini, led the way."

Meanwhile, the revival of literature in England was, even from this period, associated with a special leaning to the oracles of God. Upon the arena now appear Aungerville, Fitzralph and Wickliffe. Grossteste was not unacquainted with Hebrew and Greek literature, and, at this early day, affirmed that "It is the will of God that the Holy Scriptures should be translated by many translators, and that there should be different translations in the church; so that what is obscurely translated by one may be more perspicuously translated by another." I concur with Anderson, from whom I have quoted these rare facts, that this was the first voice in Western Europe for a vernacular translation of the Holy Scriptures.

The condition of the Papal dominions at this period may be fairly inferred from an address delivered by the Irish Fitzralph, the great pioneer in the advocacy of new and popular versions. When at Lyons, as Primate of Armagh, in the presence of Pope Innocent IV., he arraigned the Popish clergy, in the boldest terms, "for their ignorance, arrogance and flagitious conduct." In the course of his speech he affirmed that the Italian scholars did not so much as know the Greek alphabet!

He also complained to the Pope that "no book, whether of divinity, law or physic, could stir, but the friars were able to buy it up; and that his secular chaplains, whom he sent to Oxford for education, wrote to him that *they could not find a Bible in Oxford,* nor any good and profitable book on divinity for a man to study, and that they were therefore minded to return to Ireland." This conveys us down to the times of Wickliffe.

To illustrate the value and importance of Bible-translation, I will draw yet further upon my old and recent readings. Wickliffe died A.D. 1384, four years after he had finished his translation of the Roman Vulgate. Both the Greek and Roman Catholics had interdicted any translation into the living tongues of Europe and Asia. Indeed, the Council of Toulouse, one hundred and fifty years before Wickliffe's version appeared, had passed forty-five canons against heresy. One of these involved the first court of inquisition, and another forbade the Scriptures to the laity. The canon reads in the following words:—"We forbid the laity to possess any of the books of the Old or New Testament. We strictly forbid the having of any of these books translated." A Latin service in the church, and a Latin Bible in the hands of the priesthood, and none at all in the hands of the people, was the triumph of the prince of darkness in Roman Christendom, and the midnight of the so-called Christian world. The first star of hope was Wickliffe's version, though itself but the version of a version, and not of the original. Still, its appearance inflicted an incurable wound on the Man of sin and Son of perdition.

On the occasion of its first appearance commenced the era of discussion. Henry de Knyghton, a Leicester canon, affirmed that "a man could not find two people on the road but one of them was a disciple of Wickliffe;" and again, "The soldiers, with the dukes and earls, were the chief adherents of this sect. They were their most strenuous promoters and the boldest combatants; their most powerful defenders and their invincible protectors."

On another occasion he said, "This Master John Wickliffe hath translated the gospel out of Latin into English, which Christ has entrusted with the clergy and the doctors of the church, that they might minister it to the weaker sort, according to the state of the times and the wants of men. So that by this means the gospel is made vulgar, and laid more open to the laity, and even to women who can read, than it used to be to the most learned of the clergy and those of the best understanding. And what was before the chief gift of the clergy and the gift of the church is made forever common to the laity." What a comment on the value of a translation! What a portraiture of Popery!

To this adds another contemporary prelate, "The prelates ought not to suffer that every one, at his pleasure, should read the Scriptures, translated even into Latin, because, as is plain from experience, this has always been the occasion of falling into errors and heresies. It is not, therefore, politic that any one, wheresoever and whensoever he will, should give himself to the frequent study of the Scriptures."

During the controversy of two rival Popes, from A.D. 1380 to A.D. 1400, the controversy for and against translations in the vulgar tongues was very rife. A bill for suppressing Wickliffe's Bible was proposed to be brought into the House of Lords. On that occasion the Duke of Lancaster said that "he would maintain the having of this law—the Holy Scriptures in our own tongue—whoever they would be that should bring in the bill."

Still, there was no persecution instituted against the friends of a popular version, or to check the Wickliffites, already spreading all over England, until the reign of the Fourth Henry, when some members of Parliament became infected with the heresy of Bible-reading in an English version, and when the Papal clergy became alarmed lest they should introduce a public reformation.

The invention of paper, at the close of the thirteenth century or early in the fourteenth, and the invention of printing soon following the revival of learning, and the increasing taste for reading an English version, gave to the subject of translation a rapidly growing importance, which never could be annihilated—indeed, scarcely suppressed—until the seeds of a broader and deeper reformation were widely scattered and deeply rooted in the hearts of the people. This secretly working spirit prepared the way of Luther, who, with a lion-hearted courage and a herculean vigor, attacked the basis of the Papal institution. Since which time I need not tell the story of new versions or of Protestant triumphs. Bible-translations soon became the standing order of the day. Luther, Erasmus, Beza, Castalio, Junius and Tremellius, Schmidt, Dathe, &c. engaged in it with great spirit. From Luther's version soon sprang up ten others, in other states and languages on the Continent.

In the British Isles we find, in a few years, Wickliffe, Tindal, Miles Coverdale, Grafton, alias Thomas Matthew, Cranmer and the Bishops at work. The spirit spread through Ireland, Scotland and Wales, and they must severally have God speak to them in their respective tongues.

Finally, King James, borne on by the spirit of the age, is engaged in making one more acceptable to his people, and to issue it under all authority, political and ecclesiastical.

The version was soon hailed by all the enlightened men in his dominions, and appointed to be read in churches. It was in advance of all others at that day, yet wanting in some respects. Hence the number of private versions of a part, or parts, of the volume, and some of the whole New Testament, which have since that time appeared. From the days of King James down to the demise of Professor Stuart, of Andover, in Britain and America the work of translation has ever since been going on. Even Romanists themselves have been compelled, by the spirit of Protestantdom and of the age, to give sundry versions in different tongues. In the Latin tongue we have four Romanist versions of the whole Bible—that of Paginus, that of Montanus, that of Malvenda and Cardinal Cajetan, and that of Houbigant. The Scriptures, in Europe alone, are now read in some fifty languages.

Thomas Hartwell Horne has borne testimony, ample and striking, in favor of our common version, both from the orthodox and heterodox Protestants in Britain. Still, he has the candor to admit its defects and imperfections. After summoning his cloud of witnesses to attest its superior claims, he candidly adds these words:—"Notwithstanding these decisive testimonies to the superior excellence of our authorized version, it is readily admitted that it is not immaculate, and that a complete correction of it is an object of desire to the friends of religion, were it only to silence the perpetually repeated cavils of the opposers of Divine revelation, who, studiously disregarding the various satisfactory answers which have been given to their unfounded objections, persevere in repeating them, so long as they find a few mistranslated passages in the authorized version." But he did not think, some quarter of a century ago, "that sacred criticism" (I presume he meant literary criticism) "was yet so far advanced as to furnish all the means that may be expected." If we wait till "all the means," real or imaginary, that *may hereafter be expected,* be actually possessed by any individual or assembly of individuals, the work will not be commenced till about the end of the millennium!

Since Mr. Horne wrote these words, there have been issued in Europe and in America at least a hundred volumes, containing alleged errors, with their corrections. Some of these are, indeed, very minute; and, while they occasionally render the obscure more perspicuous, the defective more complete, the indefinite more precise, the ambiguous more certain, and the complicated more simple, we cannot say that any one of them is absolutely faultless in every particular. We are truly thankful that there is no version so wholly defective that an honest reader, learned or unlearned, may not understand the great scheme of salvation, and believe and obey it to the salvation of his soul.

I have never seen any English version, Romanist or Protestant, orthodox or heterodox, however imperfect, from which a man of sense and industry might not learn the way to heaven. Nor have I ever seen a country, however bleak or sterile, in which an industrious, laborious and persevering husbandman might not dig out of it the means of living. But what does this prove? That there is little or no difference between countries—between temperate or intemperate zones?

Who, having seen the fertile hills and valleys of the fairest portions of our much favored and beloved land, would think of locating himself in the barren heaths of Siberia, or in the sandy or slimy deserts of Libya? As little he who has a taste for the treasures of wisdom and knowledge, who desires the bread and the water of life that came down from heaven, who thirsts after the knowledge of God and of Christ, who prays for the full assurance of understanding the whole counsel of God, revealed in God's own book—I say, as little can he be satisfied with a mere glimpse of light—with a dim, imperfect or ambiguous version of God's own book of life, health and salvation to man. Still, they are severally and collectively useful, and some of them contain many valuable emendations; but not any one of them meets the wants of this age, or would, in the aggregate, be a proper or satisfactory substitute for the common version, notwithstanding all its obscurities and errors.

The labors bestowed upon the original text, in ascertaining the genuine readings of passages of doubtful interpretation, and the great advances made in the whole science of hermeneutics—the established laws of translation—since the commencement of the present century, fully justify the conclusion that we are, or may be, much better furnished for the work of interpretation than any one, however gifted by nature and by education, could have been, not merely fifty, but almost two hundred and fifty, years ago. The living critics and translators of the present day, in Europe and America, are like Saul amongst the people—head and shoulders above those of the early part of the seventeenth century.

As for honesty, we ought not, perhaps, to say any thing. But we may presume to say, without the charge of arrogance or invidious comparison, that we are not greatly inferior to them. And if in talent and education, compared with the moderns, they were giants still, as pigmies standing upon the shoulders of giants, we ought to see farther than those upon whose shoulders we place ourselves. Biblical criticism is now much more a science than it was in A.D. 1600, so soon after the revival of literature. A far greater number of Biblical critics has succeeded than preceded the Protestant Reformation, and of a much higher order. Before that era there was not one good Greek or Hebrew critic for one hundred at the present day. The Papal Romans were merely Roman scholars, and yet inferior to the Pagan Romans. These are facts so generally known and conceded that it is not necessary to dwell upon them. The art of printing, with the increased number of theological seminaries, and the competition between Romanists and Protestants, and between the leading Protestant parties themselves, with the facilities of a more enlarged intercourse amongst learned men, could not otherwise than elevate the standard of Biblical scholarship and afford greater facilities for acquiring Biblical learning.

Corresponding with this, the vigorous impulse given to the human mind by the rapid progress in the sciences and in the arts merely physical and intellectual, the great increase of new discoveries and general improvement in the social system, sustained by the facilities of the press, have all contributed to a higher intellectual development and a more thorough scholarship than were ever attained by the Greek or Roman schisms, or by any Protestant denomination anterior to the era of the common version. Indeed, one may affirm, without the fear of successful contradiction, that during the last hundred years, on the Continent of Europe, in Great Britain, and in the United States of America, Biblical criticism, Biblical learning and Biblical translation have advanced, in every essential characteristic and accompaniment, much more, in what is usually called Christendom, than was practicable or possible anterior to that date.

A more suitable time, therefore, has never been, since the era of the Anglo-Saxon language, since the rise of the Papal defection, than the present, for a corrected and improved version of the Jewish and Christian oracles, in the living Anglo-Saxon language of the present day.

A concerted movement of all or any of the Protestant parties in such an undertaking we cannot expect. It is not in living experience; nor is it anywhere inscribed on the pages of ecclesiastical history, that a plurality of denominations have ever agreed to make a common version, for common use. Romanists and Protestants, Episcopalians and Presbyterians, Congregationalists and Methodists, Baptists and Pedobaptists, never have agreed, and, I presume, never will agree, to make in common a new version.

Indeed, the first version in our language, as also the second—which is virtually the present commonly-used version—in the main, were made by individual enterprise and on individual responsibility. Their merit, and the course of events, providentially gave them whatever popularity and influence they have possessed.

King James's version is, at most, but a *correction*, not, indeed, always an *amended* correction, of the version of Wm. Tindal. No assembly ever made a new version of the New Testament. Conventions have met and read, have approved or condemned, have amended or altered, as the case may have been, versions made by individual men. But no convention has yet made a new or original translation.

We have already shown that those in power uniformly opposed new versions until they had already, by alleged intrinsic merit, gained an authority with the people. Those in power have always opposed innovation, for the most obvious reasons in the world. They could gain nothing earthly, in public favor, by any improvement, and might lose much by the innovations of a new version, if a correct one. And this is the reason why both Romanists and Protestants have uniformly opposed new versions.

None but pure, enlightened, conscientious, spiritually-minded men could attempt, advocate or execute an exact, faithful, perspicuous and intelligible version of God's oracles. These seldom—more probably never—have constituted a majority in any nominally Christian communion.

Majorities, in the affairs of mammon, are worthy of all respect and confidence, because in such matters they have a single eye, a clear head and a sincere heart. But in Christ's kingdom minorities are much more likely to be, and most generally have been, most worthy of public confidence, ever since the almost unanimous spiritual court of Israel delivered up the Lord Jesus Christ to be crucified. The history of mankind is full of admonition and warning on this subject. Ever since the days of Noah, Lot and Abraham, majorities are not famous—rather they are infamous—in sacred story. Still, we flatter ourselves, and will present the flattering unction to the souls of our contemporaries, that we all are exceptions to a universal rule. But I confess, I am not without fear in this matter, when I look narrowly into the volumes of church history. One thing is certain: we have as yet no version of the Christian Scriptures made by a convention.

"History," I repeat, "is but philosophy speaking by example." If history exemplifies any principle, it is that good men love light, and wicked men hate light, in all matters spiritual and eternal. Hence, as already shown, every valuable effort to give, in the vernacular of any people, an exact, faithful and perspicuous version of God's own book, has been confined to individual enterprise, or that which most nearly approaches it. "In the multitude of counsellors," Solomon says, "there is safety." But he did not say in the multitude of translators there is safety. In what regards *meum* and *tuum*, "*mine* and *thine*," there is much more facility, and much more safety, in counsel, than in making faithful versions of the doctrine of self-denial and of taking up the cross. Still, a company of select men—not selected by a king, a court, a metropolitan or an archbishop, but by spiritual and heavenly minded men selected out of a Christian community—may be found, capable and honest, single-minded and single-eyed, enough, to guarantee a version true to the original as they are competent to understand and express it. Learned in their own language they must be, as well as in the original tongues.

But it has been often asked, What may be the destiny of such a version? In other words, Who will receive it, and what will be its influence? This is a question which, however dogmatically propounded, cannot be dogmatically answered. We are neither apostles nor prophets; but we can freely express our opinion, and give some reasons for it.

In the first place, then, much will depend upon the reputed orthodoxy and piety of those who execute the version. The Society under whose patronage and by whose instrumentality it is proposed is properly called the "*Bible Union*"—not the Baptist Union.

Already it has been opposed and misrepresented as a *Baptist* Union for *Baptist* principles—a measure to carry out *immersionist* views of the action of baptism, by translating *baptism immersion*, and all its family, root and branches, by *immerse, immersing, immersed, immersion!* This is about all the logic and all the rhetoric that has appeared in one hundred and forty-four paragraphs written, printed and circulated against it, from "Dan even unto Beersheba," from Boston to San Francisco, from Mulberry Street, New York, to Old Jewry, London!

Truly, immersionists have been hard pressed, although now the largest community in the Union, and annually gaining more than any other denomination in the number of its membership, fully equalling in population, wealth and resources one-fifth of the political and moral force of this great nation!

But why have recourse to a new version for the sake of translating this family of *baptizo?* Have not all, or nearly all, the learned rabbis and doctors of the Pedobaptist communities affirmed not only that *baptism* means immersion, but also that it was so administered in the apostles' days? Ask Brenner, of the Church of Rome, what was the ancient apostolic baptism. He responds that "immersion was practised for *thirteen centuries* almost universally, and from the beginning till now" in the Greek Church. Ask the English Episcopal Church how long the church practised immersion as the representative of *baptism;* and Dr. Wall responds, For sixteen hundred years. Ask Luther what is his judgment on the premises: he answers, "I could wish that such as are to be baptized should be carefully immersed into water, according to the meaning of the word and the signification of the ordinance; as also without doubt it was instituted by Christ." Ask the great American critic, the late Professor Stuart, what is the English of "baptize;" and he affirms "that it means to dip, plunge or immerse in water, and that all lexicographers and critics of any note are agreed in this." And does not ancient history aver that both Wickliffe and Tindal were in their views immersionists? With all these venerated names—a mere cluster culled from the orthodox Pedobaptist vine—what need have Baptists themselves to form a Baptist Bible Union to inculcate their views of immersion?

But it will be whispered that other views than these—heretical and false—are cherished by the *Bible Union*, and that the version will be colored by these. This has been insinuated, nay, printed and published, by Baptists themselves opposed to it. And what is the proof, or the basis, of such suspicion? Have not the leading movers of this Bible-translation as now digested and exhibited by the Bible Union been always regarded as sound and orthodox on every vital doctrine of Christianity? Do not they believe in the fall of man, in the contamination and guilt of sin, which, as a leprosy, has infected every child born into the world? Do not they believe and teach the equal Divine nature and glory of the Father, and of the Son, and of the Holy Spirit, as developed in the great work of redemption in and through the death, the sacrifice, or vicarious sufferings, of the Lord Jesus Christ? Do not they believe and teach that the Father works, the Son works, and the Holy Spirit works, in the redemption, illumination, regeneration, sanctification, resurrection and glorification of man, through the grace of the Father, the sacrifice of the Son, and the recreative, renovating, regenerating influence of the Holy Guest of the Christian temple—the mystic house of God, erected for a habitation of God through the Spirit?

Can, therefore, our heterodoxy be alleged as an objection to any version that we may make? Then there is no vital orthodoxy, no real orthodoxy, in Protestant Christendom. My own individual orthodoxy is too orthodox for the orthodox prelates of a sectarian world. I thank God, as Paul once said of himself, in his own way of boasting, I am more orthodox than any of them. I have all their orthodoxy, and a little more besides. And I know that the next generation—or, at farthest, the one after that—will acknowledge it. But, if I know what orthodoxy means, (and I presume to think and to say that I do,) there is nothing either catholic or scriptural in the Greek, Roman or Protestant church that I do not believe and teach. There is more than a sprinkling of heterodoxy in every sect in Christendom. But that heterodoxy consists not in what are called the essential doctrines of the evangelical remedial system. It consists much more in not keeping the commandments of the Divine Redeemer, and in not scripturally observing his ordinances of worship, than in any theory of the fall of man or the necessity of sovereign and free grace or of a divinely ordained remedial system. A correct translation of the Christian Scriptures will do more to unite, harmonize and purify the Baptists, and to make them one great evangelical co-operation for God's glory and man's salvation, than any event since the Protestant Reformation. It will cause them to arise and shine in the light of God and in the beauty of holiness, fair as the moon, bright as the sun and terrible as an army with triumphant banners.

We conclude then, from all our premises—and they are both large and liberal—that any version consummated by the Bible Union can never be objected to by even the most orthodox party in Protestant Christendom because of any theoretic or practical error held or propagated by any of those who participate in its consummation. I am fully aware that the wiles of the devil will all be in requisition, ready to strangle it as soon as born. But the Lord has always taken and subdued the devil's wise men in their own craftiness, and shown that the weakness of God is stronger than man or the devil; and therefore the preaching of old, stale, quaint, spectacle-bestridden orthodoxy will be as impotent now as was Herod's decree to kill the new-born king of the Jews by the slaughter of the innocents of Bethlehem.

But, seeing that the Bible Union is not a Baptist Union, nor a heterodox Union, but a Union for a pure, chaste, exact, faithful and perspicuous version of the Christian oracles, and ultimately of the whole volume of divinely inspired truth, what is likely to be its future history, or its destiny?

An answer to this question, though somewhat in the spirit of prophecy, is not so very difficult as at first presentation might be assumed or imagined. If the version be faithful and true to the original, (and we assume that such it will be, in the judgment of all truly enlightened men,) it must, in harmony with the history of man and the progress of the age, gain a glorious triumph over its opponents. Their batteries will be silent, because they will have been silenced by the work itself. It may be condemned and reprobated—indeed, it will be—by mere sectaries, who have taken the oath of allegiance to their present prejudices, for better or for worse, and who, in advance of its appearance, have not only thought, but said, "No good thing can come out of Nazareth," and, therefore, never will. Such was the fate and the fortune of Tindal's version. He was persecuted and driven from England. He was persecuted in Flanders. He was put to death by the orthodox of that day. His translation was inhibited in England; and yet in a few years after it was virtually the English Bible, so enacted and ordained by the ecclesiastic and political potentates of England.

The present version was not, on its first appearance, a universal favorite. Some preferred the Bishop's Bible; others disliked both. One age burns heretics; the next makes them saints and martyrs, and erects monuments to their memory. No wise man, well read in civil or ecclesiastical history, can expect a different state of things. The censure of one age, is all praise in the judgment of the next; as the praise of one generation is often the shame and the reproach of the following. Christians live for immortality, for eternity, and, therefore, to them it is a matter of little or no account how their contemporaries may think or speak of them. The only happy man is he whom the Lord approveth.

But what will be the fortunes of such a version as we contemplate may be rationally anticipated. It will, ultimately, be received by all the immersionists. Some of the elders, some of the scribes, some of the popular doctors, some of the man-worshippers, will, no doubt, say of it, when issued, what they said of it before it appeared. This they will do to justify the false position which, in a fitful mood, they unfortunately took on the whole premises. This we expect, and we will not be disappointed. Human nature, in the absence of Divine grace, runs in these channels. Yet we say it will be ultimately received by all the immersionists, and by a portion of the non-immersionists. But, in some instances, it will be read with more interest to find out its faults than to perceive its fidelity or its general excellency. All who plead for perspicuous and faithful versions, into foreign tongues abroad, will be compelled to receive a perspicuous and faithful version in their own Anglo-Saxon at home. We who are now actors in the drama will soon die, and the prominent opponents of the work will soon die. Our prepossessions and antipathies will die with us, and our labors will fall into more impartial hands. In one lifetime, despite all opposition, it will be generally read by enlightened Christians of our language, probably in some points improved, but, in those points to which special reference is had, just as we give it. Many may denounce it whose children will only wish, "as duteous sons, their fathers had been more wise."

But in saying so much of a *new* version to be made in the present day, we are likely to be misunderstood. We do not really intend or wish for a literally new version. We much prefer, in all cases, the common Anglo-Saxon style and idiom, and never will capriciously change the wording, unless when defective or unfaithful to the original, or otherwise in bad taste. I am one, and have long been one, of the admirers of the Anglo-Saxon of the common version. And although often corrected and improved in its defects by such men as Campbell, MacKnight, Doddridge, &c., neither the more sonorous and elegant Latinities of the former, nor the pure, and sometimes too complaisant, Grecisms of the latter, nor the combination of them both, with less taste and vigor, by Doddridge and other modern revisionists, win my admiration, nor command my respect and affection, so much as the pure Anglo-

Saxon of the fourteenth century, as it mainly appears in the revision of King James and his forty-seven translators or revisers. With Macaulay and other distinguished writers of the present day, I believe that much of the power and effect of the common Bible, and Bunyan's Pilgrim's Progress, is owing to the fact that they are the only two good specimens of that style extant amongst us, and have, thereby, an easier and more direct passport to the understanding, the conscience and the heart of English, Scotch, Irish and Americans than any other books in our language.

Change, for the sake of change, in the oracles of God, in any language, is, in my judgment, bad taste and worse philosophy, and ought to be eschewed, rather than cultivated or adopted, by every one who desires the word of God to run and be glorified in our day and generation. Change without improvement is, in most cases, and most of all in Bible-translation, mere pedantry—more worthy of reprobation than of commendation, on the part of every lover of the Bible and of mankind. I love the phrases and forms of speech in which our venerable and venerated forefathers were accustomed to clothe their conceptions of God, of Christ and of the great salvation, when they turned their hearts to the praises of God, or prostrated themselves before his mercy-seat. I love, too, the forms of speech in which they expressed their conceptions of his grace and of his great salvation, when, in their ecstasies, they celebrated the wonders of his grace and extolled his condescension to our lost and ruined world. Magniloquence is the index of a weak and visionary mind; and a too precise and formal style, in complaisance to the verbal livery of the times, savors more of pedantry than of piety, more of the flesh than of the spirit, more of the wisdom of men than of the power of God. Much learning, real substantial learning, good common sense, much piety and spirituality of mind, and a profound humility and reverence, are essential qualifications of a good translator of the oracles of God. We are, therefore, more disposed to ask, who is fit for such a work, than to hasten rashly or presumptuously upon it, as a matter of common concern or of ephemeral duration. It is a good work, a great work, a solemn work, and must be approached with great solemnity and self-examination. It is not a task to be hastily assumed and despatched with expedition. It is as solemn as death, and as awful as eternity. If God commanded his servant Moses, when he presented himself to him at Horeb, saying, "Draw not nigh hither; put off thy shoes from off thy feet, for the place whereon thou standest is holy ground;" and if the captain of the Lord's host said to Joshua, when standing in his presence, "Loose thy shoes from off thy feet, for the place on which thou standest is holy," with what solemnity and reverence should we presume to touch "the ark of the covenant" of mercy, and to open its contents to our contemporaries and to posterity! Should not, then, such a work as is proposed be undertaken, prosecuted and consummated in the spirit of a piety the most sincere, and of a reverence the most profound?

There yet remains, my Christian brethren, another consideration, to which I would specially solicit your concentrated attention. We live in a sectarian, and, consequently, in a controversial, age. Christianity, as it is called, has degenerated into a speculative science, and, therefore, into innumerable forms of opinionism. Theories instead of *facts*, speculations instead of *faith*, forms and ceremonies instead of a *new life*, and a profession of godliness without its *vitality* and *power*, are now and long have been the characteristics of the Christian profession. As a necessary consequence, we have been, as Paul predicted, "turned away from the truth of Christ unto fables."

When we survey the motley theatre of Christendom, it resembles a badly-colored map of the Eastern or Western Continent. Shade mingles into shade, and color into color, until all the primary colors are lost, and one immense variegated field of vision spreads before us, full of mystery and of wonder. The natural and the artificial lines, rectilinear and curvilinear, which bound them and separate them, are the shades of each of the primary colors, so numerous and so faint that no mortal eye can separate them, or mark where one commences and another ends. And as upon these maps—

"Lands intersected by a narrow frith
Abhor each other:
Mountains interposed make enemies of nations
Who had else, like kindred drops, been mingled into one,"

so these shades of opinion, formalities of worship and forms of organization, alienate these sects and parties from each other, as though one were Jews and the other Samaritans.

The metaphysics of the new birth, or the speculative difference between kneeling and standing in prayer, down to the ribbons on a bonnet, or the corners of a collar, are sometimes made the badges of a holy brotherhood, more important than faith, hope or charity. A good sectary may violate, with more impunity, five of the ten commandments, than any one of the idol peculiarities of his denomination. This, too, unfortunately, has occasioned a characteristic difference in the pulpit exhibitions of the age, and has given a factitious importance to theories and customs which otherwise would have occupied little or no part in public teaching or in public edification.

In our country and in our generation, there are delivered, in the course of the year, ten sermons on the new birth for one upon the new life; as if ten times more important to be born right than to live right; and yet in the former the subject is entirely passive, and in the latter wholly active.

In the whole New Testament we have but one paragraph on the new birth for a hundred on the new life. We have had, too, a thousand sermons in behalf of sprinkling a babe, and a thousand on immersing a believer, which all depended upon the non-translation or the mere transference of a word, with the difference between blood and faith, or flesh and spirit.

For all these and many other such aberrations there is but one sovereign and grand specific—a pure, exact, definite and perspicuous translation of the Christian Scriptures. This is, in my humble conception, the great want of Christendom, the great want of the age, and the unanswerable argument in favor of the *Bible Union*.

The very name *Bible Union* has a charm in the ear of every friend of truth, of every friend of God and of man. The Bible is God's own foundation for the greatest empire in creation. It is the constitution of the empire of redeemed humanity! We have had every sort of union but a union for a perfect English Bible. The Christian world, so called, may co-operate in the great work which it proposes. And that a perfect English Bible, for an English people, is needed for three great purposes, will, I presume, on a proper exposition of the premises, be very generally conceded. The first, for the union of true Christians; the second, for the conversion of the world; the third, for the perfection of the church. To illustrate what we mean in such a broad affirmation, take an example or two. 1. Let all Englishmen read immerse for baptize, and then would not the baptismal controversy cease upon the action of baptism? 2. Let them read *congregation* for *church*, and where the basis for the patriarchy, for the papacy, or for the prelacy? 3. Let them read *love* for charity, and where that spurious tolerance of error, as a substitute for brotherly kindness and love?

First, we say, *for the union of true Christians*. The most insuperable barriers to this are the three prevailing baptisms—baptism in water, with faith; baptism with water, without faith; and baptism with the Spirit, without either faith or water. There are, therefore, three meanings attached to Christian baptism. The first is, the *immersion* of a professed believer *in* water. The second is, the *aspersion* of water *upon* a person, with or without faith. The third is, the affusion or effusion of the Spirit of God upon a spirit, antecedent to, and independent of, either knowledge or faith. Thus the word *baptize* becomes a perfect enigma.

Baptize is neither Hebrew nor Greek, neither Latin nor English. It is a modification of the Greek *baptizo,* the Roman form of which is identical with the Greek. Hence the Greek and Roman Churches practised immersion down to A.D. 1311; and the Greek Church—older than the Roman, and vast in its territory—still practises it.

The English Church, too, practised immersion down to the reign of Henry VIII., and it was so ordained by statute of said Henry, in his Holy Manual or Guide of A.D. 1530. The statute of Henry VIII., 21st, thus speaks:—"*Let the priest take the child, and, having asked the name, baptize him, by dipping him in water thrice.*"

Indulgences were given, in after-reigns, to pour water upon weak babies; and very soon after all the babies became weak, and could not even stand the shock of pouring. Then John Calvin mercifully interposed, and commuted *pouring* for *sprinkling*. The priests, English and Scotch, immediately commenced a new kind of oratory, under the shield and the star of the rhetorical figures of a *synecdoche,* which puts a part for a whole, and of a *metalepsis,* which authorizes old names to be applied to new things. And so Presbyterians, Congregationalists, Episcopalians and Methodists, liberal spirits all, in general have availed themselves of the tolerant indulgence of the falsely-styled "*intolerant Calvin.*"

The "Edinburgh Encyclopædia" is high authority in this case. Hear the article on baptism, in the words following, to wit:—

"In this country, [Scotland,] however, sprinkling was never practised, in ordinary cases, till after the Reformation; and in England, even in the reign of Edward VI., trine immersion—dipping first the right side, secondly the left side, and lastly the face of the infant—was commonly observed. But during the persecution of Mary, many persons, most of whom were Scotchmen, fled from England to Geneva, and there greedily imbibed the opinions of that church. In 1556, a book was published at that place containing 'the form of prayers and ministration of the sacraments approved by the famous and godly learned man, John Calvin,' in which the administrator is enjoined to take water in his hand and lay it upon the child's forehead. These Scottish exiles, who had renounced the authority of the Pope, implicitly acknowledged the authority of Calvin; and, returning to their own country, with Knox at their head, in 1559, established sprinkling in Scotland. From Scotland this practice made its way into England, in the reign of Elizabeth."

Baptism and *baptize* were, by the order of King James, under the caption of "ecclesiastical words," enjoined upon the translators, and were transferred into his version as representing the ideas then current. Thus the action first indicated by the adopted word *baptize* was *immerse,* but now it is made to mean no specific action; and therefore it must be translated by one specific word, to represent, in our ears, the precept of Christ.

I say, then, that, in order to *the union of Christians,* we must have a definite and unmistakable term, indicating one and the same conception to every mind. If, then, the Christian church ever become really and visibly one, she must have one immersion, or one baptism; and, if she become not one, where is the hope of a millennium? It is a dream!

Now, on observing the tendency of the two great bodies of Christian professors—immersionists and non-immersionists—let me emphatically ask, What does it show? What does it teach? Is not the manifest tendency of the past and present century towards immersion? *For every one that has renounced immersion and been sprinkled,* are there not ten thousand that have renounced sprinkling and been immersed? I speak in bonds—probably far within the limits of truth. The immersionists in America vary not much from one million. I mean not in theory, for the theorists and the realists are more than a mere plurality to one; but I mean those actually immersed.

Of this million of immersed persons, how many had been sprinkled in infancy! From having been a feeble, despised and persecuted band, in less than a century, in these United States, how stand they now? Has any one in this assembly ever seen one immersed professor renounce it, and receive sprinkling at the hand of a Protestant minister? I have never, to my knowledge, seen such a case. Has any one present ever seen such a case? If he have, we wish to know it.

Now, then, is it not contrary to theory, to faith, to experience, to history, to think of a millennium—of a union of all Christians—on Pedobaptist principles? In order, then, to pray, or to preach, or to labor, *for a millennium,* we must have a Bible that is most explicit on this great subject. There cannot be a millennium—a united church—without acknowledging one Lord, one faith and one baptism. Hence my zeal is not for water—much or little water—for dipping, pouring or sprinkling—but for one immersion, for the sake of one Lord, one faith and one church. I wish I could, by any form of utterance, so repeat these words that I might insure them a safe and a sure passport into every good heart.

The baptismal question, with me, is as much for the union of Christians as it is for the union of our hearts to the Lord, in order to the peace that passes understanding and the joy unspeakable and full of glory. Pardon the emphasis I place on this topic. If it be not the main topic of this age, it certainly will be of the next. The *Bible Union*, for a new and true and faithful version of the Christian Scriptures, is, therefore, the greatest ecclesiastic event of this our day, because the most pregnant of union, peace, prosperity and triumph to the church of Christ.

But it may be asked, Why should an English version do more to effect these great objects than a version into any other living tongue? Because, we answer, of the people that speak this language. If not more in number, they are more powerful, than any other people. Their science and arts, their religion and their general civilization, their Protestant energy of character, their great and all-pervading commercial enterprise, and especially their missionary spirit and their missionary success, give them the vantage-ground amidst all the languages and people of earth. But, better still, the Almighty Ruler of the destinies of nations has hitherto countenanced and blessed England and America more than any other people in the world, and their English Bible is more generally read all over the earth than that of any other people or language in the world.

Regarding the past as the best omen for the future—viewing what God has accomplished by English men, by English enterprise, by English Protestantism, by English Bibles—have we not in these premises enough to inspire us with a vigorous hope and with bright anticipations that the Bible Union, organized for giving free course to the Divine oracles faithfully and perspicuously translated into our vernacular, is, in its grand object and aim, co-operating with God, and, consequently, under his guidance and blessing, in the great work of redeeming man from ignorance, guilt and bondage?

The second great object of a new version is *the conversion of the world.* Our Redeemer, in his intercessory prayer, as reported by John, the beloved apostle, has declared that the union of his friends and followers is essential to the conversion of the world. "I pray, holy Father," says he, not for the apostles only, nor for those only that now believe on me, *that they may be one, as we are;* but "I pray for those also who shall believe on me through their word, [or teaching,] *that they all may be one* that as thou, Father, art in me, and I in thee, they also may be one in us, *that the world may believe that thou hast sent me*, and that I have given them the glory which thou gavest me, that *they may be one, even as we are one*, I in thee, and thou in me, that they may be made perfect in one, and that the *world may know that thou hast sent me, and hast loved them as thou hast loved me.*" Though we had a thousand arguments to offer in the advocacy of the necessity of the union of Christians in order to the conversion of the world of unbelieving Jews and Gentiles, we would not, on such an occasion, adduce one of them in corroboration of this one. They are all as the twinklings of innumerable stars in a cloudless heaven, compared with the splendors of a meridian sun blazing in all his noon-day majesty and effulgence on our world. The simple declaration of the fact that the union of Christians is necessary to the conversion of the world, by such a person, on such an occasion, is as strong as the strongest mathematical demonstration of a physical truth, subjected alike to the senses and the understanding of men.

So long as the Lord Jesus Christ—the Founder of the Christian church or kingdom—has made its union, and spiritual communion in one God, through one Redeemer, and by one Holy Spirit, a means of the conversion of the world, it could not be made more essential to that end by any enactment, ordinance or oracle in earth or heaven. It is, therefore, now, and for forty years past has been, with me, a fixed principle, that if a hundred sects or schisms in Christ's kingdom were to send out their respective myriads of missionaries into all the nations of earth, *the world*, in our Saviour's sense, could not be converted, or made to believe that Jesus of Nazareth is the true Messiah, the only Saviour of the world. I might show, in volumes, the evils of schisms, and so might another, and another, as conversant with these themes as any of us; but the simple utterance of this prayer, for the union of all the believers in the Divine person and mission and work of Jesus, *in order to the conversion of the world*, eclipses, and will eternally eclipse, them all. It is an end, a consummation, most devoutly to be wished, but which never can be gained while the Christian profession is severed and divided into innumerable parties in perpetual conflict with one another. The sword of ecclesiastic strife must be sheathed, and the halcyon flag of Zion must wave its peaceful folds on every Christian altar, from one extremity of Christendom to the other.

Whatever, then, tends to the true interpretation or translation of the living oracles into the languages of our Christendom is an object of transcendent, nay, of paramount, importance to the answer and accomplishment of our Redeemer's prayer—to the health, peace, prosperity and ultimate triumph of our most holy faith over all the superstitions and idolatries of earth. How much, then, need I ask, depends upon such a version of the holy oracles as will give an exact and perspicuous interpretation of every passage connected with each and every one of those unhappy sources of error that have occasioned, or given any countenance to, those paralyzing schisms, which have, more or less, frustrated our missionary enterprises since the establishment of the first domestic or foreign mission in Christendom?

The third great object to be gained is the *perfection* of the church. "That they may be made *perfect* in one," is a portion of the burden of our Lord's intercessory prayer. Perfection is, therefore, the glory and felicity of man.

The perfectibility of human nature, by human instrumentality, has long been the fascinating dream of visionary philosophers. A true philosopher, or a true Christian, never cherished such an Utopian vision. But there is a true, a real perfectibility of human character and of human nature, through the soul-redeeming mediation and holy spiritual influence of the great Philanthropist—the Hero, the Author and Perfecter of the Christian faith. And there is a transforming power, a spiritual, a divine energy, adequate to this end, in the gospel of Christ, as now dispensed by the Holy Guest of the Christian temple. It is first a spiritual, and finally a physical, transformation of man, in his whole physical, intellectual and moral constitution. It is, in the measure of his spiritual capacity, a perfect conformity to the perfect image of the spiritual beauty and loveliness of the Divine Father himself. This is the glorious destiny of man under a remedial economy of means and influences, expressed or suggested in the teachings of the Messiah, and fully developed in the writings of his ambassadors to the nations. Our Divine Master had this in his eye when he prayed for the perfection of Christians in and through himself.

Now, in order to this Divine scheme of redemption and transformation of a fallen and ruined world, the whole volume of the Christian Scriptures is, in the wisdom of God, inspired and fashioned as happily, as wisely and as benevolently as light is to the eye, or harmony and melody to the ear. To have the full-orbed Sun of righteousness, mercy and life shining in all his moral and spiritual splendors upon our souls, in the light of a life divine and everlasting, is the choicest boon of heaven, and the richest treasure almighty love ever imparted to any portion of God's intellectual and spiritual universe. Ought not, then, these animating and cheering rays of Divine light to be permitted to shine into our souls, in the clear and cloudless atmosphere of a pure and transparent interpretation or translation of the Divine originals of our most precious and holy faith? And what conscience purified from guilt, what heart touched with the magnet of everlasting love, and sanctified by faith, does not pant after the full fruition of the light of God's countenance, reflected upon us in the mirror of Divine revelation?

If, then, there be an object that supremely claims our concentrated energies and our most vigorous efforts; if there be happiness, honor and glory, in our assimilation to the Divine image; if the union of all the children of God in one holy brotherhood; if the conversion of the world to the obedience of faith; if the perfection of Christian character through faith, hope and love, through an ardent zeal and devotion, be objects of paramount value and importance—be pre-eminently desirable, ought not all the talents, and learning, and grace, which God has vouchsafed to his church of the present day, be consecrated and devoted to the consummation of this transcendent work?

But again: none but Baptists can do this great work. I do not mean Old School or New School Baptists. Many of both are unfit for it; not merely for the want of learning, but because they are mere Baptists—no more than Baptists. The mere Jew gloried in circumcision, and the mere Baptist, in the same spirit, glories in immersion. But there are myriads of Christian Baptists, of regenerated, enlarged, ennobled Baptists, who glory in truth and in the God of truth—men of large minds, of liberal hearts, of expanded and expanding souls, zealous for truth and for the God of truth. These all are moved and moving in the direction and under the guidance of the Spirit of Truth and of a sound discriminating mind. They never were all Israel who were of Israel. Neither are they all baptized into Christ who are baptized in water. But a portion of the Jews returned from the Babylonian Captivity. None but Baptists of enlightened understandings, of large and liberal hearts, of pure conscience, and of faith unfeigned, can cordially, zealously and perseveringly participate in such a grand and sublime enterprise.

Still, none but immersionists do discern the spirituality of the kingdom of Christ. In reason's ear, in reason's name, how can that man apprehend the spirituality of Christianity, and the spirituality of Christ's kingdom, who will, in virtue of his being flesh and blood, carry in his arms all born of his flesh to the basin, and into the church, and enroll them as *baptized into Christ?* Because wet with only one drop of rose-water, gravely affirm, that one drop is as good as an ocean! And true it is, that neither a drop nor an ocean can sprinkle or immerse man, woman or child, into a faith which he has not, and into a Christ which he knows not of. I could as soon believe that Louis Napoleon is a pure democrat, and the Pope a genuine republican, as that a sprinkled or dipped babe has been christianized by one drop or one ocean, without the knowledge and the faith of Christ. But why argue this case further?

Shall we not, then, brethren, not merely propose, approve and adopt the resolution offered, or some other one to the same effect, but, with one heart and soul, co-operate with our brethren everywhere like-minded in the prosecution and consummation of this great work, and, through good report or bad report, cleave to it, and prosecute it, until we shall have, in our own living tongue as now spoken, the words of eternal truth and love, circulating from East to West, from North to South, wherever our language is spoken, to the last domicile of man; and this, too, in the firm conviction and assurance that time, the most potent revolutionist, will make it a grand auxiliary in the great work of uniting, harmonizing and purifying the church of Christ, and of converting, sanctifying and saving the world?

ADDRESS

TO THE

AMERICAN BIBLE UNION.

NEW YORK, 1850.

MEN, BRETHREN AND FATHERS IN ISRAEL:—

Through the kind providence of our heavenly Father, and by your Christian courtesy, I have the honor to appear before you, and to address you, on this most eventful and interesting occasion. Regarding your BIBLE UNION as one of the most important events of the age—one of the most promising signs of the times, most auspicious of future good to the church and to the world—I cannot but feel exceedingly happy in being permitted to appear before you in the defence and advocacy of that great undertaking, so dear to us all, which proposes and promises to give an improved version of the living oracles of the living God in our vernacular as spoken at the present day.

The Bible is the book of God. God is not only its author, but its subject. It is also the book of man. He, too, is the subject and the object of the volume. "It has God for its author; salvation for its end; and truth, without any mixture of error, for its matter."*

It spans the arch of time, which leans upon an eternity past and an eternity to come. It came to us through the ministry of angels, prophets and apostles, and is to be transmitted by us, in all languages, to nations and generations yet unborn. It contains treasures of wisdom and knowledge beyond all the learning of earth and all the philosophy of man. It not only unveils to us the future of time, but lifts the curtain that separates the seen from the unseen, earth from heaven, time from eternity, and presents to the eye of faith and hope the

* Locke.

ineffable glories of a blissful immortality. It is to us, indeed, the book of life; the charter of "an inheritance incorruptible, undefiled and that fadeth not away." It has already measurably civilized many nations and empires. It has enlightened, moralized, sanctified and saved untold millions of our fallen and degraded race, and will continue to enlighten, sanctify and bless the world, until the last sentence of the eventful volumes of human history shall have been stereotyped forever. But alas for the unfaithful stewards, the inconsiderate and presumptuous sentinels of Zion, who, instead of guarding the ark of the covenant, set about allegorizing, mystifying and nullifying its sacred contents!

The infidel Jew and the pagan Greek first withstood its claims, resisted its evidence and denied its authority. They alike conspired to hate, to revile and to persecute its friends. But, vanquished in debate, overcome by its advocates, many of them at length formally admitted its pretensions, abjured their errors and bowed in homage to its dictates. Still, influenced more or less by their former opinions and early associations, they mystified its doctrine, corrupted its simplicity, nullified its precepts, and encumbered it with the traditions of the world. Thus, by degrees, a vain and empty philosophy beguiled its friends, neutralized its opponents and secularized its institutions.

In a little more than three centuries from the birth of its Founder, the doctrine of the cross was so perverted and corrupted as to ascend the throne of the Roman Cæsars, in the person of Constantine the Great. The sword of persecution was then sheathed, and, by an imperial ordinance, toleration was vouchsafed to the Christians, and their confiscated estates were restored.

This event was, most fallaciously and unfortunately, contemplated as the triumph of the cross over the idolatries of pagan Rome; because, forsooth, the Emperor of Rome, while commanding its armies, had seen, or dreamed that he had seen, at high noon, a golden cross standing under a meridian sun, inscribed, *In hoc signo vinces*—"under this symbol you will triumph." Thus, as a military chieftain, he was converted to the faith, and, under the banner of a painted cross, led his armies to a final triumph.

The paganizing of Christianity in the person and government of Constantine, and in his Council of Nice, inflicted upon the church and Christianity a wound from which they have not yet wholly recovered. This early defection, obscuring and paralyzing the understanding and corrupting the heart of the Christian profession, also greatly influenced Bible-interpretation, and, by degrees, introduced a new theological nomenclature; of which sundry monuments, both Eastern and Western, afford melancholy proof. Down to the first œcumenical council, the Christian Scriptures were translated into various dialects. They were not only read, in whole or in part, in Hebrew, Greek and Syriac, but also in Latin, Coptic, Sahidic, Ethiopic, Persic and other tongues.

The spirit of translating is as old as the celebrated day of Pentecost. When first the gospel was announced by the Holy Spirit sent down from heaven, it was spoken in all the languages then represented in Jerusalem. "How is it," said the immense concourse, "we do hear, every one in his own native tongue—Parthians, Medes, Persians; inhabitants of Judea, Cappadocia, Pontus and Proconsular Asia; Phrygians, Pamphylians, Egyptians, Cyrenians, Africans, Roman strangers, Cretes and Arabians—we hear them speaking, *in our own tongues*, the wonderful works of God?" Ask we any other warrant or example to inspire us with the spirit of *translation* or to guide and authorize our efforts in this great work?

The inscription upon the Saviour's cross was written in Hebrew, Greek and Latin; and certainly, for reasons at least equal, if not superior, to those which called forth this inscription, the story of his resurrection, and all its consequences, should be given in tongues as numerous and as various as the languages of those to whom this glorious message of salvation is delivered. No one denying this, we need not argue its claims as a matter of doubtful disputation. Nor need we undertake to show that the missionary spirit is essentially the spirit of Christianity, and that wherever a church is planted in any country, to it should be committed the oracles of God.

It is, however, worthy of special notice that God himself simultaneously *spoke* and *wrote* the legal and symbolic dispensation. He not only preached the law, but wrote the law, with his own hand, and gave the autograph to Moses of what he had spoken to him in the mount.

In the same spirit of wisdom and philanthropy, the apostles spoke and wrote Christianity in sermons and epistles. And our Saviour himself made John the amanuensis of the seven epistles to the Asiatic churches.

For accurate and long preservation of words and ideas, the pen and the parchment, the stylus and the wax, the chisel, the lead and the rock, are indispensable. Hence, neither the new nor the old dispensation was left to the chances of mere oral communication or tradition, but they were written by prophets and apostles, or by their amanuenses, and given in solemn charge to the most faithful depositories—

the primitive churches—with solemn anathemas annexed, to protect them from interpolation, erasure or blemish on the part of man.

But the languages in which the holy oracles were originally written died soon after the precious deposit had been committed to them. This death, however, became the occasion of the immortality of that precious deposit.

Living tongues are always in a state of mutation. They change with every generation. The language of Wickliffe, of Tindal, of Cranmer, of James I., is not the language of this country or of this generation. Wickliffe's version would need now to be translated into the English of 1850. But the Greek of the New Testament, and the Hebrew of the Old, having ages since ceased to be spoken, have ceased to change; and therefore with the languages of that age are stereotyped the general literature, the philosophy, the poetry, the history, the classics of the Greeks and Romans, together with the Septuagint, and other Greek versions of the Jewish Scriptures.

Next to the deluge, not only in time, but in its calamitous influence on the destiny of man, was the confusion of human language at the profane and insolent attempt to erect a temple to Belus, and a city to prevent the wide dispersion of Noah's progeny. The monumental name Babylon awakens in every thoughtful and sensitive heart a series of painful reflections on every remembrance of its grievous associations. But for it, as among all animals without reason and conscience, there would have been, through our whole species, but one language and one speech. It has thrown in the way of human civilization and moral progress barriers that neither can be annihilated nor overcome. It has more or less alienated man from man, making every one of a different dialect—more or less a barbarian to a great portion of his own species. Till then, the vernacular of every child was that of all mankind, and was a part and parcel of humanity itself to interest him in every one of his species as his own flesh and blood. But foreign tongues indicate a foreign origin, with which, most frequently, some ungrateful associations arise that estrange and alienate from the claims of a common brotherhood.

But, most of all to be deplored, this Divine judgment has thrown very great obstacles in the path of the evangelical ministry. It was, indeed, as observed already, miraculously overcome by the gift of tongues, instantaneously conferred on the apostles at the time of the coronation of the Lord Messiah. They had access, at once, to many nations, whose representatives returned from Jerusalem richly laden with the word of life to their countrymen. But the necessity that was overcome on the memorable Pentecost still exists, more or less, as a very formidable obstacle to the conversion of the human race to one Lord, one faith, one baptism and one communion, and must, of necessity, be overcome. And here we state our first argument in favor of translations of the Holy Scriptures into all languages spoken by man capable of receiving, in their vocabularies, the precious oracles of the living and true God.

But I am met at the threshold with the assertion that this is a subject in which all Christendom is agreed, and that it would be but a waste of time to discuss such a question. The necessity of translating the living oracles of the living God into all the nations of earth, as the means of their conversion and salvation, I am told, is universally conceded by Jew and Gentile. But have they in any other way than theoretically conceded it?

The Jews' religion and revelation, now called the *Old Testament*, was not designed for all mankind, in the same sense as the Christian revelation and religion are designed for all mankind. The Jews' religion was specially given to one nation for its own sake. It never was essentially a proselyting institution. Its genius and nature restricted it to the natural seed of Abraham. There is no precept in it commanding it to be preached or promulged to all the world. Still, the Jews' institution had in it the elements of Christianity, and, on that account, it is invaluable to all the Christian kingdom. They, too, have set us an example; for when the Jews were scattered through different countries they had their oracles translated into the language of those countries. Hence, the first translation made in Egypt by the seventy learned Jews, all natives of Egypt, assembled in Alexandria, not by command of Ptolemy Philadelphus, but during his copartnery of the throne of Egypt with his father, was designed to give to the Jews throughout the world a version in the then prevailing dialect. Thus originated the celebrated *Septuagint*. This, however, preceded the Christian era by only two hundred and eighty-five years.

But the necessity of *improved versions* is rather our present subject; and with reference to this the Jews are worthy of our regard. They were not all satisfied with this venerable and invaluable translation, though the best ever made into the Greek tongue. It is honored and consecrated, too, by the fact that it is quoted in the New Testament, and is thus sanctioned by the holy apostles themselves—a correct exponent of their own Hebrew original. Philo the Jew, Josephus and the primitive Christians also gave it the sanction of their approval.

Notwithstanding all this, many learned individuals, both Jews and

Christians, took exceptions to some parts of it, and suggested numerous corrections and emendations. Accordingly, Aquila, a Jew, who once professed Christianity, but afterwards renounced it and relapsed into Judaism, undertook and finished a new version in the fore part of the second century. His chief objection to the Septuagint was its too periphrastic character; and, avoiding this alleged defect, he became literal to a fault. It was, however, read with interest as early as the middle of the second century of our Christian era.

Almost contemporaneous with this was the version of Theodotion, an Ebionite Christian, who supposed that a rather freer version than that of Aquila was desirable. Next to his appeared the version of Symmachus. More skilled in Hebrew, according to tradition, than Theodotion, he made many alleged improvements, but borrowed too much, and rather indiscreetly, from his predecessors.

Besides these private versions of the Hebrew Scriptures into the Greek vernacular, no less than three anonymous Greek versions appeared before the middle of the second century; which, because of the columns they occupy in Origen's Hexapla, are called the fifth, sixth and seventh versions. Thus the Septuagint, which reigned without a rival for some three centuries till the close, we may say, of the first century of Christianity, has, in some one hundred and fifty years, no less than six Greek rival versions—all the fruit, we must suppose, of a desire for an improved version. It may be observed that the author of the sixth translation of this class, as arranged in the Hexapla of Origen, was evidently a Christian. So far, then, as the learning, judgment and piety of the authors of the six Greek versions of the old Hebrew Testament afford an example or argument, it is decidedly in favor of our effort to have an improved version, at least of the Christian Scriptures.

We do not, indeed, regard every new version, whether undertaken by public or private authority, as an improvement. But there is little ground to doubt that these six versions, together with the Septuagint, would enable any person of the genius and learning of Origen to furnish a better than any one of them. Hence it is that Origen's Hexapla is regarded as one of the most valuable offerings of the third century to the cause of Biblical translations.

But the necessity of original translations and of improved versions of former translations has much more to commend and enforce its claims upon public attention than the customs of the Jews or the spirit and character of their religion. Christianity, or the gospel, in its facts, precepts and promises, was divinely commanded to be promulged throughout the whole world. Neither its spirit nor its design is national or secular, but catholic and divine.

It is a dispensation of Divine grace, adapted to the genius, character and condition of men, as they now are. It grasps in its broad philanthropy the human race, and throws its benignant arms around all the nations of the earth. *It is, therefore, the sin of the church, if there be one of Adam's sons who has never heard, in his own tongue, the wonderful works of God.*

In its hale and undegenerate days the gospel was borne on the wings of every wind, and, as far and as soon as possible, it was promulged by the living tongues of apostles, evangelists and prophets, from Jerusalem to the confines of the most barbarous nations, and on equal terms tendered to Jew and Greek, barbarian, Scythian, bond and free.

It was not only spoken, but *written* and *translated* into every language accessible to those to whom were committed the oracles of God. For this purpose God gave plenary inspiration to the first heralds of the cross, and therefore it was as accurately announced to the inhabitants of the *Ultima Thule,* in word and writing, as to the inhabitants of Jerusalem, the radiating centre of the Christian church.

But it must be *written* as well as spoken, because the word in the ear is evanescent, compared with that word written and pictured to the eye on parchment. The command to preach the gospel to every creature is not fulfilled when only spoken to those whom we see and who can hear. Were speaking the only way of preaching, then the deaf could never have the gospel preached to them. In that case, Paul could not, with truth, have said that "Moses was preached every Sabbath day, being *read* in the synagogues."

We sometimes converse with the present as well as the absent by signs addressed to the eye. Words spoken are only for those present. Hence the necessity that an age of apostles and prophets should be an age of writing as well as of speaking a finished language. And such was the era of the Jews' religion; but still more emphatically such was the Christian era.

The great revelations of the Bible originated in ages and countries of the highest civilization and mental advancement. Egypt was the cradle of the learning and wisdom of the world when Moses, the prophet, the lawgiver and oracle of Jehovah, was born. From Egypt radiated the light of the world under the reign of the Pharaohs. And Moses was profoundly read in all the learning of the Egyptians. He was therefore chosen to speak to his contemporaries and to write for posterity the oracles of God.

Jesus the Messiah was born in the city of David, educated neither in Egypt nor in Nazareth, but from heaven, by a plenary inhabitation of a Divine nature and a Divine spirit. He taught in Jerusalem, in the temple, and in the presence of the Rabbis, and Scribes, and Elders of Israel. Christianity was first preached, instituted and received in Jerusalem, and thence radiated through Asia, Africa and Europe. It was written in the most finished language ever spoken on earth, so far as copiousness, richness of terms, perspicuity, precision, as well as majesty and grandeur of style, enter into the constituency of language. Hence the pen, alike with the tongue, was employed in giving utterance and free circulation to the word of life from its first promulgation to the final *amen* of the Apocalypse.

The Holy Spirit and the spirit of the gospel did not cease to work with the age of the apostles. Preaching and teaching, writing and translating from language to language, the word and works of God—the sayings, the doings and the sufferings of the Saviour—begun and prosecuted with untiring energy and assiduity by the original apostles and evangelists of Christ, was still continued with zealous diligence by the succeeding age. Peter was not the only man of his day who said, "I will carefully endeavor that you may be able, after my decease, to have these things always in remembrance." This was the spirit of all the family of God capable of such an instrumentality.

In the second century, we find the whole Bible, Old Testament and New, translated into the Syriac tongue. The oldest, most literal, simple and exact version in that language is called the *Peschito,* or the *literal,* because of its great fidelity to the original text. In after-times, other versions were published in the same tongue.

Egypt was favored at an early day with two versions—one in the Coptic, for the lower, and one in Sahidic, for the upper Egyptians. Of the Arabic, Ethiopic, Armenian, Persian, Gothic, Sclavonian and Anglo-Saxon versions we cannot now speak particularly. Suffice it to say that the philanthropy of the gospel wrought more effectually than that of the law, in giving version after version of the law and the gospel to the nations and tribes that embraced it.

At the commencement of the Christian era, the Roman empire stretched from the Rhine and the Danube, on the north, to the sandy deserts of Arabia and Africa on the south, and from the river Euphrates, on the east, to the Atlantic Ocean on the west. Over this vast extent of territory the Latin language was, more or less, spoken. Important, therefore, it was, that the *living oracles* should find in that tongue a passport to every province that acknowledged the supremacy of Rome. Versions of the gospels and Epistles, in that tongue, early began to multiply. One had obtained a free circulation through parts of Africa; but, after considerable competition, another, of acknowledged superiority, began to triumph over all its Roman rivals, under the name of the "Itala," or "Old Italic.'

When Jerome had risen to some conspicuity, the Itala was pronounced canonical. This version, containing both Testaments, was made from the Greek. Hebrew scholars capable of correctly translating the Hebrew Bible could not then be found. The first half of the second century is generally conceded to have been the time when the Old Itala first made its appearance. During that century, it was certainly quoted by Tertullian. But, as Horne judiciously remarks, before the fourth century had closed, alterations and differences, either designed or accidental, had equalled in number the interpolations found in the Greek versions before corrected by Origen. Pope Damasus assigned the work of revision to Jerome, who conformed it much more to the Greek. But this only induced Jerome to attempt a new version of the Old Testament, from the Hebrew into Latin, for the benefit of the Western church. Still, notwithstanding the reputation of St. Jerome and the authority of Pope Damasus, the version was introduced by slow degrees, lest weak minds might stumble. But through the partiality of Gregory I. it gradually rose to ascendency, so that ever since the seventh century, under the name of the *Vulgate* version, it has been extensively adopted by the whole Roman church.

The Council of Trent, convoked by Paul III., A.D. 1545, continued under Julius X. and consummated under Pius IV., A.D. 1563, after a session of eighteen years, decreed it to be *authentic*, and commanded that the Vulgate *alone* should be read wherever the Bible is commanded to be read, and used in all sermons, expositions and discussions. Thenceforth it was of equal authority with the originals: so that it was as lawful to correct the originals by the Vulgate as the Vulgate by the originals. Romanists still prefer to translate from the Vulgate rather than from the originals.

In course of time, the Old Itala and the Vulgate became so mixed up that both fell into great confusion and were interspersed with many and great errors. Hence originated Stephens's seven critical editions of the Vulgate, extending from A.D. 1528 to A.D. 1546—a period commensurate with the sessions of the Council of Trent. The doctors of the Sorbonne condemned them, and ordered a new edition by John Hortensius, of Louvain, which was finished in 1547. Still another improved version was called for, and finished in 1586, with critical notes, by Lucas Brugensis. Finally, however, it was condemned by Pope Sixtus V., who commanded a new edition, and, having himself corrected the proofs, he pronounced it, by all the authority of his chair, to be the *authentic* Vulgate, and, issuing a folio edition, commanded it to be adopted throughout the Roman church.

But, notwithstanding the labors of the Pope and the seal of his infallible decree, this edition was discovered to be so exceedingly incorrect that his successor, the infallible Clement VIII., caused it to be suppressed, and published another authentic Vulgate, in folio size, in 1592, differing more than any other edition from that of Sixtus V. These facts are a full refutation, if we had nothing else to allege, of all the pretensions of Bellarmine and the See of Rome in favor of the Vulgate. Some learned men, of much leisure, have noted several hundreds of differences between these two authentic and infallible translations—many of them, too, of very serious import. Thus the two infallibles—Sixtus V. and Clement VIII., stand in direct contradiction.

Other improved Latin versions from time to time appeared, to the number of some ten or eleven, half of them the work of Protestants and half of Romanists. Of those made by Catholics, that by Erasmus, and of those made by Protestants, that by Beza, is prominent. So far the spirit of improved versions obtained down to the era of the Protestant Reformation.

We have not yet noted the growth and prevalence of this principle in Germany or in our mother land and language. These are matters rather too familiar to deserve much notice at present. Still, that we may further demonstrate the very general acknowledgment of the moral and Christian obligation to print and publish in writing, as well as to declare by the tongue, the oracles of God, and that in the most correct and improved style of language, we must at least notice the interest that Germany and Great Britain have taken in this work.

As the art of printing is the fruit of German genius, we might, in the absence of history, presume that the Bible would have been amongst the first-fruits of the press, and that it would have a freer course through Germany than in any other country in Europe or the world. And such, in part, is the fact. The Bible was first printed and published in Germany, and in the vernacular of its inhabitants. In 1486, a German translation from the Vulgate was printed, the author of which is unknown.

In 1517, Martin Luther began to publish and print scraps of the Bible, which he continued until he got through with the whole book.

His translation of the whole Bible, from the Hebrew and Greek originals, assisted by Melanchthon, Cruciger, and other learned professors of Hebrew and Greek, was first issued from the press in 1530, and passed through three improved editions before the close of 1545.

From Luther's version of the Holy Scriptures no less than ten versions were derived; and it became the occasion of many others. But this justly celebrated work of the great Reformer was itself improved—or at least revised—by the Zuinglians and Calvinists, and numerous new editions of it circulated through Germany and its dependencies, down to the year 1659.

Besides that of Luther, other versions were printed and circulated on the continent. Among these were the Zurich version, Piscator's, from that of Junius and Tremellius, with several Romanist versions.

We pass from Germany to Britain. Authentic history we have not of the commencement of translations into the languages spoken in Great Britain. Saxon versions of parts of the holy oracles were made in that island as early as the beginning of the eighth century. Aldhelm's name is associated with a version of the Psalms as early as A.D. 706. A translation of the four Gospels, made by Egbert, appeared a few years after, and that was followed by one of the whole Bible by the Venerable Bede. Two centuries after appeared a new version of the Psalms by King Alfred. An unknown individual translated the whole Bible into English about the year 1290, copies of which are yet extant in some public libraries.

In 1380, John Wickliffe translated the whole Bible from the Vulgate into the current English of that day; it was first *printed* in 1731. To William Tindal we are indebted for the first printed English Bible. It was issued from the press at Antwerp or Hamburg, A.D. 1520. His revised English Testament appeared in 1534. In 1535 Miles Coverdale gave a new English version of the whole Bible. This was the first Bible allowed by royal authority. The fictitious *Mathew's* Bible, issued from politic reasons under this name, was, for the most part, Tindal's version disguised. This edition, printed abroad, appeared in 1537. Cranmer's version of the New Testament, with its last corrections, appeared in 1539; the Geneva version in 1557; the Bishop's Bible in 1568; the Rheims in 1582; and the Authorized Common Version in 1611. Concerning these, with the exception of the last, we will not now speak particularly.

The time usually allotted for a single address is not more than sufficient to name and describe the numerous and various versions through which the Holy Scriptures have passed. We have not even named all the versions made in our own vernacular. We have simply made selections for a specific purpose. Those named are sufficient to show that the professed church of Christ has, in all ages, acted upon the principle that the Scriptures should be accurately translated and more or less circulated amongst at least a portion of the people. Protestants say, *through all the people.* Romanists have said, and still say, *only through a portion of the people.*

But the precise question now before you, my Christian brethren, is not whether the Scriptures should be translated into every tongue spoken by mankind, but *whether they should be translated into the current language of every age.* Indeed, you take the ground that the Scriptures are not translated into any language unless the true import of the original text is perspicuously and faithfully given in the living language of the people. For this reason you justly object to the translation usually called "The Authorized Common Version." You say it is not authorized by God, because he would not authorize an erroneous version. A king, a court, a parliament, a political corporation or a secular church, *authorizing* any version, correct or incorrect, you regard as an assumption, on their part, of spiritual jurisdiction over the consciences of men; you regard it as a species of spiritual despotism, of ecclesiastic tyranny and usurpation.

That a Christian community may adopt any new version, or authorize any number of its members to prepare a version which shall correctly and perspicuously set forth, in the currency of the age, the import of the original Scriptures, you cheerfully admit. But that such is not the commonly received and frequently styled "Authorized Version," you conscientiously think and affirm.

That this is a rational, scriptural and Christian position, in our judgment, we most religiously avow. But, before proceeding further, let us summarily and distinctly state the premises already submitted.

I. It has been alleged that the command to "preach the gospel to every creature" implies that it must not only be spoken, but *written,* in the languages of all nations.

II. That such was the judgment and understanding of the apostles and primitive evangelists of Christ, is proved from the fact that both the apostles commissioned by the Saviour, and certain evangelists not directly commissioned by him, both spoke and wrote the gospel. The gospels preserved, written by John, Mark and Luke, are imperishable monuments of this fact.

III. That Jesus Christ commanded his communications to the churches to be *written,* and to be carried by messengers, called in our common version *angels of the churches*, and to be by them delivered to the churches, is also another evidence of the same fact.

IV. That the gospels and apostolic epistles were to be translated into the languages of the nations and people to whom they were sent, is evident from the miraculous gift of tongues conferred at the commencement of the church in Jerusalem, and continued to the end of the gospel ministry, contained in the inspired writings. We not only observe that this gift was instantly and simultaneously bestowed on all the apostles, for the purpose of translating the whole Christian revelation into all the languages of the people addressed by them, but also continued with them to the end of their lives. It was also bestowed supernaturally on Paul, born out of due time, and in a superabundant degree, so that he could speak in Gentile cities, in more tongues than any other member of those churches, though many of them also possessed this supernatural spiritual endowment in eminent measures.

V. The necessity and importance of translations, in order to the ends of the Christian mission, is also shown in the care taken by all the writers of the New Testament to translate every foreign word and quotation introduced into their writings. For example, the word *Messiah* is interpreted to aliens from the commonwealth of Israel; so are the words *Cephas*, *Siloam*, *Tabitha*, *Elymas*, *Talitha-cumi*, *Barnabas*, &c.

VI. The necessity is further shown, from the fact that in the primitive churches there were official translators immediately raised up for the emergency. "To one class," says Paul, "is given the gift of tongues; to another, the *interpretation* or translation of tongues."

VII. An apostolic edict is given by Paul on the subject of interpretation. 1 Cor. xix. 27—"If any man speak in a foreign or unknown tongue, let it be by *two*, or at most by three (*sentences* at a time), and let one translate; but if there be no interpreter, let him keep silence in the church."

Are not these conclusive evidences that the church of Christ, in the discharge of its duties and obligations, must have interpreters of Scripture, and make translations commensurate with the wants of mankind?

Regarding this, henceforth, as an established point, we shall advance another step toward our goal. It is, perhaps, rather a formality on our part, than a necessity imposed on us, to show that we are as much obliged, by all the reasons and authority hitherto adduced in favor of original translations, to amend, improve and correct obscure, imperfect and erroneous versions of particular words and passages in existing translations, which, in the main, are true to the original, and couched in terms well adapted to the understanding of the reader, as we are to give new versions in languages and dialects into which the gospel has never been introduced.

But this, on grave reflection, must appear to all a point already almost, if not altogether, universally conceded. Our object, in the preceding part of our discourse, (and a rather dry and irksome task it is,) in giving a summary view of the labors of the Christian ministry and the church, was to show that the necessity of *amended* versions, as well as of *new* versions, was felt and acted on in every century of the Christian church, and by the most enlightened and gifted portions of it. True, many of these amended versions were made from the original tongues, but not as the first versions from these tongues were made. These amending translators had other versions from the original, in the same language or in other languages, which they understood, and with which they compared their own version, and were, more or less, led by them on many occasions, adopting the verbiage of their predecessors. It is questionable whether we have ever had two independent and original versions in one vernacular. But this is no defect in them. It is often an advantage. For in all such cases we have two witnesses, instead of one, of the verity and appropriateness of the last version.

We have only one step further to advance in this direction. We must affirm the conviction that we are, as Christian churches, bound, by the highest and holiest motives and obligations, to use our best endeavors to have the original Scriptures exactly and faithfully, in every particular, to the best of our knowledge and belief, translated at home and abroad, into the vernacular, be it what it may, in which we desire to present them to our fellow-men. Any thing short of this is a sinful and most condemnable negligence or indiffernece. It is a clear and unambiguous transgression of the supreme law of Christian morality—viz. "All things whatsoever you would that men should do to you, do you even so to them; for this is the law and the prophets." "Speak to them all that I command thee," is the oracle of God to his prophet. "And," says Paul, "the things thou hast heard of me in the presence of many witnesses, the same commit thou to faithful men that shall be able to teach others also." We must neither add to, nor subtract from, the word of Jehovah.

But there is another attitude in which this subject must be placed before our minds. Passages of Scripture will, translated into any one language in one age, cease to be a correct and intelligible translation to the people of another age, though speaking, at least in name, the same language. Our English versions demonstrate this in a very clear and satisfactory manner.

No one unskilled in the history of our vernacular can easily appreciate the changes it has undergone during even the last three centuries. I will furnish, by way of illustration or demonstration, an example or two of these changes. We shall first give a specimen of the hundredth Psalm, found in the preface to the English Hexapla. It represents the English language five hundred years ago:—

> "Mirthes to God al erthe that es
> Serves to louerd in faines.
> In go yhe al in his siht,
> In gladnes that is so briht.
> Whites that louerd God is he thus,
> Hs us made and our self noht us,
> His foke and shep of his fode:
> In gos his yhates that are gode:
> In schrift his worches believe,
> In ympnes to him yhe schrive
> Heryhes his name for louerde his honde
> In al his merci do in strende and strende."

In 1380, Wickliffe's version, now before me, gives the Lord's Prayer —Matt. vi. 9—in the following orthography and orthoepy:—

> "Oure fadir that art in heuenes, halowid be thi name, thi kingdom come, to be thi wille don in erthe as in heuene, geve to us this day oure breed, *ouir other substaunce*, forgeue to vs oure dettis, as we forguen to oure dettouris, lede us not into temptacion; but delyuer us from yuel, amen."

We shall now add a specimen from the Rheims translation, first given to the world in 1582—two hundred and sixty-eight years ago. It is the commission, Matthew xxviii.:—

> "Al povver is giun to me in heauen and in erthe; going therfore teach ye al nations, baptizing them in the name of the Father and of the sonne and of the holy ghost, teaching them to obserue al things vvhatsoeuer I haue commanded you, and behold I am vvith you al daies."

We need scarcely say that such a style is awkward, uncouth and unintelligible; and had the holy oracles continued in this garb till this day, our language and literature, in other departments, having progressed as they have, the reading and the study of them would have been very uninteresting and unacceptable to our contemporaries. If in no other respect faulty—if every word and sentence had been a perfect exponent of the mind of the Holy Spirit—other terms and formulas of speech, or, in other words, a new and modernized version of them, would have been indispensable.

But this is not all that may or must be urged in behalf of a new, or, rather, an improved version. The word of God was not, a century or two since, as well understood as it is now, by the most enlightened and reformed portions of Protestant Christendom. Biblical literature, criticism and science, since the times of Wickliffe, Tindal, Luther, Calvin, Zuinglius, Beza, Cranmer, Coverdale, Archbishop Parker, Edward VI. or James I., have greatly advanced. The last seventy-five years have contributed more to real Biblical learning—have given to the Christian church larger and better means of translating the original Scriptures—than had accumulated from the days of Tindal to the era of the American Revolution.

We are, therefore, better prepared to give a correct and faithful version of the Sacred Scriptures, at this day, than at any former period since the revival of literature. We have also a more correct original from which to translate, than they had at any former period since the art of printing was invented. The Greek text of the New Testament has been subjected to the most laborious investigation; and, after the most rigid scrutiny and comparison, a much more accurate original has been obtained. With these advantages in our favor, we are better furnished than at any former period to enter upon a work of such awful and momentous magnitude and responsibility.

But, that we may be more deeply impressed with a sense of its necessity and importance, we must give a few samples of the aberrations and mistranslations of the commonly received version. And first, we shall read the usual title-page of the Christian Scriptures: "*The New Testament of our Lord and Saviour Jesus Christ.*"

While all the words found in this title are found in the text itself, the title itself is no part of the text or volume, but is an ecclesiastical name put upon it, as an index to its contents. It is, therefore, an index to the mind of those who prefixed it to the volume, and much affects their claim to the possession of a clear and comprehensive knowledge of the writings it contains. I assume that no one, well instructed in the volume itself, could have given to it this title.

The term *testament* or *will*, with us, is now, and for a long time has been, appropriated to one particular instrument, setting forth the final disposition of a person's estate. But in that case it indicates that the testator is dead, and that this is the last disposition he has made of his effects. How, then, does this apply to a volume containing not only the memoirs of Jesus, but the writings of six of his apostles and two of his evangelists? Again: Is the testator dead? That he died, is true; and that he continued dead a few hours, is also true; but that he ever lives and never shall die, is most gloriously true. Again: Did Jesus, during his life, make two testaments or two wills? This is called, not a New Testament, but *the* New Testament, of Jesus Christ. Where learned they the contents of the Old Testament of Jesus Christ? Have we a copy of his first will? Now, if no such document ever was, is now, or shall hereafter be, why, in reason and in truth, give it such a cognomen, rather such a misnomer? There is no such will or testament on earth as the New Testament of our Lord and Saviour Jesus Christ. He never made an old one, and he is not dead, but lives forever, a priest upon his throne, not according to the law of a fleshly commandment, but according to the power of an endless life.

Nor would it relieve the title-page from the error had it been styled "*The New Covenant of our Lord Jesus Christ,*" for that would indicate that he is the author of two covenants, which is not the fact. There is no old covenant of Jesus Christ, and, consequently, there cannot be a new covenant of Jesus Christ. It might, with both grammatical and logical propriety, be called the New Institution, or the New Covenant by Jesus Christ. But that, too, is an exceptionable use of the figure synecdoche, which puts a part for the whole, or the whole for a part. To get rid of a consecrated error is sometimes very difficult. We have chosen to designate the book "THE SACRED WRITINGS OF THE APOSTLES AND EVANGELISTS OF JESUS CHRIST." This is strictly true, and, in our judgment, enough. True, we may, after a good example found in Acts vii., briefly call the whole volume "THE LIVING ORACLES."

It would be important, could we classify under appropriate heads the different species of subordinate errors found in the common version; but in such a discourse as the present we could not give a specimen of each. It would require much more time than we have at command. I shall, therefore, as they occur, give a few cases, that may suggest to some one of more leisure and capacity the necessity and expediency of such an effort.

First, then, we shall name and illustrate an instance or two in the use of the Greek article, *ho, hee, to.* Though apparently a small matter, there are some serious errors in the use of the article. A Greek noun, with the article, is always *definite;* without it, always *indefinite.*

In Matthew xvi. 13–18, the moral and evangelical foundation of the

Christian church is stated by its founder in a very formal and inspiring manner. The question was, "*Whom do men say that I the Son of man am?*" Peter responds, "Some say John the Baptist, others Elijah, others Jeremiah, or some one of the prophets." "But whom do you say that I am?" Simon Peter answering said, "Thou art *the Christ*, the Son of the living God."

After pronouncing a benediction on Peter, he said to him, "Thou art a *stone*, and on this *rock* I will build my church, and the gates of hades shall not prevail against it." Now, to have answered this interesting interrogatory by saying, "Thou art Christ, the Son of the living God," would have given quite a different idea. It would have been merely a personal name, as Sergius Paulus, John Mark, or Simon Peter. And so has the common version made it on another and a very important occasion. 1 Cor. iii. 11, Paul is made to say, "Other foundation can no man lay than that which is laid, which is Jesus Christ." The church, according to this version, is built upon Jesus Christ, and not upon the faith "*Jesus is the Christ*," as the true original reading and the common Greek text have it.* Now, there is just as much difference between Jesus Christ and Jesus the Christ, as between John Baptist and John the Baptist, Paul Apostle and Paul the apostle, George king and George the king. It may be loyalty or treason, as the case may be, to say George is the king; but neither the one nor the other to call any man George King. Infidels talk fluently concerning Jesus Christ, but they will not, in the proper meaning of the terms, say, "*Jesus is the Christ.*"

The same law of interpretation applies to the use of the word *spirit*. *Pneuma* is simply spirit; *to pneuma*, the Spirit.

Frequently "the Holy Spirit" and "the Spirit" indicate the same person. But without the article, unless some qualifying adjunct be annexed, it means simply a spirit, or the spirit of a man, and not the Spirit of God.

There is no article in the following instances:—"If any fellowship of the spirit;" "Which worship God in the spirit;" "You live in the spirit;" "Through sanctification of the spirit;" "He carried me away in the spirit;" "Immediately I was in the spirit." In all these cases, there being no article in the original, there should be no definite article in the translation.

But in the following cases the article is found:—"The sword of the

---

* Griesbach repudiates the article; but the best Greek texts have it. It is *ho Christos* in my London Polyglot, as it is in Matthew xvi. 17, in the received text.

Spirit;" "The fruit of the Spirit;" "Let him hear what the Spirit saith;" "Keep by the Holy Spirit which dwelleth in us." In these and many such the article indicates that it is the Spirit of God that is meant. "That which is born of the Spirit is spirit." This is a striking example; *the* Spirit here means the Holy Spirit of God; and that which is born of it is spirit, a new spirit, or a new heart, disposition, or temper.

But there is a perspicacity of mind and a delicacy of taste essential to a precise and accurate transference of some ideas from one tongue to another, which is peculiarly necessary in the case of translating Greek nouns without an article, and for which no rules of grammar can be furnished.

Our translators did not always display this endowment in an eminent degree. They sometimes employed an indefinite article where they should have employed none. The dullest mind can perceive a difference between *man* without an article and *man* with an article, between assuming that *man* cannot do this, and that *a* man cannot do this; between God and *a god*, between Spirit and *a* spirit.

I will instance this in the common version:—"God is a Spirit, and they that worship him must worship him in spirit and in truth." We would render it, God is Spirit, and they that worship him must worship him in spirit and in truth. For thus translating it we might even plead the example of the same translators in other cases. For example, they render two passages from the same apostle as I have done this. "God is love," and not, God is *a* love; God is light, and not, God is *a* light. And even in the example cited from John iv. 24, they translate in this manner:—"They that worship him must worship him in spirit and truth;" not in *a* spirit and in *a* truth.

We might say as they do of God—an angel is a spirit, but not that an angel is Spirit. To say of an angel that he is Spirit is by far too august and sublime. God alone is Spirit, God alone is light, God alone is love.

We shall next give an instance or two of the mistranslation of particles or the connectives of speech. Take, for example, the particle *ote*, which occurs many hundred times in the apostolic writings. The more frequent meanings of this conjunction are, *because, for, that.* Which of these three shall be preferred in any given passage must always be discretionary with the translator, and must therefore depend upon his judgment and taste. But the sense of some passages is very much changed or impaired by the selection of an unsuitable representative of the original. Hence we have long since decided that no translator, however extensive his learning, however well read in other books, however orthodox his creed in religion, can suitably translate the New Testament, unless he have a thorough and comprehensive knowledge of the whole remedial scheme of the gospel, and the peculiar genius, spirit and character of the Christian institution. Take an example or two in the case of this particle *ote*:—

Paul to the Romans, ch. viii. 20, 21:—"For the *creature* (more properly *mankind*) was made subject to frailty, (rather than vanity,) not willingly, but by him who subjected them to it, in hope (*because*) that mankind will be delivered from the bondage of corruption into the glorious freedom of the sons of God." How awkward to say, in hope *because*, instead of, in hope *that!*

Another instance to the same effect is found in 1 John iii. 2. In the common version:—"We know not what we shall be; but we know that when he appeareth we shall be like him, for we shall see him as he is." This version indicates that our simply seeing him would transform us into his image. This is a new revelation. But how much more in harmony with the whole record to prefer *that* to *for*, and read it, We know that we shall be like him—that we shall see him as he is! There are hundreds of instances of this use of *ote* in the New Testament and Septuagint.

In the gender of pronouns we have also sundry analogies. A very remarkable instance occurs in Dr. George Campbell's version of the beginning of John. In his version it reads, "In the beginning was the Word, and the Word was with God, and the Word was God. This was in the beginning with God. All things were made by it, and without it not a single creature was made. In it was life, and the life was the light of men."

Now, although the laws of the language will justify the translation, "*this* was in the beginning," there appears no necessity to change the masculine into the neuter, especially as Dr. Campbell regards an allusion here to the eighth chapter of Proverbs, to the beautiful personification of wisdom given in that passage. The laws of rhetoric, as well as of grammar, will justify our translating it in harmony with the gender of *Logos*, and with the style of Solomon in the passage alluded to. I always dissent from this learned, candid and elegant translator of the four Gospels with great reluctance, and with much diffidence. Still, in this case, as *the Word* became incarnate and dwelt among us, and was "God manifest in the flesh," I prefer, after considerable hesitancy, to render it, "All things were made by him, and without him was not any thing made that was made. In him was life, and the life was the light of men." Paul seems to rise above himself when the uncreated glories of this most sublime personage appear before his mind. "For by him," says he, "were all things created that are in the heavens and that are on the earth, visible and invisible, whether they be thrones, or dominions, or principalities, or powers; all things were created by him, and for him; and he is before all things, and by him all things consist; and he is the head of the body, the church, the beginning, the first-fruits from the dead, that in all things he might have the pre-eminence: for it pleased the Father that in him all fulness should dwell."

But we must notice another species of errors, in the use of the auxiliary verbs and signs of moods and tenses in our language, when translating certain forms of the original verbs. For example, *may* and *can*, *might*, *could*, *would* and *should*, are used in our potential mood, for the present and imperfect tenses. Now, as there is nothing properly corresponding with these in the original Greek, it becomes discretionary with the translator whether he choose in one tense *may* or *can*, and in another tense *might*, *could*, *would*, or *should;* yet we know that there is a very great difference of meaning, with us, between *may* and *must*, *should* and *could*, &c.

We have one example of this, which, though not directly in point, illustrates how much depends on the use of proper exponents of these varieties in harmony with the sense or scope of a passage. We read it in Hebrews ii. 9:—"But we see Jesus, who was made but little lower than the angels, for the suffering of death, crowned with glory and honor, that he by the grace of God should taste death for every man." Who can see any necessity for being crowned with glory and honor that he *should* taste death, or in order to his tasting death, for all? But, properly rendered, we see a great propriety in his being crowned with glory and honor after he had tasted death for all, as Professor Stuart very properly renders the passage.

But I have wearied you and myself in thus rambling over so large a field, and shall only, on this topic, add another chapter of errors and difficulties into which most translators have occasionally fallen; and that is in the subject of punctuation. The original text itself is frequently erroneously pointed, and, of course, the translation is likely to be also at fault in this particular. As a specimen of this, and to illustrate this species of error, I will only quote one passage from the New Testament. It is found in John v. 31–47:—"If I bear witness of myself, my witness is not true. There is another that beareth witness of me, and I know that the witness which he witnesseth of me is true. Ye sent unto John, and he bare witness unto the truth. But I receive not testimony from man; but these things I say, that ye might be saved. He was a burning and a shining light; and ye were willing for a season to rejoice in his light. But I have greater witness than that of John; for the works which the Father hath given me to finish, the same works that I do, bear witness of me, that the Father hath sent me. And the Father himself which hath sent me, hath borne witness of me. Ye have neither heard his voice at any time, nor seen his shape. And ye have not his word abiding in you; for whom he hath sent, him ye believe not. Search the Scriptures, for in them ye think ye have eternal life, and they are they which testify of me. And ye will not come to me, that ye might have life. I receive not honor from men; but I know you, that ye have not the love of God in you. I am come in my Father's name, and ye receive me not: if another shall come in his own name, him ye will receive. How can you believe, which receive honor one of another, and seek not the honor that cometh from God only? Do not think that I will accuse you to the Father; there is one that accuseth you, even Moses, in whom ye trust; for had ye believed Moses, ye would have believed me, for he wrote of me. But if ye believe not his writings, how shall ye believe my words?" Though as read from the common version this address loses much of its beauty, propriety and force, it is one of the most clear, forcible and irresistible appeals to the understanding and conscience ever spoken.

1st. He modestly waives his own testimony in his own case, and submits this rule of moral decorum: that, in any matter of superlative importance, no one should use or depend on his own testimony in support of his own pretensions, and that any one so acting would be unworthy of credit.

2d. He alleges the testimony of John the Harbinger as his first argument, and enforces the regard due to it from their own respect for John, without any commendation of John to them on his part:—"You yourselves, unprompted by me, sent to John to know what he had to say of himself and the Messiah—consequently, of my claims and pretensions."

3d. After commending John as a brilliant and shining luminary, he modestly waives even his testimony, and urges a greater evidence—though, themselves being judges, John's testimony was the best human testimony ever submitted.

4th. He appeals to his miracles, which they and their contemporaries had already witnessed and tested, thereby showing and conceding that any one claiming credit on supernatural pretensions ought to submit supernatural evidence. He then recognizes and establishes a great law of evidence, viz.: that the proposition and the proof should be homogeneous; physical propositions, physical evidence; moral propositions, moral evidence; supernatural propositions, supernatural evidence.

5th. He then adduces the literal oracle of God himself, that God had actually, sensibly and audibly recognized him, and at one and the same time addressed their eyes and their ears. "Did you never hear his voice," saying, "This is my beloved Son, in whom I am well pleased"? "Did you never see his form?" alluding to the symbol of the descending dove, and its perching itself on his head, in the presence of the people. But who could learn this lesson from the common translations? The common version, and almost every other, makes our Saviour speak like a simpleton. After appealing to his Father's positive oral testimony in his favor at the Jordan, in the presence of a crowd, they make him say, "You have never, at any time, heard his voice." After appealing to the symbol of the Divine Spirit in the descending dove, they make him say, "You have never, at any time, seen his form," or any outward manifestation of him. And, further still, he is made to contradict a fact, in saying that they had not heard his declaration—that they had "not his word abiding in them;" whereas, placed interrogatively, it is, "Have you forgotten his declaration," 'This is my beloved Son, in whom I am well pleased'?"

Their position was that they had never heard God speak of him; that they had never seen him attested by any outward mark; that they had no recollection of ever hearing any confirmation of his pretensions. To all which he, knowing their thoughts and reasonings, said, "Have you never heard his voice? Have you never seen his form? Have you forgotten what he said?"*

The Saviour's climax in the argument is beautifully simple and sublime: 1. The testimony of John. 2. His miracles. 3. The public acknowledgment of his Father. 4. The visible descent of the Holy

* I have examined the London Polyglot, presented to me in Scotland, containing a Hebrew version of the New Testament, the received Greek, the Latin Vulgate, the French, the German, the Spanish, the Italian and the English. I have also examined the English Hexapla, containing the versions of Wickliffe, Tindal, Cranmer, Geneva, Rheims, and the common version—also the improved Greek text of Griesbach, of Scholz, of Mills, and sundry Latin versions, especially that of Beza, of Junius and Tremellius, with other English versions; and, judging from their punctuation, not one of them has properly understood this speech. Dr. George Campbell is the only one, in my judgment, down to his time, that properly comprehended and punctuated it.

So far as my library extends, he has been followed, in this punctuation, only by the authors of the Bible containing twenty thousand emendations, by Boothroyd, and partly by Thompson.

Spirit. 5. And; finally, the Jewish Scriptures—the law and the prophets. The common version mistakes the imperative mood for the indicative. It reads, "Search the Scriptures," instead of, "*Ye do search the Scriptures.*" "Now," adds he, "these are they that testify of me."

He then explains their unbelief. They would not come to him; they would not place themselves under his guidance, because—1. He did not seek the honor of this world. 2. They were destitute of the love of God. 3. He came only in his Father's name, seeking his glory. 4. They believed not the writings of Moses, while professing that they did. 5. Their stubborn prejudices, growing out of their notions of a worldly Messiah, a temporal political kingdom and a national hierarchy.

It would be tedious to enumerate the errors that have resulted from mis-punctuation, as well as from the other sources already named. Punctuation is a species of commentary, serving a purpose kindred to that of capitals, chapters, verses and paragraphs. Much depends upon all these, as respects our proper understanding and translating these ancient and venerable documents. We have in the above example selected a strong case, and expatiated upon it at length, to show how much depends on the proper use of points in giving significance to words.

Another class of errors in the common version, of still more serious importance, in cases of words having different significations, is the selection of inapposite and inadequate terms to express the meaning of the spirit, and the design of the original writer. In illustration of this, we will select the word *paracleetos*, so frequently occurring in our Lord's valedictory address to his apostles, reported by John, chapters xiv., xv., xvi. In the common version it is represented by the word *Comforter* in this discourse, and in another place by the term *advocate.* By Dr. George Campbell it is here translated *monitor*, and, by some other translators, *instructor*, *guide*, *&c.*

Now, of all these terms, *advocate* is the most comprehensive and generic. An advocate may guide, instruct, admonish, comfort, console, &c., but a comforter does not generally assume the character of an advocate, &c. But we have more to commend its preference in this context than its generic import. The work assigned to him by our Saviour decides his claims as paramount. He promises that when the Holy Spirit comes to act under Christ's own mission, he will reprove, convince and teach the world. He will show its sin, Christ's righteousness and God's judgment. He will guide his apostles into all the truth. He will bring all things that he had taught them to their remembrance. He will glorify the Messiah in all his personal and official relations. There is, indeed, an inelegance, an impropriety, in the sentence as rendered in King James's version:—"He will *reprove* the world of sin, of righteousness, and of judgment." It might be asked, how could he *reprove* the world of righteousness? That he might reprove the world because of its unrighteousness is evident. That he might convict the world of its sin and unrighteousness, and convince it of Christ's righteousness and of the ultimate judgment, we all can conceive.

I dwell on this passage with the more emphasis, because the office of the Holy Spirit is the most essential doctrine of the whole evangelical dispensation. The mission of the Lord Jesus by his Father, and the mission of the Holy Spirit by the Son, after his glorification in the heavens, are the two most grand and sublime missions in the annals of time or in the ages of eternity. Jesus Christ came into the world to reveal the character of his Father. The Holy Spirit came to the church to glorify Christ and to sanctify his people. Jesus came to magnify Jehovah's empire, to sustain his law and government, and to make them honorable to the universe—to make reconciliation for iniquity, and to obtain an eternal redemption for us. But the Spirit came to be the Holy *Guest* of the house that Jesus built for a habitation of God through the Spirit. He is another advocate for God, another demonstration of his infinite, eternal and immutable love.

The memorable Pentecost after Christ's ascension and coronation as Lord of all fully attests the truth and reveals the import of the special advocacy of the Holy Spirit. He opened the new reign with brilliant displays of his glory, gave great eloquence to his apostles, and confirmed his pretensions and their mission by a power that brought three thousand Jews to do homage at his feet.

We have dwelt upon this error, not so much because of its mere verbal inaccuracy and incompetency to indicate the mind of the Spirit, but because a most solemn and sublime fact is involved in it, which, when developed and established, trenches far into the territories of a cold Unitarian rationalism, and also invades the wide dominions of a frenzied enthusiasm.

If any one, however, should question its philological propriety, I will refer him to the fact that the whole family of *paracleetos* is translated, by even King James's authority, in keeping with these views. Thus, the verb *parakaleoo* is rendered *to call for, to invite, to exhort, to admonish,* to persuade, to implore, to beseech, to console. And its verbal *parakleesis* is also rendered *a calling for, an invitation, a teaching;* and *parakleetos* (1 John i. 2) is rendered an *advocate.* But no one term fully and adequately expresses all that is comprehended in the mission and work of the Holy Spirit in the remedial dispensation. It not only imparted all spiritual gifts to the apostles, prophets and Jewish evangelists of Christ, but in becoming the Holy Guest of the church he animates, purifies and comforts it with all his illuminating, renovating and sanctifying efficacy.

But there are other sources of error, growing out of the fearful apostasy which has spread its sable wings and its leaden sceptre over a slumbering world. The progress in Bible-translating, in Biblical criticism, in liberal principles, in the free discussion of all questions concerning state and church polity, has, more or less, broken the spell of human authority, roused the long-latent energies of the human mind, and begotten and cherished a spirit of inquiry before which truth and virtue alone can stand erect, with a portly mien, an unblenching eye and an unfaltering tongue. Errors long consecrated in hallowed fanes, backed by monarchical and papal authority, lauded by lordly bishops, canonized by hoary rabbis in solemn conclaves, and confirmed by the decrees of œcumenical councils, are being disrobed of all their factitious ornaments and exposed in their naked deformity to the wondering gaze of a long insulted and degraded people. The inquiry of the people is beginning to be, *What is truth?* not, Who says so? What say the oracles of God? not, What council has so decided? We must be judged every man for himself. We shall, therefore, judge for ourselves.

The Christian mind, since the era of Protestantism, has been advancing with a slow but steady pace, an onward and an upward progress. Its noble and splendid victories in physical science, in useful and ornamental arts, in free government and in social institutions, have increased its courage, animated its hopes and emboldened its efforts to find its proper eminence. It has not yet fixed its own destiny, limited its own aspirations, nor stipulated its subordination to any human arbitrament.

In the department of religion and divine obligation it has tried every form of ecclesiastical polity, every human constitution and variety of partisan and schismatic theology, and every scheme of propagating its own peculiar tenets. Nor has it yet found a safe and sure haven in which to anchor, in hope of coming safely to land. It will not surrender nor capitulate on any terms dishonorable to its own dignity, nor compromise its convictions for the sake of popular applause.

The questions of the present day are more grave and momentous, in their bearings on church and state, than any questions propounded and discussed in former times. Even the very text of the Holy Bible has been submitted to a more severe ordeal and test than at any former time. And that the holy oracles of salvation shall go forth in their primitive purity into all lands and languages is now firmly decided by the purest, most enlightened, most generous and noble-hearted men in the world. Hence the inquiry for the old paths—the ancient landmarks of truth and error.

You, my Christian brethren, assembled here on the present occasion in one of the noblest causes that ever engaged the human faculties or fired with pure devotion the human heart, have in your horizon the illustrious aim of giving to the world abroad a pure and faithful translation of the living oracles. You will have no fellowship with any compromise—with any scheme that merely builds up a party, or seeks the applause of those who have, for the sake of "a fair show in the flesh," done homage at the shrine or yielded to the false oratory and special pleadings of a self-seeking, a self-preferring, a self-aggrandizing spirit. You will show no partiality for consecrated error because of the good and learned and charitable people who advocate it, or because of the flatteries of those who fear your example as weakening their authority and impairing their hold on the smiles of the world.

You are determined to carry the work of translation to its proper metes and boundaries. You will have no privileged, canonized and time-consecrated terms, exempted by prescription, privilege or concession from the tests of language, the canons of criticism and the laws of interpretation. The most consecrated ecclesiastical terms—the aristocracy of terminology—occasionally, too, the strongholds of error—you will not exempt from the statutes of interpretation, from the umpirage of lexicography. You will pass no special statute in favor of the two houses of *baptizo* and *rantizo*, nor grant aristocratic exemptions and privileges to either, but will bring them into court and give them a fair trial, by the canons and laws of criticism, before the high tribunal of inspired apostles and prophets.

That class of errors which gives the particular currency of one age the power to nullify the legitimate and constitutional currency of another will receive no favor at your hands. For why should ordinances prescribed by Divine authority be reversed, altered, amended or adjusted by any human tribunal to suit the prejudice or caprice of worldly conformity? This species of Protestant Popery is just as abhorrent to your morals, to reason and revelation, as any other form of it.

Let us, then, still more gravely look at the issues to be made on the present occasion. Protestant Christendom has acknowledged one faith, one Lord, two baptisms, many Lord's tables, and several forms of church polity growing out of these unfortunate and unhallowed traditions; and one of the capital devices of Satan is to blink some matters of grave moment and give others a factitious importance.

Positive ordinances are belittled by most parties who have substituted human institutions for divine enactments. They enthrone their *beau-ideal* of the Christian virtues under the name of "Christian Charity," and desecrate divine ordinances under the name of "Rites and Ceremonies." But let me say it once for all, and most emphatically, that Divine ordinances are the very marrow and fatness of the Christian institution—the embodiment of its spiritual promises, joys and consolations. They are like the sun, moon and stars, those Divine ordinances of nature in which and through which God communicates light and life and health to the world. They are as the dew, and the sunshine, and the early and the latter rain, to our hills and valleys, that make them verdant and fruitful, and vocal with the praise of the Lord.

Zeal for Divine ordinances is the best criterion, and always was the most conclusive test, of a standing or a falling church. The Lord, by Malachi, said to the Jewish community in their decline, "From the days of your fathers you are gone away from mine ordinances, and have not kept them. Return unto me, and I will return unto you, saith Jehovah." The highest commendation that could be given of Zacharias and Elizabeth, the parents of the Baptist, was that they "were blameless observers of the commandments and ordinances of the Lord." What then pleased the Lord will please him now. The ordinances of sun, moon and stars differ from one another. They are, indeed, all luminaries. Each one of them, however, has its own magnitude and its specific use, as well as its own position in the universe. So of the ordinances of grace. They are all fraught with blessings to the intelligent believing recipients of them; but each one of them has its proper place and its peculiar influence upon those who scripturally submit to it. But out of that place they are unmeaning rites and useless ceremonies. They alike mock God and the recipients of them. They, therefore, not only glorify the wisdom and grace of God, who scripturally teach and dispense them, but also promote the sanctification and happiness of those who receive them. "Therefore," says the Great Teacher, "whosoever shall violate, and cause others to violate, one of the least of these my precepts, shall be of no account in the kingdom of heaven; but whosoever shall do and teach them shall be of great esteem in the kingdom of heaven."

In speaking of the classification of errors of translation, we left for special consideration one class of errors which, with the members of the Bible Union, at this peculiar crisis, is worthy of special regard. It is that to which your new institution, my Christian friends, owes its origin.

You and those who have compelled you to form a separate and distinct organization alike agree as to the necessity for an improved version. You do not say a new, an absolutely new, version; nor have I ever supposed such a thing necessary or desirable. I, as well as you, love the Anglo-Saxon Bible style; and who that has read it from infancy to manhood does not love it? *Love it,* I say; not merely *admire* its simplicity, its force, its beauty, its easy apprehension, but delight in its charms, and in its thousand agreeable associations in our memories and in our hearts.

They, too, from whom you have been compelled to separate in this particular work admire and love it.

I have long regretted that most of our approved versions, as they are called, should have needlessly changed the style and language of the Anglo-Saxon of King James. My views are that no change should be made but such as faithfulness to the original requires. True, indeed, there are many antique, quaint and ungrammatical phrases, such as, "We do you to wit;" "I trow not;" "Our Father which art in heaven;" "He purgeth it, that it may bring forth more fruit," &c., which a moderate complaisance to grammar and literary taste would correct or amend. But, while tithing these as "mint, anise and cummin," we would rather call your attention to the weightier matters of the common version.

Its authors, indeed, much more deserve the character of judicious copyists than that of learned and independent translators. King James and his ecclesiastical courtiers were much more in love with Geneva than Jerusalem, and the translators very happily copied and anglicised the Geneva version, and paid a due degree of reverence to his majesty's inhibition from touching with their unclean hands the old-fashioned and canonized "ecclesiastical words;" and by these means, as faithful servants of his majesty, they left in Greek, or in Geneva style, hosts of words, with the whole *baptizo* family, unamended and untranslated.

That *rantizo* and *baptizo* are Greek words, wanting only half a letter, no man of self-respect and of literary pretensions will deny. And that they are both of frequent occurrence in the Levitical law, is universally conceded. But our pedobaptist friends are slow to learn that in not one instance in the whole Septuagint version are *baptizo* and *rantizo* interchanged. Their families were never on friendly terms of intercommunication. They lived together for fifteen hundred years and never once intermarried, nor did *baptizo* ever employ *rantizo*, nor rantizo *baptizo*, down to the forty-third generation, to do for one another any one service. Nor did any Jew, from Moses to Christ, rantize by baptizing, or baptize by rantizing. In English, no Jew ever once tried to dip by sprinkling, or to sprinkle by dipping. This incontrovertible fact, in a law which contained many typical observances of the greatest exactness, must stand through all coming time, as it has stood through all past time, an irrefragable evidence of the folly or weakness of any one presuming that these two words can, by any grammatical, logical or even rhetorical possibility, indicate one and the same thing.

This fact is, with us, most conclusive and satisfactory proof that no man can be a faithful and competent translator of the Divine oracles, in an age of controversy, as to the initiatory *action* which Christ commanded, who does not select a term to represent it in the language into which he translates, as definite, precise and immutable as the original term *baptizo;* and that the Latin *immerse*, and the Saxon *dippan*, from the Greek *dupto*, to dive or dip, do exactly represent the original Greek, there cannot be the shadow of a doubt. There is no need whatever to multiply proof beyond this single fact, although we have volumes of evidence at our command.

With us it is, at best, but a waste of time to argue that we never can have a faithful, true and intelligible version of the Scriptures until this word is thus translated. Every intelligent Baptist, every well-educated man of no religious party, knows this to be a fact—a fact as true and veritable as that Jesus is the Christ. And shall we, knowing this, presume, before heaven and earth, to give to the world, or to circulate through the Christian church, a false or an equivocal translation, through the fear of men, or that lame and blind charity which yields to the unreasonable prejudices of society and covets the honor that comes from man, as necessary to aid either the Holy Spirit or the oracles of God in the work of converting sinners to God or the church from her idolatry?

To assume, as some of our Baptist brethren have virtually assumed, that *baptize* is an English word, and not a translation of a Greek word, is to say that the whole New Testament is translated whenever the Greek words are printed or written in Roman characters. This is, so far as I now remember its details, the pith of the whole controversy at the late meeting of the American and Foreign Bible Society, in this city.

We sometimes transfer and naturalize words, as we transfer men from one nation to another; but then we do not say that every naturalized or adopted citizen has been translated from Europe or Asia into America, as Enoch and Elijah were translated to heaven. The Romans, from whom we got the word *immersion*, did not transfer it from the Greek language. It was, with them, a translation of *baptisma;* and can we adopt this translation from the Romans, and then call both it and the word which it represents a translation from the Greek into our proper vernacular?

But, waiving, on the present occasion, any discussion of the merits of this question—any attempt to show that in the judgment of the whole literary world the term *baptizo* was translated by the Romans *immergo*, and that *immerse* is a verbal from *immergo*, ages since adopted into our language, and used as synonymous with *dip*, another naturalized Greek word, transmitted to us from our Saxon forefathers, the meaning of which every child in Great Britain and in the United States understands as well as it does the words *bread* and *water*—we proceed to state that the terms *church, conversation, communion, fellowship, repentance, charity, bishop, deacon, presbytery, angel, covenant, testament*, &c. demand the profound consideration of modern translators, as much as this now-a-days litigated sectarian word baptism.

We want no special, sectarian or national translation of the living oracles. We ardently desire a perspicuous, definite, forcible and *elegant* version of the book of life. For this great work we should desire more than the concurrence and co-operation of the whole Christian world, in its modern import; we should desire to have Jews, Greeks, Romanists, Protestants, and even well-educated antiquaries, and literary and moral skeptics, if they could be found. But this would be Utopianism—a chimerical hope. Of "the whole Christian world" we could not interest even the section called *Protestant* to unite with us. From the galleries, from the high seats of the modern synagogues of Protestant Christendom, the seven demons that pander to that trinity of lusts and passions called the lusts of the flesh, the lusts of the eye and the pride of life have not yet been exorcised. There is too much of the world in the bosom of the Protestant section of Christendom. What, then, must be done? Sit down upon the bank of the river of Babylon and wait till its waters fail—till its channel be dry?

No! You say, No! by no means! Rather let the Baptist portion of Christendom, without respect to its private opinions, come together, with its chosen men all. And make a Baptist Bible? What! a Baptist

Bible! Yes! if it should so happen that God's Bible and the Baptist Bible be one and the same book.

But we can furnish a version which we can sustain by the testimony of the mighty dead, and by a portion of the living mighty men, of the anti-Baptist Christendom. I will go one step higher and affirm that we Baptists, General and Particular, Old School and New School, Reform and anti-Reform, Orthodox and Heterodox, can make just as good, as true, as faithful, as exact, as elegant, a new version, or an improved version, out of the pedorantist or anti-Baptist versions, emendations, disquisitions and criticisms now at this moment extant, as we could make were we all, with one accord and in one place, to meet and sit upon the original text, in grave deliberation, for seven long years. This is my belief, opinion, conviction, assurance, or whatever else you may choose to call it.

But we regret to learn that not even the Baptists can be induced to come together in one fraternal phalanx to achieve this great and noble object. Since my arrival in this city I have been informed that there are some of them warmly opposed to it—that even tracts and pamphlets have been issued and put into circulation against an improved version of the living oracles. Two of these now lie before me. They were presented to me in answer to my inquiry for the reasons why the whole Baptist community did not make it a common cause and come up as one man to the work. One of them enumerates no less than *ten reasons* against an attempt to prepare a new version, and from a quarter that I could not have anticipated. Its eminent author, in the form of a very learned and laborious volume against Romanism, stands in my library on the same shelf with my Debate with Bishop Purcell of Cincinnati on the same subject. And how can it be, I asked myself, that he should now stand with that party in opposing a new and improved version, in our own language, of the words of eternal life? I opened it with much interest, curious to have this mystery revealed. To its title-page my attention was instantly turned, and fixed upon its remarkable motto—"THE OLD-FASHIONED BIBLE." While pondering upon the author's design in this strange motto, I hastily turned to its last page, and again read,—

> "The old-fashioned Bible, the dear blessed Bible,
> The family Bible, that lay on the stand."

"Is this," said I to myself, "an *ad captandum vulgus*, a lure for the unwary reader, or the great argument for the inviolability and immortality of King James's version?" I dared not, till I had read it through, answer this first inquiry. I had no sooner glanced through its ten arguments than my eyes were opened. The spirit of the motto is the soul of its ten arguments. Its body, or substance, is, "The purpose" to have and to introduce a new version "is fraught with injury" and ruin to the Baptists. Alas for the feeble Baptists, if a new version is fraught with injury and ruin to the denomination! But, combining his logic and rhetoric in two lines, he finds their salvation in

> **"The old-fashioned Bible, the dear blessed Bible,**
> **The family Bible, that lay on the stand."**

After a moment's reflection, it occurred to me that not only the motto, but the whole ten arguments, in their soul, body and spirit, were as good against a new version in the days of Tindal as now, and will be as good, as sound, as conclusive, against a new version, against every change which has been, is now or will hereafter be proposed, through all coming time.

From the printing of Tindal's version till that of James's version, there was a copy of the Bible in many Christian families, and some of them *lay* on a stand. Now, on the first motion, in the fatherland, to have an improved version, had the author of the "*Ten Reasons*" been then living and consulted, he would have raised the tune of the "old-fashioned Bible that lay on the stand," and for this good and sound reason—that good sense and good logic are immutably the same, yesterday, to-day and to-morrow. If an old-fashioned Bible lying one year, or one century, on a stand, be a sound and satisfactory argument against a new version of the Holy Scriptures, it will forever be an invincible argument against any correction, emendation or change whatever.

The ten reasons given in this pamphlet of six-and-thirty pages, arithmetically enumerated and logically arranged, are a mere dilution or expansion of this one popular and prolific syllogism.

It is again presented in the following words:—The mere purpose to have a new version is "fraught with injury to the denomination"—"destructive of brotherly love and harmony"—"suicidal to the American and Foreign Bible Society"—"and utterly uncalled for by any consideration of principle or of duty." These are the four cardinal points to which are respectively directed the ten reasons.

The ten reasons are, indeed, essentially, one and all, political or denominational. The glory, honor and integrity of the Baptist denomination, it would appear, are much more, in the eye and heart of their author, than the importance or value of a pure and faithful, a clear and intelligible, translation of the oracles of God. This I hope is not so. But he writes and reasons in such a way as to make it appear so, and thus injures his own reputation much more than he can impede the glorious enterprise. For this cannot fail, Heaven being assuredly on its side.

Now, the case stands thus:—The common version was gotten up some two and a half centuries since, under prelatical, hierarchical and royal patronage and restrictions. The vernacular of that day, spoken and written, was, in orthography, punctuation, and in much of its common wording, quite different from that of the present day. The knowledge of the original tongues then possessed, was proportionally more than two centuries behind that of the present day, and their general literature and science were still more deficient.

Since that day, there have been many changes in the common version in the use of capitals, points, verses, sections, paragraphs; some of which materially affect the sense; and, indeed, all of them are a species of notes and comments of human authority. By whose authority they were made, few can now say. But if there were any good reason or logic in favor of these changes, that same good reason and logic demand their continuance though made without the authority of King James and his forty-seven chosen men. But if the authority of King James and his hierarchical counsellors be still paramount authority in the conscience of such men as the author of the Ten Reasons, then they should repudiate all the improvements already made, and restore the identical version of King James, letter and point, for this good reason, that "he who keeps the whole law and yet offends in one point is guilty of all." Nor ought they to translate one word untranslated by these elect translators—not one single *amen, anathema* or *maranatha*. But who will stand up in defence of such a position?

If God values and will sanction and fulfil every *jot* and *tittle* of his law; if he commanded Moses to see that he made all things connected with the tabernacle and its service—even to the sockets and the tenons of its boards, and to the loops and selvedges of its curtains—according to a pattern showed him in the mount; and if the same spirit animated and guided the Jews in their best days, insomuch that they counted the words and even the letters of the Pentateuch, lest one error should find its way into the sacred text; and if after the return from their captivity in Babylon, where their language was corrupted, Ezra the scribe in reading their law interpreted every unknown term and repudiated every corruption of the text, so that he caused the people to hear and to understand the oracles of Jehovah, shall we, to whom God has committed the Christian oracles, the holy gospel and its sublime institutions, suffer it to be corrupted, obscured or rendered unintelligible, without the most strenuous effort on our part to preserve uncorrupted the precious deposit, and to extend to our contemporaries and transmit to posterity all "the words of this life?" Forbid it, reason, conscience and heaven! Has not Jehovah said that "though heaven be his throne, and earth his footstool, though he is the high and lofty One that inhabits eternity, to this man he will look with complacency, even to him that is of an humble and a contrite spirit, and who trembles at his word"?

The good sense and good taste of the Grecian poet Homer are never so impressively displayed as when introducing, as he often does, the gods of Pagan superstition into his poem. He always suffers them, without note or comment, to express themselves in their own terms. I could wish that our venerable translators had been as judicious and as discreet as this great Grecian bard.

But why argue this case any further? The many marginal readings of recondite terms in our numerous and various commentaries, and in our family Bibles and Testaments, the labors of innumerable pulpit orators and lecturers, expended every Lord's day in correcting and explaining the text in all the synagogues in our land; alike demonstrate the need of a new version, and our ability to furnish it,—first by selecting a well-authenticated original text, and then by giving an exact, perspicuous and faithful translation of it, and that, too, in a pure, chaste and elegant Anglo-Saxon style. That our age and contemporaries are equal to this, is quite as evident as that the Greek and Roman classics have been, and can again be, so translated by competent scholars.

But, according to certain learned doctors, the time has not yet come. No; nor will the time which they have imagined ever come. In all past versions the dignitaries, the prelates, the hierarchs, were compelled into the measure—though sometimes resisting till their thrones were in danger. They too, like some of our modern doctors, could see nothing but denominational ruin, dissension and disaster in such an undertaking; and, still worse, they could neither see nor feel any principle, duty or obligation requiring them to give the full sense of God's book, and, Ezra-like, to make the people understand the sacred text.

But the impending difficulties are somewhat magnified in the imagination of such desponding doctors. The pedobaptist clergy are much more friendly to us immersionists than formerly. They are sharing with us their literary and ecclesiastic honors. They desire an amicable and honorable truce, a cessation of sectarian strife, a generous league under the serene and pacific motto, "Let me alone, and I will let thee alone; for we are brethren."

But this denominational harmony, charity and truce will soon pass away should we have a new version. No, my good brethren; no such thing. They will respect you more. They will in heart and conscience honor you more. And, better still, you will be much more honorable in your own eyes, and in the eyes of Him who looks not on the outward professions, but upon the heart.

But I have not yet said that which I wish most emphatically to say. I want no *Baptist* Bible in their sense of that cognomen. Nor would I plead for a new version for the sake of the word *immersion*. We can prove Christian immersion, as Christ's own institution, against the world, and that, too, from King James's translation. We have done it on many occasions.

No one has paid less homage to sectarian tenets, prejudices and partialities—no one, it has been said, has more violently assailed the idols of the parties—than your humble servant. I have made myself vile and heretical in the esteem of their warmest defenders. And what has been the result? My experience may be profitable to others. A great revolution has been effected, our opponents themselves being judges. Myriads and myriads have, through our instrumentality and that of our brotherhood, received the gospel during the last thirty years. And, strange to tell, our very opponents who once accused us of the most heretical tenets have themselves acknowledged us orthodox, just as orthodox as themselves, in all that is deemed vital, soul-redeeming and soul-transforming in the Christian doctrine. It will be so in this grand enterprise. Those who deprecate this movement, and inveigh most loudly and bitterly against it, will, when it has achieved its object, acknowledge its value, commend your courage and magnanimity, and gratefully regard you as the benefactors of your age and country.

But we must meet with a firm reliance on the promise of Divine aid, and in an humble, sincere and prayerful spirit, free from the alloy of worldly policy, of fleshly interests, of sectarian partialities, with the love of truth and of the God of truth in our hearts, with the throne of impartial and ultimate judgment in our eye, and concentrate and consecrate all our learning, all our wisdom, all our patience, all our energies and all our devotion on the transcendent subject.

And why should we not? Is it not expedient? is it not necessary?

is it not essential to the prosperity of Zion, to the enlightenment, the consolation, of Christians, to the conviction, the conversion, the sanctification, the salvation, of the Christian world, so called, and to the illumination and rescue of Pagandom from the stupidity, the degradation, the tyranny, the abject thraldom, of the low, mean and contemptible idolatries of the regions of darkness and the shadows of death, where no vision is, and the people perish?

Let us, then, awake from this state of supineness, cold indifference, sinful apathy, reproachful cowardice, and, with an ardent zeal, a lively hope, an assured confidence in God our Saviour, concert, digest and systematize a plan of holy co-operation, of well-concerted action, of successful effort, in this benevolent, noble and godlike enterprise.

Let us make no truce with error, no covenant with guile, no agreement with hypocrisy, no league with the spirit of darkness, but, as sons of light, put on the armor of light, grasp the sword of the Spirit, and make a courageous, unanimous and brave assault on the gates of darkness, superstition and error.

And is not the object, the end in view, great, noble and divine? If human redemption cost high Heaven so much as the mission, humiliation, degradation and sacrifice of God's only-begotten and well-beloved Son, to effect the restoration of fallen, ruined, wretched man to the favor and complacent affection of his Father and his God; if the Lord Christ assumed our nature, bore our infirmities, carried our griefs, expiated our guilt by the voluntary sacrifice of himself, and descended into the grave, the regions of darkness and corruption, that he might rescue man from eternal darkness, from everlasting woe; if the Spirit of wisdom and knowledge, of counsel and might, the Spirit of the Father and of the Son, with all his powers of knowledge, wisdom and eloquence, became a missionary, sent by the Father and the Son, to inspire prophets and apostles, to animate saints and martyrs, to become the holy guest of Christ's own mystical body the church, and to sanctify, purify, and ennoble that body with the graces of wisdom and knowledge, of love and mercy, and to robe it with the beauty of holiness, to adorn it with heavenly graces, and to present it a pure and holy church, without spot, or wrinkle, or blemish, before the throne of God, amidst the congratulations and acclamations of heavenly hosts of wondering, adoring and transported angels—shall we, the subjects of Almighty grace, the ransomed sons of God, the heirs and expectants of eternal glory, be selfish, lukewarm, cowardly, faint-hearted and desponding, in the work of faith, the labor of love, the patience of hope, for the sake of any ephemeral interest, any worldly policy, any fleshly advantage accruing from our selfishess, our carnality, our earthly-mindedness? No! forbid it, reason, conscience, hope and heaven!

Now, all that faith and hope and love inspire comes from the oracles of God—comes through the words and sentences of heaven-inspired prophets, holy bards, apostles and evangelists, embalmed in Hebrew and Greek. These oracles have been committed to the church, and especially to the Baptist church, herself being judge. Her views of Christian ordinances—not merely of faith, hope and love, but of the sealing, sanctifying, animating ordinances of the Christian institution—are, in our best judgment, our most clear and forcible conviction, especially intrusted to the Baptist communities. I am aware that time was when she had not one tolerably-educated man in every hundred of her most enthusiastic, laborious and successful declaimers and proclaimers, and that still the proportion of such is but small. But, since the second conversion of the pedobaptists Luther Rice and Adoniram Judson, a great change has come upon the denomination. These noble, self-humiliating, self-denying, self-sacrificing spirits effected a great revolution in the minds of the denomination. One of them died gloriously in the harness, dragging up the rugged cliffs of worldly selfishness and parsimoniousness the car of education—literary and scientific education—subordinate to evangelical and ministerial education—a martyr, truly, in the noble cause. Meantime, his beloved brother Judson exiled himself from his own beloved land, from all the associations of his youth, from all that is dear to flesh and blood, and, in the spirit of ancient times, cast his bread and his life upon the waters of the mighty deep, crossed the broad oceans of earth, and went in quest of the lost sheep amongst the mountains and valleys of Pagan Asia, whence came the word of life to Europe and the New World. Noble spirit!—a martyr, too. Perhaps he yet lives on some sunny isle of the wild ocean, seeking to reinvigorate his shattered frame, to reanimate his fallen tabernacle, that he may yet guide a few more lost and wandering pagans to the Lamb of God, that they may be baptized in the fountain of David's house and drink the spirit of the gospel age from the golden chalice of everlasting love. With peace and love in his heart, heaven and glory in his eye, we say, "The Lord bless thee, and keep thee; the Lord make his face shine upon thee, and be gracious to thee; the Lord lift up his countenance upon thee, and give thee peace!"*

---

* Since writing the preceding paragraph, I have with grief seen the melancholy announcement of the death of the much-beloved, admired and venerated Judson. On his way to the Isle of Bourbon, while seeking health, he resigned his spirit to his Re-

Since, I say, the conversion and self-consecration of these brilliant stars of the Baptist Zion, the denomination has been annually ascending in all that gives strength, dignity and power to an evangelical ministry. Yet she is greatly in the rear of some other denominations in those literary accomplishments, in those scientific attainments, that give strength, eloquence and power to those who lead the way in the paths of public reformation. Education, without grace, does nothing in the kingdom of God. Grace, with a very little education, may, with remarkable talents, do much. But the moral, the spiritual, the evangelical power of sound learning, divine grace and eminent talents combined in one person, who can limit or define?

Still, after all the subtractions which impartial reason and justice can make, the Baptists are this day in all their force, in the addition of all their broken bands and dissociated fragments, the most numerous, the most powerful and the most proselyting denomination in America. They have, too, in their aggregate, as much talent, learning, wealth, power, political, moral and religious, as any other denomination in our country, with a little too much worldly-mindedness and a too great hankering after the idol called popularity. United in one unbroken phalanx, what might they not accomplish? Were they to go forth in the armor of light, with the holy oracles in their hands and in their hearts, not trammelled with the traditions of men, not doing homage to the false glosses and fanciful interpretations of a few rabbis baptized in the fountains of human speculations and a false philosophy, what might they not achieve?

To conclude—for we have already transcended the narrow limits of a fashionable discourse—having had only a few fragments of time, gathered up amidst many avocations and perplexities, incident to our standing in too many relations to society, I have, with a free hand, sketched but a few of the many thoughts that are now pressing on my mind for utterance.

Brethren, the time is short. Much is to be done, much can be done, and much ought to be done in the great and solemn and transcendent

---

deemer, and his body to the ocean. His work was done, and his reward is sure. For eight-and-thirty years he toiled as a missionary for Christ, and is now entered into rest.

Earth and sea are spacious burying-grounds. But the *bodies* of men, not their souls, return to dust. The sleep of souls in ocean or in earth, is the chaotic dream of sin-stricken souls. "*Bodies* of the saints," not *souls*, "came out of their graves," when the Messiah opened the portals of heaven in rising from the dead. This is an irrefragable evidence that "those who fall asleep in Jesus God will bring with him" when he comes. Let us await that day with patience, and in hope of "the resurrection of the just."

work of getting up and consummating a perspicuous, forcible and faithful version of the Word of Life, and in presenting it to the Lord, his cause and people.

Let us fear no sectarian, partisan or denominational opposition. Let us not cater to the whims, the prejudices, the pride or the partiality of any people. Let us not flatter the vain, the worldly or the proud, but, in the fear of the Lord, in the love of Zion and in the hope of a brighter and a better day, add to our faith courage, to our courage the wisdom of the serpent without its venom, the harmlessness of the dove without its timidity, and, in the humble and meek spirit of the gospel, stand up courageously, cordially and with one consent for the truth, the whole truth, and nothing but the truth; thus giving to our contemporaries and posterity an unequivocal and noble proof of our piety, benevolence and courage. Not conferring with flesh and blood, but, in the fear of God, the love of Christ and the hope of heaven, let us set about this grand and lofty enterprise, pregnant with glory to God in the highest heaven, peace on earth and good-will among men.

INDEX.

K.

L.

M.

Q.

R.

S.

T.

THE END.

www.ingramcontent.com/pod-product-compliance
Lightning Source LLC
LaVergne TN
LVHW021057110826
845150LV00001B/102